A History of

French Public Law

A LAW CLASSIC

A History of
French Public Law

by
Jean Brissaud
Late Professor of Legal History in the University of Toulouse

Translated by
James W. Garner
Professor of Political Science in the University of Illinois

With Introductions by
Harold D. Hazeltine
Reader in English Law in Cambridge University

and by
Westel W. Willoughby
Professor of Political Science in Johns Hopkins University

BeardBooks
Washington, D.C.

ISBN 1-58798-101-7

Reprinted 2001 by Beard Books, Washington, D.C.

Printed in the United States of America.

I might instance in other professions the obligation men lie under of applying themselves to certain parts of History; and I can hardly forbear doing it in that of the Law, — in its nature the noblest and most beneficial to mankind, in its abuse and debasement the most sordid and the most pernicious. A lawyer now is nothing more (I speak of ninety-nine in a hundred at least), to use some of Tully's words, "nisi leguleius quidem cautus, et acutus praeco actionum, cantor formularum, auceps syllabarum." But there have been lawyers that were orators, philosophers, historians: there have been Bacons and Clarendons. There will be none such any more, till in some better age true ambition, or the love of fame, prevails over avarice; and till men find leisure and encouragement to prepare themselves for the exercise of this profession, by climbing up to the vantage ground (so my Lord Bacon calls it) of Science, instead of grovelling all their lives below, in a mean but gainful application of all the little arts of chicane. Till this happen, the profession of the law will scarce deserve to be ranked among the learned professions. And whenever it happens, one of the vantage grounds to which men must climb, is Metaphysical, and the other, Historical Knowledge. HENRY ST. JOHN, Viscount BOLINGBROKE, *Letters on the Study of History* (1739).

Whoever brings a fruitful idea to any branch of knowledge, or rends the veil that seems to sever one portion from another, his name is written in the Book among the builders of the Temple. For an English lawyer it is hardly too much to say that the methods which Oxford invited Sir Henry Maine to demonstrate, in this chair of Historical and Comparative Jurisprudence, have revolutionised our legal history and largely transformed our current text-books. — Sir FREDERICK POLLOCK, Bart., *The History of Comparative Jurisprudence* (Farewell Lecture at the University of Oxford, 1903).

No piece of History is true when set apart to itself, divorced and isolated. It is part of an intricately pieced whole, and must needs be put in its place in the netted scheme of events, to receive its true color and estimation. We are all partners in a common undertaking, — the illumination of the thoughts and actions of men as associated in society, the life of the human spirit in this familiar theatre of coöperative effort in which we play, so changed from age to age, and yet so much the same throughout the hurrying centuries. The day for synthesis has come. No one of us can safely go forward without it. — WOODROW WILSON, *The Variety and Unity of History* (Address at the World's Congress of Arts and Science, St. Louis, 1904).

A lawyer without history or literature is a mechanic, a mere working mason; if he possesses some knowledge of these, he may venture to call himself an architect.—Sir WALTER SCOTT, *"Guy Mannering,"* c. XXXVII.

CONTENTS

INTRODUCTION

THE ORIGIN OF THE STATE

I. General Observations

II. Elementary and Composite Societies

CHAPTER I

THE ROMAN EPOCH

Topic 1. The Empire

Topic 2. Justice, Army, Finances

Topic 3. The Province

Topic 4. The City

Topic 5. Status of Persons

Topic 6. Land Ownership

Topic 7. Conclusion

CHAPTER II

THE FRANKISH OR BARBARIAN EPOCH. POLITICAL INSTITUTIONS

Topic 1. The Frankish Monarchy

Topic 2. The Nation

Topic 3. The Central Administration

Topic 4. Provincial Administration

Topic 5. Military Organization

Topic 6. Finances

Topic 7. Justice. Judicial Organization and Procedure

A. Judicial Organization

B. Procedure

CHAPTER III

THE FRANKISH OR BARBARIAN EPOCH. ORIGINS OF THE FEUDAL RÉGIME

Topic 1. Immunity

Topic 2. Status of Persons

Topic 3. Status of Lands

CHAPTER IV

THE CHURCH UNDER THE "ANCIEN RÉGIME." (THE FRANKISH, FEUDAL, AND MONARCHICAL EPOCHS)

Topic 1. Constitution of the Christian Church

Topic 2. The Clergy

Topic 3. Establishments of Religious Utility. Monasteries, Hospitals, and Schools

Topic 4. The Budget of the Church

Topic 5. Ecclesiastical Justice

Topic 6. Heretics and Jews

Topic 7. Relations of Church and State

CHAPTER V

THE FEUDAL PERIOD. THE FEUDAL STATE. SEIGNIORIES AND COMMUNES

Topic 1. General Characteristics of the Feudal System and Sketch of its Evolution

Topic 2. The Seigniories

CHAPTER VII

THE FEUDAL PERIOD (*Continued*). STATUS OF PERSONS

Topic 2. "Roturiers"

Topic 3. The Serfs

CHAPTER VIII

THE PERIOD OF MONARCHY. THE CONSTITUTIONAL MONARCHY

Topic 1. The Royal Power

Topic 2. Transmission of the Royal Power

Topic 3. Acquisition and Loss of the Crown

Topic 4. Exercise of the Sovereignty

Topic 5. The Royal Family

Topic 6. The Court

CHAPTER IX

THE MONARCHICAL PERIOD (*Continued*). THE STATES-GENERAL AND THE PROVINCIAL ESTATES

Topic 1. The States-General

Topic 2. Assemblies of Notables

Topic 3. The Provincial Estates

Topic 4. Provincial Assemblies

CHAPTER X

THE MONARCHICAL PERIOD (*Continued*). THE CENTRAL ADMINISTRATION

Topic 1. The Deliberative Organ, the Council of the King

Topic 2. The Executive Organ. The Ministry

CHAPTER XI

MONARCHICAL PERIOD (*Continued*). LOCAL ADMINISTRATION

Topic 1. The Bailiwicks and Seneschalships

Topic 2. The "Governments"

Topic 3. Taxing District ("Generalities")

Topic 4. Cities and Villages

CHAPTER XII

THE MONARCHICAL PERIOD (*Continued*). JUDICIAL ORGANIZATION

Topic 1. In General

Topic 2. The Parliaments

Topic 3. Parliaments of the Provinces

Topic 4. The Political Rôle of the Parliaments

Topic 5. Secondary Jurisdictions

Topic 6. The Judicial Personnel

Topic 7. Auxiliaries of Justice

CHAPTER XIII

THE MONARCHICAL PERIOD (*Continued*). FINANCIAL ORGANIZATION

Topic 1. Receipts and Expenses

Topic 2. The Royal Domain

Topic 3. Establishment of Taxes

Topic 4. Direct Taxes

CONTENTS

Topic 2. Principles of 1789

Topic 3. The Executive Power

Topic 4. The Legislative Power

Topic 5. Local Administration

Topic 6. Justice

TOPIC 7. FINANCES

TOPIC 8. THE ARMY

EDITORIAL PREFACE TO THIS VOLUME

By ERNST FREUND[1]

Brissaud had the uneventful career of the scholar devoted to work of research, and the annals of his life are brief and simple. The Editorial Preface to Volume III of this Series told what little could then be gleaned.[2] The following sketch is from the hand of one of his pupils, Mr. Paul Thomas (now successor to Brissaud as Professor of the History of French Law, and also Professor of Roman Law and of South French Law in the University of Toulouse), who has kindly consented to prepare it for this Volume.

"To the memory of J. B. Brissaud, Professor of Legal History in the Faculty of Toulouse.

'PIETAS DISCIPULI.'

"The 'Manual of the History of French Law,' the English translation of which is offered to the lawyers and historians of Great Britain and the United States of America, is the work of the very distinguished French professor, Jean Baptiste Brissaud. I had the honor of being his pupil, his respectful friend, and, later on, his colleague. These few lines of biographical preface, which the Editorial Committee of the Association of American Law Schools has asked me to write for this translation, are only a feeble tribute of my gratitude to the eminent master and of my admiration for the distinguished scholar.

"Brissaud was born at Puisserampion (Lot-et-Garonne, France) on December 7, 1854. He studied law at the University of Bordeaux, where he soon attracted attention by his power of work, mental vigor, and rare intellectual qualities. His thesis, written in 1879, on 'The Concept of Causa,' was a real revelation, and immediately made him known to those interested in scientific legal studies.

[1] Of the Editorial Committee; professor of Law in the University of Chicago.

[2] The present Volume represents Volume I of Brissaud's treatise; Volume III of this Series (Private Law) represents Volume II of Brissaud's treatise.

"The young doctor soon received a most flattering call to teach at the University of Berne, Switzerland. While devoting himself with zeal to the work of instruction, he prepared himself at the same time for the severe competitive tests which alone give access in France to the higher academic teaching. His efforts were crowned with success, and in 1883 he was named assistant in the law faculty of Montpellier.

"Two years later, in 1885, he obtained an appointment in the faculty of Toulouse; and in 1889 he succeeded Professor Ginouilhac in the chair of General History of Law. It was here, amidst the affectionate regard of all his colleagues, that he gave that example of untiring scientific activity to which death alone put an end. He became a member of the Toulouse Academy of Legislation, of the Academy of Sciences, Inscriptions, and Belles Lettres, and of the Archaeological Society, and his communications and observations were always received with the respect due to high scientific authority. Numerous journals in France and abroad, particularly the 'Nouvelle Revue Historique,' the 'Revue générale du droit,' the 'Annales du Midi,' the 'Revue des Pyrenées,' the 'Revue de l'Agenais,' published his writings, of which perhaps the following are the most notable: 'Gascon Folklore, and the Barbarous and Primitive Law of the Old Tales'; 'The Visigothic Legislation'; 'The Public Law of the South'; 'The Old Laws (fors) of Bearn.'

"His perfect familiarity with German permitted him to give to French students the translation of four volumes of the famous treatise on 'Roman Antiquities' by Mommsen and Marquardt. Brissaud translated the following volumes: Vol. 10, The Military Organization of the Romans, by Joachim Marquardt, translated in 1891; Vol. 12, Part I, The Worship of the Romans, by Joachim Marquardt, translated in 1889; Vol. 12, Part II, Worship of the Romans, by Joachim Marquardt; Roman Games, by Ludwig Friedlander, translated in 1890; Vol. 16, The History of the Sources of the Roman Law, by Paul Krüger, translated in 1894. Subsequently he published an excellent translation of the German work by Dickel, the Civil Code of Montenegro.

"Brissaud devoted himself at the same time with zeal to the study of provincial history and to the publications of the customs of the South of France, a complete collection of which has not yet appeared. An enthusiastic devotee of these researches, the importance of which for the history of French institutions in the South he understood so well, he prepared a valuable inventory of all publications relating to the old law of the South which had appeared from 1890 to 1900. This painstaking bibliography appeared in French in the German review, 'Kritischer Jahresbericht über die Romanische Philologie,' edited by Karl Vollmoller, Erlangen, 1901–1903, III, p. 60 ff.

"But his most perfect work, which was the fruit of the most indefatigable labor and won him a world reputation, was his 'Manual of the History of French Law,' which is now fortunately to be offered in a translation to the English-speaking world. The first part of this admirable work appeared in 1898.

"Carried away by his scientific zeal, the author far exceeded the limits which he had first set to himself. What was originally intended to be a simple manual for a student became a work in two volumes, which will remain an invaluable handbook of historical studies. This work gained for Brissaud a high tribute from the institutions of France; the Academy of Moral and Political Sciences awarded to him the Königswarter prize.

"But already the work had begun to exhaust the worker, and the excess of his labors finally undermined the health of the distinguished professor. He died on the 13th of August, 1904, less than fifty years old. By his death science lost one of its most devoted apostles; France one of its noblest reputations; and the University of Toulouse an eminent professor who has powerfully contributed to spread its influence and its fame." [1]

Brissaud's History stops with the end of the Revolutionary period. Any one who has studied law at German universities will remember that in the courses on legal history the principal stress was laid upon the medieval period, and the lectures became progressively more meager as modern times were approached. The explanation was sometimes offered that recent history was sufficiently covered by the lectures upon the existing law; which, however, was by no means the case. It was simply a bad tradition which had taken root in the legal curriculum, most easily accounted for by the greater difficulty of handling the unwieldy mass of modern material.

It is also a striking fact that of the three great histories of the

[1] (Signed) Paul Thomas, Professor of Roman Law at the University of Toulouse.

English Law, — Pollock and Maitland, Holdsworth, and Reeves, — the first is carried only to 1272, the second to the Middle Ages, and the third to the reign of Elizabeth. If it were not for the researches of the Webbs in Local Government, we should know next to nothing of some of the most significant phases of the judicial history of England.

But a French author may perhaps justify his not continuing a history of public law through the nineteenth century.

A superficial observer may get the impression that France during the past century underwent more frequent and radical changes than in any previous century. In a sense this is true: the outward form of government was overturned repeatedly; republic gave way to monarchy, and *vice versa*. And a new form of government regularly brought, in addition to the transformed executive, very important changes in the organization and exercise of legislative power. From the purely political point of view, it was undoubtedly an unsettled and restless period.

But if we look at public law from a juristic point of view the picture is very different. Governments came and went, very much as ministries come and go now, without disturbing the even course of French administrative processes; the details of the machinery are little affected by "overhead" revolutions. All that is characteristic of French public law was established before the Restoration and has since persisted. Administrative centralization; the judicial organization; the prefectoral system; the principle that to act is the function of one, to deliberate and to judge the function of a body; the doctrine of the "contentieux," securing a quasi-judicial control of administrative acts; the theory of political acts or acts of state; the organization of the audit of accounts; the function of the Council of State as representing the expert or technical and legal side of government, — all these either reach back into the old régime or are the products of Revolution and Empire.

After the downfall of Napoleon France ceased to originate and the legal history of the later 1800s is hardly of commanding interest to foreign nations. During a great portion of the past century, however, the heritage of the earlier period was the model which not only all the Latin nations, but also the countries of the nearer Orient and the German States, eagerly studied, and to a considerable extent copied or adapted to their conditions.

England and the United States, it is true, did not fall under the domination of French ideas. The tendency to systematize and to formulate precise logical categories is not congenial to the Anglo-Saxon political or legal mind. The very contrast, however, between the French and our method of treatment should prove instructive; and it would be strange indeed if the enormous mass of material brought together by Mr. Brissaud did not carry valuable lessons to English and American students.

When we remember that Norman French barons were the founders of modern English institutions, that large parts of France were for some centuries united to the English crown, and that hence the two countries started with many traditions of public law in common, we realize how interesting must be the process of gradual estrangement, and how profitable for us to be able to trace and compare the history of the public law of England and of France. The king's court and the justices; the parliament and the exchequer; the sheriffs and the bailiffs; the assizes and the juries; chancellors, writs, and jurisdictions — these and many other topics appear on the scene, under almost the same familiar terms, on both sides of the Channel, in the Norman period. And then comes the gradual melting away of common features, under the influence of different national destinies, into a new and composite picture; and the two sides of the Channel present two bodies of public law so different in their types that they have ever since furnished distinct models for the world's study and adaptation. Such is one of the chief interests which this volume has for the student of British and American law.

INTRODUCTION TO THIS VOLUME

By Harold Dexter Hazeltine [1]

Jean Brissaud's "Cours d'histoire générale du droit français public et privé," published in 1904, already ranks as one of the masterpieces of Continental legal literature It not only consolidates the results of researches by Viollet, Flach, Luchaire, Esmein, Fustel de Coulanges, and other scholars, but it also supplements the writings of these historians with the new learning that issued from Brissaud's own indefatigable study of the original sources themselves. Both in its substantial contribution to knowledge and in its literary charm Brissaud's great work will always be viewed as one of the most remarkable products of the new historical school.

The volume devoted to the history of French Private Law has already appeared in the present Continental Legal History Series. The other volume — the "History of French Public Law" — is now presented to students of Law and History in the admirable English form so characteristic of the work of the editors and translators engaged in this great undertaking. Although a complete view of French legal growth can only be obtained by reading both of these volumes together, each of them nevertheless is a distinct and separate literary work and may be studied by itself. May many a student take the present volume in his hands and read it from cover to cover thoughtfully and earnestly!

The book has lessons to teach; and each reader will best learn them for himself. While it is therefore no part of the province of the writer of these introductory paragraphs to draw attention to these lessons, a few words may yet be said as to the methods of the historian and the general contents of his work.

Brissaud's methods are those of a trained and skillful legal historian of the present-day scientific school. Master of his materials, he gives us not only detailed information, but also the great points in the life-story of institutions and of ideas. Everywhere he seeks the underlying social, economic, and political causes of legal

[1] Reader in English Law in Cambridge University.

growth itself. Everywhere he seeks the environment wherein constitutional institutions and principles have their origin and their growth, their decay, or their continuance, perhaps in altered form, down to modern times. These high purposes he has achieved by carefully marking off, one from another, distinct stages or epochs of development. His present treatise is, indeed, a notable proof of the fact that the historian of public law must distinguish, more carefully perhaps than the historian of private law, between different ages, if he would show us the main lines of development. In each one of the great periods which our historian has noted, we see the whole scheme or machinery of government, central and local, set forth in succinct and systematic manner. In each period we not only behold the various organs and instruments of government, but we are privileged to observe these organs and instruments at work, and to make acquaintance with the ideas and forces that create and propel the whole governmental machinery. Only by this historical method are we enabled to witness, for example, the origin, growth, and decay of the monarchical principle, and to behold the progress of various other principles that have shaped the public law of France throughout the long centuries of its history.

To this historical method — this tracing the whole French development by periods — Brissaud has added the comparative method. Through his intimate knowledge of the growth of European public law as a whole, he has been able to show us, at almost every stage of the French history, the similarities in and the differences between the constitutional institutions and notions of France and those of Germany, England, Sweden, and other countries. Thus do we behold the French constitution in its setting of European environment; and only by these comparisons does the French development stand out clearly. If argument were needed to prove the necessity of the comparative method in the study of legal history, Brissaud's work would be in itself sufficiently convincing. His gaze is directed at the whole of Europe and even beyond the European lands, for he draws valuable lessons from comparison of French with American and, occasionally, Oriental courses of development.

Brissaud's pages constitute, therefore, much more than a history of French constitutional government. Basing his work upon a firm foundation of comparative legal history, he reaches results as to the fundamental principles of state growth in general — not only in France, but in all the States of Western civilization.

Brissaud's results are of permanent value to students of all the countries of the Western world, for he has grasped this truth, and has taught us to see it, that no great State of modern times has arisen solely on its own territory independently of and uninfluenced by the great realm of Western institutions and ideas. Our author's grasp of the history of French public law is firm and enlightening for the very reason that he has adopted no narrow and purely French point of view, but has surveyed the whole course of history in all of Europe.

Brissaud's Introduction is a valuable contribution to comparative historical jurisprudence. Taking the origin of the State for his topic, he makes clear to us how political societies are formed, developed, reproduced, and, finally, how they pass away. This introductory chapter is an illuminating study of primitive society in general; and it places us in just the right intellectual atmosphere to understand the distinguishing features of French constitutional growth outlined in the main part of the volume. Basing his study upon this sure foundation, Brissaud then follows the fortunes of France, in their constitutional aspect, through the Roman, Frankish or Barbarian, Feudal, Monarchical, and Revolutionary Epochs. But the chronological limits of these great epochs are not drawn in any arbitrary way. We see how slowly and gradually the French State has passed from one epoch into another. In each period we get indications of the approach of the next. We see in the Frankish period the beginnings of the feudal ideas and institutions. In the feudal age we note the approach of the monarchy, and in the monarchical age itself we observe the causes already at work that will bring about the Revolution and the constitution of modern France.

Brissaud very properly makes no attempt to reconstruct the law and institutions of the Celts who in remote times occupied the territory of modern France; for, at best, such reconstruction, owing to the scantiness of really trustworthy sources, is fraught with many perils. An additional reason for passing over that remote age is found in the fact that not one of the institutions of the ancient Celts can be definitely proved to have survived in later times. By making the age of the Romans the first epoch in his history, Brissaud places his work upon solid ground; for it was the conquest and rule of the Romans which created Gaul by making it an integral part of the Roman world-state. The fall of the Western empire left a written law to the Gallo-Romans as well as to other European peoples.

A new period began with the inroads and settlements of the barbarians. Various kingdoms arose, most important of all the Frankish monarchy. The Merovingians made an heroic effort to administer the governmental machinery of the Romans; but that elaborate and delicate machinery proved to be unworkable by barbarian hands, and ultimately disappeared. By gifts and favors the king attached to himself the strong military class. Although the king claimed to be the successor of the Roman emperor, his position in the State acquired more and more a Germanic, or personal, character. He possessed the legislative power, but his direct authority came to be very materially limited by the grant of judicial and fiscal rights to great landowners. Through the alliance of the monarch and the Church, the Church became partly dependent upon the royal power, but at the same time gained new privileges for herself.

With the decay of the Merovingian dynasty and the rise of the Carolingian house, the political organism was consolidated by the growth of certain institutions which marked the beginnings of feudalism. The decentralization caused inevitably by the spread of the "beneficium" and the "commendatio" led to the reforms of Charlemagne. While recognizing and even sanctioning these institutions, Charlemagne yet reorganized the administrative machinery of the State with the object of maintaining the central authority. Chief among his judicial reforms was the establishment of the "missi dominici." Although ecclesiastical jurisdiction spread, the great king was still able to maintain, with a firm hand, his authority over the Church.

At length came the anarchy of the tenth and eleventh centuries. The old capitularies and the "leges" fell into disuse and were replaced, not by new legislation, for the legislative power was not exercised, but by territorial customs; and of real government there was little or nothing. Out of these conditions feudalism took firm root and developed rapidly. The royal power still existed, but seemed to grow weaker and weaker; while the Church, on the other hand, steadily increased in power.

This period of anarchy and of feudal growth was followed, in the twelfth and thirteenth centuries, by the age of feudal monarchy. The kingship grew in authority and position, partly owing to the revival of Roman Law, which modelled the rights of the king upon the rights of the Roman emperor. The king became the head of the feudal hierarchy and his organs of government were the institutions furnished by feudalism itself. Beaumanoir shows us clearly that the hierarchy of feudalism held complete control of the administration of justice. The doctrine he laid down at the close of the thirteenth century was that "all secular justice in France is held from the king as a fief or an 'arrière-fief.'" That "all justice emanates from the king" became the established doctrine of public law. With the rise of privileged towns a new element of feudal society came into power, an element that was at length brought under the protection of the king. So, too, in this period the process of reannexing the great fiefs to the crown was set in motion. By continuing this policy down to the very end of the "Ancien Régime" the kings at last reëstablished the territorial sovereignty of France. The twelfth century witnessed a revival of the exercise of legislative power by the crown; and in the thirteenth century this power was in full working vigor in all territories subject to the king. The growth of royal power was also manifest in changes that took place in administrative and judicial institutions. Feudal courts either disappeared or existed as tribunals of the royal authority. Royal officials everywhere rose to power..

Then came the age of limited monarchy — the fourteenth and fifteenth centuries. The direct exercise of the royal power was the object of new institutions, administrative and judicial, that now came into being. Even the old feudal institutions were shaped in harmony with crown policy. The old "curia regis" disappeared. In its place came the "parlement," a judicial body, and the "conseil du roi," a royal administrative council of non-feudal character. So too, at the beginning of the fourteenth century, arose the States-General ("états généraux") and the various provincial estates. A royal army was organized. Universal taxation by the crown became perhaps the most characteristic feature of the period.

In the period of absolute monarchy — from the sixteenth century to the Revolution — the essential principles of the old French public law were developed and defined. At length followed the Revolution itself. France became a constitutional country. Fixed and definite laws guaranteed the liberties of man. The written constitution could not be touched by the ordinary legislative power in the State.

How wonderfully illuminating to all constitutional students is this long story of government in France! And how masterfully Brissaud leads us on from one age to another, from one point to another! Even the details are enlightening when set forth for us by the great historian who views them but as parts of a living political organism! Consider, for instance, the care with which he has studied the origins and growth of feudalism from the point of view of public law. In all its manifold workings we see the feudal principle altering the whole character of governmental institutions, both central and local. Stubbs, after all his many years of labor among the medieval materials, did not see clearly the full influence of the feudal principle in the making of the English constitution. If to-day we can trace more accurately the history of the English Curia Regis and of all the central institutions that grew out of it, it is because we have learned, through the studies of Round and other present-day medievalists, that the Curia Regis of Norman times was a strictly feudal institution, and not a mere continuation of the old Anglo-Saxon witan.

Brissaud's study of the feudal constitution of France will still further instruct English and American scholars and will unquestionably show them the way to a deeper appreciation of the nature and scope of feudalism as a system of English public law. The Anglo-American school of legal historians has pretty thoroughly mastered feudalism as a system of land law, the basis of modern English real property law. Still further work should now be devoted to the study of feudalism in its constitutional aspect. English medieval public law was undoubtedly influenced by forces other than feudalism; but the feudal principle shaped constitutional institutions and rules to an extent not yet fully understood.

Brissaud's work is, then, a history of constitutional institutions and of the material and intellectual forces that shaped and worked those institutions. The historian's gaze is ever upon the living political organism of the State as it grew from age to age in its environment of Western civilization. He makes us actually see the growing fabric of the State in France, because he makes us see also the social, economic, and ecclesiastical factors that enveloped and influenced the life of the State. It is by reason of this broad viewpoint, this consideration of the history of Europe in all its main aspects, that Brissaud's work will ever be prized by students of the constitution and law of European countries outside France herself. It is by reason of this broad viewpoint that students of the history of private law and of social and economic conditions will also seek light and guidance in a work that professes to deal only with the history of public law.

INTRODUCTION TO THIS VOLUME

By Westel W. Willoughby[1]

It is not inherently impossible for abstract political speculation to produce an ideally perfect system of political organization, — one which, under ideal objective conditions, will be the best when judged from the point of view of the conception which is framed as to man's highest good. It is now recognized, however, that it is futile to attempt to construct a polity which will be the best for all peoples irrespective of their special racial characteristics, and their intellectual, moral, and industrial development, and without regard to their geographical position. Thus it is seen that it has not been a matter of historical accident or of misdirected effort that each nation in the working out of its own political destiny has constructed for itself its own peculiar governmental structure, and developed its own special rules and principles in accordance with which this machinery is operated.

This principle as to the relativity of political institutions is, however, not to be taken as indicating that political evolution should be an unplanned development, a growth undirected by ideals conscious in the minds of those in authority. Nor does it mean that nations should refrain from borrowing political methods from one another. It does declare, however, that only those foreign methods can be safely introduced which comport with the special conditions to which they are to be applied, and that when an institution is taken from another country all that is collaterally implied in that institution, the understandings as well as the explicit provisions, should also be accepted. It is not surprising, therefore, that parliamentary methods have not worked in the same manner or as successfully in European countries as in the country from which they were borrowed, when it is seen that the borrowing countries have not accepted, or at least have not been able to provide, the political conditions and legislative rules which are essential to the effective operation of cabinet government.

[1] Professor of Political Science in Johns Hopkins University; former President of the American Political Science Association.

To us in America the chief interest in the history of the political institutions which is traçed in the present volume must consist in the picture which is presented of the efforts of a great people, extending through a long period of time, to create and maintain what, in the stricter sense of the term, may be held to be a constitutional government. And, especially, our interest will be to discover in how far the constitutional conceptions which have been evolved approximate to those of our own.

In the broadest sense of the word every politically organized society has a constitution which, written or unwritten, determines the political instrumentalities which shall exist and the powers which shall be assigned to them. In a narrower sense of the word, however, a State is said to be constitutionally organized only when those who possess and exercise political authority have their competencies more or less precisely defined, and when orderly means exist for holding these functionaries politically and legally responsible for the use or misuse of their powers. This political responsibility means that the governed, or at least a considerable portion of them, have the legal power through the suffrage or otherwise to determine the form of government which shall exist, and the persons who shall administer it. 'The delimitation of constitutional powers and the enforcement of legal responsibility of public officials for all acts done under color of public authority signifies that the citizen body is protected against oppression by the government and that its members are guaranteed the possession and exercise of those rights of life, liberty, and property which the private law recognizes.

Within the broad field of constitutional government thus defined opportunity exists for a great variety of governmental structures and of political practices. Some of these differences are so important as to mark off governments into definite species. In Prussia, Italy, Austria, Hungary, and Belgium, not to mention other states, there exists what is known as constitutional monarchy,[1] and Turkey and Russia are less developed examples of the same type. Here, representative assemblies exist and participate in the enactment of laws, but their legislative powers are neither original not decisive. The law-making power is held to be vested in the monarch. He it is whose will gives legal force to all enactments. In other words, the chambers, whether popular or aristo-

[1] The German Empire exhibits certain essential features of constitutional monarchy, the "Bundesrath" possessing the characteristic functions of a constitutional ruler.

cratic, are deemed to participate in determining the content of the laws but not in giving to them legal force. Furthermore, in conformity with the general principle that all political authority springs from the monarch, the doctrine is held that such limits upon the royal power as exist are founded upon royal grant and are, therefore, only formal in character, and, in theory at least, subject to alteration or abrogation at the will of the reigning sovereign. This means, of course, that the written constitutions, whatever may have been the historical circumstances attending their creation, are, in the eyes of the law and of constitutional theory, *octroyed* rather than established by the people who, in fact, have forced their promulgation.

It is clear that while such a conception of constitutional monarchy as this exists, true parliamentary government, such as obtains in England, cannot develop. There, monarchy has not been abolished, but its fundamental basis has been changed and the European conception definitely abandoned. Since 1688 the monarchy is conceded to be a parliamentary one. Certain prerogative powers are still recognized as inhering and having their original source in the crown, but these are not such as to give the king, in fact or potentially, controlling authority. Such rights as the other organs of government possess, even if originally obtained by royal grant, are held to have been absolutely alienated by the King, and their basis found henceforth in the consent of the people. The King reigns but no longer governs. As Lowell has so strikingly expressed it, the English King no longer furnishes the motive power of the ship of state, and is but the spar upon which the parliamentary sails are bent.

In Switzerland, aside from its federal form and the democratic institutions of the initiative, the referendum, and, in several of its cantons, the "Landesgemeinde," a unique form of governmental control has been developed. Monarchy does not exist, nor, in its place, is there a president or other executive organ which exercises powers similar to those of the constitutional monarch. The legislative body has retained for itself executive as well as legislative control. The executive board, whose chairman has the title of President of the Swiss Republic, acts only as an administrative and executive board to carry out the commands of its superior, the National Assembly. Having no considerable discretionary powers of its own, it is not a political body in the sense that its personnel is determined by partizan considerations or by political majorities in the Assembly.

In the United States[1] the constitutional doctrine that no political organ possesses inherent powers is fundamental. The executive as well as the judicial and legislative branches of government derive their powers from the same source — the people. Political authority comes from below and not from above. We have seen fit, moreover, to separate the executive and legislative branches of our government, and, in a very large measure, to render them in their operations independent of one another. Also we have divided our Congress into two branches of practically coördinate powers. In practice, especially during recent years, the President has used the powers which the Constitution gives to him, and his position as the representative of the whole people rather than of a smaller constituency, to exercise an increasing *de facto* control over the legislative branch; but it is not possible, under our present constitutional arrangements, for a form of parliamentary government to develop similar to that which exists in Great Britain.

Leaving aside, however, political practice and reverting to constitutional theory, that which essentially distinguishes the American constitutional system — aside from its federal form — is that the legal omnipotence of the legislature is denied, and the courts given the power, which they habitually exercise, to refuse recognition to such legislative acts as, in their opinion, contravene the provisions of the written Constitution.

In the present volume Professor Brissaud has traced, with a wealth of detail and learning, the historical development of French political institutions until the time when France may be said to have succeeded in definitely establishing a constitutional government in the sense in which we have been using the term. For more than a hundred years, with but brief interruptions, she has been governed under constitutions which have contained the explicit affirmance of "national sovereignty" — that all political powers spring from the people. Monarchy has been abolished and, in its place, a presidency established and parliamentary institutions introduced. But, upon the one hand, the President has not been granted powers at all comparable with those possessed by our chief executive; and, upon the other hand, the legislative chambers have not been willing, as the English House of Commons has been, to grant to their cabinets those controlling powers which are essential to the effective working of the true cabinet or parliamentary system of government.

[1] I shall here speak only of the national government.

France has a written constitution, indeed, she has had many of them, but she has not deemed it expedient to grant to her courts the final constitutional interpretative power, and the authority to declare void of legal force legislative acts which are not warranted by the fundamental instrument of government. Furthermore, the French have so interpreted the principle of the "separation of powers" as to deny to the ordinary courts competency to pass upon many questions of administrative authority which, according to the practice of England and the United States, are matters for ordinary judicial cognizance. Instead, there has been created a system of administrative tribunals and courts of conflict for the determination of these questions. This practice is in harmony with the highly integrated and independent administrative system which France developed before the Revolution and which Napoleon perfected.

It is clear that where there exists no written constitution and the legal omnipotence of the legislative body is recognized, as in England; or where, as in France, a written instrument of government has been adopted, but with the final power of interpreting it placed in the hands of the legislature, — the individual has not that secure possession of constitutional rights which he has in the United States. The term "unconstitutional law" is not unknown to English and French jurisprudence, but it must have a meaning in those countries different from that which it has in the United States. That the French conception of the distinction between constitutional and ordinary laws is not a satisfactory one is made evident by such studies as those of Gajac and Santoni each bearing the title "De la distinction des lois constitutionelles et des lois ordinaires," the former published in 1903 and the latter in 1913. It is interesting to note, also, that just at the time when the American people seem to be becoming impatient of the restraints upon legislative power which their conception of constitutional law imposes, these writers urge that means be adopted in France for guaranteeing the supremacy of constitutional provisions over ordinary statutory enactments.

It is not until we are fully halfway through Brissaud's volume that we meet the term "constitution" in its modern sense, and it is not until then that the question is raised as to the existence of constitutional limitations upon the powers of the monarch in favor of the liberties of the individual. Before this the course of development of the controlling power which has been traced has been an almost uninterrupted one towards autocracy. Step by step the absolute sovereignty of the king extends over the whole domain of France. One by one the opposing powers in the realm are overcome until, in the time of Louis the Fourteenth, the proud boast of that monarch that in his person all the authority of the State is incarnate, is justified by accepted constitutional theory. But neither theory nor fact support the doctrine that the people of France are subject to a despotism in which the caprice of the monarch serves as law. All writers and statesmen are agreed that there exist "fundamental laws" such as, for example, the rules of succession to the throne, the liberties of the Gallican Church, and many others, which control the exercise of royal power; and from the jurisprudence of natural law principles, both of justice and of expediency, are derived, the controlling force of which, it is declared, should be recognized by the King and his agents. Liberalists and absolutists differ only as to the number and character of these fundamental laws. Furthermore, it may be observed, in practice there had not developed, even during the time of the Grand Monarch, that habit of obedience of administrative agents to the commands of their official superiors which, in the present, makes possible effective centralized control. It may also be added that the legislative activity of the State in the field of private law which has characterized more modern times had not then arisen, and, as a result, comparatively little attempt was made to exert the plenitude of centralized power for the arbitrary alteration of the laws by which the ordinary relations and transactions of private life were regulated.

It still remained true, however, that the citizen body as a whole was without any right to participate in the administration of its own government, or directly to exercise any influence upon its policies; and that, individually, each citizen held his rights of life, liberty, and property upon an insecure tenure. A single paragraph quoted from Brissaud describing the status of private rights prior to the Revolution will sufficiently indicate this.

"Individual liberty had no guarantees against arbitrary warrants of imprisonment ('lettres de cachet'), arbitrary arrests, justice by commissioners, or accusations for 'lèse majesté.' There was nothing which recalled the inviolability of the domicile of the English law. Private property was no more sheltered than the individual from arbitrary measures; general confiscation, expropriation without indemnity, excessive taxes, and dues demanded by the King in pursuance of his right of eminent domain. Nor did anything guarantee to individuals respect for their mutual engagements. In maintaining that the King had no right to take the property of others or to violate private agreements, Bodin invoked natural law; but the positive legislation did not afford in a like case any means of defense to subjects against the King. Freedom of labor, of commerce, and of industry existed only imperfectly; it was shackled by a multitude of regulations. Liberty of conscience was unknown, state religion, persecution of nonconformists, tutelage of the Gallican Church in such a manner as to transform the parish priests into administrative agents; that was the 'Ancien Régime.' In the place of liberty of the press, the 'Ancien Régime' did not cease to push to excess a system at once preventive and repressive; previous authorization was required to publish every writing, a censorship was exercised by the Parliament, the Sorbonne, the clergy, and the Council of States, and heavy penalties imposed against libels. The violation of the secrecy of correspondence had always existed since the establishment of the postal service. And, naturally, the 'Ancien Régime' did not recognize the right of association, of assembly, the liberty of instruction, etc."

No one who is interested in the history of human liberty, or in the institutional development of a great people, can fail to find absorbing interest in the description which our author gives of the development of the powers of the States-General, and of the Parliaments prior to the Revolution; nor read, without gaining a better comprehension of the meaning of civil and political liberty, the account given of the constitutional theories propounded and the successive popular rights asserted during the progress of that great drama which closed the eighteenth century and ushered in the régime of political liberty, — a liberty which, with some brief interruptions, the French have enjoyed to the present day.

In no other work available in English is there to be found an account comparable in learning to that which Brissaud has given us of the steps by which, from the earliest times, the political institutions of France have come into being and developed until the present constitutional period is reached. Here is set forth in detail in their processes of historical growth all the many administrative agencies, central and local, which the French people have created for the performance of the tasks which political life imposes.

GENERAL REFERENCE LIST OF TREATISES CITED

The reader will find more detailed bibliographical references in the works cited, in the general treatises indicated below, and in such bibliographical repertories as:

Camus and Dupin, "Profession d'Avocat, Bibliographie choisie des Livres de Droit," II, 5th ed., 1832.

G. Monod, "Bibliographie de l'Histoire de France," 1888.

U. Chevalier, "Répertoire des Sources Historiques du Moyen Age," 1883 *et seq.*

R. de Lasteyrie and E. Lefèvre-Portalis, "Bibliographie générale des Travaux Historiques publiés par les Sociétés savantes de la France," 1888 *et seq.*

Holtzendorff, "Encyclopädie der Rechtswissenschaft in systematischer und alphabetischer Bearbeitung," 4th ed., 1882. The systematic part, volume one, contains in a very substantial form abridged histories of Canon law, of German, French, Norman, English, and Scandinavian law. The alphabetical part, or "Rechtslexicon," gives under each name the works of the author.

O. Mühlbrecht, "Wegweiser durch die neuere Literatur des Rechts- und Staatswissenschaften," 1893.

History of Roman Law. — Public Law: *Mommsen and Marquardt*, "Manuel des Antiquités Romaines," French translation, 1887 *et seq.* *Mispoulet*, "Les Institutions politiques des Romains," 1882–83. *Bouché-Leclercq*, "Manuel des Institutions Romaines," 1886. *Mommsen*, "Abriss des römischen Staatsrecht," 1893. Private Law: *Accaria*, "Précis de Droit Romain," 4th ed., 1886. *Cuq*, "Les Institutions juridiques des Romains," I, 1891. *P. F. Girard*, "Manuel élémentaire de Droit Romain," 1896 (and numerous authors cited therein).

History of French Law. — *Laferrière*, "Histoire du Droit Français," 1845–58. *Warnkoenig and Stein*, "Französische Staats- und Rechtsgeschichte," 1846–48. *Schaeffner*, "Geschichte der Rechtsverfassung Frankreichs," 1849–50, 2d ed., 1859. *Koenigswarter*, "Sources et Monuments du Droit Français antérieurs au Quinzième Siècle," 1853. *Gasquet*, "Précis des Institutions politiques et sociales de l'ancienne France," 1885. *Ginoulhiac*, "Cours élémentaire d'Histoire générale du Droit Français, public et privé," 1st ed., 1884; 2d ed., 1890. *Viollet*, "Précis de l'Histoire du Droit Français," 1884–86. The second edition is entitled "Histoire du Droit Civil Français," 1893. *Glasson*, "Histoire du Droit et des Institutions de la France," I to VII (incomplete), 1887–96. *Esmein*, "Cours élémentaire d'Histoire du Droit Français," 1892, 2d ed., 1895. *Fustel de Coulanges*, "Histoire des Institutions politiques de l'ancienne France," 1882–92 (ed.

Julian). *Flach*, "Les Origines de l'ancienne France," 1886–93. *Luchaire*, "Manuel des Institutions Françaises," 1892. *Chéruel*, "Dictionnaire historique des Institutions, Mœurs et Coutumes de la France," 1st ed., 1855.

History of Belgian Law. — *Warnkoenig*, "Histoire du Droit Belgique," 1827, and "Flandrische Staats- und Rechtsgeschichte," 1835–42. *Defacqz*, "Ancien Droit Belgique," 1846–73. *Britz*, "Code de l'Ancien Droit Belgique," 1847.

History of Swiss Law. — *V. Orelli*, "Vorlesungen über schweizer. Rechtsgeschichte," 2d ed., 1884.

History of German Law. — *Grimm*, R. A. = "Rechtsalterthümer," 1828, 3d ed.; same, 1881. *G. Waitz*, V. G. = "Deutsche Verfassungsgeschichte," I and II, 3d ed., 1880–82; III–VI, 2d ed., 1883–96; VII–VIII, 1st ed., 1878. *Stobbe*, "Geschichte der deutschen Rechtsquellen," 1860–64; "Handbuch des deutschen Privatsrechts," 1885. *Schulte*, "Lehrbuch der deutschen Reichs- und Rechtsgeschichte," 5th ed., 1881 (French translation by *Fournier*, "Histoire du Droit et des Institutions de l'Allemagne," 1882). *Siegel*, "Deutsche Rechtsgeschichte," 1886. *Brunner*, "Deutsche Rechtsgeschichte," 1887–92. *Schroeder*, "Lehrbuch der deutschen Rechtsgeschichte," 1889. *Heusler*, "Institutionen des deutschen Privatrechts," 1885–86. *Frommhold*, "Deutsche Rechtsgeschichte," 1894. *Thudichum*, "Geschichte des deutschen Privatrechts," 1894. "Untersuchungen zur Deutschen Staats- und Rechtsgeschichte," edited by *Gierke*.

Among the old histories may be mentioned those of *Eichorn*, *Phillips*, *Hildebrand*, *Daniels*, *Zoepfl*, *Walter*. *Cf. Schulte*, translated by *Fournier*, p. 10, and *Brunner*, I, 19. On the history of Scandinavian law *cf. Brunner*, bibliography, I. 13.

History of English Law: *Glasson*, "Histoire du Droit et des Institutions de l'Angleterre," 1882–83. *Pollock and Maitland*, "History of English Law before the Time of Edward I," 1895.

History of Spanish and Portuguese Law. — *Sempere*, "Historia del Derecho Español," 3d ed., 1846. *Brauchitsch*, "Geschichte des spanischen Rechts," 1852. *Helfferich*, "Entstehung und Geschichte des Westgotenrechts," 1858. *Antequera*, "Historia de la Legislación Española," 1874. *Hinojosa*, "Historia General del Derecho Español," I, 1887. On the history of Portuguese law see *Camus*, p. 637.

History of Italian Law. — *Sclopis*, "Storia della Legislazione Italiana," 1833 (French translation, 1861). *Pertile*, "Storia del Diritto Italiano," 1st ed., 1871; 2d ed. *La Mantia*, "Storia della Legislazione Italiana," 1884. *Salvioli*, "Manuale di Storia del Diritto Italiano," 1890. *Calisse*, "Storia del Diritto Italiano," 1891. *Schupfer*, "Manuale di Storia del Diritto Italiano, Le Fonti," 1892.

TABLE OF ABBREVIATIONS MOST FREQUENTLY USED

"A. C." = "Ancienne Coutume."
"Archiv. Parl." = *Madival and Laurent*, "Archives Parlementaires," 1867 *et seq.* (The "Cahiers" of the States-General will also be found included within them.)
"Ac. Sc. Morales" = "Comptes Rendus de l'Académie des Sciences morales et politiques," 1840 *et seq.*
"Ac. Inscr." = "Académie des Inscriptions et Belles-Lettres," 1717 *et seq.*
"Ac. Législ." = "Recueil de l'Académie de Législation de Toulouse," 1851 *et seq.*
"Atti Modena," "Parma," etc. = "Atti e Memorie delle Deputazioni di Storia Patri di Modena," "Parma," "Bologna," etc.
D. Bouquet = *Dom Bouquet*, "Recueil des Historiens des Gaules et de la France," 1738–1876.
B. de R. = *Bourdot de Richebourg*, "Nouveau Coutumier Général," 1724.
"Bourg." = "Coutume de Bourgogne."
"B. Chartes" = "Bibliothèque de l'Ecole des Chartes," 1835 *et seq.*
"B. Comité hist." = "Bulletin du Comité des Travaux historiques," 1882 *et seq.*
"Bull. crit." = "Bulletin critique," 1880 *et seq.*
"B. Hist. France" = "Bulletin de la Société pour l'Histoire de France," 1834 *et seq.*
"B. Hist. Prot." = "Bulletin de la Société pour l'Histoire du Protestantisme," 1852 *et seq.*
"B. Lég. comparée" = "Bulletin de la Société de Législation comparée," 1869.
"B. Antiquaires de France" = "Bulletin de la Société des Antiquaires de France," 1817.
"Cap." = "Capitularia Regum Francorum," ed. *Boretius and Krause*, 1881.
"C. Th." or "Cod. Theod." = "Code Theodosien," ed. *Haenel*, 1842.
"C. J." or "Cod. Just." = "Code Justinien," ed. *Krüger*, 1877.
"C. J. C." = "Corpus Juris Civilis," ed. *Mommsen and Krüger*, 1866–77–95.
"C. J. Can." = "Corpus Juris Canonici," ed. *Friedberg*, 1878–80.
"Conc." = "Concilia," ed. *Bruns*, or *Massen*, or *Labbe*, etc., according to the name which precedes. *Cf. infra.*
"D. Grég." or "X" = "Décrétales de Grégoire IX" or "Extra.," ed. *Friedberg*, 1878–80.
Daremb. = *Daremberg and Saglio*, "Dictionnaire des Antiquités," 1873.
"D." or "Dig." = "Digest," ed. *Mommsen*, 1866–70.
"Dipl." = see *Pardessus*.
"Forschungen" = "Forschungen zur deutschen Geschichte," 1860.
"G. Chr." = "Gallia Christiana," 1715–1865.
"Gr. Cout." = "Grand Coutumier."
Guyot, "Rép." = *Guyot*, "Répertoire de Jurisprudence," 1775–86.
Huber = *E. Huber*, "System und Geschichte des schweitzeischen Privatrechts."
Isambert = "Recueil des Anciennes Lois Françaises de 420 à 1789," by *Jourdan, Decrusy, and Isambert*, 1822–27.
"J. Savants" = "Journal des Savants," 1665 *et seq.*
"L. Sal.," "L. Rib.," "L. Bai.," etc., or "Sal.," "Rib.," "Bai.," etc. = "Lex Salica," "Lex Ribuaria," "Lex Baiuwariorum," etc., etc.
Loysel 100 = *Loysel*, "Institutes Coutumières," Rule 100 of the *Dupin and Laboulaye* edition.
Leber = *Leber*, "Collection des meilleurs Dissertations, Notices et Traités particuliers relatifs à l'Histoire de France," 1826–42.
"L. L." = Leges.
"M. Antiquaires de France" = "Mémoires de la Société des Antiquaires de France."

"Mém. Paris" = "Mémoires de la Société de l'Histoire de Paris," 1874 *et seq.*
"M. Boica" = "Monumenta Boica," 1769.
"M. G. H." = "Monumenta Germaniæ Historica," 1826.
"M. H. Portug." = "Portugalliæ Monumenta Historica," 1870–73.
"M. H. Patr." = "Historiæ Patriæ Monumenta, Chartæ," Turin, 1836. etc.
Migne, "P. L." = *Migne*, "Patrologie latine," 1879 *et seq.*
"N. C." = "Nouvelle Coutume."
"N. R. H." = "Nouvelle Revue Historique de Droit Français et Etranger."
"Ord." = "Ordonnances des Rois de France de la Troisième Race," 1723–1849 (known as collection of the Louvre).
Pard. or *Pardessus*, "Dipl." = *Pardessus*, "Diplomata, Chartæ et Instrumenta Ætatis Merowingicæ," 1841–49.
"Paris" = "Coutume de Paris," and so generally names of places cited alone followed by numbers indicate the Custom of that place; *e.g.*, "Toulouse" = "Coutume de Toulouse," etc.
Pérard = *Pérard*, "Pièces curieuses servant à l'Histoire de Bourgogne," 1654.
"R. A." = *Grimm*, "Rechtsalterthümer," 1828, 3d ed., 1881.
"R. Brit. Scriptores" = "Rerum Britannicarum Medii Ævi Scriptores," 1858 *et seq.*
Recueils périodiques (*cf. Monod*, *op. cit.* p. 121). R. = "Revue," "Review," "Revista," "Rivista"; in German, Z. = "Zeitschrift"; J. = "Journal"; Ann. = "Annuaire"; Mem. = "Mémoires"; Jahr. = "Jahrbuch"; Mitth. = "Mittheilungen"; Beitr. = "Beiträge"; Atti = "Actes."
"R. Quest. hist." = "Revue des Questions historiques," 1866 *et seq.*
"R. H." = Revue historique," *G. Monod*, 1876 *et seq.*
"R. crit. d'Hist." = "Revue critique d'Histoire et de Littérature."
"R. H. D." = "Revue Historique de Droit Français et Etranger," 1855–69.
"R. L." = "Revue de Législation ancienne et moderne," 1870–77.
"R. G." = "Revue générale du Droit," 1877.
Schmidt, "Ang." = *Schmidt*, "Gesetze der Angelsachsen," 2d ed., 1858.
Schoepflin = *Schoepflin*, "Alsatia diplomatica," 1772–75.
Sagnac = *Sagnac*, "La Législation Civile de la Révolution Française," 1898.
S. S. = Scriptores.
"T. A. C." = "Trés Ancienne Coutume."
D. Vaissette = "Histoire générale de Languedoc," by *Dom Cl. Devic and D. Vaissette*, ed. *Privat*, 1874.
Varin = *Varin*, "Archives législatives de la Ville de Reims," 1840.
"V. G." = *Waitz*, "Deutsche Verfassungsgeschichte," I and III, 3d ed., 1880–82; III–VI, 2d ed., 1883–96; VII–VIII, 1st ed., 1878.
"Z. R. G." = "Zeitschrift für geschichtliche Rechtswissenschaft," 1815 to 1850; "Zeitschrift für Rechtsgeschichte," 1862–78.
"Z. S. S." = "Zeitschrift der Savigny-Stiftung für Rechtsgeschichte," from 1880.
"Z. V. R." = "Zeitschrift für vergleichende Rechtwissenschaft," 1882.

Treatises such as those by Stobbe, Pertile, Glasson, Pollock and Maitland, etc., which are given in the General Reference List, *ante*, p. lv, are cited by the names of their authors, followed by numerals. For example, Stobbe; Pertile; etc.

The Roman numerals following the citation generally indicate the volume, the Arabic the page. This is not invariable, however, as *Loysel* 100 means rule 100 of Loysel's "Institutes Coutumières," and "Paris, A. C.," 100, means article 100 of the "Ancienne Coutume de Paris," and in the Customs the Arabic numeral always refers to the article. By referring to the works cited or the Reference List this distinction as to the numerals may readily be ascertained.

HISTORY OF FRENCH PUBLIC LAW

Introduction

THE ORIGIN OF THE STATE

I. General Observations

II. Elementary and Composite Societies

I. General Observations[1]

§ 1. **Society and State.** — When we speak of society we mean a group of men acting collectively in a common interest. This

[1] Bibliography: *A. Comte*, "Sociologie," 1845; *H. Spencer*, "Introd. à la science sociale"; "Principes de sociologie"; *Bagehot*, "Lois scientifiques du développement des nations," 1873; *Schaeffle*, "Bau u. Leben d. sozialen Koerpers," 1874; *G. Le Bon*, "Lois psychologiques de l'évolution des peuples," 1882; *Durkheim*, "Les règles de la méthode sociologique," 1892; "Division du travail social," 1896; *Hauriou*, "La science sociale traditionnelle," 1896; *Worms*, "Organisme et société," 1895; *Vignes*, "La science sociale d'après les principes de Le Play," 1897; *Labriola*, "Essai sur la conception matérialiste de l'histoire," 1897; *E. Ferri*, "Socialisme et science positive," 1897; *Giddings*, "Principes de sociologie," 1897; *Perrier*, "Les colonies animales" ("R. encycl.," 24 avril 1897); *Espinas*, "Les sociétés animales," 1885; *Roscher*, "Politik," 1890; "Gr. Encyclop.," see "Etat"; *Orlando*, "Diritto costituzionale," 1894.

coöperation may be momentary or lasting, voluntary or forced, imposed by a higher authority or spontaneously resulting from pressing necessity. In any case, collaboration cannot take place without a certain amount of organization, however rudimentary it may be conceived; in order to secure concert of action, it is indispensable that there should be understanding and discipline, and that each one should perform his task and be able to depend on the others to do theirs. Nearly everywhere a coercive apparatus or government has been established in order to assure coöperative organization, for the advantages which it offers are so great that men have not considered that they were paying too much when they have given their independence in exchange for these advantages.

It is this coercive apparatus, this organ by means of which collective action is carried out, that is called the State or Government; but the function which this organ fulfils is also designated by the name State. In this second sense, the State is the society considered in its political function. This function cannot be precisely defined, for it has varied and still varies among different societies, and at different epochs. The jurist may attempt to give us a definition at some particular time, in order to construct a logical system of public law. The historian cannot do this, because he does not see institutions in a fixed state, but in process of evolution. The political function has its evolutionary "processus" just as the family or property has. There are societies in which collective action occurs only intermittently, and where it amounts to very little, being merely a struggle against enemies from without, and a very crude internal organization, for the purpose of attack or for defence. The State in primitive societies often takes no interest in justice and law; it is no more a creation of reason than were the primitive gods, brutal forces of nature; but like these, it develops into one. Elsewhere, on the other hand, the action of the State is very far-reaching; it regulates private life, directs industry, and presides over religion; it is at one and the same time a church and an industrial or agricultural organization. The political function of society has a marked tendency to develop, but at the same time the division of labor introduces into it departments which are distinct and almost independent, each of the other; the political, the religious, and the industrial apparatus become separated. The sovereignty, or the power of the political organ over the social body, the relation of the individual to the State, forms of government and revolutions, —

all are questions which complicate the public law of more advanced societies.

§ 2. **The Organic Theory of the State.** — There is no lack of systems which attempt to explain the origin of the State.

The theory of divine right assumes that human authority is derived from divine authority; it is a theological postulate.

The theory of the social contract is an idealistic conception, originating in the systems of natural law and standing in opposition to historical truth. For in reality, men group themselves together and submit to authority only under the pressure of necessity; the basis of society is not a free compact, but the result of compulsion from without and a reaction which results therefrom; it is for the purpose of resisting external forces that men associate themselves together.[1]

The organic theory of the State is more in accordance with the facts. Human societies, which are aggregations of individuals and of families, resemble living organisms which are groups of cells. Sociology is certainly not biology, but there are points of resemblance between them, and there are certain analogies between social facts and biological phenonema. Why not point out and utilize the elements of similarity which one observes, for the purposes of better portraying how societies are organized?[2] In human societies, as in the living body, organization is effected through the division of labor, resulting in the localization of functions, in the formation of organs and apparatus better and better adapted to the functions which they fulfil, and in an ever increasing interdependence of parts.

§ 3. **Localization of Functions.** — In the lower organisms (Protozoa), each part is at the same time stomach, breathing apparatus, and organ of locomotion; under the influence of their surroundings these functions become localized; a physiological

[1] *Fustel de Coulanges*: "Political institutions are never the work of the will of one man. Even the will of a whole people is insufficient to establish them. The human facts which give rise to them are not among those which the whim of one generation can change. People are not governed because it so pleases them, but because the totality of their interests and their convictions demand that they should be. . . ." "Hist. des instit. polit. de l'anc. France," Introd., t. I. We may add that there is nothing voluntary in these convictions; they are a product, a result. Institutions do not depend upon intentions, but upon convictions.

[2] On the condition that the establishment of a simple analogy is not to be taken as a demonstration. Social facts must be studied separately by themselves, and the laws which govern them, directly established. I shall not stop at the metaphysical objection that the individual is an end in himself, while the cell is not.

division of labor takes place; one part becomes stomach and no longer serves any other purpose; another, breathing apparatus; and a third, an organ of locomotion. Thus in primitive societies each individual hunts, fishes, wages war, builds his house, and cooks his food, while in more highly advanced societies the population is grouped into classes, or even into castes, — priests, warriors, farmers; thus a division of social labor takes place. He who is best situated or most skilful, specializes in his particular function.

§ 4. **Changes of Structure.** — Once the need has created the organ, the latter adapts itself more and more to its particular function; in order to do this it changes its form. The different parts of the living body, all of which began as simple cells, end by differing, one from the other, to such an extent that they cannot replace one another in their respective functions: for example, bony tissue differs from mucous membranes, nerves from muscles, etc. Changes of structure are less apparent in man, although there is a difference between a burly fellow of the market-place and a member of the Institute of France. But they exist, nevertheless, and they make changes from one occupation to another difficult, if not impossible, as we see in the case of unemployed laborers when a new machine has been invented.

§ 5. **Interdependence of the Parts.** — As soon as the parts of a living organism have developed differences among themselves, and each has taken on its special function, they can no longer exist independently, one from another. If we cut a sponge in two, each half will continue to live; an animal of a higher species subjected to this treatment would die immediately, and, if another example is desired, the old story of the stomach and its members supplies it. The interdependence of individuals in our civilized societies is scarcely less. A strike of miners or of bakers deprives us of fuel or bread, and thus becomes a public affair.

§ 6. **Organs and Apparatus.** — The organ, once created, develops under the action of its environment and becomes an apparatus or a collection of organs tending toward a single end. Thus the stomach is transformed into a digestive organ; that which in the lower species is merely a pouch becomes complex in animals of a higher order, and develops into a mouth for seizing the food, a stomach for digesting it, and an intestine for extracting therefrom nutritive juices. Society likewise has its organs and apparatus: 1st, *Productive (or nutritive) apparatus:* agriculture and industry, which become localized like the functions of a living being. Such, for example, are the salt and fishery industries on the sea coast, and the breeding of cattle on the plains, etc. 2d, *Circulatory apparatus:* commerce, which transports from one place to another the products of agriculture and industry, giving rise to currents more or less active, and to a circulation either slow or rapid, somewhat like the circulation of blood in warm or cold blooded animals. 3d, *Directing apparatus:* the political system, which coördinates the action of social forces in somewhat the same manner as the nervous system does in a living organism.

§ 7. **Political Forms.** — The political organs in a simple society are three in number: a general assembly of all its members for deciding questions of common interest (such as removal from one place to another, peace or war); a directing group composed of the oldest and the strongest (the assembly bases its decisions upon the opinions of this body); and a leader, more influential than the rest, to whom the final decision will be left and who will put it into execution. According as one or the other of these three forces prevails, the government is a democracy, an aristocracy, or a monarchy. Modern States, on the contrary, possess composite governments which do not, properly speaking, fall into any one of these three categories. But whatever be the system adopted, the political machinery should be only the instrument by which the instinctive feeling of the mass acts; this is what one would call public opinion if the expression were not usually limited to the present, whereas it is here a question of future as well as of past interests, of the wishes of present generations and those of the past. Personal government itself draws its strength from the harmony existing between its action and the national conscience.

§ 8. **Personal Government.** — The idea of obeying one man seems ridiculous to nations which have no chief and there are societies of this kind (the Nicobar islands, Todas, Papuans, and Fuegians). Others have chiefs only in time of war (Caribbees, Bedouins, Chinooks, Patagonians against the Spaniards, and the Indians against the English). Thus Gaul gave itself a dictator in the person of Vercingetorix against the Romans. There are peoples, and they are the most numerous, who have chiefs in time of peace as well as in time of war; these permanent rulers are often even hereditary. The first to be chosen king, said Voltaire, was a successful soldier. It was indeed personal qualities which determined the choice of the first rulers: physical strength and courage (Bedouins, Bushmen; old age means fall from power, as is shown by the example of Peleus and that of Laertes, who were dethroned by their sons; Nestor was an exception, but his case was phenomenal); age and the experience which it brings (Caribbees and Dyaks of Borneo); intelligence (the Snake Indians, Ostiaks); religious ascendency (the king is a priest or a magician in Loango and among the Amazulus; his function is especially to bring destruction upon the enemy, by means of exorcisms and witchcraft). The temporary chief becomes permanent only in consequence of continual wars and the necessity of being always prepared against surprises. In the next stage of progress, dynasties are established; the dignity of chief constitutes a kind of family possession; it is handed down from father to son, and from brother to brother, following various patrimonial systems; heredity in the family gives rise to heredity in the State, not to mention the fact that this system prevents crises, since the successor is chosen in advance. Religion has given a considerable support to monarchical power. It is not rare for kings to be high priests, vicars of God, gods upon earth; they deliver oracles, command the elements, and their subjects worship them (Peru, Egypt, Roman Empire).

§ 9. **Social Distinctions. Classes and Castes.** — In primitive societies all are equal, and class distinctions are unknown (Pueblos of North America, the Bodos of India, and the Alfurus of New Guinea). Slavery, a result of foreign war or indebtedness, gives rise everywhere to an important differentiation. Other political and social distinctions (Patricians and Plebeians) also have their source in the same causes; the division of labor perpetuates and accentuates them; sometimes, even, the food of different classes is not the same and this tends to separate them (in the Fiji Islands human flesh was reserved for the chiefs; in the Hawaiian Islands they alone could eat meat; hence they were more vigorous than their subjects). The vanquished often follow servile occupations (laborious trades), like that of farming, whereas the victors are soldiers. Privileges and distinctions become hereditary under the influence of religion or as a result of a political system which conveniently makes use of them for administrative purposes. Classes are transformed into castes (Ancient Egypt, Japan, Bambaras, etc.). In India caste forms a professional and religious syndicate, which allows its members to intermarry and eat together; neither Buddhism nor Jainism, each with its dogmas of equality, has succeeded in suppressing caste distinctions.[1] Our

[1] *Sénart*, "Les Castes dans l'Inde" ("Rev. des Deux-Mondes," 1894). "Gr. Encyclop.," see "Castes" (bibliog.). India: Brahmans, Kchatryas, Vaisyas, Soudras: priests, warriors, laborers, merchants, servants (*cf.* Persia: magi, nobles, laborers, artisans). Castes may be recognized by a large number of external signs, such as the make and color of clothing,

modern societies have taken stand against the social ideas of the ancients; they have proclaimed religious, civil, and political equality; only inequality of fortune remains.

§ 10. **How Societies are Formed, Developed, and Reproduced, and how they Pass Away.** — "In union there is strength," says the proverb. However commonplace this may be, no other cause is to be sought for the formation of human societies (and animal societies). It is not certain that man was originally a social animal, as Aristotle maintained; but there is no doubt that he has become such. The formation of groups did not take place through convention or contracts; no such fancied compact ever existed. It originated under the stress of necessity; it was spontaneous and involuntary, the instinctive reaction against external forces. It was a necessary means of defence against enemies, wild beasts, or other men; it was also necessary to obtain food by hunting and fishing in common, which is far more productive than when carried on by the individual alone. Was the primitive group a mere horde, a formless tribe which organized itself into families, clans, tribes, or towns in consequence of interior labor? Or, on the contrary, was the family the original unit, expanding by way of successive grouping into the clan and the town? These are problems whose solution is connected with the obscure question of the origin of the family. Certain it is, that among peoples of the Aryan race this latter mode is frequent; families unite to form clans, clans unite to form tribes or towns, and these last in turn unite to form large States.

Once established, societies grow by means of alliances or conquests.

(A) The alliance comprises various degrees: First, **Personal Unions**: two States have one and the same chief, yet each retains

the form of jewels, special rites, emblems, flags, flowers, etc. Caste is therefore a kind of freemasonry. It protects its members; at a word issuing from it, the merchants of a whole district have been known to close their shops, laborers suspend their work, artisans abandon their workshops on account of a slight injury done one of their number. From the moment it undertakes to defend its members, a caste is obliged to subject them to a certain amount of discipline: it exercises the function of police within its own fold and thus renders services that we are accustomed to expect from the State. Exclusion from one's caste is a severe punishment, for the individual so excluded is a pariah; his very presence is a pollution. The Hindu who comes to Europe is "ipso facto" excluded from his caste, but he is granted reinstatement upon payment of a fine, following a sentence pronounced by the tribunal of the caste. The Brahman religion has contributed toward the transformation of classes into castes; but the chief reason for this change was the lack of a strong political organization, the caste supplanting the State as an agency for the protection of the individual.

its full independence with respect to the other; for example, England and Hanover, from 1714 to 1838. Second, **Real Unions**: two States form a single one in their relation with other States, but remain distinct within themselves, for example, Austria-Hungary. Third, **Confederations of Independent States** each member retaining its own diplomatic representation, but possessing an organ, the diet, empowered to take certain measures in the common interest, for example, the German Confederation, from 1815 to 1866. Fourth, **Federal States** constituting in respect to their external relations a single State, but having internally a central power which exercises a portion of sovereignty, the rest being left with the local authorities, for example, Switzerland and the United States.

(B) Conquest occasionally results in the complete absorption of the conquered State by the conquering State. Sometimes its effects are less radical: the conquered lose a part of their independence and descend to the rank of semi-sovereign States or protectorates.

The enlargement of a society has one notable advantage. By the suppression of petty States, otherwise inevitable hostilities are obviated (thus incessant wars desolated Gaul before the Roman conquest); forces formerly wasted in internal wrangling are directed toward social co-operation; the division of labor can be carried further in a large country than in a town or a province. A nation never dies. Exterminations are rare; but it may happen that one nation is reduced to subjection by another. Sometimes a nation loses, in consequence of an unsuccessful war, a part of its territory and population; it is dismembered.

Dismemberment may also occur, as among animals, spontaneously, but it rarely takes place in this form. Societies are reproduced especially through swarming (the sacred spring-time among the Italiotes); they form colonies, images of the metropolis, to which they remain attached (Australia) or from which they separate to live independently (the United States).

§ 11. **The Factors of Social Evolution** are: 1st, the physical environment (habitat, climate, economic condition; for example, the geographical situation of England has entered largely into its history) and social environment (influence of neighboring societies, struggles, imitation). A too rigorous climate (Eskimos), a sterile soil (deserts), difficulty of communication (Alps, Caucasus), are obstacles to the formation of great States. 2d, The past which forms a race and which is itself only the result of the influence of earlier environments. From that arise habits of discipline, a certain homogeneity, kinship, language, and cult among the members of a group. The principle of nationalities, which recalls that of the fixity of species in natural history, refers too exclusively to this action of the past. It may have established a community of language, religion, and race, or at least a common existence and aspirations. It does not follow that this community is imperative and must last forever. The future may undo that which the work of the past has established.

§ 12. **Social Laws.** — Certain biological laws apply to societies. We have already stated this fact in speaking of the division of labor. Natural selection eliminates inferior societies; they disappear before those that are better armed, more wealthy, more prosperous, and of superior morality. The law of the connection of characteristics which made it possible for Cuvier to reconstruct a species which had disappeared, by the aid of a few fossil remains, appears also in society; if military institutions prevail therein one will find absolute power as a logical consequence as well as the subordination of the individual to the State and political theories in keeping therewith; free institutions are met with in industrial and commercial societies. The law of organic balancing or the law of Geoffroy Saint-Hilaire, by virtue of which the exaggerated development of one organ induces the shrinking of the others (for example, the kangaroo, whose fore quarters are so slight in comparison with its hind quarters), determines social development. The Romans were more clever politicians, better soldiers, and better jurisconsults than the Greeks, but the latter surpassed the former in fine arts and literature.

II. Elementary and Composite Societies

§ 13. **Primitive Societies.** — There are still in existence a few such societies in our day. The Vedas in Ceylon, the Todas in India, the Papuans, the aborigines of lower California, the Bushmen, the Fuegians, and the Eskimos form incoherent groups of ten, twenty, or fifty persons; chance draws them together, and accident disperses them. These anarchists, without knowing it, have realized fully the ideal of the school: the independence of the individual, liberty and equality — in poverty. Of what value is this independence which they cannot use, subjected as they are to the brutal forces of nature? What one loses in the way of liberty in our societies, one gains in power, in wealth, and in contentment, that is to say, in real liberty. The lowest serf of old

France would not have exchanged places with the free Indian of the Sierra Nevadas, who subsists only on roots and worms, nor with the Bedouin of Sinai, who for three thousand years has been wandering aimlessly in the desert. A tyrant would have rendered them invaluable service; I do not mean the good tyrant as he is pictured in the image of God (whose main defect is that he cannot exist); I mean the worst of despots. Baker, when leaving tribes who had no government, barbarians almost without clothing, was struck by the prosperity of the Unyoro, a country ruled over by a monster, who, for the least trifle, would cause his subjects to be put to death with the most frightful torture. Tyranny, indeed, is a great step in the direction of progress! And sad as it is to relate, war is also a step in advance: those tribes without chiefs are peaceful. War permits natural selection in the choice of chiefs and the elimination of the weak. We owe the strong and vigorous races and the best organized societies to the necessity of the struggle for existence. This providential rôle of war, in the beginning of societies, has nothing mysterious about it.

§ 14. **The Clan or the "Gens."** — Family communities are almost political societies; their organization is more advanced than that of the wandering hordes of which we have just spoken. The assembly of several families forms an association of the same type as these, the clan (Celts), the "genos" (Greeks) or the "gens," the "sept" (Ireland), and the "Sippe" (German). Does this association result from the natural development and dismemberment of the family, or must one see in it an artificial creation,[1] families of diverse origins grouping themselves together and, after several generations, believing themselves to be the issue of a common ancestor? Each of the two systems has its partisans, and perhaps there is in each some truth. Families having a common ancestor might admit into their group outsiders, and even these latter might admit other strangers in such a manner as to form a group as coherent as that of the family communities. To this end the form of the family community was borrowed. In any case, the "gens" is, on a large scale, what the family is on a small scale. Its members are united by a fictitious relationship or by a relationship that cannot be proved even if it exists, and which is only expressed by the use of a common name and the worship of a legendary ancestor.

[1] In Daghestan the "gentes" take the name of places or of heroes, never that of an ancestor. The Kheosures (of the Caucasus) know no other political institution than that of the "gens."

§ 15. **The Maternal "Gens" among the Iroquois.** — The tribe of Senecas had eight "gentes" bearing the name of the following animals: the wolf, the bear, the turtle, the marten, the deer, the woodcock, the heron, and the hawk. The animal for which the "gens" was named was an ancestral god, a totem; all the members of the "gens" were considered as having a common origin; they were all related, since they had the same general name and a common cemetery; they were forbidden to marry within their own "gens"; and as relationship only through a common mother was considered, the "gens" recruited its membership exclusively from among the descendants of the women. The council of the "gens," which was composed of all the adults, men and women, exercised sovereign power and decided important questions, such as those relating to the admission of new members or the practice of the vendetta. It chose and deposed the military commander, and the sachem or chief in time of peace; the latter exercised only a paternal authority, and was without any compulsory power. He was at the same time chief of the "gens" and its representative in the tribal council and in the federal council of the Iroquois. The son of the preceding sachem was never elected to succeed his father, because he belonged to another "gens" by virtue of the maternal right.

§ 16. **The Celtic Clan,**[1] such as the Gallic Codes represented it, was, on the contrary, a clan based on agnatic relationship; the wife remained in spite of her marriage, a member of her father's clan (save in some exceptional cases). At the head of the clan, which was made up of the supposed descendants of a common ancestor, was a chief whose dignity was not hereditary. He was assisted by a council of seven of the old men, by a representative of the clan charged with administrative affairs and diplomatic negotiations, and finally, by an avenger who punished offenders and led the men in time of war. The mutual responsibility of the members of the clan was minutely regulated: in case of homicide, the sum of money due as compensation ("composition") to the family and the clan of the victim was paid, one third by the murderer and his family, two thirds by his maternal clan and by his paternal clan, the latter being required to pay twice as much as the former; the relatives and the clan of the victim had a right to composition in the same proportion, but there was a deduction

[1] *Seebohm*, "The Tribal System in Wales," 1895; *Dareste*, "Jour. des Sav.," 1898; *Kovalewsky*, "Rev. de Sociol.," 1894, 199; *R. de Kérallain*, "Rev. gén. de dr.," 1890, p. 571.

of a third of the amount for the benefit of the chief who recovered it.

§ 17. **The Roman "Gens"**[1] implied: 1st, a common name; its members bore the name "gentilicium" (ending in "ius," for example, Tullius) and were distinguished from one another by the "prænomen" (Marcus) and the "cognomen" or sobriquet (Cicero); 2d, community of worship and a common burial place; 3d, common agriculture; the "gens" owned the "ager gentilicius"; the rights of succession, of guardianship and custody, which existed among the "gentiles" at a comparatively recent period, were remains of this joint ownership; 4th, solidarity among "gentiles," whether for avenging the offence of which one of them was a victim, or whether to pay expenses incumbent upon one of them (ransom, fine, expenses incident to the discharge of public duties), or whether to assist in the administration of justice, to act as surety, or to serve as witnesses for one another. The "gens" had without doubt a chief ("*ἄρχων*" in the Greek "*γένος*"),[2] the natural representative of the "gens" in the Senate, who was charged with worship, with the management of their property, and with the administration of justice within the "gens"; he was assisted in important cases by a council of "patres," which issued decrees for the punishment of and probably the expulsion of unworthy members with the "nota gentilicia." Included in the "gens" were the legitimate descendants in the male line of a common ancestry (real or imaginary) of the "gens," the adopted children or the woman "in manu" of a "gentilis," without counting clients who were only an accessory part of it. The relation of a member to the "gens" was severed by adoption, by marriage, by emancipation, or the "transitio ad plebem." The "gens" disappeared, little by little, being eclipsed by the State, somewhat as in a confederation where the parts are consolidated to form a single State. The general causes which made the building up of the State inevitable brought about the downfall of the "gens." The population became divided into classes, and the lands into districts, both being wholly different from the division prevailing among the "gentes."

§ 18. **The "Clientèle."** — The client ("cluens," one who obeys) was a freedman, a captive, or one who attached himself to a patron

[1] *Cuq*, "Instit. des Romains," 1891; *Giraud*, "R. de lég.," 1846 ("De la Gentilité"); *Lécrivain*, "Dict. des antiq.," see "Gens" (and bibliog.); *Cicero*, "Top.," 6 (according to *Mucius*).

[2] In Daghestan, there was an elective chief whose authority was primarily moral ("primus inter pares").

(" jus applicationis "). He bore the same " nomen gentilicium " as his patron, worshipped with him, and was indebted to him for " obsequium, operæ, bona," respect, services, property, that is to say: 1st, assistance in case of ransom, fines incurred, and ordinary expenses and disbursements; 2d, his succession if he died without descendants. In return, his patron, under penalty of being devoted to the infernal gods (" Sacer esto "), gave him protection before the courts and outside of them, treated him with justice in the family circle, and gave him assistance in case of need. The tie which bound the client to the patron was hereditary; the client could not renounce his patron; and the latter undoubtedly had no power to rid himself of a client except for serious cause. In the State, the client had no rights except through the mediation of his patron. The decadence of the " gentes " was the signal for the decline of the " clientèle." The clients liberated from the system of patronage made up the common people ("plebs"); they acquired the right to sue in the courts and also political rights. Towards the end of the republic, the " clientèle " was no longer an institution; it resembled the political " clientèle " of our own times.

§ 19. **The Germanic "Sippe"**[1] extended as far as relationship (" Freundesblut wallt und wenn es auch nur ein Tropfen ist "). Though Germanic law recognized both relatives through males and through females (" Gesippen," " Freunde," " Gatlinge," " Magen "), only the former, or relatives by the lance and by the sword, " Speer, und Schwertmagen," made part of the " Sippe "; the relatives by the distaff or the spindle, " Spill-, Kunkelmagen," were not included. Strangers might join the "Sippe" by attaching themselves to the families which composed it, for example, by enfranchisement or by legitimation; on the contrary they might sever their relation with it by being outlawed, or by a decision of the " Sippe," or by voluntary withdrawal with the usual formalities. The " Sippe " formed at one and the same time a political group, an agrarian community,[2] and a military division. It protected its members before the law, exercised police power over them (as a very natural consequence of its being made responsible for their acts), exercised guardianship over incompetents, women, and minors, avenged the murder of one of its members or exacted the

[1] *Brunner*, § 13.

[2] "L. Alam." 87; *Meichelbeck*, "Hist. Fris.," I, 49 (a. 750): "fines genealogiarum"; *Rozière*, "Form.," 318. The word "fara" has the same meaning and is also found in the names of places, La Fère in Picardy, etc.

" Wergeld " (compensation due from the murderer) and, vice versa, contributed to the payment of the " Wergeld " in case of murder committed by one of its members.

§ 20. **The Germanic Retinue** ("comitatus")[1] placed the free man under the service of a chief, a noble, or a free man more powerful than himself, without reducing him to the condition of a slave. It was an extra-legal institution, if one may use such an expression, one which took the place of the State as an agency for the protection of the weak. It differed from the Roman " clientèle," and doubtless from the Gallic " clientèle " (" ambacti "), about which little is known, but which filled the same need. Tacitus describes it in somewhat these terms: "The 'companion' or 'retainer' was admitted into the family community of the chief; he lived under the same roof, and ate and drank at the same table; he swore to protect the chief and to defend him in time of peace (as the vassal swore fidelity to his lord). The 'retainers' formed his escort of honor; they performed household duties; during wartime they fought on his side; if he died, it was dishonor for them to live without avenging him; they allowed themselves to be made prisoners in order to share his fate, and if necessary, served as hostages for him. If he was victorious, they received a part of the spoils, a javelin, a war horse, or other presents. The chief supported, armed, equipped, avenged, and protected them. The bond between the chief and his 'retainers' was not, however, indissoluble; if one wished to withdraw, for example, to return to the house of his father (home), he might do so. It was an honor for the chief to have a large number of 'retainers'; any free man might have 'comites,' but all do not have them, for that implied riches, military glory, or an illustrious name. It was not

[1] *Tac.*, "Germ.," 13. *Cf.* the poem of Beowulf, Icelandic Sagas; *Cæsar*, 23, speaks of the chiefs of the band who may be compared to the "principes" with their "comitatus," but the first attached volunteers to themselves only during an expedition. The "comitatus" was not an institution exclusively military; the Germanic names that were given after the invasion to the "comites" clearly show this; they are servitors, "degen," companions, "gasinde," relatives, "gatlinge," "freunde": *cf.* the "antrustions" of the Frankish kings. The "companions" were not entirely vassals, whatever *Montesquieu* may say in the "Esprit des Lois," 30, 33; but they were precursors of them. They formed a part of the household (in quality of free servitors), whereas the vassals were outside the household. *Cf. Brunner*, I, 137. The "retinue" and the "clientèle" prepared the way for the division of society into classes by making servitors of free men. There is much argument, wrongly, I think, as to whether the right to have a "comitatus" was a privilege of the king, of the "dux," or of the "principes." *Esmein*, p. 41 *et seq.* The "comitatus" was not numerous enough for me to be able to see in it the origin of the expeditions which caused the fall of the Roman Empire. *Kohler*, "Germania," 1868, 143.

rare for nobles with their 'retainers' to make war on their own account."

§ 21. **The Tribe**, an aggregation of clans or "gentes," had no other organization than that of the units which composed it; it differed from the clan only in its greater size, which was an advantage in itself; and by its purely political character, whereas the clan or "gens" sometimes resembled the family so much that they were confused with it. Among the members of the tribe, there was no question of relationship, even artificial; at most, they were united by a common religion. The Iroquois "gentes" formed the "phratria" and these the tribe. The tribe of the Senecas was composed of only two thousand persons; the territory which it occupied was surrounded by a neutral zone; it had its own religion, and its own council composed of sachems and of chiefs of the "gentes." The five Iroquois tribes (numbering in the neighborhood of twenty thousand persons) were themselves confederated, forming a permanent league (as all leagues are) directed by a council in which voting was by tribes and where the decisions had to be unanimous. In 896 the seven Hungarian tribes were united under the leadership of Arpad.

§ 22. **The Gallic and Germanic Towns.**[1] **Political Divisions.** — Neither Gaul nor Germany constituted a State. Neither were they mere geographical expressions. The peoples of these regions, while entirely autonomous, were yet closely enough related to be designated by the same name. Cæsar maintained, it is true, that the Belgians, Aquitanians, and Celts (or Galli) had neither the same language, the same institutions, nor the same laws, but he was guilty of exaggeration, for when he came to describe the Celtic institutions, he found no differences to point out. Religious unity had been realized by the Druids, and several facts indicate that they were on the road to political unity. The Gallic towns placed themselves under the protection of each other. At the time of Cæsar's arrival the whole country was grouped about the Eduii and the Sequani, who were disputing among themselves for leadership and supremacy. In Germania this tendency was not so marked: however, there were dependent States, such as the Ubii, who paid tribute to the Suevi, and confederations such as

[1] *Bulliot et Roidot*, "La Cité Gauloise," 1879; *Lefort*, "R. gén. du Droit," 1880, *et seq.* *D'Arbois de Jubainville*, "R. hist.," 1886, 3, does not seem to me to have established the existence, about the 400 s B.C., of a great Gallic Empire extending from Thrace to the Atlantic Ocean. We cannot apply our knowledge of the Galates of Asia to the Gauls. *Strabo*, XII, 5; *Robiou*, "Hist. des Gaulois d'Orient," p. 153.

those of the Franks and Alamanni, at the time of the barbarian invasions.

The territory of each town was divided into districts or cantons ("Pagi"), each of which included a certain number of villages or small towns ("Vici"). It is presumed that the "Pagus" (or "Gau") was the territorial division occupied by the "Millena" or group which furnished one thousand fighting men; at least it seems that such was the case with the Suevi. As for the group known as the "hundred," whose existence Tacitus endeavored to establish in his "Germania," although without producing direct proof, it must have been a subdivision of the "Pagus," if we should regard it as a territorial division, and then we would be tempted to compare it to the "Vicus"; but the silence of the sources does not permit us to see anything in it except a military division, a district containing a certain number of families or "Sippen." In proportion as the organization of the "gens" weakens, this personal grouping (with which one may compare those formed around the Icelandic "godis") tended to transform itself into a territorial division; it is no longer the family, but as in Rome and in Greece, residence in a given place, which stands as the base of social structure. But in the time of Tacitus the change had probably not taken place. We read in the "Germania"; first, that the judges had a hundred assessors; second, that each "Pagus" furnished foot soldiers, at first to the number of one hundred, and later an indeterminate number; but the name of "centeni," the hundred, remained with them as an honorary title (thus it was once customary to say "the hundred-guards," etc.). These numerical divisions of military origin were not at all peculiar to Germania.[1]

§ 23. **Classes of Population.** — Gaul and Germania were covered with forests and swamps; the population, rather sparse,

[1] The town of the Helvetii had four "pagi," twelve "oppida," and four hundred "vici"; the "oppida" and "vici" were burned. *Cæsar*, I, 5, 12 (the "pagus" of the "Tigurins" made war alone); IV, 1 (the Suevi had one hundred "pagi," a strip of uncultivated land along the frontier of the Suevii). *Mela*, 3, 3. *Tacitus*, 6, 12, 16. As to the geography of Gaul see *Longnon*, "Atlas hist.," 1888; *Desjardins*, "Géogr. de la Gaule," 1878; *Deloche*, "Mem. des Savants étrang.," 2d S., t. IV, I, 365. — Among the Anglo-Saxons the division was carried as far as the "ten" ("dizaine"). The Salic Law speaks of the "Centenarius." *Cf. infra* on the personal or territorial character of the Frankish Hundred. "Lex Wisig.," II, 1, 26: "millenarius," "quingentarius," etc. Rome had its tribes, its centuries, many other peoples analogous numerical divisions. *Alamans*, 36, 1; *W. Sickel*, "Der Deutsche Freistaat," 1879; "Mitth. d. oest. Instituts"; *Ergänz.* I, 7; *Waitz*, "Verfass." I, 201; *Stubbs*, "Constit. Hist. of England," t. I; "J. Hopkins Univ. Studies in History," 3d S., 143, 342.

was largely engaged in the raising of cattle, hunting, and fishing, agriculture being very little developed. Tacitus tells us that the heavy labors in Germany fell to the women and old men; in time of war the men were entirely occupied with carrying it on; in time of peace they remained idle ("ipsi hebent"). In Gaul, in the time of Cæsar, the population was divided into several classes; first, the Druids, a powerful clergy having special privileges, such as exemption from military service and holding annual assemblies in the country round about Chartres with a certain hierarchy existing among its members ("si quis . . . excellit dignitate"), and having a chief chosen by the priestly body.[1] In Germania, the religious function was not yet specialized; it was exercised there, to be sure, by political leaders. It is only in the time of Tacitus that we find priests with whom the Scandinavian "godis" (but not the Icelandic ones, for the latter had also political attributes) may be compared. Second, the knights, "equites"; they constituted the military class and the nobility; they alone took part in the political assemblies, and they derived their influence from the number of their slaves, debtors, and clients.[2] Among the Germans, the nobility, the old families, did not form a distinct class with legal privileges; their clientèle and their wealth gave them an actual superiority over mere free men. It resulted from this that their family could claim a large "Wergeld" and that it was from among them that the kings and chiefs were usually chosen.[3] Third, the plebs[4] having no political rights

[1] *Cæsar*, VI, 13. In Ireland the purely literary men, "file," "brithem," or jurisconsults, were distinguished from the priests. *Diodorus of Sicily*, 5, 31, separated also the "Druids," the "Bards," and the "Vates" in Gaul. *Ritterling*, "Hist. Tasch.," 1888, 195.

[2] *Cæsar*, I, 31; VI, 13.

[3] *Cæsar*, VI, 23; *Tac.*, "Germ.," 7, 8, 13, 25; "Ann.," 11, 16; *Jordanes*, "De Reb. Get.," 5; *Greg. of Tours*, 2, 9. In the 900 s it was stated that there were among the Saxons, as formerly, three classes of people: nobles, "edlingi," simple folk, "frilingi," "servi," or "lazzi." M.G.H., S.S., II, 361. "Frisons," I, 5, 11, 15. "Bavarois," 2, 20. "Angles," 1, 10 (differences in the amount of "Wergeld"). "The Edda" of *Soemund*, III. p. 173, attributed a divine origin to the three classes of men; the "thrael," "servus"; the "karl," "vir"; the "jarl" or noble, warrior. Bibliog. detailed in *Brunner*, "D. Rechtsg.," S. 14. From what was this nobility derived? Perhaps from long exercise of public functions which presupposes notable actions.

[4] *Cæsar*, VI, 13; "plebes pæne servorum habetur loco, quæ per se nihil audet nullo adhibetur consilio" (*Viollet*, p. 13). "Plerique, cum aut ære alieno aut magnitudine tributorum aut injuria potentium premuntur, sese in servitutem dicant nobilibus; in hos omnia sunt jura, quæ dominis in servos." Were the "Ambacti" or clients of the chiefs free men? *Cæsar*, VI, 15; *Festus*, see "Ambactus," N.R.H., 1890, 709. The "devoti" or "solduri" were chosen soldiers devoted to the chief whom they accompanied, and who supplied them with food. Their devotion was

and being scarcely more than slaves, grouped around the knights and formed their clientèle. In Germania, there were no "plebs"; society, as yet, comprised only two classes, free men and slaves, which was an indication of a less advanced social status. Fourth, the slaves. Among the Germans they were somewhat like free men: indeed, scarcely any distinction was made between them and free men; the master had the right of life and death over them, but it was very unusual for him to exercise it. He gave them land to cultivate and a separate dwelling place; he treated them rather like tenants, being content to exact of them a part of their earnings.[1]

§ 24. **The Political Function** was still greatly circumscribed. It was entirely external in character as is the case in a league, and consisted primarily in the organization of measures against attack and for defence against the enemy. Within, clans and families retained their independence, and collective action, when it took place, was the result, in Germania at least, of the deliberation of an assembly of free men. The maintenance of order within was not an affair of the State. It belonged to each individual to avenge his own wrongs. The only procedure known was private war, the feud or vendetta, which was carried on from generation to generation until families were exterminated, or until, weary of struggling, the two parties made peace, just as to-day arbitration or mediation is resorted to for ending differences between States. The Druids in Gaul and the Brehons in Ireland played the rôle of arbiters. Both enjoyed a sort of magical power; it was this which caused them to be chosen, and this explains the fact that their decrees were respected. Cæsar maintained that they had the power to excommunicate those who disobeyed them. Already, however, alongside of these priests in Gaul a secular system of justice meted out by the magistrates of the cities had made its appearance. In Germania, elected "principes" dispensed justice in the cantons and villages: they also were magistrates, and the common people assisted them in their duties.[2] This popular

such that they did not allow themselves to survive their chief. — In Ireland we find free clients and vassal serfs. The "clientèle" was connected with the concession of the lease of cattle made by the patron.

[1] *Tac.*, "Germ.," 24, 25, 20.

[2] *Cæsar*, VI, 23; *Tacitus*, 12. One might bring a capital accusation before the national assembly; to each one of the chiefs ("principes") who dispensed justice "per pagos et vicos," were joined, to serve them as counsel, and to lend their "auctoritas" to their decisions (that is to say, to guarantee them and make them valid), one hundred assessors, chosen from among the people. ("Centeni singulis ex plebe comites consilium simul et auctoritas adsunt.") Interpret the word "centeni" in whatever sense you will, whether as applying to the family chiefs of the political

intervention, quite natural at a time when political power was weak, was one of the most striking features of Germanic justice. The assessors of the magistrate did not limit themselves to giving him their advice as they did in the Roman tribunals; they pronounced the sentence which the magistrate carried into execution. If we may judge by tradition and subsequent law, outlawry seems to have been the most severe penalty which could be inflicted by the Germanic tribunals, or rather by the highest of them, the popular assembly (later, by the king).[1] This was a sort of secular excommunication, more lay than religious, entailing at one and the same time, death, banishment, confiscation of property, and the burning of the offender's home. An individual who was put outside the pale of the law (" ex lex," outlaw) might be killed with impunity by the first comer; whoever sheltered him was punished, even his parents and his wife; he was an enemy of the community and had only one resource left — to flee, to take to the jungle, as the Corsicans say, and there he was hunted like a wild beast (" wargus," wolf), exiled and compelled to live abroad.

§ 25. **The Political Organs** of each town were: first, the popular assembly; second, the senate or council of chiefs; third, the king or magistrates.

I. *The popular assembly*[2] in Germany was composed of all free

division called the hundred, to the assembly of a hundred, or to any person whatsoever, it is none the less true that the popular element had its place in the rendering of justice. Concerning the rôle played by the "centeni comites," compare *infra*, the Frankish "rachimbourgs." *Brunner*, I, 143; *Vanderkindere*, 100; *Beaudouin*, N.R.H. To the contrary, *Fustel de Coulanges*, "Rach.," 361.

[1] Compare as to Gaul, *Cæsar*, V, 56 ("hostem judicat . . . in concilio"); "Lex Sal.," 56. Edict of Chilperic, 10: "homo qui per silvas vadit." —Z.S.S., XI, 625.

[2] *Montesquieu*, "Esprit des lois," XI, 6: "If one will read the admirable work of Tacitus concerning the German customs, he will see that it is from them that the English have drawn the idea of their political government. This excellent system was found in the forests." *Guizot*, "Civilisation en France," 1, 7: "the Germans have given us the spirit of liberty." Comparative jurisprudence has justified these opinions. At a certain period of their civilization, other peoples have had the same political institutions as the Germans.

F. de Rocca, "Les ass. politiques dans la Russie ancienne" ("R. Hist.," 1895, vol. 59, p. 241). Ancient Russia had its classes: nobles ("boyars"), and among them courtiers, "kniajić," in the service of the prince, merchants, villagers, and slaves. The nobles did not enjoy hereditary privileges. Every free man had the right to be present at the "Vétché" or popular assembly and to speak in it (but by reason of the paternal power the son could not take part in these assemblies during the lifetime of his father). The "Vétché" deliberated on all questions, unanimity being required for its decisions. This was obtained by a friendly agreement or by force, the majority imposing its will upon the minority. At Novgorod the dissenters were drowned in the Volga. The meetings were not periodic, the convocation was made by the prince, or by a group of men capable of bearing arms.[1] They came to it, grouped, no doubt, in families and in clans ("propinquitas," "sippe") as though it were a military expedition. They sat fully armed[2] in the open air. The priests commanded silence and compelled it, if necessary. The king or chief spoke, seeking rather to persuade than to order. The crowd expressed its disapprobation by groans, its approbation by the rattling of arms.[3] There were ordinary sessions at the new and full moons, and extraordinary sessions whenever circumstances made it necessary. The assembly[4] decided upon the most important affairs of the town, chose the chiefs who administered justice in the "pagi" and the "vici," heard, to the exclusion of the latter, important accusations, such as high treason, cowardice, crimes against nature, and inflicted penalties of death, or outlawry. It was in its presence that the political enfranchisement of young men took place; when they were able to fight, a chief or a relative solemnly armed them with the shield and the lance.

This assembly was, therefore, at one and the same time, the army, the judicial tribunal, and the political organ, exercising

citizens, but attendance was not obligatory. The "Vétché" had a seal and officers who executed its decisions. This political organ was, however, powerless to maintain internal order or to safeguard its independence without. It was necessary, therefore, to call upon the princes with whom the "Vétché" negotiated somewhat as the Italian cities negotiated with their "podestas." The "Vétché" appointed and removed the prince, and decided upon war and peace. The prince commanded the troops, administered justice, attended the sessions of the "Vétché," and caused its decisions to be executed. The invasion of the Tartars brought about the ruin of the "Vétché" and gave the Moscovites sufficient power to solidify Russia.

[1] The Norwegians who emigrated and settled in Iceland, taking their old customs with them, had a popular assembly or "Althing." It met in a vast plain on an isolated block of lava called the "Mountain of the Law": there was an altar, a lake from which they drew water to wash away the blood of the victims, and a rock from which the condemned were hurled. The sacrifices were followed by solemn banquets; during the session of the Diet, private warfare was suspended, the priests proclaiming a holy truce. *Brunner*, I, 30, thinks that, in the "Germania" of Tacitus, the assembly was accustomed to open its sessions with religious ceremonies.

[2] The army was the nation under arms. *Cæsar*, V, 56. Military service was for the free man quite as much a right as a duty. Also the handing of arms was a method of freeing slaves among the Lombards (*Paul Diacre*, "Hist. Langob.," I, 13), and the taking of arms for the young man was the ceremony by which he entered upon political life.

[3] General usage among the Germans (laws, the election of kings). Vápnatak in Norway. *Greg. Tours*, "H. Fr.," 2, 40; "*Rotharis*," 386.

[4] Perhaps unanimously. According to primitive usage, a mere majority scarcely ever sufficed (Russian "Vétché," Montenegrin assemblies, the Ossetes, and the Abyssinian). *Viollet*, I, 286; "Cap. Saxon.," c. 26, 27.

direct government and leaving to the kings or chiefs only matters of secondary importance.[1]

Among the Gauls, popular assemblies did not occupy so important a place as they did in Germany. However, there were meetings in every town, composed of all the men who bore arms.[2] Cæsar spoke also of a national assembly[3] which he himself convoked annually and in which only the "principes civitatum" took part; but he is not certain that this "concilium totius Galliæ" existed before his advent; it was perhaps an institution which came into existence from the necessity of resisting the Romans; they convoked national assemblies as one would appoint a dictator; Gaul was compelled to establish its unity just as Greece had to do to resist the Persians.[4]

II. *The Senate.* — As soon as the territory was extended so the population increased, it became impossible to hold general assemblies; where they still existed, they were held only at rare intervals and for the consideration of vital questions. Ordinary affairs were placed in the hands of a less numerous body, a senate or assembly of notables or elders. The assembly of the "principes," in the "Germania" of Tacitus, was of this character ("de minoribus rebus principes consultant, de majoribus omnes"). The Gallic senates, composed no doubt of the élite of the knighthood, seem to have played a more important rôle and almost to have superseded the popular assembly. Among the Nervii it was composed of six hundred members; among the Eduii, two relatives could not occupy a seat in it, which would lead one to suppose that it included only family or clan chiefs represented just as in States made up of an aggregation of "gentes" or clans. The senate resembled, therefore, the diets of

[1] These assemblies reappear, after the invasion, among nations of the German race, under the following names: "Thing" (Scandinavian), "Ding," "Gedinge" (German), "Mallus" (Frank), "Gemot" (Anglo-Saxon), "Werf" (Saxons, Frisons). The "Landsgemeinde" of the little Swiss cantons such as Uri and Appenzell is nothing more than the old popular assembly which found there a congenial environment and has been perpetuated to our own times. Compare the Kabyle "Djemaa." *Masqueray*, "Formation des cités chez les pop. sédent de l'Algérie," 1886; *Zimmerman*, "Volksversamml. dd. alt. Deutschen" in "Brandes. B. üb. d. germ. Gesellsch.," II, 1863. The Italian cities and the French communes of the Middle Ages had also their popular assemblies.

[2] *Cæsar*, V, 6 ("concilium Æduorum"), 56; VI, 20, 23; *Cougny*, II, 499.

[3] *Cæsar*, I, 30; IV, 6; V, 27, 54, 56; VI, 3, 44; VII, 1, 2, 63, 75; II, 4 ("concilium Belgarum"). Compare *D'Arbois de Jubainville*, "Les Assemblies Politiques de l'Irlande," 1880; they may be compared to the annual assemblies of the Druids in the country of Chartres. *Post*, "Bausteine," II, 81.

[4] Another symptom: Oregetorix meditates getting possession of the "imperium totius Galliæ." *Cæsar*, I, 2.

modern confederations. In countries where a noble class existed, as in Hungary, it was the lords who composed the political assembly; until the beginning of the 1500 s, they were accustomed to assemble on the race course of Rakos, near Pesth. This was also the practice in Poland.

III. *Kings or Chiefs.*[1] — The authority of the chiefs was in harmony with the development of the political function and was consequently very weak. "Reges habent, quorum tamen vis pendet in populi sententia," is said of the ancient Swedes. The same may be said of the kings of Germania, chiefly powerful by reason of their "clientèles."[2] Half hereditary and half elective, the practice was to choose them from certain families because of their rank, whereas military chiefs in countries where there were no kings to command the army and, no doubt, also where the kings were too old, were appointed because of their courage ("reges ex nobilitate, duces ex virtute sumunt"). They had no right to punish as the military chiefs in the time of Cæsar had; this right was reserved for priests, who were the supposed executors of the will of the gods. They were distinguished from the people, somewhat as the chiefs of savage tribes are distinguished, by the arrangement of their hair, which was such as to give them a more martial air and to frighten the enemy (Suevi, Franks). It was customary to offer them presents and a part of the composition due in case of murder was paid to them, whereas the town received it where there were no kings. The "principes" or local chiefs had still less power (*cf.* "reguli," "ealdormen" among the Anglo-Saxons and "duces" among the Lombards). They were chosen, ordinarily, from among the nobles; but there was this difference between them and the kings: the latter inherited their office, whereas the chiefs were elected, but it is not certain whether the election was for life.

Gaul had kings[3] and especially magistrates: the "vergobret,"

[1] *Braumann*, "Principes der Gallier u. Germ.," 1883; *Sybel*, "Entstehung d. deut. Koenigthums," 1881; *Dahn*, "Koenige der Germanen," 1861–85; *Voss*, "Republik u. Koenigthum im alt. Germ.," 1885; *Waitz*, "Forsch.," II, 387; *Brunner*, sec. 17 (bibliog.); *Cæsar*, I, 31; II, 5, 28; III, 16, 17; IV, 11; V, 54; VII, 32, 33; VIII, 21; *Hoffmeister*, "Das Koenigt. i. altg. Staat," 1886.

[2] The king or "principes civitatis" (*Tac.*, 10) was called "thiudans," from "thiuda" meaning people (*cf.* "Lex Sal.," 46: "antetheoda," meaning "ante dominum"): "chunning," "konungr" ("koenig") from "chunni," "künne," meaning race, nation; "leod" (Anglo-Saxons) word which also means people. M.G.H., S.S., VII, 377. *Waitz*, I, 322; *Grimm*, R.A., 231; *Cæsar*, VI, 23.

[3] *Val.*, "Maxime," 9, 6, 3. *Cæsar*, I, 3; II, 4; IV, 21; V, 26, 25, 54; VII, 4.

who was the chief magistrate among the Eduii,[1] was elected by the priests and the other magistrates for one year; he had the power of life and death and could not leave the territory of the town, which in time of war necessitated the appointment of an additional military chief. The authority of these magistrates seems to have been greater than that of the German chiefs; nevertheless, they complained that simple individuals had more influence than they in the State. The military aristocracy with its "clientèle," and the Druidic priesthood, counterbalanced their power.

§ 26. **Composite Societies.** — Political machinery here becomes complicated. The central organ includes various elements: thus in a monarchy one finds associated with the king a council composed of officers or ministers, chosen from among the relatives or servitors of the king, for example the eunuchs [2] under the Later Empire, and bureaus by the side of the ministers. In proportion as the attributes of the State grew, the authority of the ministers increased; the king, physically incapable of attending to everything, kept in his hands only the general direction of public affairs; often, even, the real power passed to a prime minister or a grand vizier. The king reigned but did not govern. At the head of the territorial divisions there were the local organs, which were the reproduction, on a small scale, of the central organ, and were superordinated hierarchically one to the other.[3] The central organ was charged with coördinating the action of the local organs, and also that of the special machinery which came to be formed little by little alongside of it and at its expense: judicial, military, financial, — all with the same hierarchy and the same centraliza-

[1] *Cæsar*, I, 4, 16; VII, 32, 33 ("intermissis magistratibus," that is to say, with the intervention of the other magistrates of the town and of the "vergobret" in office); others translate "in the absence of the magistrate"; *Strabo*, 4, 4, 3. The "Lexovii" had also a chief alderman ("vergobret"). *Cf. Robert*, "R. archiol.," 1886.

[2] Mistresses of the king (Louis XV), lovers of the queen (Catherine II), favorites of both, have an important political influence in monarchies. Nepotism in modern régimes is a survival of the past.

[3] The local organs are sometimes created directly by the central organ (colonies, etc.). At other times, the latter is content to subordinate to itself powers already existing, by transforming the local chiefs into simple functionaries. In confederated States, the chiefs surrender only a small part of their powers. In India the English have allowed petty potentates to remain, rajahs with great nominal power. Whatever their origin, the local organs tend to resemble the central organ. In the Persian monarchy, the satraps arrogated to themselves the power of life and death. In Greece, Sparta propagated aristocratic institutions, Athens, democratic. The "municipes" adopted in the Roman Empire the constitution of republican Rome which, in appearance, had always remained in vigor.

tion. The separation of powers was a consequence of the division of labor, and it was even more pronounced than in modern societies; the industrial and religious machinery was distinct, and in a large measure independent, of the political machinery. This is not saying that there were not protests against this tendency. The socialistic theory of the organization of labor made the State a great manufacturer and even the only possible manufacturer. In religious matters, the ultramontanes like Auguste Comte desired a State religion; some would have restored to the State the religious function which it had so long exercised throughout antiquity and almost everywhere even to our own time; others wished to restore to it the economic function of which it had been deprived. Even when we set aside these radical theories, there remains the open question of the relation of the Church and the State, and of the intervention of the State in industrial and commercial matters.

Ancient patriotism demanded the entire devotion of the citizen; it is necessary to picture to ourselves ancient States as villages in a state of siege, and to remember that an act innocent in time of peace became a crime in the presence of the enemy. In our own time there is, as it were, a return towards militarism; the State takes possession of the telegraphs and the railroads; it enacts laws against drunkenness; we aim to make men happy and virtuous by decree of the State, whether they like it or not. But liberal institutions, free trade, liberty of conscience, liberty of the press maintain on the whole the upper hand. The modern State has gained in strength almost as much as the individual has gained in independence, — a circumstance that has solved a problem as difficult in appearance as the squaring of a circle. If the régime of State control rather than that of anarchy is to be the régime of the future, it does not follow that the State ought to be everything and the individual nothing. The body draws its strength from the vitality of its cells; these must have a life of their own; it is the same with society; the more vigorous the individual, the more powerful the society. It is not the atrophy of the individual that should be sought, but his full development.

§ 27. **The Ancient Town and its Revolutions.**—The small Greek cities, and even Rome itself, were originally organized according to the type of the Gallic or German city, with their popular assemblies, senates, kings, or magistrates. But in time, their constitution became more complicated and was transformed. The history of their public institutions shows great uniformity;

the ancient writers, Polybius among the others, noticed it and described the course of their revolutions. They passed, for the most part, through the following stages: first, patriarchal monarchy, Rome for example; second, aristocracy of race, the patriciate taking the place of the monarchy which had become tyrannical; third, aristocracy of wealth which replaced the old nobility (constitution of Solon at Athens, and of Servius Tullius at Rome, political rights being dependent upon wealth); fourth, democracy based upon equality between the common people and the patriciate. Military and financial burdens fell upon the plebeian as well as upon the patrician class, upon the poor as well as upon the rich. Those who shared the burdens desired to share also the privileges. Artificial divisions, purely territorial, replaced the old ethnical or family divisions (tribes and "demes" in Athens); the assembly of citizens voting by tribes had the last word concerning all matters of importance. The magistrates were temporary; they were responsible to the people and might be recalled by them; they were chosen by means of the lot, election retaining an aristocratic character (compare the Athenian jury of the Heliastes who were chosen by lot and the Roman judges who were taken, up to the time of the Gracchii, from among the Senatorial order); the fifth stage was Tyranny. The social question proved to be the rock upon which the ancient democracies were wrecked. After having attained equality in political matters, the people demanded equality of wealth. In the pursuit of this end, which was as fantastic as equality of strength or intelligence, rich and poor, fat and lean, struggled without respite. If the latter were stronger, they profited by it to obtain from the State distributions of wheat and food, the cancelling of debts, and the division of land. The disturbances arising from these measures cost the city its liberty and political rights. A tyrant, a Cæsar, usually the leader of the democratic party, was at hand to reëstablish order and repress anti-social tendencies. His rule was submitted to, as to the lesser of two evils, the greater being anarchy.

Chapter I

THE ROMAN EPOCH[1]

Topic 1. The Empire

Topic 2. Justice, Army, Finances

Topic 3. The Province

Topic 4. The City

Topic 5. Status of Persons

[1] Bibliography: "Corpus inscriptionum latinarum," t. XII (Narbonnaise); Vol. XIII contains the inscriptions of the three Gauls; *Desjardins*, "Géographie de la Gaule romaine," 1878 *et seq.*; *Longnon*, "Atlas historique de la France," 1884; Roman histories of *Duruy*, of *Mommsen*, etc.; Manuals of Roman public law by *Marquardt* and *Mommsen*, *Mispoulet*, *Bouché-Leclercq*, etc.; *Fustel de Coulanges*, "La Gaule romaine"; "L'Invasion germanique et la fin de l'Empire," 1891; *C. Julian*, "Gallia," 1892; *Viollet*, "Hist. des instit. polit. de la France," I, 25 (detailed bibliog.); *Glasson*, "Hist. du dr. et des inst. de la France," I, 155; *Viollet*, "Ac. Inscr.," XXXII, 2, 79; *Giraud*, "Essai s. l'hist. du dr. fr.," 1846; *Chauveau*, "Le droit des gens" (N.R.H., 1891, 393); *Daremberg*, "Dict. des Antiquitès."

TOPIC 6. LAND OWNERSHIP

TOPIC 7. CONCLUSION

TOPIC 1. THE EMPIRE

§ 28. **The Conquest of Gaul.** — Gaul, after its conquest by Cæsar, was quickly Romanized. A number of the Gauls received the right of citizenship,[1] and in A.D. 212 Caracalla conferred citizenship on all aliens.[2] This general act completed the assimilation of the Gauls by the Romans.[3] Druidism fell under the ban of the law forbidding human sacrifices, prohibiting associations not recognized by the State, and punishing the practice of magic; so it disappeared.[4] Nothing remained of the Celtic language and institutions. However, Gaul left us two things: its geographical divisions and the genius of our race. "The old Gallic States, in fact, preserved, almost to our own day, their name, their boundaries, and a sort of moral existence in the memories and affections of men. Neither the Romans, nor the Germans, nor feudalism, nor monarchy have destroyed these ancient units; they are still found in the provinces and the countries of France to-day." As the Romans judged the Gauls, regarding them as unsteady, light-hearted, easily turned toward new things, having a pronounced taste for disputation and agitation, good soldiers, clever talkers, so foreigners judge us, Mommsen, for example: "You see them always the same, made of poetry and of shifting sand, with weak heads, with deep sentiments, credulous and eager for novelties, amiable and intelligent, but devoid of political genius." [5]

[1] *Cf.* the "senatus-consultum," rendered upon the Oratio of Claudius in the year 48, and granting to the "primores Galliæ" entrance into the senate. *Tacitus*, "Ann.," XI, 23; *Desjardins*, III, 280; *Julian*, p. 172.

[2] Dig., 1, 5, 17.

[3] *Gaius*, III, 96, 120, and *Chénon*, "La loi pérégrine," 1890. Gaul does not seem to have preserved, as did the East, the national customs. *Mitteis*, "Reichsrecht u. Volksrecht," 1891.

[4] *Suetonius*, "Claud.," 25; Pliny, "H.N.," 30, 4, 13. Were the Druids persecuted? *Fustel de Coul.*, "R. celt.," IV; *d'Arbois de Jubainville*, "R. archeol.," 1879, p. 374, and "Etudes de dr. celt.," p. 172; *Duruy*, "Ac. sc. morales," 1880, p. 896.

[5] *Mommsen*, "Hist. rom.," VII, 111 (tr. fr.). *Cf.* "R. celt.," Jan., 1893.

§ 29. **The Roman Empire** presents the type of a powerful unitary society having a strongly centralized organization, and most of the characteristics of the great modern States. Under its republican form, the ancients considered it as a mixed government — monarchy because of the imperium or authority of its magistrates, aristocracy because of the rôle which the senate played, and democracy from the sovereignty which the popular "comitia" reserved to themselves. The strict dependence of the individual upon the State did not result, however, in the annihilation of liberty; there were limitations upon the power of magistrates (especially in penal matters); however absolute their "imperium," the principle of annual terms of office and the responsibility of the magistrates in connection with their administration prevented much abuse. The division of functions among the great magistrates, the rule of collegiality, and the right of intervention between colleagues or equals, were excellent guarantees for the citizens. This nice mechanism did not, however, save Rome from demagogic anarchy and the tyranny which results therefrom. The Empire concentrated in the hands of a single man the various powers which the republican constitution had separated.[1] We might suppose that this revolution would have done away with the impersonal conception of the State and of the public functions. There was, however, no such result; it existed in the general conscience by force of habit and because the idea was still true in many respects. The division of the Empire into two parts, the East and the West (A.D. 395), did not impair it; the laws were common and the State remained one.

§ 30. **The Central Power.** — Augustus held his power from laws or special decrees ("senatus-consulta");[2] his successors held

[1] What became of the great powers of the Republic? The comitia lost the election of magistrates under Tiberius, the voting of the laws under Nerva, and are scarcely recognizable in the assemblies of the Campus Martius where the emperor was acclaimed. The republican senate was an independent body selected from among former magistrates, appointed by the comitia; the censors inscribed them on the senatorial list after having established their honorable character; the imperial senate depended upon the will of the prince, who constituted it according to his own discretion ("allectio inter consulares"), and convoked it when he pleased and made it vote as he wished. This assembly, for show only, dragged out a useless existence during the whole period of the Later Empire. Magistrates, consuls, prætors, had no more effective power than had the senate, and their functions, all a matter of form, constituted the degrees of a "cursus honorum" which appealed only to the vanity of the wealthy. *Lécrivain*, "Le Sénat Romain depuis Dioclétien," 1888. *Cagnat*, "Cours d'épigraphie," 2d ed., 1890. (Senatorial and equestrian career.)

[2] Monument or inscription of Ancyre: "Res Gestæ divi Augusti," ed. *Cagnat et Peltier* (terminated in A.D. 14).

it by virtue of a general law, pronounced at the time of their accession, itself a decree which the people voted by acclamation.[1] In theory, the Empire was elective; the prince was appointed by the senate whose authority apparently counterbalanced his own (Dyarchy); in reality, he arrived at his power by inheritance, his successor sharing the throne with him, or by usurpation, thanks to the support of the army. He bore the religious title of Augustus,[2] worship of him was a part of the religion of Rome during his lifetime, and he was placed among the number of the gods by the senate, after his death ("divus"). He had, by virtue of his quality as sovereign pontiff, the supreme management of the official religion, exercised the powers of the ancient censors, and consequently prepared the list of senators (which was equivalent to the right of creating the senate at his will); prepared the census of the citizens, which permitted him to grant the right of citizenship, exercised the tribunitial power ("sacrosanctus," the right of coercion over all, the right of intercession, the right to preside over the senate and the popular "comitia") and the proconsular power (supreme head of the army, right of peace and of war, administration of the provinces, the right to levy taxes upon them, and the right to exercise the supreme judicial power). If he did not possess, properly speaking, the legislative power, he caused decrees to be made by the senate at his command, pronounced edicts and rescripts, and finished by legislating directly himself. He did not appoint the magistrates before the 400 s, but he recommended candidates to the senate, and his recommendations were equivalent to orders. The republican laws of sovereignty, that is to say, laws in relation to the public safety, permitted him to reach all suspects. By virtue of these he had the right of life and death ovet all. A special clause by which he was appointed authorized him to do whatever he believed expedient for the safety of the republic.[3]

[1] "Lex de imperio Vespasiani," A.D. 69–70. *Girard*, "Textes," 81. *Ulpian*, Dig., 1, 4, 6: "Quod principi placuit legis habet vigorem cum lege Regia quæ de ejus imperio lata est, populus ei et in eum omne imperium et potestatem suam conferat." *Cf.* the rule; "princeps legibus solutus est," *Krueger*, "Hist. des Sources du dr. Romain," 138.

[2] *Dion Cass.*, 53, 7; *Lampride*, "Al. Severe," 6; Dig., 14, 2, 9.

[3] The soldiers were bound to him by oath by virtue of his quality as military chief, conformably to the usages of republican Rome (*Liv.*, 22, 53); but it seems that all his subjects similarly bound themselves at his accession. C.I.L., II, 172 (oath of the inhabitants of Arithiun in Lusitania, the 11th of May, A.D. 37, to Caligula). "Eph. epigr.," V, 154. *Herodius*, 2, 9, 5; *Duchesne*, "Lib. pontific," I, 408.

§ 31. **The Later Empire.** — These rights of the magistrates of the republic, united in the hands of the prince, blended with one another and finally became undistinguishable. The monarchical régime was sanctioned by law as it was accepted in fact. The practice of the Emperor in associating his heir with him on the throne assured the regular transmission of power (cases of forcible seizure excepted). To the emperor belonged directly and solely all power and all right in regard to legislation, justice, army, and finance. In his palace, surrounded by a brilliant court, clothed in gold and purple, crowned with diadems, isolated from his subjects by a ceremonial almost religious in character ("adoratio"), he was treated as a god on earth. He resembled the Oriental monarchs, and, too often, like them, was a weakling or indolent king ("roi fainéant"), who allowed his favorites, eunuchs, and women to govern.

§ 32. **The Representatives of the Central Power.** — The State being incarnate in the emperor, his personal servants became functionaries: the prefect of the pretorium, or chief of the imperial guard with criminal jurisdiction in Italy, in reality often prime minister or vice-emperor; prefect of the city,[1] who was charged with the police of Rome; bureaus ("scrinia"); chancellery of which the employees ("ab epistulis," correspondence; "a libellis," reception of petitions; "a cognitionibus," reports to the emperor; "a memoria") were chosen at first from among the slaves or from those who had been enfranchised by the prince, later from the equestrian order, like the procurators or financial agents who were sent into the provinces; the council of the prince,[2] at first without official character (his friends and servitors), but from the time of Hadrian, a part of the machinery of the State (with a staff of functionaries). The Later Empire developed and became better organized. The council of the prince became the sacred consistory, a true council of State, with its members ordinary and extraordinary, and with notaries who kept the records of the proceedings of the sessions. The entourage of the prince formed the "Palatium."

In this we may distinguish, first, a civil household under a master of offices, who exercised surveillance over the palace and its personnel, directed the bureaus ("scrinia"), had charge of the correspondence, which gave him an opportunity to participate in the administration, introduced ambassadors, and was at the

[1] *Vigneaux*, "La præfectura urbis," 1897.
[2] *Cuq*, "Le Conseil des empéreurs," 1882.

head of the "officium admissionum" ("marshals"), despatched "agentes in rebus," or couriers (among which were the "curiosi" or "policiers"), managed the movements of the court, and had as subordinates the sergeant-majors, equerries, etc. There was also in the private service of the emperor a large personnel of "cubicularii," "ministeriales," "silentiarii," and "ostiarii," all under the orders of the grand chamberlain ("præpositus sacri cubiculi"). The questor of the sacred palace, a sort of minister of the interior, prepared the laws, received appeals, and addressed the senate in the name of the emperor. The finances were intrusted to the count of the sacred largesses, and to the "comes rerum privatarum."

The "palatium" contained, in the second place, a military household including the "scolæ," or body of palace guards, at the head of which was the master of offices, and the body-guards ("domestici" "protectores") commanded by the count of domestics and a "comes stabuli" under whose orders were the "stratores" or equerries who followed the court on its journeys. The masters of the militia were at the head of the rest of the army.

§ 33. **Officialdom ("Functionarism"), Separation of Powers and the Hierarchy.** — Insignia, honors, subordinate employees or "officiales," bureaus, distinction between honorary service, active service, and reserve service: one finds in the administration of the Later Empire all the characteristics of our officialdom ("functionarism"). A division of labor followed, resulting in the creation of seven ministerial departments: the service of the palace, the private service of the prince, legislation ("quæstor s. p."), the army, the finances, the administration of which was divided into two parts ("comes sacrarum largitionum, c. rerum privatarum"), and administration (which included justice). In each of these the inferior functionaries were hierarchally subordinated one to the other, and placed under a chief of service who alone was in direct relation with the prince. The Empire was divided into four prefectures: Gaul, Italy, Illyria, and the East. The two capitals, Rome and Constantinople, were not included, each occupying a special situation. Each was governed by a prefect who provided for their subsistence and exercised important judicial powers. The four pretorian prefects directed the administration and justice. Each prefecture was divided into dioceses administered by vicars (fourteen in all), and each diocese in turn into provinces (one hundred and twenty in all); the governor of the province ("præses," "corrector," "judex") resided in the chief town of one of them ("metropolis"). This was a model administrative organization, but, for lack of equilibrium, was easily turned to despotism and fiscal oppression.

Topic 2. Justice, Army, Finances

§ 34. **Justice.** — First: all justice emanated from the State; but this principle was attacked under the Later Empire by the creation of a rival jurisdiction, that of the Church, and by the rise of the system of private justice.

Second: justice was administered by administrative functionaries; in default of the separation of judicial and executive power, one finds here a distinction between the magistrates who prepare the cause for trial ("jus"), and the judge who pronounced the sentence ("judicium"). Every lawsuit thus passed through two phases of procedure ("ordo judiciorum"); if by exception the magistrate conducted the case to the end, he proceeded "extra ordinem." This extraordinary procedure, as it was called, began with Diocletian, and legal controversies of minor importance were assigned to the "pedanei" (petty judges), these being delegates of the magistrates, "judices dati," in contradistinction to the former jury-judges, who were inscribed on a list or "album" which included only senators or decurions. The magistrates under the Empire administered justice both in civil and criminal cases.[1]

[1] *Auxiliaries of justice.* The advocates ("advocati," "scholastici," "togati," "causidici," "patroni," "defensores") formed a corporation as early as 319, for each tribunal; they were inscribed on a roll "matricula fori"; some were "statuti," others, simple licentiates ("supernumerarii"); they had a president, "primas," who was chief of the corporation; they took the professional oath, and were ranked in order of seniority. From among them the assessors of the magistrates were chosen, and they were exempt from onerous charges, such as the service of the curia. The magistrate before whom they practised exercised a disciplinary power over them (fine, suspension, removal) and supervised their appointment. Only those were admitted who fulfilled certain conditions, such as a prescribed course of study, and a statement by their professor that they possessed the necessary knowledge. Their fees could not exceed the amounts fixed by law. "Mél. d'arch.," 1885, p. 276; *Bethmann-Hollweg*, "Civilpr.," III, Sec. 143; "Dict. des Antiq.," see "Advocatio"; *Grellet-Dumazeau*, "Le barreau romain," 1845.

The "advocatus fisci" ("Mél. d'archeol.," 1885) represented and defended the public treasury in cases in which it was involved. This function was a public office from the time of Hadrian: Cod. Theod., 10, 15. Cod. Just., 2, 7, and 8; it has been compared to our State's Attorney or public prosecutor. There was no profession corresponding to our solicitors ("avoués"). The "procuratores" or "actores" conducted the case in the absence of a party. The "officiales" of the magistrates, their scribes ("exceptores," "chartularii"), performed the functions of our recorders and bailiffs, executed judgments, and prepared the judicial papers.

Third: suitors had certain guarantees, such as public procedure (the magistrate sat in the forum, surrounded by assessors that he himself had chosen and whom he consulted if it pleased him to do so,[1] and in the 200 s he sat in the basilicon, the audience chamber, "auditorium," "secretarium" the doors of which remained open); equality of all before the law (except in criminal procedure, "cives et peregrini, honestiores et humiliores"); gratuitousness of justice (but the employees of the tribunal received fees from the 300 s on);[2] liberty of defence; trial face to face with accusers; a good system of proof; and, finally, the right of appeal. Through the system of assizes or "conventus,"[3] held by the governor in the cities of the provinces, the courts were brought to the doors of all; the municipal magistrates were on the ground; the emperor and the superior magistrates, such as the prefects of the pretorium, were, no doubt, far away, but they were not appealed to except in rare cases.

Fourth: there were, however, some abuses: The emperor had the prerogative of bringing before his tribunal all cases or of submitting them to commissioners or special judges. The members of the senatorial class also had jurisdictional privileges.

Fifth: on the criminal side the punishments were atrocious, unequal, and to a certain extent arbitrary.[4] Accusation by a private individual was the preliminary step in every process: however, there were crimes which the magistrate might prosecute "ex officio,"[5] and there were functionaries ("stationarii," "irenarchæ," "curiosi") who were charged with hunting them out and laying informations. The employment of torture increased by reason of the operation of the crime of high treason, since it applied to all who were accused of this crime. In the end all persons (except the "honestiores") accused of any crime whatever were put to torture.

§ 35. **Military Institutions.** — By reason of the division of labor, the standing and paid imperial army replaced the national militia. It was all at Rome or on the frontiers. Thirty legions sufficed

[1] The plenitude of judicial power resided in the magistrate; the assessors, although they might be jurisconsults, had no official status.

[2] *Ammianus Marcellinus*, 15, 13, complained, however, in the 300 s, that all rich defendants were acquitted. Cod. Theod., 1, 16, 7; *Girard*, "Textes," p. 144.

[3] *Festus*, see "forum": the president "forum agere dicitur."

[4] The principle was, indeed, that of a fixity of penalties, but, by way of exception, the judge might increase or reduce the legal penalty (Dig., 48, 19, 13) and punish misdemeanors for which the law made no provision. Dig., 47, 2.

[5] The "quæstiones perpetuæ" (permanent commissioners), a real criminal jury, disappeared in the 200 s.

to repel the Barbarians, and, at the same time, to maintain order among a hundred million subjects — sure proof of the popularity of the imperial government. The army was recruited first by voluntary enlistment, or by enrolment with the privilege of finding substitutes. In the 300 s, by generalizing and systematizing the practice of substitution, military service became a sort of tax on landowners; they were compelled to furnish conscripts in proportion to the extent and value of their lands, — unless they furnished money with which to hire barbarians — a circumstance which deprived the army of its national character. Besides the masters of the militia, its chiefs were, first, the "duces" (the title was official since Gordian) who, in the 300 s, commanded the troops cantoned on the frontier;[1] and, secondly, the "comites," who were friends or relatives of the prince, afterwards functionaries of various orders ("comes stabuli," "comes sacrarum largitionum," "comites consistoriani," "comites rei militaris").[2]

Among other peculiarities of the Roman military régime may be mentioned the benefice and the "hospitalitas." The military benefices[3] were the lands granted in hereditary right and upon condition of military service ("fundi limitani," lands situated on the frontier of the empire; "laetio lands" granted to the Laeti, Germans in the service of the empire and forming military colonies, for example at Chartres, Bayeux, etc.).[4] The troops of federated nations, allies of the Romans, were lodged among the inhabitants, received a "pittaccium," or ticket of lodgement, and became guests of the Romans who lodged them. Their food was furnished by the inhabitants by means of the "annona militaris." This system, called "metatum" (storehouse, lodging by rations), was applied by Arcadius and Honorius to the legions and to all the auxiliaries. It was by this means that the Barbarians acquired ownership of land.[5]

[1] The Italian dukes of the 500 s all had civil and military powers.

[2] "Comites 1, 2, 3, ordinis." The title of count was given to professors, to assessors of the magistrates, to members of the curia, "omnibus honoribus in patria functi," and was bestowed so lavishly that in the 500 s in the East there were no longer at the palace any counts and in the army it was an inferior rank. "Dict. des Antiq.," see "Comes," "Dux."

[3] These benefices were collective concessions, institutions of the State, in this respect different from the Carolingian benefices. The word "beneficium" under the Later Empire was applied only to lands. The "beneficiarius" was a soldier attached to a special service. *Lampride*, "Al. Sev.," 53; Cod. Theod., 7, 15, 12, 19; Cod. Just., 11, 59; *Maine*, "Ancient Law," c. 8.

[4] The "Gentiles" do not differ from the "Laeti," although it is said that the former were of Slavic origin (Scythes, Garmates) while the Laeti were Germans.

[5] Cod. Theod., 7, 4, 8; Nov. 25 of *Theod.* II; Cod. Just., 1, 2, 3, 38, 41.

§ 36. **Finances.**[1] — The public expenditures, much smaller than those of our modern States, included neither the public debt nor public instruction, nor the salaries of magistrates like our judges or diplomats. Most of the public works were constructed by the city or by the soldiers in time of peace. The greater part of the budgetary resources went to pay the army (fifty millions under Tiberius for twenty-five legions, "donativa," lands for the veterans), the Court, and the cost of administration. Public assistance was also expensive; in antiquity it assumed the most diverse forms: discharge of debtors, grants of public land by agrarian laws, planting colonies, workhouses (Rhodes), pension establishments like those of Trajan, curious combinations of land credit institutions and of public assistance (for example 200,000 francs were lent at 5% to fifty-one landowners for the purpose of rearing 300 poor children).[2] At Rome the distribution of wheat and other allowances (oil, wine, meat, clothes, money) was constantly increased. With this "budget of indolence" the number of unemployed increased to an alarming extent. State socialism has perhaps a splendid future, but its past is unquestionably a sad one.[3]

§ 37. **Same: Revenue.** — The revenue, which formerly came chiefly from the public lands, consisted of what we call direct taxes (those directly collected by the State from the taxpayers) and indirect taxes (those levied by reason of some act, such as the transfer of a commodity). The ancients did not have the same notion of a tax that we have. It did not appear to them as an assessment levied upon each citizen in proportion to his resources, for the expenses incurred in the common interest; neither was the

[1] *Viollet*, "Hist. des Inst.," I, 103 (detailed bibliog.); *Thémis*, X, 270. "R. hist. de dr.," 1861, 365; *Lecrivain*, "Mél. d'archeol.," Vol. VI, p. 91; *Humbert*, "Essai sur les finances chez les Romains," 1887.

[2] At Veleia, near Plaisance in A.D. 103, *Girard*, "Textes," 715.

[3] An Edict of Diocletian in the year 301 established a maximum scale of prices in the Roman Empire in order to put an end to the increasing cost of commodities; the emperor complained of the illicit profits due to avarice and of the passion of gain; nothing stopped the speculators, neither the quantity of the imports nor the abundance of the harvest. According to Mr. *Waddington*, who has given us a publication of the edict ("Edict Diocletien," of the year 301, 1864) this maximum price scale differed little from the prices of our times: Rye, 1 hect., 21 francs 75; oats, 1 hect., 10 francs 75; chickens, 3 fr. 72; a hundred eggs, 6 fr. 20; one day's work of a mason 3 fr. 10; one day's work of a laborer in the country, 1 fr. 55 (plus his food), avocat for a petition, 12 fr. 40, and for a judgment, 62 fr. *Lactance*, "De mort. persec.," 7, maintains that in spite of the penalty of death against those who violated it the edict was not observed. Its enforcement caused troubles; the markets were no longer provisioned and in the end it was necessary to repeal the law.

vote of the budget by the taxpayers known to them, nor the equality of all in the matter of taxation recognized. According to their ideas, the tax was a tribute imposed by the conqueror upon the conquered, the price of liberty and of property which was left as a favor to the "dedititii." In general, the citizen did not owe money to the State; he owed it his services (gratuitous performance of public duties, maintenance of public roads, etc.)[1] and he paid it by personal service.

§ 38. **Direct Taxes**, in conformity with these ideas, were levied upon the inhabitants of the provinces only and not upon those of Italy, the conquering country. Several Gallic cities (Lyons, Vienna, etc.) received by way of privilege the "jus italicum," or assimilation with Italy:[2] their lands became in consequence susceptible of full private ownership ("dominium ex jure Quiritium") and were exempt from the land tax. The immunity of Italy from direct taxes lasted until the time of Diocletian. Direct taxes were sometimes paid in kind — ("annonæ") — sometimes in money; sometimes as land taxes, sometimes as personal contributions; "stipendium" paid by the senatorial provinces and turned into the "ærarium," or treasury of the people; "tributum" paid by the imperial provinces and turned into the "fiscus" or treasury of the prince. In the beginning, they were diverse, but were reduced to a certain uniformity by measures taken by Augustus and Diocletian. Augustus had a general census taken of the population and property and a kind of register or survey (chorography or "breviarium totius imperii").[3] Every five years, the municipal magistrates made a new census based on the declaration ("professiones") of private individuals themselves; the results being brought together in the provinces and later in Rome. In the 300 s there was a revision at intervals of fifteen years (borrowed probably from Egypt); also the cycle of "indiction,"

[1] Among the prestations (payment in kind) or Corvées which were required of the citizens by reason of this principle may be cited the postal services. The imperial post, "cursus publicus," the operation of which might be farmed out to private individuals by a "tractaria" or "evectio," had as agents the "tabellarii" or the "veredarii;" it had stations, "mansiones," requisitions of spare horses for relays, and for reënforcement ("paraveredi," palfreys, "pferd"), and it exacted ordinary or extraordinary team service ("angariæ," "parangariæ"). "Mèl. d'archeol.," 1889, 249; Dig., 1, 4, 18; Cod. Theod., 8, 5; *Karlowa*, "Roem. Rechtsg.," I, 874; *Dahn*, "Koenig. d. German," VI, 286, and *Gaupp*, "Ansiedlung.," p. 348, as to the post of the Visigoths and the Burgundians.

[2] *Gaius*, 2, 7; *Beaudouin*, N.H.R., 1881; *Heisterbergk*, "Jus italicum," 1885; *Beaudant*, thesis, 1887; "R. crit. de litt." 1884 (Feb. 4).

[3] *Jullian*, "Mèl. d'archéol.," 1883, 149. The colonies had a plan ("forma,") and a commentary of this plan ("libri," "scriptura").

or budgetary period of fifteen years beginning the first of May, 312, and which served for the reckoning of the years until the Middle Ages. The word "indictio" signified a declaration by the emperor of the total product of the tax, the sum that was required of the taxpayers.[1] This sum was apportioned among the provinces, then in each province among the cities, and finally in each city, the curia fixed the quota of each taxpayer. Diocletian created the taxable unit, "jugum" or "caput," employed in all the empire and embracing a quantity of land which varied with its fertility and the state of cultivation; each unit paid the same amount.[2] This wise measure did not succeed, however, in putting an end to the arbitrariness and to vexations.

§ 39. **The Later Empire.** — Under the Later Empire the direct tax is split up into a variety of special impositions which reached every class of society: 1st, the "Capitatio terrena"[3] or land tax on the "possessores," in addition to the "annona" and various "prestations" (construction of roads, transport of provisions, lodgement of the emperor or his suite, etc.);[4] 2d, the "Capitatio plebeia," "humana," personal contributions levied upon the plebeians, particularly the cultivators, the "plebs urbana" having been exempted by Constantine; this was in the nature of a poll tax (so much "per caput" or group of men); 3d, "Chrysargyre" ("lustralis collatio"), a license tax on merchants or manufacturers apportioned by the notables; 4th, "Crown Gold" voluntary gifts, which became the tax of the decurions;[5] 5th, "Gleba senatoria," imposed upon the senatorial class who still paid the "oblatio votorum" every year, and the "aurum oblatitium" on the occasion of every happy event.

§ 40. **Indirect Taxes.**—1st, The principal, "portorium," "vectigal" or "teloneum," a toll levied on merchandise which circulated in the interior of the Empire[6] or which crossed the frontier,

[1] Reductions or "Superindictiones," additions to the rate of the indiction.

[2] "Capitastrum," "catastrum" (register of the survey), assembly of heads. The register of taxes called "libri," "censuales," "vasaria," "publica," "polyptycha," *Marquardt*, "Org. fin.," p. 285–287 (assessment rolls).

[3] *Ulpian*, Dig., 50, 15, 4.

[4] Cæsar imposed on Gaul a tax of at least ten million francs (40 million sesterces). It is calculated that under Julian, it paid nearly 150 million francs. *Viollet*, 1. 84, "Hist. de droit," 1861, 375. 6 N.H.R., 1893, 172 (La "lucrativa descriptio").

[5] *Vigie*, "Etude s. les imp. indirects romains," 1881. "Soc. languedoc. de geogr.," 1882, 467, *Cagnat*, "Et. hist. s. les impots indirects chez les R.," 1882. *Kneip*, "Societas publicanorum," 1896. Customs duties among the Gauls, *Cæsar*, I, 18, III, 8. Cod. Just., 12, 47, 1.

[6] It was forbidden to export arms, gold, wheat, or wine.

was at first a payment to the State for the use of the "loca publica"; it was employed and extended for fiscal purposes and only incidentally for protection of national industry.[1] The tax varied in amount,[2] in Gaul it was $\frac{1}{40}$ of the value of the objects taxed, and, in principle, all were taxed except those intended for the personal use of travellers. The tax was farmed out to societies of publicans whose employees collected it on the basis of declaration ("progressiones") of travellers, seized merchandise found circulating fraudulently, and had power to compromise in case of dispute. A "procurator" examined and judged. 2d, "Vicesima libertatis" ($\frac{1}{20}$ of the value of a freed slave). 3d, "Vicesima hereditatum" (until the time of Constantine); 5 % on inheritances, this tax, intended for the "ærarium militare," was paid by citizens only. 4th, "Centesima rerum venalium," 1 % at first, and in the 400 s 4 % of objects sold.

§ 41. **Appendices.** — The Regalian rights of the Middle Ages may be compared to certain rights existing at Rome for the benefit of the Prince: such as the monopoly of salt;[3] the coinage of money; (which was left at first to the cities);[4] mines, which the emperors appropriated to themselves nearly everywhere, and which they exploited by the labor of condemned criminals under the direction of "farmers" and procurators;[5] the right to pillage, to succession in case of escheat, to "caduca," and to confiscated property.

Topic 3. The Province

§ 42. **The Province**[6] was a territorial district embracing several cities situated outside of Italy, and under the direction of a governor (proprætor or proconsul for the provinces of the senate where there was no army, legate of Augustus for the provinces of the emperor where there were troops). The proconsuls of the republican epoch exploited the provinces on their own account though at the risk of being prosecuted for extortion (Verres, Fonteius). The contrast between them and the governors

[1] *Roziere*, "Formules" 32 bis (500 s).

[2] Tariffs: List of Marcian, Dig., "de publ," 39, 4, 16; Nov. of *Valentinian III* 445. Inscr. of Palmyra, April 137.

[3] Dig., 50, 15, 4; Cod. Just., 4, 61, 11.

[4] Mints in Gaul, at Lyons, Arles ("Notitia Dign.").

[5] Table of Aljustrel (Portugal), "Lex metalli Vipascensis," N.R.H., 1878.

[6] "Provincia" signifies the totality of the powers of a magistrate, for example, the command exercised by the magistrate over a conquered territory, and, finally, the territory itself. *Herzog*, "Galliæ Narbon. prov. historia," 1869. "R. archéol." 1866, 377 *et seq.*

of the imperial epoch, who were closely watched, was striking, for the latter were punished and dismissed for the least abuse and were compelled to be content with their salary. The imperial administration was beneficial to the provinces. Under the Later Empire administrative uniformity was complete, there was no longer any differentiation between Italy and the provinces. Souvenirs of the past remained only in the classes of governors, proconsuls, "consulares," "correctores," and "præsides."

§ 43. **Provincial Assemblies,**[1] institutions of liberty under a most despotic régime, were indeed born of the very excess of despotism.[2] They were a product of the political religion of the empire, the cult of Rome and her fortune personified in the prince.[3] Each year delegates from the cities of a province assembled at the most important of them to celebrate the birthday of the emperor.[4] The three Gauls joined together for this purpose and the delegates of their sixty tribes held their assembly at Lyons ("Concilium Galliarum"). The powers of these assemblies were chiefly religious in character, and included the choice of the flamen charged with the conduct of provincial worship, the sacrifices and games which he celebrated,[5] and the administration of the budget supplied by the contributions of each city.[6] But in addition they also possessed political attributes, which had not been anticipated, and which, if they had had the importance that has been wrongly attributed to them, would have made of these assemblies provincial estates like those of ancient France. They granted pardons to the retiring governor against whom complaints had been preferred and sent a delegation to the prince to transmit them to him. By means of this power the diets were able to exert a certain influence over the governor.

Under the Later Empire these assemblies lost their religious character with the triumph of Christianity; for some time, however,

[1] *Guiraud,* "Les assemblées prov. dans l'emp. romain," 1887; *R. Dareste,* "J. des sav.," 1891; *Beurlier,* "Bull. crit.," March 15, 1888; *Beurlier,* "Le culte impérial," 1891; *Carette,* "Les ass. prov.," 1896.

[2] Precedents: Gallic diets, "conventus" or assizes held by governors and provincial deputations to frame indictments against governors at the end of their term. *Viollet,* p. 106, *n.* 2.

[3] *Suetonius,* "Aug.," 90; *Saint Simon,* "Mémoires," II, 20.

[4] "Lex concilii prov. Narbonensis," C.I.L., XII, 6308, N.R.H., 1888, page 353.

[5] *Pliny,* "Ep.," 10, 60, 101. "Bronze of Italica" ("Senatus consultum" of Marcus Aurelius concerning the gladiatorial combats). C.I.L. II, "Suppl. Eph. epigr.," VII, 385.

[6] A complete organization of the functionaries was found in Gaul: "Judex arcæ," judge of legal disputes, "allector arcæ," receiver general, and "exactor," "inquisitor Galliarum."

they continued to be convoked as consultative bodies,[1] somewhat as the notables of the "ancien régime," who deliberated on local affairs, formulated complaints, and sent delegations to the prince in case of serious affairs.[2] In Gaul they had disappeared when Honorius in 418 reëstablished the assembly of the seven provinces at Arles (diocese of Vienna). This latter assembly had two kinds of members, public functionaries, ("honorati," "judices") and landed proprietors ("curiales," "possessores"). The meetings were held annually and the attendance of the deputies was required under penalty of a fine. These assemblies had in other respects the same powers as those which had preceded them.[3]

Finally, these assemblies had nothing democratic about them; the central power favored their establishment, or itself created them; the population, obliged to maintain the deputies, saw in them only a burden to be cast off at the first favorable opportunity. They had no power in regard to public affairs and were not, as one might suppose, a serious counterpoise to the power of the governor.

Topic 4. The City

§ 44. **The Municipal Régime.**[4] — In the early days of the Empire there were three principal classes of cities: 1st, subject or stipendiary cities, which were absolutely dependent upon the governor; 2d, free cities, some of which had no treaties with Rome, others having treaties, these cities furnished a military contingent and dues or services in return for which they were allowed to retain their autonomy, in appearance at least; 3d, cities with Roman constitutions, either colonies of citizens such as Narbonne, Lyons, Cologne, or Latin colonies like Toulouse, Carcassonne, Nimes, Avignon, Aix, etc.[5] In the 100 s these different types, which gave the Empire a variegated or heterogeneous character like English India, were unified by

[1] Dig., 17, 14, 1; 49, 1, 1; 5, 1, 37. "Amm. Marcell.," 28, 6.

[2] Cod. Theod., 12, 12, "de legatis."

[3] "Judices," provincial governors. "Honorati," ancient imperial magistrates. "Possessores," proprietors who did not form part of the curia, but who might be summoned ("subjecti curiæ"); *cf. Viollet*, p. 125, who compares them to the most heavily taxed. *Hincmar*, Op., II, 200, (ed. *Migne*) adds the bishops (wrongly). *Haenel*, "Corpus legum," 238.

[4] *Houdoy*, "Le droit municipal," 1876; *Klipfel*, N.R.H., 1878, p. 555; and 1879, p. 171; *Duruy*, "R. Hist.," I, 1, 321; *Kuhn*, "Die städtische Verfassung d. r. Reichs," 1864; *Viollet*, p. 146, (bibl.); *C. Jullian*, "Transform. politiques de l'Italie," 1883; and *Willems*, "Les élections à Pompéii," 1887.

[5] Certain of these cities did not in reality receive "colons."

the adoption of a municipal régime,[1] which was nothing more than the constitution of republican Rome;[2] not that the imperial policy systematically imposed it upon them, but uniformity arose from other causes: the spirit of imitation which sought the title of colony, the right of citizenship conferred upon aliens, the real advantages of the municipal régime.

§ 45. **The City or "Municipium"** ("res publica") had an extended territory (somewhat like that of one of our departments). It contained the city or most important place (curbs), the "pagi," "vici," "fora," "conciliabula," "castella," small market towns, villages, small agglomerations or meeting places scarcely organized.[3] Three authorities governed the city: 1st, the "comitia" or popular assembly, 2d, the curia or municipal senate, 3d, municipal magistrates.

I. *The Comitia.* — The population included two elements: 1st, the "cives," the middle class (bourgeois), attached to the city by birth, adoption, emancipation, or the "adlectio inter cives" (by virtue of a decree of the curia); 2d, the "incolæ," or resident foreigners, subject to the same charges ("munera") as the "municipes" but without political rights; like the plebeians of ancient Rome they ended by acquiring the right of admission to the comitia and in proportion as political rights lost their importance equality triumphed. The comitia had two principal powers: the election of magistrates[4] and the enactment of local

[1] From "*municipum,*" "*munus capere*" allusion to the submission to public burdens, "Aulus Gellius," N.A., 16, 3. This word designated at first cities without political rights, then, in general, subject cities.

[2] Under the name of municipal laws is understood: *1st,* The "leges rogatæ," voted by the comitia, for example "Lex Rubria," 705–712, of Rome. *Fr. d'Este, id.*, "Lex Julia municipalis" ("Table of Heraclitus"), 709, a general law concerning the municipal régime. *2d,* The "leges datæ," laws given through delegation of the people by a Roman magistrate, or, under the Empire, by the emperor by virtue of his proconsular power (for example, the military diplomas). Such were the "*Lex coloniæ* Genetivæ Juliæ" (bronzes of Ossuna), a municipal statute of the colony of citizens established at Urso, in Andalusia, 710, and the Tables of Salpensa and of Malaga, under Domitian, A.D. 81–82, statutes of two Latin colonies. *Girard,* "Textes," p. 108. Add N.R.H., 1896, 404; and 1897, 113: "*lex municipii* Tarentini." 3d, The laws voted by the municipal comitias. *Cicero,* "de leg.," III, 16, 6.

[3] *Isidore,* "Etym.," 15, 2; *Salvien,* "*De gub.*" Dei V, 4 Dig.; "de leg.," I, 73, I; Cod. Just., 2, 58, 1; *Esmein,* p. 6; *Houdoy,* p. 204; *Schullen,* "Philologus" 1894, vol. 56 ("*pagi*" their "magistri," etc.). Likewise the "*conventus*" or groups of citizens domiciled in a foreign country, 1892 the camps, "Hermes," 1896, 429; *Mommsen,* "Hermes," xvi, 447; xix, 36.

[4] The elections of this period greatly resembled those of our day; official declaration of candidature, placards, measures against electoral corruption, convocation of electors, meeting of these in the separate enclosures by tribes or curias, deposit of the ballots ("tabella") in a box ("cista")

laws, but their legislative power was necessarily very restricted under a monarchical régime and at the beginning of the 200 s the election of magistrates passed to the senate.

II. *The Municipal Senate.* — ("ordo," "senatus," "curia"; "decuriones conscriptivi," and, after the 200 s, "curiales"). This body often included as many as a hundred members. Every five years the "*quinquennales*" proceeded to the "*lectio senatus*" (like the censors at Rome) by inscribing in the place of the dead and unworthy the names of the retiring municipal magistrates and, in default of these, of private individuals ("pedanei") who fulfilled certain conditions of age and property. At the beginning of the 200 s there was a strike among the candidates for the municipal magistracies whose duties had become too burdensome. The magistrates were chosen of right by the senate ("creatio") upon the nomination ("nominatio") of those whose terms had expired, the names being taken from among the decurions. Later the senate recruited itself through coöptation by choosing its own members from among the "possessores" or landed proprietors, giving preference to the sons of the decurions.[1] The decurions had the privileges of the "honestiores" (insignia and places of honor) and were treated like them; convocations, meetings, and voting were sometimes public ("per secessionem"), sometimes secret ("per tabellas") and took place as in the case of the Roman senate.

In general, the senate had to be consulted by the magistrates in regard to all affairs of interest to the city: religion (fêtes, games), public expenses, public works (expropriation, days of prestation), the arming of the citizens, nomination of patrons, the award of statues or honors, and concessions to the bourgeoisie.

III. *Magistrates.* — 1st, *Duumvirs* ("duoviri juridicundo") performing the functions of consuls, censors, and pretors at Rome. Every five years, under the name of "quinquennales," the duumvirs of the year prepared the "lectio senatus" and took the census of the population. They convoked and presided over the comitia and the senate, executed their decisions, administered affairs, and exercised (though in the territory of the city only)

placed at the entrance of each enclosure and watched over at the same time by electors taken from another tribe or curia, and by representatives of the candidates, counting of votes by the electoral bureau, proclamation of the result by the presiding magistrate, and the necessity of an absolute majority of votes for election.

[1] The "Album decurionum" of *Canusium* ("Apulia"), (C.I.L., IX, 338; *cf.* Dig. 50, 3, 1, and C.I.L., VIII, 1, 240), made known the hierarchical order among municipal senators.

(*a*) the "imperium" and in consequence military command ("tribunus militum a populo") and criminal jurisdiction (except for crimes affecting the security of the State), (*b*) civil jurisdiction until the 100 s at least,[1] though their competence was limited to a certain amount not known. 2d, *Ediles,* who were charged with the police of markets, control of weights and measures, maintenance of public buildings, highways, games, victualling. 3d, *Quæstors* or "duumvirs ab ærario," who administered the municipal funds. 4th, *Prefects,* who in case of vacancies took the places of the absent duumvirs, or of the emperor, called duumvir. The municipal priesthood ("sacerdotes") resembled the magistrates except as to their life tenure. There were "sacerdotes" for the local gods, such as the "Tutela," or protecting spirit of the Bituriges Vivisci at Bordeaux, pontiffs and soothsayers for the official Roman religion, and flamens of Augustus for the imperial religion. To this last cult were attached the Seviri,[2] a college of freedmen, whose ex-members made up the "Ordo Augustalium" below the decurions and above the plebeians.[3]

§ 46. **Résumé.** — Summarizing, we may say that the municipality or city was an autonomous State which had adopted the constitution of republican Rome and which gravitated within the sphere of attraction of the imperial monarchy. It administered itself through its senate and its magistrates; it had its own budget, its militia, its religion, its system of justice. It was a little republic, but an aristocratic one, because the curia was an assembly of the richest; the service of its magistracies was gratuitous, even more; the first object of the magistrates was to make largesses to the people, to provide games for them and, in case of need, to furnish them with the means of subsistence. This régime of decentralization brought great prosperity to the Empire, or, at

[1] These were the same general principles as governed the Roman magistracy: hierarchy of magistracies, collegiality, or two incumbents for each office, intercession, annual tenure and unpaid service, conditions of eligibility (ingenuousness, military service, age: 30, 25, 18 years and payment of taxes), oath, right of entry, insignias, honorary privileges, "apparitores" (that is to say, "lictors," scribes, "viatores," etc.).

[2] C.I.L., XII, 4333 ("ara narbonensis"), *Beurlier*, p. 194.

[3] Contradistinguished from the municipal honors that we have just enumerated were the "munera" or burdens, some personal like those of a representative of the courts of justice ("syndicus," "defensor," "actor") of the city, curator of the "annonæ," delegates near the prince (they received in this case a "viaticum," travelling expenses, etc.); others patrimonial, for example, reception and support of public functionaries, horses, chariots, and means of transportation, furnished to the post, etc. Cod. Theod., 11, 16, 15. Immunities or "vacatio munerum," for the benefit of pontiffs, veterans, rhetoricians, grammarians, physicians, philosophers, etc.

least, coincided with a period of prosperity due chiefly to the "pax romana" of which numerous monuments are still witnesses. The municipal liberties in the provinces had the same fate as the political liberties of Rome; they disappeared toward the end of the 200 s. The governors interfered more and more in the local administration, the logic of the monarchical system required it. Christianity discouraged the acceptance of municipal honors, for the government of the city was not distinct from the ceremonies of religion.[1] The troubles of the 200 s destroyed the municipal aristocracy, which formed in the Empire a middle class intermediate between the senatorial nobility and the plebeian class.

§ 47. **Decadence of the Municipal Régime.** — There were no more comitia. The decurionate became hereditary and obligatory, it was even imposed as a punishment; when necessary whoever possessed twenty-five arpents was attached to the curia;[2] the legitimate children of the members of the curia were members by right, their "liberi naturales" were legitimized by being offered to the curia.[3] Once members, the senators were attached to the curia permanently;[4] if they fled, they were pursued as deserters; if they took refuge in the army, in the public service, or in the clergy, they were forced out; if they succeeded in escaping, their property at least answered for them, for the curia had a right to such property. The reason for the repugnance to service in these bodies was due chiefly to the responsibility for the collection of the land tax, which was imposed on members of the curia. This responsibility, which constituted a personal burden, tended to become a patrimonial charge and to fall only on the decurions, that is to say, on the rich. They chose ordinarily from among themselves the collectors ("susceptores" and "exactores") who were responsible not only for their negligence, but even for the insolvency of the taxpayers. The curia was secondarily responsible because it had appointed them.[5] This system presented another inconvenience: the decurions who were charged with the apportionment and collection of the tax[6] overwhelmed

[1] For a contrary view, see *Bossier*, "La fin du paganisme," 1894; Cod. Theod., 16, 2, 2.

[2] The twenty-five arpents was equal to more than six hectares (about 15 acres).

[3] Cod. Theod., 12, 1, 122; Cod. Just., 5, 27, 3.

[4] *Ibid.*, 12, 1; Cod. Just., 10, 32, 34, 38.

[5] *Lécrivain*, "Mél. d'arch.," 1889, p. 381. The collectors of the "taille" during the monarchical epoch were often compared in this connection to the members of the curia under the Later Empire.

[6] The most important members of the curia were distinguished as the "principales," the "decemprimi," and the "primus curiæ." *Lécrivain*, "Mél. d'arch.," 1889; *Viollet*, p. 126.

the poor and feeble with vexations both in order to spare themselves and because they were obliged to treat the powerful and rich with consideration. The curia was transformed furthermore into a bureau of registry of private acts. The municipal magistracies finally disappeared or their incumbents became simply agents of the central power (thus the duumvirs were often appointed by the governor of the province) and had rivals in 1st: the "curator reipublicæ,"[1] a guardian whom the emperor was compelled to impose upon the cities on account of the disorders in their financial administration, as guardians are put over spendthrifts, and whose powers, exclusively financial at first, were finally extended until they took the place of other magistrates, particularly the ediles, as soon as an expense was incurred, that is to say, in the majority of cases. Thus he exercised a surveillance over the service of victualling, fixed the maximum price of provisions, and regulated the business of public markets, for neither commerce nor industry was free. 2d, the "defensor civitatis,"[2] who was appointed at first by the prefect of the pretorian guard, later by the people,[3] and was taken, not from among the plebeians, but from among the "nobilitores"; he was the patron of the city, defended it against the "injuriæ potentium," corresponded directly with the emperor, had free access to the presence of the governor, assisted in the preparation of the tax lists, and ended by transforming himself into a true municipal magistrate (appointed for five years) with police powers, civil jurisdiction, and the preparation of the "gesta" in coöperation with the duumvirs, whose rôle disappeared more and more into the background. The city thus became an administrative division, the curia a society of collectors, the municipal magistrates subordinate functionaries. In the East, Leo the

[1] Concerning the "curator reip.," see "Mél. d'archéol.," 1884, pp. 133–357; *Cassiod.*, "Var.," 7, 12; Cod. Theod., 12, 1, 20; Dig., 50, 8; *Ulpian's* treatise "de off. curat."

[2] On the "defensor civitatis," *cf. Lécrivain*, "Mél. d'archéol.," 1884, p. 133; *Chénon*, N.R.H., 1889; Cod. Theod., 1, 29. A constitution of Valentinian I, 364, was the first document which mentions the "defensor." It was believed, wrongly, however, that he was taken from the plebeians and he has been compared to the tribunes of Ancient Rome. The bishops were never "defensores." See Nov. XV of *Justinian*. Concerning the "defensores" in Gaul, see "Lex romana Wisigoth.," C. Th., 1, 10, 1, 29, 6. *Papinian*, 22, 4, 36, 8. "Lex romana Wis.," 1, 7, 2. During the same period, there were "defensores ecclesiæ," "senatus."

[3] Cod. Theod., 1, 29, 6 (year 387). Cod. Just., 1, 55, 8 (year 409). The constitution of 409 speaks only of the bishop, the clergy, the "honorati," the "possessores," and the curiales. It is probable that the aristocracy always had a large part in this choice, but that the people were not debarred from it. "L. Wisig.," 12, 1, 2: the bishops and the people.

Philosopher (886–911) by Novel 46 abolished what remained of the municipal régime; this shadow of liberty offended the imperial majesty, whose solicitude, like that of divine Providence, extended over everything. In the West, the establishment of the Barbarians had destroyed municipal institutions long before.[1]

TOPIC 5. STATUS OF PERSONS

§ 48. **Class System.** — The Roman State was always a régime of privileges, it never knew equality. Social distinctions disappeared only to be replaced by others (patricians and plebeians, citizens and aliens, "honestiores" and "humiliores").[2] The Later Empire exaggerated this system, multiplied classes and strictly held every person to his class. There were upper classes, such as the senatorial order and the functionaries; and lower classes like the city plebeians (working-classes), coloni (agricultural classes), freedmen, slaves, and a middle class which was in process of disappearing, "curiales" and "possessores."

§ 49. **Functionaries**, with their brevets, insignia, solemn installation, salary, employees ("officium," "officiales"), fiscal and judicial privileges, and rights of precedence, formed a hierarchical nobility[3] which recalls the Russian "tchine" embracing in fourteen classes all the civil and military officers. In the highest rank were the "nobilissimi" or members of the imperial or patrician families; then the "illustres," the first dignitaries of the court, prefects of the pretorians and of the city, and masters of the militia; the "spectabiles," chiefs of divisions at the palace, such as the dean of the notaries, the vicars, the counts, and the dukes; the "clarissimi," senators and governors; the "egregii," mem-

[1] The mention made of the curia, of the "defensor," and of the "Gesta," that are found up to the 800s and 900s no more prove the persistence of the municipal régime than the custom of counting by sous proves to-day the preservation of the monetary system of the old régime. The curia existed in some towns to the 500s and 600s, *Fr. de Gaudenzi*, c. 15. But after that the curia whenever it is spoken of is meant a judicial assembly presided over by a judge who was qualified as a defensor. *Menard*, "Hist. de Nimes," 1, 19. B. ch., 5th Cent., 1, 440; "R. de. leg.," 1872, p. 155; *Martel*, "Etudes s. l'énregistr. des actes dans les Gesta," 1877; *Daremberg*, "Dict. des ant." see "Acta"; *cf. Raynouard*, "Hist. du dr. municipal en France," 1829; *Viollet*, I, 315.

[2] Concerning the "honestiores" and the "humiliores," *cf. Duruy*, "Acad. inscr.," Vol. 29, p. 253; "Hist. des Romains," V, 487; *Mispoulet*, "Institut. polit. des Romains," II, 149; Dig., 48, 2, 10; 48, 19, 28, 2; 50, 2, 2, 2; *Paul*, "Sent.," 5, 4, 10. The imperial rescript forbade the striking of the "honestiores" with rods. The plebeians were ineligible to public office.

[3] But not hereditary; heredity only existed for simple employees ("officiales").

bers of the equestrian order (which ceased to exist after the 300s); the "perfectissimi," which included various employees, such as the "primicerii scriniorum," "actuarii" after ten years of service, and decurions in certain cases. This "mandarinat" possessed a beautiful symmetry.

§ 50. **The Senatorial Class** was constituted in two ways, 1st, by inheritance of the senatorial dignity; 2d, by grant of this title from the prince to the large provincial landowners who were too distant to take part in the assemblies and who ultimately lost the right of sitting in the senate, — these were the honorary senators scattered throughout the Empire. The senatorial families formed an aristocracy of the great landed proprietors, who were the rivals of the public functionaries in power and influence and who furnished bishops for the dioceses of Gaul. Besides honors, insignia, and the title of "clarissimi," they enjoyed certain privileges of a judicial character and in regard to taxes.[1]

§ 51. **Associations of Laborers.**[2] — From the earliest days of Rome, the working-classes were organized in "collegia," which had a monopoly of industry. But with the exception of these associations, protected by their antiquity and by their religious character, the "collegia," from fear that they would become political clubs, were subjected to a régime of previous authorization, and of public control.[3] The Empire allowed especially industrial or commercial associations (mariners of the Seine, "nautæ parisiaci," butchers of Périgueux,[4] etc.), and the "collegia tenuiorum" which were principally designed to procure burial for their members.[5] Lawful associations were all, moreover, of the same type,

[1] (A.) In Judicial matters: (*a*) civil; they were tried by the prefect of the city, at least, when they were defendants, for they were reckoned as having their domicile at Rome ("Actor sequitur forum rei"); (*b*) criminal; it was still this prefect who tried them, subject to the right of appeal to the emperor. The punishments to which they were liable were of the lightest kind and they were exempt from torture (except in case of lèse-majesté). (B.) In respect to taxes, they enjoyed various immunities such as exemption from servile charges ("munera sordida"), and from coronation gifts, but they gained less by this than might be supposed, for they were subject to special taxes and restrictions in regard to their lands, in respect to the payment of the land tax. The Later Empire was obliged to provide them with a defender ("defensor senatus").

[2] BIBLIOGRAPHY: *Levasseur*, "Hist. des classes ouvrièrs," 1859; *Vauthier*, "Etude sur les personnes morales," 1887; *Waltzing*, "Les corporations chez les Romains," 1895; *Liebenam*, "Römische Vereinswesen," 1890; *Matthias*, "Römische Zwangsverbände," 1891.

[3] Dig., 3, 4, 1, 47, 22, 1, and following; *Girard*, "Textes," p. 111.

[4] *Desjardins*, "Géog. de la Gaule romain," III, 261; *Pigeonneau*, "Hist. du commerce," Vol. I.

[5] Statutes of the "Collegium funeraticium" of Lanuvium, A.D. 133; *Girard*, "Textes," p. 735; C.I.L., III, 924; VI, 10234; *Bossier*, "Reli-

and they were above all religious brotherhoods.[1] They were in some sense comparable to a family, all the members being regarded as brothers, one could no more belong to two associations than to two families. The right of membership was hereditary, passing from father to son, at least under the Later Empire. Viewed from its internal constitution the association ("respublica") had, like the municipalities, its magistrates elected by the "Collegiati" or members ("duumvirs" "quinquennales"), its inferior employees (treasurers, "actor," or syndic to represent it before the courts of justice), its patrons ("pater," "mater collegii"), and the "populus" of the members. The treasury was supplied by a monthly assessment. Juristic personality was possessed only by societies recognized by the State and ceased as soon as the authorization was withdrawn.[2]

(A.) Under the Later Empire and from the 200 s, instead of treating the members of labor associations as suspects, the State incorporated them and utilized them for purposes of government. Alexander Severus, for example, organized the trades of Rome into corporations as a means of assuring the victualing of the city. This example was followed until there was official regulation and almost official organization of labor. It was to the interest of the workmen to be enrolled in the corporations in order not to be sacrificed in the assessment of the "chrysargyre," a fact which made the collection of this tax easier. The workman thereby found himself and his children attached by an indissoluble bond to his corporation, as the "curialis" to the curia, the "colonus" to the land, the "officialis" to his bureau, and the soldier to the army.[3]

1st. *Manufactures of the State*[4] (such as the manufacture of arms, etc.). The workmen were in the strictest sense of the term bound like serfs to their workshop, they were branded with hot irons, and their daughters were not allowed to marry outside of their trade.

2d. Certain *trades* necessary to the subsistence of the people

gion romain," II, 308. It was under the protection of these societies that Christianity grew. "The respect for the dead was the reason for the momentary toleration accorded to Christians."

[1] The association afforded a pretext for banquets, fêtes, and distribution of provisions and money; but it was the chiefs, that is to say, the richest, who received the most. The Roman "colleges" were therefore only remote analogies to our mutual aid societies.

[2] Dig., 50, 16, 85; 47, 23, 1; Cod. Theod., 12, 1; 14, 3, 16; 10. 20; 1, 21, 22; *Wilmann's* "Exempla," 1745 (Boatmen of Ostia, A.D. 152); Cod. Just., 8, 6, 24 (year 291).

[3] Cod. Theod., 12, 1, 179; 4, 2, 4; 7, 1 and 2; 8, 2; Cod. Just., 11, 42.

[4] About the year 400, there were in Gaul eight establishments for the manufacture of arms.

(bakers, butchers, and seamen)[1] were scarcely less strictly regulated, but they were assured in turn a monopoly of their industry and certain privileges, such as exemption from military service.

3d. The *free trades* (blacksmiths, carpenters, etc.) were also enrolled in corporations and subjected to the tutelage of the State, though the principle of heredity and obligation did not become well established among them.[2]

§ 52. **The "Colonat."**[3] **Status of the "Coloni."**—The "coloni" were cultivators ("colere")[4] attached from father to son to the lands which they exploited for the benefit of others. They were half slaves, yet free men, since they could marry ("justæ nuptiæ"), have legitimate families, become proprietors,[5] creditors, and plead in the courts; but free men who were bound to the land of others became a kind of real estate by destination, serfs of the glebe ("membra," "servi terræ") as they were already called under the Later Empire (Cod. Just., 11, 52, 1). If they escaped they were pursued, reclaimed, and taken back to the land which they had no right to leave. The proprietor was thus assured of having enough cultivators and the State was assured of collecting the tax, since the land was always occupied by cultivators. But this dependence, which seems altogether in favor of the master, was at the same time a guarantee for the "colonus"; he could not be expelled, nor could the land be alienated without him. "The land holds him but he holds the land." The slave might be sold, but not the "colonus"; the proprietor might change, but the "colonus" remained and could plan for the future. His situation in that respect was therefore better than that of the modern tenant. It

[1] The "nautæ," "navicularii," "caudicarii," transported the wheat from the provinces and the "saccarii," "portitores," unloaded it. Cod. Theod., 14, 3; Cod. Just., 11, 2. *Symmachus*, "Ep.," 10, 34.

[2] The Cod. Theod., 14, 7; 12, 19, 1 applied only to the municipal services, for example firemen.

[3] TEXTS: Cod. Theod., 5, 9; Cod. Just., 11, 47, 48 *et seq.* BIBLIOGRAPHY: *Daremberg*, "Dict. des Antiq.," see "Colonus"; *Savigny*, "Verm. Schriften," 1828; *Fustel de Coulanges*, "Recherches," 1885 (*cf.* "J. des Sav.," 1886, 512; "R. de quest. hist.," 1886; "Bull. crit.," 15 Aug. 1886). *Segré*, "Archivio giur.," vol. 42 *et seq.; Viollet*, "Hist. du dr. civ.," 309 (bibl.); *Heisterbergk*, "Entstehung d. Colonats," 1876; *Esmein*, "Mélanges," 293; *Karlowa*, "R. Rechtsg.," I, 918; *Hermes*, 1885, 3.

[4] The names given the "coloni" recall certain peculiarities of their condition: inscription on the census registers, obligation to pay the personal tax, etc. Compare the "Romanus tributarius," "L. Sal.," 41, 6, 7; *Zeumer*, "N. Archiv.," XII, 392. Concerning the "Inquilinus," *cf. Haenel*, "L. rom. Wisigoth," p. 460; N.R.H., 1897, 388; Dig., 43, 32, 1. The condition of the "coloni," different at the beginning, continued to tend toward uniformity.

[5] But they could not alienate their own property without the consent of the proprietor. Cod. Theod., 5, 11, 1; Cod. Just., 11, 49, 2.

was also better because the dues that he had to pay, "canon," "pars agraria," were invariable; usage ("consuetudo prædii") fixed the amount of the assessment and its nature, as did the rules for the imperial domains ("Lex Hadriana"). It was a sum of money or a portion of the crop, perhaps a third as in the inscriptions of Ain-Ouassel or of Henchir Mettich, a fifth, or a seventh as Hygin says concerning the "ager vectigalis." [1] The master could not increase the amount; if he attempted it the "colonus" was allowed, by exception, to make a complaint against him. The inscriptions of Souk-el-Khmis and of Henchir Mettich imposed on the cultivators of the great African domains the burden of the "corvée," harvesting, and weeding, in all six days of work per year; but no text subjected those properly called "coloni" to this obligation.[2] The property occupied by the "colonus" was subjected to the land tax and the "colonus" himself to the "capitatio plebeia"; the master paid the first and advanced the money for the second. The "colonus" was also subject to military service in the sense that the landed proprietors were required to furnish recruits and these recruits were taken from among the "coloni" occupying their lands.

§ 53. **How One became a "Colonus" and how he Ceased to be One.** — (A) One became a "colonus": 1st, by birth;[3] 2d, by

[1] The "colonus" who married outside of the domain paid a sort of tax for the privilege of marrying a person belonging to a different master ("commodum nuptiarum"). In case of a mixed marriage between "coloni" and free persons, the children acquired the status of the father, since the marriage was regular. If the father was free, it was held that the children were "coloni," following the status of the mother. (Cod. Just., "de agric.," 11, 47, 16, 21, 24.) If the father was a "colonus" and the mother free, the children were "coloni" before the time of Justinian; this prince declared the children free, but with power of the master of the husband to demand the divorce (Cod. Just., 11, 47, 24, Nov. 54); then he annulled the marriage (Nov. 22, c. 17) and obliged the children to remain with the land. It is apparent that Roman legislation, little favorable to liberty, tended to apply the rule that was later formulated: "In the case of marriage between serfs belonging to different masters, the inferior status governed." If one of the parents was a slave, the child acquired the status of the mother. If the husband and the wife were both "coloni" and occupied domains belonging to different masters, the children were "coloni," the master of the mother being entitled at first to a third of the children (Cod. Theod. "de inq.," 5, 10, 1), later, to all the children (Cod. Just., 11, 53, 3). In the law of the Novels (156, 162, c. 3, *cf.* Cod. Just., 11, 47, 13 pr.) the children were divided equally between the two masters; if the number was odd, three or five, for example, the third or fifth went to the mother. Novel 157 gave to the master of the husband the children and even the wife, but Cujas finds this a local law.

[2] *Salvien,* "de gub Dei." 5, 8; Cod. Theod., 14, 18, 1; Cod. Just., 11, 48. 18, 22–23; 51, 1.

[3] *Cf.* however, Digest., "de instr. legato," 33, 7, 20, 1 (Scævola a contemporary of Marcus Aurelius); "de leg." I, 30, 112 (Marcian, time of Alexander Severus); Cod. Theod., 5, 9, 1. (year 332).

convention; 3d, by prescription, that is to say, by the fact of having lived as a "colonus" for thirty years; 4th, as a result of punishment (for example, in the year 382 all healthy beggars). (B) The rule was: once a "colonus," always a "colonus," for attachment to the soil was a part of the public system; there was neither freedom nor limitation for the "colonus" (at least after the time of Justinian), he could escape only in some exceptional manner, as, for example, by elevation to the episcopacy, by thirty years of service in the curia, or by leave after having performed his military service.[1]

§ 54. **Origin of the "Colonat."** — This revolution in the condition of agricultural laborers passed unobserved, not a document assigns a date to it, not an author has investigated the causes of it. The "colonat" had obscure beginnings. Its legislative organization was the work of Christian emperors; there were scarcely any positive traces of its existence before the time of Constantine (332). Certain sections of the Empire formerly, or at this time, had farm laborers in a condition similar to that of the "coloni," such as the Egyptian fellahs, the Penestes or Helots in Greece, but "coloni" were unknown in ancient Rome. According to the testimony of Varron, agriculture was intrusted to the slaves or to the free farmers, without taking into account the small proprietors. The transformation of these peasants into "coloni" was general under the Later Empire, the preceding epoch only preparing the way for it. The Digest which contains the law of the first three centuries A.D. is silent concerning this institution; on the contrary the Code, which embodies the subsequent law, regulates it.

§ 55. **Causes.** — 1st, *Economic Causes.* It was especially the slow operation of these causes which created that intermediate rank between slavery and freedom to which the agricultural slaves were raised and to which the free peasants were reduced. The insufficiency of slave labor and its unproductivity in comparison with that of free labor led the master to endeavor to interest the slaves in some manner in his affairs; attached in fact to the soil, inscribed like the domain and with it on the census registers, they became definitely fixed to it.[2] On the other hand, the insecurity of the small proprietors led them to settle on the domains of the rich and to become their "coloni."[3] The insolvent farmers,

[1] *Revillout,* "Cours de droit égypt.," I, 129. "Gr. Encyclopedie," see "Colonat" (*Guiraud*).

[2] *Cf.* the "Servi casati" with individual tenure and domicile. Cod. Theod., 9, 42, 7; Cod. Just., 11, 48.

[3] *Columelle,* "de r. r.," 1, 3; *Salvien,* "de gub. Dei," 1, 5.

not being able to pay the arrears due to their landlords, lost the right to leave his lands.[1] The double evolution which resulted from these causes was sanctioned by the fiscal legislation of the Later Empire. In like manner, serfdom in Russia was organized by Boris Godounov, who only regulated the condition of the slave cultivators and of the farmers who were ruined by the wars and were obliged to replace money rent by forced labor or payment in kind.[2] Perhaps the situation of the "colonus" was modeled after that of the cultivators of the great imperial domains, who were inhabitants of the country, former proprietors, who had been dispossessed and were held in strict dependence by the agents of the prince, whose rights and obligations were not fixed by free contract but by administrative rules.[3]

2d, *A Fiscal Measure.* This being the economic situation, it was no great task for the Later Empire to bind the cultivator to the land. By this means good cultivation of the land and consequent payment of the taxes were assured. Moreover, it was nothing more than an application of the general policy of the government which was to make every one the serf of his profession. But it did not create the "colonat," the birth certificate of this institution is not found in its laws.

3d, *A Political Measure.* The slaves in Germany were almost like "coloni," this was enough to give rise to the supposition that the Barbarians transplanted into the Empire had brought the "colonat" with them. These transplantations "en masse" had taken place rather early as, for example, the Marcomans under Marcus Aurelius. But the historians who narrated these facts do not say that the Barbarians were treated as "coloni." It was only under the Later Empire when the "colonat" existed officially that this was so. The transplantations did nothing more than maintain an institution already existing.

[1] *Fustel de Coulanges, Schulten,* etc.

[2] *Kovalewsky,* N.R.H., 1889, p. 411.

[3] African documents recently discovered. 1st, The inscription of Henchir-Mettich, A.D. 115–117, under Trajan. (N.R.H., 1897, p. 373; *Schulten,* "Die römisch. Grundherschaften," 1897; *Cuq,* "Le colonat partiaire dans l'Afrique romaine," 1898; *Beaudouin,* "Les grands domaines," N.R.H., 1897 and 1898; *H. Monnier,* N.R.H., 1898, p. 391.) 2d, The inscription of Souk-el-Khmis (rescript of Commodus relative to "Saltus Burunitanus") and that of Kasv Meznar, first years of Commodus. (*Girard,* "Textes," p. 151; C.I.L., VIII, 10570 and 14428; *Esmein,* "Journal des Savants," 1880, 686.) 3d, The inscription of Aïn-Ouassel, under Sept. Severus. (N.R.H., 1892, 117; "R. Arch.," 1892; *Schulten,* "Hermes," 1894, 204.) The "lex Hadriana," mentioned in several of the documents, seems to have been a common rule in several imperial African domains.

TOPIC 6. LAND OWNERSHIP

§ 56. **Roman Theory.**—(A) As to Italian lands. Private individuals enjoyed full ownership ("dominium ex jure Quiritium"), that is to say, the use, the enjoyment, and the right of disposal (of selling, giving, or devising). The State did not enjoy superior rights over the land in the sense that it could, for example, arbitrarily confiscate or expropriate it.[1] By means of a tax on inheritances it affected ownership, but it did not dare levy the tax on the nearest relatives. (B) As to provincial lands. These lands belonged to the Roman people or to the Emperor, but were leased to private individuals by precarious tenure and in consideration of the payment of a tax.[2] In fact, however, except for the question of the tax, there was not much difference between the Italian lands and those of the provinces so far as ownership was concerned; under the Later Empire, this assimilation was recognized by law and was absolute, at least after the time of Justinian.

§ 57. **Large Estates.**—Large estates were established as early as under the Republic. The competition of foreign wheat ruined Italian agriculture and caused the abandonment of petty ownership and cultivation on a small scale. The occupation of the "ager publicus" on a large scale and by revocable tenure lent itself to the substitution of pastures for tillage. The rural population flocked to Rome. These political and economical causes operated throughout the Empire.[3] But the most important of the large domains,

[1] On Expropriation, see *Liv.*, 40, 51; *Cic.*, "de leg. agr.," 2, 30; *Suet.*, "Aug.," 56; *Frontin*, "de aquæd.," 6; Dig., 8, 4, 13; Cod. Theod., 15, 1, 50, 53.

[2] *Gaius*, II, 2; "Institutes of Justinian," 1, 40. *Cf.* in Mussulman law, *Van Berchem*, "Etude sur l'impôt du Kharadj," 1886: lands acquired by conquest were returned to the conquered in consideration of a tribute of a fifth of the products.

[3] The rural domain called "fundus," "ager," "prædium." "Villa" means house, and by extension, domain; "curtis," farm yard, and in the 400s, domain. Dig., 50, 16, 198. The "fundus" bore the name of its original proprietor: "cornelianus," that is to say, lands of Cornelius, etc. It was divided into "unciæ," twelfths, like the ace and the foot, and formed a certain unity. *Lécrivain*, "Mél. d archéol.," 1885; "Hermes," 1884, 393; *Fustel de Coulanges*, "L'Alleu," 1889. The "massa" was a group of domains, *Cassiod.*, "Var.," XII, 5; *Gregory the Great*, "Ep.," I, 41; V, 44; IX, 30; xiv, 14; *Pliny*, N.H., 18, 6, 35: "Latifundia perdidere Italiam, jam vero et provincias." *Columelle*, 1, 3; *Frontin*, "Gromatici veteres," ed. *Lachmann*, p. 53. *Ausone*, "Idyll.," III had near Bazas a "parvum herediolum" of more than 1050 arpents (250 hectares); *Salvien*, "de gub. Dei," 5. 8. Petty ownership did not, however, disappear. In the 1100s, it existed in Italy (*Girard*, "Textes de droit romain," p. 717), and we know how under the Later Empire, in order to be a decurion, it was necessary to be the owner of twenty-five arpents of land at least.

the "saltus," uncultivated lands which had not been assigned at the time of the foundation of the colonies and which had remained in the "ager publicus," whether they belonged to the emperor as was ordinarily the case, or to private individuals, were autonomous and independent of the municipalities and of the municipal authorities, because they were considered from the beginning as being outside their territory. They may be compared to seigniories.[1]

§ 58. **Mode of Exploitation.**[2] — The lands were cultivated by slaves, by "coloni," by farmers, and by the "emphytéotes" (tenants who had a perpetual lease). There is little to say about the slaves[3] and the farmers, but the "colonat" and the "emphytéose" were new institutions destined to a great future.

§ 59. **The "Emphytéose"** (ἐμφυτεύω)[4] was a perpetual or very long lease of land made on condition that the land be cleared, cultivated, and improved. It is still practiced to-day in many countries; it was a means of improving uncultivated lands since the cultivator was willing to make the necessary outlay only when he was sure of not being dispossessed. Feudal institutions, the fief, and the manor seem to be modeled on it.

The perpetual lease, in use among the Greeks[5] from the 400 s B.C., was applied to the property of cities and of temples. In the Roman State the cities also made perpetual leases, the lessee having almost as many rights as the proprietor so long as he paid the "vectigal," that is, rent due in silver or in kind.[6] Under the

[1] *Schulten*, "Die röm. Grundherrschaften," 1896; *Beaudouin*, N.H.R., 1897 (bibliography and discussion); *Cf. Esmein*, p. 6, *n.* 3; "Mélanges," p. 299–309; N.R.H., 1892, 336; *Blumenstock*, "Ensteh. d. Immobil.," p. 126.

[2] *Julian*, "Gallia," p. 125 (description of the "villa").

[3] The agricultural slaves ("familia rustica"), "instrumentum fundi" were grouped in decuries, under a monitor, or in trades (bakers, masons, etc.), or under a "magister." The women worked in the gymnæceum. The butler ("cellarius") distributed the food and the wine; the steward ("dispensator") kept the accounts; the "vellicus" (of "villa") manager, was at the head of the "familia rustica," and above him was found the commissioner ("intendant") ("actor procurator"). The slaves were branded or marked as a punishment and were shut up in the "ergastulum."

[4] BIBLIOGRAPHY: *Vuy*, "De origine et natur. juris emphyteutici," 1838; *Pepin le Halleur*, "Hist. de l'emphytéose," 1843; *E. Lattes*, "Studi s. il contr d'enfitensi," 1868; *Le Fort*, "Histoire des contrats de location perpét.," 1875; *Garsonnet*, "Hist. des locations perpétuelles," 1879; *Tocilesco'*, "Thesis," 1883; *Lécrivain*, "De agris publicis," 1887; *Beaudouin*, N.R.H., 1898, 310, 545 (and the other authors cited). On the "jus perpetuum" and the "jus privatum salvo canone" see this author.

[5] "Rev. archéol.," 1886, p. 253 (lease of Munychie), C. I. Gr. III, 5774 (Table of Heraclitus), 1886; *Caillemer*, "Le contrat de louage à Athènes"; *Beauchet*, "Hist. du droit privé athénien," 1897.

[6] *Gaius*, III, 145; *Hygin*, "Gromat," ed. *Lachmann*, p. 116; 205; Dig., 63; *Girard*, "Manuel de droit romain," p. 373.

Later Empire, perhaps from the 200 s, the emperors applied the "emphytéose" to their patrimonial properties remaining uncultivated, which was nothing more than a variation of the vectigalian lease of cultivated lands.[1] Private individuals imitated them, which was quite natural at a time when the régime of large ownership prevailed and when the decadence of agriculture led to an increase of waste lands.

§ 60. **Formation.** — The "emphyteusis" was formed "solo consensu," without delivery and without written instrument (except for the ecclesiastical "emphyteusis"). It was a sort of renting, but it was also somewhat like a sale, for there was little difference between a purchaser and a perpetual lessee. In the East, Zeno, between 476 and 484, declared it to have been an agreement "sui generis."

Rights of the "Emphytéote." — These were somewhat analogous to what was later called the right of use or usufruct, a real right as against all, even against the proprietor, while the ordinary farmer had only a trust. The right of the "emphytéote" was perpetual (or of long duration), hereditary, either "ab intestat" or testamentary; he might even sell and, in general, alienate "inter vivos" subject to heavy burdens; but before the time of Justinian, there were no rules governing these transactions and it was necessary to pay well for the consent of the proprietors. Justinian decided that the proprietor must be notified of proposals of purchase and that he might have the choice between preëmption in two months ("jus prelationis," "protimeseos") and a right of two per cent on the price of sale ("laudemium," from "laudare," to approve).[2]

Obligations of the "Emphytéote." — These were: (*a*) to clear the land, to cultivate it, to keep it in good condition, to improve it, without the right to make any claim for his improvements, since the long lease permitted him to profit therefrom; (*b*) to pay the rent ("pensio," "canon"); Zeno decided that it was due in

[1] The Theodosian Code speaks only of the domanial "emphytéose" (imperial possessions), but already, no doubt, the custom had been introduced for private individuals to consent to "emphytéotic" leases. The private "emphytéose" was regulated only in the Justinian Code, IV, 66, Novels 7 and 120 (ecclesiastic "emphytéose"). It is generally asserted that the Theodosian "emphytéose" was known only in Gaul. This seems to me very doubtful. *Haenel*, "Lex roman. Wisigoth.," 460; *Tardif*, B. Ch., 1857, p. 45; "Capit.," I, 421; Exc. "Petri," I, 60; "Form. d'Angers," c. 37; *Lécrivain*, "Le Senat," p. 125, 3. *Cuq*, "Le colonat partiaire dans l'Afrique romaine," p. 43, and *Beaudouin*, *op. cit.*, p. 560, who recognized in the inscriptions of Henchir Mettich the essential characteristics of the "emphytéose."

[2] Cod. Just., 4, 66, 3. 11, 62. 1. 11. 59, 2. *Lécrivain*, "Le Senat," p. 83.

case of partial loss and not in case of total loss; (*c*) to pay the land tax.[1] Forfeiture took place in three cases: sale without the knowledge of the proprietor, deterioration of the property, non-payment of the "canons," or of the land tax, after a period left at first to the discretion of the judge, later fixed by Justinian at three years, and at two years for church property.[2]

TOPIC 7. CONCLUSION

§ 61. **The Decadence of the Empire** must not be imputed to the administrative system, which rather retarded it, and, in the East, prolonged the existence of the Empire for several centuries. It was causes of a political character which ruined it, by assuring the success of the Barbarians. The fiscal burdens were too heavy[3] and badly apportioned; the troubles of the 200 s led to a general impoverishment; the maintenance of the court and the army became more and more burdensome.[4] The middle class was ruined and with it perished local liberties and municipal life. Excessive regulation paralyzed individual liberty. Despotism was everywhere, but in the presence of the general suffering it no longer had the same force. Public authority became enfeebled, and it was this that strengthened the power of wealth and of the great proprietors. The army, composed chiefly of Barbarians, was a menace to the State and was so poor a defense that it became

[1] The simple farmer had only a right of personal action against the lessor, and not a real right opposable to everything; he did not have possession "ad interdicta," nor could he alienate or mortgage his right. The lease was ordinarily for a term of five years. Precarious tenure was a gratuitous concession, revocable "ad nutum," implying neither the payment of dues, nor the establishment of a right, real or hereditary. Differing from the "colonus," the "emphytéote" was not attached to the soil, but he could not, upon leaving the property, be exempted from his personal obligations.

[2] Forfeiture took place legally and of full right without notice, nevertheless, if the proprietor did not use his right, the "emphytéote," was not deemed dispossessed and the Canon law permitted an avoidance of the forfeiture "celeri satisfactione" before the proprietor had declared his intention to make use of his right or to resort to legal proceedings, X. 3, 18, 4 ("de loc.").

[3] Among the facts which show it, there is none more striking than the legislation concerning abandoned lands ("agri deserti") and the system of "adjectio" which was applied to them. *H. Monnier*, N.R.H., 1892. Proprietors of fertile lands were forbidden to abandon sterile portions which were contiguously attached to them. Taxpayers or curials took abandoned fields in their charge, if they formed part of the same fiscal unit as their lands. Lands not attached to others were offered for sale to the first comer (with exemption of taxes) in default of being attributed to collectors and curials. Cod. Theod., II. 1; Cod. Just., 11, 59.

[4] Cod. Theod., 1, 7, 1; 12, 1, 146, 1, 16, 1; Cod. Just., 9, 39, 2; Novel, *Majorian*, t. 2.

necessary to fortify cities and in consequence fortresses sprang up everywhere.

§ 62. **The Potens** of the 400 s was a Roman senator in his "villa" who had become a feudal lord. He was independent of the local public authorities such as the municipal magistrates, though not of the imperial power: it was forbidden to hold courts in his domains; if malefactors or fugitive slaves were found therein, the first step was to call upon his intendants to deliver them up; the agents of the treasury were stopped when they attempted to enter his domains to collect the taxes. He exercised authority over the inhabitants of his estates, his "homines"; his "coloni," and his "emphytéotes" paid him regular dues like taxes. In spite of prohibitions to the contrary, he maintained a private militia. He tried his slaves for offenses, exercised the right of correction ("castigatio moderata") over his "coloni" and his agricultural freedmen, and was the patron of his free farmers.[1]

The peasants separately or by "vici" put themselves under the protection of a functionary ("dux," "comes") or of a large proprietor; they purchased his patronage by presents or even by periodic dues. From that time the fiscal authorities were paralyzed and had no power of action against the taxpayers, or else the taxpayers paid the tax twice, first to the patrons then to the public treasury. Prohibitions of these contracts of tutelage, which reduced the power of the public authorities, were too often renewed for us to believe that they were efficacious. At all times, moreover, the cities had had patrons who received them "in fidem clientelamque suam" and with whom they were united by a

[1] Cod. Just., 12, 1, 4; 11, 58, 7; 9, 12, 10. Concerning the private militia *cf. Lécrivain*, "Mél. d'archéol.," 1890, 267; Novels of *Valentinian*, III, 18, 14. The military chiefs were also private soldiers (*cf.* "beneficiarii" of the early Empire), "buccellarii" ("buccella," military bread, biscuit) in the 400 s. Among the Visigoths ("Wisigoth," 5, 3, 1) they were freemen who promised the "obsequium" to their patron, received arms and lands from him, returned them to him when they left, and transmitted them to their children, if the children had the same patron. On private jurisdictions, *cf. Lécrivain*, "Le Senat," p. 110; *Esmein*, "Mél. d'archéol.," 1886, p. 416; Cod. Just., 11, 48, 24; Cod. Theod., 16, 5, 52; 54, 6, 8; 9, 6, 4. *Sidonius Apollinarius*, "Ep.," 3, 1, *cf.* 4, 18, caused grave-diggers who violated a sepulcher to be tortured and excused himself to the bishop of the place for having usurped the latter's proprietary rights. *Brunner*, II, 285. The jurisdiction of landed proprietors was explained perhaps by the fact that they frequently received the function of "assertores pacis" ("lex. Rom., Wisig.," Cod. Theod., 2, 1, 8), officials resembling the "eirenarchs," of the West, who were judges of peace competent for "causæ minores." ("L. Rom. Cur.," 2, 16, 2, edition *de Clot.*, 614, c. 14.) At Angers at the beginning of the 600 s an ecclesiastical functionary had the right of "assertor pacis" and of "defensor civitatis" (Z.R.G., V, 74).

pact of hospitality ("hospitium"), and the very emperors who prohibited the "patrocinia" did not hesitate to grant to ordinary individuals in the villages ("metrocomiæ") the taxes which citizens were paying to the State, not as a matter of ownership, but as beneficiary grants under the title of land dues.[1]

[1] *Salvien*, "De gub. Dei," 5, 8: "Tradunt se ad tuendum protegendumque majoribus, dedititios se divitum faciunt Cum domicilia atque agellos aut pervasionibus perdunt aut fugati ab exactoribus deserunt, quia tenere non possunt, fundos majorum expetunt et coloni divitum fiunt." Cod. Theod., 11, 24; Cod. Just., 11, 53, 54; *Haenel*, "Corpus legum," index, see "Patrocinium"; *Libanius*, "Orat.," I. ("De patrocinii"); *Zachariae de Lingenthal*, "Gesch. d. griech.-röm. Rechts," 1877, p. 277. The Egyptian documents of the 200 s and 300 s testify to the administrative disorder. A cavalry commandant ruled as absolute master over the nome Arsinoïte. In 203–207, twenty-five inhabitants of a borough of this nome, Socnopéonèse, addressed a petition to a centurion as if they could not depend upon the civil power. "R. archéol.," 1894–1896, p. 34. On the patronate and the clientèle of the cities, see the Spanish inscriptions. *Girard*, "Textes" and *Berlanga*, "El nuevo bronce de Italica," 1891.

CHAPTER II

THE FRANKISH OR BARBARIAN EPOCH. POLITICAL INSTITUTIONS[1]

TOPIC 1. THE FRANKISH MONARCHY

§ 63. Introductory Remarks.
  1. Establishment of the Barbarians in Roman Gaul.
  2. Immediate Consequences of the Invasion. Were the Roman Gauls reduced to a State of Slavery?
  3. Were the Roman Gauls dispossessed of their Lands?
  4. Inequality of the "Wergeld."
  5. Public Taxes.

§ 64. The Frankish Monarchy.
§ 65. The German Chief.
§ 66. Personal Power.
§ 67. The King's Peace and the Royal "Mundium."
§ 68. The King's Ban.
§ 69. The Successor of the Roman Emperors.
§ 70. The Oath of Fidelity.
§ 71. The Elect of the Church. The Anointing and the Coronation.
§ 72. Kings by the Grace of God.
§ 73. Change of Dynasties. Substitution of the Carolingians for the Merovingians.
§ 74. Temporal Power of the Popes. Pepin Defender of the Holy See.
§ 75. The Reëstablishment of the Western Empire.
§ 76. Consequences.
§ 77. Universal Monarchy and Christendom.
§ 78. The Papacy and the Empire.
§ 79. The Elective Principle and the Capetians.

TOPIC 2. THE NATION

§ 80. The Nation. Popular Assemblies. The March Encampments ("Champs de Mars") and the May Encampments ("Champs de Mai").
§ 81. Assemblies of the Notables. Carolingian Courts.
§ 82. The Legislative Power of the King.

[1] BIBLIOGRAPHY: Bibliographical details in *Viollet*, *Glasson*, *Brunner*, *Schröder*; *Guizot*, "Hist. de la civilis. en France," 1828; *Lehuérou*, "Hist. des instit. méroving. et caroling.," 1842; *Péligny*, "Et. sur l'époque méroving.," 1851; *Léotard*, "Essai sur la condition des Barbares," 1873; *Waitz*, "Deutsche Verfassungsgeschichte," 3e éd., 1882; *Sohm*, "Die altdeutsche Reichs- und Gerichtsverfassung," 1871; *Sybel*, "Entstehung des deutschen Königthums," 2e éd., 1881; *J. Tardif*, "Et. sur les inst. polit. et admin. de la France," 1882; *Fahlbeck*, "La royauté et le droit royal francs," 1883; *Brunner*, § 59 *et seq.*; *Fustel de Coulanges*, "Hist. des instit. politiques de l'ancienne France": "L'Invasion germanique," 1891; "La Monarchie franque," 1888; "L'Alleu," 1889; "Les Origines du syst. féodal," 1890; "Les transform. de la royauté," 1892; *Vanderkindere*, "Introd. à l'hist. des inst. de la Belgique, jusq. 843," 1890; *Lamprecht*, "Deutsche Geschichte," 1894; *Amira*, "Recht" in *Paul's* "Grundriss"; *Lecoy de la Marche*, "La Fondation de la France," 1893;

TOPIC 3. THE CENTRAL ADMINISTRATION

§ 83. The Court.
§ 84. The "Antrustions."
§ 85. The Mayor of the Palace.
§ 86. The Counts Palatine.
§ 87. The Royal Chancellery.
§ 88. The Administration of the Domain.
§ 89. The Personal Service of the King.
§ 90. The Council of the King.

TOPIC 4. PROVINCIAL ADMINISTRATION

§ 91. Functionaries according to the Salic Law.
§ 92. The Public Function.
§ 93. The "Pagus" or County.
§ 94. The Count.
§ 95. Subordinates of the Count.
§ 95A. The Viscount.
§ 96. The Merovingian Dukes.
§ 97. The Hundred.
§ 98. The Centurion or Provost.
§ 99. The "Missi Dominici."
(1) Origin.
(2) Organization under the Carolingians.
(3) Powers.
(4) Decadence of the Institution.

TOPIC 5. MILITARY ORGANIZATION

§ 100. The Armed Forces.

TOPIC 6. FINANCES

§ 101. Finances among the Germans.
§ 102. Persistence of Roman Taxes.
§ 103. Indirect Taxes.
§ 104. Corvées, Lodgement, Subsistence.
§ 105. Germanic Institutions.
§ 106. The Domain of the King.
§ 107. The Right of Coinage.
§ 108. Feudalization of Taxation.

TOPIC 7. JUSTICE. JUDICIAL ORGANIZATION AND PROCEDURE

A. Judicial Organization

§ 109. Classes of Tribunals.
§ 110. Popular Justice.
§ 111. The "Rachimbourgs."
§ 112. Royal Justice.
(A.) Ordinary Jurisdictions: the Count and the Centurion.
(B.) The Tribunal of the King.
§ 113. The Jurisdiction of the King's Court.
(A.) Original Jurisdiction.
(B.) Appellate Jurisdiction.

B. Procedure

§ 114. The Régime of Private Vengeance and Composition.
§ 115. Primitive Procedure.
(A.) Extra Judicial Procedure.
(B.) Judicial Procedure.
§ 116. Proof.
(A.) Written Testimony.
(B.) System of Negative Proofs.
§ 117. The Carolingian Inquest.
§ 118. The Purgatory Oath.
§ 119. Judicial Trials or Ordeals.
§ 120. The Judicial Combat.

Prou, "La Gaule mérovingienne," 1897; *Longnon*, "Géogr. de la Gaule au VIe siècle," 1878, and "Atlas historique de la France"; *Monod.*, "Bibliogr."

TOPIC 1. THE FRANKISH MONARCHY

§ 63. **Introductory Remarks 1. Establishment of the Barbarians in Roman Gaul.**[1] — It was readily believed in former times that the victorious Barbarians had ruined the Roman world. The Count De Boulainvilliers in 1727 adopted this opinion in order to justify the privileges of the nobles whom he recognized as the descendants of the conquering race. The Abbé Dubos in 1734, making himself the organ of the third estate against the nobility, answered him by saying that there had been no conquest but only a peaceful establishment. Montesquieu attempted to take a middle ground between these two extreme opinions. In our day the question is still discussed; there is as yet no agreement either as to the immediate consequences, nor as to the remote results of the invasions. For the Germanists, it was an event which regenerated society. The Romanists consider it an accident which did not sensibly modify the course of events. They seek to discover in the decadence of Rome the beginnings of the feudal world. The truth is the invasion was not a single act. The Barbarian incursions, even when they failed, were a cause of troubles; they ruined "Roman civilization materially and morally." At the same time a peaceful penetration of the Barbarian element was in operation: Germans entered the Empire sometimes as soldiers in the service of Rome ("Fédérés," "Lètes"), sometimes as "coloni," and they brought new customs with them. Thus the way was already prepared for the definite establishment of the Visigoths, the Burgundians, and the Franks. These three peoples, at first mercenaries in the service of Rome, became, toward the end of the 400 s, independent of the Empire.[2] It was they who introduced Germanic institutions into Gaul. Two currents or tendencies, one Roman, the other

[1] *Boulainvilliers*, "Hist. de l'ancien gouvernement de la France," 1727; *Dubos*, "Hist. critique de l'établiss. de la monarchie franç. dans les Gaules," 1734; *Montesquieu*, "Esprit des lois," 30, 24; *Littré*, "Él. s. les Barbares," 1867 ("R. des q. histor.," 1869, 225); *Geffroy*, "Rome et les Barbares," 1874; *Fustel de Coulanges*, "L'Invasion germanique," 1891; *Viollet*, p. 194; *Junghans*, "Hist. crit. des règnes de Childéric," etc., 1857 (tr. fr., 1879); *Jahn*, "Gesch. d. Burgund.," 1874; *Binding*, "Das burgund. Koenigreich," 1868.

[2] Concerning these invasions, *cf. Viollet*, p. 195, and the bibliography cited above. The causes were want in Germania and internal strife. *Tacitus*, "History," 4, 73. There was a great invasion in 406. The Burgundians were in Savoy in 413, at Lyons and in the Valley of the Rhone in 470. The Visigoths in 376 appeared on the banks of the Danube to the number of 200,000. The Franks were defeated by Aurelius about 240. "Læti" of the 400 s were cantoned on the Scheldt and the Rhine. From the middle of the 400 s the Breton refugees, pursued by the Anglo-Saxons, were established on the Armorican peninsula. *Loth*, "L'émigration bretonne en Armorique," 1883.

Barbarian, were formed in public and private law; they became united little by little and their fusion resulted in the establishment of feudalism.

2. **Immediate Consequences of the Invasion. Were the Roman Gauls reduced to a State of Slavery?**—Neither the laws nor the writings of the time indicate that they were deprived of their liberty. On the contrary, they enjoyed the same civil rights as the Barbarians, and like them were called to the exercise of public functions. The personal theory of the law left them their own rights. Besides, the Barbarians were too few in number to be able, even if they had wished, to subjugate completely the Gallic-Roman population.

3. **Were the Roman Gauls dispossessed of their Lands?**—There was neither a general confiscation nor a reservation of a superior right of ownership for the benefit of the State. The public lands, like the domains of the treasury, passed naturally to the Barbarian chiefs, who kept a part of them and distributed the remainder to their followers. In this respect the Franks restrained themselves, although the Vandals and the Anglo-Saxons stripped the inhabitants of the countries which they occupied of their lands. The Goths, the Burgundians, and the Lombards made use of a modified form of the Roman system of the "hospitalitas."[1] The Barbarians established themselves as guests on the lands of the Romans; but while in the beginning they shared only the revenue because they were there only temporarily, they finally claimed a share of the property itself and established themselves on it by virtue of a definite title. The division was so made that the Barbarians were the gainers by the change; the law of the Visigoths gave to the Romans only a third;[2] that of the Burgundians gave the Barbarians a half of the house, two thirds of the tillable lands, and a third of the slaves, the forests and the meadows remaining undivided; in a supplementary division they were given a half only of the houses and lands.[3]

[1] Cod. Theod., 7, 8, 5: "Duas dominus propriæ domus, tertia hospiti deputata, eatenus intrepidus ac securis possideat portiones ut in tres domo divisa partes, primam eligendi dominus habeat facultatem, secundam hospes quam voluerit exsequatur, tertia domino relinquenda." If the host was illustrious he took half of the house. In Africa, the Vandals dispossessed the inhabitants; in Italy, the Herules and the Ostrogoths took a part of the lands (*Cassiod.* "Var.," 1, 18); the Lombards compelled the Romans to pay them a third of their income. *P. Dicare*, 6, 32. Concerning the "tertiatores" of the "Land of Labor" (end of 700 s) *cf.* N.R.H., 1893, 701.

[2] "Visig.," 10, 1, 8, 9 and 16; 10, 2; "Antiqua" of *Bluhme* c. 277, 303.

[3] According to *Fustel de Coulanges*, there was only one division. The "tertiæ" ("Wisig.," 1, 10. 8; "Burg" 54, p. 52) was a farming of the rent,

4. **Inequality of the "Wergeld."** — The Salic Law fixed at two hundred gold sous the "wergeld" or "composition" due for the murder of a free-born Frank, and at one hundred sous the "wergeld" for the killing of a Roman, from which it appears that according to the ideas of the Franks a Roman was worth only half as much as a Frank because the amount of the "wergeld" was, in general, determined according to the social rank of the victim. But Brunner has shown that the amount of the "wergeld" did not imply the least inferiority of condition; this is explained by the fact that the part of the composition due to the "Sippe" did not have to be paid for a Roman who had been killed. We have there, in effect, a Germanic institution unknown to the Romans; in the latter case the murderer paid only the half due to the heirs.[1]

5. **Public Taxes.** — It is generally admitted, though the point is disputed, that the Gallic Romans continued to pay, under the Merovingians, both the land and the personal tax, while the Franks, following the Germanic tradition, were satisfied to offer presents to the king.

§ 64. **The Frankish Monarchy.** — The Frankish Monarchy was absolute neither in fact nor in law.[2] It must be regarded as an institution badly defined, an incoherent mixture of different elements. The Frankish Prince was a king with three personalities, the Barbarian Chief, the Roman Cæsar, the Lord's Anointed of the Holy Scriptures. Let us analyze this trinity, notwithstanding

a third of the income which the Barbarian guest received from the Roman proprietor. *Cf.* on this point an obscure passage from *Sidonius Apolinarius*, ("Necdum enim quicquam de hereditates ocruali vel in usam tertiæ sub pretio medietatis obtinuit"); the "Eucharisticum," a little poem of *Paulin de Pella.*; *Saleilles*, "Rev. bourguignonne de l'enseign. sup." 1891, p. 44., (see detailed bibliography); *Gaupp*, "German. Ansiedlungen" 1844; *Caillemer*, "L'établissement des Burgondes," 1877; Léouzon-le-Duc," N.R.H., 1888, 232; *J. Havet*, "R. Hist." Vol. VI. p. 87.

[1] *Fustel de Coulanges*, who is alone in his opinion, maintained that the Roman "Wergeld" was the same as that of the Franks. According to him, the word "Romanus" in the Salic Law, vol. 41, sec. 6, was understood to mean "freedman," and according to the other Barbarian laws, the "wergeld" of the freedman was half that of the free man.

[2] For participation of the nation in the legislative and judicial power and the rôle, of the aristocracy of the 500 s see *Viollet*, I, 250 and *Lavisse*, "R. des Deux-Mondes," 15 October, 1885. The Frankish kings did not have the power of life and death over their subjects in time of peace. The abuse of power of which they were guilty does not prove anything, and it has been exaggerated by Gregory of Tours, who regarded as an abuse the application of the law to (Count Becco and the Salic Law, 10, 3. "De Virt, S. Juliani" 10, 3, M.G.H., S.S., I, 571), the case of illegal murders, acts of war or the chastisements inflicted on those who were not faithful to the king, the very act authorizing the death punishment without other action.

the fact that such an operation is more or less arbitrary, in order that we may acquire a just idea of its powers.

§ 65. 1st. **The German Chief. Struggle between the Principle of Election and that of Heredity. Division of the Kingdom.** — The situation of the petty long-haired Barbarian Prince [1] was no longer as precarious as formerly when he was subject to overthrow on account of defeat or even a bad crop; successful wars and conquests rendered his position more stable and brought him increased power. Authority was centered in certain families, like that of the Merovingians among the Franks, and became hereditary in them. Nevertheless, even when there were kings by right of birth, the principle of election sometimes still defeated the principle of heredity; it was thus that the Franks deposed Childeric and elected Egidus as his successor, and that the Ripuarians elected Clovis king. The raising of the prince on the shield was a feature of popular election and an indication of the military character of the Frankish monarchy.[2] After Clovis, the principle of heredity prevailed, but the great nobles, whose power was strengthened by civil wars, interfered in the designation of the kings; then came the revolution which dethroned the Merovingians, and the new dynasty based its claim upon popular election [3] no less than upon consecration by the church. The same facts were repeated under the second race: heredity had the advantage at first, then gave place to the system of election which was definitely established in Germany, although in France the Capetians were successful in transmitting their power from father to son.

The hereditary principle led to the treating of the kingdom as a domain, as the patrimony of a family; the sons of Clovis and those of Clothair divided their towns among themselves as they divided the royal treasure.[4] The right of primogeniture did not

[1] *Viollet*, I, 248, *n.* 2. To cut off the hair of a member of the royal family was to degrade him; it was to signify his deposition by a material sign.

[2] Germanic (and Byzantine) usage see below; *Tacitus*, "Hist." IV. 15; *Gregory of Tours*, 2, 40. 4; 52. 7, 10; *Cassiod.*, "Var.," 10. Another sign of the military character of the monarchy consisted in regarding the lance as the symbol of power. Gontran invested Childebert with his kingdom by restoring his lance to him and making him sit on his throne.

[3] The people intervened only nominally in recognition of the old tradition; in reality the aristocracy alone participated actively in the choice. We may say then, that a mixed system partly hereditary and partly elective was followed; the prince being elected, but from the royal family. *Huhrich*, "Fränk Wahl und Erbstammesstaaten," 1889.

[4] These partitions "æqua lance" were the cause of numerous wars. Their inconveniences were quickly felt and large divisions were established: *Austrasia, Neustria, Burgundy*, and *Aquitaine*. In 656 the eldest son of Clovis II alone succeeded his father. *Cf. Viollet*, I, 243. The same

exist; it was not known in the private law.[1] The right of succession among women was not recognized and hence females could not succeed to the crown; since the Salic Law excluded women from inheriting land, the reason was all the greater why they should not have the right of succession to political power.[2] In default of male issue[3] the brothers of the king succeeded him. If one of the brothers died first, his children were not considered with their uncles as heirs, for the private law did not admit the principle of representation. The regency, in case of the minority of the king[4] was in the nature of a guardianship except where the great nobles or the mayors of the palace had preponderating authority.[5]

§ 66. **Personal Power.** — The German chief exercised a public function but he was at the same time the head of a group of followers who freely attached themselves to his fortunes.[6] His authority over them was entirely personal in character, they obeyed the man, not the king. This was a very precarious authority, for upon the slightest pretext the followers withdrew. The only means of retaining their attachment was by bestowing

rule of division prevailed among the *Burgundians*, the *Alamanni*, the *Bavarians*, and the *Thuringians*. The partitions had applied to the royal authority as well as to territory and revenues. Nevertheless, the kingdom being treated like private property, it retained, in spite of the division, a certain unity. Every king was called "Rex Francorum" and not king of Austrasia or of Neustria. The towns were sometimes left in joint possession. Unity was much better safeguarded among the Goths and the Lombards where the kings were elected.

[1] Seniority among the Vandals, *cf.* Pepin the Short and Charlemagne, who excluded from the throne the children of their brothers. *Cf. Viollet*, I, 246, 244; *Gregory of Tours*, 7, 36, 38; *Lehuërou*, "Just. Cavol," p. 92.

[2] Salic Law, 59, 8.

[3] Bastards sometimes succeeded like legitimate children, but the influence of the Church caused them to be set aside under the second race, in principle at least. "Div. imp.," 817, 15, 18. *Viollet*, I, 242. A king without issue could transmit his kingdom to one of his relatives.

[4] The Merovingians attained their majority at the age of twelve years according to the Salic Law, 24; they were not so until fifteen, according to the "Lex Rib.," 81; and according to the "Lex Burg.," 87; when they were able to carry arms. (*Childebert* II; *Gregory of Tours*, 7, 33; *Pertz*, "Dipl." 23.) As for the Carolingians, the "Lex Ripuaria" was applied. "Cap." 817, c. 16, I. 273. M.G.H., S. S., II 643: "Imperator filium Karolum (Charles the Bald) armis viribus cinxit." *Pardessus*, "L. Salique," p. 452.

[5] The regency was exercised: 1st, as a guardianship, tutelage by the nearest agnate, following the Germanic law, or by the queen mother, following the Roman law and certain Barbarian legislations; 2d, in a manner differing from tutelage by the palace and grandees, or by the mayor of the palace. If the king was young, it was in his name that the government was carried on and legal documents prepared.

[6] By the acts which they signed, they considered themselves attached only to the person of the chief of state with whom they contracted, not to his successors. *Lavisse*, "Rev. des deux Mondes," 1885, p. 408.

benefits upon them; but this was a dangerous policy, and pursuing it meant ruin to the chief. Under such a policy, his domains were torn to tatters and the day when the chief was without fortune, his authority was gone. The Frankish kings allowed themselves to be guided, nevertheless, by these ideas; in their subjects they saw faithful friends; their power was understood above all as a personal power; they relied on the oath which all took at their accession, the violation of which carried with it, in principle, death or exile and confiscation of property.[1]

§ 67. **The King's Peace[2] and the Royal "Mundium."**—According to the old Germanic law, he who violated the public peace, by committing murder, for example, was exposed to retaliation on the part of the relatives of the victim, or more rarely, on the part of the entire community. The State was obliged to maintain the peace only in certain places and at certain times, as during the holding of political and judicial assemblies. In such cases it was the duty of the king to see that the peace was respected. With the extension of the royal power, the right of royal police was developed to the point where the public peace was transformed into the king's peace; whoever violated it was lacking in the fidelity due to the king. The king was substituted for the community in punishing political offenses and for the family in avenging private wrongs; he reserved the right to declare a man outside the pale of the law ("extra sermonium regis ponere,"[3] "Friedlosigkeit"). We may say then that his first duty was to establish and maintain peace in the kingdom. The popular and limited origin of his police power was forgotten. Of the old system there continued only the special peace which was enjoyed by the king's property, his palace, sometimes by the town in which he happened to be,[4] and by the churches and monasteries.[5] Offenses against these kinds of property or those committed in these privileged

[1] "Lex Rib.," 69. *Cf.* the crime of lèse-majesté at Rome. But every free man recognized the right of taking oath to the king whom he preferred.

[2] *Lehmann*, "Der Königsfriede der Nordgermanen," 1886.

[3] "Lex Salic," 56. 78. 106 (*Hessels*).

[4] In the case of the king's property the composition was double at first ("Sal.," 25, 3 and 4; 38, 2. Mss. 5 and 6. 3, 5, Mss. 5 and 6. *Lombard's* "Aist.," 17) then triple (Sal. Herold., 79, "Rib.," 11, 3, 60, 8. "Alam.," 31, 7). *Cf.* "Capitularia regum Francorum," I, 92, c. 4. I, 285, c. 20. The king's palace, "Roth.," 36, 37. "Ina," c. 6 (*Schmid*, "Ges. d. Ang.," pp. 385, 411) "Leges Henrici, I," 13, 7. 12, 3. *Cf. Pollock*, *Lehmann*, p. 215. On the word "scandalum," *cf. Brunner*, II, 45, n. 21; "Alam." 28. 33. 30; "Fris.," 17, 2; "Baiuv.," 2, 10, 12; *Bened. Levita*, VI.; 97, 383. Road of the king, "Alam." 28; "Roth.," 17, 18; "Saxon.," 37. "Capitularia regum Francorum," 779, c. 17, I, 51.

[5] *Church*, "Capitularia regum Francorum," 818–819, c. 1, 2, I, 281.

places were punished with a special severity (the composition was increased, the death penalty was inflicted, or the offender was put beyond the pale of the law).[1]

Some analogous effects resulted from the royal "mundium,"[2] or protection accorded by the king to the members of his household, to his officers, to his personal "clientèle," to those who were without patrons (clerks, monks,[3] widows, orphans, Jews, and foreigners), and finally to private individuals who placed themselves under the protection of the king and obtained charters of "mainbour"[4] ("cartæ de mundeburde")[5] similar to the letters of protection long used under the "ancien régime." The person so protected gained thereby the right to a higher composition (for himself, his family, and even for his property) and the privilege of carrying his suit to the king's court.[6] The protector was entitled to the "Wergeld" due in case of the murder of his protégé, and had the right to certain services and rents; women could not marry without the consent of the king, for marriage had the effect of withdrawing them from his patronage (protection) and of placing them under that of their husbands.[7]

[1] It is probable that whoever waited upon the king enjoyed by full right the same favor; by a very simple extension of this idea, it was maintained in the 1200s that jurisdiction of misdemeanors committed on the great highways or on the royal roads belonged to the officers of the king.

[2] Detailed bibliography in *Brunner*, II, 48; *Sickel*, "z. Gesch. d. Bannes," 1886; "Rechtslexicon" of *Weiske*, see "bann."

[3] Can it be said that the Frankish king was the protector of all his subjects? Yes, in the sense that he maintained peace among them. But, in general, he was the protector only of those who were "in verbo regis," who had no defenders and who could not protect themselves. The Salic Law permitted him to exact the "wergeld" of those who did not have relatives, Vol. LX.

[4] On churches and monasteries, *cf. Brunner*, II, 50.

[5] *Marculf.*, I, 24, and add., 2. *Cf. Rozière, op. cit.* Perhaps the king specially charged one of his officers to protect the person placed under his "mundium." *Mulbacher*, No. 89. Ostrogoths: "Sajo" appointed by the king as defender. *Cassiod.*, VII, 39. II, 29. IV, 27. In the Roman epoch, the magistrate could designate an "apparitor" to assist one in law. *Mommsen*, "Ostgot. Studien" (N.A., XIV, 531).

[6] In general, the patron represented his protégé in law; but as the king did not appear personally before the tribunal, he was replaced at need by a defender whom he designated. *Marculf.*, I., 24. "Form Bitur.," 14. Above all, he allowed the right of appeal to his tribunal which had equity jurisdiction.

[7] "Lex Rib.," 35, 3. 58, 12. "Lex Wisigoth.," 5, 3, 1. *Cf.* "Ant.," 310. It was an abuse under the Later Empire when an order of the public authority displaced the consent of the wife and her relatives. "Lex Rom. Wisigoth.," Cod. Theod., 3, 6, 1; 10, 1; 11, 1. There was a reaction under Clothair, who forbade these forced marriages (614). "Capit. regum Francorum," I, 19. 23. Council of Tours, 567, c. 20. "Lex Rom. Cur.," I, 3, 1. *Cf.* Feudal Epoch, the Great Charter (Magna Carta) of King John, c. 8. *Viollet*, I, 251, 3.

§ 68. **The King's Ban.**[1] — This was the order of the king and also the fine imposed upon him who was guilty of disobedience thereto, the amount being collected if necessary by seizure and without the employment of judicial formalities. Did the right to issue a ban, that is to say, to command and to prohibit under penalty, a right which Sohm calls the Germanic "imperium," have its source in the military powers of the king, or in his authority as magistrate charged with the maintenance of the public peace? It is difficult to answer this question. In the course of time, he greatly extended his power, but it was never unlimited nor absolutely arbitrary. His exercise of power was legitimate only when it was in conformity with the laws, or at least with the requirements of public order, and so elastic was this rule that it sufficed to prevent much abuse. Viewed from the standpoint of its principal applications the ban of the king served to put under a special peace and protection people like widows and orphans, and certain property like that of "the exempt";[2] it permitted the king to exercise executive power in the enforcement of military or judicial service (convocation for military service, pleading). In short, it was by the ban that the king could, by a kind of regulatory authority, strengthen, complete, and correct the popular law.[3] The law of the Ripuarians fixed the usual (normal) penalty for infraction of the king's ban at 60 sous per free man, and 30 for the half free.[4]

§ 69. **The Successor of the Roman Emperors.** — In the eyes of the Romans, the authority of the head of the State had something of the abstract and impersonal; obedience was due rather to the office than to the person. The regular succession of magistrates for centuries had accustomed them to this point of view. This idea did not prevail in the Frankish State; although the king was considered in many respects to have inherited the rights of the Roman Cæsars. His own power was often doubled and fortified by means of it (royal ban, unfaithfulness, and lèse majesté). He took the Roman titles: "vir gloriosissimus," "Ex-

[1] N.R.H., 1893, 23 (*d'Arbois de Jubainville*): Etymology. *W. Sickel*, "z. Gesch. d. Bannes," 1886.

[2] The oldest application, according to *Brunner*. "Capit. regum Francorum," I, 171. "Alam.," I, 2.

[3] "Capit. regum Francorum," 779, I, 51, c. 19. "Rib.," 64 and "Angl.," 10, 9. The eight bans (the principal ones) of the Carolingian Capitularies relate to the church, widows, orphans, "minus potentes," rape, burglary, incendiarism, and refusal to perform military service. "Capit. regum Francorum," V., I., p. 157, 224, etc.

[4] "Rib.," 35, 60, 65. "Capit. regum Francorum," I. 17, c. 9. *Ansegis*, III. 66. "Capit. regum Francorum," V., I., p. 72, 284.

cellence," "Sublimity," "Majesty."[1] He governed according to the Roman method, held his Court, appointed and dismissed functionaries like the dukes and counts in the towns. In many ways, the Frankish State recalls the Roman world (somewhat as the rude Latin of the Merovingian deeds recalls the language of the imperial constitutions). The tendency to Romanize was strong enough to bring about the reëstablishment of the Empire. The unity and indivisibility of the title of emperor modified the rules of succession to the throne; primogeniture appeared in the **Divisio imperii** of 817, to the benefit of Lothaire, son of Louis the Debonair. He had the title of emperor, was the lord of kings, who were his brothers, as well as his vassals, and they were forbidden to make war or peace without his consent. If he should die without issue the people were to choose one of his brothers as his successor. The kingdoms dismembered from the Empire of Charlemagne were declared indivisible and at the death of each king the people were to choose a single successor from among his children. This act, the charter of the Carolingian State, remained in many respects a dead letter, but is none the less important as an indication of the mind of the times. For some time when there were divisions the princes formed a "fraternitas" thus leaving to the empire a kind of ideal existence, and the divisions were made along political lines, by nationalities. After the treaty of Verdun, 843, France was never divided.

§ 70. **The Oath of Fidelity,** required of all free men whatever their race at the accession of the king, was of Roman origin, a similar one having been taken to the emperors. The Frankish epoch[2] would have invented it if it had not existed because it indicated the personal character of the royal power. The subject stood in relation to the king as a vassal did toward his lord. It was already said under the Merovingians that the oath pledged fidelity and homage ("fidelitatem et leudesamium").[3] The Carolingian formulas of 802 and 854[4] resembled the oaths of

[1] The formula "rex Fr. vir in luster." *J. Havet*, BCh., 1887. *Brunner*, II, 14. Clovis received of Anastasius the title of consul. *Duc de Nivernais*, "Mém. Acad. Inscr.," 20, 143. The Burgundian kings were masters of the militia.

[2] Ostrogoths, *Cassiod.*, 8, 2 to 7. Wisigoths, 5, 7, 19 (*Egica*), 2, 1, 6. Lombards, *Frédeg.*, IV, 70. Anglo-Saxons, *Edmund*, III, 1. For the Franks, the oldest text is that of *Gregory of Tours*, 314 to 532.

[3] *Marculf.*, I, 40. Etymology, *Brunner*, II, 60, p. 16.

[4] Charlemagne appeared to have reëstablished the abandoned practice of the oath; his successors abused it. "Capit. regum Francorum," 789, I, p. 63, 65 (*Brunner*, II) 59, 10, 92. 101, 124. 131. Formulas of 789, 802, 854, 858, 872. The duty of fidelity was here understood in so broad

vassals; fidelity to the king was sworn "sicut debet esse homo domino suo." The detailed commentary that Charlemagne took care to have made on the formula of 802 is a catechism of the duties of chivalry. Afterwards the feudal character was more emphasized; the oath was reciprocal, for after the subject had sworn, the king swore in turn so that a reciprocal contract united them.[1] The king could scarcely make an important resolution without the approval and assent of the aristocracy.[2]

§ 71. 3d. **The Elect of the Church. Anointing and Coronation. Formula, "by the Grace of God."**—The Church held up the king as the living image of God on earth. "It invented an eighth sacrament, the sacrament of royalty." The Carolingian king was anointed[3] following the examples of Saul and David, of the Wisigothic (600 s) and the Anglo-Saxon (700 s) kings, and of the bishops. His office was quasi-religious, he was a member of the priesthood; he was an unattached bishop and the chief of the clerical hierarchy; he governed by the bishops as much as by the counts. His first duty was to impress on all his subjects, laymen or clergy, the duty of observing Christian precepts; he himself was bound to govern according to justice, that is to say in accordance with Christian morals, under pain of being considered a tyrant.

The first Frankish king to be consecrated was Pepin the Short, who was anointed by the Anglo-Saxon, Saint Boniface; Charlemagne and Louis the Debonair were consecrated by the popes; Charles the Bald by the Archbishop of Sens, at Orleans (848). The prerogative of the archbishops of Rheims was not claimed

a sense that its violation was punished in very diverse ways, depending upon the nature of the case, "Capit. reg. Franc." 818, I, 285, c. 20: arbitrary punishment. Concerning the origin of English felonies, see *Brunner*, II.

[1] Thus in 858 the oath required of the subject was: "according to my power, with the help of God, without fraud or deceit, I will be faithful to you and will aid you with counsel and help, in order that you may keep the royal crown which God has given you and that you may govern according to his will and in the interest of your faithful followers." That of the king was: "And I, according to my power, with the help of God, promise to each one of you benefit and protection without deceit or injustice and I will guard the right of each one of you as a faithful king ought to assure to his faithful subjects protection and rights; if by human weakness I am diverted from my duty, I will take care to make amends."

[2] Intervention of the grandees and of the people at the treaty of Verdun, 843. *Nithard*, 3, 5, 4, 3.

[3] Concerning the ceremony of the sacrament and the coronation, *cf.* acts of 869 and of 877. M.G.H., L.L., I, 512, 542. Coronation of the daughters of kings. *Th. and D. Godfroy*, "Le cérémonial français," 1649. *Du Mont* and *Rousset*, "Le cérémonial diplomatique des Cours de l'Europe," 1739; *Leber*, "Des cérémonies du sacre," 1825; *Prou*, "Gr. Encycl.," see "Coronation"; Leviticus viii, 2, 12; Kings i, 16.

until the end of the second dynasty and was due, perhaps, to the great influence of Hincmar (845–882), though it was recognized only in the 1100 s.[1]

The coronation was united with the consecration from the time of Charlemagne. In the East, Leo 1st or Anastasius had been crowned at Saint Sophia by the Patriarch of Constantinople. After having been elevated on the shield and acclaimed, the emperor was dressed in purple, mass was celebrated, the patriarch made a cross on his forehead with holy oil and pronounced the word "saint," then he crowned him, saying "worthy." The ceremony was terminated by the "adoratio" at the palace. For the Carolingians, the anointing was followed by the coronation and the elevation to the throne (according to the Merovingian usage). The popular will, however, made itself felt; although in the Byzantine ceremonial there were only acclamations, the Frankish usage was to go through the form, at least, of consulting the people by means of an election after hearing the promises and the oath of the prince.

The assumption and exercise of the royal power did not depend in the least upon these solemnities, as logic would have required; the king was king before being anointed and crowned. Certain kings (*e.g.* Pepin the Short) were anointed several times; others (like Louis the German) not at all. But when the elective principle prevailed, this was no longer the case; it was because of this fact that the Capetians took care to have their sons crowned during their lifetime.[2]

§ 72. **Kings by the Grace of God.** — Charlemagne and his successors called themselves "kings by the grace of God," an expression like "episcopus dei gratia" or "dei misericordia."[3]

[1] When Charles the Bald was crowned at Rheims by Hincmar, the latter declared that it was done with holy oil brought to Saint Remi by an angel for the consecration of Clovis. It is to be observed that the legend of the Holy Phial was very highly regarded, M.G.H., "L.L.," I, 514. The Holy Phial was broken in 1793 at Rheims on the public square by Rhul, the member of the convention. It was pretended that a portion of it was saved and was used for the consecration of Charles X.

[2] The coronation acquired for a moment the same effect under Pepin and Charlemagne. Thus Charlemagne dates his reign only from his elevation to the throne, October 9, 768, and not from the death of Pepin, September 24.

[3] This formula, used since the time of Charlemagne (*Viollet*, I, 271, *n.* 6; *cf. Pertz*, "Dipl.," 28, 29), was derived, it is believed from England, where something analogous to it had been employed from the 600 s. Prelates, counts, and dukes adopted it at the close of the 800 s ("Monumenti Ravennati," I, 90, 179. *D. Vaissette*, V, 190, no. 77), and for a stronger reason, throughout the feudal epoch until the 1400 s, at least, the kings retained it.

This pious formula was employed without a single political afterthought. Later it came to symbolize the divine right, and served to justify the absolute and hereditary power of the monarchs. It was a weapon in the hands of the king both as against the pretensions of the Church, which claimed that royal authority came from God but through the Church as intermediary, and as against popular rights and the elective system. The phrase signified simply that the authority of the king existed because God had permitted it; but it excluded neither election [1] nor the intervention of the Church, for the will of God could manifest itself through these channels as well as through heredity; neither did it exclude a system of limited monarchy, for the power conferred by God is not necessarily absolute; it might have limits in the intervention of the Church, the people, or the aristocracy. Thus we see how much it was perverted from its original sense by interpreting it to mean that the king received from God *directly* an *absolute* power. This interpretation, entirely in favor of royalty, made progress, however, from this epoch. Wise men, says Hincmar, maintain that the prince is not subject to any law, that he is bound to obey only God who has established him as king on the throne which his father left him. But this thesis was that of a minority, according to the view which prevailed the formula "dei gratia" was justly opposed to hereditary right; [2] it held that the king might derive his authority from election as well as from inheritance. Louis the Stammerer, elected in 877, called himself: "Misercordia Domini et electione populi rex constitutus." Odo, in 888, was elected king, although he did not belong to the Carolingian family, and in Germany only the elective principle was applied. It held in the second place that the bishops who crowned the king exercised a control over the government; they were the thrones of God, they judged the king and deposed him at need; thus Louis the Debonair was deposed.[3] In 859, Charles the Bald made the following declaration at the council of Savonnières: "After having elected me, conformably to the will of the other bishops and of the faithful of our Kingdom, Wénilon, in his diocese at Orleans, consecrated me king according to ecclesiastical tradition; he anointed me with holy oil; he gave me the diadem and the

[1] The pope held his power by election.

[2] *Jonas*, "Inst. reg.," 7 (*Migne*, "Patr. l.," 106, 295).

[3] Louis the Debonair, after a general confession, was reclothed with the robe of the penitent; as a result, since his penitence must endure for all his life, he ceased to be emperor. At the time of his restoration, the bishops "reconsecrated" him. *Viollet*, I, 278.

royal scepter, and made me ascend the throne. After which I must not be driven from the throne by any one without having been heard and adjudged by the bishops by whose ministry I was consecrated king, who are called the thrones of God, in whose persons God himself sits and through whom He makes known His judgments, to whose reproaches and chastening judgments I am ready to submit myself."[1] Behind the bishops, who in the document are in the foreground, we can easily see the papacy. Nicholas I, — the same who showed so much energy in the affair of Lothair's divorce, excommunicating this prince because he repudiated without cause his wife Teutberga and annulling the decisions of the councils which had been favorable to him, — Nicholas I wrote in 863 to the Bishop of Metz: "See that the kings govern well, first themselves, afterwards their people; if they do not rule according to law they must be regarded as tyrants, and it is a right and a duty to resist them." From that it is seen that they were dependent upon the clergy, whether as men or as kings. The Christian character of their office made them dependent upon the Church. The Pope Gelasius had declared a long time before in a celebrated formula: "There are two powers which govern this world, the sacred authority of the pontiffs and the royal power; of these two the authority of the pontiffs has the greater weight, for on the day of judgment, they will be considered responsible even for the conduct of the kings themselves" (492–496).

§ 73. **Change of Dynasties, Substitution of the Carolingians for the Merovingians.**[2] — The mayors of the palace disposed of the throne at their will. One of them, indeed, Charles Martel, made bold to govern without a king. His son, Pepin the Short, "dux et princeps Francorum" took the title of king in 751, as did later Hugh the Great, father of Hugh Capet. The dispossession of the Merovingians had been for a long time an accomplished fact; the mayors of the palace exercised the royal power and the office became hereditary in the Heristal family whose territorial wealth gave it an exceptional situation. Pepin had scruples, however, about changing the dynasty; he was anxious to have legality on his side and the annalists state that he was appointed king on the advice of the pope and by virtue of election

[1] M.G.H., L.L., I, 463. A supreme test of Saint Remi (apocryphal), *Migne* t. 135, c. 67. Among the Wisigoths of Spain, the government became entirely theocratic. Here the councils and bishops governed the State.

[2] As to the facts cited, *cf. Mülbacher*, "Regesten," 751–918, 1889.

by the Franks. Pope Zachary when consulted, replied: "It is better that the one who exercises supreme power should also have the name of king." Without great importance in itself, because the reply of the pope was evidently known in advance, this consultation created a precedent most dangerous for the royal power. The head of Christendom gave only counsel, but the faithful were bound to believe that he spoke in the name of God: from this to disposing of the crown was not a long step. All the more since, like Samuel among the Hebrews, he gave holy unction to the king, he made him a sacred personage and marked him with the priestly sign, implying that monarchy was sacerdotal in character. Thus the Church found that it had created for the benefit of the second dynasty a counterfeit of the Jewish Kingdom, from which the pagan origin of the Merovingians had preserved them. Election among the Franks was reduced to obtaining the assent of the great personages of the kingdom. Even under these conditions it was the popular right which reappeared; another danger for the new dynasty which might find itself at the mercy of a sudden change of opinion. The Church tried to avert the peril in advance. Pope Stephen II himself, in 754, consecrated Pepin, his wife, and his children — the family and not the man alone — and forbade the "Francorum proceres," under penalty of excommunication, to take a king outside of the descendants of Pepin.[1]

§ 74. **Temporal Power of the Popes. Pepin Defender of the Holy See.** — By giving his moral support to the Frankish princes the pope obtained the right to their protection for which he had the most pressing need. Rome and the neighboring territory ("ducatus Romanus") no longer formed part of the Empire except in a nominal sense; the pope was the real sovereign. The Lombards now menaced the duchy, which could not count on the support of the Greeks. The popes turned to the powerful Frankish chiefs, the only ones who could give them effective aid, to Charles Martel in 739,[2] to Pepin in 754. The latter received from Stephen II the title of Patrician of the Romans [3] and after two interviews,

[1] *Bayet*, "R. Hist.," 1882, 90; *Viollet*, I, 258 (bibliog.); *Lavisse*, "R. des Deux Mondes," December 15, 1886; *R. Weyl*, "Das fränk. Staats-Kirchenrecht z. Z. d. Meroving.," 1888.

[2] *Fredeg.*, "Cont.," 22 (consulate, that is to say, duchy).

[3] The representatives of the Greek Empire, the exarchs, were patricians; likewise the Duke of Rome, a Byzantine functionary, bore the title of patrician. There was still the question of a Duke of Rome in 743. In decreeing this dignity to Pepin, the pope did not act by delegation from Byzantium, but he acted in his own name and as representative of the Roman people. *Duchesne*, "Lib. pontif.," I, 426; *Diehl*, "Etude sur l'administration byzantine," 1888; *L. Hartman*, "Unters. z. Gesch. d.

at Pontion and at Kiersy, he promised the pope the Exarchate and the Pentapolis then occupied by the Lombards. In spite of the protests of the Greeks he donated these to the Church of Rome and the act of donation was deposited on the tomb of the apostle Peter with the keys of the twenty-two towns; thus the temporal power of the Holy See was definitely founded. In 774 Charlemagne renewed to Pope Hadrian I at Rome the pledge of Kiersy and later, in 962, Otho I confirmed these donations.[1] According to a tradition, accredited to the 800 s and accepted during the Middle Ages, the donation of Pepin was only the renewal of a previous donation made by Constantine to Pope Sylvester. By this act Constantine, after having been cured of leprosy and baptized by Saint Sylvester, delivered to him the golden crown and the imperial insignia, and surrendered to him the sovereignty of Rome, of Italy, and of the entire West. This audacious forgery,[2] one of the most celebrated in history, must have been conceived with the object of assuring to the papacy the temporal power that it held as the patrimony of Saint Peter, and at the same time of justifying its claims to suzerainty over the princes of the West. The temporal power did not need to rely upon this title, for it was established in as regular and as legitimate a way as that of most of the sovereigns of that time. The impotent Greek Empire no longer defended Rome, which was independent in fact. The popes, spiritual chiefs and large proprietors, were obliged to act as political chiefs, to repel invasions and to protect, feed, and govern the City; their authority was accepted by the Romans and lacked only official recognition.

§ 75. **The Reëstablishment of the Western Empire**[3] was the crowning achievement of this policy. Charlemagne had reunited

byzant. Verwaltung," 1889; *H. Cohn*, "Die Stellung d. byzant. Statthalter," 1889.

[1] Among the pacts between the Carolingians and the Holy See, the only one available for us is that of 817 between Louis the Debonair and Pope Pascal, and even it is an altered copy. "Capit. reg. Francorum," I, 352. Bibliography in *Brunner*, II, 83. The promise of Pepin at Kiersy is found in *Waitz*, III, 87, but we have not the act of donation itself, neither that of Charlemagne. *Sickel*, "Privileg. Otto I, für d. Röm. Kirche," 1883, established the authenticity of the privilege of Otho.

[2] This forgery was probably made at Rome, according to *Brunner*, between 813 and 816, in order to justify the second coronation of Louis the Debonair in 816. Pope Stephen pretended to give him the crown that Constantine had given to Pope Sylvester. *Brunner* and *Zeumer*, "Die Constantin, Schenkungsurkunde," 1888; *Brunner*, "D. Rechtsg.," II, 90, *cf. Viollet*, I, 267 (bibliog.). Other dates suggested are: 750–755, 778, 840–850.

[3] *J. Bryce*, "The Holy Roman Empire"; *Gasquet*, "L'empire byzantin et la monarchie franque," 1888; "De translata a Græcis apud Francos

under his dominion nearly all the provinces of the old Empire; he reigned over Rome and was emperor in fact; it was natural that the title that the Roman Cæsars had borne should have been bestowed upon him and that the coronation should have taken place at Rome where the "imperial idea" was more alive than elsewhere. The disputes between the Roman aristocracy and pope Leo III took Charlemagne to Rome in the year 800. On Christmas Day he went to the basilica of Saint Peter and as he knelt before the altar to pray Leo III placed the crown on his head. The crowd of Romans present cried out: "To Charles Augustus, crowned by God, great and pacific emperor of the Romans, life and victory!" These were the forms that had been observed at Constantinople for the creation of emperors. The pope next prostrated himself ("adoratio") before the emperor as the Byzantine ceremonial prescribed. Was this a coup contrived by Leo III unexpected by Charles,[1] or was it a scene arranged in advance between the two principal actors? It is impossible to say.

§ 76. **Consequences.** — The great event of the year 800 was surrounded with ambiguities. It gave rise to controversies and conflicts concerning the origin of the Empire, its relations with the papacy and with the Eastern Empire, to new rights as over against subjects, etc. Charlemagne did not believe that he held the Empire from the pope who had crowned him and he himself passed the crown on to his son without the participation of the Holy See. The Roman people had acclaimed him, but he did not regard this action as an election; the coronation was for him only the consecration of his possession of the State. It is none the less true that the initiative had the appearance of coming from the pope, and while the latter only imitated, perhaps by order, the patriarch of Constantinople the act appeared to Christendom as that of a dispenser of crowns. In any case in the middle of the 800 s the imperial dignity was regarded as having its source in the consecration and coronation by the pope;[2] the latter did not even feel under an obligation to take the emperors from the Carolingian house (Lambert of Spoletus).

imperiali dignitate," 1879, and "R. hist." t. 26; *Lavisse*, "R. des deux Mondes," April, 1887, and May, 1888; *Bayet*, "Ann. de la Faculté des lettres de Lyon," 1883, 173; "Rev. historique," 1882, 1884; *R. Weyl*, "Die Beziehungen d. Papstthums u. Karoling.," 1892; and *Himly*, "De sancto rom. imperio," 1849.

[1] *Einhard*, "Vita Karoli," 28.

[2] Louis the Debonair and Lothair were crowned at first without the intervention of the Church; but the popes proceeded to a second coronation. In Russia, the czar crowns himself.

§ 77. **Universal Monarchy and Christendom.** — In his relations with the emperor of the East the Roman emperor was independent and on a footing of equality; Charlemagne called the Eastern emperor brother, and the latter permitted his ambassadors to address Charlemagne as "Basileus." It was even proposed to reëstablish the unity of the Empire under the two emperors; but the schism between the Greek and Roman churches was one of the causes which contributed to the failure of this project. But there remained the idea of universal monarchy, of the suzerainty of the Emperor over all kings, the Eastern Empire being as though forgotten. This idea was still expounded by Alciat as late as the 1500 s and combated by Lebret in the 1600 s. "Western Europe, in its political and religious unity, appeared as a great Christian family presided over by two powers, the one spiritual, the other temporal," both associated in the pursuit of the same end, the propagation of the faith and the salvation of souls. The theocratic character of the State was accentuated, the Roman Empire had become the Holy Empire ("sacratissimum imperium");[1] the prince was a *very Christian* king; his essential rôle was to protect the Church, to lend it his support and to aid it by force to accomplish its mission. Moreover, by virtue of his new title he gained in prestige though not in real power; his rights over his subjects were the same as in the past; the advance toward feudalism was not retarded by a day.

§ 78. **The Papacy and the Empire.**[2] — The restoration of the Empire which in one way exalted the papacy, in another had a disastrous effect upon it. The pontifical State formed a part of the Empire and was so regarded. Of the temporal power of the popes there continued only the rights enjoyed by the great churches, charters of immunity; but this led to feudal autonomy and from the middle of the 800 s, the feebleness of the imperial power left the pope in possession of authority which would have been very great had not the Roman aristocracy disputed it. The election of the pope was now dependent upon the Emperor; formerly the newly elected pope advised the Byzantine "patricius"; now he must advise the emperor and take an oath between the hands of an imperial "missus" who assured himself of the regularity of the election; consecration was possible only after the oath had been taken. Thus there came about a contradictory state of affairs

[1] A title that it received from the time of Frederic Barbarossa.

[2] *Lapôtre*, "L'Europe et le Saint-Siége à l'époque carolingienne," 1895 *Cf. Leroux*, "Rev. Historique," 1892, 241; *Blondel*, "Frédéric II," 37.

in which the pope created the emperor and the emperor created the pope.[1]

§ 79. **The Elective Principle and the Capetians.** — In Germany with the title of emperor the principle of election prevailed over that of hereditary right; in France, there was a struggle between the two systems. In 771 Charlemagne excluded the son of his brother Carloman, "consensu omnium." The "divisio imperii" of 806, confirmed by the oath of the great nobles, allowed the people to choose the nephew in preference to the uncle. In that of 817 it was declared that if Lothair died without issue the people would choose his successor. The word people was for form's sake; in reality it was only the nobles who were consulted. Thenceforth the principles of heredity and election were combined. After the deposition of Charles the Fat by the diet of Tribur in 887 the Western Franks chose as king Count Odo, son of Robert the Strong, though he did not belong to the Carolingian family. After him his brother Robert, and Raoul, duke of Burgundy, son-in-law of Robert, also owed their crowns to election. Finally, with the accession of Hugh Capet in 897, the dynasty was changed. This fact was due to different causes: such as the abasement of the Carolingians by the rising feudalism, the power of the Capetian house, the services which it had rendered in the wars against the Normans, the central situation of its fiefs, and the greater independence which the accession of a national dynasty assured to France. The political ability of Hugh the Great and Hugh Capet did the rest. Under the initiative of Adalbero, Bishop of Rheims, an assembly held at Senlis supported the candidacy of Hugh Capet to the throne of France over that of a Carolingian prince, Charles, duke of Lower Lorraine. The throne is not reached by hereditary right, Adalbero declared, but only he should be placed upon it who is distinguished not only by nobility of birth but by wisdom; and he endeavored to prove that Charles was unworthy to wear the crown.[2]

[1] As early as 774 Charlemagne exacted oaths at Rome and in the Exarchate in his quality as patricius. Leo III informed him of his election and promised him fidelity (795) by giving him the key to the tomb of St. Peter and the standard of the City of Rome. Roman constitution of Lothair in 824, "Capitularia regum Francorum," I, 323. *Th. Sickel*, "Privil. Otto," 1883; M.G.H., S.S., III. 722; *Einhardi*, "Ann." 827; *Bayet*, "R. Historique," 24, 49.

[2] *Klackstein*, "La lutte des Robertiens et des Carolingiens," 1877. (In German); *F. Lot*, "Les derniers Carolingiens," 1891. Concerning the title of "Dux Francorum" of Hugh the Great, and concerning the "Francia," *cf. Viollet*, I, 245, and the authors cited. It was also claimed that the crown was elective in the collateral line. *Richer* 4, 11, and following.

TOPIC 2. THE NATION

§ 80. **The Nation. Popular Assemblies. The March Encampments ("Champs de Mars"), and the May Encampments ("Champs de Mai").**[1] — In the Germania of Tacitus the people played the principal part in the government. The assemblies through which the sovereign power was exercised doubtless never ceased to be held. They are alluded to in the laws of the Barbarians after the invasions. The edict of Rothair was promulgated at Pavia in a national diet. The system of representation among the Saxons was evolved from old usages; thus deputies, to the number of twelve for each "pagus," assembled every year at Marklo in the center of Saxony to deliberate on affairs of common interest.[2] Among the Franks a similar tradition likewise persisted; thus it was in a general assembly of the Ripuarians that Clovis was chosen king. The "Mallus," held by the centurion according to the Salic Law, was a local popular assembly. However, after their establishment there were no regularly organized assemblies of the whole people; for it would have been impossible for them to come from all parts of Gaul to the place where the king resided, and his powers increased to such an extent as to absorb almost all those belonging to the people.

Gregory of Tours speaks of the military assemblies or the great March encampments ("Champs de Mars") of Clovis. To be sure, these were military reviews, but reviews at which the old custom of assemblies, at the same time military and political, was not unknown: they decided for peace or for war, refused to follow their king, or compelled him to undertake an expedition of which he disapproved.[3] Without doubt there was a vast difference between these reviews and the Germanic assemblies with their unlimited powers, which met periodically and which every free man had the right to attend. The assembly of the March encampments never met except when convoked by the king; he might take advantage of it to consult the people, but it does not appear that it was generally done. His faithful followers attended by his order, it being a duty which they fulfilled rather than a

[1] *Waitz*, "Forschungen," 13, 489; *Prou*, "Hincmar" p. 71; *W. Sickel*, "Mitth. d. Inst. f. oest. Geschichts f.," 1885, 220; 1888, 295; *Prenzel*, "Beitr. z. Gesch. d. Kriegverfassung," 1887; *Viollet*, I, 199; *Brunner*, II, 125.

[2] M.H.G., S.S., I, 361.

[3] *Gregory of Tours*, 2, 18. 27. 28. 31. 37. 4, 11. 14. 24. 3, 7 and 11. M.H.G., S.S., I, 192. Thierry and his incursion in Auvergne, Clothair II, and his war against the Saxons. These facts show in their true light the "reviews" and "proclamations" of the Frankish kings.

right which they exercised. Fallen into desuetude in Neustria,[1] reëstablished by the Pipinides for the entire kingdom the assembly of the March encampments became in 755 the assembly of the May encampments; the meeting coincided with the opening of the campaign,[2] but was delayed when the cavalry was numerous, since Pepin the Short wanted to wait until the season was far enough advanced for it to live on the country.[3]

§ 81. **Assemblies of the Notables. Carolingian Courts.** — A reduced form of the ancient popular assemblies, preserved in form at least in the "Champs de Mars," an imitation of the ecclesiastical synods, and an extension of the king's council, the assemblies of the nobles held under the Merovingians were partly all of these. In Austrasia they coexisted with the May encampment and were often hardly distinguished from it, which explains the fact that powerful kings in the commencement of their edicts spoke of the consent of the entire people. Their aristocratic character corresponded with the increasing influence of the men whose chief ended by usurping the throne. Following the example of the Church[4] Charlemagne[5] established two annual courts of pleas or hearings: the first and most important in the spring or summer ("placitum generale") was merged with the May encampment; the second, in the autumn, was for matters of urgency and the

[1] Edict of Chilperic, 573–75. Decree of Childebert II, 596; M.G.H., S.S., I, 320.

[2] The bishops were sometimes constituted into a council by the side of the political assembly in which they took part.

[3] M.G.H., S.S., 16, 495. There was no longer an assembly of the "Champs de Mai" after Louis the Debonair, says *Brunner*, II, 129. From that time there was a complete separation between the army and the political assembly.

[4] The Synod, *Vern.*, c. 4 ("Cap." I, 34), in 755 prescribed the holding of two councils per year.

[5] It has been claimed that he had restored to the nation its imprescriptible rights; this would have made him the real creator of the States-General. This was the burning question of the 1700s. The third estate was then like a "parvenu" who searches for his ancestors. It was claimed that the third estate had been despoiled of its liberties; those who have written about it agree that the "Champs de Mai" was modeled on the type of the English Parliament with the three orders of State, nobility, clergy, commons. Charlemagne, says *Mably*, taught the French to obey their laws by making them their own legislators. Were the people represented in these assemblies? A capitulary of 820 c. 2 (I, 295) seems to indicate that they were. The count brought to the assembly twelve "échevins" (aldermen) from each district, and in default of these, twelve of the "better men" ("meliores hommes"). These "boni hommes" were the judges whom the count led to the pleas held by the "missi dominici." The Capitulary of 820 did not deal with the "Champs de Mai." If the people were represented, it was purely local representation, and it is difficult to see in this duty, accepted reluctantly by those on whom it was imposed, anything which recalls our public liberties. *Anseg.* 2, 24.

preparation of others. To the first he summoned the principal functionaries, the higher clergy and the great landowners ("potentes"). All the nobles assembled, says Hincmar in his "de Ordine palatii," the more important to deliberate and render decisions, the lesser to give their assent. The king received the annual presents from them and the great affairs of the kingdom were discussed.[1] The assembly was especially political and military in character; it was at the same time a high court of justice summoned to pronounce judgment in exceptional cases by supplementing in a way the king's court in cases of *lèse-majesté* and in cases involving high personages or grave political interests.[2] Did it have authority of a legislative character? Yes, if we take into account the more and more marked preponderance of the aristocracy. Louis the Debonair agreed to do nothing without the advice of the council of the Great Nobles.[3] Under Charles the Bald the edict of Pistoa and the Capitulary of Quiersy were dialogues between the prince who proposed and the "conventus" which approved or disapproved. It was described as "an exchange of diplomatic communications between two powers." Let a favorable occasion arise and these assemblies will make and unmake kings; one of them will elevate Hugh Capet to the throne in 987.

§ 82. **The Legislative Power of the King** was limited both in law and in fact. (A) *Popular law* ("Volksrecht"), and national custom he could alter only in exceptional cases and with the consent of the people; according to the formula of the Edict of *Pistoia,* 864, c. 6: "lex fit consensu populi ac constitutione regis"; the king must content himself moreover with consulting the diets or general courts.[4] (B) The *Capitularies,* which, in contradistinc-

[1] *Fustel de Coulanges* held that the king commanded and that the assembly was summoned only in order that his will could be made known to it. "La Monarchie franque," p. 63.

[2] Brunhilda was so judged. Under Charles Martel, an assembly pronounced judgment on the question of a disputed succession between a duke and his sisters. *Cf.* also the judgment of Tassillon in 788, of Pepin in 792, of Judith, wife of Louis the Debonair in 831.

[3] M.G.H., S.S. II, 555. "Capit." t. II, p. 166.

[4] The Salic Law contemplated that summonses to appear in court should be made at the domicile of the person whose presence was desired. The inhabitants of regions pillaged by the Normans no longer having a domicile could not be summoned; the procedure of the Salic Law had, therefore, to be modified. It was for this purpose that the formula of the Edict of *Pistoia* was introduced. The Capitulary of 803, c. 19 (I, 114) and the preamble of the Capitulary of 803 (I, 111) relate only to the publication of the laws. *Seeliger,* "Kapitul.," p. 40; *Viollet,* I, 281; "Capitulari regum Francorum," I, 201. c. 10; *Liutp.* 118; *Bonnaire de Pronville,* "Pouvoir législatif sous Charlemagne," 1800; "Fustel de Coulanges," "R. historique," III, 22. *Cf.* Cod. Just., 1, 14, 8.

tion to the "leges," were acts of public authority ("Amtsrecht"), formed, like the latter, general and permanent laws; in principle they emanated from the king alone; nevertheless, the most important measures were submitted to the same popular Consultations.

TOPIC 3. THE CENTRAL ADMINISTRATION

§ 83. **The Court** ("aula," "palatium," and much later, the "Curia regis") was a Barbarian copy of the Byzantine sacred palace and served both as the residence of the prince and the seat of the central administration. It is well known that the Frankish kings had no fixed residence nor capital; they went from one palace to another accompanied by a household which included the following: 1st, the "antrustionat," a military body which doubtless had its origin in the Germanic "comitatus"; and 2d, the "ministerium," entire body of the servants of the prince. The chief of the latter were at the same time servants of the State, public functionaries, sometimes holding a special office like that of the mayor of the palace, sometimes exercising a temporary mission like that of an Ambassador.

§ 84. **The "Antrustions"**[1] (from "trustis,"[2] aid, protection, *cf.* "Trost") formed the bodyguard of the prince and were, in the 600 s at least, under the orders of the mayor of the palace.[3] By their name they recall the "schola protectorum" or guard of the Byzantine emperors, but we must recognize in them above all the followers of the chiefs in ancient Germany. One formula shows them with their hands in those of the king swearing fidelity and assistance ("trustem et fidelitatem").[4] By this act they promised a more strict devotion than that which was required of simple followers. Between them there existed such a solidarity that one "antrustion" could not testify against another. They enjoyed privileges in matters of judicial procedure and a "Wergeld" three times the amount of that of simple freemen.[5] Perhaps in

[1] *Deloche*, "La trustis," 1873. *Brunner*, Z.S.S., 1890, 210.

[2] "Trustis" means troop, escort, "Sal." 66. *Hessels* glossary h. v.

[3] They are called "scholares" "bellatores." *Fortunat*, 7, 4. Vita Aldegundis, *Mabillon*, "Acta" S.S., s. II, p. 807. "Eph. epigr." V, 121. "Hermes," 24, 221. *Jullian*, "De protectoribus et domesticis Augusti," 1883. "R. qu. hist.," 61, 490, and 62, 546.

[4] *Marculf.*, I, 18. "Lex Sal." 42. *Tacitus*, "Germ.," 14. The "antrustionat" was not hereditary. *Cf.* the Hirdmenn of the Norwegian kings. (*Viollet*, I, 231), Guards of the Kaffir chief (*Post*, "Afrik. Jurisp.," I, 165).

[5] "Lex Rib.," 11, 1. "Recapit. Lex Sal." 30. Formerly only "lites" and slaves could be "antrustions." "Sept. causæ," 8, 7. "Antrustions" resident outside the court. "Lex Salic" 106, 7 (*Hessels*), 42, 1. "Antrustions" of the queen, *Fortunat*, 6, 5.—"Salique" 41, 5.

the beginning the Barbarians alone could serve as "Antrustions"; but the Romans themselves in turn received this title. The Edict of Chilperic appears to have confused them with the "optimates" and made them councillors of the king as was already doubtless the case with the "Romanus conviva regis."[1] In the 700s the "antrustions" no longer existed; the "vassi regis" had taken their place.[2]

§ 85. **The Mayor of the Palace** ("major domus"[3]), the oldest of the servitors, the chiefs of the household in the palace of the king,[4] became, when individual servants of the king were public officers, the first of the royal agents and the head of the central government, or as we would say, the prime minister. About the year 600 he became the commander of the "antrustions," that is to say, the chief of "the Frankish aristocracy whose 'antrustions' formed a military nucleus." His power increased with the royal power because he supplemented the king in many of his functions. He was the chief judge at the royal courts and ultimately came to preside over them in the place of the king.[5] During the minority of the king (and there were numerous instances) he acted as regent. From the day that the nobles gained his adherence in that duel between the royal power and the aristocracy which fills the history of the first dynasty, the mayor of the palace became the equal, if not the superior of the king, because he was in alliance with the "leudes" and directed them.[6] In 613 Clothair, establishing Warnachair in Burgundy, swore not to deprive him of his office, thus creating an irremovable mayor.[7] Some of the mayors were elected by the nobles. The mayoralty finally passed into the powerful family of Pepin of Heristal (after Testry, in 687); it was no longer a simple dignity deriving its power from the personal valor of him who exercised it; it was a dignity clothed with great territorial possessions and, like them, inherited; the impoverished royal power gave way before this new dignity and the nobles discovered that they had given themselves new masters ("subreguli"[8]).

[1] Cod. Theod., 6, 13, 1. Cod. Just., 12, 1, 1, "Nutritii," *Gregory of Tours*, 9, 36. [2] Capitulary of Kiersy, 877, c. 20. *Cf.* above, "Vassalage."

[3] Older dissertations: *Pertz*, 1819; *Zinkeisen*, 1826; *Schoene*, 1856; *Bonnell*, 1858; *Hermann*, "Hausmeieramt," 1880.

[4] "Lex Sal." *Herold*, 11, 6, 7. This was without doubt originally the same personage as the seneschal or the dean of the seneschals.

[5] *Marculf.*, I, 25. Every part of the kingdom, Neustria, Austrasia, Burgundy, had its mayor of the palace.

[6] "Lex Rib." 88. *Cf.* "Burg." 1ª const. c. 4.

[7] *Fredeg.* IV, 42, "Fredeg. Cont.," 7 (104), 23 (110).

[8] The other so-called Barbarian monarchies had their mayors of the palace but the concurrence of circumstances which among the Franks

§ 86. **The Counts Palatine.**[1] — The Count Palatine[2] was the auxiliary of the king in the administration of justice. He was the official witness to acts executed in court (taking of oaths, judicial sentences, etc.).[3] The official records of judicial proceedings ("placita") were prepared by the royal chancellery upon his attestations and under his guarantee. Under the Carolingians he had a record-office distinct from that of the royal chancellery. It is probable that from early times he had been charged with the examination of cases brought before the king's court and with the execution of the decisions which it had rendered, perhaps upon his motion. In any case, under the second dynasty, the king's court was divided, the Count Palatine holding a tribunal distinct from that of the king.[4] Like the king he exercised equity jurisdiction, though the king reserved for himself cases involving the notables and questions upon which precedents were lacking.[5] The Count Palatine was therefore, above all, a great judge, but at the same time he was charged with the general management of secular affairs which, under the Merovingians, had belonged to the mayors of the Palace.[6] He was thus a viceroy in temporal matters, as the arch chaplain was a viceroy in spiritual affairs.

§ 87. **The Royal Chancellery.**[7] — From the time of the Merovingians this was placed under the direction of referendaries or functionaries charged (in the 400s) with making reports to the emperors upon petitions addressed to them.[8] Royal acts or instruments were drafted under their direction or dictation, by scribes

gave to these mayors such a high position, did not take place anywhere else. "Burg." 1ª C. c. 4. Extr., 21, 14; *Mommsen*, "Ostgoth. Stud." ("N. Arch.," 14, 514); *Schupfer*, "Instituz. polit. Langob.," p. 255; *Schmid*, "Ges. d. Angels.," p. 665.

[1] *A. Pernice*, "De comitibus palatii commentatio," 1863; *Th. Sickel*, "Acta regum Karol.," I, 360; *Brunner*, "Festg. f. Heffter," 1873. *Cf.* above, Cod. Theod., 6, 16 ("comites sacri palatii") 6, 35 and 6, 22, 8, 1 (Counts of the consistory).

[2] Or the Counts Palatine, for there were several of them ordinarily. *Pertz*, "Dipl." 23, 78. The king confided to them all kinds of duties, for example, the command of an army, etc. Italian Counts Palatine under the second race. *Cf.* Counts Palatine of the Empire of the time of the Othos, *Ficker*, "Forschungen," I, 312.

[3] *Marculf.*, I, 37, 38; *Pertz*, "Diplom." 22, 35, 41, 49, 60, 78.

[4] *Thévenin*, no. 71 (a. 834) "Reg. Farfense," no. 161, 165 (a. 801).

[5] "Capitularia de just. fac.," 811–813, c. 2 (I, 176).

[6] *Hincmar*, "De ord. Palat.," 19, 21.

[7] *Th. Sickel*, "Acta r. Karol.," I, 72, 215, etc., "Beitr. z. Diplom." ("Wien Sitzb.," 36, 39, 93); *G. Seeliger*, "Erzkanzler u. Reichskanzler," 1889; *Brunner*, § 74; *Bresslau*, "Urkundenlehre," 1889.

[8] *Mommsen*, "Ostgoth. Stud.," p. 482. Code Just., I, 50. *Cassiod.*, "Var." 6, 17.

called "cancellarii," "notarii," or "commentarienses."[1] The referendaries certified their accuracy and authenticity after verification, and sealed them with the royal seal, the custody of which was intrusted to one of them, the "gerulus anuli regalis," who doubtless enjoyed a certain superiority over the others. The chancellery was reorganized under the Carolingians. The dukes of Austrasia, like those of the Alamanni and of the Bavarians, had ecclesiastics as chancellors and when they became kings continued this practice. The title of referendar disappeared. The chancellery had a chief, "summus cancellarius," "archicancellarius," who alone was authorized to certify to the authenticity of royal acts[2] although formerly each referendar had had this right.[3] He soon became an important personage; at the same time archchaplain and archchancellor,[4] he was the head of the ecclesiastical personnel of the palace and minister of worship and of religious affairs, a sort of viceroy like the Count Palatine.[5]

§ 88. **The Administration of the Domain**[6] under the Merovingians was confided to intendants called "domestici," some of whom resided at the court, others, who were simple stewards placed under the orders of the intendants, were to be found on the lands of the king.[7] Under the Later Empire the title of "domestici" was given to chief clerks of various functionaries, to those of the "comes rerum privatarum" or minister of crown lands, and probably to those of provincial tax-collectors who were his subordinates.[8] Under the Carolingians the higher admin-

[1] The "cancellarius" was a sort of usher who received the petitions of private individuals at the chancel "cancelli" which separated them from the "secretum" reserved for the magistrates. Cod. Theod., 9, 19., 1, (Int.).

[2] The archives followed the king to his various residences, a fact which led to the loss of a large number of important documents.

[3] In 819, Fridugis caused the acts to be certified in his name.

[4] Under Louis the German, 856; "Capellanus" from "capella," cape of Saint Martin, the most precious relic of the king. "The kings possessed numerous relics; they took them along on their journeys and it was on these relics that they took their oaths; it was also on the relics carried from the palace to every town that the subjects of the king swore fidelity to him at the time of his accession." "*Pron.*," p. 53.

[5] *Hincmar* calls him an "apocrisiary," from the name that was given under the Later Empire to the legates of the pope, or of the patriarchs at Constantinople (since the 500s, Nov. VI, 2 and 3).

[6] *Sohm*, I, 13, *Ersch und Gruber*, "Encyclo. d. Wissensch.," see "Graf," "Domesticus"; *Fahlbeck*, p. 317; *Lamprecht*, "Wirthschaftsleben," I, 719, 804; *Brunner*, § 75 (bibliography).

[7] *Marculf.*, 1, 39. 2, 52; *Pertz*, "Dipl.," no. 29; *Fortunat*, 7, 16. "Vita Arnulfi," c. 7; *Gregory of Tours*, 9, 36; "Vita Eligii," 1, 17.

[8] *Mommsen*, "Neu. Arch.," 14, 507; *Cassiod.*, "Var." 10, 11. 12. 5, 14. Cod. Just., 1, 42, 1. 51, 3, 4. 9. Cod. Theod., 1, 11, 2 (Int.).

istration of the crown lands belonged to the seneschal and the cupbearer.[1]

§ 89. **The Personal Service of the King.** — The seneschal [2] was subject to the orders of the mayor of the palace during the Merovingian period, the latter dignitary reserving for himself all political prerogatives, but leaving to the seneschal matters of a domestic character. This was the rôle which the seneschal played under the Carolingians, exercising a general surveillance over the palace and having charge of the king's table ("dapifer").[3]

The **Treasurer** or **Chamberlain,** "cubicularius" under the Merovingians, was custodian of the treasury and received offerings made to the king.[4] The **Marshal** became under the Roman name "comes stabuli," the high **Constable** or chief of the royal stables and other marshals were under his orders.[5] The **Cupbearer** ("buticularius," [6] "princeps pincenarum") also had subordinates, "scanciones" or "pincernæ." Of these four officers the first two (seneschal and treasurer) became the most important; they were to be found in every great household because every such establishment consisted of four parts: the treasury, the table, the cellar, and the stables. These offices appear to have been of Germanic origin, but the mixture of names attests Roman influence.[7]

§ 90. **The Council of the King** did not exist under the Merovingians, though the king consulted the principal officers of the court, and the dignitaries of the kingdom.[8] To those who enjoyed his confidence was given the Roman title "consiliarius." [9] Under the second dynasty there was a beginning of organization.[10]

[1] "Capellanus de villis," c. 16, I, 84. *Hincmar*, "De ord. palat.," 23. In the provinces, the intendants (commissioners?) were called "actores," "judices," "fisci," "procuratores," "villici," (*cf.* the Lombard "gastaldio"). Every "fiscus," or collection of property, was divided in "ministeria," at the head of which were the mayors, "majores," subordinates of the "actor." Among these subordinates ("ministeriales") were the "decani," charged with guarding a group of manses, "decania."

[2] "Alam. Law," 74: "Senescalcus, sius scalc," old servitor.

[3] Inferior personnel: "infertores," "pistores," "coqui" (cook).

[4] *Hincmar*, "De ord. Palatine," 17, Inferior officers: "cubicularii," "cubiculium," private apartment. The chamberlain was under the orders of the queen, or mistress of the house.

[5] "Capitularia regum Francorum," 801–813, c. 10, I, 171. "Mariscalcus," "mara," horse; "scalc," servitor.

[6] A word of the Carolingian period.

[7] To mention only the subordinates: "spatarius" or "armiger," sword bearer, "archiater" and "medici," masters of the hounds, falconers, runners, "mansionarius," "ostiarii" (porters), "summus ostiarius" (master of ceremonies).

[8] *Cf.* the duty of giving counsel during the feudal epoch.

[9] "Lex Burg.," 1 const., § 4; 107, 13.

[10] *Hincmar*, "De ord. Palatine," 21, 26. "Capitularia regum Francorum," 790–810, c. 2, 1, 208.

TOPIC 4. PROVINCIAL ADMINISTRATION

§ 91. **Functionaries according to the Salic Law.**[1] — Under this law we are concerned with popular functionaries, the "thunginus" and the centurion ("centenier") and with royal functionaries, the "sacebaro" and the "graf." The "thunginus" and the "sacebaro" soon disappeared, but the centurion and the "graf" were retained in the definitive organization of the Frankish State. The "**sacebaro**" or "sagibaron" was an agent of the king (since he had the right to a triple "wergeld") charged with the collection of fines, like the Burgundian "wittiscalci." There were not to be more than three "sacebarones" before the same tribunal. If it is true that the "sacebaro" was an agent of the royal treasury, it would lead us to suppose that at the time of the Salic Law the ordinary functionaries of the "pagus" and of the hundred were independent of the king. The latter did not yet have any permanent representatives; he sent temporary delegates to places at which judicial assemblies were held, to demand his share of "compositions" and to establish his rights. It was natural that these "missi" should have disappeared when there were no longer popular officers.[2] The prevailing opinion sees in the "thunginus" the chief of the hundred and does not distinguish him from the centurion. As it is admitted at the same time that the count did not yet possess judicial powers, the result is that the Salic Law would have known only judges of hundreds. This would be an organization different from that of the Germania of Tacitus, where the "principes" went on circuit holding their courts, and from that of the Frankish State where the jurisdiction of the count extended over the entire county and where he traveled from one hundred to another administering justice. For this reason it has been contended that the "thunginus" was distinct from the centurion, that his jurisdiction extended over the entire "pagus" like that of the count later, and like that of the "principes" earlier. He was a popular functionary because he did not enjoy the right to a triple "wergeld," as did the royal officers.[3]

[1] On this subject where nearly everything is questioned, *cf.* bibliography above, "Justice."

[2] *Koegel*, "Sagibaro" (Z. f. D. Alt, 1889, 33, 13). Etymology questioned: "Sace = Sache," causa, "compositio" or "sagja," "sequens," "socius," *cf.* "sagio" Visigoth. "Baro = vir." The most varied opinions in regard to function: jurors, judges of appeal, "asega," etc. *Sohm*, "Reichs. und Gerichtsv.," I, 67, and "La procédure de la Lex Sal.," p. 152; *cf.* "Lex Burg.," 49, 4; 76, 1. On the subsequent texts, *Brunner*, II, 153, 23.

[3] "Lex Salica," 44, 1; 46, 1. 4. 6; 50, 2; 60, 1. Etymological meaning of "thunginus": one who holds the "thunchinium" or "placitum"?

The **Centurion** (or "Hunne"), also a popular functionary, for the same reason bore the same relation to the "thunginus" that he did later to the count; he was intrusted with the administration of the hundred and replaced the "thunginus" in the administration of justice but only in extraordinary judicial assemblies (" gebotene Dinge ").[1]

The "**Grafio**"[2] of the Salic Law, who was confounded with the count,[3] was a military chief, and an executive functionary (for example he seized property by way of distraint, expelled foreigners, etc.); he was not a judge any more than was the count. But from the 500 s the latter became the ordinary judge in the place of the "thunginus"; he was no longer distinguished from the "graf" and became a subordinate of the centurion (" centenarius comitis ") who had become a royal functionary. In brief, the suppression of the popular element in the administration, the simplification of royal officialdom, — these sum up the history of the changes in organization as shown by the Salic Law.

§ 92. **The Public Function,** "actio," "officium," "militia," was confided to agents who were designated in a general way as "judices," "actores publici," and, under the Carolingians, as "ministeriales." Already under the Empire the provincial governors bore the title of "judices." The Merovingian officer, although a representative of the public authority, was, in consequence of the absorption of the State in the person of the king, considered as a servant of the Sovereign. He was a part of the

The Salic Law says "thunginus aut centenarius." Is it necessary to understand "aut" in a disjunctive sense? This is the opinion of *Brunner* and this savant remarks that everywhere where there is a question of "mallus legitimus" ("das echte Ding"), only "thunginus" is mentioned. For the extraordinary assemblies ("gebotene Dinge") that the centurion had the right to hold, it is no more used. The plural used also by the Salic Law would lead us to believe that the "thunginus" and the centurion were two distinct personages.

[1] "Hunne" (later text) is a word which is connected with "hundert," "hundertschaft," a hundred. *Baiuv.*, 2, 5 (military chief). *Alam.*, 36, 1, 3 (judge) and 27, 3. "L. Rib.," 50.

[2] Disputed etymology: perhaps from "rôva," "numerus," group of soldiers furnished by the "pagus," the old "millena" (*cf.* "Hunne" and "Hundert").

[3] The common opinion does not distinguish the count and the "grafio." In favor of a distinction, the following arguments are given: the Salic Law speaks only of the "grafio" and not of the Count (Salic Law, 54, 1, cod. 2: altered); according to the documents, the "grafio" was appointed after the count (*Pertz.*, "Dipl.," 66. "L. Rib.," 88). By admitting the conclusiveness of these arguments — and the second, at least, is debatable — "grafio" and count are confused. In the "capitularia extrav." of the Salic Law, *Hessels*, 72, 74, we read: "judex, hoc est comes aut grafio." It is difficult not to assimilate in this passage "graf" and count. *Paul Diacre*, "Histoire Langob.," 5, 36.

"ministerium" of the king and sometimes a simple freedman.[1] Disobedience to the orders of the king was punished as "lèse-majesté," the penalty being death, mutilation, or confiscation of property.[2] His tenure of office depended entirely on the will of the sovereign;[3] but the royal agents, more and more powerful, tended to acquire a life interest in, and even a hereditary right to their offices. The edict of 614, elaborated by an assembly of nobles and published by Clothair II, declared that henceforth no "judex" should be sent from one region to another, that is to say, the king would be bound to select his representatives from among the inhabitants of that portion of the country in which they exercised their functions, so that if they were guilty of extortion their property could be seized by way of reparation. This measure, through which the royal power tied its own hands, served at the same time to strengthen both the local aristocracy and the higher functionaries. The great local proprietor, already very powerful, derived from his office a new authority. The edict perhaps was enforced only incompletely, but it was none the less very significant.[4] We need not be surprised to see that in 642 the dukes and bishops of Burgundy extracted from the mayor of the palace, Flaochat, a written agreement made under oath, that he would leave to each of them his office and dignities during his life.[5] At the beginning of the 700 s the mayoralty of the palace and the title of duke had become hereditary. The Carolingians temporarily repressed this tendency by means of the institution of the "missi dominici." But the tendency quickly reasserted itself anew with increased strength; as most of the functionaries were vassals of the king, the office became transformed little by little into a fief; and the public function was feudalized in order that it might gradually become the property of its incumbent. It was conferred, in principle, for the life of the prince who gave

[1] "Lex Sal.," 54. 2. *Gregory of Tours*, 5, 48, *cf.* "Rib.," 53, 2. "Adrevaldi Mir. S. Bened.," c. 18. M.G., S.S., 15, 1, 486.

[2] "Capitularia regum Francorum," I, 7, 23. *Brunner*, II, 78. Chilperic, threatening to have the eyes of disobedient functionaries plucked out, modified the usual punishments and showed himself more humane than did the Roman law. (Cod. Just., III, 26, 9: "publice vivus concremetur.") *Marculf.*, 1, 11, "Form. imp.," 21. "Capitularia regum Francorum," 802, c. 21, 28, I, 95 and 257, 2. *Gregory of Tours*, 8, 6, 10, 5. "Form."; *Merkel*, 51.

[3] Duration fixed in the 500 s. Roman precedents, *Cassiod.*, "Var.," 7, 2. *Gregory of Tours*, 5, 36. 47; 4, 42; 7, 15. *Karlowa*, "Roem. Rechtsg.," I, 870. *Marculf.*, I, 8, does not fix any term (600 s).

[4] "Capitularia regum Francorum," I, 22. It is held, contrary to the general language of the text, that the edict was applied only to subordinate functionaries. *Cf.* "Vita Leodegarii," c. 4.

[5] *Frédégaire*, 4, 89.

it, and for that of the functionary who received it; but in fact heredity[1] was introduced and became the customary rule. How was it possible to dispossess a count or his son without losing the support of a powerful family? The prince would not have dared do such a thing even if he had wished. The famous capitulary of Kiersy-sur-Oise, in 877, promulgated during the reign of Charles the Bald, assumed that the office of count passed ordinarily from father to son.

§ 93. **The "Pagus" or County.**[2] — The Roman Province no longer existed; the territory was divided into counties which corresponded to the Roman "civitas" with this difference, that they were much more numerous. Imperial Gaul included about 120 "civitates," in the 900 s the Carolingian counties numbered about three hundred. The Barbarians were as powerless to govern vast territories as they were to establish great States. The county was first called "pagus" (country, German "Gau"[3]) later "comitatus," a term which originally meant the territorial area of a count. Sometimes several counties were united under the authority of a military chief in such a manner as to form a duchy, but the duchy had no regular boundary, nor was the territory entirely divided into duchies.

§ 94. **The Count.**[4] — At the head of each town or "pagus" was a count appointed by the king. From the 400 s one finds in the Roman Empire military counts established in some towns.[5] Thus the Merovingians had only to develop a practice already in existence. But differing from the Roman count, the Merovingian count united in himself both civil and military powers and exer-

[1] *Meichelbeck*, "Histoire Frising.," u. 299, a. 814.

[2] *Guérard*, "Essai sur le system des divisions territoriales de la Gaule," 1837; *Longnon*, "Geog. de la Gaule au VIe siècle," 1878; "Etude sur les pagi de la Gaule" ("Bibl. Ecole hautes Etudes," 2d and 11th fascicules); *Jacobs*, "Geog. de Gregoire de Tours," 1862; *Bladé*, "Le Sud-Ouest de la Gaule franque," 1894.

[3] By the side of the official "pagus" administered by a count, the existence of other divisions also called "pagi" (for example the Ardennes), was sometimes maintained.

[4] *A. Pernice*, see "Graf"; *Ersch* and *Gruber*, "Encyl. d. Wiss."; *W. Sickel*, "Goett. gel. Anz.," 1888, 440; *Ch. Mortet*, "Gr. Encycl.," see "Comte."; *Marculf.*, I, 8, "Alam.," 41.

[5] *Esmein*, "Mélanges," p. 387; *Fustel de Coulanges*, "Monarchie," p. 197; *Viollet*, "Instit.," I, 74. The bishop of Toul, Auspicius, writes to a "comes Trevirorum," c. 457; *Sid. Apoll.*, ep. 7, 2, 5, mentions in 475 a "comes civitatis" at Marseille. *Brunner*, II, 163, 12, observes that it is not proved that these counts had united civil and military attributes. *Cassiod.*, 3, 34. 4, 12 and 46. *Mommsen*, "N. Arch.," 14, 499: Ostrogoths. On the Wisigoth "comes civitatis," *cf.* "L. antiq.," 322. "Comites civitatum" or "pagorum" among the Burgundians. *Bethmann-Hollweg*, IV, 190.

cised the judicial authority of the "thunginus" of the Salic Law.

The counts unlike Roman functionaries received no salary, but they enjoyed certain privileges, such as the triple "wergeld," [1] the title of "vir inluster," certain revenues, a third of all fines,[2] and rights which were later called "gîte" and "procuration," that is to say, board and lodging and means of transportation for themselves and their servants when they traveled in the county. Did they receive in addition a portion of the revenues from the royal lands situated in the county? Perhaps. In any case, under the Carolingians, certain of these domains were assigned to them as benefices.[3] Ordinarily an endowment of land was attached to the office. The powers of the count were, in a general way, the same as those of the king. He was the king's representative in the "pagus," the commandant for all the inhabitants both Roman and Barbarians, exercising his authority over the entire territory ("pagus"), with the exception of two reservations ("enclaves"): the royal domains and the "potestates" of the "immunistes." He received the oath of fidelity in the name of the king.[4] As military chief he convoked in the king's name the troops of the "pagus," put himself at their head, and led them to the royal host, where ordinarily, they did not cease to be under his orders. As financial agent he received all that was due the royal treasury (taxes and fines) and transmitted it to the treasurer (except the part that belonged to him personally).[5] As judge his jurisdiction extended over the entire county; he was a common law judge in the sense that he did not possess the extraordinary powers of the king or of the "missi," such as the right of equity jurisdiction, the power to punish arbitrarily or to grant pardons;[6] likewise in the sense that he traveled from one hundred to another to hold court. His judicial powers were doubled on account of his extensive power of police. He was charged with the maintenance of the public peace and to this end he could issue a ban the violation of which was punishable by a fine of

[1] "L. Sal.," 54, 1. "Rib.," 53, 1, 2. Cham. 7.

[2] "Capitularia regum Francorum," 790, c. 5, I, 201. "Capitularia Bonon.," 811, c. 2, I. "Dialog. d. scaccario," I, 17.

[3] *Brunner*, I, 203, 3; "Capitularia miss.," 832, c. 8, II, 64; "Capitularia regum Francorum," 898, c. 8, II, 110.

[4] *Gregory of Tours*, 7, 12. *Marculf.*, I, 40. "Capitularia Kiersy," 873, c. 5, 6.

[5] On the collection of the "héribau," *cf. Gregory of Tours*, 7, 42, and 5, 26. "Capitularia regum Francorum," I, 207, c. 13 and (811) I, 166, c. 2.

[6] "Capitularia Aix," 801–13, c. 13, I, 172, p. 225.

15 sous among the Franks and Saxons and of 6 sous among the Alamanni; sometimes also he exercised the king's ban, that is to say, he could issue a command in the name of the king with a penalty of 60 sous, sometimes by virtue of special delegation, sometimes without delegation for the protection of the widow and the orphan, to distrain real property, and to arrest criminals.[1] The possession of so much authority made the count a sovereign and consequently too often a despot. No other personage in the county, except the bishop — and sometimes a great privileged landowner — had an authority or influence comparable to his. He abused his authority and the extortions of which he was guilty arose from two circumstances: he had obtained his office by making presents to the king and he desired, therefore, to reimburse himself for the outlay; he was entitled to a portion of the fines and consequently he was interested in multiplying the occasions for collecting them. He was, it is true, responsible to the king, but the king was far away. The Carolingian "missi" for a time made his responsibility effective but, as is well known, this institution soon fell into decadence.

§ 95. **Subordinates of the Count** ("juniores," "ministri")[2] were: 1st, the "missi" or "legati" who were charged with a special mission; 2d, the viscounts, vicars, or lieutenants, who replaced the count in the exercise of all his powers; 3d, the centurions or provosts ("viguiers"), who were charged, under the count's direction, with the administration of the hundred which was a subdivision of the "pagus"; 4th, the "tribunus," an officer who sometimes commanded bodies of police and in this capacity was allied to the tribune of the Later Empire, placed at the head of a "numerus," and who sometimes collected taxes (for example among the Alamanni). In this capacity he acquired somewhat the character of a Lombard "Schultheiss" ("seuldasius") who was assimilated to the centurion after the Frankish conquest;[3] 5th, the "sagio" or "saio" in the Wisigothic or

[1] "Capitularia miss.," 802, c. 57, I, 104; Cap. 1. add., 803 c. 2, 1, 113; Cap de pact, Saxon., c. 31; Cap. Sax., c. 3. 4; L. Sax., c. 36; Chamav., 34 (4 sous). Alam., 27, 1 (ban of the duke 12 sous; ban of the count, 6 sous); Baiuw., 2, 14 ad 2, 13. Sec. Niuh., c. 15 (40 sous); "Capitularia regum Francorum," Aix, 813, c. 11: that the count has a prison, the "vicarius" a gibbet.

[2] Bibliography and details in *Brunner*, II, 180. "Capitularia regum Francorum," 802, c. 25, I, 96.

[3] "Schultheiss," the one who exacts what is due ("Schuld"). At the beginning of the 800 s, the bishop of Coire had "Schultheissen," by virtue of his character as an "immunist." This title was preserved in Switzerland to the Middle Ages. *Luitp.*, 25.

Ostrogothic country, a court bailiff in the service of the count; and 6th, the scribe or clerk (who was rather the count's personal secretary).[1] There was little left of the bureaucracy of the Later Empire, no mere "officium" with its division of labor, its hierarchy, its traditions and administrative experience. The household service of the counts had taken its place by means of an unfortunate reversion, for the "officium" had likewise been originally the household service of the Roman magistrate.

§ 95A. **The Viscount** ("vice comes")[2] appeared in France and in Italy during the Carolingian epoch.[3] The Edict of Pistoa, 864 declared that every count should have his viscount.[4] This functionary was a lieutenant of the count and had the same powers, the same jurisdiction over "causæ majores," and the same general authority over the entire county; whereas the provost, "vicarius," did not exercise authority outside the hundred, nor jurisdiction of "majores causæ." There were in the county as many provosts as there were hundreds, but ordinarily, there was only a single viscount. Hence one need not be surprised that the title of provost was not to be found, like that of viscount, in the feudal hierarchy. Certain counts who were set over the frontier provinces ("marca," "limes") bore the title of **Marquis** ("comes" or "dux marcæ," "marchio," "marchisus"[5] in German, "Markgraf," margraves). Unlike the ordinary count the marquis already had, under Charlemagne, several counties to administer.[6]

§ 96. **The Merovingian Dukes**[7] were military chiefs[8] who mustered under their orders the troops of several counties; they had, in the 600 s, the same powers as the count and the formula of appointment was the same for one as for the other.[9] Only the duke administered a more extensive territory; he governed several towns, and in each of them there was a count who was hierarchically

[1] The law of the Ripuarians, 59, 88, speaks of a scribe officially attached to the "mallus": "cancellarius," "Capitularia regum Francorum," 803, c. 3, I, 115, same, 805, c. 4, I, 121. On the "honorarium" due for the acts, same, 801–4, I, 145. It is difficult to know to what point these measures decreed by Charlemagne were applied in France; it seems that in Italy they were put into execution. In the 800s, the official notaries and administrators of oaths had a monopoly of the drawing up of authentic acts, "Capitularia Mant.," 781, c. 3, I, 190.

[2] "Vice dominus," "vidame," in "Septimania," *Thévenin*, no. 71.

[3] *Mühbacher*, no. 171, a, 774.

[4] C. 14, *cf.* "Capitularia regum Francorum," 884, c. 9.

[5] *Hincmar*, "De ord. Palat.," c. 30.

[6] M.G.H., S.S., 2, 736.

[7] *Bornhak*, "Forsch.," XXIII, 167; *W. Sickel*, "Histor. Z. n. f.," 16, 407, and "Goett. gel. Anz.," June 1, 1888; *Whittmann*, "Akad. Bay.," 8, 1.

[8] *Gregory of Tours*, 8, 30. 12. 9, 7. 12. 14. 10, 9. 5, 18. 4, 24. 43.

[9] *Marculf.*, I, 8. "Rib.," 50, 1.

his inferior. How was the administration of the duke combined with that of the counts? It is difficult to say. It is probable that there was no count in the "pagus" where the duke resided and that in the other "pagi" aside from military matters the duke intervened only in exceptional cases. In the 700s the remote provinces like Thuringia, Bavaria, Alamannia, and Aquitania had hereditary dukes;[1] but the Carolingians dethroned these petty sovereigns. The title of duke, however, continued to be applied to commanders of the armed forces, or to certain counts. Toward the end of the 500 s new dukes appeared in consequence of incessant wars. Like the dukes of Austrasia the Frankish dukes ultimately reached the throne as kings. The "**Patrice**" (patrician) was simply a duke with a higher title borrowed from the Roman hierarchy (for example, in Burgundy and Provence).[2]

§ 97. **The Hundred.** — During the ascendancy of the second race the counts were divided into hundreds or provostships ("vicariæ").[3] Had this not already happened during the Merovingian epoch? The question is much discussed. According to the Romanist School, the hundreds which were mentioned in the texts of the time[4] were groups of a hundred persons organized for police purposes and who were held responsible for thefts committed within their territory. Their chief, the centurion, commanded the armed forces ("trustis") furnished by the group for the purpose of pursuing offenders. In the end, the name "hundred" was applied to the territory inhabited by the group and thenceforward constituted an administrative unit. This theory is based on an act whose meaning is obscure and whose date is disputed, namely, the pact between Clothair and Childebert, 511–558.[5] It is more probable that the hundred, a personal group

[1] *Fredeg.*, 4, 87; *Perroud*, "Origines du premier duché d'Aquitaine," 1882; *D. Chamard*, "R. d. q. histor.," 1884, 5.

[2] In Provence, the subordinate functionaries were called "priores." *Fr. Gaudenzi*, c. 18; *Mommsen*, "N. Arch.," 14, 501.

[3] "Capitularia," 818, c. 10, 283. "Polypt." of *Irminon*, 12, 1. 1, 43.

[4] Formulas: "in pago illo in centena illa," for example, *F. Bignon*, 29. "Condita," Normandy and Brittany; *F. Andeg.*, 78; *F. Turon*, "Ager," "finis," Burgundy, "Aicis," Auvergne, Rouergne, Septimania; *Viollet*, I, 294, 4. — "Alam.," 36 (who seems to regard the hundred as an old institution.

[5] Concerning this pact, c. 8 and 16. *Cf. Waitz*, II, p. 402; *Sohm*, p. 211; *Schröder*, Z.S.S., IV, 86; *Brunner*, II, 147. The establishment of hundreds was here prescribed and the choosing of centurions as heads of groups for the purpose of pursuing thieves and those responsible for thefts committed in their territory. Was this an innovation, or an extension of an institution already existing? Was it not desired to create centurions there where the Frankish organization of the hundreds did not exist? The documents throw no light on this point. Analogies are found in the Swedish and

among the ancient Germans, was transformed among the Franks into a territorial division. As early as the Salic Law it constituted a judicial unit. In the following period, it became generalized and spread over the entire Frankish kingdom, perhaps in consequence of the pact of Clothair and Childebert.

§ 98. **The Centurion or Provost** ("Vicarius").[1] — These two functionaries were not distinguished one from the other, at least not under the Carolingians.[2] The centurion was appointed by the count with the assent of the local assembly.[3] He was a lieutenant of the count with military, financial, and judicial powers; he commanded the armed forces of the hundred,[4] exacted the payment of fines,[5] pursued and punished offenders,[6] and administered inferior justice.[7]

§ 99. **The "Missi Dominici."**[8] 1st, **Origin.** — The Roman Empire had maintained legates, commissioners, or ambassadors[9] and so had the Merovingian kings in their turn. They had in their "entourage" ("a latere regis") delegates ("missi," "legatarii") whom they intrusted with missions and invested with special powers; these delegates enjoyed the privilege of triple "wergeld";[10] and they received the "tractoria legatariorum," or diploma which permitted them to be lodged at the expense of the inhabitants. Those who were sent abroad as ambassadors went as magicians, holding in their hands a staff consecrated according to the pagan rites;[11] whoever laid hands upon them in-

in the English laws. *Glasson*, "Inst. de l'Angl.," I, 60. The "trustis" included all the men of the hundred qualified for police service and who owed it under penalty of a fine of five sous. "Electi centenarii" did not comprehend members of the "trustis," for "centenarius" was never understood in that sense. Under the name of "centenarius," the Later Empire had a police official charged with seizing the property of debtors to the treasury, somewhat like the Lombard advocate ("sculdasius," "scultelus," "Schultheiss") who was also a judge.

[1] It seems that in the south of France, during the Merovingian epoch, there were no centurions, but "vicarii comitis," lieutenants of the county, sometimes having jurisdiction over the entire county and sometimes over only a part of it. Even under the Carolingians, the title "viguier" (provost) was used rather than centurion, and this term finally came to prevail in all France.

[2] "Conc. Cabil.," c. 21, *Mansi*, XIV, 98. *Sohm*, p. 215.

[3] "Capitularia Aix," 809, c. 11, I, 149; "Capitularia miss.," 809, c. 22, I, 151. The Saxon "Gograf" which corresponded to the Frankish centurion was elected by the judicial assembly. *Schröder*, 171.

[4] "Capitularia," 808, c. 3, I, 137. *Ibid.*, 811, c. 2. 3. I, 165.

[5] "Capitularia," 801–13, c. 5. 6, I, 171. Ed. Pistoa, 864, c. 28.

[6] "Capitularia," I, 96, c. 25.

[7] See above "Justice."

[8] *Krause*, "Gesch. d. Inst. d. Missi dominici," 1890 ("Mitth. d. Inst. f. oest. Geschichtsforschung," XI, 193). *Thèodulphe*, "Paraenesis ad Judices." *Cf.* in general the "Capitularia missorum."

[9] Cod. Theod., 1, 10, 7.

[10] "Sept. caus.," 8, 6. 7.

[11] *Marculf.*, 1, 11, "Capitularia," 819, c. 29, I, 291.

curred divine wrath. Others were commissioners dispatched into the interior of the country, for example, to receive oaths of fidelity to the king [1] or to organize a conquered province like those whom Pepin the Short sent into Aquitania in 768.[2]

2d, **Organization under the Carolingians.** — Extraordinary commissioners ("missi discurrentes") were sufficient in a state like the Frankish kingdom under the first dynasty. Out of these casual assignments given when circumstances required, Charlemagne found himself obliged to make a regular institution, in consequence of the vast extent of his empire and the increase of his power. This he did in 802 with a view to rendering his authority effective even in the most remote provinces.[3] The "missi" made annual tours, they were sent throughout the whole empire, the territory of which was divided into inspection districts ("missatica," "legationes") with varying limits and numbers. They recalled the Merovingian "missi" only in one respect, namely, that their powers ceased as soon as the inspection was complete. Further progress would have made permanent functionaries of them hierarchically superior to the counts, as the Roman vicars were to the provincial governors.

3d, **Powers.** — The "missi" went out, two by two, one a bishop, the other a count. They held great assizes upon which the counts, vicars, centurions, sheriffs, bishops, abbots, ecclesiastical solicitors, and vassals of the king were obliged to attend.[4] At these assizes they promulgated the orders of the king, received oaths of fidelity, addressed to the people "admonitiones,"[5] one might say sermons, somewhat like this: "My brothers, give alms, be hospitable, receive strangers under your roof, ransom captives, avoid drunkenness, respect your parents, observe the Sabbath, fast, attend mass, receive the sacrament"; after which they performed their work of inspection and administered justice.

(A) **Control of the Administration.** (*a*) *Lay Functionaries.* — The Chroniclers represent these as oppressors of the poor, taking their property from them and reducing them to slavery.[6] Some of them sold justice, others rendered their judgments while under the influence of intoxicants.[7] The "missi" discharged the sub-

[1] *Gregory of Tours*, H. Fr., 7, 32. [2] *Marculf.*, 1, 40.
[3] "B. Ch.," v. 48, p. 29, "Capitularia regum Francorum," I, 91; same, 853, II, 271, *passim.*
[4] *Ibid.*, I, 291, 295, 309, and following. Investigation of 804 on the Istric, *Waitz*, II, 488.
[5] *Rozière*, "Form," II, no. 521. [6] *Thégan*, "Vita Lud.," 13.
[7] "Capitularia regum Francorum," 802, in f., I, 103.

ordinate functionaries, vicars, centurions, solicitors, and "vidames" and made reports to the king concerning the dukes and counts.[1] (*b*) *Ecclesiastics.* The public and private conduct of ecclesiastics was also subject to the surveillance of the "missi." They made sure that the bishops and priests lived lives in conformity with the canons, that they did not keep packs of hounds, falcons, or goshawks, that no women dwelt in their houses, and that they possessed the books prescribed by the councils (good editions, perhaps from fear of heresy). They also inspected the monasteries and property of the church.

(B) **Direct Action.** — In both the general or special courts which they held at their pleasure they rendered justice; it was as if the King's Court was transported into the provinces; recourse was had to them as to the king himself, in cases of denial of justice, or in cases which fell within the jurisdiction of the royal tribunal.[2] Like the king they exercised an equity jurisdiction; they were charged to look after the interests of the churches, of widows, orphans, the poor, and the infirm; they were instructed to make inventories of the royal domain and of the benefices granted by the king;[3] and in case of necessity they served as chiefs of the army.

4th, **Decadence of the Institution.** — The "missi" were very restraining censors under an energetic prince, but from the time of Louis the Debonair the enfeeblement of the royal power had its effect upon the institution of the "missi." The nobles managed the choice of these surveillants, who were chosen on the spot. One of the principal functionaries of the district was charged with the inspection of the count's neighbors; in Italy the bishops inspected themselves.[4] From time to time extraordinary commissioners were charged with special missions, as under the Merovingians. And so the circle is complete and we have come back to the starting point. The institution disappeared, but not without leaving any traces; in the "justitiarii itinerantes" of Normandy and of England, it is not difficult to recognize the ancient "missi" of the Carolingians.

[1] *Ibid.*, I, 51 (779, c. 21); 124, c. 12, 144; c. 4, II, 8, 15.
[2] *Ibid.*, I, 308, 314; *Zeumer*, "Form," 4, 326.
[3] "Capitularia de justit. fac.," I, 177, 250.
[4] "Capitularia of 876," II, 103.

Topic 5. Military Organization[1]

§ 100. **The Armed Forces.** — The Germanic system of the "levée en masse" in time of war took the place of the permanent army of the Romans maintained by the state.

1st, **The Nation in Arms.** —As in primitive times every free man[2] was required to perform military service and to equip and support himself at his own expense. No distinction of race was recognized, Romans as well as Franks were enlisted. At the summons of the king ("summonito," "bannito") the inhabitants of the provinces whom he had designated (since it was rare that the inhabitants of the entire kingdom were called out) betook themselves to the host under penalty of a fine of sixty sous for disobedience to the "heriban"[3] and, according to the Capitularia, reduction to slavery in case of non-payment of the fine. Receiving no pay for their services the men who were called into the army nevertheless enjoyed certain privileges, such as the triple "wergeld," exemption from all other public duties, immunity from judicial prosecution, a share of the booty and of the royal largesses. This method of recruiting the army was never abolished in theory and was always resorted to in time of defensive wars. The Edict of Pistoa in 864 laid down the principle: "ad defensionem patriae omnes sine ulla exceptione veniant." The "levée en masse" was designated by the name of "landwehr" ("lantwêri").[4]

2d, **Carolingian Reforms.** — The Merovingian troops were almost entirely composed of foot-soldiers, but after the wars against the Saracens the cavalry came to constitute the principal branch of the army.[5] "Miles" and "caballarius" were synonymous terms. This change of tactics reacted upon the methods of recruiting since the equipment of a horseman was more expensive than that of a foot-soldier. It was henceforth necessary to exempt the poor and require military service from the rich, especially from landowners, for the obvious reason that they alone were capable of rendering it. But who were the rich during these times? There was no definite standard. A capitulary of 807 declared that it

[1] *Bontaric*, "Institutions militaires de la France," 1863; *Brunner*, § 87; *Baldamus*, "Das Heerwesen u. d. spät. Karoling.," 1879; *Viollet*, I, 436. — See particularly the "Capitularia" of 807, 808, and 829 (I, 134, 137; II, 7).

[2] Concerning the free men and the non-free *cf. Brunner*, II, 213.

[3] This word is applied to both the summons and the fine. "Lex Rib.," 65; "Capitularia de exerc. prom.," c. 3; 811, c. 1 and 9.

[4] "Capitularia regum Francorum," 847, c. 50, II, p. 71.

[5] It was because of this that in 755 Pepin the Short changed the "Champs de Mars" to the "Champs de Mai."

was those who possessed four or even three "manses." Small landowners who possessed only a half, one, or two "manses" were grouped together in such a way as to make up the minimum requirement and one of them equipped himself for the campaign at the expense of the others. The possession of personal property worth 600 sous was officially regarded as the equivalent of three or four "manses"; those who possessed only 100 sous' worth of personalty were grouped together by sixes for the purpose of furnishing a soldier. Simple free men were able to obtain exemptions from military service by reason of their poverty, but in many instances the exemption was more apparent than real, since most of them were vassals of some lord and were obliged to render military service to him; they were his private soldiers and the benefices which they received put them in a condition to serve in the royal army, their lord took them and was responsible for them. The bishops and abbots, who were at the same time great landowners, were compelled equally with lay proprietors to perform military service, but clerks (inferior clergy) were generally exempt, since the canons of the church prohibited them from bearing arms and from shedding blood.

3d, **The Army was Feudalized.** — At the end of the 800 s the royal army was composed of scarcely anything but private troops; most free men were enrolled under some lord. For those who held benefices from the king and who joined the army under the orders of the counts, military service was regarded as a land tax rather than a duty of a subject.

TOPIC 6. FINANCES[1]

§ 101. **Finances among the Germans.** — Among the Germans, free men paid no taxes because that was a mark of servitude; but they owed services to the state. The Roman Empire, on the contrary, had an ingenious system of taxation: a land contribution paid in kind or in money by the owner, a personal tax paid by non-property owners, and indirect taxes imposed upon everybody. In the hands of the Barbarian kings this system was deranged and public taxes similar in every respect to private dues were mingled in the royal treasury with the revenues of the royal domain. Their significance was no longer understood.

[1] BIBLIOGRAPHY: *Guérard*, "B. Ch.," I, 336; *Vuitry*, "Etude sur le rég. financier de la France," 1876; *Fustel de Coulanges*, "Monarchie franque," p. 243; *Viollet*, I, 319; *Brunner*, § 90; *F. Dahn*, "German. Abhandl.," dedicated to *Maurer*, 1893.

"They were no longer a necessary charge to which the people submitted for the general needs of the state and even in the interest of the community. Although still designated as public revenues, they were in fact only the private income of the king." Everybody considered them odious, those who collected them as well as those who paid them. Henceforth, they were often renounced by the kings, who no longer maintained assessment lists of current taxes, and the rate became invariable.

§ 102. **Persistence of Roman Taxes.** — No document contains a record of their abolition; on the contrary many speak of the public tribute, of a public rating, of the "functio publica," of the "inferenda," and of the land register ("libri censuales," "polyphyci"); under Clothair I, under Childebert, and under Chilperic new "descriptiones" were made.[1] But the tax was not changed, as it should have been, with the changing needs of the state; it was a customary charge analogous to interest of the rent of a farm. The Edict of Clothair II in 614, ch. 8, prohibited the preparation of a "census novus" since this would have been an act of impiety. The collection of the tax devolved upon the count who was responsible therefore; if necessary he advanced the amount to the treasury.[2] Did the Franks pay a direct tax? Not in our opinion, for a personal contribution was a mark of subjection. The Merovingian kings attempted without success to impose tribute upon them; but they owed land taxes for the lands obtained from the Romans, they acquired the charges along with the lands. On the other hand, the estates which came to them from the king, being exempt from taxes before they were acquired, never ceased to be exempt.[3]

§ 103. **Indirect Taxes** were more enduring; far from disappearing, the "portorium" or "teloneum" (market tolls) were multiplied and aggravated under various names, such as, "partaticum," "ripaticum," "rotaticum," "pontaticum," "pedagium" (tolls),

[1] *Gregory of Tours*, 4, 30; 5, 35 (*cf.* 10, 7). A revolt broke out at Limoges when Chilperic attempted to levy new taxes; the king's children died, which was construed as a warning from heaven; Chilperic then destroyed the registers.

[2] *Marculf.*, I, 8; *Gregory of Tours*, 10, 30. 7. The "exactores" were perhaps subordinate to the count, analogous to the Lombard advocate, and perhaps to the Frankish centurions.

[3] *Gregory of Tours*, 10, 30. 7. There was no idea of an eminent domain on all the lands of the kingdom, for this would have legitimized the levying of a tax on all landowners Frankish or Roman. It is evident that much of the land was not subject to the payment of the tax, for it was disposed of freely, while the transfer of the "terra tributaria" was not free. *Brunner*, II, 237; "Capitularia regum Francorum," I, 177, 187; *Wartmann*, I, 302, no. 328.

etc.[1] There was always a toll farmed out and levied in connection with the transportation of merchandise over the highways, on the rivers, or across bridges. Dues were also collected on commodities brought to the market; such were the Roman "siliquaticus" which reappeared in Italy during the Middle Ages, and market stall fees, which were analogous to the Roman "proponenda."[2] Moreover the erection of new markets was permitted only with the consent of the king[3] and the count exercised public authority over such places, either himself or through a "judex fori."[4]

§ 104. **Corvées, Lodgment, Subsistence.** — So many Roman usages could have been preserved only in a society like that of the Frankish epoch. Public works, roads, and bridges were constructed by means of forced labor (the corvée).[5] The service of the past was disorganized. Franks and Romans were subjected to the burden of providing lodgings for ("mansio," "lodgment") and defraying the expenses ("paratae," "fodrum," "procuration") of the prince during his journeys, as well as for his "legati," his "missi," his counts and those who had secured from him this privilege. A letter from the king, "tracteria," fixed the quantity of commodities which they were authorized to demand: so many hogsheads of white bread, so many of brown bread, so much wine and beer, so much bacon, eggs, pepper, etc.[6] Among other dues may be mentioned requisitions of chariots and of horses ("angariae" "veredi" and "poraveredi"). The rights of lodgment and subsistence brought with them a thousand abuses: murder, pillage, spoliation were committed at the very doors of the houses in which hospitality was extended.[7]

[1] These names, for the most part, explain themselves well enough: "pedagium," a tax on pedestrians; "volutaticum," tax on transportation of goods; "passionaticum," transit tax; "saumaticum," tax upon beasts of burden, etc.; "pulveraticum," tax on powder, etc. "Laudaticum," "salutaticum," "foraticum," "mestaticum," these various names may designate the same imposition. "Stationes" were offices in the interior of the kingdom. Objects destined for the personal use of the traveler were exempted.

[2] *Cassiod.*, "Var.," IV, 19. *Godefroy* on the "Cod. Theod.," 7, 20, 2.

[3] *Esmein*, "Mélanges," p. 366; *Huvelin*, 1897; *Lehmann*, "La paix du marché" ("Kauffriede") and *Mayer*, on the markets between the Rhine and the Loire, "Germ. Abh."

[4] Subordinated to the count, without doubt. "Monumenta Germaniae historica," "Scriptores," XV, 496, c. 35.

[5] "Lex Chamav.," 38, 39. "Capitularia regum Francorum," I, 288, 290, c. 17, 306, c. 22. II, 16. 84. 87. *Anség.*, 4, 11. 58.

[6] "L. Rib.," 65, 3, "Burg.," 38, 1; *Marculf.*, I, 2, 11; *Anség.*, IV, 70; "Capitularia reg. Franc.," I, 85, c. 27. 138. 291. 306. 315. II, 88. "Scara" service of messengers, "Capitularia reg. Franc.," I, 166. Analogous usages in Morocco.

[7] *Gregory of Tours*, 6, 31, 45. 8, 42. Is it not from this that the "jus spolii" of the Middle Ages is derived by virtue of which the lords appropriated the furniture found in the house of dead bishops?

§ 105. **Germanic Institutions.** 1st, **Voluntary Gifts.** — The Franks gave presents to their princes as the Germans did to their chiefs in the time of Tacitus. The custom was established of bringing them every year to the May Encampment. But scarcely any except the nobles were able to conform to the custom (and then at least, both Romans and Franks without distinction of race). The voluntary gift was the beginning of taxation; under Charlemagne it was obligatory for the churches and probably also for those who came to the May Encampment.[1] It appears that gifts were made to the king at the time his son was solemnly initiated into the army, or on the occasion of his daughter's marriage, in the latter case the donations for her dowry.[2]

2d, **Composition,** a portion of which was assigned to the state (for example, in the time of Tacitus). Fines, particularly those which were imposed for the violation of the king's ban (60 sous)[3] went also to swell the royal treasury; but the rule was as much Roman as German. The Frankish prince succeeded also, like the Roman emperor, to confiscated property and to certain inheritances through escheat.[4] 3d, **Tribute exacted of Conquered Races.**

§ 106. **The Domain of the King.**[5] — The Frankish kings possessed, like the Roman emperors from whom they received their property, vast domains.[6] They spent the income therefrom on the land from which it was derived and to this end the Merovingians went from one villa to another. The celebrated capitulary "de villis" gives some idea of the administration of these do-

[1] *Hincmar*, "De ord. palat.," c. 29. "Capitularia Kiersy," 877; *Muhlbacher*, no. 1369.

[2] *Gregory of Tours*, VI, 45; "Lex Rom. Cur.," 84.

[3] "Lex Rib.," 65; "Chamav.," 2.

[4] "Lex Salica," 60, 3; 62, 2. 44, 10. He collected the "wergeld" of those who died without relatives, the king's "wergeld" and the succession of foreigners, and the "servitia" of Jews. "Capitularia regum Francorum," 801–13, c. 7, I, 171.

[5] The king's domains were withdrawn from the authority of the functionaries of administrative order and confided to special agents. On special rules which apply here, representation at law, inquisitorial procedure, etc., *cf. Brunner*, II, 73.

[6] The king had the right to appropriate all lands without owners, but he often allowed private persons to clear them or to occupy them in return for the rent. "Praec." of Clothair II, c. 11, and Edict of Clothair II, c. 23. He could reserve, under menace of the royal ban, the woods and rivers, and particularly the hunting and fishing: "foresta piscationis et venationis." Mines and salt works belonged, for the greater part, to the king; if there was no exclusive right to his benefit, this right tended to be formed by the application of the same rules as those for property without ownership.

mains.[1] Under the first two dynasties the principle of the inalienability of the domain was unknown; the kings disposed of it with a prodigal hand, giving to the church for the salvation of their souls, and to their subjects to secure their support, so that almost none was left to the last representatives of the two dynasties.

§ 107. **The Right of Coinage** preserved its character as a royal privilege, but the coiners ("monetarii") who exercised the right under the supervision of the public authority went from place to place in the discharge of their functions. Concessions to the churches and monasteries, however, impaired the monopoly of the state and ultimately it was transformed into a feudal right.[2]

§ 108. **Feudalization of Taxation.** 1st, *Exemptions and delegations.* The kings despoiled themselves of their revenues by exempting from the payment of taxes (direct or indirect) certain individuals, churches, merchants, and even Jews. At other times they retained the tax but sold or gave away the proceeds; thus in 629 Dagobert gave the market toll paid by merchants attending the fair at Saint-Denis, to the monastery of this name.[3] 2d, *Public functionaries kept the proceeds of the tax.* A third of the ban and doubtless other fines belonged to the counts. Some concessions were made to them, too, and in the absence of regular assignments they were able to profit by circumstances to appropriate to their own use the public revenues. Thus, usurpation completed that which an imprudent liberality had begun. 3d, *The tax was confused with the domanial revenues.* The direct tax became fixed like rent. The texts of the Carolingian period speak of the "census regalis," "de rebus," and "de capite" in such terms that we do not know whether the taxes were in the nature of rent collected by the king in his quality as a proprietor, or whether they were public taxes imposed by the sovereign as such, without reference to his lands.[4]

[1] *Guérard,* "B. Ch.," 1853; *Garcis,* in the "Germ. Abhandl.," 1893.

[2] "Capitularia de moneta," of 820, I, 299, Edict of Pistoa, 864; *Anség.,* 2, 18. 3, 13. 90. 4, 31. 53; *Prou,* p. 72, 174; *Brunner,* I, 213; *Vanderkindere,* 178.

[3] "Form. imp.," 30, 31, 37; "Gesta Dagob.," 34; "Capitularia," 820, c. 3, I, 294; *D. Bouquet,* VIII, 538, no. 130. Sometimes private persons collected taxes, in virtue of a tacit concession of the king; thus, one who built a bridge or who kept it in repair, claimed the passage toll for his expenses. The workers who helped him were naturally excused from paying.

[4] "Capitularia regum Francorum," 811, c. 2 (I, 166); Edict of Pistoa, 864, c. 28; *Anség.,* 3, 15. 85, 4, 35. 37.

Topic 7. Justice. Judicial Organization and Procedure[1]

A. Judicial Organization

§ 109. **Classes of Tribunals.** — During the Frankish period justice was administered by four sorts of tribunals: 1st, the popular tribunals; 2d, the royal courts; 3d, the patrimonial courts ("immunités"); and 4th, ecclesiastical courts. The last mentioned were outside the general system; the other three succeeded one another in the order in which we have enumerated them. The judicial evolution was only one phase of the evolution of public law: first, a foundation of primitive institutions, then an attempt at centralization according to the Roman idea, and finally, the dead weight of feudal institutions which, in the end, destroyed the Roman veneer behind which they were formed.

§ 110. **Popular Justice.** — The Germanic system in which the people participated in the administration of justice persisted among the Franks. Without mentioning the national assemblies, or the assemblies of nobles whose judicial functions were exercised only in exceptional cases, ordinary processes were brought before the assembly of the hundred or "mallus."[2] It was the duty of all free men of the hundred to attend this assembly; judicial service was the same in nature as military service. There was a distinction between ordinary courts (the "Echte Dinge" of the Germans)[3] held at times fixed by usage, and extraordinary courts ("Gebotene Dinge") held only upon special convocation at which only those who had been summoned were obliged to attend.[4] An ordinary court presided over in each hundred by the judge of the "pagus," the "thunginus" or count, depending upon the epoch, lasted three days among the Salic Franks and took place

[1] "Lex Salic," 597; *Waitz*, "Das alte R. d. sal. Frank.," 154; *Siegel*, "Gesch. d.d. Gerichtsverfahrens," 1857; *Sohm*, "Reichs und Gerichtsverfassung," 1867, and "Prozess d. l. Sal.," 1867 (translated into French, "La Procédure de la Lex Salica," 1873); *Bethmann-Hollweg*, "Civilprozess," t. 4 ad 5; *Amira*, "Recht," § 83 and following; *Thonissen*, "L'Organis. judic. de la L. Salique," 2d edition, 1882; *Fustel de Coulanges*, "Recherches," 1885, p. 357; "Monarchie franque," p. 304; *L. Beauchet*, "Hist. de l'organis. judiciaire en France," 1886; *Beaudouin*, N.R.H., 1887; *Brunner*, § 88; *Platon*, "Le Mallus ante theoda vel thunginum," 1889.

[2] "Mál" (*cf.* "Gemahl") in the sense of to confer. The "mallus" was the judicial assembly, the tribunal; the "malloberg," the place where it met; the "gemallus," one who belonged to the same judicial community; "mallare" means to lodge a complaint. The assembly was still called, "Thing," "Gemot," "Warf."

[3] "Mallus legitimus m. publicus." The convocation was general in this case.

[4] The "Afterding" or complementary plea did not exist among the Franks.

regularly, apparently every forty or forty-two days.[1] The centurion could act as a substitute for the judge only in extraordinary courts.[2] The assembly was held in the open air ordinarily on elevated ground with no other protection against inclement weather or the heat of the sun than that afforded by the trees.[3] The assembly and the place at which it was held were, during the pagan epoch, committed to the protection of the gods; the session was opened with ceremonies; silence was commanded;[4] sacramental questions were put;[5] and then the president ordered every one to respect the religious peace which must prevail in the assembly.

§ 111. **The "Rachimbourgs."** — Judgment was pronounced by the "rachimbourgs," the popular assembly, and the presiding magistrate, all acting together.[6] The "rachimbourgs,"[7] or "boni homines" ("prudhommes") were local dignitaries who made known the usage by a public declaration; they did not judge in the modern sense of the word, sentence and order of execution

[1] "Lex Salic," 56; "Form. Sen.," rec. 2 and 5; *Bignon*, 12. *Cf.* "L. Sal.," 47, 1. 5; 50, 1; 56. 74. 78, 7. 106. "L. Rib.," 30, 2; 33, 2; 31, 1; Chamav., 44. Delay of fourteen days among the Ripuarians. *Cf.* "Alam.," 36 (every fourteen days or every eight); *Bavarois*, 2, 14 (every month or every fourteen days); *Brunner*, II, 218, proves that this delay of six weeks corresponds to the phases of the moon. Edict of Pistoa, 864, c. 32. The ordinary plea was held Mondays or Thursdays.

[2] "Capitularia Missi," 819, c. 14, I, 290.

[3] Charlemagne caused the place where the "mallus publicus" was held to be covered with a roof. "Capitularia regum Francorum," 809, c. 13, I, 149.

[4] *Tacitus*, "Germ.," 11.

[5] "Lex Salic," 44, 1: "tres causas demandare." *Tacitus*, "Germ.," 10. "The three sacramental questions were perhaps these: Has the time come to open the session? Shall the tribunal be regularly constituted? Shall silence be ordered? Analogous questions of mere form are found again in the old ritual of Free-masonry." *Vanderkindere*, p. 267; *Warnkoenig*, "Flandr. Staats, u. Rechtsg.," III, CLXVIII; *Burchard*, "Die Hegung d. d. Gerichte," 1893.

[6] Analogies: The "ésago" or "judex," proposed the sentence, the more important personages acquiesced, and the people ratified it. In Friesland the function of the "asega" was only to give advice. Among the Saxons, the "vicinantes" or "pagenses" sometimes consulted men of known learning. The Anglo-Saxon "sapientes" or "witan" dictated, in a fashion, the sentence to the people. It was the same personage, who in Iceland merely gave information on the law, in Norway pronounced the sentence which was ratified by the people, and who in Sweden judged alone. *Brunner*, I, 150.

[7] From "ragin," counsel, and "purgjo" surety, bail. Wide differences existed in regard to the rôle of the "rachimbourgs," *cf.* "*Beaudouin*," *op. cit.*, who enumerates and discusses the proposed systems. There is nothing certain concerning their number. The Salic Law, 57, indicates that the minimum was 7, but in a special case where they were experts. "Lex Rib.," 32, 3. *Cf.* "L. Sal.," 50, "Form. Senon," rec. 6. On the so-called four benches where they would have been seated, and the Flemish name of the tribunal, "vierschare" = "quatuor scamna." "Septem causæ," 7, 6, and "Récap.," B, 31; *Fustel de Coulanges*, "Recherches," p. 384.

being pronounced by the president of the tribunal; but this order was based upon the declaration made by the "rachimbourgs" and approved by the assistants, that is, the free men ("Volbart") composing the judicial assembly, but whose rôle was in other respects continually receding into the background. The "rachimbourgs" thus occupied a peculiar position. They resembled neither the assessors of the Roman magistrates, who had no official rôle and who were consulted by the magistrate or not as he willed, nor modern judges who are functionaries. They may be compared to our jurors, to whom they were in reality analogous. Among the free men who attended the assembly the more important took a place apart or were chosen by the president or the parties. They gave advice and on account of this function they came to be called "rachimbourgs"; judges for the time being only, they could attend one assembly and be absent from the next.

§ 112. **Royal Justice. (A.) Ordinary Jurisdictions: the Count and the Centurion.** — The counts and the centurions were the ordinary judges; both the latter, former popular magistrates, and the former, agents of the king without judicial power, ended by becoming royal judges with this peculiarity that the centurion was subordinate to the count and had jurisdiction only in minor cases. The count was not yet a judge at the time of first writing of the Salic Law, but had become one when the first capitularies were added to this law. He held assizes in the hundreds of his county, for the hundred (and not the county) constituted the judicial unit.[1] The centurion substituted for him, but only in his own hundred. Ordinarily the count was assisted by the "rachimbourgs" (and later by the "échevin"), but when there was a question of inflicting public punishment rather than the fixing of a composition, particularly in cases of flagrant offenses, sometimes even when resort was had to a procedure of denunciation against notorious criminals whom their victims did not dare to accuse,[2] the count, in imitation of the Roman magistrates, prosecuted them of right and passed judgment alone.

[1] *Gregory of Tours*, 8, 18. Even under the Carolingians, although it is held by some that there was then a county tribunal.

[2] *Beaudouin*, N.R.H., 1888, 112; *Siegel*, "Wien. Ak.," 125. Under the Merovingians these were measures for cases in which there was neither accusation nor flagrant misdemeanor. "Sal.," 74. "Capitularia de latron." c. 15. I, 180, and "Kiersy," 873, c. 7. Procedure of denunciation ("Rugeverfahren") under the Carolingians was that employed for grave crimes, homicides, thefts, adultery, incest. "Capitularia of Pepin," 782, c. 8, I, 192. "Conv. Silv.," 853. The Church adopted it, and the bishop, in his

The capitularies reserved for the assizes presided over by the count the trial of crimes involving capital punishment, cases affecting immovable property, and those involving liberty (" causæ majores"). These cases were tried at ordinary sessions over which the count alone had the right to preside. The others (" causæ minores ") fell within the jurisdiction of the centurion who had the right to preside only at extraordinary sessions.[1] There we find a distinction analogous to that made during the feudal epoch between superior and inferior justice. Charlemagne is entitled to credit for two correlative and doubtless simultaneous reforms (about 770–780 ?): a reduction in the amount of the judicial service required of the inhabitants and the creation of the office of " échevin." Attendance upon the judicial assembly, like the obligation of jury service to-day, was a heavy burden for free men, but the counts and the centurions aggravated it; they multiplied the sessions unnecessarily with the sole object of collecting the fine imposed upon absentees, a portion of which went into their pockets. Charlemagne decided[2] that not more than three general sessions should be held annually,[3] " propter pauperes," and that free men should be obliged to attend only these.

The curtailment of this service was not allowed to impede the course of justice. In order that the reform might work no prejudice to suitors it became necessary to establish the " échevinat "; to judges who served on occasion, the " rachimbourgs," there were now added, and consequently substituted in their places, permanent professional judges, who were real functionaries, the " scabini " or " échevins."[4] They were chosen for life

pastoral visits, also made an inquisition on the morals of the faithful. The king alone or his special delegates had the right to organize this abnormal procedure. In Italy, the counts received this power in a general way. In France, it was accorded to them only by way of exception.

[1] Concerning the origin of this distinction, *cf. Brunner*, II, 178; regarding the distinction that he established between the "neufränkische" and the "altfränkische Graf," see II, 164; Cod. Theod., 2, 1, 8; "Form. Andeg." 47; *Bignon*, 7, 13; *Merkel*, 29, 30; "Lex Salic," 74, 67; "Rib.," 77, 58. Is it necessary to distinguish between the tribunal of the centurion and the justice of the "vicini" or "pagenses"? "Præceptum pro Hispanis," 815, c. 2. "Capitularia Saxon." 797, c. 4, I, 71.

[2] "Capitularia regum Francorum," 819, c. 14, I, 290; *ibid.*, 769 (?), c. 12, I, 46; "Capitularia franc.," c. 4, I, 214. The capitularies enacting the reform have not reached us. *Brunner* observes that it was easy to realize it by administrative means; it sufficed to prohibit public functionaries from holding more than three general pleas and from summoning simple free men to attend any but these three.

[3] By hundred or by county.

[4] From "skapjan," "schaffen," to decide. In Germania, the "échevins" were called "schoeffen," "Formulas" of 770–775; *Bignon*, 7; *Merkel*, 32; *cf.* Lindenbrog, 19, 21; "Carta of Saint Victor," I, 43; *Brunner*, "Forsch.," 248; *W. Sickel*, Z.R.G., 19, 1; *Hermann*, "Entwick. d. Schoeffeng," 1881; *Saleilles*, "R. historique," 40, 286.

by the counts with the assent of the people, and consequently in the assembly of the hundred, or "mallus," and they took an oath to render judgment according to law.[1] They were obliged, usually to the number of seven, to attend all the sessions of the judicial assembly.[2] In the "placita generalia," they sat by the side of the "rachimbourgs," whom no one had thought of excluding; at the other sessions they were alone with the centurion or the count.[3] By this means the "rachimbourgs," without losing in theory the right of participating in the administration of justice, passed to a lower plane or disappeared entirely, like the judicial assembly itself. Moreover, the choice of "échevins" had to be made from the "rachimbourgs," who sat oftenest and who were the best qualified, already these were summoned by the counts in preference to others. The division of labor brought about the creation of the "échevinat." The change was not very apparent, the reform was a simplification rather than a radical innovation. More especially as the "échevins" only declared what the law was, while the count gave in some way an executory force to their sentence. The rôle of the count and that of the "échevin" (or that of the "rachimbourgs") was clearly distinguished in documents in which were found formulas like this: "conformably to the judgment of the 'échevins' and upon the order of the count." The count was not bound absolutely by the decision of the "échevins"; he could reject it upon his own responsibility though he rarely did so. The counts and their vicars, so the capitularies declared, must know the law in order that no one might be judged unjustly in their presence.[4]

(B.) **The Tribunal of the King**[5] already foreshadowed in the Salic Law, Vols. 18 and 46, had a double origin. The Frankish king, following Roman tradition, had assumed the judicial authority of the emperor and, in accordance with Germanic traditions, also that of the popular assembly. Can it be said that he exercised the judicial power in all its plenitude? No more than that he possessed the legislative power in all its plenitude. How-

[1] "Capitularia Aix," 809, c. 11, I, 149. *Cf.* 150, "Cap.," 22.

[2] "Capitularia regum Francorum," 803, c. 20, I, 116; *ibid.*, 820, c. 2, I, 295; *ibid.*, 817, c. 14, I, 290.

[3] *Ibid.*, 803, c. 20, I, 116; "Capitularia Aix," 809, c. 5, I, 148; "Capitularia reg. Franc.," 809, c. 13, I, 150.

[4] *Ibid.*, 801–814, c. 4, I, 144. *Ibid.*, 813, c. 13, I, 172.

[5] *Barchewitz*, "Das Koenigsgericht," 1882; *Esmein*, N.R.H., 1887, 545; *Brunner*, II, 133. "Mallus, stappulum regis" (terrace at the entrance of the palace) under the first dynasty. "Lex. Rib.," 50, l. 33, l. 67, 5. 75. We find in *Pertz*, "Dipl.," 20 "placita" of the Merovingian kings, and 6 "placita" of the mayors of the palace.

ever, the extension which the royal authority had received permitted the king: 1st, to judge in equity without conforming strictly to the law and by this means to bring about useful innovations;[1] and 2d, to establish at the expense of the ordinary jurisdictions a judicial competence almost unlimited. It is not necessary, however, to believe from this that he judged as he liked and in an arbitrary manner; as a general rule, he rendered judgment in accordance with the laws and his competence was determined by certain principles. The composition of the king's tribunal was at the same time out of harmony with and in accord with the idea of the royal omnipotence: the king constituted at will his tribunal, appointing as its judges the principal officers of the court and other important personages who lived at the palace, though there was no fixed or precise rule in this respect. It was a rule, however, that the king should never judge alone; he was always attended by these assessors and their rôle was not merely passive, the judgment of the court being as much their work as that of the king.[2] The count of the palace, who had already played an important part at the court of the king under the Merovingians, became the ordinary president during the second dynasty, the king reserving for himself only the more important cases. During the same time the administration of justice by the "missi dominici" in the provinces supplemented that of the king's court; it was the court of the king traveling in circuit.

§ 113. **The Jurisdiction of the King's Court** was rather badly delimited than unlimited. Above all should we regard the jurisdiction of this tribunal as exceptional and extraordinary.

(A) **Original Jurisdiction.** — As a court of first instance it had jurisdiction of cases which involved the interests of the king as the representative of the State, such as: lèse-majesté, refusal to take the oath of allegiance, repeated violations of the public peace, high treason, and fiscal questions.[3] As a general principle,

[1] Ex: the procedure of inquisition. Charters of "mundium"; *Hincmar*, "De ord. pal.," c. 21; "Capitularia regum Francorum," 803–13, c. 1, I, 143. *Brunner*, II, 136, cites the Roman precedents. Cod. Theod., 1, 2, 3, and Cod. Just., 1, 14, 9; the origin of this equity jurisdiction is believed, however, to be Germanic because of the analogies offered by the Anglo-Saxon and Scandinavian laws. The arbitral jurisdiction was always inspired by equity rather than by positive law; the Frankish king was a powerful mediator who imposed on the parties arbitral sentences.

[2] *Gregory of Tours*, 7, 23. 8, 12. 9, 19. *Cf. Eginhard*, "Vita Kar.," c. 24. The king's tribunal was ambulatory, like the court itself.

[3] "Capitularia Aix," 810, c. 13, I, 153; "Capitularia Kiersy," 873, c. 10.

cases in which great personages were parties fell within the competence of the ordinary tribunals,[1] but this principle suffered many exceptions, especially in criminal matters; thus crimes committed by the bishops were judged by the king. Charlemagne and Louis the Debonair likewise decided cases involving *homines boni generis*, abbots and counts.[2] Persons under the protection of the king were in every case allowed to bring their suits before his court; this was the origin of the privilege later known under the name of "committimus," the effect of which was to withdraw certain suitors from their natural judges.

The right of removal ("évocation") likewise existed, it being optional with the king to transfer a case from the jurisdiction of the ordinary tribunals to his own court for trial; in such a case he issued an "indiculus commonitorius" (*cf.* the Anglo-Norman "bref"), which was a written order, sometimes addressed to the interested party himself, sometimes to the judge, enjoining the defendant to give satisfaction to the plaintiff, in default of which the latter had a right of recourse to the king.[3]

(B) **Appellate Jurisdiction.** — The king's court had also an appellate jurisdiction, at least a jurisdiction akin to that of appeal, since procedure by appeal strictly speaking was not known:[4] 1st, in cases in which there was a denial of justice, though in such cases it was not wholly a matter of appeal since there had been no first judgment;[5] 2d, in cases in which the judgment was false; but here also it was not a question of appeal, since it was the judges who were attacked, they were accused of having given many judgments, fraudulently rather than erroneously, and hence it was rather a taking to task than an appeal;[6] 3d, in cases of "reclamatio a regis sententiam" by persons placed under the

[1] "Capitularia regum Francorum," 822, c. 7, I, 319; "Capitularia Mant.," 781, c. 13, I, 191; *ibid.*, 801, c. 10, I, 210; "Capitularia regum Francorum," 884, c. 11, II, 374.

[2] *Ibid.*, 811, c. 2, I, 176; "Capitularia Aix," 801, c. 12, I, 171. Certain churches and certain private individuals received the privilege of exemption from condemnation except by the king.

[3] The expression "évocation" is of a later date. Roman precedents, *Cassiod.*, "Var." 4, 39. 44. 40; *Marculf.*, I, 26. 27. 28; "Carta Senon": 18.

[4] This took either the arbitral character of the primitive jurisdictions or a form depending upon the nature of the methods of proof employed; there was no appeal from an arbitral decision, nor from the result of a judicial combat; neither was there any appeal from the judgment pronounced by a popular assembly.

[5] "Cap. Mant.," 781, c. 2, I, 190; "Capitularia Worm," 829, c. 14, II, 17; "Capitularia Missi," c. 19, I, 101; "Capitularia regum Francorum," 810, c. 5, I, 155.

[6] "Cap. Pepin.," 754, c. 7, I, 32. "Capitularia," "Baiw.," c. 7, I, 159 and "Sax.," 797, c. 4, I, 71. *Cf.* Edict. Chilperic, c. 8, and "Lex Rib.," 32, 4; *Gebauer*, Z.S.S., 1896, 33.

royal "mundium"; but their petition might not be received, the king was not obliged to give a hearing in such cases; it was a privilege rather than a regular institution.[1]

B. Procedure

§ 114. **The Régime of Private Vengeance and of Composition.**[2] — The ancient Germanic law like that of most primitive peoples made it the duty of the family to avenge crimes committed against one of its members and, as relatives were responsible, the one for the other, the family of an offender found itself in a state of war with that of the victim ("Faida");[3] thenceforth private vengeance or reprisals were directed either against the guilty party or a relative innocent of the crime. The only thing necessary to make revenge legitimate in such a case was that it should be public. The Franks fixed the head of their dead enemy on the end of a stake and hung his body on a gibbet, or placed it on a gallows in the middle of a crossroads. Private wars were terminated ordinarily by a treaty of peace or an arrangement in the nature of a compromise; the offender adjusted matters with the injured family and paid it a sum of money, "compositio"[4] ("multa," "Busse")[5] in consideration of which the family renounced its right of revenge.[6] In case of murder the "composition" was

[1] "Cap. Theod.," 805, c. 8, I, 123; "Cap. Sax.," 797, c. 4. "BCh.," 39, 197.

[2] A state of things frequent among primitive people: India, Persia, Hebrews, Slavs, etc. *Cf.* system of the "delicta privata" at Rome. *Festus*, lex Talionis: "si membrum rupit, ni cum eo pacit, talio esto"; *Cf. Kovalewsky*, "Coutume contemporaine et loi ancienne," 1893. *Dahn*, "Fehdegang und Rechtsgang"; *Bausteine*, 2, 90; *Del Giudice*, "La vendetta n. d. langobard.," Studi, 246; *Kohler*, "Shakespeare vor dem forum d. Jurisprudenz," 1884.

[3] "Rothair," 74; "faida, id est inimicitia." The "faidosus" who was killed in a legitimate feud was "sine vindicta"; "Lex Rib.," 79: "jaceat forbatatus." Vengeance was exercised primitively for slight offenses as for grave crimes. *Günther*, "Idee d. Wiedervergellung," 1889; *Brunner*, "Forsch.," 467.

[4] "Iliad," 9, 632, 18, 497; "Law of Gortyne," c. 6 to 9. N.R.H., 1886, 241; *Ireland*, N.R.H., 1887, 66; *Dareste*, "Etudes," *passim*.

[5] The system of compositions tended to be introduced in Roman society at the eve of invasions in consequence of administrative anarchy; after the invasion, it easily spread among the Romans. The compromises in criminal affairs (Cod. Just., 2, 4, 18) increased under the influence of the Church, which was horrified at the shedding of blood and had a feeling of repugnance toward corporal penalties. *Cf.* the penal clauses in the Frankish laws "Capitularia regum Francorum," 803, c. 7, I, 114.

[6] The Frankish and Thuringian laws fixed the "wergeld" including the "fredus" in the amount, whereas the other Barbarian laws did not include this part of the composition in the amount which they fixed. The "fredus" was half in the Lombard law, and a third in the other laws where the amount was fixed, 12, 14 under "Rib.," 36, "Sal.," 41. In case of

known as "wergeld" (man money); it varied according to the rank and nationality of the victim and the circumstances under which the homicide was committed. The State retained a portion of the composition, a half or a third, which was known under the name of "fredus" (*cf.* "Friede," peace), doubtless as the price of its intervention in bringing about the conclusion of peace;[1] the remainder of the amount was called "faidus."

The right of private revenge had not disappeared at the time of the writing of the Salic Law nor under the Merovingians (Clotilda, and the Burgundian kings, Fredigunda and Brunhilda).[2] It was not even abolished in principle under the Carolingians.[3] The exercise of the right however was limited by tolerating it only for grave crimes like homicide, rape, and adultery; by prohibiting inhuman procedure, like burning; by sheltering the relatives of the guilty party except the nearest; and by not permitting acts of violence in various places, such as the courts, the army, the vicinity of the king, at church, and in going to and returning from various places.[4] The Roman system of public punishment gradually developed and crimes came to be regarded not merely as an injury to individual rights but as violations of the public order, — crimes which society was interested in repressing.[5] In every case where the right of private revenge disappeared without being replaced by public punishment the

offenses against property, there was due in addition: 1st, the "capitale," or reparation for damage caused, 2d, the "dilatura" ("wirdira") which was probably a sum in the nature of an indemnity for the deprivation of a thing. *Vanderkindere*, "La dilatura," 1888 (Acad. Belgique); *G. Tamassia*, "La delatura" ("Arch. giur." 58 and 1st Veneto, 1897–98).

[1] According to others, because of the disturbance to the public peace. "Sal.," 35.

[2] "Lex Salic," 41, 8 (Some one whose enemies have cut off his hands and his feet and who is in a "quadruvium," is killed) "Capitularia regum Francorum" I, 39. 175. 201; II, 86. 96. 107; *Monod*, "Les aventures de Sichaire" ("Revue historique," 1886); *Mansi*, XIII, 371. In 745, a bishop of Mainz killed his father's murderer. *Cf.* "Capit. reg. Franc.," I, 59. *Gregory of Tours*, "Vitæ patrum," VIII, 7 (Lyon: Roman and Burgundian law).

[3] Many admit the contrary. The "Capitularia regum Francorum," 789, c. 67, I, 59 contains only a pious counsel. No text punishes the murder of the "faidosus."

[4] "L. Bav.," 7, 1. 2, "Capitularia regum Francorum," 866, c. 7. II, 96; "Sax.," 19, 27; "Alam.," 44, "Wisigoth," 6, 1, 7.

[5] "Burgund.," 2, 1, "Wisigoth," 6, 1, 7. Childeb. II, 596, decreed death as a punishment in case of murder, of rape and of theft; he abolished at the same time the collective responsibility of the family for the payment of the "wergeld"; the murderer, reduced to his own resources, could not easily evade death, since he would not have sufficient means with which to pay the "wergeld." Already, according to the Salic Law, the murderer who could not pay the wergeld was put to death. "Lex Salic," 59.

offender was obliged to pay the composition and the injured to accept it. The Carolingian Capitularies endeavored to enforce peace [1] and the right of private revenge would have been actually abolished, if the wise measures decreed against it could have been executed.[2]

§ 115. **Primitive Procedure** [3] had its origin in private revenge; it consisted in doing justice for one's self according to the forms consecrated by usage. Aside from the practice of private revenge much of this system remained in the Barbarian laws. Procedure was much more the work of the parties than of the public authority; the plaintiff was obliged to act according to the established forms, under these conditions he was certain of triumphing over his adversary. The formal act functioned mechanically, but it was a two-edged sword which returned against him who employed it if he had recourse to it wrongfully, or if he committed irregularities; the fine was the same for the recalcitrant defendant as for the plaintiff who lost.

(A) **Extra Judicial Procedure.** — The Barbarian law authorized individuals to seize trespassing animals,[4] to require security from those who committed offenses prejudicial to their interests,[5] to follow on the track of ("vestigii minatio") stolen animals and to make domiciliary searches in order to discover them.[6] In case of a flagrant offense the victim gave an alarm in order to summon his neighbors to his aid; [7] if vengeance was permitted he killed the aggressor in the presence of the spectators and exposed his body to the public; in other cases the offender was seized, put in chains [8]

[1] The count obliged the parties to pay or to accept the composition and to make peace; recalcitrants were taken before the king and condemned to exile or to have their property confiscated. "Capitularia Héristal," 779, c. 22, I, 51.

[2] Individuals, in times of violence, were loath to appeal to the judges, who were, besides, strongly suspected. Gregory of Tours speaks of a litigant who, supplied with presents for the judge, was robbed on the way and arrived empty-handed and lost his suit.

[3] *Siegel*, "Die Gefahr. v. d. Gericht" (Wien. Ak., 1865); *Behrend*, "Zum Process d. L. Galica"; *Gaudenzi*, "L'antica proced. germ.," 1884; *Brunner*, "Forsch.," 260; *Immerwahr*, "Die Verschweigung," 1895.

[4] "Lex Salica," 9 (*Hessels*, ref.); "Lex Rib.," 82; "Lex Wisigoth," 8, 3.

[5] "Vie de saint Landelin" (A.S.S., jun. III, 542).

[6] "Lex Salica," 37, 47. "L. Ribuaria," 33, 72.

[7] Later sources acquaint us with the cries used, for example the "haro," an Anglo-Norman word, signifying "this way." *Cf.* the old high German "hara," *Diez*, "Etym. Woerterb." *Glasson*, "Etude hist. sur la clameur de haro," 1882. *Cf.* the Latin "huc," the low Latin "huccus," cry, the old French "hucher." In the case of crimes which put the guilty party outside of the law, those who had assembled could kill him. They formed a "Notgericht," as the Germans say and as might be said of lynch law.

[8] "Lex Rib.," 41. "Form. Turon.," 30; *cf.* "L. Rib.," 77.

and brought before the judge. The plaintiff then swore with six or twelve of his friends, that the accused was guilty; if the "legatio" was regular, that was sufficient to convict; if he resisted while in chains, he might be killed.[1] According to the procedure of the Salic Law in an action against an "homo migrans" for "fides facta" and "res præstita" the plaintiff invoked the intervention of the public authority, not for the purpose of obtaining a judgment, since he was considered as already having that, but rather to eject the defendant or obtain possession of his property.[2]

(B) **Judicial Procedure.** — Here, as in extra-judicial procedure, the parties took an active part in the proceedings and much importance was attached to formalities. The judges effaced themselves in the presence of the suitors, who directed the trial at their risk and peril. Adjournment took place upon the demand of the plaintiff himself under the form of "mannitio" or notice addressed to the defendant at his domicile.[3] The capitularies substituted (in most cases) in the place of this clumsy "in jus vocatio," which was often an occasion for fights and quarrels, the "bannitio," or order of the judge, employed at first to bring an individual before the king and later made general. The defendant was obliged to appear unless he was able to offer a valid excuse, such, for example, as absence in the service of the king.[4] The plaintiff waited until sunset and established undeniably the defendant's absence when his counsel was liable to a fine; if absent several times, he was summoned to appear before the king and, as a punishment for his contumacy, he was outlawed and his property confiscated.[5] Assuming that the parties were all present, the next step was for the plaintiff to make his complaint, sometimes after having taken an oath;[6] he then pronounced the "tangano"[7] (constraint) against the defendant, holding in

[1] "Lex Salica," 32 (*Hessels* ref.); "Lex Rib.," 73, 77, 79. "Pactus pro ten. pacis," c. 2. 4. 10; "L. Henrici," 9, 1 and 6; "Capitularia regum Francorum," I, 180, c. 2. 3. The person caught in the act of committing a flagrant crime was not allowed to take the purgatory oath. "Lex Rib.," 41, 2.

[2] *Ibid.*, 45, 50, 1, 52.

[3] *Ibid.*, 1, Edict of Pistoa, 864. For suits other than those involving liberty or rights of inheritance the "Capitularia" of 816, c. 4, I, 268, prescribed the seizure of the property of the defendant who did not respond on the second summons of the court. "Capitularia regum Francorum," 818–819, c. 12, I, 283. — *Opet*, "Gesch. d. Prozesseinleitungsform," 1891.

[4] "Sunnis," "Essoine," "L. Salica," 1, 47.

[5] "Solsadire, solem collocare." "Lex Salica," 37; 40, 56, 106 (*Hessels*); "Lex Rib.," 32; *Cohn*, "Justizverweigerung," 1876.

[6] "Wedredus," "widereid," "voreid," "Lex Salica," 106; "Lex Rib.," 67, 5; "Capitularia regum Francorum," I, 217.

[7] "Tangano" = I compel.

his hands, it seems, a weapon or a staff. The defendant was required to answer by a confession or a denial; he must say "yes" or "no" without restrictions or conditions. If he refused to respond, he was liable to punishment for contumacy. So far was the rigor of this rule pushed that the law of the Ripuarians had to permit the "tangano" to be passed over in cases where a master was prosecuted for offenses committed by his slave; in such cases the master was allowed to declare that he knew nothing of the affair since it would have been clearly too unjust to compel him to say "yes" or "no."[1] Where such formalism prevailed each word had its weight, and to avoid errors the parties were allowed to have the assistance of a "prolocutor" or "für sprecher," the "avant-parlier" of the feudal law, who was their guide in the preparation of legal instruments and formulas of procedure.[2] By means of a new "tangano" the plaintiff invited the judge to pronounce judgment[3] and according to the procedure of summons already described the magistrate concluded by addressing the same invitation to the "rachimbourgs." If the defendant confessed, or if he had been taken in the act of committing a flagrant offense, he was condemned without further proceedings. Otherwise the judges determined the proof, which, as a general rule, the defendant must furnish and upon which his judgment and condemnation depended. Among the Scandinavians they rendered only a judgment awarding proof; among other Germanic peoples, however, they pronounced a conditional sentence, that is, one which conditioned the conviction on the evidence submitted. In that case the judgment took into consideration both the evidence and the merits of the action. The defendant was required under penalty of contumacy to promise upon oath ("adramire," "fidem facere") to furnish on a certain day the prescribed proof.[4] The

[1] "Alsaccia," entire dispute ("all-sakjo"), "Lex Rib.," 30, 1. 50, 19, 59, 8. This principle has been contested under the pretext that it often tended to sacrifice the rights of the defendant. Thus, when he was asked if he had committed a murder, he had to reply *yes*, without the power to add, that it was for legitimate defense, and he would be condemned contrary to all justice. Let us reply that the system of the "legis actiones" of Rome did not admit exceptions either; the deficiency was here made up by cross-questions. *Cf.* the procedure in the "Saga" of Nial. Exceptions were possible when the judge and not the plaintiff addressed himself to the defendant.

[2] "Capitularia regum Francorum," c. 3, I, 281. The "prolocutor" differed from the attorney, "advocatus," "muntporo." The latter had the right to appear in court in the place of his client in exceptional cases, or where this was found permissible. *Brunner*, "Forsch.," 389, and "Z. f. vergl. Rechtsw.," I, 321; *Lass*, "Die Anwaltschaft," 1891.

[3] "Lex Salica," 57.

[4] *Ibid.*, 50.

process ended, the suitors must acquiesce in the judgment or challenge it as wrong (" blasphemare," " fausser le jugement "); if they did neither, ancient custom analogous to that followed by the French to-day in Tunis, required their imprisonment until they were able to pronounce themselves either in favor of acquiescence or rejection of the judgment.[1] If the judgment was attacked as false, an ordeal or duel followed in early days or, during the Carolingian period, recourse was had to the court of the king.

§ 116. **Proof.** — The varieties of testimony admitted by the Roman law were rational: witnesses, written instruments, and confession. Hardly any other means of bringing about a conviction were recognized by the judge. Proof was furnished by the plaintiff; this was entirely just, since it was for him who wished to change the "status quo" to show that his complaints were well founded. Barbarian law, on the contrary, introduced a principle which was the reverse of that established by Roman legislation (which, moreover, resembled modern law). It organized a system of illogical proof, the oath, the ordeal, the duel, and others that cannot be discussed; from the moment at which they were regularly furnished the judgment followed, whatever might be the opinion of the judge. In the second place, it was the defendant who, in most cases, was obliged to furnish the proof. This system, singularly odd in our eyes, appeared very natural to the men of the Barbarian epoch.

(A) **Written Testimony.** — Written proof or proof by witness was not possible in most cases; these, in fact, were concerned with crimes and misdemeanors, but there were acts which could not be proven by writing; moreover, the use of writing was little known. Members of the family of the accused could not testify against him without violating the most sacred duties, nor in his behalf, because no weight was attached to testimony which custom almost obliged them to give. The same was true in regard to the members of the family of the accuser; and as to those who were not relatives of either party they dared say nothing for fear of exposing themselves to the enmity and vengeance of one or the other of the two families. Confession alone remained, but this

[1] "Lex Salica," 57, 3; "Lex Rib.," 55; "Lex Wis.," 2, 1, 19, 23; "L. Burg.," 90, 2; "Cap. Theod.," 805, c. 8; *Esmein*, N.R.H., 1887, 545; *Skedl.*, "Die Nichtigkeitsbeschwerde," 1886; *Gebauer*, Z.R.G., 30, 33. Among the Ossetes (Caucasus), the execution of judgments was insured by the surety whom the tribunals required of the parties and because they drew infamy upon themselves in case of inexecution. The arbitral character of the ancient jurisdiction, is well shown in these facts.

was very rare. Reasonable proof being lacking, in nine cases out of ten recourse was had to an appeal to God and to Him the judgment was deferred by means of the oath, the ordeal, or the duel. In the belief of the time this was a supreme and sure resource and everywhere it came naturally to the front.

(B) **System of Negative Proofs.**[1] — It is less easy to explain why this sort of evidence had to be furnished by the defendant, that is, by him who denied the charge, contrary to the Roman axiom "negantis nulla probatio."[2] A simple denial on his part it seems would have offset the simple affirmation of the plaintiff, but this affirmation, or to speak more accurately, this accusation, was made ordinarily under such conditions that the judge was bound to give it serious consideration.[3] At times it was accompanied by an oath, at other times it was supported by strong evidence, and in bringing it in the accuser risked his life, his fortune, and even the lives and fortunes of his family, because an

[1] *Grimm*, R.A.," 839 (and *Michelet*, "Origine du droit français"); *K. Maurer*, "K. Viertelj," 16, 97; 18, 32. "Das Beweisverf. Kr. Uebersch.," 5, 180; *Zorn*, "Beweisverf. n. langob., R.," 1872; *Beaudouin*, "Remarq. sur la preuve par le serment" (Ann. Grenoble, 1897); *Declareuil*, N.R.H., 1898.

[2] "Roth.," 364; "Burg.," 45; "Lex Rib.," *passim* (and the greater part of the other laws): "juret aut componat." "L. Salica," 14, 2. 39, 2. 42, 5; "Burg.," 45. *Agobard*, "Adv. l. Gundob.," c. 6, declares that a guilty person taken in the act, could clear himself by oath; it is admitted, however, on the faith of other texts, that flagrant offenses were an exception to this rule. The expressions of the Salic Law: "si probatio certa fuerit" or "non fuerit et ei adprobatum fuerit" do not prove that the Salic Law had reversed the procedure and placed the proof on the plaintiff. The defendant was "adprobatus" or "convictus," in case of flagrant offenses, "Lex Salic," 21, 2, by witnesses (if they were allowed), by a proof to which he submitted and which went against him, "Lex Salic," 53, 1. 2. 4., by an ordeal submitted to by the plaintiff, "Lex Salic," 93. 94. "Capitularia regum Francorum," I, 6, and in the case where the "probatio" properly called, waived the oath, "Lex Salica," 39, 2. The law of Gortyne admitted an intermediary system: witnesses and, in default thereof, an oath with co-swearers.

[3] The current formula: it is the right of the tribunal to determine the character of the proof and to decide upon whom it shall be incumbent to produce the evidence, by ascertaining the party most nearly brought to it (for example, the plaintiff if there were documentary evidence, or in case of flagrant offenses), was accepted with difficulty because the judges were bound, by the declaration of the parties, and the laws usually imposed the burden of proof on the defendant. Germanic proofs were different also from the Roman, in that they were not debated, for how could an oath be debated? They could be attacked only exceptionally, as, for example, by impeachment. From this point of view, it can be said that it was an advantage to furnish the proof and not a burden, as in Roman law. The one who gives proof, it has been said, is like the one who, in a duel, shoots first. There is, at least, some exaggeration in this manner of view. It was not always easy for the defendant to procure the number of joint swearers required by law; often one recoils before an ordeal or before a duel when it is to be fought with a redoubtable adversary. (Ex.: Saga of Nial.)

accusation was equivalent to a declaration of war between the two families. The accuser who failed to establish his accusation was liable to the penalty which he wished to have inflicted upon his adversary. Against a complaint made under such conditions it was entirely natural (and the historians have shown this to be true) that the accused should cry out and protest his innocence by means of an oath, and the law sanctioned this practice. The defendant could not be convicted in the absence of positive proof, nor could he be acquitted, because he was suspected of being guilty; he was therefore requested to swear, in the presence of the court, that he was innocent. Thus, in principle, the accused cleared himself by means of an oath; [1] the ordeal was resorted to only in a subsidiary manner and by virtue of an agreement, or when joint swearers could not be found, or when persons belonging to the servile class were involved (because an oath taken by them was distrusted).[2] The duel was resorted to chiefly as a means of attacking an oath, or a sentence alleged to be unjust. The law of the Burgundians allowed the plaintiff to challenge the defendant to single combat at the moment when the latter was in the act of clearing himself by oath.[3] Confession,[4] written proof,[5] and witnesses [6] were not unknown, however, to the Barbarian law. But witnesses as they were known to the Germanic laws were not generally comparable to those of modern times. There were: 1st, documentary witnesses ("testes rogati") called to establish a

[1] The plaintiff sometimes had the right to prevent the defendant from taking the purgatory oath by establishing his guilt through the testimony of witnesses. *Cf.* "Lex Rom. Cur.," XI, 14. *Troya*, nos. 340, 641, 677, 703.

[2] Decree of Gratian, c. 15, c. 2, q. 5.

[3] "Lex Alam.," 43. The Salic Law, 53, 82. 106. 94 (*cf.* "Pactus pro ten.," p. c. 4) permitted a direct challenge to the ordeal by boiling water, which seems to have taken the place of the duel. "Burg.," 45.

[4] The Salic Law did not authorize the use of torture except for slaves. Nevertheless, *Gregory of Tours* refers to its application rather often, "Lex Salic," 40, "Lex Burg.," 7, 39.

[5] "Lex Rib.," 59, 1. *Brunner*, "Das Gerichteszeugniss u. die fränk. Urk." ("Festg. f. Heffter," 1873). The royal charter gave faith. When two royal charters were opposed to each other, an attempt was first made to reconcile them, but usually the oldest was given the preference. "Lex Rib.," 60, 67. A private instrument drew its force from the oath of the scribe and the witnesses; the German "urkunde" which designated the written instrument, signified witness. "Lex Rib.," 58, 5. 59, 2. "Sal. Extrav.," B, 3. Alam., 2, 2. Lib. Pap. Wid., 6. The Ripuarian law distinguished the simple contestation and the false accusation which supposed and decided it by duel or the comparison of handwriting.

[6] *Ibid.*, 60, "Bav.," 16, 2. When land was sold, the children were boxed on the ears or their ears were pulled in order to better fix the fact in their memories. The Salic Law established it by means of witnesses. To what extent did it deviate in this respect from the common Barbarian law by admitting witnesses on occasion?

fact, such as a summons to appear in court, and to declare under oath that this fact had taken place,[1] and, 2d, witnesses of notoriety summoned to establish a known fact, such as the fact that a stolen hog was "votinus," that is, consecrated to the divinity.[2]

§ 117. **The Carolingian Inquest.** — In this last category of witnesses are perhaps to be found those who took part in the Carolingian inquest.[3] This procedure could be prescribed only by the king (the count of the palace, or the "missi") who issued an "indiculus inquisitionis," or letter, enjoining the judge to make an inquiry and transmit the results to the king by means of a report, or to decide the controversy himself. The royal treasury and, consequently, the benefices and monasteries belonging to the king, many churches, and Jews under royal protection, were entitled to demand procedure by inquest without the royal letter. Under it proof was more easy to establish and the results of the "inquisitio" could not be vitiated through resort to the duel. This procedure, moreover, was applied only in actions relative to landed property, to long-term usufructuary rights, and to questions affecting the State. To conduct the inquest the judge chose men from the vicinage, "pagenses," "infra patriam habitantes," who were known for their uprightness, "bonos," "veraces"; he made them promise under oath to decide according to truth ("vere dictum," verdict), after which they were asked what they knew of the facts. There was no rule which fixed the number of jurors, or which regulated the examination or the verdict. It was this procedure which, as it developed, gave birth to the Anglo-Norman trial jury, to the English jury, and consequently to the modern jury; it is found again in the "inquest of bystanders."

[1] "Lex Salica," 1, 3. 39. 1. 45. 2. 46. 47. 49. 52.

[2] *Ibid.*, 2, 13. 33, 2. In our time the value of the testimony is chiefly considered and weighed "ponderantur, non numerantur." *Cf.* "Lex Salica," 39, 2 (cod. 3) and "Extrav.," B, 2; on the contrary weight is given to the number of witnesses. "Cap. reg. Franc.," 816, c. 1, I, 268.

[3] *Brunner*, "Entstehung d. Schwurgerichte," 1872; "Forschungen," 88; and "D. Rechtsg.," II, 524; "Rev. gen. du droit, Orig. du jury," 1881; "Cap. Worms," 829, c. 8, II, 713. The "inquisitio" also took place in the procedure of information. It was a question of reaching notorious criminals whom no one dared accuse. Then the most worthy of confidence were summoned and they were made to swear to inform against crimes committed in their district. Those against whom they informed were treated as if they were under formal accusation; they had to clear themselves by oath or by ordeals. This procedure was applied eventually, in the greater part of the Germanic countries. "Communes vérités dans le droit flamand" (Lameere, 1882), Vehme in Westphalia, grand jury in England.

§ 118. **The Purgatory Oath.**[1] — Proof by oath was the proof recognized by the common law.[2] The accused cleared himself by swearing that he was not guilty.[3] The oath was considered as a judgment of God; God, being called upon to witness the truth of an affirmation, would not fail, if it were false, to strike down the one who uttered it; the perjurer would die at once, or later in the year.[4] The oath included: 1st, a consecrated formula;[5] 2d, a solemn act coupled with the customary words; thus a material object having some relation to the gods or to the saints to whom appeal was made was touched by the accused. The pagan oath was taken upon arms or upon a ring dipped in the blood of an animal that had been sacrificed;[6] the Christian oath was taken upon the relics of a saint, upon the altar where these relics were kept, upon the gospel, or upon the cross.[7] The oath of the accused was ordinarily required to be accompanied by the oath of a certain number of cojurors or fellow swearers ("conjuratores," "sacramentales"), first, the relatives, who were bound to swear for him on account of the family solidarity;[8] then, neighbors, including

[1] *R. Loening*, "Reinigungseid," 1880; *Beaudouin*, "Ann. Grenoble," vol. VIII.

[2] "Lex Salica," 14, 2. In default of "probatio certa" they swore with fellow swearers ("cojureurs"); if none could be found, they must submit to the ordeal of boiling water, or pay composition.

[3] "Purgatio canonica" in contradistinction to the duel; and to ordeals, "purgatio vulgaris," rejected by the courts of the Church.

[4] *Gregory of Tours*, 8, 16. 40. 5, 50; "De gloria confess.," 93. (91) 94. "Patr. lat.," vol. 87, p. 582 ("miracula Eligii"): a crime was committed; father and son were accused; each charged the other with the act; the bishop and the duke, "cum non possent rei veritatem cognoscere," had the case judged by Saint Eloi: "tibi, sancte Eligi, hoc judicium committimus"; the two accused persons were placed before the tomb of the saint, and "expectabant per sacramentum Dei fore judicium"; scarcely had the son begun to take the oath when, seized by the demon, he fell to the earth.

[5] "Lex Rib.," 67, 5. The accuser and the accused had to use, in general, the customary formulas. The accused was not free to swear as he wished; his adversary was not authorized to dictate to him the formula of the oath. Often, doubtless, the plaintiff dictated the formula which the defendant repeated word for word. The Norman law had a "juramentum escariatum," whose formula was dictated by the judge; the English law, a "juramentum factum," which was contrary to the "juramentum planum," taken without being dictated.

[6] Arms were perhaps consecrated to the gods. *Ammien*, 17, 12, 21; "L. Alam.," 86; "Rothair," 364; "Bavar.," 16, 5; "Lex Rib.," 67, 5: "in circlo et collore" or "hasla," ring or switch of hazel tree. "Frisons," 3, 5; 22, 2. Alam., 5, 4.

[7] *Marculf.*, I, 38: "in palatio super capella (cope) S. Martini," "Alam.," 6, 4 (on a shrine; if it is empty, the oath was void), "Cap.," 803, c. 11. Where was the oath taken? In the church: "Lex Rib.," 67, 5, and "Cap., add. l. Rib.," 803, c. 11. "Form. Turon.," 39. In the palace: *Marculf.*, I, 35. "Jurare in harao"; "L. Rib.," 32, 72. 77, means to swear on a consecrated object (relics, etc.); of "haruc," consecrated place.

[8] The custom of joint swearing is explained by this solidarity: it was desired to establish the collective responsibility of the family, and it was

any free men whomsoever, provided they were of the same race and condition. The number of joint swearers varied according to the different laws, the importance of the action, and the status of the persons; the "plenum sacramentum" of the Saxon law contenting itself with twelve.[1] They took the same oath as the accused or they swore that his oath was credible; if he was guilty of perjury, so were they. According to the law of the Alamanni they all placed their hands on the shrine containing the relics; the accused pronounced the words of the oath and the fellow swearers said: "Sic Deus nos adjuret."[2] The penalty for false swearing was mild enough at first, it being left to God to wreak vengeance upon the perjurer; but when it was seen that the effects of the divine wrath made themselves felt too tardily, many rendered themselves liable to the penalty. The capitularies punished the perjurer by cutting off his hand, a sure means of preventing a repetition of the offense if he had not been allowed to save his hand through the payment of composition.[3] The purgatory oath fell into disuse rather than was abrogated; it had lost in the public mind its character as judicial proof. It was realized that there was no good reason for supposing that he who would not shrink from committing a criminal act would hesitate to take a false oath. There was nothing to be seen in the oath except a solemn affirmation to which religious faith gave a certain weight; finally, the practice of inquest, or inquisitorial procedure (toward the end of the 1100 s in the ecclesiastical courts and at the end of the 1200 s in the secular tribunals), rendered the oath useless and led to its abandonment.[4]

required that the accused submit himself and his property to the malediction contained in the oath. When the old organization of the family was gone, the neighbors were taken; if they were suspects, the plaintiff sometimes chose them; sometimes each party chose half (*Marc.*, I, 38: "Medii electi"). *Cf.* "Lex Sal.," 60; "Burg.," 8; "Rothair," 360; "Capit. reg. Fran.," I, 315; *Cosack*, "Die Eidhelfer," 1885.

[1] Multiples or submultiples of 12: 3, 6, 24, 36, 48, 72. The expressions to swear "duodecima manu," "sibi tertius," are not clear. The accused swore sometimes as twelfth with eleven joint swearers, sometimes as thirteenth with twelve: sometimes with two, sometimes with three. On the "tres seniores," "Sal.," 48, 2, cod. 5. 6. 10; on the "three aloarius," "Cart. Senon.," 17, 21.

[2] Subsequently, they vouched for the honesty of the accused; but the certificate of morality which they thus delivered to him did not hold them responsible in case of perjury. "Form. Turon.," 31, X, 5, 34, 5 ("juram de credulitate").

[3] *Liutpr.*, 144. "Capit.," 779, c. 10, I, 49. 789, c. 64, I, 58 ("nec testis nec ad sacramentum accedat").

[4] X, 5, 34. In case of grave rumor ("diffamatio") one cleared himself by oath with the compurgatores (canonical law). "Inquisitio," 1198, 1199. X, 5, 3, 31. The oath of the 1200s: "Olim," I, 320, 7. "Cont. de Toulouse," 46, 47, 48.

§ 119. **Judicial Trials or Ordeals**[1] have been in use among nearly all peoples. Wherever animistic beliefs have prevailed, suitors have desired to appeal to wise spirits scattered about in all material objects to assist them, to take sides with them, and to make known on what side law and right were to be found.[2] With more exalted conceptions, whether polytheistic or monotheistic, it was thought that the gods intervened in human affairs by a spirit of justice.[3] The Christian Church adopted the Barbarian practice of tests;[4] according to the common belief God could not refuse a miracle to those who invoked his aid, in order to insure the triumph of right and justice and, as though he were not able to accomplish this alone, they had the "naïveté" to prepare the elements for him. The principal tests during the Frankish epoch were: 1st, the *ordeal by boiling water*, which is the only one mentioned in the Salic Law.[5] After mass and an adjuration to the accused not to receive the sacrament if he were guilty, after an exorcism and a benediction of the water that it might escape the power of the devil, after orisons and prayers over the boiling water, the judge hung a stone in it and the culprit drew it out; his hand was then wrapped with linen and the seal of the judge was affixed; three days later the cloth was removed and if no traces of burning remained on the hand, or if it was in a state of convalescence, the innocence of the accused was established; but if the wound appeared in a bad condition, the case went against him. The popular saying, "I would put my hand into the fire for it,"

[1] "Ordeal," Anglo-Saxon; "urtheil," German. "Judicium Dei, Examen aquæ frigidæ," etc. *Kaegi*, "Festschr. f. d. Versamml. d. Philologen in Zürich," 1887; *Patetta*, "Le Ordalie," 1890; "Gr. Encyclop.," see "Epreuves."

[2] Most of the ordeals are satisfactorily explained only by reference to these primitive ideas; the spirit of fire burned the guilty and spared the innocent; the spirit of water repelled one who had injured it; the spirits which were found in foods could cause sickness and death (consecrated foods, bitter waters among the Hebrews to establish the adultery of the woman); the soul of the dead denounced the assassin ("Bahrrecht," trial by coffin, the corpse bled at the approach of the assassin), etc. The desire for vengeance or an appropriate exorcism caused the spirits to act.

[3] God or the gods, conceived as Justice itself, naturally intervened in favor of right and justice, but was it in this world or another?

[4] Christian rituals of the 900s and 1000s, "Ordines judiciorum Dei": *Zeumer*, "Form.," p. 608. See *La Mantia*, "Ord. judic. Dei nel messale gallicano d. XII s. d. cattedr. d. Palermo," 1892. *Schmid*, "Ges. d. Angels.," 414.

[5] "Judicium aquæ ferventis, æneum or ineum." Caldron, "caldaria." "Lex Sal.," 14. 16. 53. 56. Except under the Salic Law, ordeal by boiling water was reserved for slaves. "Lex Rib.," 30, 1. 3. 31, 5. "Cham.," 48; "Fris.," 3. 6. 14, 3; *Liutp.*, 50; "Wisig.," 6, 1, 3. Charlemagne here substituted the duel.

comes from these old ideas. 2d, the *ordeal by red-hot iron,*[1] with the same ritual, consisted in the accused's carrying a red-hot iron in his naked hand a certain distance, ordinarily nine steps, or in walking with naked feet on red-hot plowshares; 3d, *trial by cold water*[2] according to which the offender, bound by a cord, was plunged into a vat filled with water; if he sank, he was innocent, but if he floated, he was guilty, on the theory that pure water would refuse to receive him; 4th, *ordeal by consecrated bread,*[3] which was given the accused to eat; if it stopped in his throat, he was guilty; 5th, *trial by lot;*[4] 6th, *trial by the cross,*[5] an ordeal probably of monastic origin, which consisted in the holding an immovable position with arms extended in the form of a cross during the recital of certain prayers; the one of the two adversaries who first allowed his arms to fall was declared guilty. This form of trial, the most recent of all, was abolished in 818–819, for the reason that it was considered to be a profanation of the Passion. The issue in these methods of trial by ordeal depended upon the physical vigor of the culprit, upon the frauds which he was able to practice,[6] and upon an anæsthesia which was produced in certain persons of a nervous temperament, similar to hysteria and hypnotism. The more enlightened minds soon perceived this, and in the end even the credulous populace came to realize that miracles were rare and frauds frequent. But in spite of the discredit into which trials by ordeal fell they reappeared in the 1100s and 1200s, only to be condemned by the Church about the middle of the latter century; at the same time the revival of the Roman law and the progress of judicial procedure had the effect of creating a preference for written proof and proof furnished by witnesses.

§ 120. **The Judicial Combat.** — A simple recourse to force, trial by single combat, was considered from early times as an appeal

[1] Customs of Barcelona and of Montpellier. In 1815, it was still used in Flanders for the trial of sorcerers.

[2] The "Capitulary of Worms," 829, c. 12, II, 16, prohibited only the pagan form of trial. Until the 1700s, it was employed in actions against sorcerers.

[3] "Judicium offæ, caseus exsecratus" (cheese). A consecrated wafer was sometimes used for the same purpose (ex. Gregory VII). The popular expression was: May this piece of bread choke me if I do not tell the truth.

[4] The lot. "Lex Rib.," 31, 5. "Capit. reg. Fran.," I, 5, c. 5 and 11: "ad plebium seu ad sortem"; subjecting the slave to torture on the pledge of the plaintiff to pay his worth to the master, or trial by lot ("sortiariæ," sorceress).

[5] "Cap. reg. Franc.," 758, c. 17, I, 41. 816, c. 1, I, 208. 818, I, 279. *Cf.* II, 23.

[6] Doubtless a modern conjurer would extricate himself without much difficulty by means of such a procedure.

to God.[1] Although the Salic Law did not speak of the duel there is no doubt that it was a form of procedure employed among the Salic Franks[2] as it was among other Barbarian peoples.[3] It was resorted to especially when an oath or a judgment was to be contested.[4] The two parties entered into an agreement to engage in single combat and for this purpose threw down what were later called " gages of battle " (" vadiare pugnam "). The combat took place in public before the judges after the two parties had sworn not to make use of magic.[5] Among the Ripuarians the parties fought with a long sword or " gladius," among the Salians with pike and shield, " cum scuto et baculo." [6] From the time of Louis the Debonair persons of quality fought on horseback and with lances, as they did during the feudal epoch, although the common people in accordance with ancient custom fought only with staves and shield. The duel might continue until sunset, at which time it always came to an end and the defendant who was not vanquished won his case; it ceased sooner if one of the adversaries declared himself defeated, if he were killed, or if one of the judges put a stop to the combat.[7] Many laws permitted the parties to employ substitutes to act as their champions.[8] The judicial combat was regulated with more detail during the feudal epoch but except in certain particulars relating to procedure, the institution remained unchanged.[9] The Church did not condemn it

[1] "Judicium pugnæ," "campus," "batalia," etc., "L. Alam.," 81; *Pron*, "Gr. Encyclo." (and bibliography); *Gelli*, "Il duello," 1886.

[2] "Lex Salica," 93, *Hessels. Gregory of Tours*, 7, 14, 10, 10.

[3] *Tacitus*, "Germ.," 10; "L. Rib.," 57, 2. 59, 4. 32. 4; Alam., 54; "Bav.," 2, 1. 8, 2. 17, 2; "Burg.," 8, 2; 45; 80. 2; *Liutp.* 21. Scandinavian "sagas." Conventional duel in ancient Ireland. Slavs of the 900s. The Anglo-Saxons practiced ordeals, but not the judicial duel; the Normans introduced it into England. Wisigothic laws are silent; but *cf.* "Vita Hludow.," c. 33, M.G.H., S.S., II, 625. *Baist*, "Roman. Forsch.," 5, 1890.

[4] "Thuring.," c. 56. "Cap.," 816, c. 1, I, 268: duel against witnesses or between witnesses; the defeated champion lost his hand. *Cf.* "Bav.," 12, 8.

[5] "Bavar.," 2, 1 and 11. "Rothair," 368 (371).

[6] "Capit. reg. Franc.," I, 117, 150, 172, 180, 268, 283. The "baculus" of Frankish law, the "baculus cornutus" of Norman law ("Summa," c. 68) was doubtless a pike, a stick with a point of iron. *Du Cange*, "Baculus," "Fustis." *Gregory of Tours*, 10, 10.

[7] "Fris.," 14, 4; "Bav.," 2, 11.

[8] "Rothair," "Fris. sup. Bav.," 2, 12. 9, 4. 12, 8. *Gregory of Tours*, 10, 10.

[9] "Biblioth. Med. Ævi" of *Gaudenzi*. "Summula de pugna. Stylus Parlam.," 16. *Beaumanoir*, 39, 4. 61. 65, 4. *Artois*, 40, 41. *Loysel*, "Inst. Cont.," no. 108 and following (with bibliog.). *Brunner*, "Rev. crit. de législ.," 1871. The duel was always regarded as a privilege of nobles and of free men; sometimes it was allowed serfs. Combatants, common in Normandy (*cf.* "Fris.," 5, 1. 14. 7; "Roth.," 368), were admitted only exceptionally in France (minors, sexagenarians, women, sick

at first; Saint Augustine saw in war, which was but a duel between nations, a judgment of God.[1] But from the 800 s[2] a party opposed to the duel was formed within the Church; the Council of Valencia, in 855, pronounced the one who was killed in a duel as a suicide and the one who killed him as an assassin. Nicholas I and his successors forbade the "judicium sanguinis" in the Church tribunals and by churchmen; Innocent II in 1140, and Adrian IV in 1156 condemned it even in the secular courts of the bishops and abbots; the fourth Lateran Council in 1215 prohibited it completely. Among the lay tribunals the duel resisted for a long time the opposition of the Church and the action of the Roman law. Abolished among the privileges of certain cities like Saint-Omer in 1127, abolished on the royal domains by an ordinance of Saint Louis of 1258 or 1260, regulated in the constitutions of Sicily, Frederick II, 2, 25, and in the ordinance of Philip the Fair in 1306, it disappeared only about the 1600 s.[3] Philip the Fair authorized the duel only in capital cases (except larceny), on the supposition that the accused could not be convicted upon the testimony of witnesses. It continued to exist in an extra-judicial form; numerous edicts of kings (embodying the most rigorous measures, particularly the edict of 1769) were not successful in extirpating this relic of barbarism.[4]

people). The person attacked had the choice of arms only in combats by challenge and not in those which took place on the order of the judge. The procedure comprised several phases: 1st, *Appeal;* complaint before the judge with right to private combat if the adversary refused to give justice. For less than grave crimes calling for imprisonment of the parties, the judge required the necessary security to insure their presence at the trial; 2d, *Presentation;* on the day and at the place fixed, the parties presented themselves before the judge; 3d, *Record of the appeal;* oath of the parties confirming their pretensions, oath that they would not make use of sorcery; the judge had three bans called out ordering those present not to disturb the king's peace; 4th, *Battle;* the dead was in the wrong, and the defeated paid the fine; in case of murder the conquered was hung if he survived, and all his property was confiscated.

[1] Process between Saint Benoit and Saint Denis.

[2] *Liutprand,* 118: "incerti sumus de judicio Dei."

[3] *Loysel,* 818. In 1574, duel of Jarnac and La Chastaigneraie before Henry II. In England, the judicial duel had been practically disused when an eccentric person took it into his head to demand it. This occasion was seized for its abolition (1820).

[4] *Savaron,* "Traicté des duels," 1610; *Ragueau* and *Laurière,* "Gloss," see "Gage de bataille." "BCh.," I, 552; N.R.H., 1889, 729; *Esmein,* "Hist. de la procéd. crim.," 1882 (English translation by John Simpson, Boston, 1913). *De Smedt,* "Le duel judiciare et l'Eglise," 1895; *P. Fournier,* "Yves de Chartres," p. 25; *Isambert,* "Table," see "Duel"; Tribunal of honor under Richelieu (Edict of 1626); *D'Avenel,* "Richelieu et la Monarchie absolue," II, 69.

CHAPTER III

THE FRANKISH OR BARBARIAN EPOCH. ORIGINS OF THE FEUDAL RÉGIME

TOPIC 1. IMMUNITY

TOPIC 2. STATUS OF PERSONS

TOPIC 3. STATUS OF LANDS

TOPIC 1. IMMUNITY[1]

§ 121. **Roman Immunity**, an exemption from taxation and from public services, was applied under the Later Empire to the imperial domains, and, by virtue of special privileges, to the domains of certain individuals and to those of the Church. If the inhabitants of the domain were guilty of serious offenses, the agents

[1] BIBLIOGRAPHY: *Waitz*, II, 2, 339; *Fustel de Coulanges*, "Le bénéfice," p. 336; *Prost*, N.R.H., 1883, 113; *Flach*, "Orig. de l'anc. France," I, 91; *Beauchet*, "Organis. judic.," p. 418; *Salvioli*, "Storia d. immunità . . . in Italia," 1889; *Chamard*, "R. q. hist.," 1877; *Bonvalot*, "Hist. du dr. Lorrain," I, 120.

of the domain were required to bring them before the governor of the province; in case of resistance or delay the governor had the right to seize the malefactors of his own accord. Minor offenses and civil controversies among the inhabitants of the domain were judged by the agents; those between the inhabitants and foreigners, by the ordinary judges, but in the presence of an agent of the domain.[1]

§ 122. **Frankish Immunity**[2] produced more radical consequences; it was a royal privilege which exempted a great landowner, or rather his domain and its inhabitants, from the jurisdiction of the royal functionaries. The royal domains enjoyed this privilege without a special concession;[3] most of the churches and abbeys obtained diplomas of immunity[4] and so did many laymen.[5] The concession was perpetual but this did not hinder the grantees, for greater security, from having it confirmed by successors of the grantor when considerations of greater security were opposed thereto.[6]

1st, **Negative Effects.** — The charter delivered to a great landed proprietor contained one essential provision, namely, a prohibition upon the royal officers from entering the lands of the immunist ("absque introitu judicum"). If the count presented himself, he was stopped by showing him this charter; he was no more authorized to exercise his functions upon the domains entitled to immunity than upon the lands belonging to the king. His authority ended at the boundaries of the territory belonging to the immunist owner; he could enter them neither to judge nor

[1] Dig., 50, 4, 18; Cod. Theod., 11, 12; Cod. Just., 10, 25; Cod. Theod., 11, 16, 15. 18 and Nov. *Valent.*, III, 10, 3 ("munera sordida"), and Cod. Theod., 11, 16, 1. 2, and following. Church, Nov. *Valent.*, III, 10; Cod. Just., I, 2, 5, 8, and Cod. Theod., 2, 40. 11, 1. 33. Concerning the obligation of "repræsentatio," see Cod. Just., 3, 26, 8; Cod. Theod., 10, 4, 3. 1, 11, 2. 2. 1, 11; Cod. Just., 3, 26, 7, 11.

[2] THE OLDEST TEXTS: *Marculf.*, I, 3 (*Rozière*, no. 16). Dagobert's diplomas for Resbach and St. Denis. *Th. Sickel*, "Beiträge zu Diplom.," 3, 19; Conc. Orléans, 511, c. 5.

[3] Property given by the king in full ownership did not enjoy immunity unless the donation carried the clause "sicut fiscus tenuit, cum emunitate"; that which the king gave as a benefice, belonged to him of right, and consequently was entitled to immunity without the special clause. *Pertz*, "Dipl.," 21, 25, 71, 75; "Capit.," 779, c. 9 (I, 48); "Cap. Kiersy," 877, c. 20; *Brunner*, II, 292; *Esmein*, p. 142.

[4] This is what certain documents declare, from which it would be incorrect to conclude that in principle all churches and all abbeys enjoyed immunity. *Mühlbacher*, n. 184; 755. "Capit.," vol. II, p. 177; Clothair II referred only to private dues or impositions.

[5] "Rib.," 65; "Capit.," v. I, p. 22, c. 14; *Marculf.*, I, 14. 17. II, 1; *Mühlbacher*, no. 1751. The charters granted to laics have not been preserved with the same care as have those of the clergy.

[6] *Bonvalot*, p. 123: Charter of Treves, Saint Dié.

to collect the "freda," nor judicial fees, nor to exercise any restraint over the men of the privileged domain ("homines distringere"). He could collect no taxes there and no one was obliged to furnish him lodgings or subsistence; he could not raise troops thereon for military expeditions nor exact the "hériban." The domain so privileged henceforth had the character of an inclosure ("enclave") in the administrative network of the times; it was outside the county, but not outside the State. But if it was independent as against the royal officers, it was not independent as against the king; the exempt person was under authority and, at the same time under special protection, that is, under the "mundium"[1] of the king.

2d, **Positive Effects.**—On his own lands the privileged person enjoyed the powers of the royal officer; he levied troops and conducted them to the army of the king, he collected the taxes[2] and forwarded them to the royal treasury, but in most of the diplomas he was authorized to keep them for himself. His privilege was doubled by means of a delegation of the taxing power. Since the count, that is to say, the ordinary judge, was excluded from the privileged domain, it was very necessary that some one else should judge of the men on the domain or "potestas"[3] in his place. Thus a system of patrimonial courts was the necessary consequence of the immunity described above.

§ 123. **Patrimonial Courts.** — The private judge, the agent of the immunist, was called "vidame" ("vice dominus") or advocate ("advocatus").[4] Like the count and the centurion

[1] At least, the immunity accorded to ecclesiastics was protected by a "composition" of 600 sous. "Cap.," 803, c. 2 (I, 113); *Thévenin*, no. 96.

[2] The inhabitants of a privileged domain ("immunité") were not exempt from taxes. In Italy they were bound to assist in the construction and maintenance of roads and bridges. Cod. Theod., 15, 3, 6. *Cf.* "Capit.," 782–86, c. 4 (I, 192).

[3] The existence of the system of justice of the immunist is contested. But the Merovingian acts declared that the inhabitants of the privileged domain were responsible to the proprietor ("redhibere mithium"). *Brunner*, II, 298; *Flach*, I, 117, n. 1, charter of Gorze, in 775 ("cartul. de Gorze," p. 37), "Cap.," 779, c. 8. 9. 802, c. 13, I, 48, 93 and 88, "de villis," c. 56. The domainal agents were judges to the exclusion of ordinary tribunals in the king's domains.

[4] Concerning the "avoués," "judices privati" ("L. Rom. Cur.," 2, 16, 2), "actores," "præpositi," *cf. Brunner*, II, 302; *Wickede*, "Die Vogtei," 1886; *Viollet*, p. 372; *G. Blondel*, "De advocatis ecclesiasticis in rhenanis region," 1892; *Bonvalot*, "Hist. du dr. de la Lorraine," 1897; and N.R.H., 1893, 270. The "avoué" had, ordinarily, a double rôle: on the domain he was a judge; externally, as over against the State, he was the "mandataire," the representative of the immunist; thus, in matters of justice, he took oath for him, and fought duels for him (because of which, it was necessary that the "avoués" of the Church should be laymen). It was by way of exception, as for counts and the vassals of

he held sessions in which suits were judged by persons of quality ("communi sapientium judicio"), as in the "mallus" by the assessors ("rachimburgs," "boni homines").[1] The jurisdiction of the tribunal embraced controversies between the men of the domain, "commanentes" (peasants); in case of disputes between them and outsiders the tribunal of the count or of the neighboring centurion had jurisdiction. At the end of the 700 s this rule was abandoned for the general principle: "Actor sequitur forum rei."[2] If the defendant was an inhabitant of the exempt estate, he drew before his own judge those owing jurisdiction to the count or to the head of the hundred; and, conversely, if he were the plaintiff. Public and private courts were put on the same footing; the latter multiplied and were no longer regarded as an anomaly in the political system of the times. The judicial competence of the privileged person was extended in regard to both persons and things; restricted at first to civil actions, or to criminal actions involving private penalties, it was extended by a capitulary (exceptional, it is true) to include offenses punishable by public penalties.[3] Cases involving personal liberty also came within the jurisdiction of the privileged person.[4] The judgment pronounced in all such cases could be reversed only by the court of the king. The patrimonial courts of the Frankish epoch prepared the way for the system of feudal courts; at the same time there appeared the jurisdiction of the lord over his vassals, this

the king, that he was allowed to represent the churches and abbeys before the courts. From this rôle, which prevailed under Charlemagne, came the title of "advocatus." Already, under the Later Empire, the Church had "defensores." Council of Carthage, 419. Cod. Theod., 16, 2, 38. Conformably to the rule: "Nemo militans Deo implicet se negotiis sæcularibus," the Capitularies of Charlemagne compelled the churches and abbeys to have "avoués." This prince appointed, or had his officers appoint, the "avoués" of the laical or ecclesiastical immunities, foreshadowing thereby the tendency toward autonomy, which was accentuated, on the contrary, under his feeble successors. The office of "avoué" became hereditary only during the feudal epoch. The hereditary "avoués" were troublesome and oppressive protectors. Among them all the emperor was the most powerful. ("Ecclesiæ Romanæ defensor.")

[1] Edict of Clothair, 614, c. 19; "Cap.," 779, 9 (I, 48); "Cap.," 802, c. 13; 801–813, c. 14 (I, 93, 172).

[2] *Bouquet*, V, 756 (dipl. of 796). "Capitulary of 779," c. 21 (I, 51).

[3] Edict of Clothair, 614, c. 15; "Cap.," 815, c. 3 ("de Hispanis"); capitulary relating to the churches of Bavaria (I, 158): "tam in vita quam in pecunia." In principle the immunist had only to deliver up the malefactor ("Cap.," 779, c. 9 (48); 803, c. 2 (I, 113), Edict. Pist., 18, "Kiersy," 873, c. 3 and, in like cases, he sat beside the public judge when the latter pronounced sentence.

[4] *Brunner* believed them competent only for "causæ minores," as the centurions, "Const. de Hispanis," 813, c. 2.

being a continuation and development of the courts of the "potentes" during the Roman period. These private courts performed their functions, it is true, under the authority of the king, but feudalism freed them from royal control.[1]

§ 124. **Causes which produced the Immunity.** — The great landed proprietors solicited charters of immunity in order to escape from the spoliations and abuses of the counts and public officers; these latter often received their appointments through purchase and, since they received no salaries, we need not be astonished that they respected neither the liberty nor property of those over whom they ruled. How could one defend himself against them? There was but one way: to stop them at the gates of the domain. It was too late to apply to the king after one had been a victim of their exactions; the great landholders took their precautions in advance and with the aid of a diploma succeeded in forestalling the evil. The requests for immunity are easily understood, but it is less easy to understand the shortsightedness of the king who granted them and thereby destroyed his own power. If one recalls, however, that the privileged person was freed from the authority of the count but not from that of the king it is not so difficult to explain. The power of the king was, according to the conception of the times, a personal power, the bond between him and his subjects was a personal bond, a weak power and a bond easily broken. The king had only one policy: to secure the loyalty of his subjects by means of favors, one of which was immunity. He hesitated all the less to abridge the authority of the counts over the bishops and abbots since, in his own domains, his intendants were a sort of privileged class, the count could not enter, and the "judex fisci" took his place; it was not rare for a slice of the royal domains to pass to bishops and abbots and in their hands it preserved the privileges it had possessed.

Topic 2. Status of Persons

§ 125. **In General.** — Equality no more existed in the Frankish State than it had in the Roman. There was a distinction between

[1] Many seigniorial courts were only royal courts that public officers, counts, or others appropriated themselves. Because of its double origin, the seigniorial court was extended even over the inclosed lands ("enclaves") in the fief and over which the lord had no right of ownership; but he was none the less regarded as a judge in the same manner as was the royal officer whom he succeeded. The immunist had rights only on his lands, in his domain. The inclosed lands ("enclaves") belonging to others were not under his jurisdiction.

slaves, those who were *half free* (freedmen, "coloni," and "lites"), and *free men,* Barbarians or Romans, who themselves were divided into *seigniors* and *vassals.* Foreigners and Jews[1] occupied a position apart from the rest, as did the clergy and monks. The *nobility,* that is, the class having hereditary privileges, like the senatorial class of the Later Empire or the feudal nobility, had not yet come into existence, though the feudal nobility was in process of formation. It will be recruited from this aristocracy of great landowners and public functionaries, who, although very powerful, have, as yet, only personal prerogatives.[2] The old nobility of family of Germania did not exist among the Franks, but it was continued among the other Barbarian peoples with the right to a higher "wergeld."[3]

§ 126. **The Slaves**[4] — prisoners of war,[5] free men who sold themselves[6] or their children,[7] debtors who were unable to pay their

[1] Measures for isolation of lepers, for example, "Roth.," 176; *Viollet,* "Dr. civ.," 377.

[2] "Leudes," the faithful of the king — subjects in general and specially, the king's men, public functionaries or "antrustions." By this term are meant, also, the grandees of the kingdom, "proceres," "optimates." "Leudes" is rarely employed under the second dynasty.

[3] "L. Thur.," 1. 1; "L. Edw. Confess.," 35. 1; To define: "erl," Saxon; "eorl," Anglo-Saxon; "jarl," Scandinavian. "Sax.," 14; "Fris.," 1, 1. 3, 10; 15, 1, 2; "Bav.," 2, 1; "Pact. Alam.," 2, 37: "wergeld" of the "minofledi," 160 s., of the "mediani," 200 s., and of the "primi" or "meliorissimi," 240 s. "L. Alam.," 69; "Sal.," 74 (*Hessels*): "minoflidi" in opposition to the "meliores": The "minoflidi," possessors of a small domain ("flid," "flet" = "area," "aula") were simple, free men. "Burg.," 2. 2; 26, 1. 2; 101. 2 (three classes; 150, 200, 300 s). "Cham.," 3, 17–20. *Savigny,* "Verm. Schr.," 41; *K. Maurer,* "Wesen d. aelt. Adels," 1846; *Naudet,* "Acad. Inscr.," 1827; *Brunner,* D.R., §§ 14, 29, 32.

[4] BIBLIOGRAPHY: *Potgiesser,* "De statu servorum," 1736; *Perreciot,* "Etat civil des personnes," 1845; *Wallon,* "Hist. de l'esclavage," 2ᵉ éd., 1879; *P. Larroque,* "De l'esclav. chez les nations chrét.," 1864; *Allard,* "Les esclaves chrétiens."; *Guérard,* "Polypt. d'Irm.," 277; *Pardessus,* "L. Sal.," 517; *Fustel de Coulanges,* "Mon. fr.," 76; "l'Alleu," 273; "N. Rech.," 361; *Yanowski,* "Abol. de l'esclav. ancien," 1860; *Jastrow,* "Forsch. d. Gesch.," 19, 626; *Thévenin,* "Textes," table.

[5] "Servi," "mancipia," "ancillæ," called "Sclavi" or "slavi" following the wars of the emperors of Germany against the "Esclavons" or Slavs in the 900 s.

[6] In consequence of extreme misery in times of distress, *Grég. Tours,* 7. 45; "Capit.," I, 40, c. 9, 317, c. 3. Edict of Pistoa, 864, c. 34; "L. Fris.," 11, 1; "Bav.," 6, 3; *Beaumanoir,* 45, 19. "Acta S. S," Jan. 1, 330. *Grég. Tours.* "Glor. conf.," 101; "Form. Andeg.," 25. It is known that the Roman law did not allow the transfer of liberty. Sales of men, free in spite of them. "Sal.," 392; *Liutp.,* 48; "Alam.," 46, 47; "Bav.," 15, 5. Liberty was recovered by returning the purchase price. Current value in the 500 s, 12 sous, "Wergeld," 36 sous. "Rib.," 8; *cf.* "Sal.," 10; "Thur.," 3; "Sax.," 17; "Alam.," 8; "Cham.," 6; "Fris.," 15; "Bav.," 6, 12; "Cap.," 808, c. 2, I, 139. The Church councils forbade the sale of Christians to pagans or Jews.

[7] Edict of Pistoa, 864, c. 34. Cod. Just., 4, 43, 1, 2; Nov. XI of *Valentian.* Exposure of children. *F. Sirm.,* 11; *Mabillon,* 48; Cod. Theod., 5, 7, 1, 58. 1; Cod. Just., 8, 52, 2. 3. 4. Nov., 153.

debts,[1] criminals who lost their liberty as a punishment,[2] and the descendants of all these [3] Slaves were numerous during the Frankish period and there were slave markets at which even eunuchs were sold. At law the condition of all was the same but it varied in fact; thus slaves belonging to the Treasury ("Fisc") or to the Church were better treated than were ordinary slaves, and even among these latter there were distinctions according to their occupations; an artisan was worth more than a simple shepherd ("wergeld").[4] In principle the rights of the master over his slaves were the same as at Rome: the right of life and death,[5] the right to pursue and demand fugitives,[6] the right to permit slaves to marry, the right to exact services and dues,[7] and the right of

[1] "Obnoxiationes." *Marculf.*, 2. 26; "Form. Andeg.," 18. Temporary slavery, "Bav.," 1, 11 ("usque dum se redimere possit"); partial, "F. Andeg.," 37; *Marculf.*, 2. 27; "Wis.," 6, 4, 2. Right of a person to free himself by his work, "Cap." "l. Ribb. add.," 803, c. 3, I, 117.

[2] "Burg.," 36 (adultery); "Wis.," 3, 3. 1, 3, 4, 14; "Alam.," 38, 4 (violation of Sunday repose); "Bav.," 6, 2 (fire, abortion, sorcery, poisoning, etc.); "Rib.," 58, 18. The free man who degraded himself by marrying a slave woman was reduced to slavery: "servus trahit ad se francum." Prescription, *Langob.*, 2, 35, 2.

[3] Mixed marriages between slaves and free: "the worse carries with him the good" (Int. Cod. Theod., 4, 11, 1, 3, 7) and, consequently, the children were slaves. "Rib.," 58, 15, 16; "Sal.," 13, 8, 25, 5; "Burg.," 35. Conventions in contrary sense, "Polypt. d'Irminon," p. 80, 143, 361. "Epistola conculcatoria," *Marculf.*, 2, 29. *Cf. Rozière*, "Rec. de form." "Culcare" means to lie down. "Carta triscabina" "Form. Sal." *Lindenbr.*, 20. "Cap." 801–804, c. 8, I, 145. Marriage between slaves belonging to different masters: three system, division, preference to the master of the father or of the mother.

[4] "Servi casati," slaves with a tenure which allowed them to live with their family and to which they were attached as "colons." Cod. Just., 11, 47, 7. *F. Merkel*, 30. "L. Cham.," 42; "L. Rom. cur.," 8, 5. "Div. imp.," 806, c. 11, I, 129; "Div. regni," 831; c. 7, II, 22. "Ministeriales" (from "ministerium," service), "pueri," "vassi ad ministerium": slaves charged with a service in the house or near the person of the master. "Sal.," 10, 76, 9. 79, 2 (*Hessels*): seneschals, mayors ("major," oldest), marshals, cupbearers, chamberlains. "Alaman.," 74. They accompanied their master on his travels, and to the army. "Burg.," 10, 1; "Alam. Pact.," 2, 45. "Recap. l. Sal. H.," 22. Under the second dynasty they served on horseback, carrying the lance, receiving the benefices. "Cap.," 792 or 786, c. 4, I, 67. "Pueri regis," or "ministerials" of the king. "Sal.," 13, 25, 4. 42. 54. 79. M.G.H., L.L., III, 460. "Wergeld" of the "lites." They were sometimes counts. "Fiscalini," "Cap.," 803, c. 2, 10, I, 115, or "servi casati" of the king. "Alam," 8. Slaves of the Church: Triple "wergeld," "Alam.," 8; "Rib.," 58, 20; "Bav.," 1, 5, 13. Like the "fiscalini," they ended by being confused with the "colons" of the Church.

[5] *Tacitus*, "Germ.," 25; *Grég. Tours*, 3, 15. 5, 3; "Sal.," 10, 1. Domestic jurisdiction of the master over the slave. "Wis.," 7, 2, 21. *Marculf.*, 2, 28. *F. Turon*, 9, F. Sen., 9; *Marculf.*, 2, 2 (enumeration of redhibitory vices). *Lindenbr.*, 15; "Sal.," 35, 5. 40. 7. 8. 9. *Leseur*, N.R.H., 1888; *Girard*, *ibid.*, 1886.

[6] *Marculf.*, 1, 38; "Rib.," 72; "Burg.," 6; "Alam.," 20.

[7] *Cf.* slaves in the "Germania" of *Tacitus*, also Frankish "colons."

ownership over their property, since all that they acquired belonged to the master.[1] If the master allowed the slave a fund it was understood that this did not cease to belong to him and he might repossess himself of it whenever it pleased him, and that at the death of the slave it passed to his children only with the consent of the master.[2] The slave did not have political rights any more than civil rights. He was incapable of rendering military service,[3] of appearing in court [4] or of taking holy orders.[5] His only judge was his master, who was held responsible for the offenses of the slave. The penalties to which he was liable were more severe than those which were inflicted for the same offense when committed by a free man and so he was always put to the torture.[6] There was, however, improvement and progress; the Church, like the Roman State in earlier times, sought to prevent mistreatment by masters,[7] and by proclaiming the equality of all men before God attacked the very foundations of slavery. Marriage among slaves was a sacrament the same as among free men, and the Church caused the legitimacy of such marriages to be recognized contrary to the Roman law,[8] and from that time a slave might have a family, his personality was redeemed. At the same

[1] "Burg.," 6, 10, 2; *Papian*, 2, 4; "Rib.," 8, 9, 10, 21.

[2] "Wis.," 5, 4, 13. 16; 9, 1, 18. 10, 1, 17; *Marculf.*, 2, 32, 33; "Bav.," 15, 67. In the donations, the savings were transmitted with the slave. *F. Lindenbr.*, 20. The Penitentials forbade the master to take away from the slave what he had acquired by his own work. "Poen. Thèod.," 3, 13, 2.

[3] "Faux Capit.," 5, 247. Cod. Theod., 13, 8, 11.

[4] He was represented by his master. "Rib.," 58; "Sal.," 43, 1. 2; "Rib.," 29. 30. 22. *Leseur*, N.R.H., 1888; "Pact. Child.," 5; "D. Chlot.," 11, 12; "D. Child.," 10; "Cap.," 803, c. 5, I, 117; "Wis.," 6, 1, 4; *Liutp.*, 21.

[5] It was forbidden to confer upon the slave ecclesiastical dignities if he was not freed. If he had been ordained without the consent of the master, the ordination was invalid, unless the master accepted a compensation. *Gratian*, p. 1, "Dist." 54; "Cap.," 805, c. 11; 789, c. 23 and 57; 794, c. 23; I, 122. 57. 76; "Capitul.," c. 23, and 55; c. 106; 1, 5, c. 380; 1, 6, c. 261; 1, 7, c. 51.

[6] "Dec. Childeb.," 596; "Sal." 40; "Wis." 3, 4, 14. 3, 3. 8; *Jastrow*, "Zur strafr. Stellung d. Sklaven," 1878 ("Unters.," of *Gierke*, 2).

[7] "Wis.," 6, 5, 12; Conc. of Agde, 566, c. 62; of Orléans, 538, c. 13. Edict. 614, c. 22.

[8] Marriage was a sacrament for slaves as well as for free men. Contracted with the consent of the master, it was indissoluble, although the master reserved the right to separate them when selling them, for example, Adrian IV (1154–1159) validated marriages concluded without the knowledge of the master; the latter could not sell the slave in order to indirectly annul the marriage by separating the husband and wife. Saint Leo wrote to Rusticus of Narbonne that marriages between freemen and slaves were not permissible, though eventually he allowed it; but if there was a mistake on the side of the free woman, she could demand divorce first, and afterwards when the doctrine of the indissolubility of marriage came to prevail, the annulment of the marriage. *Yves de*

time slavery tended to disappear; emancipation increased (it was regarded as an act of charity); numbers of slaves became "coloni," so many that during the feudal epoch "coloni" were known only under the name of serfs.[1] Towards the 1100 s slavery no longer existed, although slaves were still to be found in the south of France until the 1400 s.[2] The Church did not actually abolish slavery, it was content with proclaiming the religious equality of master and slave; nor did it condemn slavery, but merely urged masters to treat their slaves kindly and humanely and the slaves to obey their masters.[3]

§ 127. **Negro Slavery in the Colonies.**[4] — Contact with the Moslems and reprisals against them were responsible for the maintenance of slavery in Spain until the 1500 s. At this time the discovery of America developed these germs under the form of the negro slave trade; the African blacks, physically more vigorous than the Indians, were destined to displace the latter, decimated or maltreated by their conquerors. Thus odious African slavery was established in a Christian land. However, it was permitted only in the colonies, for as soon as a slave touched French soil he became free, as Loysel said and this principle was affirmed by the law of September 28, 1791. The abolition movement did not take form until the 1700 s, then inspired by the philosophic spirit of men like Voltaire and Montesquieu and by the Christian spirit of sects like the Quakers (1751) it had as its leading representatives Wilberforce in England and the Abbé Gregory in France. The law of the 16th Pluviôse, year II (February 4, 1794), abolished slavery in the French colonies though Bonaparte reëstablished it in 1802. Arrested in France the movement continued in England. The slave trade was abolished in 1815 by the Congress of Vienna at the instigation of Lord Castlereagh; slavery itself was abolished in the English colonies in 1833, and in France on April 24, 1848.

Chartres, "Ep." 221. 242; Nov. 22, C. 10; Decretal of Gratian, c. 6, C. 29, 9. 2. X, 4, 9, 2; *Esmein*, "Le mariage en dr. canon.," I, 317; *Meynial*, "Le mar. ap. les invasions," 1898.

[1] "Cap.," 801–14, c. 1, I, 145 (concerning the marriage of a "servus" and a "colona").

[2] *Brutails*, N.R.H., 1886, 388; *Viollet*, "Hist. du dr. civ.," p. 329; *Loisel*, "Inst. Cout.," I, 40.

[3] *Saint Paul*, to the Ephesians, vi, 9; to the Colossians, iii. 11; *cf. Seneca*, Ep. 1, 31. 47. 73; *Saint Augustin*, "De civ. Dei," 19, 14–15: slavery, unjust according to natural law, was a consequence and a penalty of sin, like sickness and death.

[4] BIBLIOGRAPHY: in *Viollet*, "Hist. du dr. civil," p. 336; *Cochin*, "Abol. de l'esclav.," 1861; *A. Desjardins*, "R. des Deux Mondes," 1891, p. 864; *Moreau de Saint-Mery*, "Lois et Constit. de l'Amerique sous le Vent," 1784; *Duvergier*, "Lois," v. 33, p. 104; *cf. Farbstein*, "Recht d. unfreien Arbeiter," 1896.

§ 128. **The Emancipated Class.**[1] — Slavery ceased ordinarily by enfranchisement and this act might take place either in consideration of a price[2] paid to the master by the slave himself which was saved from his earnings or furnished by other persons, or as a reward, or as a purely gratuitous act ("pro remedio animæ") for the salvation of the master's soul. In ancient Germania the freedmen constituted an intermediate class between the slaves and freeborn,[3] they were not assimilated to the latter class. During the Barbarian period the position of the freedmen was not uniform; some were assimilated to the "lites" (or nearly so) with attachment to the soil, a "wergeld" paid to the master, services and dues fixed by custom, then limited, and consequently the chance to save up and become landowners;[4] others had the freedom of going and coming, but a patron replaced for them the "Sippe" that they lacked;[5] finally there were some who acquired absolute equality with free men, in Sweden by solemn admission before the "Thing" into a family, among the Anglo-Normans, by the delivering of their arms at the popular assembly[6] and this reception into the body of free men seems to have dated from remote antiquity. Among the Franks *emancipation by a coin* in the presence of the king had the same effect.[7] The procedure was as follows: the slave held a coin ("denarius") in his hand whereupon the master caused it to fall as a sign that he renounced all services due from the slave; that done the slave was given his free liberty. This gave rise to the supposition that this method of emancipation was employed at first to enfranchise "lites" who were compelled to pay dues to their master. From the end of the 800 s it was the king, to whom the slave was delivered, who himself practiced the "excussio denarii" and who became the patron of the "denarialis."[8] Emancipation likewise took place according

[1] *M. Fournier*, "Essai sur les formes et les effets de l'affr.," 1885; "R. hist.," v. 21; *Roth*, "Feudalität," p. 289; *Vinogradoff*, "Die Freilassung zu voll. Unhab."; *Brunner*, I, 95, 238; *Zeumer*, "Beerb. d. Freigelass."

[2] Prescription. "Wis.," 9, 1, 9. 10, 2, 2.; "Loth.," 1, 95.

[3] *Tacitus*, "Germ.," 25.

[4] "Burg.," 57; "Roth," 225; "Faux Cap.," 6, 159.

[5] "Roth," 216. 224. 225. 257; *Liut.*, 9. 23. 55.

[6] Probably also among the Lombards ("manumissio per gairethinx"). Emancipation "in pans," "Roth.," 224, that is to say, "per votum regis," corresponded to the Frankish emancipation by denarius (money). "Pact Alam.," 2, 45.

[7] "Rib.," 58, 61 and following; *Marculf.*, 1, 22; *Bavarois*, M.G.H., L.L., 3, 465.

[8] Other Germanic methods were: (*a*) "Per bantradam, Cham.," 11, 12: the master, who was the twelfth, swore that his slave was free. *J. Havet*, N.R.H., 1877; *Froidevaux*, "L. des Fr. Chamaves," p. 91; (*b*)

to *Roman Methods* (and in the final reckoning they were the ones followed): (*a*) *in "ecclesia."* in the presence of the bishop where the record of the proceedings of enfranchisement, "tabulæ," were drawn up, from which the name of "*tabularii*" was given to this class of freedmen. They were dependent upon the Church[1] and frequently were obliged to furnish candles for the lighting of the church; (*b*) by *testament;*[2] (*c*) "*per cartam*" or "*epistolam,*"[3] a document containing the most diverse provisions. There were also the "*chartularii*" who were held to the payment of all sorts of dues and to the performance of a variety of services either to their former master or to the Church into which the weak flowed like a river.[4]

§ 129. **The Agricultural Class** was composed chiefly of "coloni" and "lites," without counting the slaves. The "*coloni*" of the Frankish epoch[5] differed but little from the "coloni" of the Later Empire.[6] Their attachment to the soil[7] was perhaps less indissoluble; thus the "coloni" of a monastery passed sometimes

"Per manum"; the master delivered his slave to a free man, who delivered him to a second, and this consecutively to the fourth who conducted him to a place where the roads crossed and delivered him to a surety; he was allowed to choose the one of the four roads which pleased him. *Roth*, 224; (*c*) "Per sagittam," *P. Diacre*, "Hist. Langob.," 1, 13; M. Fournier holds that the Germanic methods were based on the idea of tradition, an ingenious explanation, but difficult to accept.

[1] Cod. Just., 1, 13, 1, 2; Cod. Theod., 4, 7, 1. It was forbidden to emancipate a "tabularius" before the king, because one of his protégés was raised to the Church. *Marculf.*, 2, 32. It was to the interest of the Church to encourage emancipation in order to increase the number of its protégés. "Alam.," 22.

[2] "L. Fufia Caninia"; *Paul*, "Semt.," 4, 14; *Savigny*, "Hist. du dr. r.," 2, 89.

[3] Cod. Just., 7, 6, 1; "Burg.," 88, "Chartularii libellarii." *Cf. Rozière*, "Rec. de form."

[4] If the emancipated slave died without issue, his succession reverted to his patron, or to the Church, if it was a question of a "tabularius"; to the king if it was a question of a "denarialis." The same for his "wergeld" in general. "Wis.," 5, 7, 12, 13; "Cap.," 803, 9 and 10; 801–13, c. 49, I, 118, 158.

[5] *Guérard*, "Polypt. d'Irminon," "Cart. Sen.," 10, 20. The "tributarius" of the Frankish laws was only a "colon." *Vanderkindere*, "Les tributaires" ("Ac. Belgique," 1897). *Cf.* Bavarian "Parscalci," *Meichelbeck*, "Hist. Fris.," *n.* 481; M.G.H., L.L., 486.

[6] One became a "colonus" by birth, by agreement or convention, and by thirty years' prescription. If the parents were of different status, the offspring took the status of the inferior; thus the children of a marriage between a free man and "colonus" were "coloni." If the parents were both "coloni," but belonging to different masters, the rules were diverse; the children followed the status of the mother ("partus ventrem sequitur") or that of the father, or they were divided equally with preference for the master of the father or of the mother, if the number was uneven.

[7] The "colonicæ" were places cultivated by groups of "coloni." Regarding their liberal charters, *cf. Hanauer*, "Const. des camp. de l'Alsace," 1865.

from one piece of land to another. Their emancipation, impossible at Rome, was permitted and in fact practiced. But these were small matters in comparison with the increased burdens which weighed upon the "coloni," and one may say that on the whole their condition was much worse.

1st, **The Dues**, which were fixed by custom, included: (*a*) the "capaticum" or "census de capite" (later called "chevage") which was collected by "hearth or by head" — it was the "capitatio plebeia" which was formerly paid to the Roman State and which was now paid to the landowner; (*b*) the ancient *canon*, already called predial rent, "agrier" ("agraria pars"), field rent paid in kind, "champart" ("campi pars"), and "terrage" ("terragium"); [1] (*c*) fees for the use of property belonging to the master ("herbaticum," "lignaritia," "pastio," etc.); and (*d*) supplies for the army, beeves, carts, horses, and small cattle; but money payments might be substituted for these.[2]

2d, **Services**, unknown to the Romans, were required in addition to the dues (described above). Such were: plowing ("riga," "curvada" from which the word "corvée" was derived), manual labor ("manuoperæ") such as the felling of trees, and carting ("carroperæ," "angariæ," and "paraveredi"). This labor was performed on that part of the domain which the master had reserved for his own exploitation; the number of days of labor owed by the "coloni" varied in different places; sometimes they gave three days per week without pay or subsistence. In reality their condition differed little from slavery. Formerly the "colonus" was contrasted with the slave by saying that the "colonus" was a person, the slave was a thing, but this distinction was no longer true, for the slave was a person; and even if the slave was owned entirely by his master, what was left to the "colonus" after he had paid his dues to the king, to the Church, and to his master? Abstractly speaking the relation of the "colon" to his master was, according to the law, that of a free man, he could bear arms, appear in court, even sue his master; in fact, however, the master was often an "immuniste" and in this capacity was the judge of his coloni.[3]

[1] Chickens, eggs, wax, silver, cheese, pork, honey. *Cf.* "Alam.," 21.

[2] "Hostilitium," "ad hostem" (oxen, etc.), "carnaticum" (small cattle).

[3] The "Colliberts," "culverts" ("cum liberti") were slaves who had been collectively emancipated; they were the half-free, as the "colons" of the Carolingian epoch and the serfs of the Capetian epoch, but they seem to have been in a situation superior to that of ordinary serfs. They were found only in the center of France and toward the end of the 1100s

§ 130. **The "Lites" or "Lides"**[1] were "coloni" of Germanic origin[2] who were found among the Franks, the Frisians, and the Saxons; they were a half-free class attached by a similar bond, and subject to similar obligations;[3] they were capable of entering into contracts, but could not marry without the consent of the master, they might be emancipated, or might purchase their freedom, and they had the right of private vengeance like free men.

§ 131. **Seigniorage and Vassalage.**[4] — Free men ("ingenui") had the right to go and come, to dispose of their persons and property, and were dependent only upon the State; they were numerous at the beginning of our period, but had begun to decrease. The State did not furnish them the security necessary for their protection; their lives and their property were exposed to such an extent that they descended to the rank of servitors of a powerful neighbor, to a position where he would defend them; they became his vassals, that is, his clients, and he became their lord ("seignior"), that is, their superior.[5] The more powerful one became the more numerous was his clientèle: kings, counts, bishops, abbots, great landowners, certain vassals themselves, were found at the head of groups formed outside the regular political framework; by this means society was reconstituted and emerged from anarchy.

§ 132. **How One became a Vassal.** — One became a vassal by recommending himself ("commendatio") to a seignior, or by

were entirely confounded with the serfs. Concerning the controversies relative to the "colliberts" *cf. Luchaire*, "Man. des inst.," p. 313; *Lamprecht*, "Et. sur l'état écon. de la France," trans. *Marignan*, 1889. The "hospites" were foreigners provided with land; their tenure was called "hostise," *H. Sée*, N.R.H., 1898, 116.

[1] *Boos*, "Liten u. Aldionen," 1874; *Thonissen*, "Org. jud. de la L. Sal.," p. 143, no. 2; *Schupfer*, "Encicl. giurd.," see "Aldi."

[2] "Letus" = "maneus." "Fris.," 2, 5. 8. 11, 2; "Sax.," 65; "Liut.," 139; "Sal.," 42, 26. 50; "Cham.," 5. 14; "Roth.," 205. 206; "Rib.," 62; 10. 36. 5; and "Cap.," 803, c. 2, I, 117 ("wergeld" of 100 sols); *Brunner*, I, 238. The Lombard "aldion" (*Pertile*, 3, 26) was in a more strict dependence upon the master. "Wergeld" of 60 sols. "Roth.," 129; "Capitulary," 801, c. 6, I, 205, likens them to the "lides." The "mansi lidiles" were contradistinguished from the "mansi ingenuiles" of the "colons," and from the "mansi serviles" of the slaves.

[3] "Lidimonium," personal rent of the "lite" corresponding to the "capaticum."

[4] BIBLIOGRAPHY: *Waitz*, II, 1, 241; *Ehremberg*, "Commendation u. Huldigung," 1877; *Flach*, "Orig. de l'anc. France," 1886; *Fustel de Coulanges*, "Le Bénéfice et le Patronat," 1890; *Beaudouin*, "Annales Grenoble," 1889 ("Et. sur les orig. du r. féodal"); *Dippe*, "Gefolgschaft u. Huldigung," 1889.

[5] From the Celtic "gwas," young man. From "vassus" are derived "vassallus," "vasseletus" (valet). "Vassus" at first signified slave, servitor, "Sal.," 35, then free man dependent upon others, "Rib.," 31; "Alam.," 36, 5. Other expressions: "amici," "gasindi," "pares," "fideles." "Senior" was the opposite of "junior," inferior.

promising under oath to assist him and to serve him as became a free man ("obsequium," "servitium ingenuili ordine"); whereupon the seignior in turn promised to protect him.[1] It was a true reciprocal contract between the protected and the protector. Conformably to the formal customs of the time the vassal did not bind himself by simple consent; the ceremony designed to symbolize the dual relation established between the parties was fixed later by homage and fealty. It had already appeared in a Germanic form: the vassal swore fealty by placing his hands in those of his seignior, which signified that he put himself under the power, and the protection of the seignior; the latter, on his part, restored his arms to the vassal and gave him presents.[2]

§ 133. **Obligations of Vassals.** — The vassal owed his seignior constant devotion, assistance under all circumstances, and a great variety of services (such as guarding his house, following him when he changed his residence, and defending him when he was attacked). These were not at all obligations that were precisely fixed or well determined. At times they went very far and recall the time when the vassal was a servitor, clothed and fed by his master who compelled him to marry and who took oaths for him. In general, however, the vassal was more independent; he lived apart from his seignior and came to his court only when he was summoned; he was a free man and owed only the service of a free man.[3] As such he was obliged to render military service and it was especially for this, with a view to being able to exercise the right of vengeance in case of need, that the seignior and the vassal associated themselves together; furthermore, the seignior was obliged to bring his vassals to the royal army.[4] Thus vassalage

[1] "Form. Turon," 43: "I have nothing with which to feed and clothe myself. . . . Being put under your care, you must help me and sustain me. As long as I live, I must render you obedience and the service of a free man. I have no right to withdraw myself from your power. If one of us fails in this present agreement, he will pay to the other so many sous." "Commendare," *cf. Gregory of Tours*, 4, 46; "Antiqua Wis.," 310.

[2] "Cap.," 804, c. 9, I, 124: "ut nulli alteri persacramentum fidelitas promittatur nisi nobis et unicuique proprio seniori." Presents of the "seignior" to the "vassus"; arms, horses (*cf.* military service on horseback), *Stubbs*, "Select Charters," 91: "Lib. Pap." (M.G.H., L.L., 4, 583), or "wadia," or pledge, symbol of the engagements that he entered into with him. The lance, or the standard, served afterwards as symbol of the feudal investiture.

[3] "Form. Tur.," 43 (*supra*); "Cap.," 758–768, c. 9, I, 41; *Hincmar*, "Ad Ludov. Balb.," op. II, 183, 611, 823.

[4] *F. Lot*, "Chron. de Saint Riquier," 1894, pp. 96 and 308; "Cap.," 811, c. 7, I, 165. 847, c. 5, II, 71. The "vassi regales" were held more strictly to military service and must march at every requisition. If the seignior was a count, the "vassus" had to assist at his pleading. "Cap.," 808, c. 5, I, 148. The "vassus" was often charged with a mission or a service

took its place in the public law, became a political instutition, and it can be understood why the same capitularies which compelled the vassal everywhere to attach himself to his seignior prohibited him from breaking the bond that united them, except in very serious cases, such as attempts upon his life, or against the honor of his wife or daughter, or an injury like a blow with a stick, or an attempt to make way with his property, or refusal of protection. In principle the association was entered into for life, thus differing from the Germanic "retinue" which created only a fragile bond under which the chief and his retainers had the right to separate whenever it pleased them.[1] Perhaps it is necessary to see in this a result of the Roman customs of the patronate, a sequel in the political character of vassalage or an infection of benefit.

§ 134. **Duties of the Seignior.** — Above all the seignior was bound to assist and protect his vassal. He furnished him in the beginning with the means of living; afterwards he assisted him rather by grants of land (benefices). He was bound to defend him against every injustice, to take vengeance against those who injured him, to sue in his behalf in the courts [2] and at the same time, by a just reciprocity, to answer for him when prosecuted.[3]

§ 135. **Was the Vassal Subject to the Ordinary Obligations which Free Men owed the State?** — In the beginning there was hardly any doubt as to this because the act of commendation was merely a private contract; it created only a personal relation between man and man. But little by little the vassal, who had

by the seignior; he took oath for him, etc. The seignior was authorized to leave two men in his house.

[1] "Form. Turon," 43 (*supra*); "Cap.," 813, c. 16, I, 172, 215 ("quod nullus seniorem suum dimittat, postquam ab eo acceperit valente solido uno, excepto si. . . ."). "Cap. franc.," c. 8, I, 215; *cf.* "Wisig.," 5, 3, 1; 5, 3, 4 (right to leave the lord if all that had been received from him had not been returned). "Kiersy," 856, c. 13; "Rib.," 31, 1: "eodem tempore." The French law did not admit in principle the resolution of the contract of fief on the demand of the vassals and by means of the restitution of fief; the German and Lombard law did, on the contrary. *Cf. Beaumanoir*, 61, 29.

[2] "Form. Tur.," 43. Vassals were sometimes called "suscepti" and "sperantes": *i.e.* those who were received under the protection of the "seignior" and who counted on him. Superior "wergeld" for the vassals of the king.

[3] "Mitium Redibere," "Rib.," 31, 1; Edict of Clothair, II, 614, c. 13. "Mitium" signifies: 1st, responsibility for the acts of the vassal, obligation to deliver him up to justice; 2d, clientèle for which one is responsible; 3d, domains (occupied by the clients). If a man was sent on a mission by the king, his suit and those of the people for whom he answered remained in suspense. The master was responsible for all his men, slaves, half slaves, and even free men. The Anglo-Saxon law held the host responsible if he harbored a person three nights. "Cap. ital.," c. 11, I, 218; "Cap.," 820, c. 5, I, 298; *cf. Brunner*, § 93.

two masters, the one, his seignior, near by, the other, the State, far away, forgot the latter. The State itself encouraged this transformation by accepting the seignior as the intermediary between itself and the vassal; moreover, the seignior had in fact more authority over his vassals than did the count and the other royal officers. The Capitularies affirmed nevertheless that the vassal always owed to the king the oath of fealty, military service, and judicial service.[1] But the seignior became the military chief of his vassals; he was bound to conduct them to the royal army and to compel their attendance upon the courts of justice when they were summoned. Did he become likewise their judge (as among the Scandinavians)? No, except when he was a privileged person and the vassals inhabited his own domains. The intendants of the royal domains likewise were the judges of the king's vassals who resided thereon and the latter, as such, enjoyed special privileges such as the right of appeal to the king and the right of representation before the courts.[2] Before ordinary vassals could be judged, their seigniors must be addressed, who, bound to produce them in court or to settle for them, had a special interest in preventing all suits. In fact, therefore, it happened in most instances that their cases were submitted to the seignior without there being any definite recognition of a right on his part to administer justice, such as he possessed during the feudal period; but it is clear that its possession was not very far distant.[3]

§ 136. **Origin and Development of Vassalage.** — Germanists and Romanists debate the question of the origin of vassalage. The "clientèle" and the patronate were found wherever public authority was feeble. The Germanic "comitat" and the Roman patronate responded to needs of the same kind in different societies, and the two institutions were continued in the "antrustionat" and in the "commendation" during the Merovingian period when the protection of the great was more necessary than it ever had been for the small. From the 700 s the patronate of the weak was greatly extended under the name of vassalage. From which

[1] "Cap.," 873, c. 6; "Cap.," 807, c. 1, etc.; "Cap. Mersen," 847, c. 5; "Cap.," 786, c. 4.

[2] *Ibid.*, 884, c. 4, 11; 801-10, c. 10, I, 210; "Worms," 829, c. 7, II, 13.

[3] *Ibid.*, 811, c. 9.; *Marculf.*, 1, 24. "Carta de mundeburde: cognoscat magnitudo vestra quod nos viro illo de civitate . . ., cum omnibus rebus vel hominibus suis aut gasindis vel amicis, seu undecumque ipse legitimo reddebit mitio, juxta ejus petitionem, propter malorum hominum inlicitas infestationes, sub sermone tuitionis nostræ visi fuimus recepisse," 27. "Cap.," 869, c. 11; 853, c. 4; 883, c. 3; II, 336, 268, 37. "Cart. Senon.," 27, 30. *Brunner*, II, 266: nothing of the kind in Italy or in Germany. *Cf. Migne*, "Patr. l.," 135, 1035. 1050.

did it receive the greater contribution, from Roman practice or Germanic custom? The obligation of the parties and the forms of contract furnished more evidence in favor of a Germanic origin.[1] Contrary to the Roman Emperors, who proscribed the patronate, the Carolingians, finding themselves powerless to repress abuses, encouraged seigniorage and utilized it for purposes of government. They themselves had numerous vassals ("vassi dominici") scattered throughout all the kingdom and not forming a petty restricted group like the "antrustions." They believed that, as a result of the intervention of the seigniors, the recruiting of the army would be easier and that justice could be better rendered; thus the seigniors acquired, with their connivance, a share of the public authority; the power of the counts and functionaries became enfeebled, the king lost what the seignior gained[2] and in obeying the king it came to be habitual to regard him only as a seignior. Personal subjection and the contractual relation of individual with individual thus took the place of general subordination to the State.[3]

Topic 3. Status of Lands

§ 137. **In General.** — Full ownership of property like complete liberty was rare, and for the same reason. Aside from the king, the churches, and certain powerful personages, most free men ultimately came to have no property of their own but held it only by concession. The small estate gradually became lost among the great ones. The "proprium," free land, called the *alod*[4] ("allodium") during the feudal period was transformed into

[1] The "antrustions" were followers of the king, as the "gasindi" or "amici" were followers of private individuals. They received lands, were removed, and replaced in the 700 s in their rôle as followers, by servitors, "vassi." *Brunner*, II, 262: analogous evolution among the Anglo-Saxons; the "gesith" left the court; the thane who exercised a "ministerium" replaced him as companion (he was called "vassallus"); the thanes formed, in their turn, a class of proprietors; the king and lords then had as follower the knight (*cf.* "knecht"), who corresponded to the German "ministerialis," who, after the Frankish epoch, took the place of the vassal at the lord's court. *Cf. Esmein*, p. 125, and N.R.H., 1894, 523; *Flach*, "Orig.," I, 76 and II, 435.

[2] The seignior attended the royal muster but commanded the vassal not to leave his lands, or the seignior did not go, when the vassal remained with him because he could have services rendered for him. "Cap.," 808, c. 9, I, 138; 811, c. 7, I, 165.

[3] The "Cap. de Mersen," 847, c. 2, did not impose on all free men the obligation of having a lord; it stated simply that each person could take whom he pleased for his lord. *Cf.* "Cap.," 817, c. 9, I, 272.

[4] The word "alodis" signifies: 1st, (Salic Law, 59), succession; 2d, by extension, land acquired by succession: it was, then, contradistinguished from "comparatum" or "conquisitum," acquisition, land acquired by

the "*précaire*" (land held by tenancy at will) and the *benefice*. A great domain at this time[1] was composed of several parts: 1st, the master's manor ("sala") and land which he kept for his own exploitation by his slaves or servants ("mansus dominicus," "terra salica"); 2d, lands held subject to servile tenures, or manses of "coloni," "lites," and slaves (these were detached from the dominical manse and were not cultivated under the direction of the master; they were, however, in a condition of strict dependence on account of the charges due the master and on account of the work which the tenant was obliged to do on his manse); 3d, lands held by free tenure or by a tenure at will, subject to quit rents, annual rents, and similar compulsory dues, but less burdensome because the tenant was a free man; 4th, benefices or lands held by a tenure which imposed on the tenant the obligation of military service to the grantor. These benefices were sometimes parcels detached from the domain, sometimes they were entire domains themselves, distinct from the domain proper, the dependence upon the principal manor being much reduced in that case, since the grantee was obliged merely to render service to his proprietor. The tenant at will ("précariste") and the holder of a benefice ("benéficier") were both only half proprietors; they held the land only as tenants, the grantor retaining important rights over the land thus granted. The two institutions (the "précaire" and the "benéfice") differed especially in the fact that the one was rather economic in character, the other was rather political; the tenancy at will was a method of exploitation, the benefice, a means of creating a clientèle.

§ 138. **Tenancy at Will**[2] ("Précaire") a form of tenure in which lands were granted subject to the payment of a quit rent ("cens") was employed especially in the case of lands belonging to the Church. Did it originate in the Roman "precarium," which

purchase; 3d, by extension, land possessed in full ownership, free of all encumbrance; it was contradistinguished from land granted subject to a charge, that is to say, as a benefice or by tenancy at will. The land that was held in full ownership was ordinarily inherited land. Edict of Pistoa, 864, c. 36; "Cap.," 802, c. 10, I, 100. This last meaning, still rare, appeared only under the second dynasty. The etymology of the word "allodium" is disputed. The "allodium" was not, as was formerly believed, the land or lot of the Frank in the division which followed the conquest. The supposed drawing of lots at that time did not take place.

[1] "Mansi vestiti," "absi," depending upon whether they were held by hereditary tenure or were occupied only temporarily. *Cf.* above Feudal epoch.

[2] *G. Demante*, "R. hist. dr.," 1860, 54; Z.S.S., G.A., 1884, 69; N.R.H., 1885, 249; *Viollet*, "Hist. du dr. civ.," p. 673; *Brunner*, I, 201, 210; *Loennig*, "Kirchenr.," I, 703.

was a gratuitous and essentially revocable concession? This had been doubtful, because this institution disappeared from the texts under the Later Empire, and the Frankish "precarium" was neither revocable "ad nutum" nor gratuitous; it resembled more nearly the Roman lease ("bail"). It is more probable that the folk law assimilated the "precarium" to the lease and that the Frankish institution is the result of the fusion of two Roman institutions. Otherwise its name cannot be explained. The Church granted its lands by tenure at will[1] to the clergy to enable them to live, to laymen in order to attach them to itself or as a means of getting the lands cultivated, to a donor who gave his lands to the Church subject to the condition that he should conserve them during his lifetime ("precaria oblata" of the commentators as contradistinguished from the "precaria data"), or to a donor to whom it gave back twice as much ("precaria remuneratoria").[2]

(A.) **Constitution.** — According to the general practice two deeds were drawn up to establish the "précaire"; 1st, a "precaria" ("epistola," understood) or petition;[3] 2d, a "præstaria" or letter of concession.[4] The first was delivered to the grantor, the second to the grantee.

(B.) **Effects.** — The "précaire" was sometimes revocable "ad nutum,"[5] sometimes temporary in duration,[6] sometimes for life,[7] and sometimes it was perpetual and hereditary.[8] The "précaire à temps" was a sort of lease by consent ordinarily for five years, as at Rome, but renewable indefinitely. A clause dispensing with the necessity of renewing the lease was contained in the deed, thus making easy a natural transition from tenancy at will to perpetual tenure.[9] This last form was particularly proper for a person who surrendered his estates to the Church upon condition that he might resume possession by tenancy at will. Whatever may have been

[1] Dig., 43, 26, 1; "L. rom. Wis."; *Paul*, 5, 7, 8, Cod. Just. ("ad tempus"), 8, 9, and 7, 39, 2.

[2] Conc. d'Agde, Mansi, XIII, 325; M.G.H., L.L., 4, 543; "Cap.," 846, c. 22.

[3] Already at Rome. *Paul*, 5, 6, 9. "Securitas," means of proof for the grantor. *Marculf.*, 2, 4 and 5.

[4] At Rome in the matter of lease. Cod. Just., 4, 65, 24; "Epit. Mon.," *Paul*, 5, 7, 9; *Marculf.*, 2, 40. "Cart. Sen.," 16, 33. Bignon, 22.

[5] *Marculf.*, 2, 41. "F. Tur.," 7.

[6] "Wis.," 10, 1, 12. *Rozière*, "Recueil," 320.

[7] "F. Andeg.," 7. *Marculf.*, 2, 3, 39.

[8] "F. Ang.," C.B., 8. *Zeumer*, 352.

[9] *Marculf.*, II, 41; "Cart. Sen.," 15; *Esmein*, "Mélanges," 1886, p. 219; Cod. Theod., 4, 13, 1; "Cap.," 818, 9, c. 4, I, 287; *Guérard*, "Cart. de Saint-Bertin," p. 113 (year 867); *Warnkoenig*, I, 13.

the duration of precarious tenure the tenant or grantee was obliged to pay an annual charge in money (or in kind) to the grantor.[1] The amount sometimes corresponded to a rent charge ("fermage"); sometimes, on the contrary, it was merely nominal, its purpose being simply a means of affirming the right of the grantor ("cens récognitif"). In default of payment the tenant lost his right: "qui negligit censum perdit agrum." By special provision in the grant, however, this rule was often set aside and a fine was imposed in lieu of forfeiture.[2] In this way the right of the tenant "précariste" over the land was limited; also in another way since he could not dispose of the property that he had received for the benefit of a third party, the grantor alone having authority to do this and even then subject to the condition that he must respect the rights of the tenant.

§ 139. **The Benefice.**[3] — The word benefice ("beneficium") signified at first simply a benefit or favor, a gracious concession, and especially a concession of land; by extension it came to be applied to the land thus granted. Lands were possessed "ex beneficio" as a result of an act of liberality as they were held "ex alode," by inheritance.[4] The benefice was not a means of exploiting the land, it was rather a political invention designed to create rights to services or as a recompense for those already received.[5] The institution is closely connected with the system of donations made by the kings under the first two dynasties.

[1] *Guérard*, "Cart. de Saint-Bertin," 68, 70, 72, 111, etc.

[2] "Form." of Angers and of Tours; *Esmein*, "Mélanges," p. 393; "Form. Sal. Merk.," 5; *Marculf.*, 2, 41 (Revocation if the "precarist" tried to make himself master of the property). "Form. Merk.," 34 (Engagement to pay within a certain time).

[3] BIBLIOGRAPHY: *Waitz*, "Hist. Z.," 1865; *Roth*, "Gesch. d. Beneficialwesens," 1850; "Feudalität u. Unterthanverband," 1863; *Brunner*, Z.R.G., VIII, 7; *Menzel*, "Entstehung d. Lehnwesens," 1890; *Garsonnet*, "Hist. des locations perpétuelles," 1879; *Fustel de Coulanges*, "Le Bénéfice et le Patronat," 1890; *Ch. Mortet*, "Gr. Encycl.," see "Bénéfice."

[4] "Beneficium," in contradistinction to "proprium," "hereditas." "Cap.," 817, c. 9. The terminology is not fixed; the words "précaire" and "bénéfice" are often employed the one for the other. *Tertullien*, "adv. Hermog.," 9; Dig., 43, 26, 14; "Form. Andeg., 7; Merk.," 35. Nevertheless, it seems that one avoided designating the royal benefice by the term "precaria," perhaps because the king did not need to have a "precaria" constituted in order to guarantee his right.

[5] The ecclesiastical benefices were the lands which constituted the endowment of the offices of the Church; thus in investing a clerk with a benefice, the bishop set aside for his maintenance a portion of the property of the Church. From the 1100 s the term "précaire" is no longer employed. Ecclesiastical benefices did not become patrimonial as did ordinary benefices. The property of the Church was inalienable; the canonical law forbade private persons from appropriating them. The recipients of benefices having no family, and enjoying them only by reason

§ 140. **Donations of the French Kings.** — According to the old Germanic conception the donation conferred on the donee only restricted and revocable rights; it was addressed to him personally, or at most to his children and descendants. Consequently, the donee could not alienate the lands to others and they returned to the donor in case of the death of the donee without issue. Such, doubtless, were most donations of lands made by the Merovingian kings to their subjects.[1] Charles Martel disposed of the lands of the Church,[2] which for the most part had come from the royal domain,[3] in order to establish a cavalry service. His sons, Carloman and Pepin,[4] restored some of these lands and left others, with the consent of the Church, in the hands of the soldiers who had received them by a tenure at will ("precariæ verbo regis"); the Church received ground rent from them.[5] The beneficiary did not become the proprietor, as under the Merovingian donations, because the lands of the Church were inalienable according to the canon law. Henceforth donations affecting the royal domain itself did not carry full ownership, but only possession by tenure at will, or rather by benefice, to save the trouble of drawing up a "precaria" since the king had sufficient authority to make good his rights without a legal document. Great nobles followed the example thus set by the king.

§ 141. **Origin of the Military Benefice.** — The military benefice resembled neither the Celtic clientèle nor the Roman benefice (a concession of lands to veterans or to "Læti" for military service, collective and not individual). It originated rather in Germanic customs and in the gifts made by chiefs to their followers. And yet one cannot speak of a direct connection, since the military benefice did not exist under the Merovingians. It was the association of the military reforms of the second dynasty with these ancient customs which gave to the benefices their new character and which explains their development. Many difficulties were

of their spiritual function could not cede them or transmit them. We shall see later that the Frankish benefice was derived from them.

[1] *Brunner*, "Die Landschenkungen d. Merow.," "Berlin Ak.," 1885, 1175); *Marculf.*, 1, 14. 15. 17. 30. 31; *Grégory of Tours*, 6, 12; 7, 22; 11, 38; 10, 31; 9, 35; "Burg.," 1, 3, 4. Donations made on account of a service were returned to the donor when the service ceased. Confirmations were made by the prince who succeeded the donor. "Burg.," 1, 3; Edict of Clothair, c. 16.

[2] *Roth*, "Die Saekularisation d. Kirchengutes," 1864; *Kaufman*, "Die Saek. d. Kirch.," ("Jahrb. f. Nationaloek.," 22, 73); *Beugnot*, "Ac. Inscr.," 19, 2. [3] *Grégory of Tours*, 4, 2; Cod. Theod., 11, 20, 4.

[4] "Cap.," 742, c. 1, I, 25; *Lipt.*, c. 2, I, 28; *Mabillon*, "Acta S.S.," s. II, p. 100, c. 4; "Cap.," 768, I, 42, c. 1, and following.

[5] Double tithe ("decima et nona"), according to "Cap.," 779, c. 13, I, 50.

experienced in recruiting the army; the king sought to create a soldiery more closely bound to himself by granting them benefices; in this way he furnished them the means of equipment. The seigniors, upon whom were imposed the obligation of bringing their vassals to the royal host, did likewise, for they had no other means of discharging this obligation. Military service ceased to be required as a duty of the subject to the king or of the vassal to the lord, it was purchased by concessions of land.

§ 142. **How the Benefice was Created.** — The benefice was created: 1st, by direct grant or concession conformably to the old Germanic custom according to which the chiefs made presents to their followers; and, 2d, by the "recommendation of lands."[1] Small proprietors were frequently despoiled of their land and exposed to loss of life; the possession of property was a danger because of the covetousness which it excited, and recourse to public authority for protection was an illusion. There was no possible security except by putting themselves under the patronage of a powerful man; so they gave up their lands to him and, as he did not expect to cultivate them, it was understood that he should restore them immediately; but he reserved certain rights, he acquired consequently only a partial ownership and the former owner was reduced to a condition of tenancy. The "recommendation" of persons often brought about the "recommendation" of lands; vassalage and benefice were confused and thus gave rise to feudalism.

§ 143. **Obligations of the Recipient of a Benefice.** — The grant of a benefice did not imply that the grantee was subject to the same duties of fealty and of assistance which were required of a vassal, but as he was almost always a vassal he owed fealty as a vassal. The personal "recommendation" might exist independently of the benefice, but, on the contrary, the grant of a benefice was rarely made without a "recommendation." Besides, the recipient of a benefice might be required to render certain services in consideration of the grant made to him. These services were of various kinds: 1st, the duty of performing official duties (ministerial benefices); 2d, payment of dues and labor (benefices by ground rent[2] which were held only by a tenure at will); 3d, mili-

[1] The expression "Recommendation of lands" is not employed by the texts, *Marculf.*, I, 13 (cession of lands on condition that they should not be owned during lifetime, "beneficio"). Spoliations were made by ecclesiastics or laymen: "Cap.," 811, c. 3, 5, I, 163; 2, 165; "Cap.," 850, c. 5, II, 88; "Form. Turon.," 1.

[2] "Form. Andeg.," 7; "Wisig.," 10, 1, 11; "Cap.," 768, I, 43.

tary service (this was, properly speaking, the benefice, the one which became the fief). Benefices of the latter kind were found only during the ascendancy of the second dynasty when the seignior was obliged to lead his vassals to the host of the king. To be sure that they would follow him, he granted them benefices to enable them to equip and support themselves and to provide themselves with horses.[1]

§ 144. **Rights of the Recipient of a Benefice.** — He had a right to the income from the land that had been granted to him, but, unlike the proprietor, his right was neither absolute nor perpetual. The donations of the Merovingians were ordinarily revocable in case of default by the grantee and were for life (or, at least, they reverted to the grantor if the grantee died without issue). Under the Carolingians benefices were also granted for life, a new grant being necessary upon the death of the grantor as well as upon the death of the grantee.[2] The grantee had no right to alienate his benefice; only the grantor could do that.[3]

§ 145. **How did the Benefices become Hereditary?**[4] — That is to say, how they were transformed into fiefs, because the fief was nothing more than the benefice for military service which had become hereditary. At the death of the grantor the benefice rarely reverted to his heirs. At the death of the grantee it ought to have been otherwise, but the grantor had no interest in resuming possession of the land, the son of the grantee, already known to

[1] The recipients of benefices from the king were obliged always to be ready to march and for all time if it so pleased the king. "Cap.," 807, c. 1, I, 134; "Cap. Bonon," c. 5, I, 167. Inspection by the "missi"; reports to the emperor were required to be made concerning the condition of the benefices. "Cap.," 807, c. 4, I, 136; "Cap.," 802, c. 6, 9; *Anség.*, 3. 19, 20, 82.

[2] Forfeiture of the benefice was the penalty for the vassal who failed in his duty of fidelity, or for him who neglected it, or cultivated it poorly ("Cap.," 768, c. 5, I, 43; 818, c. 3, I, 287; "Worms," 829, II, 14; "Pap.," 865, c. 4, II, 92; *Loersch and Schr.*, "Urk.," no. 38); or who abandoned his peer while marching against the common enemy ("Cap. Bon.," 811, c. 5, I, 166); or who refused to perform judicial service ("Cap.," 782, c. 7, I, 192); etc. The refusal to perform military service appears to have involved only the penalty of banishment, but without doubt the persistent refusal would have caused the loss of the benefice. "Cap. Thed.," 805, c. 6, I, 123; 818–9, c. 16, I, 284.

[3] With the consent of the recipient of the benefice, if he wished to transmit the possession, "Berlin Ak.," 1885, p. 1186; *Roth*, "Bénéfice," p. 426. The grant of a fief in arrears was permitted to the recipient of the benefice.

[4] Following the "Libri Feudorum," 1, 1, 1, the benefices would have been: 1st, revocable "ad nutum"; 2d, temporary; 3d, for life; 4th, hereditary. This traditional opinion would, perhaps, be more exact for the offices than for the benefices. The donations of the Lombard kings were revocable "ad nutum," and void at the death of the donor. *Roth*, 177, 223; *Liutp.*, 43; "Cap.," 776, c. 3, I, 188.

him, was in possession and naturally had the preference over all others in a new concession; to have refused it to him would have been a violation of the promise made at the time the benefice was established by the recommendation of the lands.[1] It was thus by virtue of custom that the tenure of benefices became hereditary. From the 1700 s, at least, the opinion has been common that the feudal régime had been established by Charles the Bald in the Capitulary of Quierzy or Kiersy in 877,[2] but there is no truth in it. All are agreed in recognizing in this capitulary a law of circumstance implying and tolerating the rule of heredity without sanctioning the principle in a definite manner; it established no new right, and it is impossible to fix a precise date at which the feudal system was established.[3]

§ 146. **Heredity of Offices.** — The Capitulary of Quierzy dealt at the same time with benefices and public functions or offices.[4] Revocable "ad nutum" at first, public offices soon came to be held by a tenure for life; the hereditary principle was then introduced, so that they passed from father to son like private property. This change, so contrary to the nature of a public function, was due to various causes. The aristocracy of the great landholders laid hands on public offices and their pretensions were recognized, as we have seen, by the edict of Clothair in 614. To his functionaries the king often assigned a portion of his territorial

[1] *Migne,* "Patr. l.," 125, 1035, 1050; *Esmein,* p. 138.

[2] *Bourgeois,* "Le Cap. de Kiersy," 1885. Neither the treaty of Andelot in 587, nor the Edict of Clothair, in 614, rendered benefices hereditary. "By the treaty of Andelot, Gontran and Childebert II bound themselves to restore to the churches and to the "leudes," the property that they had unjustly confiscated or of which they had illegally or violently taken possession, limiting the right to revoke their donations to cases where the holder was guilty of treason. In 614, Clothair II guaranteed to his subjects the peaceable possession of property that they had received from his predecessors or from himself.

[3] Custom of offering presents ("exenia"). Fraud foreseen by the Capitulary of Nimwegen, 806, I, 131, c. 7. Benefices for life in the 900 s and 1000 s. *Flach,* "Orig.," I, 127.

[4] "Cap.," 877, c. 9 and 10. Charles the Bald, on the point of leaving for Italy, proposed certain measures to the nobles, c. 9: if a count should die and his son follow the king on his expedition, a provisory administrator for the count should be appointed until Charles the Bald had been informed. In the same way, if he should leave a son of minor age, or if there were no children. Same rules for the benefices of the king or of others. From this, it follows that Charles the Bald reserved the right to regulate the heredity of offices; he did not wish that the sons of counts who had followed him to Italy be despoiled of the paternal earldom; but although this was favorable to heredity, it did not less establish the right of the king (or of those who had conceded the benefices), c. 10. After the death of the king, those of his faithful subjects who renounced the world for love of God and for the king, could dispose of their honor at will, if they left a son or a relative capable of rendering service to the State.

domain in the form of a benefice, all the more readily, because they were in most instances his vassals. It became the practice to recognize no distinction between a public charge and the land which was an accessory to it and whose income served to compensate the functionary; both came to be designated by the term "honor." Finally, the king considered the public offices as his property the same as his other possessions. Under these conditions the appropriation of the public offices by those who exercised their functions was accomplished with little difficulty.

CHAPTER IV

THE CHURCH UNDER THE "ANCIEN RÉGIME."[1] (THE FRANKISH, FEUDAL, AND MONARCHICAL EPOCHS)

[1] BIBLIOGRAPHY: Treatises on canonical law cited, p. 145 [French edition] and following; particularly *Thomassin*, *Van Espen*, and in our time *Hinschius;* also the collections of *Héricourt*, *Durand de Maillane*, and "l'institution" of Fleury. Concerning the ancient literature, *cf. Camus* and *Dupin*, "Biblioth.," nos. 2604 and following, which contains a large number of monographs. For a more recent bibliography, *cf. Viollet; Glasson; Martigny*, "Dict. des antiq. chrétienne"; *Gams*, "Series episcoporum ecclesiæ catho-

TOPIC 5. ECCLESIASTICAL JUSTICE

TOPIC 6. HERETICS AND JEWS

TOPIC 7. RELATIONS OF CHURCH AND STATE

TOPIC 1. CONSTITUTION OF THE CHRISTIAN CHURCH

§ 147. **Political Evolution of the Church.** — The first Christian communities passed through an inorganic state similar to that which primitive societies went through; "ubi tres, ibi ecclesia," according to the words of Christ; the only distinctions which existed resulted from the gifts conferred by the Holy Spirit ("charismes").[1] They formed coherent groups ("ecclesiæ") from the main body of which the **clergy**[2] were separated (bishops, presbyters, servitors) thus recalling the "ordo" of the municipal constitutions, and the common people who constituted the **Laity**. From this body of notables and dignitaries one of the bishops was set apart and, about the middle of the 100s, at least, all au-

licæ," 1873; *Eubel*, "Hierarchia catholica medii ævi," 1898. On the Roman epoch, see *Loening; Sohm; Duchesne*, "Les origines chrétiennes," 1880; and *Renan*, "L'Eglise chrétienne." On the Frankish epoch, see *Fustel de Coulanges*, "La monarchie franque," 525; *Loening; Waitz*, etc. On the feudal epoch, see *Luchaire*, "Manuel des inst. fr.," 1892. On the Church in 1789, see *Taine*, "L'Ancien Régime," 1882; *cf.* for the epoch of Richelieu, *d'Avenel*, "Richelieu," III, 27; *Lavisse* and *Rambaud*, "Hist. génér.," III, 352, etc.; *Isambert*, "Table," see "Eglise," "Culte catholique," "Ecclesiastiques," "Pape," "Puissances," "Ordres," "Monastères," etc. Code Hénri III, liv. I, "R. q. hist.," 50, 397; 58, 5; 60, 369. "Mémoires du clergé," 1768–1781.

[1] *Cf.* the organization of the Protestant sects, such as the Quakers.

[2] From the Greek "χλήρος," lot, the share of the seignior, as in the case of the Levites. Laics, from "λαός," people. *Cf.* Jewish communities.

thority became concentrated in his hands. The unitary episcopacy was gradually established;[1] it came into existence as did the monarchy in civil society, through the need of order and through the necessity of a government to combat heretical anarchy, or to defend itself against persecution by the public authorities. The state of war in which the Church found itself drove it toward a monarchical organization; at the same time, the Eucharist, which was the principal rite of worship, presupposed the intervention of a single person and in the long run this was always the same one; moreover, the management of ecclesiastical property which was intrusted to him accommodated itself equally well to this régime.

Each Christian community, then, constituted a petty independent State with a monarchical constitution and Christendom as a whole had the appearance of a confederation with its diets (**councils**). It only remained to become a unified State, and under the influence of the political organization of the Roman Empire it proceeded in this direction. The towns formed dioceses or parishes; the chief cities of the provinces became the seats of **metropolitan bishops** who took precedence of ordinary bishops in the councils; and the Oriental **patriarchs** and the Occidental **primates** corresponded somewhat to the imperial vicars. In his turn the bishop of Rome, the **pope**,[2] occupying the capital of the Empire and being at the head of the most important of the churches, naturally came to be regarded as the head of Christendom. As if

[1] *J. Réville*, "Les origines de l'épiscopat," 1894; The *Abbot Duchesne*, "Les origines chrétiennes," 1879–1880; *de Smedt*, "Introd. ad eccles. histor. et R. d. q. hist.," 1888, 339; *Sohm*, "Kirchenrecht," 1892. *P. Fournier*, N.R.H., 1894, 286; *Beaudouin*, N.R.H., 1896, 105. Textes. *cf. Harnack*, "Altchristl. Literatur," 1886. There is no direct proof of the existence of the unitary episcopacy before the 100s; toward the end of this century, it appeared entirely formed, from which it was concluded that it originated earlier. The inference is not certain; it may be that there were germs in the anterior organization which had only to be developed. It did not undergo revolution, else traces would have been left; it was rather a matter of evolution. The Abbe Duchesne admits the existence of presbyterian colleges in the primitive churches, connecting the unitary episcopacy which would have succeeded them according to apostolic tradition.

[2] The title of pope was common to all Eastern bishops. The pope was elected, not by the entire Church, but by the clergy and the people of Rome. The primacy of the pope was distinctly recognized by the council of Sardica, 343. *Viollet*, "R. crit. d'hist.," 1880, p. 33. The primacy of the bishops of Rome was recognized aside from any motive of theological order: 1st, because Rome, as the center of the Empire, tended, naturally, to become the center of Christianity; 2d, because of the wealth of the Roman Church; 3d, because of the talent for organization, entirely Roman, of the popes, and because of the idea of unity and of catholicity to which it gave satisfaction.

to supply the last element in a resemblamce already so marked the Church divided itself, after the manner of the Empire, into the Eastern Church and the Western Church, just at the moment when the papal authority had reached its zenith (857–1054).

§ 148. **The Catholic Monarchy.** — The Western Church developed then in the direction of a monarchical organization. 1st, **Centralization of spiritual power:** (*a*) the pope enjoyed a primacy in respect to honors (precedence, etc.); he was the vicar, not of St. Peter, but of God; (*b*) he possessed the legislative power in full; he could, so the canonists said, change the nature of things, could make just that which was unjust; if he was assisted by a council, it was from him that the council derived its authority, for the council gave only counsel; (*c*) he possessed a primacy of jurisdiction (reserved cases, major causes, exemptions); he was the supreme judge who judged all others but whom no one might judge; (*d*) he was the universal bishop, other bishops derived their power from him and were only his delegates for the conduct of religious worship and the administration of their churches.[1]

2d, **Seizure of the temporalities of the individual churches:** (*a*) by taxes (tithes, "annates") levied for the benefit of the papacy; (*b*) by the conferring of ecclesiastical benefices (charges, expectancies, reservations) — the pope controlled at the same time both the property and the functions of each Church.

3d, **Seizure of the secular power:** (*a*) the pope had his states (patrimony of St. Peter[2]); churches, monasteries, principalities, and

[1] "Dictatus papæ" of Gregory VII; the Roman Church could not err; the pope alone was universal pontiff; he could judge everybody; he could make laws concerning ecclesiastical organizations; he could remove and transfer bishops; no council was œcumenical unless it was convoked by him; his legates had precedence in the council; the pope could remove kings and absolve their subjects from the oath of fidelity; he alone could wear the imperial insignia. *Jaffé*, "Mon. Greg.," p. 174; *Viollet*, "Inst.," II, 272; *Delarc*, "Grégoire VII," 1889.

[2] The patrimony of St. Peter was formed by the vast possessions that the Holy See had held for a long time in central Italy; the pope, as a great proprietor, and a political sovereign like the "immunists," the counts, and the dukes. The Church of Rome collected rent from those who cultivated its lands. From the 800 s, the monasteries "recommended" themselves with their property to the Apostle Peter for the purpose of enabling them to withdraw from the authority of their diocesan bishops; the Holy See acquired the right of eminent domain over their property and received an annual rent as a sign of its ownership. (Ex: Vézelay paid a pound of silver.) About the 1000 s, not only the monasteries, but also seigniories and kingdoms were offered to Rome. The new powers relied upon the support of the Holy See and were legitimized by it, by paying rent. (Robert Guiscard promised to pay 12 "deniers" for a pair of oxen, 1059.) Whoever wished to escape a troublesome sovereign did the same (Hungary and Poland in order to escape from the Empire). The "denier" of St. Peter (Peter's pence) paid by England

kingdoms all were united to it by the feudal bond of homage in becoming vassals of the Holy See; (*b*) where it did not secure so strict a dependence the papacy attempted, at least, to make the State the servant of the Church; but it only half succeeded and soon it encountered resistance even in spiritual matters. The great schism of the West (1378–1429) was a blow to its prestige from which it was difficult to recover; its omnipotence was attacked. The councils of Constance and of Basel failed to make a representative government of the papal monarchy by giving the councils of the Church precedence over the Holy See.[1]

§ 149. **The Reformation.** — For the papacy the Reformation substituted: 1st, the **episcopal system** and the authority of synods; this was a return to the aristocratic institutions of former times, but by a remarkable contradiction the political sovereign was made the head of the Church, the "summus episcopus;"[2] 2d, the **presbyterial system**, which was more democratic, since the laity sat by the side of the ecclesiastical element in the consistories or councils of the parish and in the synods or general assemblies of the delegates of the Church. **Gallicanism** with its national Church, its principle of the superiority of the councils over the pope, and its dependence upon the State approximated the episcopal system. At the time of the Revolution an attempt was made through the **Civil Constitution of the Clergy** (July 12, 1790), but without success, to democratize the Church by giving the political electors the power to elect the curés and the bishops. Ultramontane Catholicism, already attacked by the Reformation and by Gallicanism, attacked anew by the Revolution, was obliged to retire within itself and concentrate its strength in order to be stronger for the struggle. In reaction against the Reformation which broke up and scattered the creeds, its leaders submitted to the strictest unity of faith and discipline. The clergy despoiled of its property by the Revolution now found itself strictly dependent upon the papacy, the State no longer had any hold over it.

from the 700 s to 1534 was an analogous imposition. *Cf. Blumenstock*, "Der Paepstliche Schutz i. M.," 1890; N.H.R., 1894, p. 145; *Viollet*, "Inst.," II, 277 (Alexander VI gave the West Indies to the king of Spain); 289 (international arbitration of the popes); *J. de Salisbury*, "Metalog.," 4, 42.

[1] The councils judged and removed popes. This was necessary when no one was able to tell who was the real pope. *Cf.* the constitutional systems of elective monarchies.

[2] Others held that the head of the State was, for this reason (and not by reason of a delegation of episcopal power), also head of the Church (*Grotius*, *Thomasius*, *Böhmert*); or indeed the whole Church which as such was a mystical body, conferred his rights on him.

The council of the Vatican, in 1869, crowned the Catholic edifice by proclaiming the infallibility of the pope in doctrinal matters.[1]

TOPIC 2. THE CLERGY

§ 150. **The Central Government of the Church.** — The choice of the pope,[2] like that of ordinary bishops, passed through three stages: 1st, election by the clergy and the people of Rome; 2d, confirmation of the election by the Eastern emperor or the Western emperor; 3d, election by the cardinals, that is, by the higher Roman clergy, from the time of Nicolas II (1059).[3] After the quarrel over investitures the imperial confirmation disappeared, but there still remained a right of diplomatic intervention on the part of the great Catholic States like Austria, Spain, and France, that is, a right of exclusion which could be exercised only once against a single papal nominee.

§ 151. **Œcumenical Councils.** — From time to time the pope convoked Œcumenical Councils to assist in the government of the Church. Under ordinary circumstances he was advised by the **Sacred College** composed of cardinals[4] whose plenary meetings were called *consistories* when convoked during the lifetime of the pope, and *conclaves* at his death. The cardinals, who were formerly the chiefs of the Roman clergy, represent to-day the Church universal. The consistories have degenerated into assemblies for mere pomp and show. The government of the Church is carried on, in reality, 1st, by commissions, the congregations organized by Sixtus V (1587), to which the pope summons only such cardinals as he pleases;[5] 2d, by the Curia (bureaus of employees); and 3d, by the legates or nuncios.

[1] Constit., "Pastor æternus," July 18, 1870.

[2] *Bignon,* "Tr. de l'élection des papes," 1655, 1874; *Travers,* "Essai hist. sur l'él. des papes," 1875; *Bayet,* "Elec. pontif." ("R. Hist.," v. 24); *L. Lector,* "Le conclave," 1894. Exclusion of the people, 1154; of the inferior clergy, 1179.

[3] The rigorous seclusion of the conclave dates from the 1200s, Bulls of 1274; 1562; 1732. Bull "consultari," October 10, 1877. Since the great schism, it has been the custom to elect an Italian; the majority required was ⅔ of the votes, the electors being the cardinals present.

[4] There are now seventy-four cardinals, of whom about thirty are not Italians.

[5] The principal ones are: The Holy Office (inquisition), the College of the Index (censure of books), the College of Studies, the College of Bishops and regulars (appeal of ecclesiastical causes), the College of the Council (ecclesiastical discipline), the College of the Propaganda, and the College of Rituals (ceremonial, canonization). The Holy See has also its Chancellery, its Datary (collation of benefices); its secretarial office (for diplomatic negotiations), its supreme tribunal or Rote, its "signatura justitiæ" (appeals, challenge), its "signatura gratiæ" (privileges), its

§ 152. **Bishops, Metropolitans, and Primates.** — The ecclesiastical unit is the diocese of which the chief is the bishop. But there is not complete equality among all the bishops; a hierarchy has been established among them as among the clergy of the diocese. The **Metropolitan** — the bishop whose seat was in the metropolis or chief place of the province ("archiepiscopus," 600s)— presided over the provincial councils, ordained the bishops of the province, decided disputes between bishops, and heard appeals from their decisions.[1] In the 700s we see one of them, Hincmar, assuming the right to depose his suffragans (case of Rothade). The popes opposed these pretensions [2] and reduced the superiority of the metropolitans to a mere trifle. The **primates**,[3] whose situation recalls that of the oriental **patriarchs**,[4] possessed hardly any privileges not honorary.[5] The provincial and national **councils** did not cease to meet any more than did the œcumenical councils, but these representative institutions were so often opposed to the monarchical principle that they lost much of their importance.

§ 153. **Episcopal Elections.**[6] — The bishops were elected at first by the people of the episcopal city and the clergy centered in this city; they were ordained by other bishops (those of the same province) and particularly by the metropolitan.[7] Occasionally,

penitentiary office (dispensation), its apostolic chamber (for the management of the budget: Peter's Pence, products of dispensations and indulgences, and gifts). This group of bureaus and of ministers, like a great State, constitutes the Roman Curia. In foreign countries the pope is represented by legates, nuncios, internuncios, for, by a peculiarity that tradition only can explain, he constitutes an international personage, although he has been deprived of his States. Concerning the Roman Curia, *cf. Goyau, Pératé,* and *Fabre,* "The Vatican," 1895; *Benoist,* "Le gouvern. du Saint Siège" ("R. des Deux-Mondes," 1895); *Aymon,* "Tableau de la Cour de Rome," 1726; *Viollet,* "Gr. Encycl.," see "Congrégations."

[1] Council of Antioch, 341, c. 9.

[2] Nicholas I reëstablished in his place Rothade, bishop of Soissons, who was removed in 862 by a provincial council and excommunicated by his archbishop, Hincmar. *Varin,* "Arch. leg. de Reims"; "Coutumes," 5.

[3] Curacy of Arles in the 400s; primacy of Mayence over Germany; Bourges, primacy of Aquitania, second half of the 800s; Lyon, primacy of the Gauls (894). *Bladé,* "Prétentions primatiales des métropol. de Vienne, Bourges, Bordeaux," 1896. *Viollet,* I, 343; II, 319. "Ann. du Midi," 1895, 141.

[4] Antioch, Constantinople, Alexandria, Jerusalem.

[5] Ecclesiastical circumscriptions: ecclesiastical provinces, dioceses, archdeaconries, deanships, parishes, annexes.

[6] *Gratian,* "1ª pars," D. 63; *Imbart de la Tour,* "Les elections épiscopales," 1891; *Esmein,* "Cours. d'hist. du dr.," 3d ed. p. 150, no. 1; *Duchesne,* "Orig. du cult chr.," 329. The Jewish "community" also had elected heads.

[7] *Saint Cyprien,* "Ep." 68; Conc. Laodicée, 372; Arles, 452, 42; Orléans, 538, 3; Cod. Just., 1, 3, 41, pr. Nov. 123, 1, 15.

however, the Emperors intervened. The canonical customs persisted after the invasions, but the Frankish kings took a more active part in the episcopal elections;[1] hardly anything more was left to the people and the clergy than the right of presentation to which the king paid little attention. The bishoprics (and the abbeys) were bought by gifts to the king (simony), or were given as rewards to his servitors. Charlemagne promised to the young men of the palace who should distinguish themselves by zeal for study, bishoprics and *monasteria permagnifica;*[2] he believed, moreover, that he was all the more authorized to dispose of them because the vast territorial possessions of the Church came to it for the most part from kings and were badly distinguished in his mind from the functions to which they were joined. It was from this state of affairs, and from the conflict between the pretensions of the secular power and the customs of the Church that the **quarrel over Investitures** arose; it ended in the victory of the Church, which recovered its right to elect the bishops, but the composition of the electoral body was no longer what it had been in the ancient Church. Little by little, the aristocracy of the urban clergy, the chapter of canons, which exercised a preponderating influence in the elections, dispensed completely with the people, that is to say, the laity and the rest of the clergy (1100s). The intervention of the king and the seigniors no longer appeared except in a feeble way. But the intervention of the popes[3] which had been necessary for a return to canonical rules had as a remote result the complete abandonment of these rules. The popes, being called upon to express an opinion in regard to irregularities or contests, came little by little to confirm all episcopal elections;[4] they substituted themselves for the electors by appointing directly to bishoprics in more and more numerous instances;[5] they required the bishops to take an oath of fidelity to the Holy See and to visit it "ad limina." They also assumed the appointment to

[1] Council of Orléans, 538, c. 3, 549, c. 10; Edict of Clothair of 614. *Gregory of Tours*, 6, 7; "Bav.," 1, 11; "Can. Apost.," 131; Council of Antioch, 341, c. 12; "Cap.," I, 25, 29 (742 and 744).

[2] M.G.H., S.S., II, 732; "Cap.," 818–9, c. 2, I, 276. The king had to authorize the people and the clergy to proceed with the election, approve its action, and put the bishop in possession of the temporalty of the bishopric. In fact, the election was in his hands. *Gratian*, "1ª pars," D. 63, c. 22; *Hauck*, "Bischofswahlen u. d. Meroving.," 1883.

[3] At first unknown, canonical elections required. *Gratian*, "1ª p.," D. 62, c. 2. Lateran, 1215, c. 23. Decretal of 1169. *Hinschius*, II, 603, 3. X. 1, 6, 42, s. "Sexte," 1, 6, 10.

[4] "BCh., Extrav. Comm.," 1, 3, 1 (Boniface VIII).

[5] For example, in case of a change of seat: the chapter postulated the pope instituted ("Postulation"), X, 1, 5; 1, 7, 3. *Viollet*, II, 325.

a multitude of benefices: 1st, by virtue of the right of **devolution**,[1] that is, when the election had not occurred during the prescribed period, the hierarchical superior supplied the place of the negligent electors; 2d, by **apostolic mandates**, by charging the collator to appoint to an already vacant benefice a person whose choice was obligatory upon him; 3d, by **expectative favors** (1100 s), enjoining the collator to assign the first vacant benefice to the person indicated; 4th, by **reservations**, that is to say, by reserving for themselves the conferring of benefices vacant "in curia" (of which the titulary was at Rome at the time of his death).[2] Urban V thus reserved for himself all the important benefices of Christendom. Under these conditions the Court of Rome had no trouble in having the first year's income ("**annates**") of newly granted benefices paid to itself, as if they were fiefs of the papacy (1100 s).[3] The resistance of the Church came out at the Council of Basel, and in France it expressed itself in the **Pragmatic Sanction of Bourges** (1438) prohibiting reservations, expectancies, and annates. The **Concordat of 1516** completely deprived the chapters of their electoral rights and divided them between the pope and the king.[4] This permitted Louis XIV to make of his confessor "a sort of minister of worship by giving over (1670) to him the *list of benefices*," that is to say, by intrusting to him the appointment of the incumbents of these benefices. The Council of Trent made appointment by the pope the law of the Church, at least outside of France.

§ 154. **Powers of the Bishops.**[5] — In his diocese the bishop possessed full spiritual authority; he alone baptized, confirmed, ordained, and excommunicated; he administered the entire patrimony of the Church; he paid the clergy and was their judge. Through his clergy, through the poor inscribed on the register ("matricula"), of the church, through the freedmen, "tabularii," through the numerous slaves or "coloni" who lived on the lands of the Church, and through the weak who sought his patronage,

[1] The "Dévolut" differed from devolution in that it supposed that the titulary of a benefice was unworthy; that one who caused this to be known, the informer, in short, took his place by virtue of recompense; the superior of the ordinary collator conferred it on him, "jure devoluto."

[2] 1200 s. "Sexte" (the sixth book of Pope Boniface VIII's "Decretals"), 3, 4, 2; "Règles de la chanc. apost.," 5, 18 (1362–1370).

[3] "Extrav. Comm.," 3, 2, 10. *Cf.* "Précedents," *Viollet*, II, 332.

[4] The bishop appointed by the king received the canonical investiture from the pope; Rome delivered to him the bulls, for which he paid certain fees and which he had registered by Parliament; after which he took oath between the hands of the king and entered upon the possession of his diocese.

[5] *V. Mortet*, "Maurice de Sully, bishop of Paris" (1160–1196), 1890.

he had, under the first two dynasties, an authority at least equal to that of the counts and the dukes. The capitularies enjoined the latter, moreover, to aid the clergy in the discharge of their duties; and they lent a helping hand to the bishops.[1] To their spiritual powers the latter usually added vast estates with the privilege of immunity. Feudalism strengthened their situation.[2] They held important seigniories which were sometimes real States like the pope's; such were the archbishop-electors of Mainz, Treves, and Cologne. Six of them bore the title of peers of the realm; the bishop-dukes of Reims, Laon, and Langres; and the bishop-counts of Beauvais, Châlons-sur-Marne, and Nyon. A number of prelates were counts, barons, or seigniors; the bishop of Grenoble was a prince; and the bishop of Lescar was the first baron of Bearn. Under the monarchy they were all mediatized and if they preserved their titles they no longer carried with them any temporal authority.[3] The French prelates alone, who were at the same time princes of the Holy Empire, such as the archbishops of Cambray and of Besançon, the bishops of Metz and of Strassburg, and the abbot of Gorze (Lorraine), were able to preserve beyond the frontier the subjects and the rights of sovereignty. The spiritual rights of the bishops were split up into fractions during the Frankish period, as a result of the division of labor as we shall see in speaking of the diocesan clergy.

§ 155. **The Diocesan Clergy.** — Exclusively urban at first,[4] later, including also rural priests, the diocesan clergy increased and was organized hierarchically. The council of the bishop was divided into a permanent oligarchic assembly, the **chapter of canons** [priests living in common and subject to a rule in the 700s, afterwards abandoning at the same time community life and the

[1] *Viollet*, "Inst.," I, 380; Nov., *Just.*, 86, 1, 4; *Chlot.*, "Præc.," c. 6, I, 19; N.R.H., XI, 556 (revision of the sentences of the count); "Wis.," 2, 1, 29, 30; *Anségise*, 2, 23; "Cap. Pap.," 876, c. 12, II, 103; "Cap.," I, 257, c. 2; Conc. Meaux, 845–6, c. 71.

[2] *Viollet*, p. 388, cites the case of a bishop-count of the 600s; there were some such, especially from the end of the 800s to the 900s. *Bouquet*, 3, 635; *D. Vaissete*, 5, 221; 146; 147.

[3] There were great inequalities among the bishops at the end of the Old Régime, ecclesiastical circumscriptions having changed little since the Roman epoch. Brienne received 120,000 pounds as bishop of Toulouse, and 572,000 on other accounts. The bishop of Fréjus received only from seven to eight thousand pounds. The plebeian was almost excluded from holding the office of bishop.

[4] Priests in the places of prayer ("oraison") (for example at Rome, where every cardinal was attached by virtue of his title) at first administered the sacrament only in cases of urgency, then, in a measure, as the numbers of the faithful increased, they became inferior bishops. "R. q. hist.," 56, 493; 64, 180.

monastic rule in the 1100s], and a **diocesan synod**, or assembly of the clergy of the diocese. The **archpriest**, the chief among the priests, administered a part of the diocese; the **archdeacon** was intrusted with the service of worship, the discipline of the clergy, and the distribution of revenues and ecclesiastical stipends, and was an even more important personage. The diocese was divided into archdeaconries and these were again subdivided into archpresbyteries or deaneries. The **vicars-general** of the bishops did not become permanent until the 1400s; they administered the diocese and the **official** rendered justice therein.

§ 156. **The "Chorepiscopus."** — The country districts had rural bishops about the 300s; but in consequence of rivalries and quarrels with the bishops they disappeared in the 900s and were replaced by country *curés*.[1] The **rural parishes**[2] (from the 200s) resulted for the most part from foundations of private oratories on their estates[3] by the great landowners. The founder or patron had, aside from various honorary rights, the right to present a curate to the bishop, who could not, in principle, refuse to confer the curacy.[4] Once appointed, the curé could not be removed; "he could be dispossessed only by virtue of a sentence rendered after a formal trial, from which he had a right of appeal." Each grantee of a benefice thus intrenched in his ecclesiastical fief was much less dependent upon the bishop than the priests of our day.[5]

§ 157. **The Clergy in General** were distinguished externally from the laity by their tonsure;[6] a clerk was one who had received the tonsure in a regular way, but this did not always establish the clerical character, it was only presumptive evidence. Celibacy[7]

[1] "Cura animarum." *Viollet*, "Inst.," I, 355; II, 363 (elections of curés by their parishioners).

[2] Council of Orléans, 541, 7, 33; *Gregory the Great*, "Ep.," 11, 12 (dotation); *Marculf.*, 1, 19; *Anségise*, I, 114, 125; Cod. Theod., 16, 2. 33.

[3] *Imbart de la Tour*, "Les paroisses rurale" ("R. hist.," 63. 19).

[4] "The patron went first to the offering, he was the first to receive incense and holy bread, he led the processions, had his seat and sepulcher in the choir, and his coat of arms was placed in the Church above even those of the seignior." X, 3. 38; "Sexte," 3, 19. Concerning his rights, compare no. 26 following, and on German theories see *Blondel*, "Frédéric II," p. 241; *Heusler*, "Inst. d. d. R.," I, 314.

[5] *Abbé Mathieu*, "L'Anc. Rég. en Lorr.," p. 192; *Viollet*, II, 364. Below the parish were found simple chapels with an income.

[6] In olden times, the shaved head was a sign of servitude. The use of the tonsure, introduced by the monks, was applied to the secular clergy (500s). "Cap.," 817, c. 8. *Anségise*, I, 114. *Beaumanoir*, 11, 43 ("couronne de clerc").

[7] Ecclesiastical celibacy was associated with the ideas of the Jews concerning the impurity that marriage implied, ideas widely prevalent among primitive peoples (Matt. xix, 11; Paul, 1 Corin. vii and following), and with the fact that marriage did not allow a person to give himself

was not required of the inferior clergy (the minor orders were: porters, readers, exorcists, and acolytes), but it was obligatory upon bishops, priests, deacons, and subdeacons (the major orders). The qualifications for taking orders were chiefly: the attainment of a certain age (25 or 30 years for the priesthood), a certain amount of learning, the rank of free man, and often the authorization of the civil power.[1]

§ 158. **Personal Immunity.** — The personal privileges of ecclesiastics originated in part during the Roman epoch and are to be explained by two ideas: honors due to the clergy, and the necessity of leaving them free to discharge their religious duties.[2] The principal privileges which they enjoyed were: (A.) precedence over the laity,[3] the clergy forming under the monarchy the highest order in the State; a higher "wergeld" than that of simple free men during the Barbarian epoch;[4] and exemption from torture and from arrest on account of debt;[5] (B.) exemption from military service (except that they could not profit from this when they held benefices or fiefs, because if they enjoyed immunity and were forbidden to shed blood by virtue of their character as clergy, this would not hold when they were regarded as grantees of benefices or feudatories);[6] exemption from personal burdens ("munera

completely to religious works. The most zealous Christians, particularly the clergy, turned away from it. For a long time, however, married men were allowed to enter the ecclesiastical state, but they were recommended to live in continence. After ordination, "Can. Ap.," 25, inferior clerks (readers, etc.) only could marry; bigamy, that is to say, second marriages, or marriage with widows, was alone forbidden to them, as it was among the Jews. In the Eastern Church, priests were married before ordination; bishops, who had to live in celibacy, were taken from the black clergy, and from among the monks who had taken the vows of chastity (Conc. of Elvire, 324); in 440, the prohibition was extended to deacons. These prohibitions were poorly respected. It was necessary, in the 1000 s and 1100 s, to take more radical measures and to annul the marriages of clerks, and to restrain them by prohibiting them from the exercise of their offices. Conc. of Lateran, 1122; 1139; "Sexte," 3, 2; 1, 12; *Esmein*, "Le Mariage," I, 282; II, 130. *Viollet*, "Inst.," II, 367; *Bocquet*, thesis; *Viollet*, "Gr. Encycl.," see "Célibat." The Church allowed the Maronite clergy to marry.

[1] Cod. Theod., 16, 2, 6 and 7; *Marculf.*, I, 19; "Cap.," 805, c. 15, I, 125; *Anségise*, 1, 114, 125. At the end of the 800 s the rule was repealed. "Kiersy," 877, c. 10; *Loening*, II, 171.

[2] *Saint Paul*, 2 ad Tim., ii, 4: "nemo militans Deo implicat se negotiis sæcularibus." Nov., 123, 6; *Anségise*, 1, 22; *Pothier*, "Des personnes."

[3] Declar., Feb., 1580; L. pat. 1st May, 1596, etc. *Domat*, "Droit public."

[4] "Rib.," 36; "Cap.," 803, etc; "Baiuw.," I, 8 and following.

[5] *Ferrière*, "Dict. de Droit," see "Contrainte par corps." Ord. Blois, Art. 57.

[6] Clerks were forbidden to carry arms. (*Cf.* "Cap.," 742, 769; "Ep. ad Folradum," "Faux Cap.," 6, 370.) In the 1000 s and 1100 s also bishops

personalia sordida" of the Roman law, the "corvée" of the feudal and monarchical period);[1] and exemption from burdens like guardianship; but in return for these privileges they were forbidden to engage in trade, and could not perform public functions because these were incompatible with the clerical character.[2]

§ 159. **Appendix. Local Immunity or Right of Sanctuary.** — This pagan practice was adopted by the Christian churches from an early time. Under the Frankish kings the right of sanctuary was extended to the inclosure around the Church, to the cemeteries, the monasteries, the dwellings of the bishops and to places where crosses were erected on the roadside.[3] It was a form of the right of grace which was justifiable in an age of violence.[4] The culprit was surrendered when his pursuer had promised not to put him to death nor to mutilate him. But the remedy was sometimes greater than the evil, the churches became asylums for malefactors, and criminals went unpunished. The capitularies had therefore to restrict the right of sanctuary by refusing it to great criminals, like murderers, as did the laws of the Later Empire.[5] But in spite of the restrictions the privilege continued through the centuries; it did not entirely disappear until the 1400s in France,[6] until 1794 in Prussia, and until 1850 in Sardinia.

and abbots who warred with their men. *Teulet*, "Layettes," I, 567. "Acad. Inscr.," 5 Feb., 1892; Ord. IX, 530. The monarchy put them under ban and arrear ban; in order to escape therefrom, they paid a contribution in the 1600s; but they no longer paid it in the 1700s. They had always been exempt from performing sentinel duty, from doing guard service, and from furnishing lodging to warriors. *Durand de Maillane*, "Dict.," I, 250; *Viollet*, "Hist. du dr. civ.," 275; *La Roque*, "Tr. du Ban"; *D. Vaissete*, VI, 843; *Fleury*, "Inst. au dr. eccl.," part I, ch. 29; *Pollock and Maitland*, I, 422.

[1] Cod. Theod., 16, 2. 8. 9. 10 (repairs of roads, bridges, carting, wood, flour, etc.); Cod. Theod., 13, 1, 11 and 16; Cod. Jus., 1, 3, 3. *Cf.* "Faux Capit.," 6, 116.

[2] Ord. 1287, I, 316.

[3] Cod. Theod., 9, 45; Cod. Just., 1, 12; 1, 25; Nov., 17, 7; "L. Rom. Wis.," p. 210. *Papian*, 2, 3 and 6; 4, 2. "Alam.," 3, 1; "Dec. Childeb.," c. 4; "Dec. Clothair," c. 14; "Capit.," 779, c. 8, I, 48; *Viollet*, "Inst.," I, 402; "Gr. Encycl.," see "Asile"; *Beaurepaire*, BCh., 1852–1854; *Fuld*, Z.V.R., 1, 887, 102.

[4] Arcadius suppressed the right of sanctuary at the instigation of Eutropus; Saint John Chrysostom protected the latter, who sought refuge in the Church, against the emperor (399). *Saint Augustine*, "De verb. ap.," 18; *Haenel*, "Corp. leg.," p. 235. Intercession of priests, Cod. Theod., 11, 30. 57; 9, 40, 15–24; 9, 3, 7; Cod. Just., 1, 4, 22; "Cap.," 779, 11; *Thonissen*, "Une controv. du XIII s. sur la légitimité de la peine de mort."

[5] Conc. Orléans, 511, c. 1; Mayence, 813; c. 39.

[6] *Beaum.*, 11, 14; 25, 24; *Boutillier*, 2. 9. *Des Mares*, 4, 7, 99. "Gr. Cont. de Norm.," 81. Parliament caused criminals to be delivered up, agreeing to return them after examination, but in fact they were not reintegrated. Ord. Villers-Cotterets, 1539, Art. 166, and Ord. 1547. Council of Trent, sess. 25, c. 20. Later acts, of which the last was in 1852, by which the Church gave way to modern law.

TOPIC 3. ESTABLISHMENTS OF RELIGIOUS UTILITY; MONASTERIES, HOSPITALS, AND SCHOOLS

§ 160. **The Regular Clergy.**[1] — In the 200s the most zealous of the Eastern Christians withdrew to the desert in order to practice asceticism; these were the monks (hermits) or anchorites (who separated themselves from the rest). But, as if to demonstrate how necessary the régime of association is to man, it was not long before they united themselves into communities of **Cenobites** (people who live together) under an abbot (father)[2] of their own choosing. The hermits renounced their property and families; the Cenobites agreed, besides, to obey the abbot and to follow a rule (in the East, that of Saint Basil; in the West, that of Saint Benedict of Nursia, in 543, reformed by Saint Benedict of Aniane in 817). The practice of perpetual vows dates from the 400s and 500s; until then the monks were free to withdraw at will from their monasteries. For a long time the monks belonged to the laity; the State, however, assimilated them to the clergy (except under a particular régime to which we shall return), and most of them received orders about the 900s or 1000s.[3] The monasteries, each independent of the others, and each having its own property, its own elected chief, and its own rules, were subject to the disciplinary power of the bishop of the diocese in which they were situate; but in the 500s they became detached therefrom, tended to become autonomous, and obtained exemption from the episcopal authority, or ecclesiastical immunity.[4] Nicolas I, in 863, granted this immunity to all the monasteries of Gaul. At the same time the monastic establishments were united by a confederation and formed **religious orders** (congregations, Cluny, 910, and Cîteaux, 1098); at the end of the 1200s Cîteaux had seven hundred abbeys dependent upon it. For all

[1] *Richer*, "Tr. de la mort civile," 1755; *Thomassin*, *Héricourt*, *Durand de Maillane*, *Guyot* ("Répertoire"); *Du Bois*, "Max. du dr. canon.," 1681; *Isambert*, "Table," see "Monastères"; *Beaune*, "Droit coutumier fr." The condition of persons, 1882, *Viollet*, "Hist. du dr. civ.," p. 283; "Inst.," I, 370; *Abbé Mathieu*, "L'Ancien Rég. en Lorraine," p. 43 and following. "Annuaire histor." for 1838, p. 66.

[2] The title of abbot was given to every clerk (not bishop) because he was qualified to receive an abbey.

[3] The monasteries were not exclusively religious establishments; they were agricultural, industrial, and literary republics.

[4] Council of Arles, 554, c. 2; of Orléans, 511, 538; Arles, 455; Carthage, 525. *Weiss*, "Die Kirchl. Exempt. d. Kloester," 1893, X, 5, 33; "Sexte," 5, 7; *Viollet*, I, 371. Interminable struggles between the regular clergy and the secular clergy concerning the subject of exemptions.

the more reason the military orders (Hospitalers, who became the order of Malta in 1530, Templars,[1] and the Teutonic Knights) took this form of organization. In the 1200s the mendicants, Franciscans or minors, Dominicans or friars, and later, in the 1500s, the Jesuits (1540), had each its constitution in accord with the spirit which prevailed at the time of its foundation.[2] Whatever it was, it was by this means alone that they were organized into international associations and these latter were formidable powers with which the State and even the Church had to reckon. In France, the State arrogated to itself considerable powers of police over religious communities; the authorization of the king was necessary before they could be established (edicts of 1659, 1666, 1695, and especially of 1749); and the king had the power to suppress those which he regarded as useless and dispose of their property.[3] As for the inmates of such establishments they had a special status: they declared themselves dead to the world and were taken at their word.

§ 161. **Civil Death of the Monks. Results.** — 1st, They were disqualified from exercising civil functions; 2d, from appearing in court and consequently from entering into contracts, because those who contracted with them could not bring actions against them; 3d, from being witnesses to deeds; 4th, from receiving gifts; and 5th, from possessing property, in consequence of which their relatives succeeded to their estates when they

[1] *Langlois*, "R. des Deux-Mondes," 1891, 383; *De Curzon*, "Règle du Temple," 1891; *Delaville le Roulx*, Thesis, 1885; "Cartul de l'ordre de Saint-Jean," 1891.

[2] Religious congregations, like civil societies, were sometimes constituted by "swarming," sometimes by affiliation, and, in this latter case, they were attached to the principal abbey (head of the order), sometimes spontaneously, sometimes against their will. Cluny had an archabbot, priories who depended on the mother abbey, abbeys prescribed or subject, abbeys simply affiliated, associated and keeping their autonomy. *Chénon*, "La France chrétienne," p. 187. Cîteaux had an abbot in each of its monasteries; a general chapter, assembled every year, had the direction of the congregation. The militant orders had a military organization somewhat like that of the Army. "Arch. f. Litt. u. Kircheng.," I, 169; VI, 5; *Viollet*, II, 392. The constitution of the Jesuits, with its general elected for life, its superiors, its prefects, was monarchical and absolute in character. "Edict. nov. 1764" and brief of Clement XIII, 21 July, 1773, suppressing this last order. *Holstenius*, "Codex regul. monast.," 1875.

[3] Suppression of a great number of congregations by the Commission of regulars, 1766, presided over by Brienne, and the Commission of the Union, 1779. *Cf.* Joseph II in Austria. In 1789 there were 15,000 members of religious orders in 300 houses. The noble chapters were secularized convents, for example, Remiremont; the abbey of Saint Cloud became likewise, in 1740, a chapter of canons. *Abbé Mathieu*, "L'Ancien Régime dans la Lorraine," 1878. Concerning the benedictions of the 1700s, *cf.* "La France chrétienne," p. 450.

took religious vows.[1] Everything which they acquired thereafter belonged to the community (with the exception of savings from property which they managed, which they were free to dispose of among the living).[2] Hence it was very important to know who was a monk according to the civil law. The monarchical law demanded that they should attach themselves to some order approved by both the Church and the State. It was not the garb which made the monk, so it was said, but the profession. Regulated at first by ecclesiastical law alone, members of religious orders were later required to submit to certain conditions prescribed by the civil law (1500 s) such as: 1st, the taking in a regular manner of vows before their ecclesiastical superiors and the recording of their professions upon a register;[3] 2d, the attainment of a certain age, 16 years by a rule of the Council of Trent; 21 years for men and 18 years for women, according to the edicts of 1768 and 1779;[4] we find in these requirements of the civil law a reaction against the ancient custom of admitting children of tender years ("oblats") to the monasteries and of compulsory religious vocations (daughters or younger brothers of the great houses); and 3d, a period of probation, one year from the date of taking the vows. The Oratorions, who did not take vows, were not treated as civilly dead, nor were the Lazarists, who took only simple vows (without the prescribed solemnities); as to the Jesuits[5] the course of decisions varied because they took simple vows at first and later solemn vows. The law of February 19, 1790, suppressed the religious orders.[6]

§ 162. **Public Assistance.** — (A) **The Church** took under its protection the poor and the indigent. Its property, "res pauperrima" was applied in part to the alleviation of misery. In the course of time there was established in every church by means of gifts of individuals a fund for the relief of the poor ("mensa

[1] *Beaumanoir*, 56, 1; "Gr. Cout.," 2, 370; *Loysel*, "Inst.," 345; *cf.* Nov., 5, c. 5 and 6; Cod. Just., "de sacros. eccl.," 1, 2 (their succession was opened for the benefit of the monastery and not for their relatives). "Faux. Cap.," 6, 110.

[2] At what epoch? From the time of the Frankish epoch, allusion seems to have been made to this civil death. "Gr. Cout. de Norm.," 25. *Isambert*, XII, 359; *Richer*, p. 663.

[3] X, 3, 31, 13. Ord. Moulins, 131; 1667, 20, 15; Decl. 1736.

[4] Ord. 1569, 19; 1579, 28; March, 1768, and January 17, 1779.

[5] Expelled in 1594; reëstablished, 1603. By virtue of the Edict of November, 1764, the order of Jesuits was dissolved, and its members allowed to remain only as private individuals on French soil.

[6] *Cf.* Decree of 19–26 March, 1790; Decree of October 9, 1793. *Cf.* Loi 24 May–2 June, 1825, Art. 5. *Loranger*, "Comm. s. le Code civil du Bas Canada," 1873, maintains that members of religious orders are still liable to civil death.

pauperum "), a sort of charity bureau, the administration of which was intrusted, like that of the church buildings, to special curators. But long before the ecclesiastical guardianship of the poor had been expressed in this way, bishops and private individuals had founded charitable establishments: "xenodochia," "nasocomia," during the Frankish period; lazar-houses, houses for lepers, during the feudal period; and "hospitalia," charity hospitals in general. The bishop had them administered through ecclesiastics under his direction and the kings took them under their protection. The clergy charged with the management of hospitals received them as benefices or fiefs; but as they appropriated the revenues, allowed the buildings to fall into decay, and wasted the property, it became necessary to transfer the administration to laymen who were required to render account to the bishops.[1]

(B) The **Secularization** of this public service. The State thus took the place of the Church and proceeded to reform the hospitals at the same time that it enacted measures of repression against impostors, that is to say, against beggars and vagabonds. In the 1500 s only, and after long opposition, the supervision passed to bailiffs, seneschals, and the grand almoner of France. An edict of June, 1662, established general hospitals throughout all France. The communal hospitals, it appears, were better administered than those of the State and we find in the cities along with the communal council a sort of charity bureau.[2] The Revolution sanctioned the right of public assistance, attempted to centralize all charitable resources, and to organize a complete system of public assistance with the abolition of begging. From England was taken the system of poor rates and workhouses; but few of the Revolutionary innovations were put into execution.[3]

[1] Numerous provisions in the capitularies (for example, *Anség.*, 2, 29) and the collections of the acts of the councils (Vienne, 1311). Hospital orders, for example, "Saint Lazare," X, 3, 36, Clem. 3, 11.

[2] Edicts of December, 1543, January, 1545, February, 1546, and especially Ord. Blois, May, 1579. Edict of 1612 on the reformation of the hospitallers. Edict of June, 1662, the Declaration of 1693, 16, 98, the "*Reglement*" of the Council of April 20, 1656, the act of parliament of December 30, 1740, constitute the "code hospitallier" of the old régime, Provisions against mendicants, Ord. February, 1350. Decl. July 18. 1724, Aug. 2, 1764 (confinement in houses of correction and of labor). *A. Monnier*, "Hist. de l'assist. publique," 1866; *D'Avenel*, "Richelieu," 4, 340; "Gr. Encycl.," see "Assistance publique"; *Isambert*, "Table," see "Hôpitaux" and "Méndicité"; *Tollemer*, "Les Origines de la charité catholique," 1863; "R. q. hist.," 63, 98; "Econ. fr.," 21 May, 1898. Code Henry III, I, 29.

[3] Reports of La Rochefoucauld-Liancourt to the constituent assembly. Const. Sept. 3, 1791, I, 25; Decree of March 19, June 24 and 28, 1793; 24 Vend. year II; 22 Flor. year II; 23 Mess. year II; 16 Vend. year V; 7 Frim. year V.

§ 163. **Public Education**[1] began merely as an appendage of religious services and for a long time the school was annexed to the church or the abbey; the clergy alone had the right to teach, and until the end of the "ancien régime" this monopoly had important consequences. The educational organization grew larger and was divided, forming universities, or establishments for higher instruction, and small schools and colleges for what we now call primary and secondary education. The universities acquired a life of their own and passed from under the tutelage of the Church to that of the State. The secularization of the schools proceeded apace, at least from the end of the 1300 s, with the establishment of communal schools.[2] Gradually a large number of communal or royal *collèges* (grammar schools) were established, the personnel being largely ecclesiastic, often even members of some order. As to laymen the bishops conferred upon them and withdrew at will the authority to teach. At Paris the grand precentor of Notre-Dame had the direction of the lower, or grammar schools. Education was not therefore an affair of the State; the State merely exercised a right of police over what it regarded as an ecclesiastical or municipal monopoly. With the Revolution public education, like poor relief, became a national duty; it belonged to the State to instruct its citizens; scientific and teaching orders were suppressed and their property confiscated; primary education was declared to be free and obligatory, and Napoleon I completed the work of the Revolution by creating the University (1806).

TOPIC 4. THE BUDGET OF THE CHURCH

§ 164. **The Tithe;[3] Origin; How the Tithe became Obligatory.** — It was from the Bible that the idea of the tithe was borrowed, for it is well known that the Hebrews were required to give a tenth of their crops to the Levites.[4] Among the early Christians the tithe was merely a voluntary offering, but by the end of the 300 s the custom had become law and the payment was declared to be

[1] *Luchaire*, "Manuel," p. 126; *D'Avenel*, "Richelieu," 4, 166; *Babeau*, "Le village sous l'Ancien Régime," 1879; *Abbé Sicard*, "L'éducation avant la Révolution."

[2] The teacher hired by the municipality received a fixed salary.

[3] *Salvioli*, "Dig. ital.," see "Decime"; *Camus*, "Biblioth.," no. 2939 (Treatises of *Duperray*, *Fréminville*, *de Jouy*, etc.). X, 3, 30, "Sexte," 3, 13; *Clem.*, 3, 8.

[4] Precedents in pagan antiquity. "Dict. des Ant.," of Daremberg, see "Decumæ"; *Viollet*, "Inst.," I, 376; Genesis, xxviii, 22; xiv, 20; Leviticus, xxvii, 30; Deuteronomy, xiv, 22; Exodus, xxii, 29; Numbers, xviii, 21; *Paul*, 1 Cor., ix, 13, 16; Matt., x, 10; Luke, x, 7.

obligatory in conscience.[1] In the 500 s (second council of Mâcon, 585, c. 5) the penalty of excommunication was pronounced against those who refused to pay it. Tithes and first fruits were the share of God; by paying them one drew upon his crops the divine blessing; at the same time one assisted the poor and helped support the clergy. The Carolingians made the payment a civil obligation and organized measures of repression against the refractory: summons, prohibition from entering the church, fines for the benefit of the Church, closing of the house, imprisonment, and fines for the benefit of the State.[2] During the feudal period the most common means of coercion were: excommunication, seizure of property or at least of the crop subject to tithe, fine, and in case of need, extraordinary penalties.[3]

§ 165. **In what the Tithe Consisted.** — We may distinguish: 1st, the **real tithe** or the tithe of the products of the soil. The principle was that the tithe was due on all such products, but local custom often changed it[4] and determined only the quota to be paid (10th, 11th, 12th, 13th, 20th)[5] and the tithable products (great tithe for wheat, cereals, wine, and hay; lesser tithe for vegetables; a slaughter tax for lambs and sucking pigs). Nobles and ecclesiastics owed the tithe from their lands equally with the common classes. It was paid in kind; the tithe gatherer took it the first from the field without deducting the expenses of cultivation and before any claim of the seignior or proprietor was allowed. This privilege was justified by the idea that it was reserved by God as a sign of His universal ownership.[6] 2d, the **personal tithe** was one collected on the products of labor and industry;[7] in the 1700 s it ceased to be enforced.

[1] In the West, but not in the East, where the tithe did not exist. *Origène*, "Homél.," 9; *Saint Augustine*, on the Psalms, 146, 17. "Décret," c. 8, C. XVI, q. 7; c. 26 and 65, C. XVI, q. 1; *Dodu*, "Inst. mon. de Jerusalem," 316 (tithe in Palestine).

[2] Epist. Pipp. to the Bishop Lulle, 755–768; "Cap. Héristal," 779, c. 7; "Sax.," 775–790, c. 17; "Worms," 829, c. 5 and 7, II, 13; *Anségise*, 2, 37; 4, 38. In many places the institution of the tithe met with strong resistance. Thuringia, 1073; England, 835.

[3] *P. Fournier*, "Officialités," p. 102; Ord. Blois, 1579, Art. 49; *Isambert*, "Table," see "Dîmes."

[4] The "Philippine," often cited by the Ordinance of 1303, forbade the levying of unusual tithes. But by this was not meant the "Novales" or tithes on lands newly cleared.

[5] *D'Avenel* estimates the average assessment of the tithe at 4% of the income, remarking, however, that all crops were not subject to it and that this amount was often less than the tenth.

[6] The quota and the method of payment of tithes was prescribed for a period of forty years. The tithes were not permitted to be in arrears, that is to say, they could not be exacted on the crop of a previous year.

[7] "Cap. Sax.," 775–790, I, 90, c. 16. 17. X. 3, 30, 20. Products of theft, of usury, and even of charity.

§ 166. **To what Church was the Tithe Payable?** — Originally the tithe was paid to the bishop, in whose hands were concentrated all the revenues of the diocese. In certain countries he retained all the tithes, but in France they passed to the parish priest, who claimed them by right of his bell tower.[1] Real tithes were paid to the church of the parish in which the lands were situated; personal tithes to the church at which the faithful received the sacraments.

§ 167. **The Great Tithe Owners.** — In the division of the property of the Church, the bishop, the cathedral chapter, and the monastery kept certain tithes by virtue of their character as *original parish priests* and left to the officiating curate only a small portion of their revenues (or paid him an allowance in money hardly sufficient for his maintenance). To remedy this abuse, against which complaints were made as early as the time of Yves of Chartres, the minimum of this part, or suitable allowance, was fixed at 120 livres in 1571, 300 and 150 in 1686, 700 for parish priests and perpetual vicars, and 350 for simple vicars, in 1786.[2]

§ 168. **Enfeoffed Tithes.** — These were met with from the end of the second dynasty and here the abuse was more striking because the ecclesiastical tax was diverted from its destination into secular hands. Many churches had to purchase seignioral protection with their tithes, or submit to usurpations which they were powerless to curb. The Council of the Lateran, in 1179, prohibited for the future these transformations of the revenues of the Church into fiefs, but it succeeded so much the less in preventing them because the origin of enfeoffed tithes was often obscure.[3] Some of them were only feudal dues badly defined and the rights of the seigniors could be defended.

§ 169. **Evaluation of the Tithe.** — The tithe was a tax on income that was payable in kind and that followed the variations of the crop. Vauban regarded it as the most firmly established and the best-collected tax of the "ancien régime" since he wished to substitute a royal tithe in place of the various contributions

[1] "Cap.," 803–4, c. 2, I, 119; "Worms," 829, c. 6, II, 13; *Anségise*, 2, 45. Exception for churches by the king or lords in their lands. "Cap. de villis," c. 6, I, 83; 856, c. 11. Division: "Cap.," 801, c. 7; 803, c. 11; *Ben. Levita*, 3, 375.

[2] *Isambert*, "Table," see "Portion congrue"; *Rousseau de la Combe*, "Jurisp. canon. h. v." The first curés were so called because they had first administered the "curé." The permanent vicars elected by the chapters, scarcely differed from the curés except in name. On the contrary, the simple vicars appointed by the bishop were revocable "ad nutum" as are our curates.

[3] X, 3, 18, 2; 3, 30.

levied at his time for the support of the State. Why, therefore, the unpopularity with which it was regarded? A word of Voltaire explains it: "I pity," said he, "the lot of a country curé who is obliged to dispute with his unhappy parishioner over a sheaf of wheat, to sue him, to demand the tithe of his lentils and his peas." [1] The controversies and legal actions to which the collection of the tithe gave rise led to its abolition in Holland, in parts of Germany, and in the Scandinavian countries. By the tithe commutation act of August 13, 1836, a tax on real estate was substituted in its place in England. In France it was abolished by the Revolution.[2] The present compensation of the priests is uniform (except inequalities resulting from surplice fees, foundations, and property belonging to the rectory); under the "ancien régime" it varied infinitely because it depended upon the extent of the benefices, the rights of the seigniors and of the great tithe owners, upon the number and object of the tithes, and upon the fertility of the lands which were subject to them. In this respect there has certainly been a very useful simplification. But it might be worth while to know what the relation is between the product of the tithe and the present actual budget for religion. The clergy receives to-day about 50 million francs from the State and 22 million from the communes.[3] Vauban, about 1695, estimated the income from tithes at 134 million francs, the same evaluation as in 1789.[4] Without concerning ourselves with the purchasing power of money, which was then greater than now, we see that the clergy was better paid than at present, much more so if we add to this sum the enormous revenues derived from the possessions of the Church.[5]

§ 170. **Oblations and Surplice Fees.** — The practice of making voluntary gifts to the Church did not disappear when the tithe became obligatory; out of it grew the surplice fee. It was simony to demand pay for administering the sacraments, but there was nothing to prevent the clergy from accepting gifts and they

[1] *Voltaire*, "Dict. Philos.," see "Curé de campagne." Vauban says that it did not give rise either to an action or to a complaint. "Sécus," *Champion*, "La France et les Cahiers de 89," p. 182.

[2] The Decree of 17 July, 1793, suppressed all tithes without provisions for indemnity. Previous legislation concerning infeudated tithes had varied: The Decree of Aug. 4, 1789, Art. 5, declared them redeemable. D. Sept. 14–22, 1790, Art. 3; D. Oct. 23; Nov. 5, 1790, v. 5, Art. 14; D. Aug. 25, 1792, Art. 5.

[3] No longer true, of course, since the separation of Church and State in 1905. — Translator.

[4] *D'Avenel*, "Richelieu," 3, 302.

[5] "R. des Deux-Mondes," 1891, 571 (the Tithe in Wales). The amount in England was in the neighborhood of 172 million francs.

ended by being voluntary only in name; the Church rated them as an obligatory contribution, a sort of indirect tax.[1]

§ 171. **The Property of the Church. Constitution of the Ecclesiastical Patrimony.**[2] — The churches received from the Christian Emperors the capacity to acquire estates "inter vivos," or by testament (without authorization or intervention by the State); they were treated like cities or pagan temples. Monasteries and foundations, or charitable institutions (hospitals and orphanages), viewed as organs of the Church, likewise possessed a civil personality. But this personality was recognized as belonging only to each individual church and to each monastery, and not to the Church universal.[3] From that moment possessions flowed toward the clergy: 1st, endowments by the State, with the property of cities and of temples, under the Christian Emperors; the privilege of a manse under the Carolingians;[4] 2d, donations by the French kings so abundant that already the avaricious Chilperic complained that the treasury was being ruined;[5] 3d, donations by wealthy individuals; there was no testament which did not provide a bequest for the salvation of the soul of the testator, or for the redemption of his sins. One compounded with God as with men, some acres of land would appease his wrath[6] and secure for the donor a place in heaven; also the intestate was sometimes assimilated to the condition of a *déconfès* or even to that of a suicide; a will was before all a religious act.[7] 4th, each church inherited

[1] "Const. apost.," 2, 25; *Tertullian*, 39; Ord. Orléans, 1560, 15; Blois, 1579, 51; Edict, April, 1695, 27; Organic articles of 18 Germ., year 10, 68 and 69.

[2] Luke, vi, 38; xviii, 22; John, xii, 6; xiv, 30; Acts, ii, 45; iv, 34; v, 1. At Rome, the Church, which was a sort of funeral college, had a fund for establishing cemeteries. In the 100 s, the Roman church was rich. *P. Fabre*, "De patrim. rom. Eccl.," 1892. Its vast domains were the foundation of the temporal power of the popes (system of the "domuscultæ"). *P. Fournier*, N.R.H., 1897.

[3] Cod. Theod., 16, 2, 4; Cod. Just., 1, 2, 1, 13, 26; Edict of Clothair, 6, 14, c. 10, 13; "Bav.," 1, 1; *Anségise*, 1, 135. *Esmein*, "Mélanges," p. 398; *Geouffre de Lapradelle*, "Fondations perpétuelles," 1895.

[4] "Mansus integer absque omni servitio," to every church. "Cap.," 819, c. 10; *Anségise*, I, 85.

[5] *Pardessus*, "Diplom.," 191, 249, 269, etc., *Gregory of Tours*, 6, 33.

[6] "Dono vobis parva pro magnis, terrena pro cœlestibus." Pious deeds were performed for saints, the patrons of churches, in order to secure their protection, for monks for their prayers, and for the churches for masses. Pretended miracles were the occasions also of large donations. A.S.S., sept II. See *Bertini*.

[7] *Saint Augustine*, "De div. Serm.," 49. The capitularies complain of the avidity of the clergy (811, *supra*, p. 590; 814, 827, c. 7, 8). Charities or pious donations; testamentary executors, "erogatores, eleemosynarii." X, 3, 26. "Etabl. de Saint Louis," I, 93; *Loysel*, 837, 838; *Bourquelot*, BCh., v. IV, "R. h. dr.," 1884, 39.

from its bishop, at least the property that he had acquired during his episcopate; he could leave to his relatives only the family possessions and often he preferred to leave them like a dowry to the Church which he had espoused. The property of the clergy and of monks went also to swell the ecclesiastical patrimony.[1] Already during the Frankish period the bishops and abbots were the greatest landed proprietors in the kingdom; the pope, from the time of Gregory the Great, had acquired extensive possessions in the whole of Italy and even in Sicily.

§ 172. **The Régime to which the Estates of the Church were Subject.** — These estates could not be bequeathed, were inalienable,[2] and were almost imprescriptible by reason of their purpose; they had to be devoted in reality to the maintenance of religious edifices, the needs of the clergy, and the assistance of the poor and the sick. The ecclesiastical budget was at the same time the budget of public assistance; the possessions of the Church were the patrimony of the poor. From the Later Empire a struggle was made to secure the exemption of such property from taxation; the financial system of the Frankish régime rendered the attempt a success and the Church found itself in the enjoyment of a **real immunity.** During the monarchical epoch the claims of the royal power and those of the Church were adjusted by a compromise; the clergy paid the tax under the form of a free gift in order to preserve in appearance their immunity. The administration of the patrimony of each church belonged exclusively to its bishop; of each monastery, to its abbot. It was the custom, in the West only and from the 400 s, to divide the revenues into four parts:[3] one fourth for the bishop, one fourth for the clergy of the diocese, one fourth for the poor (inscribed by the "matricularii"), and one fourth for the maintenance of the Church ("fabrica").[4] From

[1] Council of Carthage, 398, 31; Agde, 506, c. 6. 48; "Cap.," 794, c. 39; Cod. Just., 1, 2, 14; Nov. 131, 13; "Cap.," 810–13, c. 11; "Cap.," 817. Reaction, *Loysel*, 343: Ord. 1386, the ecclesiastics could dispose of all their property. X, 3, 13, 19 and following. "Sexte," 3, 9.

[2] Council of Carthage, 398, c. 31. 32; Agde, 506, c. 7; *Anség.*, 1, 77; 2, 29; *Gratian*, c. 23 and following, and 52, c. 12, q. 2; Nov., 7, 1. 3. 6; 120, 3; Cod. Just., 1, 2, 23; Nov. 9; 111; 131, 6 (Prescription of 100 years, or for 40 years).

[3] *Gélase*, "Ep.," 9, 27 (year 494); "Can. Apost.," 3, 4; *Gratian*, c. 27, c. 12, 2. 2.

[4] The "fabriques" were auxiliaries of the Church and were established at the moment of its greatest development. The expenses of worship (the maintenance of buildings, etc.) were from the first a charge upon the property of the churches, and upon their sole administrator, the bishop. When the property was divided, the curé took the place, in

the end of the 800 s this system was definitely abandoned, ecclesiastical property was divided into as many portions as there were offices, each priest had his special revenue which he used according to his conscience without rendering an account; this revenue, joined to the ecclesiastical function of which it was the endowment, was called a "benefice." It was like the régime of private property substituted for collective ownership; or rather it must be regarded as an application to the Church of the feudal system; the benefice being, in fact, a sort of ecclesiastical fief. The revolution which was thus brought about in the status of the ecclesiastical patrimony came from this; after the invasions a large number of churches, founded by simple individuals, had been regarded as the property of the founders; they had exploited them, somewhat as they exploited the other portions of their domains, by granting them as benefices to priests who "chanted the mass by virtue of the same obligation by reason of which some other beneficiary worked the field, or pruned the vineyards." It was the same even when the proprietor of a church was a monastery instead of a layman or the king.[1] The division of the ecclesiastical patrimony tended also to simplify the administration of the bishop. Even at the seat of the bishopric a distinction was made between the episcopal income and the capitulary income, or property attributed to the canonical chapter, 900 s, and when, in the 1100 s, the canons ceased to live in common, they divided their possessions among them (prebends).[2] Likewise for the property of the monasteries the revenue of the abbey was contradistinguished from the revenue of the convent or the possessions of the monks.

§ 173. **Ecclesiastical Benefices,** such as they appear to us in the decretals of Gregory IX and in the classic doctrine of the

general, of the bishop. The necessary funds were derived in part, from ecclesiastical revenues, in part, from donations made by private individuals, or from contributions of communes; these latter constituted the special funds of the fabric, administered by the curé and by the laymen, "provisores," "vitrici." It was often the custom for the curé to maintain the choir; the tithe owners and the patrons, the nave; and the commune, the clock. *Walter*, § 267; "Cap.," 825, c. 8, I, 327; *Viollet*, "Inst.," II, 327; *Isambert*, "Table," see "Fabrique," "R. q. hist.," 63, 406.

[1] *Gross*, "Recht an Pfründe," 1887; *Stutz*, "Gesch. d. kirchl. Benefizialwesens," 1895; "Die Eigenkirche," 1895; N.R.H., 1897, p. 486 (*P. Fournier:* the appropriation for the churches was generalized at the same time as the appropriation for justice and for taxes, and for the same causes; it was not derived from Germanic usage; there were private churches in the Roman world before the invasions). "Cap.," I, 195, 8; "Cap.," 855, c. 5; "Cap.," 802, c. 19, and 810, I, 1, 95, 207. *Hincmar*, "Collectio de ecclesiis"; in *Gaudenzi*, "Bibl. juris. med. ævi," II, 9.

[2] "Cibi ac potus portiones quæ monachis canonicis præbentur." *Pertz*, II, 55.

canonists, were no longer the private property of a seignior conferred by him upon a priest, but a portion of the patrimony of the Church assigned, in principle, by the bishop. But there remained some characteristics of the Frankish benefice: the right of règalia, the right of patronage, perhaps the parochial right of the parish priest, or the duty of their parishoners to address themselves to their parish priest to the exclusion of all others (*cf.* "banalites"). The irremovability of the holders of benefices, afterwards simple parish priests, was also derived from the benefice; they had their guarantees, and could not be turned out without just cause.[1] Benefices were either secular or regular.

1st, **Secular benefices** (bishoprics, canonries, priories, rectories) had three ordinary collators: the bishops, the chapter of canons, and the patron (who had built, endowed, or founded the Church) according to whether they were dependent upon the episcopal revenue, the revenue of the chapter, or upon the founder. But they were also granted exceptionally: (*a*) by the pope, upon whom the collation of the benefice was devolved by virtue of his character of superior, if the ordinary collator did not exercise his right within six months (**devolution**) and who even dared, by reason of the plenitude of his powers, to take upon himself the presentation by way of priority, without there having been any negligence on the part of the ordinary collator (expectancies, reservations); (*b*) by the king, sometimes in virtue of an **indulgence** or concession of the pope (conveyance of expectancies), sometimes directly, on the occasion of a joyous event or in virtue of the royal prerogative. The Council of Basle reserved, besides, a third of the vacant benefices occurring during the year, to the graduates of the universities.[2]

2d, **Regular benefices** (abbeys, priories, monastic offices, for example, chamberlain, cellarer, etc.). The ordinary collators of regular benefices were the abbots; they were granted by the pope and the king in exceptional cases. The granting of vacant benefices became a veritable traffic although it was prohibited as simony. It was forbidden to the titulary to dispose of them,

[1] *Abbé Mathieu, op cit.*, p. 110: "Feudalism, by giving ecclesiastical property its imprint, communicated to it also its privileges, its tenure, its independence, but also its inequalities and sometimes its injustices. Moreover, it annoyed it often by its violence and always tried to confiscate it for its own use."

[2] The "pays d'obédience" where the concordat did not apply (Britanny, Lorraine, etc.) left to the pope benefices which were vacant for a period of eight months ("months of the pope"). The titularies were designated by examination.

but change of title having been admitted, renunciation for the benefit of third parties was tolerated as was resignation "in favorem" by means of a money payment; and saving the presentor a power which he rarely used, of rejecting undeserving persons. In the 1400 s this practice was general and had its counterpart in the venality of public offices. This was not the only abuse from which the Church suffered. The scandalous cumulation of benefices was prohibited in vain by the councils of the Church (*e.g.* the Lateran, 1179).[1] Abbeys were given in "commendam," that is to say, into their keeping, to bishops, to priests, or even to laymen who, at first, were simply charged with administering them while they were vacant and awaiting the appointment of a titulary. The abuse dated from the time of the Carolingians. Some abbeys were possessed by laymen, by children, and by Protestants. The commendatory abbot had as few friars as possible and gave them barely enough to live on. The "commendam" resulted, like the cumulation of benefices, in the diversion of the possessions of the Church from their true use. If the higher clergy was very wealthy numbers of churches and monasteries were miserably poor.

§ 174. **Ecclesiastical Possessions and the Feudal Law.** — The acquisition of feudal estates (fiefs and manors) by the Church was very prejudicial to the seigniors because it deprived them of the transmission fees "inter vivos," or at death, which laymen paid. The Church was likewise little fitted to render feudal duties. From this arose the very old disfavor with which acquisitions for the benefit of persons in mortmain (churches, religious communities) were regarded.[2] The suzerain could compel the Church to dispossess itself of its lands in a year and a day,[3] but he did not always exercise this right. The Church paid him a sum of money or redemption fee in consideration of which the suzerain would renounce his right of dispossession; sometimes it assigned to

[1] Under the second dynasty, Theodulf, bishop of Orléans, was abbot of Saint-Aignan; Anségise, of three abbeys, etc.

[2] "Mortua manus" ("manus" in the sense of power; "mortua," without strength, incapable of disposing). "Cap. Worms," c. 5, II, 15; "Cap.," 865, c. 6.

[3] "Coutume de Toulouse," 144, c. Must we see in this only a comminatory disposition? In fact, yes, without doubt. In law, no; for in law the seignior could oppose every alienation which was prejudicial to him. "Et. de Saint Louis," I, 129; *Beaum.*, 12, 5; "Sexte," 3. 23, 1; *Viollet*, II, 406 (countries where all acquisitions of immovable property by the Church were forbidden: Portugal, Bohemia, Strasbourg, etc.). *P. Meyer*, "Textes bas-latins," 1874, p. 174; *Bladé*, "Cout. du Gers," p. 49; *Britz*, "Anc. dr. belg.," I, 122.

"a living and a dying man" who represented it; at the death of this man the Church was obliged to pay "relief," or the customary fee for change of ownership (mutation fee). It was not always sufficient for the Church to deal with the immediate seignior; the superior seigniors often complained of these acquisitions and, under pretext that there had been an "abridgment" of the fief, that is to say, an infringement of their rights, seized the legacies which had been left to the Church. The Church was obliged to pay a second time or surrender its lands within the year. Logically, it would have been necessary to redeem the lands from seignior to seignior up to the highest and even to the king himself when the king was regarded as the supreme suzerain. So extended, the price of redemption would have been a ruinous tax for the Church. Philip the Bold, by the ordinance of 1275, decreed that if three successive payments had been made, without counting that which had been paid to the alienator, the property should be definitely redeemed; at the same time he reserved to the barons, who had always possessed it, the right of redemption. Aside from these two cases and except in case of prescription for thirty years, it was necessary to pay to the king the revenues for two or three years from the property acquired; thus was established the principle of the 1300 s: "to the king alone and for the whole belonged the right of redemption throughout all the kingdom." Gradually the payment ceased to be made to the seigniors intermediate between the alienator and the king. The seignioral right of redemption was transformed into a domainal fee; it was applied even to freehold estates, and the jurisconsults of the monarchical epoch maintained in principle that religious establishments were incapable of acquiring real property.[1]

§ 175. **Ecclesiastical Estates and the Monarchy.** — As the Church acquired property without ceasing and never alienated it,

[1] "Amortissement" appeared as early as the 1000 s, *Mabille*, "Cartul. de Marmontiers," no. 621, but was not general until the 1200 s. *Du Cange*, see "Amortizatio." *Isambert*, Table, see "Amortissement"; *Laurière*, "Orig. du dr. d'amort.," 1692; Bacquet and the jurisconsults who have written of the domainal laws. *H. de Pansey*, "Diss. féod.," 1789; *Chénon*, "Alleux," 69 and following; *Viollet*, II, 408 (and a manuscript treaty of the 1400 s which he cites); *Cauwès*, "Gr. Encycl.," see "Amortissement"; *Langlois*, "Philippe le Hardi," 206, 235. If the heritage had not been redeemed, the holders were subject to the tax called "nouveaux acquêts" (new acquisitions) which was renewed from time to time as a penalty for having acquired property contrary to the laws (for the possession which they had had of the inheritance to the time of redemption). "Instr.," May 8, 1372, Art. 11; *Isambert*, 5, 372; "Table," see "Mainmorte." "Olim," II, 108, 32; Ord. I, 303. Lett., Oct., 1402: the fee was one third of the value of the fief redeemed. *Mesdach de Ter Kiele*, "Du dr. d'amortisation," 1890.

it was feared that all the land would gradually pass into its hands. In the Middle Ages, when land constituted the principal source of wealth, the danger was not chimerical. Under the first dynasty the kings were not far from regarding the lands of the Church, which, for the most part, were derived from their liberality, as half belonging to themselves. So, Charles Martel, in obedience to military necessity, did not scruple to secularize ecclesiastical estates.[1] Even the institution of tithes did not escape infeudation. From time to time the idea of expropriating the lands of the Church for the benefit of the State was broached (Arnaud of Brescia, 1100 s; P. Dubois, about 1307;[2] Wycliff, 1300 s; and John Huss, 1400 s). In the Estates of 1560 such a proposition was made and L'Hôpital, in 1563, appropriated the income of the Church to the extent of 100,000 "écus" [an obsolete French coin]. Louis XIV in his memoirs affirmed the right of the State to do this; and, finally, in August, 1749, the edict relating to lands in mortmain concerned at the same time with the interests of families who had been too easily despoiled of their possessions and with the interest of the State which suffered from the withdrawal of too much property from commerce, prohibited all acquisition of real estate by religious establishments without the authorization of the State, if it was by act "inter vivos"; and if it was by testament the prohibition was absolute.[3] In 1764, at the time of the suppression of the Order of Jesuits, its possessions were sold for the benefit of the State.

§ 176. **Real Immunity.** — We understand by real immunity the exemption of the property of the Church from taxation. From Roman times the tendency had been in this direction, for it was exempt from the "munera" for the public services, though not

[1] *Cf.* "Synod. ad Theod.," 844, c. 3-5; "Cap.," II, 114; 385; 387. It is not necessary to believe that these measures were general and systematic; using a right which the Merovingian kings had exercised, the mayor of the palace took a part of the ecclesiastical domains. Louis the Debonair, "Cap.," 818-819, c. 1, I, 276, promised to no longer interfere with the property of the Church. *Pertz*, "Dipl.," I, 28.

[2] "De recuperatione terræ sanctæ," ed. *Langlois*, p. 35. "Dubois," says M. Langlois in his Introduction, "was a man devoid of criticism and of prejudices; he proposed the most radical measures: suppression of the temporal power of the popes, confiscation of the property of the churches and convents, international arbitration to assure perpetual peace, the putting of the United States of Europe under the suzerainty of the king of France, suppression of ecclesiastical celibacy, 'lycées' (schools) for young girls where medicine was taught, etc."

[3] The edict recalled that it was necessary to have authority from the king in order to found monasteries. Decl., 21, Nov., 1629; June, 1659; Dec., 1666. *Tardif*, "R. d. lég.," 1872, 492; *Bourgain*, "Et. s. les biens ecclés.," 1890.

from the "capitatio terrena." Under the first two dynasties exemptions and the assignments of taxes for the benefit of the churches and abbeys were multiplied; the "mansus integer" assigned by Charlemagne to every Church was exempt from public or private charges. The feudal Church declared its property to be exempt from taxation; the theologians found no difficulty in justifying this privilege on the theory that what was given by one hand to the Church for the support of worship or for the benefit of the poor ought not to be taken away by the other. Nevertheless, the right of regalia gave to the king and the seigniors the income from vacant benefices. The political revolution which restored the central authority brought about the reappearance of taxes. Should the possessions of the clergy escape?[1] The pope, who exacted a tenth for himself, was in a bad position to object if the State did the same thing. Nevertheless, he encouraged the clergy to resist (Boniface VIII and Philip III the Fair) and they succeeded in securing exemption from the royal "taille" (poll tax);[2] and as regards the subsidies and the tax on salt ("gabelle") the ecclesiastics were better treated than the laymen. Finally, in 1560, threatened with spoliation, the clergy agreed to contribute to the support of the State, but, in order to save appearances or to bring about a return to their former immunity, they reserved the right to vote their contribution and it was called a free gift. It is, therefore, not exact to say that the people contributed of their property, the nobility of their blood, and the clergy of their prayers to the needs of the State. But the burden of the clergy was much less heavy than that of the Third Estate.

§ 177. **The Regalia**[3] was the right of the king, during the vacancy of a bishopric, to receive its revenues and to make appointments to the benefices which were dependent upon it (from the 1100s). Notwithstanding its name, the right belonged also to others than the king, as certain seigniors also enjoyed it. It appeared under

[1] Lateran, 1179 and 1215. X, 3, 49, 4 and 7. Every assessment on the clergy was prohibited without their consent and that of the pope; this had the effect of diverting the patrimony of the Church from its true purpose. The first "decimes" (tenth of a franc) had a religious purpose. "R. q. hist.," 1890, p. 62.

[2] Ecclesiastics were exempt from the personal taille. In countries where the real taille was levied (Provence, Dauphiné, Languedoc) the property of the Church only was exempt from the tax, but not the property of ecclesiastics.

[3] *Viollet*, "Inst.," I, 370, 5 ("regalia"); II, 345. The "regalia" or "régales" comprised the entire temporalty of the bishop, landed property, and seigniorial dues which were attached to it. Ord. 1334, II, 102.

the second dynasty in the form of a guardianship of vacant bishoprics by the public authorities for police purposes,[1] and its extension was justified by the origin of ecclesiastical property, most of which came from the king. It is singular that it disappeared as early as the 1300s for the monasteries.[2] The bishoprics of the South had never been subject to this régime; royal officers as early as the 1200s attempted to extend it, and, under Louis XIV, two prelates only, the bishops of Pamiers and of Alet, dared resist the edicts of 1673 and 1675 which made the right general.[3]

§ 178. **Ecclesiastical Tithes. Free Gifts.** — From the time of the Saladin tithe levied by Philip Augustus to meet the expenses of the crusades, the clergy often paid to the State a tenth of their revenue ("décimes," tenths). The papacy was consulted at first and gave its consent, as did the clergy. From the time of Philip the Fair, the authorization of the Holy See was often dispensed with. Tithes were granted to the king repeatedly, but the contribution of the clergy became permanent only in the 1500s when the assembly of the clergy, held at Poissy (1561), promised to the king, for six years, an annual sum of 1,600,000 livres. The contract was renewed every ten years and the clergy engaged to pay in the place of the *décimes* the sum promised once, and afterward free gifts. In the main, it was the king who fixed the amount of the contribution to be paid by the clergy and almost in arbitrary fashion.[4] But the clergy had three privileges: 1st, on the occasion of making free gifts its assemblies were called together every ten years, thus forming a real ecclesiastical parliament in which the

[1] "Cap. Kiersy," 877, c. 8; *Hincmar*, in *Migne*, "Patr. l.," I, 1123.

[2] *Cf. D. Vaissete*, 6, 880; 5, 1443; *Boutaric*, "Alf. de Poitiers," p. 460; *A. Maury*, "Assembl. du clergé" ("R. des Deux-Mondes"), Aug. 1, 1880; *D'Avenel*, "Richelieu," III, 298 (holds that the rule imported nothing). *Isambert*, "Table," see "Régale." Edict Jan. 14, 1682; Ord. Feb. 1303 (I, 402), Art. 18. Ancient literature on this subject is very rich. *Le Vayer de Boutigny*, "Diss. sur . . . la régale," 1682; *Phillips*, "Das Regalienrecht in Frankreich," 1873; *Fouchier*, "Hist. du dr. de Régale," 1893; *P. Desjardins*, "Etudes relig.," v. 45, 481; v. 46, 65; July, 1889, 507.

[3] The right of spoliation ("jus spolii") was the right to plunder the house of the bishop who had just died (perhaps by virtue of the right of patronage). It appeared at the time of the Merovingian bishops, was abolished in the 1000s and 1100s, and in the 1400s was reëstablished under a less brutal form as one of the sources of income to the papacy. *Luchaire*, "Actes de Louis VII," nos. 119, 222; Council of Chalcedon, c. 22; Lateran, 1139, c. 5; Ord. XVI, 217; *Viollet*, II, 350; *D. Vaissete*, 5, 685 and 1025.

[4] In 1641, Richelieu forced the assembly of the clergy to promise him 2 millions. The archbishop of Toulouse, Montchal, asserted that a horrible sacrilege had been committed; the new tax would put an end, he said, to more than 100,000 masses per day; Calvin heresy did not bring so much injury to souls in purgatory.

clergy, in their several grades, were represented by means of election, and at which their deputies could deliberate upon the interests of their body and formulate their grievances; 2d, these assemblies gave their consent to and voted the tax; 3d, the apportionment, the collection, and the decision of controversies relative to the tax were left to the Church; the assembly appointed receivers; contests were submitted to the diocesan bureaus, to general bureaus, or sovereign chambers; and every five years a petty assembly, a sort of commission of the general assembly, met to receive the reports of the general agents. The treasury of the clergy was rich enough to lend to the State. The administration of ecclesiastical finances was good; the apportionment alone left anything to be desired since it allowed inequalities to creep in to the detriment of the lower clergy.[1]

§ 179. **The Law of the Revolution. Conversion of Ecclesiastical Property into National Property.** — The bad condition of the public finances in 1789 led to a movement for the seizure of the property of the Church. Upon the proposition of Talleyrand the constituent assembly took the matter into consideration; the cause of the Church was defended by the Abbé Maury and combatted by Theuret, Le Chapelier, and Mirabeau. The measure was one of delicate application; fears were expressed of jobbing, of the sale at a low price of property thrown en masse upon the market, of the ruin of credit. The Abbé Maury went so far as to speak of a great conspiracy of Jews who wished to acquire at the same time the rights of citizens and the property of the Church; but the discussion turned principally on the legality of the operation. The partisans of the clergy maintained that the right of property was as sacred for the Church as for individuals, and even more so, since its estates were the patrimony of the poor. The answer made to this was that the State bore the expense of public services (worship, salaries of the clergy, and the relief of the sick and the poor) which the Church conducted very badly;[2]

[1] The foreign clergy, that is to say, the clergy of the provinces recently united to the crown (Alsace, Roussillon, Artois, etc.), were exempt from the "taille," but paid the twentieth and the capitation tax; they did not attend the assembly and did not vote free gifts. "Collection des procès-verbaux des Ass. génér. du clergé de France," 1767–80.

[2] The Church was the first to divert its property from its true purpose; in place of being devoted to the relief of the poor, ecclesiastical revenues too often served the pleasures of worldly men like the spiritual Boufflers, the abbé-commandant of Belchamp, or of worldly prelates, like the cardinal of Rohan. The abuse that it had made of its property put it in a very bad position for defense against the State. It was ludicrous to refuse to the latter for public services, what it had the weakness to accord

the nation, on that account, had the right to dispossess the clergy; their estates would pass into other hands but without changing their destination. The clergy as a political order had ceased to exist; if its property were left to it, it would retain its influence and would constitute, as in the past, a body within the State.[1] The ecclesiastical estates were accordingly put at the disposition of the nation and they constituted about one fifth of the land of France. Treilhard, in 1789, estimated the income at 120,000,000 francs; Necker estimated the capital at 4,000,000,000 francs.[2]

Topic 5. Ecclesiastical Justice

§ 180. **Ecclesiastical Jurisdiction.**[3] **Origin.**[4] — Like an ordinary society, the Church having its own laws must have a system of justice in order to make them respected. It was by this means that it maintained internal discipline; thus it imposed penances upon believers[5] and even went so far as to excommunicate them. The **jurisdiction** of the Church in spiritual matters (faith, discipline) is necessary to its existence; it is legitimate and it will last as long as the Church exists; but as the spiritual and the temporal are so closely united it is often difficult to separate them. The Church during the days of its power drew to itself, under the pretext that religious questions were involved in them, a large number of

to an abbé of the court for complimentary fêtes. Other complaints against its proprietorship were that its possessions were withdrawn from trade (mortmain) and they escaped taxation. Reasons of a religious order on which this ownership was based had been shaken by the philosophers.

[1] *Cf.* the Italian law of July 17, 1890, concerning charitable works. *Vauthier*, "Personnes morales," p. 150.

[2] A precise evaluation is almost impossible. *Cf.* ecclesiastical registers of benefices or other statistical documents. *Taine*, "L'Ancien Régime," p. 530; *D'Avenel*, "Richelieu," 3, 278. According to the latter, the net revenue amounted to 120 millions. To this should be added 123 millions of "dîmes" and approximately 100 millions that the ecclesiastics would have received as feudal lords, and we shall then have some idea of the wealth of the Church. The properties of the Church yielded less than other property, for leases were terminated by the death of the lessor. *Cf. Pelletier*, "Recueil des bénéfices de France en 1690." "Add.: Almanach royal, France ecclésiastique," etc.

[3] *Fleury*, "Inst. du dr. ecclésiast."; *Beauchet*, "Hist. de l'org. jud.," p. 87, 354; *Loening*, "Gesch. d. d. Kirch.," 1878; *Nissl.*, "Gerichtst. d. Clerus i. fr. R.," 1886; *Salvioli*, "La Giurisd. d. Chiesa," 1884; *Flach*, "Orig. de l'anc. France," I, 295; *P. Fournier*, "Les Officialités," 1880; *Viollet*, in the "Encycl. des sc. relig." of *Lichtenberger*, 7, 630, *Camus*, no. 2660, X, "Sexte," Clem., 2, 1 and following, *Dodu*, 325.

[4] *Beauchet*, N.R.H., 1883, 387.

[5] Indulgences or remissions of canonical penalties in favor of pious works, as alms. On occasions of jubilees: plenary indulgences were granted to all the repentant faithful (Boniface VIII). *Friedberg*, § 136; *Hinschius*, § 203; *Walter*, § 287.

secular lawsuits; it acquired a temporal jurisdiction which, during the Middle Ages, rivaled that of the secular tribunals. This abnormal jurisdiction had already made its appearance in pagan Rome; following the counsel of Saint Paul[1] and fearing the judges who persecuted them, the believers (the faithful) had chosen the bishops to act as arbitrators for the settlement of disputes arising among themselves.[2] Under the Christian Emperors the bishops held a public "audientia" in which they exercised a sort of patriarchal jurisdiction; they sat surrounded by their clergy; the parties appeared in person before them; the procedure was limited to oral explanations; the cases were examined simply and with good faith, without strict adherence to the law, and an especial effort was made to conciliate the parties. The bishop therefore had always appeared in his original rôle as arbiter,[3] but he was an arbiter much occupied, a quasi-official, designated in particular to hear cases between clerks because the Church councils made it the duty of the latter not to have recourse to the secular tribunals.[4] Did not the bishop therefore become a real judge? In civil matters the first constitution of Sirmond,[5]

[1] *Paul*, 1 Cor., vi, 1 and following. "Const. Apost.," 2, 43. *Cf.* Decretal of *Gratian*, C. XI. 1. c. 7. (*Hinschius*, "Decret. Pseudo-Isid.," p. 221).

[2] Same custom among the Jews. Cod. Theod., 2, 1, 10.

[3] Ordinary jurisdiction was imposed on the parties; arbitral jurisdiction implied an agreement of the two parties to submit their differences to an arbitrator chosen by them. This arbitrator was not obliged to follow strictly the law, for he was an equity judge. As the parties had agreed in advance to be bound by his sentence, there was no possible appeal; finally, since the arbitrator was only a private individual, his sentence was not enforceable. The condemned party was liable for damages or for a pecuniary penalty stipulated in the arbitral agreement.

[4] "Counc. Chalcedon," 451, c. 9. The Nov. *Valentinian III*, v. 34, year 452, required a "compromise"; the "interpretatio" states that it was repealed.

[5] It enacted that every action might be brought before the tribunal of the bishop if one of the parties so requested, notwithstanding the opposition of the other (it was then no longer a question of arbitral justice); the ordinary judges could renounce jurisdiction even if they had already begun to pronounce sentence. This rule was in opposition to the subsequent law; it may be said that the successors of Constantine ignored it; they decided that the bishop was competent only if the two parties agreed to appear before him. It would have been singular if they had withdrawn such an important privilege from the Church without a trace of it being left in subsequent documents. Likewise was there not often seen in this constitution a false document made to justify ecclesiastical jurisdiction, and which the compiler of the False Capitularies did not fail to take advantage of? *Godefroy*, "Com. sur le t. de episcop. jud. Cod. Théod.," remarks that it was not dated and that it did not figure either in the Justinian Code or in the Breviary of Alaric. *Haenel*, in the Introduction to his edition of the "Const. de Sirmond," defends its authenticity. There is an eighteenth century manuscript of it, and *Eusèbe*, "Vit. Const.," 10, 27, makes allusion to it. *Krüger*, "Hist. des sources du dr. rom.," French translation, p. 393, and the authors cited. *Cf.*

attributed to Constantine (331?) appears to have so regarded him. But if this constitution must be considered as authentic, it remained in force only a short time and consequently it has little interest for us. In **criminal matters** the bishops were judged only by bishops [1] and it is probable that petty offenses and simple disciplinary faults of the clergy belonged exclusively to the ecclesiastical tribunals,[2] although grave offenses were within the competence of the tribunals of the State.[3]

§ 181. **Composition of the Ecclesiastical Tribunals.** — During the Frankish period the bishops (or the abbots who were assimilated with them as the monks were assimilated with the clergy) became real judges, either by virtue of royal concessions, or as a result of usurpations sanctioned by usage.[4] The judicial authority being derived from the sacerdotal authority, resided, like the latter, in the person of the bishop; the custom of calling for assistance from the clergy did not become a rule of law. The bishop being unable to discharge all the multifarious duties which devolved upon him was often under the necessity of delegating certain of his judicial functions to the archdeacon;[5] this dignitary in the end became irremovable and no longer judged in the name of the bishop but in his own name (Carolingian epoch), and after the fashion of counts who became feudal lords and independent of the king; he left to the bishop only cases of especial importance. During the 1100s archdeacons and bishops wrangled in regard to their jurisdiction; the latter got the better of it and, in order to make sure of not having rivals in those who judged in their place, they selected them from among humble employees, "officiales." The one who was charged with the functions of judge, the "official," as he was customarily called, was a deputy, removable "ad nutum," [6] without ecclesiastical title, and chosen by reason of his knowledge of canon and of Roman law. [7] Hence the name "officialités" given to the ecclesiastical tribunals. In fact,

"Const. of Sirmond," 17 (Cod. Theod., 27, 1, 1, year 318, 321); Cod. Just., 1, 4, 7 (year 398); 8 (year 408) Nov. *Valent. III* (452), 34, pr. § 2; Nov. *Justinian*, 79, 83, 123; *Schulte*, "Constitutio Constantini ad Ablavium," 1888. The emperors had accorded a real jurisdiction to the Jewish patriarchs. *Matthias*, "Festschr. f. Windscheid," 1888, 132.

[1] Cod. Theod., 16, 2, 12 (year 355); 23 (year 372).

[2] "Const. of Sirmond," 15 (year 412). Cod. Just., 1, 2, 12.

[3] "Lex. Rom. Wis."; Cod. Theod., 16, 1, 3; Nov. *Valent. III*, N.R.H., 1889, 310. [4] "Capitulary," 782–6, c. 6, I, 192 (Italy).

[5] The archpriest also acquired a jurisdiction which the councils of the 1200 s restricted to unimportant cases.

[6] Only if there was a just cause, in the 1600 s.

[7] The principal official and an itinerant official. Vicars-general with clemency jurisdiction, 1400 s. X, 1, 23, "Sexte," I, 14; Clem., 1, 8.

therefore, the division of labor had done its work and had substituted for the bishop a man learned in the law. This was a guarantee for the clergy, since their judge was no longer at the same time their master. In law, since the "official" was a simple deputy, the bishops had maintained (as against the Parliaments) that they might act as judges in his place, reserve certain cases for themselves or delegate them to others. As in the case of the secular tribunals, the "official" was assisted by a certain number of auxiliaries: assessors with a purely consultative voice, sealers, recorders or notaries,[1] "procurators," and especially a "promoter" (1300s), who represented the bishop in a permanent manner, accused criminals, and corresponded, therefore, to our public prosecutors, advocates, apparitors, and beadles or sheriffs. In contradistinction to the ordinary judge, who was the official principal, the Church had extraordinary judges or delegate judges, such as the papal legates, and the inquisitors of the faith. From the principal official no appeal lay to the bishop, since the official judged in his name and was his representative, but an appeal might be taken to the metropolitan and from him to the pope.[2] There was even a possibility of direct appeal to the pope, "omisso medio," and this practice which the Parliaments considered contrary to the liberties of the Gallican Church caused the jurisdiction of the metropolitan and of the provincial councils to lose much of their importance.[3]

§ 182. **Competence of the Ecclesiastical Tribunals.** (A.) *Ratione personæ.* — 1st, clergy (or monks). The Church councils forbade the clergy to bring their cases before the secular judges; in the 500s and 600s they threatened with excommunication the secular judges who took jurisdiction of cases, in which the clergy were parties, without having referred them to the bishops.[4] How did the secular authorities come to adopt these rules? The texts are obscure and are disputed. The edict of Clothair II in 614 appears to have attributed exclusive jurisdiction to the bishop

[1] In the 1300 s and 1400 s the notaries of the "officialités" were both apostolic and imperial, that is to say, they were invested with their office by both the pope and the emperor, and, consequently, were authorized to exercise in all places the jurisdiction of the pope and that of the emperor which extended everywhere.

[2] Concerning justice in the court of Rome, *cf. Fabre, Goyau,* and *Pératé,* "Le Vatican," 1897.

[3] These appeals were suspensive (false decretals) and the pope was the exclusive judge of the major cases of the bishops. X, 1, 7, 2 (Innocent III). *Beaumanoir,* 61, 65, *cf. Glasson,* "Hist. des Inst. de l'Anglet.," IV, 386; V, 131.

[4] "Orléans," 541, c. 20; "Macon," 585, c. 10; "Paris," 614, c. 4.

over crimes committed by priests and deacons, and to the civil judges, those committed by the inferior clergy in case the offense was flagrant or confession was made; otherwise the civil judge could not act without having referred it to the bishop with whom it was optional to smother the affair at that point.[1] "A fortiori," it was the same for all "causæ minores." Concerning actions affecting real estate and condition (liberty, family), the edict was silent; but they were regarded as "causæ majores" and under this head they were no doubt reserved for the civil tribunals.[2] Bishops accused of crime were, in principle, taken before a council and, if they were adjudged guilty, punished by the king.[3] Under the Carolingians the same principles prevailed, with an extension of the powers of the Church. The bishops judged simply the "causæ minores" of the clergy. For grave offenses which could not be suppressed by means of canonical penalties the ordinary judges lent to the ecclesiastical sentences the support of the secular arm; they inflicted upon the guilty cleric the chastisements pronounced by the laws of the State.[4] In civil matters the bishop was competent unless it was a question involving real estate or status; in this case the clergy were represented before the secular tribunal.[5] If a case arose between a layman and an ecclesiastic the bishop had the right to take part in the proceeding before the count.[6] During the feudal period the privilege of the forum was fully recognized;[7] the clergy, that is to say, all those who had

[1] Was his sentence obligatory upon the secular judge? This question is controverted.

[2] The "civiles causæ" of the edict were secular affairs in contradistinction to ecclesiastical affairs. Cod. Theod., 16, 2, 23. Criminal and civil jurisdiction were not distinguished one from the other at that period as they are to-day. Concerning the various interpretations of this edict, *cf. Beauchet*, p. 90.

[3] *Cf.* Nov. Just., 83, pr. § 2, 123, c. 8, 21 (known in Spain before 600). *Viollet*, "Inst.," II, 395.

[4] "Cap.," 789, c. 28, 38, I, 56 (*Anség.*, I, 38); 755, c. 18; 769, c. 17, I, 36, 46. *Hincmar*, "de preb. crimin." (*Migne*, "Patr. l."), I, 1093. *Caillemer*, "Florus et Moduin," 1882.

[5] *Viollet*, "Inst.," I, 398; *Esmein*, N.R.H., 1887, 401. "Cap. Mantoue," 787, c. 1, I, 196. Preliminary to conciliation before the bishop for actions relating to real estate. *Hincmar*, *Migne*, "Patr. l." vol. 125, p. 1047. "Lex Rom. Cur.," 16, 1, 3.

[6] The layman was not obliged at first to go before the bishop. Nov. *Valent.* III, 34, 1; Cod. Just., 1, 3, 25; 1, 4, 13; Council of Agde, 506, c. 32. Justinian desired that the bishop should decide, subject to the right of appeal to the civil judge. Nov. 79, 1, and 123, 21. "Cap.," c. 30, I, 77. *Cf. Hincmar*, "Quales jud. const. deb. ad caus. inter eccles. et sæc. dirim." *Viollet*, I, 398.

[7] Already the same in *Hincmar*, "ad Carol. Calv.," *Migne*, "Patr. l.," 125, 1047. Decretal of Gratian, II, c. 11, q. 1. Decretals, 2, 2, "de foro compentente." *Beaumanoir*, 43, 13. Ord. I, 39. 340. 402. *Isambert*, "Table," see "Justice ecclésiastique."

the tonsure and wore the clerical garb were amenable only to the ecclesiastical tribunals, save for the fiefs which they held.[1] There were even laymen who were assimilated to them and who might claim that they belonged to the courts of the Church. Such were crusaders,[2] students,[3] and "miserabiles personæ" (widows and orphans).[4]

(B.) *Ratione materiæ.* — Spiritual cases between all persons, clergy, and laity alike, were within the competence of the Church tribunals and, as a consequence, temporal cases which were accessory to or dependent upon them. Thus the courts of the Church had exclusive jurisdiction (about the 900 s) in cases involving the following matters: (*a*) sacramental matters and particularly matrimonial cases,[5] such as obstacles to marriage, separate maintenance, legitimacy of children, and civil status; (*b*) suits involving tithes and ecclesiastical benefices. The parties had an option between the ecclesiastical jurisdiction and the secular jurisdiction in: (*a*) cases involving wills (alms or pious legacies);[6] and (*b*) promises made under oath. The ecclesiastical tribunals became also competent in case of negligence on the part of the secular judge or in pursuance of agreements between the parties. Some went so far as to say that the ecclesiastical tribunals were the natural judges in all actions, since every suit supposed a sin, or an injustice committed by one of the parties. For the trial of criminal cases the bishops traveled on circuit throughout their dioceses from the 800 s to the 1000 s, holding genuine assizes, and, with the aid of the count, repressing notorious crimes.[7] Afterwards, the ecclesiastical judges were alone authorized to pronounce judgment in the case of crimes against God and the

[1] *Brussel*, "Us. des fiefs," II, 27. *Isambert*, see 481 and following. Same if they had a suit with a layman. *Beaumanoir*, 43, 13. Exceptions: 1st, Flagrant offenses; the secular judge could arrest a clerk taken in the act, to prevent him from escaping, but he was required to turn him over to the "official"; 2d, atrocious crimes, involving the degradation of the clerk; 3d, unworthy clerks (usurers, merchants, bigamists, that is to say, persons married the second time, or to widows). Ord. 1302, Art. 1; Ord. I, 39, Art. 2.

[2] Ordinance of Philip Augustus I, 34, Art. 6, 7; 1188, XI, 255; 1303, Art. 11, I, 399. "Etabl. de saint Louis," I, 89. [3] Ord. I, 21, Art. 7.

[4] *Beaumanoir*, 43, 14; *cf.* c. 11, "Des Cours d'Eglise."

[5] *Ibid.*, 11, 3; *Beungot*, 2, 121; *Esmein*, "Le Mariage."

[6] Because of the connection between the testament and the last sacraments, to die unconfessed and to die intestate were often regarded as the same thing. *Beaumanoir*, 11, 10, 12, 60; "Grand Cout.," p. 615. "Des Mares," 68, 69, "Britanny," 614. *Cf.* Decree of Parliament of 1376, cited by *Viollet*, "Inst.," II, 309. In England until 1857, testaments were submitted to the Church judges.

[7] *Viollet*, I, 391; II, 307; "L. Delisle," "Cond. de la cl. agr. en Norm.," p. 118.

faith [1] (sacrilege, heresy, sorcery, blasphemy, etc.); but the guilty party sentenced by them was delivered to the secular arm.[2] It was by this means that the gravest sentences of these tribunals were executed. Spiritual punishments, monition followed by excommunication,[3] served also frequently to compel respect for them. Direct execution by the beadles of the officialities was even practiced;[4] but in France, ordinarily, the ecclesiastical judge was denied all jurisdiction over the temporal property of the laity. The secular power dealt rigorously by different means with recalcitrant excommunicants: exile and imprisonment according to the capitularies, confiscation of property according to the statutes of Saint Louis.[5] This was onerous assistance for

[1] General texts: "Capitulary," 801–813, c. 1, I, 170; 846, c. 6, II, 66. Incest, adultery, and other crimes were punished by both the civil and ecclesiastical law. "Capitulary," 743, c. 3; 779, c. 5, 758–768, c. 1; 802, c. 33 (I, 28. 48. 40. 97). Suits against sorcerers (Basque sorcerers in 1609, etc.; and the books of *De Lancre*, *Leloyer*, *Sprenger*, etc.). *Ferrière*, "Dict.," see "Sortilège," "Maléfice," "Magie." *Beaumanoir*, 11, 25; c. 68, of usurers, *Langlois*, "Phil. III," 269.

[2] *Beaumanoir*, 11, 2, Edition of Feb., 1580; Sept., 1610; *Isambert*, XIV, 471; XVI, 10.

[3] Excommunication or exclusion from the Church in ancient law, Matt. xviii, 17; *Paul*, 1 Cor., v, 11; 2 Thess., iii, 14. "Const. apost.," 8, 4, had to be changed when there were only Christians. The Middle Ages distinguished two degrees of excommunication: 1st, the *minor*, involving deprivation of the sacraments; 2d, *major*, or anathema, which involved interdiction of all intercourse with the faithful. ("Os," "orare," "vale," "communio," "mensa negatur"), the wickedness of an excommunicated offender spread like that of a leper, to those who approached him, even to his wife and children; access to the courts was forbidden him; he could not act as a witness or exercise any right; and excommunicated sovereigns lost their authority. Sometimes this penalty was incurred in full right, sometimes it was pronounced by the ecclesiastical judge after several warnings. Concerning the ceremonial, *cf. Réginon*, II, 431. "Pontif roman.," 1, 344 (ed. Rome, 1752); *D. Martène*, "De antiq. eccl. rit.," *Gratian*, 2, 11, 3. Decretals, 5, 39; *Isambert*, 2, 797. Early constitutions: *Martin V*, 1418, and of our time, *Pius IX*, 1869. The Church abused its power of excommunication ("quasi omnes sunt ligati," it was said in the time of Saint Louis) to such an extent that this punishment, terrible at first, lost all efficacy. The secular power refused to proceed against an excommunicated offender. The interdict was employed from the 1000s against seigniors who defied excommunication; the clergy rebelled and refused to administer sacraments to the full in their domains. *Friedberg*, § 104; *Viollet*, II, 297. On these abuses, *cf. Vaissete*, VIII, 1470, 1419. Excommunication for debts: *Varin*, "Arch. de Reims," I, 2, 775 (1275); *Viollet*, "Et. de saint Louis," IV, 50. — Mitigation of excommunication: "Sexte," 5, 11, 9; "Concordat of 1516," v. 14.

[4] Ord. 19 Nov. 1549. Is XIII, 134.

[5] Decretal Childeb., 596, c. 2, I, 15; "Capitulary," 869, 10, 883, 10; "Cap.," 755, c. 9; "Olonn.," 825, c. 1, I, 35. 326; 853, c. 10, II, 269, 19. "Etabl. de saint Louis," I, 127 (vol. I, p. 256, ed. *Viollet*). *Cf.* Const. of Frederic II, 1220, c. 6 (M.G.H., L.L., 2, 236); Ord. "Cupientes," 1228, I, 62; *cf.* XI, 439 and I, 432; *Viollet*, "Ac. Inscr.," 18, 444; *Friedberg*, § 104; *Isambert*, "Table," see "Excommunications." "Cout. de Bayonne," 101, 1; *Pollock and Maitland*, I, 461.

the Church because the civil power did not accord it without examination and often made itself the judge of the ecclesiastical authority.[1]

§ 183. **Decadence of the Ecclesiastical Jurisdiction.** — The extension of the jurisdiction of the Church courts resulted not only from the fact that the ecclesiastical power expanded in developing like all forces, but also from the fact that better justice was rendered by these tribunals at less cost, according to a more learned procedure, and by more enlightened judges. The secular tribunals did not without resistance see themselves deprived of a considerable source of profit from the administration of justice; the 1200 s was a period of fierce struggle[2] and in the 1300 s the crisis became so acute that the question of delimitation between the two jurisdictions was made the subject of an official debate, the Conference of Vincennes, held in 1329 in the presence of Philip of Valois, between P. de Cugnères, the royal advocate, and P. Bertrand, bishop of Autun, produced no result. But from this time the courts of the Church receded gradually before the advance of the royal jurisdiction. In the 1500 s their competence was greatly reduced; on the eve of the Revolution it was known vaguely that there was an "official"; in our day one is unconscious of his existence.

The secular tribunals regained from the Church the ground it had taken possession of: 1st, by the **appeal by writ of error**;[3] we understand by this the practice of impeaching acts of the ecclesiastical authority (judgments or others) before the Parliament or the council of the king which reversed them as contrary to the laws and the customs of the kingdom, or to the canons of the Church as received in France. The ground upon which the intervention of the State was justified was that the ecclesiastical authority had encroached upon the temporal jurisdiction. The author of the act or decision was punished by an arbitrary fine; and even his temporalities[4] were attached as long as he refused obedience. Through this means the ecclesiastical tribunals lost their independence and became subordinated to the royal jurisdiction. Tradition ascribes the invention of this procedure to

[1] The "Saxon Mirror" 3, 54, 3 (excommunicated "mit Rechte").

[2] *Viollet*, "Inst.," II, 314; *Labande*, "Hist. de Beauvais," p. 69; *Teulet*, "Layettes," II, 298; *Boutaric*, "Actes du Parl.," I, no. 6; "Saint Louis et Alf. de Poitiers," p. 424; *Roy* in the "Mélanges Renier," 1887.

[3] *Fevret*, "Tr. de l'Abus," 1653; *De Foy*, "Tr. des 2 puiss.," 1752; *Richer*, "Tr. des appellations comme d'abus," 1763; *Viollet*, "Inst.," II, 301, 413; I, 408 (and the authors cited); *Isambert*, "Table," see "Appel comme d'abus." Foreign countries, *cf. Friedberg*, tr. *Ruffini*, p. 435, n. 10.

[4] *Cf. Isambert*, II, 719, 721; V, 484.

Pierre de Cugnères. The most ancient decisions known date from the 1300 s, but the institution itself appears to have been much older, the name only is modern. 2d, by the restriction of the ecclesiastical judges to spiritual matters. Wills and contracts were secularized; pious legacies were no longer regarded as the essential part of a will, and the oath which corroborated a contract was omitted. In questions of marriage a distinction was made between the sacrament and the civil contract; the Church retained only a Platonic sphere of action in respect to the sacrament; questions of practical interest (separate maintenance, impediments to marriage, etc.) were restored to the lay judge. In matters relating to benefices and to tithes the distinction between possessory and petitory action had the same results; the royal judge took jurisdiction in the case of possessory suits under the pretext that they involved the public order and required a prompt settlement in order that the public peace might not be disturbed; in reality, the action for possession was prolonged to such an extent that the discouraged parties never made use of their right to submit anew the affair " in petition " to the ecclesiastical judge.[1] Crimes against God, even cases of heresy, came to be regarded as under royal jurisdiction, as crimes against the State. As to offenses committed by the clergy, only those of a minor character were left to the Church, under the name of " délit commun "; serious offenses, designated as privileged cases, were reserved to the royal judges[2] in the interest of the public security. It was desired only that the inquiry should be made conjointly by the ecclesiastical judge and the royal judge,[3] the cleric being regarded, at least in the 1600 s, as degraded by the crime itself. The jurisdictional privilege was thus greatly abridged[4] because it was especially in criminal cases that the clergy feared the bias of the lay judges. In civil matters the lay judge had little difficulty in establishing his competence in real actions, through the analogy of feudal matters; in personal actions,

[1] "Gr. Coutumier," p. 254; *Fevret*, "Abus," 4, 8, Ord. 1493 I s, XI, 214.

[2] *Viollet*, "Hist. d. dr. civ.," 273, shows that in 1469 (the affair of Cardinal La Balue), the Court of Rome did not know that it was a privileged case. *Isambert*, II, 655; *Guyot*, "Rép." — Cod. Just., 1, 3, 33, and Nov., 83.

[3] *Muyart de Vouglans*, "Inst. crim.," 3, 3, 2; *Fleury*, 3, 14; Edict of Melun, Feb. 1580, Art. 22; Feb. 1678; Edict April, 1695, Art. 38; *Isamb.*, 14, 471; 19, 449; 20, 255; *Ferrière*, "Dict.," see "Délit commun."

[4] Restrictions on this privilege: Ord. 1563, Art. 21, *Isamb.*, 14, 165. Edict 1695 concerning ecclesiastical jurisdiction, "Table," see "Justice ecclésiastique."

the clergy, in spite of the canons which prohibited it, deserted their own judges, because justice was more prompt in the lay tribunals, and their sentences were executed without further formalities, while those of the ecclesiastical judges needed the "visa" or "pareatis" of the secular judges.[1]

TOPIC 6. HERETICS AND JEWS

§ 184. **In General.** — The persecuted Church[2] preached tolerance; but having attained power it retaliated against the pagans, and St. Augustine,[3] a former Manichæan, in order to justify the measures taken against the Donatists, formulated the theory of legitimate persecution which was, during the whole of the Middle Ages, the guide of the Church, which was applied to the reformers of the 1500 s and 1600 s and which even the reformers themselves, who had had to suffer so much from it, invoked without hesitation.[4] The great Arnold, persecuted and a refugee at Brussels, demanded that the Huguenots be smitten.

§ 185. **Paganism.** — Public worship was forbidden during the reign of the son of Constantine; Gratian, in 382, suppressed the

[1] The law of the 16–24 August, 7–11 December, 1790, abolished the officialities.

[2] See the works of *d'Aubé*, *Le Blant*, *Cuq*, *Mommsen*, *Allard*, *Duchesne*, *M. Conrat*, and a critical analysis of *Beaudouin*, "R. hist.," 1898; *Guérin*, N.R.H., 1895, 601; "Dict. des Antiq.," see "dilectus," p. 219: "non possum militare, christianus sum" (year 195), said a soldier. Pliny the Younger, "Ep.," 10, 47 and Bull of Trajan; Bull of Hadrian in 124 to Minicius Fundanus; *Eusèbe*, "H. eccl.," 4, 8, 9. Edict of Milan, June, 313, in *Lactance*, "De mort. persec.," 48; and *Eusèbe*, 10, 5; *Plato*, Laws, liv, 10; *Cicero*, "de leg.," 2, 8.

[3] "Ep.," 93: "Compelle intrare" in the sense of material constraint exercised by the secular arm; he who binds a distracted person, torments him, but loves him. God does not cease to mix with the mildness of His instructions the terror of His menaces; it is not necessary to consider if one is forced, but to what he is forced, whether to good or to evil; no one can become good in spite of himself, but fear puts an end to self-will and by impelling him to study the truth leads him to discover it. Let us not spare our brother; God himself did not spare His Son. *Cf.* in favor of tolerance, *Tertullian*, "ad Scap.," 2; "Apol.," 24, 28; *Lactance*, "Div. Inst.," 5, 20. Moreover, St. Augustine did not demand the death penalty, but the civil authority did not have the same scruples as he.

[4] Plurality of religions in a State is only possible when the religions do not differ too much from each other. To-day, the immoral practices of certain religions are not tolerated. When we speak of liberty of conscience, we understand that it exists only within certain limits. Religious unity is an element of cohesion and, consequently, of strength. This explains why J. J. Rousseau was able to make of it one of the principles of his political philosophy. But as it is scarcely realizable except at the price of the sacrifice of individual consciences, it becomes an obstacle to religious progress and is rather an evil than a good. Persecution has, besides, great disadvantages; it is easy to go too far with it; the laws of violence react on those who demand them.

budget for pagan worship, confiscated the lands of the temples, and caused to be removed from the hall where the Senate held its sessions, the statae of victory (polemic between Symmachus and Saint Ambrose).[1] Theodosius, in 392, forbade both public and private worship. From this time there was complete proscription: destruction of temples, exclusion of pagans from civil and military offices, death, and confiscation. The most rigorous measures, however, were not successful in annihilating pagan superstitions, and Frankish legislation reproduced them.[2]

§ 186. **Heretics.** — Under Constantine and his successors punishment of heretics was limited to canonical penalties like excommunication and banishment. From the time of Theodosius II there was systematic legislation against them, including: (*a*) *general laws* decreeing the penalties of infamy, incapacity to hold public office, pecuniary penalties, confiscation of property, and banishment; (*b*) *special laws,* and, in particular, those which were directed against the Manichæans and which decreed punishment by burning as early as Diocletian.[3] After the invasions these laws were rarely enforced; Arianism disappeared without persecution and there were dangerous heresies only during the 1000 s among the Cathars.

§ 187. **The Inquisition.**[4] — The insufficiency of ordinary justice against heresy led the popes to establish an extraordinary tribunal, a sort of court-martial, called the Inquisition. It was especially the Dominicans who were charged with pursuing heretics ("in-

[1] *Allard,* "R. q. hist.," 1894; *Boissier,* "La fin du paganisme." The reasonings of St. Ambrose recall those of modern radicals who demand the suppression of the budget of worship and of respect for liberty of conscience. "Christian priests," he said, "do not receive a salary, why should pagan priests receive any? The presence of the statue of Victory was an offense to Christian senators. Symmachus protested against the spoliation of the pagan clergy: what one prince has given, another should not take away; it is, above all, unrighteous to meddle with property willed to the pagan religion; is it not a menace for private fortunes?"

[2] Cod. Theod., 16, 10; Nov. *Theod.*, II, 3, 8; *Valent.*, 26; Cod. Just., 1, 11; "Lex Rom. Wis."; Nov. *Theod.*, II, vol. III; "Præcept. Cap. Carlom," 742, 743; "Indiculus superstit.," "Cap.," I, 222; "Cap. Sax.," 789; "Cap.," 794, 805.

[3] "Lex Dei," 15, 3, 6; Cod. Theod., 16, 5; Cod. Just., 1, 5; Nov., 119, 132, 144; "Wis.," 1, 2, 2; "Cap.," 744, c. 7, I, 40. "Coun.," 794; *Beaumanoir,* 11, 2; 30, 11; "Etabl. de Saint Louis," I, 90; "Assises de Jérus.," I, 522; X, 5, 7, 9. 13; Ord. "Cupientes," 1228 and 1250; Const. of *Frederic II,* 1220.

[4] *Ch. Molinier,* "L'Inquisition," 1880; *J. Havet,* "L'hérésie et le bras séculier au moyen âge," 1881; *Tanon,* "Hist. des tribunaux de l'Inquisition en France," 1893; *Eymeric,* "Directorium inquisitorium," 1578; *Bernard Gui,* "Pratica inquisitionis," ed. *Douais,* 1886 (composed about 1321–23).

quisitio hereticæ pravitatis"); the civil and religious authorities were required to lend their assistance under penalty of incurring excommunication and the punishment which overtook abettors of heresy. The procedure followed by these exceptional tribunals[1] was arbitrary and secret; they proceeded "simpliciter et de plano," without advocates, in such a way that the judge was not bound by any form either as to extension of time, or defense, or proof. Arrests were made upon the slightest suspicion; informing was the duty of the faithful and informers were rewarded by bounties. The accused was subjected to detention while awaiting trial; at the beginning of the examination he was required to swear to tell the truth even against himself.[2] In order to extract confessions from him every artifice was regarded as justifiable and ingenuity expended itself in devising tortures.[3] The worst evidence (infamous persons, etc.) was received against him and it was the practice not to communicate their names to him. Advocates could not defend him without being liable to the same treatment themselves as abettors of heresy. Condemnations and "auto-da-fés"[4] were inevitable under such inhumane rules, to which must be added suits and penalties against the bodies of the dead. After having pronounced spiritual penalties against heretics the Church delivered them to the civil courts which applied to them the penalties of the Roman law, particularly fine and banishment. The canonical laws were silent in regard to the death penalty because the ecclesiastical tribunals had no right to inflict it. These latter tribunals in delivering heretics to the secular arm requested that they be spared from mutilation and death: not that they wished that mercy should be shown, but

[1] Inquisitorial procedure and the procedure of the tribunals of the Inquisition must not be confused. The criminal procedure of the Church courts was from the first accusatory, oral, and public. Following the procedures of transition, evangelical charge, synodal procedure, and defamation, inquisitorial procedure was resorted to (it was based on inquiry or "inquisitio"), it was secret, written, and was instituted of right. The inquisitors employed an inquisitorial procedure which was anterior to them, and they exaggerated its severity. X, 3, 3, 1 (1199) and X, 5, 1, 17 and 24 (1206). Council of Lateran, 1215. "Sexte," "de hæret.," 20. Ord. "Cupientes," April, 1228, Art. 5.

[2] *Esmein*, "Le serment des inculpés en droit canonique," 1896.

[3] Concerning the employment of torture by the ecclesiastical tribunals, *cf. Tanon*, p. 370, and "Formulaire de Guillaume de Paris." *Gratian*, II, 15, 6, 1; 5, 5, 4; 23, 5, 4 and 8, 30. X, 5, 41, 6; 3, 16, 1 ("duris quæstionibus" in the original). "Sexte," 3, 24, 3. *Guill. Durand*, "Specul. jud.," 3, 1, "de accus.," 1, 24; "de præs.," 2, 8.

[4] "Auto-da-fé" act of faith, designated the proclamation of the sentence and the pious exhortations which accompanied it. It was made synonymous with execution, because, in effect, execution followed it.

solely because they did not wish to fall under the threat of the prohibitions addressed to the clergy nor to take part in the infliction of capital sentences. The judge who would have been so simple as to comply literally with these requests would have himself incurred the penalties for abettors of heresy. Burning was the penalty for the impenitent and for him who had relapsed into heresy, banishment for ordinary heretics; perpetual imprisonment (liberal confinement, close confinement) for penitents; the badge of infamy (a cross on the clothes), pilgrimages and fines, and the purchase of penance for less serious offenders. Confiscation of property was a consequence of imprisonment and for all the more severe punishments.[1]

§ 188. **The Protestants.**[2] — At first the measures prescribed during the Middle Ages against heretics, particularly burning by fire, were applied to Protestants. But the Church tribunals were almost deprived of heresy cases under the pretext that since there had been a public scandal it was the duty of the civil power to intervene. The parliaments did not show less rigor than the former Inquisition. Even more, the Reformers, persecuted in France, became persecutors themselves in those countries where the State sustained them. In 1553 Calvin burned Michael Servetus at Geneva. But this execution was the signal for a reaction against the policy of intolerance. A French refugee, Sebastian Castellion, wrote in favor of liberty of conscience which Theodore de Bèze, like him also a refugee, called a diabolical dogma. Thenceforth it had a considerable number of partisans, among them, L'Hospital, La Noue, Pasquier, and Bodin.

With the **Edict of Nantes**, in 1598, it was believed that a régime of toleration was about to be definitely established. It provided, 1st, that Protestants could not be disturbed on account of their religion and they were to be capable of exercising all public functions; 2d, they were given the right of worship in their houses, but public worship was permitted only in places designated in the Edict: thus the Protestants of Paris were compelled to worship

[1] Toulouse had an inquisitor until 1706. The Spanish Inquisition, an institution both political and religious, directed against Jews and Moors, differed but little from the French Inquisition in its procedure and the penalties which it inflicted.

[2] *Buisson*, "Séb. Castellion, 1515–63" (1891); *Martinus Bellius* (pseudonym of *Castellion*), "De hæreticis," 1554; *Th. de Bèze*, "De hæreticis a civili magistratu puniendis," 1553 (tr. into French by *Colladon*, 1660). Before Castellion, Marsilio of Padua was, perhaps, the only one who, in the Middle Ages, had been a partisan of the liberty of conscience. In the 1600s, *Milton* (*cf.* his "Civil Power in Ecclesiastical Causes," 1657) went so far as to demand the separation of Church and State.

at Charenton; 3d, the Protestant Church was given the capacity to acquire property in the same way as the Catholic Church (under reserve of amortissement) and could have its own budget. The Protestants (compelled to pay the tithe to the Catholic priests as the Methodists in Wales to-day pay it to the Anglican clergy) assembled under the presidency of a royal judge and voted the amount necessary for the expenses of worship and the salaries of their ministers. The latter were, like Catholic priests, exempt from the payment of poll taxes and personal charges; 4th, their marriages were valid when celebrated by their pastors, and they had special cemeteries for their dead; 5th, law suits in which a Protestant was the principal party were judged in the parliaments by a tribunal called the "Edict Chamber" composed half of Catholics and half of Protestants.[1] This régime, against which neither the Church nor the State had reason to complain, lasted less than a century.[2] After Richelieu had ruined the Protestant party as a political party the Catholic clergy never ceased to demand, in return for the gifts and subsidies that it gave the king, repressive measures against the reformers. Louis XIV was already disposed by temperament to comply with this demand; he was hardly able to understand how political unity was possible without religious unity, and he believed, as was then the general belief in Europe, that subjects ought to adopt the religion of their prince, dissenters being regarded as seditious. After a series of measures against the Huguenots (in 1662 they were prohibited from holding their national Synod which met every three years, and in 1669 the Chamber of the Edict was abolished) the **Edict of October 1685** revoked the Edict of Nantes. All Protestant ministers were required to leave the kingdom within fifteen days under penalty of being sent to the galleys. On the contrary, it was forbidden to ordinary members to depart from France under the same penalty for men and confiscation for women; those who expatriated themselves were punished with civil death (as were later the "émigrés"). The public exercise of worship was forbidden to

[1] *Cf.* Edicts, declarations, and treaties following religious wars; *Isambert*, "Table," see "Culte protestant"; *P. de Beloy*, "Conférence des édits de pacification," 1600; Edict of Nantes, *Isambert*, XV, 174. The edict embraced ninety-five Articles published and verified, fifty-six secret Articles, and twenty-five second secret Articles, relating especially to places of safety (there were in the neighborhood of 150 defended places). Concerning the political organization of the Protestant party, *cf. Anquez*, "Hist. des Assemblées politiques des réformés," 1859.

[2] The Treaty of Westphalia, 1648, secured to the Protestants of Alsace an exceptionally favorable situation. *Cf.* the works of *Hanotaux* and of *d'Avenel* on "Richelieu." *Gachon*, "L'Edit de Béziers," 1888.

Protestants, and they were not even allowed to assemble in private houses. The reformers were excluded from holding public office and were obliged to baptize their children and bring them up in the Catholic faith. In spite of the Edict it was estimated that 250,000 Protestants left France. Others were converted to Catholicism in great numbers by dragonnades and at the end of the reign of Louis XIV the ordinances and decisions recognized as legal truth that there were no longer any but Catholics in France; officially the Protestants were recent converts.[1] The result of this fiction was: 1st, to subject to the penalties prescribed for the offense of relapsing (death, confiscation) all Protestants who exercised their cult; 2d, to render impossible marriage among them except by a Catholic priest; if he refused to perform the ceremony, they could not marry and had no civil status; their children were considered bastards and they themselves were accounted as living in concubinage.[2] On the eve of the Revolution, the Edict of November 19, 1787, in spite of the opposition of Parliament, reinstated Protestants in their civil rights. They were permitted to contract marriages before the law officer of the place or even before a priest, but the latter acted in regard to them only as a civil officer. By that means the civil status became secularized.

§ 189. **Liberty of Conscience.** — The persecution of the Protestants was no less rigorous than that of Catholics. To cite only England, all public officials were compelled to swear that they recognized no other head of the Church than the prince. Catholics were excluded in that way from holding public office; they were expelled, their property was confiscated, and they were prosecuted for high treason under the pretext that they recognized the authority of the pope. Presbyterians and Independents were hardly better treated (they were imprisoned, pilloried, and mutilated, and many, like the Puritans, fled to the United States). This violence had a result entirely contrary to what was expected.

[1] The Edict of 1685 was completed by other acts. *Cf. Isambert.* The "nouveaux convertis" were exempted from providing lodgings for soldiers; on the contrary, they were enjoined to lodge the greatest number possible of them at the homes of the Protestants; in this way the dragonnades are explained. *Saint-Simon,* "Mémoires," v. 8, ch. 11; "Parallèle," p. 222. In the funeral oration of Letellier, *Bossuet* calls Louis XIV "nouveau Théodose" for having exterminated the heretics. *Monin,* "Essai s. l'hist. admin. du Languedoc pendant l'int. de Basville, 1685–1719" (1884).

[2] *Beauchet,* N.R.H., 1882, 671; *Esmein,* "Le Mariage," II, 201. *Cf.* decree of the Council of State of Sept. 15, 1685; Declaration, Dec. 13, 1698. The use of the "billet" of confession dates from this time; the "nouveau convertis" were suspects and guarantees were demanded of them. "Consultation of Portalis on the marriage of Protestants," 1770.

The royal power was shaken by it; in France the Protestants Jurieu and Ancillon appealed as early as 1689 to the States General. The public conscience revolted against such persecutions and it found expression in the writings of the philosophers of the 1700 s in favor of toleration.[1] In Holland and in Pennsylvania the religious sects were tolerant toward one another. Finally, the French Revolution proclaimed liberty of worship.

§ 190. **The Jews.**[2] — The Jews, scattered over the Roman world, especially after the wars of Vespasian and of Hadrian, lived in communities[3] with their own magistrates and their own national laws.[4] During the Later Empire a régime of disfavor and persecution began ("abominandi Judæi," said the laws); which was aggravated after the Crusades: their own courts were no longer recognized by the State (but persisted under the name of arbitral tribunals); and they were declared incapable of holding public office, of owning Christian slaves, or, at least, of endeavoring to convert them, and of marrying Christians.[5] During the Frankish period Childebert I forbade them to show them-

[1] *Voltaire*, "Traité sur la tolérance," 1763. Trial of Calas, 1762; of Sirven, 1763. *Ath. Coquerel*, "J. Calas," 1858. *Cf.* "Gr. Encycl.," see "Emancipation des catholiques."

[2] BIBLIOGRAPHY: *Viollet*, "Hist. du dr. civil," p. 364; *Beurlier*, "Le culte impérial," p. 263; *Th. Reinach*, "Hist. des Israélites," 1890; *Loening*, "Kirchenr."; *Brunner*, "D.R.," I; *Giraud*, "Hist. du dr. fr."; *Malvezin*, "Hist. des Juifs à Bordeaux," 1875; *Saige*, "Les Juifs en Languedoc," 1881; *Bardinet*, "R. hist.," 12, 1; 14, 1; "R. des ét. juives," 1883 (Comtat Venaissin); *R. de Maulde*, "Les Juifs dans les États fr. du Saint-Siège," 1887; *B. Lazare*, "L'antisèmitisme," 1894; *A. Leroy-Beaulieu*, "R. des Deux-Mondes," 1891; "Gr. Encycl.," see "Juifs"; *Pollock and Maitland*, I, 451.

[3] Following the model of Greek cities with the elders ("gérousia") and the elected magistrates. They enjoyed certain privileges, such as exemption from military service or from the curia.

[4] Sources of Jewish law: 1st, the Pentateuch; 2d, the "Mischna" (Repetition, 2d law), a collection of the works of the doctors of Palestine, composed by Rabbi *Juda* at the end of the 100 s; the "Tosefta," a collection of the same kind completing the "Mischna"; 3d, the "Gnemara" (complement or tradition), which adds to the "Mischna" subtle commentaries: (*a*) issued at Jerusalem at the end of the 200 s; (*b*) at Babylon at the end of the 500 s. The "Mischna" and the Gnemara together form the Talmud. The Talmud of Babylon was "the Code, or rather the Digest, of medieval Judaism"; 4th, in the 1000 s, the Commentary of Raschi, inseparable from the text; 5th, Talmudic codes, systematic abridgments from the Talmud (for example, that of Maimonide, 1100 s) the Code of Quaro, 1567, is the one which prevailed. Talmud of Jerusalem, French translation by *Rabbinowicz*, 1873–1882, and by *Schwab*, 1871–1888; the Talmud of Babylon, German translation by *Wünsche*, 1886–1888. Rabbinical Code, translation *Sautayra*, and *Charleville*, 1868–1869. *Dareste*, "Etudes," p. 18.

[5] Cod. Theod., 16, 18; Cod. Just., I, 9; Nov., 45, 146; "L. Wis.," 12, 2; "Burg.," 15; "Cap.," I, 5, 152; Edict of Clotair, 614, c. 10; "Cap.," 809, 845; X, 5, 6; *Josèphe*, "Ant. jud.," 19, 5, 3.

selves in public between Holy Thursday and Easter. They were already required, as in the Middle Ages, to live in their own special quarter (ghetto); in the 1200 s the obligation was imposed upon them of wearing a strip of saffron-colored cloth on the breast and back in such a way that they could be recognized as bigots at sight.[1] Their testimony was not received in the courts against Christians, but only when they themselves were parties and then they took an oath "more judaïco." The popular prejudice against "deicide" people caused them to be accused of atrocious crimes (such as the crucifixion of infants) like those which the pagans imputed to the early Christians. From time to time the populace rose against them and destroyed their synagogues. The State was sometimes a party to these acts or forestalled them: 1st, by compelling the Jews to be baptized (*e.g.* Chilperic and Dagobert); 2d, by confiscating their property (as did Philip the Fair in 1306); 3d, by expelling them (Louis II in Italy, 855; Philip Augustus in 1182, Saint Louis in 1250, and Philip the Fair in 1306), as was done in a definitive manner by Charles VI in 1394. From this time Jewries were merely tolerated in France. During the periods which intervened between persecutions the principle was that the Jews should be closely assimilated to the serfs ("Judæi sunt servi principium servitute civile," as Saint Thomas said).[2] The seigniors of the king and, in the end, the king alone, had them under their protection; they profited from this by exploiting them and exacting arbitrary dues from them ("census Judæorum," corporeal tolls in Alsace), to such an extent that if a Jew was converted to Christianity his property was confiscated on account of the resulting injury to the king who lost thereby an important source of revenue (abolished 1393). It was because the Jew could be taxed that Christian society did not eliminate him entirely, and also because he was an indispensable economic agent as a money lender, a business prohibited to Christians. Jews were usurers, which means lenders for interest, not by vocation, but by necessity, because other careers were closed to them.[3] They were prohibited from acquiring real estate and the isolation for which they are

[1] *U. Robert*, "Les signes d'infamie au moyen âge," 1880; *D. Vaissete*, II, 485; *Beaumanoir*, 18, 8; 39, 63; "Olim," "*pass.*"; *Giraud*, II, pp. 19, 29, 67, 126, 244, etc.

[2] In Morocco, certain Jews are tolerated, and allowed a special quarter with their wealth which they gain from usury; others, outside the law, are obliged to put themselves with their property under the ownership of a master.

[3] The "Songe du Verger" reproached the Jews for reducing the Christians to misery. In the south the condition of the Jews was exceptionally

reproached was likewise imposed upon them. The idea of the **emancipation of the Jews** made progress with difficulty in the 1700 s (Mendelssohn). Louis XVI exempted, it is true, the Jews of Alsace from the personal tax, in 1784, but at the same time, he allowed them to marry only with his consent (Prussia and Austria). The Revolution gave them the same rights as other citizens (Sept. 28, 1791).[1]

TOPIC 7. RELATIONS OF CHURCH AND STATE[2]

§ 191. **The Priesthood and the Empire.** — Unlike the national Churches of antiquity, which were organs of the State, the Christian Church was born independent and international. But after it had traversed the period of persecutions it formed with the State an alliance which soon became burdensome. The Emperors, "external bishops" to it,[3] did not remain strangers (in the East) to questions of faith. In the West, the downfall of the Empire gave the Roman Church more liberty. The Pope Gelasius was able to write to Anastasius in 493: "in spiritual matters everybody, even kings, ought to submit to the priests, and, in particular, to the Church of Rome." The Barbarian kings, and especially the Carolingian Emperors, put themselves at the service of the Church,[4] of which they declared themselves the protectors; they proscribed pagan practices and caused religious precepts to be respected, such, for example, as those relating to the observation of the Sabbath, and overwhelmed the clergy with privileges and riches. But in return the king appointed the bishops and abbots, paid them as though they were public officials and did not permit the councils of the Church to meet without his

favorable; at Narbonne, the Jewish community had a king; elsewhere there were to be found colonies of Jews with elected consuls. There they were allowed to hold public office.

[1] The Jews of Alsace, however, occupied a special situation by virtue of the treaties of Westphalia, 1648. Ord. 1784, *Isambert*, 27, 440 and "Table," see "Juifs"; *Guyot*, "Rép.," see "Juifs"; *Mirabeau*, "Sur la réf. polit. des Juifs," 1787; *Abbe Gregory*, "Mém. sur l'émancip. des Juifs," 1787. Dec., Sept. 28, 1789; April 16, 1790; Jan. 28, 1790. Dec., May 30, 1806; March 17, 1808.

[2] *Hinschius*, "Staat und Kirche" in the "Handb. d. oeffentl. Rechts" of Marquardsen, 1887, vol. I; *Viollet*, "Inst.," II, 267 (bibliog., p. 414); *Gasquet*, "L'authorité imp. en mat. rel. à Byzance," 1880; *Seresia*, "L'Eglise et l'Etat s. les rois francs," 1890; *Laboulaye*, "R. de Lég.," 1845; *Dodu*, thesis, 331.

[3] *Eusebius*, "Const.," 4, 24. Valentinian and Marcian annulled all civil law which was contrary to the canons. X, 2, 26, 20. *Cf.* Cod. Theod., 4, 14, 1; Cod. Just., 7, 39, 3.

[4] Under the Merovingians the Frankish Church was nearly independent of the pope. It governed itself as a general rule. *Cf. Viollet*, I, 340.

authorization. The appointment of prelates led to the **quarrel over Investitures** (1075–1122) between Gregory VII and Henry IV. To every bishopric and abbey were attached fiefs, and regalian rights ("regalia") arising from royal concessions. The prince chose his vassal and invested him by delivering into his hands the cross and the ring, which were the emblems of spiritual power.[1] The Church saw in this practice simony and traffic in holy things. By the **Concordat of Worms**, in 1122, the Emperor renounced the right of appointing high ecclesiastical dignitaries, of investing with the cross and ring, but he retained the right of conferring the regalia by means of the scepter and standard as for laymen.[2] In France the quarrel was less lively, but the same principles were applied; the king could demand from the bishops only the oath of fidelity and not homage.[3]

§ 192. **Theocratic Systems.** — The supremacy of the Church over the State was maintained during the Middle Ages by the most celebrated popes, Gregory VII, Innocent III, and Boniface VIII. This supremacy resulted, it was said, from the Christian doctrine of the superiority of the soul over the body, of the city of God over the earthly city, and consequently of the Church, which represented the former, over the State, which existed only for it. In order that the plan desired by God might be realized, it was necessary that the temporal power should be subject to the spiritual power.

1st, **The Theory of Direct Power.** — The pope, the vicar of God on earth, had the same power as God himself. The texts of the Holy Scriptures gave St. Peter the plenitude of authority without distinguishing between the spiritual and the temporal;[4] these

[1] "The ring was the symbol of the mystic marriage of the bishop to his church, and the cross represented the pastor's crook." M.G.H., S.S., 6, 374; 14, 209; 2, 770, c. 11. (Remission of the "baculus pontificalis" in the year 865.)

[2] *P. Fournier*, "Yves de Chartres," 1897. The Golden Bull of Egea, 1213.

[3] *Viollet*, II, 343, 4 (Councils of 1078, 1102, 1110, etc.), and 344, 3 and 4.

[4] Other textual arguments: Levi preceded Juda, Samuel deposed Saul, incense and gold were offered to Jesus Christ by the magi. His disciples presented him with two swords: "Whatsoever ye shall bind on earth shall be bound in heaven: and whatsoever ye shall loose on earth shall be loosed in heaven." Saint Paul says: "If you judge the spirit why should you not judge the world?" The adversaries of the papacy restricted these arguments to spiritual matters. Decret. of Gratian, comment 1st part D. 10. X, 1, 2; 2, 1, 13. The word "beneficium," in a letter of Pope Hadrian IV to Frederic I, excited lively protests (1157–1158); the pope gave the appearance of saying that the empire was a fief of the Holy See. The pope had to withdraw the expression. Let us observe that: "the pope who regards kings as his vassals is not always sure of his life in Rome." *J. Bryce*, "The Holy Roman Empire."

texts were confirmed by the false decretals, and particularly by the donation of Constantine; it was by virtue of this that the popes were able to transfer the Empire of the Greeks to the Germans, to depose the last Merovingian, and to anoint all kings.

2d, **Theory of Indirect Power.** — The princes were subject to the Church "ratione peccati": (*a*) in respect to their private conduct like ordinary members of the Church; (*b*) by reason of the office which they had received from God; the Church, responsible to God for all their acts, had the right and the duty to chastise them if they did not reign according to the teachings of Christianity, even to excommunicate them (Nicholas I and Lothair,)[1] and consequently to depose them, if necessary. As the question of sin was raised apropos of every political act, the Church and the papacy came to take a hand in the internal politics of every State and the Holy See found itself the arbiter of the Christian world; the State was in the service of the Church.

§ 193. **Imperialists. Gallicans.** — The defenders of the secular power did not contend that the State could not be inspired with religious doctrines; but they desired that this should be of its own accord and in so far as was judged opportune; the passive obedience which the Church insisted upon was repugnant to them. They invoked important passages from the Scriptures in support of their contentions: 1st, those of the Gospel where Jesus said: "My kingdom is not of this world," and better still: "Render to Cæsar the things that are Cæsar's and to God the things that are God's," from which followed the distinction between the two powers, or as was said in the Middle Ages, the two swords, in allusion to those offered to Jesus Christ; 2d, the words of St. Paul, "the powers that be are ordained of God," [2] and therefore the clergy and laity must be subject to the powers; the prince did not hold anything from the Church but from God alone. It is true that one reads in the Acts of the Apostles: "it is better to obey God than man," but this is not to be understood as giving subjects the right to resist the prince with armed force; Christians resist only by prayers and, if necessary, suffer martyrdom. According

[1] Lothair, king of Lorraine, nephew of Charles the Bald, had married Teutberg; he turned her out in 856, accusing her of various crimes. Teutberg justified herself by the ordeal of boiling water to which she submitted through a champion. Nevertheless three councils annulled her marriage and permitted Lothair to marry Waldrade, a relative of the archbishop of Cologne and of Trèves. Nicolas I repealed the acts of the councils and forced Lothair to take back Teutberg as his wife.

[2] John, xviii, 36; Matt., xxii, 21; Luke, xxii, 38; *Paul*, Romans, xiii, 1.

to the pure Christian doctrine bad kings were given to the people by an angry God in order to punish them for their sins. With these theological arguments the Ghibellines coupled the idea of the perpetuity of the Roman Empire and that of the universal monarchy; ancient tradition was combined with divine right in order to shipwreck the attempts at theocracy of the great popes of the Middle Ages. The Church, conquered, surrendered slowly the ground which it had occupied in order to retire gradually to the domain of spiritual matters. The bad use which the clergy made of its wealth during the Middle Ages contributed not a little to the enfeeblement of its moral authority; as to the papacy, its cosmopolitan character was too much opposed to the feudal system and the national tendencies to obtain the political sovereignty of Europe.

§ 194. **St. Thomas and the Theologians after the 1300s.** — The saying of St. Paul: "omnia potestas a Deo" may be understood in different ways: 1st, **The theory of Divine Right.** According to this theory, God created a special form of government, for example, a hereditary monarchy in France and an elective empire in Germany; this authority, established and organized directly by God, was the divine right; God commanded all to obey it; 2d, The principle of authority alone was the divine right. God created man a social being and made authority a necessity in human society, but he did not establish any special political organization, hence no form of government exists by divine right; it belongs to men to organize the State according to the needs of the time and place. This interpretation, which prevailed in the school following St. Thomas, opened the way to political speculations of every kind. In this way the political problem became secularized. The theologians were able to bring to the examination of the problem the same liberal spirit as the learned scholars of our day. Moreover, they were not confined to any particular régime; universal monarchy, national States, absolute or limited monarchies, aristocracies, democracies, popular sovereignties, and the social contract theory, all had partisans among them.[1]

§ 195. **The Holy See and the Frankish Royalty.** — To St. Louis, who exhibited in his relations with the Holy See a remarkable firmness, was attributed an act, the **Pragmatic Sanction of 1268**, by which he affirmed the independence of the Church of France in the matter of appointments to ecclesiastical benefits

[1] *Cf. Chénon,* "Théorie catholique de la souveraineté nationale," 1898.

and forbade the Roman Curia from levying taxes on the churches of France without the consent of the king. But the authenticity of this Act is very doubtful.[1] Shortly afterwards occurred the **controversy between Boniface VIII and Philip the Fair.** The pope protested against the taxes which the king levied on the clergy and claimed for the Church the right to judge kings (" ratione peccati ").[2] The arrest of the pope at Anagni and his death (1303) terminated the dispute in favor of the king of France. In the 1400 s, following the great Councils of Constance and Basel in 1414 and 1431, appeared the **Pragmatic Sanction of Bourges** (July 7, 1438), in which Charles VII promulgated the reform decrees adopted by those Councils: supremacy of the general councils over the popes and the regular meetings, the suppression of the privileges attributed to the Holy See in the collation of ecclesiastical benefices (reservations and expectancies), prohibition of the papacy from collecting fees like the annats, or those for the bull of confirmation of ecclesiastical dignities, the prohibition of appeals " omisso medio " to the Roman Curia. The papacy left no stone unturned to prevent the application of this liberal charter, which attacked at the same time the spiritual power and the temporal rights of the pope. After long negotiations a treaty was concluded, the **Concordat of Bologna**, on the 18th of August, 1516, between Leo X and Francis I.[3] By the terms of this agreement the right of appointment to the principal benefices, bishoprics, abbeys,

[1] Because appeal to it would not have been neglected at the time of the contest between Philip and Boniface VIII, whereas there was no resort to it before the time of Charles VII. At this time it served to overcome the resistance which the Pragmatic Sanction of Bourges encountered. It is silent concerning the regalia which gave rise to so many difficulties in the 1200 s. The original was never found though there are fifteenth century manuscripts of it. Text in *Isambert, Viollet*, "La Pragm. Sanction de Saint Louis," 1870.

[2] The bull "Clericis laicos," 1296, forbade the levying of taxes on the clergy. The bull "Ausculta fili," 1301, declared that the king of France was subject to the sovereign pontiff and that a council would be called together to deal with the reformation of the kingdom of France. The little bull, "Scire te volumus," which is a counterfeit of it, reads: "Know thou that thou art subject to the temporal as to the spiritual." The States-General of 1302 affirmed that the king is responsible only to God for the exercise of his temporal power. The bull "Unam Sanctam," Nov. 13, 1302, declared that there are two swords, and the temporal must be employed by the kings on the order of the pontiffs. "R. q. hist.," 1879, 26, 91. *Cf.* the dispute of Louis XII and Julius II, 1510–13. *Viollet*, II, 283.

[3] *Isambert*, XII, 1, 75; *Boutaric*, "Explic. du Conc.," 1747. Concerning the other concordats, *cf.* "Gr. Encycl.," see "Concordat"; *Bruck*, "Coll. de Concordats"; *Nussi*, "Conventiones int. S. Sedem," 1870. Germany: concordat of the princes, 1447; of Vienna, 1448. Italy: law of the guaranties, May 13, 1871.

and priories was given to the king and the pope; the king chose the incumbent from among those who fulfilled the conditions of learning and age (twenty-seven years and the degree of licentiate or doctor of theology or of law) and the pope confirmed the appointment by means of a bull. It was thus that the transition was accomplished from the régime of free election by equals to that of the royal good pleasure, that is, to the régime of favor. The higher dignities of the Church came to be more and more the monopoly of the nobility. The papacy abandoned its privileges in respect to the granting of benefices (reservations, expectancies, and apostolic mandates), and appeals direct to the Roman Curia remained abolished in principle. But there was no longer any question of general councils, and, as the Concordat said nothing of annats, the papacy continued to collect them but with more moderation as to the amount. The Parliament, the University, and the French clergy itself protested against this rupture of Gallic traditions.

The Germanic Concordat of 1448, admitting the right of election by the chapters and monasteries, was applicable in Alsace, at Metz, Besançon, and Cambray (except for the cathedrals). In Brittany ("pays d'obédience") the pope appointed to benefices eight months out of twelve, since no concordat had been concluded for this province and some others.

The ultramontane tendencies prevailed still more in the Council of Trent (1545–63), whose decrees were not received and published in France, except in so far as they related to matters of faith. The publication of the **Liberties of the Gallican Church**[1] in 83 Articles (1594) by Pierre Pithou was in the nature of a response to ultramontanism, these "liberties," it is said, were derived from two fundamental maxims: 1st, our kings are independent of the pope as regards temporal powers, therefore the pope cannot levy taxes in France; the subjects of the king cannot be relieved from the oath of fealty; the officers of the king cannot be excommunicated on account of their official acts; the pope cannot understand the rights of the crown, he cannot exercise criminal

[1] Ed. *Dupin*, 1844 ("Manuel du dr. publ. ecclésiast. fr."); *P. Dupuy*, "Preuves des Lib. de l'Egl. g.," 1639 (edition 1715, 1731); *Bouchel*, "Decr. Eccl. gallic," 1609; *P. d. Marca*, "De concordia sacerd. et imp.," 1641; *Fleury*, "Disc. s. les lib. de l'Egl. gall."; *J. de Maistre*, "De l'Eglise gall.," 1821; *Picot*, "Hist. d. états gén.," III, 355. Declaration of the Third Estate to the States General of 1614; *cf. Mariana*, "De rege," 1599 (tyrannicide) and *Bellarmin*, "De pot. S. pont.," 1610. The Sorbonne and the Parliament condemned the book of the Jesuit Sautarel on the power of the pope, 1625. *Tardif*, "Privil. acc. par le Saint Siège," 1855.

jurisdiction; and the bulls of the pope cannot be executed in France without authorization from the secular authority;[1] 2d, the power of the pope was limited by the Holy canons; he was a sort of monarch, we may say, limited by the terms of a charter. Thus the Church of France did not admit indiscriminately all the decretals;[2] the kings had the right to convoke the church councils in their States and to make regulations concerning matters of ecclesiastical discipline.

Richelieu and Louis XIV did not deviate from the traditional policy toward the papacy. Under Louis XIV the **affair of the regalia** gave rise to a very serious conflict.

The king wished to extend the right of "regalia" to all the bishoprics, but the bishops of Alet and Pamiers, Pavillon and Coulet, protested. Condemned by their metropolitan, the archbishop of Toulouse, they appealed to the pope, who sustained them and launched against the king briefs which the Parliament condemned as libelous. An assembly of the French clergy, in which Bossuet played the principal part, voted the celebrated **Declaration of 1682**: 1st, the popes had no authority over princes in temporal affairs; 2d, the apostolic power was limited by the supremacy of the general councils; 3d, the pope must respect the customs of the Gallican Church; 4th, in matters of dogma the decisions of the pope were irrevocable only with the consent of the Church universal. The teaching of these four maxims was made obligatory upon the faculties of theology and did not cease to be required until 1789.[3] In the 1700 s, the quarrel between Gallicanism and ultramontanism reappeared in the form of interminable discussions on the subject of the bull "Unigenitus" in 1713,[4] prosecutions against the Jansenists, and the suppression of the order of Jesuits (1764).[5]

§ 196. **Catholicism, the State Religion** found itself subjected to a régime of privileges and servitudes, to honorary privileges

[1] Or "Placet," a right which existed in most of the States, but which did not appear as a general measure until near the 1400 s, *Viollet*, II, 292.

[2] The bull "In Cœna Domini," the collective work of the popes since Boniface VIII, was not accepted in France.

[3] *Mention*, "Doc. rel. aux rapports du clergé avec la royauté (1682 to 1705)," 1893; *Bossuet*, "Def. decl. cleri. g.," 1730; *Gérin*, "Rech. hist. s. l'ass. du clergé de 1682," 1870. *Cf. Febronius*, (Hontheim) "de statu ecclesiæ," 1763; *Isambert*, "Table," see "Libertés gall."

[4] *Isambert*, "Table," see "Jansénisme." Decree of the Council, Sept. 5, 1731.

[5] Brief of Clement XIV, July 21, 1773. Edict, Nov. 1764; *cf.* decree of Parliament, Aug. 6, 1762. *Isambert*, "Table," see "Jésuites"; *cf.* "Monod.," nos. 4538 and following. "Assertions des Jésuites," 1762 (collection of propositions, extracts from their writings).

and to personal, real, and judicial immunities which have been treated before. The first duty of the prince was to enforce the laws of the Church (but in the Gallican Church he owed only filial obedience): laws for the observance of the Sabbath, for the punishment of usury, against blasphemy and especially against heresy (there must be civil sanction for excommunication as long as excommunication was taken seriously), and for religious marriage. But he possessed considerable rights over the Church and these he attained in various ways: 1st, as a political magistrate. The Church was a body politic which formed a part of the State and which had as its head the head of the State, the temporal sovereign. 2d, As the protector of the Church, a mystical body whose chief was the pope. 3d, As feudal lord to whom belonged the right of eminent domain over all the land of the kingdom and consequently over the lands of the Church. 4th, As the patron and founder of a large number of churches. By virtue of these latter titles the property of the Church was often dependent upon the king. It was always dependent upon him if the king were looked upon as a political magistrate, because this property was required to serve for the defense of the State and it was for the prince to decide whether it was necessary to take it for this end, or whether it was possible to allow the Church the liberty to acquire property, especially real estate. The clergy depended upon the king as the protector of the Church who, as such, saw that the canons were observed and who might enforce them (for example, the obligation of residence) by pecuniary penalties and even by seizure of temporalties.[1] It was dependent upon him as a political magistrate because in this capacity the king had the right of appointment to the bishoprics and abbeys, to require the oath of fealty, and to exclude foreigners from ecclesiastical dignities; and it belonged to him to permit or refuse the establishment of religious communities, to control their statutes, and to authorize monks to open colleges.[2] Even in matters of ecclesiastical discipline and in matters of faith the king did not always lack jurisdiction. He ordered public prayers, watched over the administration of sacraments, the application of the laws regulating marriage, stood in the way of the printing and publication of reli-

[1] Ord., July 10, 1336, II, 117: the king ordered that the bishop of Amiens should be restrained by the seizure of his temporalty from levying taxes on newly married men who lived with their wives. "Olim," II, 138, no. 28.

[2] The curés read from the pulpits the acts of the civil power, recommending the methods of worship prescribed by the intendant, etc.

gious books, forbade the use of the pulpit to preachers or to university professors, and authorized or prohibited assemblies of the clergy. The decisions of church councils in matters of discipline had the force of law only when approved by the king. It is not astonishing that enlightened men like Jurieu characterized such a régime as slavery.[1]

§ 197. **The French Revolution. Civil Constitution of the Clergy.** — With the outbreak of the Revolution Catholicism ceased to be the State religion. Liberty of worship was proclaimed and logic would have required, it seems, the separation of Church and State and the abolition of the budget for the maintenance of worship. The Convention (Constitution of 1795, Art. 74) actually did this; it declared that since religion was only a matter of individual conscience no one could be compelled to contribute to the support of any worship whatsoever. But the members of the Convention believed themselves authorized, like Louis XIV and Joseph II (of Austria), to legislate concerning ecclesiastical discipline by virtue of the police power which the State had over the churches and in general over all associations. The **Civil Constitution of the Clergy** of July 12 and December 26, 1790, was nothing more than a logical application of the principles of the "ancien régime" to the relations between the Church and the State and was the last victory of the Jansenist and of the Gallican spirit. The ecclesiastical divisions were harmonized with the political divisions and the number of bishoprics was reduced to one for each department. The bishops and curés were to be elected like public officers by political assemblies (and consequently by reformers or unbelievers as well as by Catholics). The nation undertook by this means to substitute itself for the king (or in the place of lay patrons who might not be Catholics), and it was not to be supposed that the Church could complain of it. Moreover, bishops and curés were required to receive the canonical institution from the metropolitan, that is to say, from their hierarchical superior whose place the pope had wrongfully usurped. The bishops could write to the pope in testimony of the unity of communion between them and him. When required to take an oath to support this constitution, the clergy, for the most part, refused. Henceforth France

[1] *Abbé Mathieu, op. cit.*, p. 155: the pope was scarcely anything but a sort of constitutional king of the church, rarely intervening in its affairs and always with the good pleasure and subject to the control, accepted by all, of the Parliament and of the sovereign. *Le Vayer de Boutigny*, "Traité de l'autor. des rois touchant l'admin. de l'Eglise," 1753. *Cf.* Reforms of Joseph II in Austria.

had two clergies: the clergy which had taken the oath, or the "constitutional" clergy, and the refractory clergy.[1] The Legislative Assembly and the Convention instituted a veritable persecution against catholicism, and, in 1794, there were almost no communes in France where mass was said. The worship of Reason, the worship of the Supreme Being which they attempted to substitute for the Christian religion had little success. Little by little, during the last days of the Convention, under the Directory, the priests reappeared and the churches were reopened. The First Consul, by the **Concordat of July 16, 1801**, restored religious worship and reëstablished the union between Church and State, but with the preservation of the principle of liberty of conscience.

[1] Decree of July 12, 1790; Nov. 1790; May 7, 1791. The analysis of subsequent laws would lead us too far. *L. Sciout*, "Hist. de la Const. civile du clergé," 1879; *Jaeger*, "Hist. de l'Eglise de France pend. la Révolution," 1878; *Méric*, "M. Emery," 1881; *Sicard*, "La France chrétienne," p. 476.

CHAPTER V

THE FEUDAL PERIOD. THE FEUDAL STATE. SEIGNIORIES AND COMMUNES [1]

In General.

TOPIC 1. GENERAL CHARACTERISTICS OF THE FEUDAL SYSTEM AND SKETCH OF ITS EVOLUTION

TOPIC 2. THE SEIGNIORIES

[1] BIBLIOGRAPHY: Besides general works like those of *Viollet, Glasson, Esmein, Schröder*, etc., *cf. Camus* and *Dupin*, "Biblioth.," nos. 1566 and following; treatises of *Brussels, Salvaing*, etc., already cited; *Championnière*, "De la propriété des eaux courantes," 1846; *Secrétan*, "Essai s. la féod.," 1858; *Odier*, "Rhdr.," t. 14; *Fustel de Coulanges*, "R. des Deux-Mondes," t. 105, p. 436, et t. 92, p. 274; *Boutaric*, "Origines du rég. féodal," 1875; *Garsonnet*, "Locations perpétuelles," 1879; *Seignobos*, "Le rég. féodal en Bourgogne," 1882; *Menzel*, "Lehnswesen," 1890; *Flach*, "Orig. de l'anc. France," 1886; *Esmein*, N.R.H., 1894, 523; *E. de Rozière*, "J. des Sav.," 1894; *A. Molinier* dans *D. Vaissete*, "Hist. de Languedoc," t. VII; *Luchaire*, "Manuel d. inst. fr." (Capétiens directs), 1892; *Ch.*

TOPIC 3. TOWNS AND COMMUNES

In General. — Feudal society was not simple; it was a composite of heterogeneous elements, monarchical, ecclesiastical, seigniorial, and communal institutions. To better grasp the logic of its structure the jurist needs to put aside the consideration of the monarchy and the Church which are to him, in some sort, external institutions, if not altogether foreign; it would seem to be necessary to do the same with regard to the communes; but if they are antifeudal in origin, they remained, nevertheless, a part of the feudal organization; they were collective seigniories. We shall consider here, therefore, seigniories and communes, leaving the study of the royal power and its development to be treated when we come to the monarchical period.

TOPIC 1. GENERAL CHARACTERISTICS OF THE FEUDAL SYSTEM AND SKETCH OF ITS EVOLUTION

§ 198. **Division of the Sovereignty.** — From a unitary régime such as was Carolingian France, we pass with the establishment of feudalism to a system of petty States, or of groups having a principal State around which gravitated satellite States. The territory of France was divided into seigniories connected with one another by the loose bond of fealty and homage. They belonged: (*a*) to former public functionaries, dukes, counts, and viscounts who had appropriated their offices for their own use and handed them down from father to son; (*b*) to holders of "immunities" who were exempt from the royal authority (the bishops of Laon, Beauvais, and others); and (*c*) to adventurers who, under cover of anarchy, had usurped the public authority. The royal power, to be sure, had not disappeared; nevertheless, if we wish properly to understand the feudal system, we must put aside this disturbing

Mortel, "Gr. Encyclopédie," see "Féodalité"; *Ciccaglione*, "Encicl. giur. ital.," see "La Feudalità"; "Dig. ital.," see "Feudo" (*Pasq. del Giudice* et *Calisse*); *L. Delisle*, "Cond. des classes agric. en Normandie," c. 1 (schéma de la féodalité), 1851.

element and view the king at most as a feudal lord, more powerful than the others, the universal suzerain or sovereign fief holder of the kingdom.[1] In the petty States thus formed by the splitting up of the kingdom the political authority proceeded: (*a*) from a contract,[2] the grant of a fief by a lord to his vassal; and (*b*) from the protection exercised by the nobles over the lower classes. Feudalism was at once a régime of contract and a régime of patronage.[3]

§ 199. **Constitution of Landownership and the Political Powers.** — Between the former and the latter there were close relations, which are explained by the origin of the sovereign rights of the seigniors (domains of holders of "immunities" and benefices of counts) and by the fact that land was the principal source of wealth in an age when commerce and industry scarcely existed. The seignior was the only landowner intended to become such; his ownership was doubled by political rights and there was such confusion between the attributes of ownership and those of sovereignty that they were poorly distinguished and were often treated in the same way. Thus the right of administering justice regarded as belonging to the domain was handed down, sold, exchanged, divided, and entailed. The lands of the seignior were divided into two parts: those which he reserved for his own direct exploitation, the domain properly speaking, and those which he granted by enfeoffment to his vassals or leased to the common people ("roturiers"), the enfeoffed domain. Over the latter he had a superior ownership, the right of **eminent domain**, or direct seigniory; this carried with it certain prerogatives such as the right to military and judicial service from the occupants, the right to certain taxes or dues, to transmission fees, to quit rents, that is to say, rights closely resembling those which a sovereign has over his subjects. The noble vassal as well as the commoner to whom he had granted

[1] *Beaumanoir*, 34, 41: "each baron is sovereign in his baronetcy; he is sovereign above all and has, of right, the general guardianship of his domain, by which he may tax establishments as he pleases for the common good." *Luchaire*, 457: "the action of kings as heads of the feudal edifice is scarcely manifested in facts before the commencement of the 1200 s." *Cf.* German Empire, Kingdom of Jerusalem, England.

[2] *Esmein*, p. 176: "veritable social contract in the sense in which Rousseau used the word, although under conditions quite different from those that he dreamed of." "The feudal constitution rests on the concession of the fief and the obligations that proceed from it for the vassal." *Flach*, "Orig. de l'anc. France," vol. II, erroneously considers this concession as secondary; in primitive feudalism he sees only personal relations, as in the Frankish seigniory. For a contrary meaning, *Esmein*, N.R.H., 1894, 523.

[3] *Imbart de la Tour*, "Ac. sc. mor.," 1896, vol. 146, p. 395.

a part of his lands in the form of a fief or quit rent, had the domain of use ("domaine utile"), that is to say, a badly defined usufructuary right involving enjoyment and disposal in variable measure. The Romanists regarded this right as a "jus in re aliena" because the real ownership appeared to them to reside in the seignior. The Feodists made of it a sort of inferior ownership so that the same property had two masters (sometimes, indeed, several when there was a suzerain). This system of divided ownership outlived the political authority of the seigniors; but manifested itself as a slow dispossession to the benefit of the vassal and the renter; in the 1700 s the "domaine utile" became the true ownership, the eminent domain a servitude, a mere honorary right to which the Revolution had only to give the last blow.[1]

§ 200. **The Hierarchy of Fief Possessors.** — Among the members of the landed nobility there was a bond which resulted from the granting of the fief; by this bond the vassal was allied with his seignior, as the seignior himself to his superior seignior or suzerain, and consequently a hierarchy was established among them. It should be remarked, however, that this hierarchy differed from that of the public functionaries of the Frankish period, although in appearance there had been few changes, since the old titles (dukes, counts, and marquises) remained. Among the feudal lords rank depended less upon the titles than upon the extent of possessions and the number of vassals; the counts of Flanders and of Toulouse, for example, were not inferior to the dukes of Burgundy.[2] We must take care, moreover, not to assimilate this hierarchy to that which exists among the public functionaries of to-day, in which the subordinate is dependent upon his imme-

[1] The "L. Feud.," 2, 8, 4, designated the right of the vassal by the terms "possessio," and "usufructus"; the glossarists called it "dominium utile," applying to the vassal the texts which accord a claim "utile" to the "emphytéote" (tenant on long lease); the seignior retained the direct action and remained "dominus directus." *Landsberg*, "Gloss. d. Accursius," p. 97; *Stobbe*, "Handb. d. d. R.," II, § 80 (texts of 1276, 1307, 1313, southern Germany); "Gr. C. de France," 2, 11; *Pontanus*, s., "Cout. de Blois," Art. 33; *Hévin*, "Quest. féod.," c. 4, no. 18; *Pothier*, "Tr. des Fiefs," no. 8.

[2] Details in *Luchaire*, "Man.," p. 236. In Germany there was a hierarchy of the military bucklers ("Heerschilde"), (originally king, princes, or "capitanei," "Regis valvassores"); superiors only were able to give fiefs to inferiors: 1st, the king; 2d, ecclesiastical princes, holding their fiefs immediately from the king; 3d, laical princes; 4th, counts and free lords ("Freiherr"), holding their fiefs from nos. 2 or 3; 5th, "Mittelfreien," that is to say, free men who were not lords ("schoeffenbarfreien") and the vassals of lords; 6th, "Ministeriales" ("Dienstleute"); 7th, citizens of the towns. "Sachsensp.," I, 3; *Ficker*, "Vom Heerschilde," 1862; *Blondel*, "Frédéric II," p. 86.

diate superior and, for a stronger reason, upon the superior of the latter. The vassal, on the contrary, was dependent only upon his immediate seignior because his contract was with him alone. He was not the man of the suzerain; in principle the latter could not reach him except through the medium of his own seignior, but there was a strong tendency in the direction of "immediatization." [1]

§ 201. **Causes of the Establishment of Feudalism.** — The feudal system was a type of social organization which is found in most countries, such as China, Japan (until 1867), and ancient Egypt. It was not at all peculiar to the Middle Ages nor to Western Europe. Even there it originated under varying conditions. It was imposed upon England by the Norman Conquest; it was introduced into the Byzantine Empire in the 900 s by the government as a means of offering greater resistance to the enemy and later by the Ottomans, who were few in numbers in the midst of a hostile population,[2] where it was a question of control.[2] In France the system grew up spontaneously with the decadence of the Carolingian power. The diversity of customs, language, and interests, the difficulty of communication, the habits of violence and insubordination, the invasions and incessant wars, were almost insurmountable obstacles to the maintenance of a unitary State. The royal power committed itself to a policy of which the most marked result was the strengthening of local and eccentric sovereignties.

The establishment of the feudal system is therefore explained by the general causes which, ruining the Roman administrative structure, led to a renewal of the State on a small scale. The peculiarities of this régime, its details and its physiognomy, were derived from immediate precedents: the immunity, the seigniorat, and benefices, or from the more remote origins, Roman or Germanic, of these very institutions. The fief itself originated in the fusion of the institutions of vassalage and the benefice; from the 800 s this fusion was in a fair way to take place, and during the 900 s it was complete.[3]

§ 202. **Appreciation of the Feudal System.** — Feudalism was the only possible régime in the anarchical condition of French

[1] "Vasallus vasalli mei non est meus vasallus." *Joinville*, "Hist. de Saint Louis," c. 26; *G. Durand*, "Spec. de feudis," no. 28.

[2] *Maspero*, "Hist. anc. de l'Orient," I, 297; *Tischendorf*, "Lehnw. in mosl. Staat," 1872.

[3] In the letters of Fulbert de Chartres, 1007, the fief appears to have been definitely constituted. *Cf. Yves de Chartres*, "Ep.," 71, 208.

society after the end of the 900 s. Incessant wars, pillaging, burning, devastations, paint the chronicles of these times in the saddest colors. The seignior was a saviour; his châteaus, his strongholds, "firmitates," were places of refuge for the people. Taine compares the seignior to "the American lieutenant in a blockhouse of the Far West in the midst of the Sioux Indians; under his protection the peasant plowed and sowed his lands; he would not be killed, nor taken captive with his family in droves, the neck under the yoke; he gladly agreed to the most onerous feudal conditions in return for protection, what he had endured every day was worse. It was in this way that petty feudal States grew up around the nobles, and it remained only for the royal power to transform them into a great national State."

The work of the seigniors was good, if viewed from a distance and as a whole; they established a new public law based upon feudal contract, upon reciprocal engagements, and therefore on a principle of liberty. This good is overlooked if viewed from close range; the baron who defended his peasants was almost as rough and as coarse as the enemy; the military régime made him despotic and, as the domain was so small and his subjects at his door, it was easy for him to multiply exactions, arbitrary sequestrations, and other abuses. The pettiness of his State also led to other evils: frequent wars, restraints upon trade, and a strict and inflexible routine instead of progressive legislation. Finally, there was nothing more unstable than the bond between the lord and his vassal.

§ 203. **Decadence of the Feudal System.** — The smaller States increased their territory by means of conquest or formed confederations among themselves; these federations in turn drew closer together and became centralized and unified, and so came about the feudal world. At first great fiefs were formed (in the 1200 s) and these in turn were annexed to the crown. Concentration was facilitated by the confusion of landownership with political sovereignty. Fiefs were transmitted like ordinary property, by inheritance, purchase, and marriage. Powerful families thus rounded out their domains and adopted measures to prevent their dismemberment. More especially as the great seigniories were not always new groupings but former administrative divisions maintained by the force of tradition; this facilitated the "immediatization" of subvassals, which was to their benefit.

To this internal evolution which the feudal world underwent must be added the action of other forces. The royal power had been enfeebled but not annihilated; it had kept, along with its prestige, certain pretensions it was ready to push forward on every occasion. It had an ally in the ecclesiastical body with its unified organization; it had another in the Third Estate, although the cities, enriched through trade and industry, had powerful corporations and a communal organization. The nobility succumbed in the struggle. It is true that the Church and the Third Estate were hardly more fortunate. The unified State of former times with its formidable administrative mechanism was reconstituted at the expense of these powers of the past. Feudalism was eliminated from public law and relegated to the domain of private law; this was the work of the monarchy. The Revolution expelled it from this latter domain and reëstablished in its place full and complete individual ownership.[1]

TOPIC 2. THE SEIGNIORIES

§ 204. **In General.** — The seigniories or feudal States had, like all States, sovereign rights,[2] especially financial rights and the right to administer justice, but also the rights of war and of peace, legislation, police administration, rights over the Church, and the right to coin money. But the sum total of these rights belonged only to the important seigniories;[3] the petty seigniories had only a small portion of them, and simple fiefs none at all.[4]

§ 205. **Right of Peace and of War.**[5] **Feudal Armies.** — Disputes among feudal seigniors were supposed to be settled by judi-

[1] In Germany, allodification laws, so called (transformation of fiefs into freeholds, *Stobbe*, § 117), have almost supplanted feudal ownership; but they still exist in England.

[2] *Viollet*, "Inst. pol.," II, 237 (feudal reaction under Louis the Quarrelsome).

[3] The seigniory was a fief to which were attached sovereign rights. Concerning baronies *cf. Beaum.*, 34, 41.

[4] Concerning castellanies (castlewards), *Touraine*, c. 5, *Luchaire*, 279. **Coseigniories and Pariages.** As a result of succession and of other facts, it happened that a seigniory was sometimes divided in two or several parts. "Pariage" was a convention or agreement which produced the samo result; it was a real association between seigniors who were peers ("paréage"), equal among themselves. It was most frequent between the king and the ecclesiastical lords, and was an advantage to both sides, the latter gaining a powerful protector, the former obtaining by it a means of increasing his domain. It happened also that the "pariage" was sometimes concluded between two seigniors, for example, the valley of Andorra was divided between the bishop of Urgel and France, by virtue of a "pariage" concluded between that bishop and the Count of Foix, to which France succeeded. *Viollet*, "Inst. pol.," II, 171; *Luchaire*, 384, 449; *Dognon*, "Inst. pol. du Languedoc," 16; *A. Molinier*, *op. cit.*

[5] *Huberti*, "Gottesfrieden und Landfrieden," 1892 (with bibliography); *Luchaire*, p. 228. *Du Cange*, "Diss. 24" on Joinville; *Laurière*, "Ord.,"

cial process before the superior lord, but usually they preferred to fight it out (" Faustrecht," fist right). The habits of violence, the anarchical tendencies, the right of the seigniors to raise troops and exact military service from their vassals of noble rank,[1] and from the common people themselves,[2] the right which they granted themselves, to erect fortresses [3] — all united to revive among the seigniors the system of the Germanic " faida " (feud).[4] Custom recognized the right of private war among them.[5] War should be declared by a **challenge** (by letter or by a herald), or begun by an affray; it was suspended by a truce (" treuga ") and terminated by a peace concluded under oath.[6]

§ 206. **The Chronicles** [7] show how frequent and barbarous were these wars between the feudal lords; no other calamity but famine can be compared with them. The sad thing about it was that those who suffered most were the lords' men who took no part in the wars, or who took only a small part; everything on their lands was ravaged and destroyed. (A) **The Church** took up again the work of the Capitularies and endeavored to limit the evil: [8] (*a*) by the **peace of God** which neutralized to some extent the churches, the clergy, merchants, women, the aged, children, defenseless peasants, the property of the clergy, and work animals (Councils of Charroux, 989, of Limoges, 994, etc.); (*b*) by the **truce of God** which forbade hostilities at certain times of the year, namely, from Advent Sunday to the eighth day of the Epiphany,

I, preface; *D. Vaissete*, 7, 552; 8, 1462 and 1691; *De Mas Latrie*, "Dr. de marque" (BCh. vol. 27 and 29); *Boutaric*, "Inst. milit.," 1863.

[1] "Gr. C. Norm.," 22 and following. "Artois," 56, 8.

[2] By reason, not of the fief, but of the right to administer justice. *Beaum.*, 59, 21, "Et. saint Louis," I, 65; "L. des Droiz," § 443; *Boutillier*, I, 84; *Boutaric*, "Inst. milit.," p. 141.

[3] "Capit.," 847; 863; 887. Interesting details in *Flach*, vol. II; *cf. Blondel*, 186. "Mir. de Saxe," 66.

[4] The families were, as formerly, in a state of war only in the sense that there was open war between some of their members. To what degree of relationship did solidarity exist? *Beaumanoir* limits it to impediments to marriage (59, 20); but it is doubtful if this was the primitive rule, or the rule that prevailed in general. According to *Beaumanoir*, also, 59, 18, a declaration of neutrality made under oath before the tribunals allowed a relative to remain a stranger to the war. Case of legal neutrality, 59, 22.

[5] The right existed only between nobles and not between the common people (although the contrary was formerly held. *Esmein*, 244, 2, according to a text which seems to me to aim at only legitimate defense). *Beaum.*, 59, 5; 60. "Et. saint Louis," I, 31, 52; "Jostice," 112, 305; Ord. 1316, Art. 22; *D. Vaissete*, X, 547.

[6] "Gr. C. Norm.," 71, 74; *Viollet*, "Et. saint Louis," vol. I, p. 180; *Mazure*, "Fors de Béarn," 279.

[7] *Raoul Glaber*, ed. *Prou*, "Guibert de Nogent."

[8] *Du Cange*, "Gloss."; see "Treuga Dei"; "Diss. 29 sur *Joinville*"; *Sémichon*, "La Paix et la Trêve de Dieu," 1869; *Luchaire*, p. 231 (bibl.); "Tr. Anc. Cout. Norm.," 71; *Pfister*, "Robert le Pieux," p. 160; X, 1, 34.

from the first day of Lent to the eighth day of Pentecost, and, throughout the entire year, from each Wednesday evening to Monday morning (Councils of Elne, 1027, of Clermont, 1095, etc.). But these institutions in the interest of peace were badly respected, although the bishops, not limiting themselves to canonical penalties, went so far as to compel by means of force their observance by the seigniors.[1] (B) **Popular Associations**[2] continued the work of the Church either by combating the seigniors ("En capuchonnés du Puy," 1182) or by the maintenance of a sort of gendarmerie, "gentlemen police officers," charged with enforcing peace by a tax called the "pezade" or "peace common."

§ 207. **The King** alone succeeded in destroying the evil by making himself the great peace officer of France: (*a*) through the "**King's Quarantine.**"[3] Philip Augustus forbade the attacking of the relatives of belligerents before the expiration of forty days after the act which caused the war (unless they had been witnesses to the act); by that means he prevented surprises and odious ambushes, for they had had no scruples in attacking those who were not on their guard. (*b*) Through **assurance**[4] ("assecuramentum"), that is to say, an agreement entered into by one of the parties not to attack the other. The superior lord, and especially the king (through his officers), required such an engagement, at least in the 1200 s, whenever one of the parties requested it; it was therefore a forced truce. Beaumanoir required it in certain cases even when neither party requested it. (*c*) By the **prohibition of private wars.** The first two mentioned were only halfway measures. During the 1200 s private wars were forbidden while the king was engaged in war, and during the 1300 s, when he was always at war, they were forbidden absolutely.[5] There remained to the

[1] Louis VII, 1155 (*Isamb.*, I, 152). *Yves de Chartres*, "Ep.," 44, 50, etc. The Church made the lords swear to peace.

[2] *D. Vaissete*, VII, 161 (*A. Molinier*) *Guiraudet*, "Soc. Lett. Aveyron," X; *Ragueau*, see "Commun de paix."

[3] *Beaum.*, 60, 13 (Philippe, doubtless Philip Augustus); *Boutillier*, I, 34 (Saint Louis; Ord. 1245, lost as was the other); Ord. April 9, 1353; Ord. I, 56. *Cf.* Ord. January, 1257, I, 84, "G. C. Norm.," 74, "Bourbon," 51; "Champagne," 32; "Sens," 159.

[4] *Beaum.*, 60; "Olim," "Table," see "Assecurationes." "Et. saint Louis," I, 31; II, 29, 35; *Boutillier*, 1, 3, and 5 (pp. 15, 30, edition 1603); *Masuer*, vol. 12; "Fors de Béarn," r. 53; "Jostice," 2, 6, 2; 4, 12, 1; *Loysel*, 276.

[5] "Tr. Anc. Cout. Norm.," 31. Ord. Jan. 1257 ("guerras omnes inhibuisse in regno"); 1303; 1319. Ord. I, 344, 701; III, 294. *Isamb.*, I, 357; II, 671; *D. Vaissete*, X, 547. Louis le Hutin established and regulated the right of private war. The number of ordinances of the 1300 s and even of the 1400 s prohibiting private wars, shows how little they were respected. See especially the Ord. 1367, V, 19.

nobility only the duel, against which the "ancien régime" displayed so much severity without much success. The feudal armies disappeared and no one but the king could maintain troops. Richelieu caused a number of châteaux to be razed.[1]

§ 208. **The Legislative Power.**[2] — The task of the feudal lord was especially to enforce and apply custom. Nevertheless he had police powers, the ban right,[3] and consequently the ability to make police regulations ("établissements") which sometimes became real laws and which he often drew up by mutual consent with his vassals in his feudal court, especially when there was a question of applying them outside of his domain in the fiefs which had been detached from it.[4] The "bourgeoisie" itself had been represented in the 1200 s in these courts or feudal assemblies, to which were joined the provincial estates of the 1300 s.

§ 209. **The Administration.**[5] — This word is properly employed only in the case of the great seigniories; in the petty fiefs it is necessary to use the term *domanial exploitation.* There were no administrators, but only intendants and servants; but whether intendants or functionaries, they all sought to feudalize their offices, that is to say, to convert them into fiefs which were transmissible from father to son.

(A) **The Central Administration** was in the seigniories the same as in the royal domain, that is, a reduced form of the Carolingian administration with its offices, seneschal, chancellor, chamberlain, constable, and cupbearer.

(B) **The Local Administration** was made up of "ministeriales" or servitors: (*a*) provosts ("præpositi") in the north, beadles ("bajuli") in the south;[6] (*b*) mayors ("majores"), road

[1] The Ord. of 1627 prescribes the destruction of the fortresses (as did the Edict of Pistoia). *Anség.* 4, 27.

[2] "Hist. de France," vol. XI, pref.; *Du Cange*, "Coll. Leber," vol. 8; *Flammermont*, "De concessu legis," 1884; *Laferrière*, "Lois de Simon de Montfort" ("R. crit. de lég.," vol. 7). *Luchaire*, p. 250, (bibl.) above, "Etats prov. Communes" (grant of charters by the lords). *Petit-Dutaillis*, "Louis VIII," 424.

[3] *P. de Font.*, 16, 1. "Jostice," 2, 2; "Fors de Béarn," r. 56; *Fleury*, "Dr. public," 1, 2 (right of ban and of public cry, ordinary seigniors published only by placards). "M. de Saxe," "Landr.," I, 59; "M. de Souabe," "Lehnr.," 41; *Blondel*, 181. *Cf.* feudal rights, following, "ban vin" (right to sell wine), "ban de moisson" (right of harvest), "nemus bannitum." "Gr. Cout. Norm.," 8. "Et. saint Louis," I, 111.

[4] "Et. de saint Louis," I, 36; *Beaum.*, 34, 41; *Frommhold*, 169, 127 ("Sent. de jure statuum terræ," 1231).

[5] *Luchaire*, 260; *Molinier*, VII, 128 and following; *Seignobos*, c. 7; *D'Arbois de Jubainville*, "Hist. des comtes de Champagne," II, 85 and following.

[6] To the provosts or "bailes," corresponded the viscounts in Normandy, the "chatelains" in Flanders, Champagne, and Burgundy, the

surveyors ("viarii"), sergeants ("servientes"), and other inferior officials. The provosts and beadles ("bailes") combined the most diverse powers, military, judicial, and financial. Unlike the inferior officers, they did not generally succeed in making their offices hereditary. At the end of the 1100 s and at the beginning of the 1200 s an intermediate piece of machinery appeared in the great seigniories, namely, the **seneschal**, or great bailiff ("bailli"), who was interposed between the seignior and the provosts, and who was the hierarchical superior of the latter; in his hands were concentrated the affairs of several provosts.

The seneschals of the court, at first charged with this care, were too far removed from the provosts to exercise efficacious supervision over them; it was necessary therefore to send out inspectors (from the time of Louis VII), who soon became permanent officials under the name of bailiffs.[1] The multiplicity of affairs led therefore to a division of this office and the creation of secondary centers; Philip Augustus appears to have established "the first of the great bailiwicks in his own domain a little before 1190." It thus came about that there were three kinds of administrative divisions: 1st, the seneschal's jurisdictions and bailiwicks; 2d, provostships, castellanies, etc.; and 3d, cities, or, in the country, parishes and villages.

§ 210. **Seigniorial Courts.**[2] — The "Saxon Mirror" presented the king as still the grand justiciar of the kingdom, "communis judex omnium"; as soon as he appeared every other jurisdiction was suspended; the inferior judges were only delegates to whom he had given a portion of his powers.[3] In France, as in Germany, the administration of justice was regarded as the essential attribute of political sovereignty. But the theory of the "Saxon Mirror" which was far from being exact for Germany was still less so for France. From the beginnings of feudalism the seigniors administered justice in their own names. The Frankish period already had its **domestic courts** of the master for his slaves, its **domainal courts** of the great privileged landowner for his "coloni"

"bailles" in Flanders, Brittany, etc., the "viguiers" in Toulouse, etc., "Gr. Cout. Norm.," c. 3 and following, *Lot*, N.R.H., 1893, p. 293; *Bonvalot*, "Hist. des Inst. de la Lorr.," pp. 263, 270, 276.

[1] Ord. 1190 or Testament of Philip Augustus. "Gr. Cout. Norm.," c. 4 and following. *Petit-Dutaillis*, "Louis VIII," 365.

[2] *Viollet*, "Inst. pol.," II, 212, 453; *Esmein*, p. 175, 413; *Luchaire*, p. 204, 331; *Tanon*, "Hist. des just. des anc. églises de Paris," 1883; *Beautemps-Beaupré*, "Cout. de l'Anjou et du Maine," vol. I, p. 1890; *Pollock and Maitland*, I, 559.

[3] 3, 26, 1. *Cf.* 1, 58, 2 and 3, 60, 2; M.G.H., L.L., II, 96, 183, 199, etc. *Blondel*, p. 169.

and the inhabitants of his lands; perhaps also its **seigniorial courts**, if we admit that the *seniores* judged their "*vassi*." With the advent of feudalism private courts developed; whether he had a charter of immunity or not, the landowner judged the men of his domain; the contract of fief gave to the seignior the administration of justice over his vassals; and, on the other side, the successors of the Carolingian officers (dukes, counts, etc.), who administered justice in the name of their sovereign, converted this right to their own use.[1]

§ 211. "**Fief and Justice have Nothing in Common.**" — In Beauvasis and Normandy in the 1200 s every feudal seignior had the right of administering justice on his fief.[2] On the contrary, according to the "Saxon Mirror," a seignior could not administer justice without special permission from the prince, as his ownership did not imply the right of administering justice.[3] Of these two systems, one distinguishing the fief from the right of dispensing justice, the other confusing them, which one came to prevail? This question has been the subject of lively discussion. The maxim, "fief and justice have nothing in common," has been, in the hands of the jurists, a weapon against the seigniors; the fief was left to them, that is to say, the ownership, but the right to administer justice was taken away, that is to say, the sover-

[1] "Justitia" signifies: 1st, justice; 2d, profits of justice (fines, etc.); 3d, (by extension), administrative and financial powers ordinarily connected with justice, the procuring of revenues or even seigniorial dues and revenues. *Du Cange*, see "Justitia"; *Guérard*, "Polypt. d'Irminon"; "Gr. Cout. Norm.," 3. "Vicaria" is the equivalent of "justitia" and does not mean inferior justice only as is ordinarily believed. *F. Lot*, N.R.H., 1893, 283. Beginning with the 1200 s "viaria" was used in preference to "vicaria," "vigeria," but this word has two meanings: 1st, justice in general ("Et. Saint Louis," ed. *Viollet*, III, 14, 18, 20, 34, 52, etc.), and territory over which a seignior exercised it; policing of the streets, squares, markets, and consequently inferior justice was attached to it. Concerning the etymology, *cf. Lot*, p. 296; concerning the various functions of the "vicarius," *cf.* p. 292. *Laurière* on "Loysel," 272.

[2] *Beaumanoir*, 10, 2 and following. In Beauvaisis, every feudal lord administered superior and inferior justice in his fief, except actions which belonged to the count by reason of his sovereignty. *Cf.* c. 58. "Et. Saint Louis," I, 115. "Tr. Anc. C. Norm.," 59: "quilibet dominus habet placita in terris suis." "Gr. C. Norm.," 2, 2 ("solus autem princeps plenam habet jurisdictionem"); 27, 7. *Cf. Clermont*, 3, 22; *Epinal*, 1, 29; *Loysel*, 271; "Olim," "Table," see "Justitia."

[3] "Saxon Mirror," 3, 53, 3; 64, 5. *Blondel*, pp. 54, 169. Every seignior who administers justice over a fief or an allode must obtain special permission which was completed by the collation of the royal ban which was distinct from the investiture of territory. "Gr. Cout. of France," I, 3, and IV, 5. To the king only belonged the right to create new jurisdictions throughout his kingdom. Many "customs" had two distinct titles; the one on justice, the other on fiefs (for example, Eu, Bretagne, Maine, Anjou, etc.).

eignty, the political rights. The distinction which the laws of the Revolution made between **dominant feudalism** and **contracting feudalism** was only a variation of this formula. But if we consider only primitive feudalism and if we stick to the administration of justice, properly so called, without concerning ourselves with the rights of sovereignty in general, the embarrassment is great. In reality, seigniorial courts were not born from a simple situation; their origin was too complex for us to dream of a perfectly logical theory. The maxims, "fief and justice are only one," and, "fief and justice have nothing in common," express two tendencies both of which made headway under the feudal régime. The seignior who granted a fief acquired thereby the right to judge his vassal; in case of failure on the part of the vassal to perform the contract of infeudation, he had the right to take the law into his own hands and take possession of the fief. On this fief were to be found holders who were not nobles, and serfs, and it was entirely natural that he should have claimed the right to judge these tenants, at least in so far as questions of their tenure were concerned. Once vested with the administration of feudal or domanial justice he set aside all other judges, if he could, and himself administered justice in all its plenitude; in that case his justice was not merely contractual or feudal but it was seigniorial. In the process of this evolution the administration of justice by the seignior exceeded at times its natural limits and encroached upon that of less powerful seigniors or allodial proprietors who were his neighbors.[1] He judged cases arising outside his lands, that is, he judged persons who were not bound to him by the feudal tie.[2] Inversely, it sometimes happened that the old dispensers of justice arrested his progress and reduced him to the position of a simple domanial or landed judge, or even despoiled him of all right to administer justice. Thus we find fiefs without their courts just as we find courts without fiefs.[3]

[1] The administration of justice was attached to many allodes; the Feudists held, nevertheless, that there was no allodial justice; they meant by this that the holders of allodes who administered justice received this right from the king by virtue of the fief; their lands were allodial in respect to ownership, but feudal in respect to justice. *Beaum.*, 11, 12; "Miroir de Souabe," 101.

[2] The same land might be a fief held of one lord and at the same time be in the justice of another. Many little fiefs, allodes transformed into fiefs, had no courts. It was rare that a seignior had a right of justice independently of a fief, but his right to administer justice often extended beyond the limits of the fief and included the lands that he had not granted.

[3] *Cf. Esmein*, p. 252, who distinguishes: 1st, seigniorial justice, which was exercised even outside of the fief and extending in general to all actions;

§ 212. **Superior and Inferior Jurisdiction; "Medium" Jurisdiction; Land Jurisdiction.** — Among the seigniors some had superior jurisdiction, that is to say, they exercised civil and criminal jurisdiction without restriction (thus they had the right to impose the death penalty, a gibbet with two or more posts, with a pillory and carcan, was the sign of a superior jurisdiction);[1] others had only an inferior jurisdiction, limited ordinarily to simple police offenses (punishable by a fine of ten sous) and to civil cases (involving sixty sous). This distinction, which seems to be very old, was doubtless connected with that established during the Frankish period between the jurisdiction of the count and that of the centurion or privileged person.[2] Moreover, it was never precisely delimited and so we need not be surprised to see the appearance in the 1200 s, and certainly in the 1300 s, of a system of intermediate ("moyenne") courts for all civil cases and for criminal offenses punishable by a fine not exceeding sixty sous (generally speaking because the limits varied according to custom);[3] and also a system of land courts ("justice foncière") which were less courts than the exercise by the seignior of the rights of ownership; it permitted him by virtue of his private authority to seize the property granted by him as a fief or copyhold, for lack of the fulfillment by the vassal or the copyholder of his obligations.[4]

2d, feudal justice: (*a*) over the vassals of the seignior by virtue of the contract of fief (at least if the homage was "liege"); (*b*) over the disputes relating to the fief (or even to the profit of the seignior renter in respect to litigation relating to the "censive"); it was "justice foncière" (land justice) but interpreted in a broad fashion. The texts cited do not convince me. "Jostice," 19, 26, 2; "Gr. C. Norm.," 29, and 30, 53; *Beaum.*, 50, 15, and following; *Artois*, 3, 17; *Bout.*, I, 84. It does not seem to me to be established that originally the possession of a fief had always carried the right of feudal justice over the extent of the land that it comprised. *Cf. Beaum.*, 10, 2; 58, 1; "Gr. C. Norm.," 2; *Boutillier*, I, 84 (exceptions according to *Esmein*). I doubt if one could translate "fief and justice have nothing in common" as "fief and seigniorial justice have nothing in common, but every fief involves feudal justice."

[1] "Tr. Anc. Cout. Norm.," 53 ("placita ensis"), 59, 70; "Jostice," 2, 5, *Beaumanoir*, c. 58 (superior and inferior justices). *Des Mares*, 295. *Cf.* "Gr. Cout.," 1, 4, and 4, 8 and following; *Loysel*, 274 and following. "Et. de saint Louis," I, 34, 42, 115; II, 8; *Bacquet*, "Dr. de justice," c. 2; *Ragueau*, see "Justice"; *Fleury*, "Dr. public," 1, 2; *Bonvalot*, 346.

[2] "The right of administering justice went with the land; the most powerful lord of the kingdom, if he acquired land of inferior justice, could not exercise superior justice over it." *Viollet*, "Inst. pol.," II, 459. For Lorraine, see *Riston*, Thesis, p. 188.

[3] *Viollet*, "Inst. pol.," II, 458, cites an act of 1252. *Des Mares*, 296, 297; "Gr. C. of France," l.c. *Loysel*, 273.

[4] *Bacquet*, "Tr. des droits de justice," 3, says that in his time (end of the 1500 s) there was no system of land and manor justice in the provostship and the viscounty of Paris. *Ragueau*, see "Justice foncière"; *Flach*, I, 276; *Brutails*, N.R.H., 1896, 532; *Bourdot de Richebourg*, III, 507, 570; "Gr. Cout. Norm.," 28, 2; *Boutillier*, 2, 91; *Fleury*, "Dr. public," 1, 2

§ 213. **Organization of Seigniorial Courts.** — These courts had, if we may so speak, two sides: the seignior held a feudal court (high court, baronial court) for the nobility and a bourgeois court for the common people.[1]

1st, **The Feudal Court.** — (A) *Composition.* This court was presided over by the seignior (or by one of his officers in his stead, for example, a bailiff); it was composed of his vassals or men of the fief (to the number of three or four at least) in virtue of their obligation to attend court (and such of his officers as he had summoned).[2] However, it had neither a fixed composition nor seat, nor were its sessions held periodically; the seignior was bound by no rule except that of rendering justice to his vassals under penalty of losing them, and that of judgment by their peers. (B) *Competence.* The jurisdiction of this court embraced: (*a*) cases between the seignior and his vassals, or between the vassals themselves, and for this purpose cities and religious orders were likened to vassals; (*b*) cases involving denial of justice by vassals and those in which wrongful judgments had been pronounced by them; (*c*) actions between nobles which had already been tried by the seignior's officers if it pleased him to allow an appeal.[3]

2d, **Inferior Tribunals.** — Those not belonging to the nobility, the serfs and common classes ("roturiers"), were judged sometimes by the seignior himself or by the feudal court [described above], but more often, it appears, by the seignior's officers (bailiffs, provosts, etc.), sometimes alone, sometimes presiding over a group of upright men ("prud'hommes"), well-known local representatives of the common people (*cf.* the Châtelet of Paris).[4]

§ 214. **Judgment by Peers.** — In both classes of seigniorial tribunals the parties were generally judged by their peers, the

(very rare). According to *Esmein*, p. 414, this would be a residue of the justice inherent in the fief which would have permitted the judging of all suits relating to this fief, and not merely the act of seizure. *Loysel*, 272; "Gr. Cout. of France," 4, 11, p. 645. *Loyseau*, "Seigneuries," 10, 43; *Valois*, 6, "Sens," 18; following "Saisie d'authorité privée."

[1] *Marnier*, "Cout. Picardie," p. 1. England: feudal courts and manorial for the copyholders. Germany: "Lehns-" and "Dienstgerichte," "Hofgerichte" (domanial courts).

[2] *Langlois*, "Textes rel. à l'hist. du Parlement," no. 21 (1224).

[3] *P. de Font.*, 21, 10, 22, 37; *Beaum.*, 67, 2, "Et. saint Louis," I, 76. If there were not enough vassals, he addressed himself to his suzerain who sent his or who retained the affair and judged it in his court ("mettre sa Cour en Cour souveraine"). "Fors de Béarn," r. 5. Women judges, *Viollet*, "Inst. pol.," II, 456; "roturiers," 457. Itinerant judges in Normandy and in England; ambulatory magistrates who held feudal assises, somewhat after the fashion of the Carolingian "missi."

[4] *Beaum.*, 1, 13, 15; "Artois," 3, 20; 52, 12; 36, 11 and following. *P. de Font.*, 21, 8; *Boutillier*, 1, 2, 3, 84; "Lille," 1, 22; *Dodu*, "Inst. Jérusalem," p. 281.

president only pronouncing the sentence and ordering its execution.[1] The judgment of their peers afforded guarantees to suitors against the arbitrary action of the seignior or his officers; it was not an innovation, but a continuation of customs prevailing during the preceding period ("rachimbourgs," "échevins," or aldermen) and which were favored by the customary character of legislation. Feudalism made the custom of judgment by peers a right of the vassal. As to the common people and serfs, the old custom had less force; for serfs it had not existed everywhere, and in many places, doubtless, the seignior was their only judge; the common people themselves in the 1200 s were often judged by seigniorial officers who were content with asking advice of the notables; thus judgment by one's peers became a customary or conventional privilege. During the 1500 s a complete change took place: the king alone had peers; the seigniorial tribunals were composed of men learned in the law; the feudal and customary elements were eliminated; and there remained in them only jurisconsults such as there must have been from early times, in the persons of certain seigniorial officers. The change had its causes in the progress of the law and of judicial procedure under the influence of the revival of the Roman law. The duel and the ordeal gave place to examinations and written procedure[2] (Council of the Lateran, 1215; ordinance of St. Louis, 1260 or 1258); vassals and customaries feeling their incapacity in the presence of this legal learning and finding the duty of attending court irksome withdrew and were replaced by professional jurists; the seignior himself had himself replaced by his bailiff or seneschal, and the latter by a lieutenant; from the 1400 s this latter official was the ordinary judge.[3] The legislation of the 1500 s forbade the barons themselves to sit, just as it was forbidden to the royal bailiffs, and for the same reasons.[4]

[1] *P. de Font.*, 15, 33; "Gr. Cout. Norm.," 9; *Beauman.*, 67, 2, 17: "li segneur ne jugent pas en lor cours, mais lor home jugent." "Et. saint Louis," I, 76; *Beautemps-Beaupré*, "Cout. de l'Anjou," I, 82; *Tanon*, p. 81; *Viollet*, II, 463; in Lorraine, gentlemen were judges, the "baille" did not even deliberate. *Dodu*, "Inst. Jérusalem," p. 261: the king could not himself render justice. "Grand Charter," 21, 39: "nullus liber homo capiatur aut disseisiatur nisi per legale judicium parium suorum vel per legem terre," 52. *Bonvalot*, p. 295, *Amiens*, 75, *Bouillon*, 1.

[2] X, 5, 35, 3. *Esmein*, "Hist. de la procéd. crim.," p. 46 (English translation by John Simpson, Boston, 1913).

[3] *T. Basin*, "Projet de réf. procédure" (1455), ed. *Quicherat*, IV, 57. In Artois, in the 1700 s, the men of the fief still judged under the presidency of the bailiff. *Viollet*, II, 463; *Beaumanoir*, 1, 13; *Boutillier*, 1, 3; *Loysel*, 565; *Danty*, "Preuve par témoins," I, 345. Code Henry III, 16.

[4] *Loyseau*, "Offices," 5, 1, 43. The seignior could, according to common opinion, remove the judge that he had appointed, unless the latter had acquired his office by paying for it. "Ord. Rousillon," 27; *Loyseau*,

§ 215. **Feudal Procedure.**[1] — The system of pecuniary "compositions" was abandoned and gave way to a system of fines paid to the seignior. But of the custom of private vengeance there remained the necessity of accusation on the part of the victim; prosecution, "ex officio," took place only in cases of flagrant offenses. In a general way the procedure was still almost the exclusive work of the parties. The methods of proof were still those of the Barbarian period, namely, the oath, ordeals, and especially the duel. Procedure was both oral and public; its formal character, a natural consequence of the oral pleadings, also recalled the Barbarian epoch. The judgment was based solely on the words pronounced by the parties, words which, once uttered, could not be retracted, corrected, nor supplemented; they were interpreted literally and the judgment was based on what was actually said and not on intention according to the adage: "oxen are bound by their horns and men by their words." The slightest error caused the loss of the case, as, for example, where one said "Brachton" instead of "Bracton"; thus a formal error in the appeal rendered the judgment open to attack in its entirety and was punishable by a fine.

§ 216. **Decadence of the Seigniorial Courts.** — At the opening of the monarchical period the seigniorial tribunals were no longer feudal in their composition, since men of the law were now the judges; they underwent the same transformations as the royal courts, and, at the same time that the principle of uniformity was established on this side, they lost much of their importance on another through the theory of the **royal cases** and that of **priority**, and were subordinated to the tribunals of the king through the system of appeal.

§ 217. **Royal Cases.**[2] — The tribunals of the king claimed from an early time, in accordance no doubt with Roman ideas, the exclusive jurisdiction of certain causes called *royal cases*. There

"Offices," 5, 4. These offices did not become hereditary. The seigniors had attached to their tribunals, fiscal procurers whose situation was analogous to that of the public prosecutors of the royal courts.

[1] *Brunner*, "Wien. Akad.," 57, 738 (French translation "R. crit.," 1871–72); *Esmein*, "Hist. de la procéd. crim." (English translation by John Simpson, Boston, 1913).

[2] *Viollet*, "Inst. pol.," 2, 221 (and bibliog.); *Tardif*, "Procéd.," 10; *Tanon*, "Justices des Egl. de Paris," 93; *Langlois*, "Phil. III," 275; *Aubert*, "Hist. du Parlement," I, 264; "Le Parlement," II, 8 and following; *Luchaire*, 571; *Glasson*, "Inst. Anglet.," 3, 277. *Esmein*, p. 420, holds that the theory of the royal case did not have its point of departure in Roman law ("Pratique de Jacobi," r. 35). Its development coincides, nevertheless, with the diffusion of Roman ideas. *Cf. Blondel*, p. 61.

had never been a definite list of these, a fact which permitted their multiplication as the authority of the king increased.[1] At first the theory applied only to the Roman crime, "crimen majestatis," which included every assault upon the person or honor of the king, or upon his domainal rights, crimes on the great highways or royal roads,[2] and even every violation of the public peace of which the king was the guardian (for example, possessory actions).[3] At the beginning of the 1300 s the nobles were alarmed, so many reserved cases encroached upon their right to administer justice. Louis X, the Quarrelsome, endeavored to reassure them by this rather unsatisfactory definition: "The royal 'crimen majestatis' is understood to include every case which by law and ancient custom may and must belong to a sovereign prince and to none other."[4] Gradually, during the 1300s and 1400s most serious crimes came to be included in the category of royal cases; such were rebellion, unlawful assemblies, heresy, the bearing of arms (which the ordinances of 1487 and 1532 prohibited except by gentlemen and officers), counterfeiting money, usury, etc.[5]

§ 218. **Priority ("Prévention").** — If the royal judge had taken cognizance of a case before the seigniorial judge, he retained the jurisdiction, especially for offenses of which the repression was urgent, under the pretext that there had been negligence on the part of the inferior judge ("supplet superior inferioris negligentiam"). By this means the royal courts continually encroached

[1] *Beaumanoir*, 34, 41; 10, 2 and following: a case which belonged to the Count of Clermont by reason of sovereignty. "Tr. Anc. C. Norm.," 15, 53, 59, 70; "Gr. C. Norm.," 2, 2; *P. de Font.*, 32, 17; "Gr. Cout. of France," 1, 3; *Boutillier*, 1, 51; 2, 1; *B. de Richeb*, 2, 652; *Valois*, 9; *Perche*, 8.

[2] *Beaumanoir*, 25 (royal road); the public highways, or jurisdiction of offenses committed on the roads, 25, 5; "C. de Norm.," *supra*.

[3] Which supposes assault. *P. de Font.*, 32, 1. *Cf.* following, Possession.

[4] Ord. I, 606; "Olim," I, 626. The theory of the royal case was developed out of the various means by which the jurisdiction of the royal courts was extended especially before the 500s: 1st, the safeguard or special protection of the king, following the "mundium" of the Frankish epoch; 2d, the bourgeoisie of the king; 3d, the royal seal; the acts to which it was affixed fell within the competency of the royal courts; *Boutillier*, 2, 1; "Gr. Cout. de Fr.," 1, 3, 15; *Loyseau*, "Seigneuries," 14, 13; 4th, royal letters also permitted the royal courts to take jurisdiction of affairs which would not have belonged to them necessarily; *Guy Coquille*, "Hist. du Nivern.," 1, 508; 5th, the "évocation au Parlement." *Cf.* German "privilegia de non evocando."

[5] *Imbert*, "Pratique," I, 23, 2; *Lecoq*, 198. Enumeration in the criminal Ord. of 1670, I, 11; *Ferrière*, "Dict.," see "Cas royaux"; *Fleury*, "Inst. au dr. fr.," I, 112; *Muyart de Vouglans*, "Inst. au dr. crim.," 1, 4. During the monarchical epoch the royal cases were within the competence of the bailiffs and seneschals; the provosts or inferior judges could not judge them. *Isambert*, "Table," see "Cas royaux," "Anjou," 65.

upon the jurisdiction of the seigniorial courts. Sometimes the "priority" was absolute, that is to say, the royal judge necessarily retained jurisdiction of the case (cases of dowry and others); sometimes it was relative, that is to say, the seignior had the right to ask that it be sent before his own judges.[1]

§ 219. **Appeal.**[2] — (A) On account of **default of the law,** that is to say, the denial of justice. If the seignior refused to decide a case brought before him, the vassal was freed from his obligations toward him, he ceased to be the seignior's man although keeping the fief, and might declare war against him or demand justice from the suzerain whose immediate vassal he then became;[3] thus he sometimes reached even the king. (B) On account of **writ of false judgment** (by means of an action against the magistrate for damages on account of abuse of power). The losing party declared that the judges had pronounced a false and wrongful judgment, that he was ready to uphold this with his life against each of them and to put them to death or make them declare themselves vanquished.[4] Ordinarily the judges pronounced their sentences in a loud voice and it was necessary to demand a duel as soon as the majority had given their opinion. "Whenever the judges did not deliberate in public the losing party could say after the pronouncement of the judgment: 'Which one of you did this?' If one of the judges replied: 'I did it,' the party could attack him only. If, on the contrary, the reply was: 'the court did it,' the appellant must show that the court as a whole was wrong in order to gain his cause and it was necessary to conquer all the judges on the same day, otherwise he would be hung or beheaded." This was, at least, what the assizes of

[1] The old idea that the king was the justiciary "par excellence" contributed to the acceptance of the system of "prévention," X, 1, 10; *Loyseau*, "Seigneuries," c. 13; *Viollet*, "Inst. pol.," II, 221; "Artois," 11, 1; *Beaumanoir*, 10.

[2] *M. Fournier*, "Essai s. l'hist. du dr. d'appel," 1881; *Viollet*, II, 214. Appeal signifies, properly speaking, provocation to a duel. *Loysel*, 877 and following.

[3] *Beaumanoir*, 62; 61, 53, 70; 10, 2. "Et. de saint Louis," I, 53, 56. "Gr. Cout.," p. 594; *Langlois*, "Textes Parl.," table, see "Défaute de droit," *Brussels*, p. 235, 349.

[4] If one said "and" instead of "or," it was necessary to kill his adversary in order to make the appeal a success. "Styl. Parl.," 16, 8. The plaintiff who confined himself to the statement that the judgment was bad without adding that he would prove it with his body, was liable to be fined; and his appeal was not valid. *Beaumanoir*, 61, 45 and following, 51; 67, 9; 10, 3. *J. d'Ibelin*, 110, 187. "Et. de saint Louis," I, 83, 86, 142; "Jostice," 20, 16; *Artois*, 7, 8; 56, 27. According to *P. de Font.*, 22, the villain could not falsify the judgment, unless by a special privilege. *Tardif*, *op. cit.*

Jerusalem decided; the French "customaries" (collections of customs) of the 1200s substituted for the death penalty a fine of 60 pounds for the baron and each of the judges.

(C) **Demand of Better Judgment** (later petition or writ of error). This was a means of recourse which recalls our bill of review (petition for recall of a judgment which is not appealable). A petition was addressed to the tribunal which had pronounced the sentence asking for a revision of the judgment, that is, an appeal was taken from a badly informed tribunal to one which was better informed. This resource was the only one which the losing party had when he did not wish to impute felony or disloyalty to the judges as in the case of perversion of judgment. This procedure was used in particular for the decisions of the Parliament (letters of grace were necessary).[1]

(D) **Appeal properly Speaking** ("appellation"), or recourse to a superior tribunal for the purpose of obtaining a revision of the judgment of the inferior court, was unknown to ancient law,[2] either on account of the composition of the tribunals, or by reason of the character of the procedure followed. The popular element which entered into the composition of the tribunals and their arbitral character made them independent of one another. The judgments which they rendered were based on a procedure which excluded almost every possibility of error, at least in the minds of those who employed it, namely, the oath or the judgment of God. Often, however, the party who lost his suit complained. Even to-day suitors always believe that it is through malevolence that they are condemned; in the worst times of the Middle Ages these suspicions were often justified. Perversion of judgment with judicial combat was recommended for this situation. But the

[1] *Beaumanoir*, 67, 7. "Etab. de saint Louis," II, 16, Ord. 1331, II, 80; 1344, II, 217; *Viollet*, "Et. de saint Louis," vol. I, p. 218. "Jostice," 20, 16.

[2] Concerning appeal in the Frankish epoch, see above, p. 564. In Germany, the "curia regia" ("Hofgericht") heard appeals from the ordinary tribunals (except in case of delegation to the tribunals of the power of "privilegia de non appellando"). We find cases of appeals from the end of the 1100s. *Blondel*, p. 50, "Saxon Mirror," 2, 12, 4 and following. But this related especially to the "reprobatio sententiæ" ("Urtheilschelten"), or falsification of judgment. The limitations upon the royal jurisdiction were increased. In France, traces of appeal were found in the 1000s and in the 1100s; at Noyon under Philip Augustus; *L. Delisle*, "Cat. des Actes de Philippe-Auguste," no. 2232. Ord. 1254, I, 75, Art. 30. In the Midi, the right of appeal had perhaps always been in use. *Tardif*, p. 128; "For de Morlaas," 7, 100, Art. 298; r. 111, Art. 226; *Petrus*, 4, 1. It was especially in the 1200s that the institution became general. *Viollet*, II, 214; *Langlois*, "Textes Parlement," 13; *Luchaire*, "Ann. Fac. Bordeaux," 2, 176. "Gr. C. of France," 3, 72, p. 577. "Ass. Jerusalem," I, 537.

customs changed; the parties, more enlightened, became less suspicious, and the conduct of the judges justified the lessening suspicion. As they were no longer barons but men learned in the law, their decisions were attacked only by way of procedure. Only involuntary errors were imputed to them and a judgment was impeached without a charge of bad faith.[1] The Roman law and the practice of the ecclesiastical tribunals favored the right of appeal in the modern sense of the word. A hierarchy of superior judges (bailiffs and seneschals) and inferior judges (provosts) was established in the courts of the king and the seigniors. Thus in the royal courts appeal lay from the provost to the bailiff and from the bailiff to the *Parlement* (1200 s). Appeals were even taken from the seigniorial courts to the king. This practice was established with little difficulty in the case of judgments rendered by the seigniorial courts on the royal domains; but it was more difficult to extend it to judgments rendered by the courts on the lands of the great feudatories.[2] Here the practice became definitely established only during the 1300 s. In the charters of confirmation or of concession of jurisdiction the king reserved for himself the resort or the right to hear appeals on account of default of the law, or on account of bad or erroneous judgments. It has been supposed that there were tacit reservations of the same

[1] *P. de Font.*, 22, 23, appeal without battle the first known instance of which is in Vermandois. The Ordinance of Saint Louis which abolished the duel prescribed appeal without battle. "Olim," I, 200, 10; *Beaumanoir*, 1, 14, 35; 61, 65 and following; "Jostice," 1, 4, 4, "Const. of Châtelet," 24, 34, 55 (no longer speaks of the errors of the court). The appeal retained some archaic characteristics: (*a*) the judgment had to be declared false and bad; without one of these words, the appeal was not admissible. "Etabl. de saint Louis," II, 16. "Olim," I, 402, 6; (*b*) the appeal was directed against the judge and not against the party, who was simply invited to appear if he was interested in it. *Boutillier*, I, 3. But in the end, the procedure was the same as in the countries with written law, where the case was postponed, the judge being notified to appear for the purpose of seeing his sentence corrected if necessary. "Olim," II, 278, 15; I, 731, 18; "St. Parl.," 4, 1, 2; 3, 28, 3; (*c*) the judge of appeal did not know anything of the facts of the case, but simply declared that it had been judged badly. *Imbert*, "Prat.," 2, 7, 4; (*d*) the appeal had to be lodged before the judge had left his seat. "St. Parl.," 20, 2, 3; *Bout.*, I, 20; II, 14. In the counties with written law, the appellant had ten days after the judgment in which to present the "apostoli" or "libelli appellatorii." "Olim," 2, 39, 3 (*cf.* Roman law); Ord. II, 51. *Cf. Isambert*, "Table," see "Appel." These various points were reformed in the 1500 s and 1600 s. *Cf. Lange*, "Pratique"; *Pothier*, "Procéd. civil.," etc.

[2] *Langlois*, "Textes Parlement," Table, see "Appellation: Phil. III," 275. Annoyances inflicted by the seigniors on those who appealed and protection of the appellants by the king. *Cf. Viollet*, 2, 218; *Beaumanoir*, 11, 12; "Olim," I, 453; II, 38 (1286, in criminal matters to the "Parlement"). "Et. saint Louis," 2, 78. *Tanon*, p. 70. Arbitrations of the king, *Petit-Dutaillis*, "Louis VIII," 352.

kind in respect to all seigniorial courts. The appeal was taken first to the superior seigniorial tribunal if the seignior had the right to hear the appeal, that is to say, the right to create two degrees of jurisdiction;[1] then to the tribunal of the suzerain and from one degree to another up to the king (that is to say, to his judges of appeal, his bailiffs and his *Parlement*).[2] Direct appeal, "omisso medio," from the seignior to the king was not permitted. Since the number of appeals was not limited and the right of appeal was always open to the parties whatever the amount at issue, one evil followed another. There were sometimes as many as six degrees of jurisdiction and hence suits were long drawn out. However, the seigniors lost the right to hear appeals in criminal cases.[3]

§ 220. **All Justice emanated from the King.** — From the end of the 1200 s, Beaumanoir (11, 12) affirmed that all lay jurisdiction belonged to the king in fee or in "arrière-fee." It was asserted that seigniorial justice was an emanation from the sovereignty of the king but at the same time that the king had delegated it to the seigniors as an irrevocable property right. The monarchy did not interfere with this right and left to the seigniors their profits from the administration of justice because the wretched condition of the royal finances did not permit the king to indemnify them. The crying abuses to which these village courts gave rise created a demand for their abolition by jurists like Dumoulin and Loyseau.[4] The monarchy contented itself, however, with the

[1] *Langlois*, 276 (1278: prohibition against having a second degree of jurisdiction except by contrary usage), Ord. of Louis le Hutin. "Gr. Cout. de France," 1, 4, c. 51, no seignior could, in the exercise of his right to administer justice, create a jurisdiction. Ord. of Orléans for Languedoc, Art. 14 and following. *Boutaric*, "Droit seig.," p. 502.

[2] *Beaumanoir*, 2, 30; 11, 12; "Olim," III, 2d p., 867, 42; 123, 12; 314, 6. "Gr. Cout. of Rousillon," 1560, forbade the seignior to create various instances or degrees of jurisdiction in the same place. Ex. six degrees of jurisdiction: Rameau, Prépalteau, Montigny, Châteaudun, Blois, Parlement. *Fleury*, "Dr. public," 1, 2; *Imbert*, "Prat.," 2, 3. "Appeaux volages," "Appellationes Laudunenses" (of Laon), appeal to the bailiff before judgment. "Olim," I, 875, 26; II, 398, Ord. II, 81, *Bout.*, 2, 14. Authorized and forbidden successively. Ord. 1413, X, 144 (interdiction).

[3] *Esmein*, "Hist. de la proc. crim.," p. 153.

[4] **Abuses of village justice.** They were so called, because there remained scarcely any seigniorial courts except in the villages. 1st, they developed among the peasants the mania for chicanery; long drawn out procedures, numerous degrees of jurisdiction, and, consequently, a great deal of expense for unimportant affairs; 2d, the judges were corrupt and ignorant; as they earned little, they engaged in all sorts of collusions; the cabaret was the annex of the tribunal; the same judge was bailiff here and clerk of the court or procurator somewhere else; 3d, the seigniors were masters of the judges and of justice. There was only one remedy for these abuses, namely, to abolish the village courts, but it would have been necessary to indemnify the seigniors and the state shrank from this expense. The encroachments of the royal judges weakened their power every day.

policy of diminishing the abuses by means of appeal, priority and the reservation of royal cases, and by gradually including these courts in the framework of the royal judicial system. In reality, the revenues, if we may so speak, remained with the seigniors, but the office had almost returned to the king. Many seigniorial courts had even disappeared through the enforcement of the maxim: "all maxims emanate from the king." The consequence was, says Dumoulin, that no seignior could pretend to administer justice without a royal concession established by title or immemorial possession. The Revolution finally abolished this institution which had so long survived its usefulness.

§ 221. **The Right of coining Money**[1] and of fixing the value of that coined belonged to a number of seigniors from the end of the 900 s.[2] The only coins which were current in the seigniory were those struck by the seignior himself, all others were excluded except for a frequent toleration of the best-known coins.[3] The alteration of the coin was for the seigniors and the kings a source of profit the legitimacy of which was hardly questionable in their eyes.[4] Uniformity of the monetary system was the only remedy for the evil and this the royal power partly brought about under Saint Louis. This prince improved the royal money thus causing it to be preferred to the money struck by the seigniors, and he enacted that it should circulate throughout the kingdom concurrently with the seigniorial coin although the latter was excluded from the royal domain. The extension of this domain annihilated the seigniorial rights which the king had not com-

Fleury, "Dr. public," I, 2; *Loyseau*, "Tr. des justices de village." In England, feudal courts had been at a very early time almost annihilated.

[1] *Luchaire*, p. 270, 591, 600 (bibliog.); *Blondel*, p. 152; *Petit-Dutaillis*, "Louis VIII," p. 381; *Prou*, "Introd. au Catalogue des monnaies carol.," 1896.

[2] There were three systems for the coinage of monies: farming, infeudation, and direct exploitation. Coinage dues ("seigniorage") were levied on the occasion of the coinage of the monies. *D. Vaissete*, 5, 1228; 8, 1040. Hearth-money ("focagium") was a royalty paid to the seignior or to the king to insure that he would not change or alter the monies, "Gr. Cout. Norm.," c. 14. Counterfeit money was widely circulated in the Middle Ages. "Enciclop. giur. ital.," see "Moneta."

[3] It is for the economists to explain how this fact was reconciled with the law known as Gresham's law. *Gide*, "Principes d'écon. polit." In the south good money such as that of Morlaas, of Melgueil, of Toulouse, of Agen, drove out bad money from regions where the seigniors imposed it upon the people.

[4] The alteration was made either materially, for example, by mixing copper with silver, or nominally by changing the value of the coins which was a great deal simpler than it would have been if there had been a fixed standard (pound, sou); it was decreed, for example, that the coin which was worth a pound, should be worth two.

pensated them for, but now the seigniors, short of cash, especially since the time of Philip the Fair, by the assay-marks of the royal officers, agreed voluntarily to the redemption. Philip the Fair, who never ceased to alter his own coins, did not permit the seigniors to do the same. Thus the rule came to prevail that to the king alone belonged the right to coin money, a rule which in England dated from Edward I.[1]

§ 222. **Seigniorial Finance. Feudal Dues.**[2] — (A) The seigniorial treasury included the sum total of the revenues of the seignior, the products of his domains; these were: (1) domanial rents collected by virtue of his character as proprietor; (2) judicial fees which belonged to him as justiciary or sovereign, and among which were veritable taxes, since the right to levy a tax was a seigniorial prerogative. From the judicial fees were taken the regalian fees, that is to say, fees which after having belonged for some time to the seigniors reverted in good time to the king (1300s and 1400s).[3] (B) The distinction which we have just established cannot be traced in detail because feudalism had precisely the effect of con-

[1] Ord., May, 1263, 1313, I, 93, 519, and later ordinances. *Langlois*, "Philippe III," 368; *Isambert*, "Table," see "Monnaie"; *Vuitry*, "Etudes," I, 443; II, 181; BCh., 1876, 145; *Fleury*, "Dr. public," II, 4; Code Henry III, liv. 15.

[2] Concerning seigniorial dues see: *Renauldon*, 1765; *Boutaric*, 1741; *La Place*, 1757; *Loysel*, I, 2, vol. 2; (*Boncerf*) "Les inconvénients des droits féodaux," 1776 (burned by a decree of Parliament), 1789; *Tocqueville*, "L'anc. Rég. et la Révolution"; *Taine*, "L'Ancien Régime"; *L. Delisle*, "Class. agric. en Norm."; *Viollet*, "Inst. pol.," II, 448; *Flach*, "Orig. de l'anc. France," I, 381; *Vuitry*, "Et. s. le Rég. financier de la France av. 1789," 1878; *Fournier de Flaix*, "L'impôt dans les div. civilis.," 1897. *Cf.* the "Glossaires" of *Du Cange*, *Ragueau*, etc. Their designation as feudal dues is scarcely exact, for these exactions were far from being derived wholly from the fief. They varied infinitively according to places and epochs. We mention only the best known. *Isambert*, "Table," see "Droits seigneur," etc.; *Despeisses*, "Tr. des dr. seign.," 1659.

[3] The celebrated "Constitutio de regalibus" of 1158 (Frederick Barbarossa). "L. Feud.," 11, 56, enumerated the regalian rights (without providing any means for preventing the seigniors from themselves appropriating them): public roads, and navigable rivers with the tolls or dues levied for the use of the same, "angarius" and various "prestations" on the occasion of the expeditions of the prince, the right to coin money, fines, confiscations, and vacant properties, fisheries, mines, and salt deposits, the right to half of the treasures found, appointment of magistrates charged with dispensing justice. *Blondel*, 73; *Britz*, 607. *Cf.* in England, the "Prærogativa regis" of Edward II; *Glasson*, "Inst. Anglet.," 3, 64. In the 1500s *Bacquet* in his "Traité des droits de justice," showed that the king had the rights of "aubaine" (escheat), of bastardy, of amortization; he disputed with the seigniors the rights of police, of watch, of "voirie"; banalities, rights over the rivers, tolls and markets; the seigniors were obliged to obtain a concession from the king. *Boutillier*, 2, 1; *Heusler*, "Inst. d. d. R.," I, 364: sovereign jurisdiction of the routes and rivers under the Carolingians (*Waitz*, 4, 114, n. 1). Text of the constitution of Frederick I in M.G.H., L.L., "Const.," I, 244.

fusing the two kinds of ideas from which it was derived. Seigniorial dues were classified differently according to places and times. The feudal seignior and the justiciary seignior disputed with each other, the one by reason of his ownership, the other by reason of his sovereign rights; the inferior justiciary and the superior justiciary did the same for those rights which were reserved to them, and the king also laid claim to many of them. Here was a source of endless controversy.

In the 1300s the royal tax came to be superimposed upon the seigniorial tax. It was a question whether the king could levy subsidies on the lands of his barons without their consent. Philip the Fair, in an instruction of 1303, said to his officers: "Do not act against the will of the barons, but regard this instruction as secret, because if the barons knew it, it would result in too great an injury to us." Therefore, the baron alone had the right of taxation on his domains; the right of the State was not established until much later, as we shall see.

§ 223. **Dues collected by the Seignior by Virtue of his Proprietorship.** — Many of these dues were nothing but ancient public taxes which had become private property (for example, the land tax and the personal tax). The seignior exacted them ordinarily as rent by reason of the tenure that he had granted; but sometimes it was also an account of the personal condition of those who owed it because they were serfs (former slaves). (A) *Dues and Services* ("consuetudines," "exactiones"), 1st, (*a*) quit rents ("cens") paid in money; (*b*) "champart" (a tax on crops) (*e.g.* clayage and terrage) paid in kind; (*c*) "regards," or accessory dues (on hens, capons, eggs, etc.);[1] 2d, the "corvée," or compulsory servile labor on the land of the seignior. The nobles were not subject to these obligations. (B) *Transmission*, 1st, on fiefs: (*a*) relief or purchase (a year's income); (*b*) "quint" and "requint" (24%); 2d, on manors ("censives"): (*a*) relief or "recension"; (*b*) "lods et ventes" ($\frac{1}{12}$ of the price); 3d, on servile tenures (mortmain), etc. [see discussion of these feudal terms in *Luchaire*, "Manuel," § 176 ff.]. Certain dues falling in this category, such as redemption charges (amortissement) and the "franc-fief" were, in time, transformed into regalian rights and reverted to the character of a tax. (C) *Dues from the Church* (patronage, spoils, perhaps also the regalia). (D) *Personal*

[1] Curious dues which were, doubtless, only the remains of old obligations more serious. *Michelet*, "Orig. du dr. fr.," p. 228 and following; *L. Delisle*, p. 89.

exactions from the serfs ("chevage," payments for marriage between serfs of different seigniories, etc.).[1]

§ 224. **Judicial Fees or Fees Exacted by the Seignior in his Character as Sovereign.** — I. The administration of justice was the principal attribute of sovereignty and it was for the seignior a source of profit. These profits included fines ("justitia," "placita," the one arbitrary in amount, the other fixed by custom),[2] proceeds of confiscation,[3] fees for affixing the seal, registration fees, and notarial charges.[4]

[1] Concerning the seigniorial dues the only scientific work is the "Jus primæ noctis" of *K. Schmidt*, 1881 (c. r.); *Viollet*, "R. crit. d'hist.," 1882, 90; Z.S.S., G.A., 3, 241; *Bernhoeft*; Z.V.R., 1883, 279; 1884, 397. *Add Schmidt*, "Z. f. Ethnol.," 16, 18; *Slav.*, "Geschichtsq. z. d. hist. Ger. f. Posen," I, 323). In order to prove the existence of these exactions only the scattered texts, small in number and relatively recent (1400 s and 1500 s) are cited, whereas we should expect witnesses of the earliest feudal times. It seems then that we can, at most, give credence to a local abuse, a débris of slavery. Schmidt sees in the seigniorial tax a legend which came into existence toward the 1500 s through the aid of travelers' narratives or traditions of antiquity, and which served to give a reason for certain seigniorial taxes poorly understood. See "Marquette," "Cullage"; *La Curne* of Sainte-Palaye, see "Cuissage"; *Merlin*, "Rép.," see "Markette"; *Ferrière*, "Dict. de dr.," see "Nopçages." The greater number of these texts assumed the consent of the seignior to the marriage of the serfs with the fees that it implied, in default of payment of which the exercise of the seigniorial right was permitted; here was a provision that was purely comminatory, says Schmidt, for it was the parties and not the seignior, who had the choice between the payment of the fee and the exercise of the right. From that time, this right was never exercised. The seignior had a right to marriage viands (a piece of pork, a gallon of drink) or to the "cullage" (from "culeus," leather bottle, allusion to the beverage); he had a right to the "brachionagium," or embrace in token of the authorization of the marriage; to the "jambage" or "cuissage," or right of placing, in the presence of witnesses, a leg in the nuptial bed in recognition of his seigniory, as in case of marriage by proxy. The dues of the seignior have been confused with the price for dispensing with the obligation imposed on the husband and wife to be continent during the first three days of marriage. *Boutaric*, "Dr. seign.," ed. 1775, says: "I have seen seigniors who pretended to have this right, but who had been, as well as many others of this kind, proscribed by the decrees of the court." *Gallenga*, "St. d. Piemonte," I, 321.

[2] *Beaumanoir*, 30, 20 and following; *Boutillier*, 2, 4; *Loysel*, 6, 2, 2. The old royal "ban" often fixed the amount at 60 sous in the tariff of fines of the "Coutumes." *Viollet*, "Et. saint Louis," vol. I, p. 245. For the same misdemeanor, the fine inflicted on a noble was higher than that imposed on a common man ("roturier"); the one paid in pounds, the other in sous. *Loysel*, 6, 2, 30. "Gr. Charte," 20 and following ("amerciamenta").

[3] *Boutillier*, 2, 15; *Loysel*, 839: who confiscates the body, confiscates the property. "Paris," 183, "Gr. Cout. of France," I, 11, p. 205; *Isambert*, "Table," h. v. *Cf.* Roman law.

[4] "Tr. Anc. Cout. Norm.," 56 (fines); "Gr. C. Norm.," 22, *Boutillier*, 2, 15 and 40. The fee for sealing was the price for the authenticity given to the acts. No act could be produced in a judicial trial without being sealed, and often the seal had to be, as it were, legalized by a superior seal; for that, a double fee was charged. Richard the Lion-hearted, at the end

II. The justiciar had a right to vacant properties, inclosed lands, strays,[1] treasure trove,[2] successions in escheat, to which the inheritances of aliens and bastards should be added,[3] the tax on Jews, and, finally, mines and salt works,[4] all this following the example of the Roman Emperors and because they were regarded as a consequence of the right to administer justice, a compensation to the seigniors for the expenses imposed upon them in the administration of justice.

of his reign, changed the seal in order to be able to levy a new tax for affixing the same to all acts; and this example found imitators, as do all bad examples. *Infra*, Royal finances. The clerks' offices were sometimes farmed out, sometimes put into the keeping of some one. In the 1300s, the king tried to reserve for himself the clerk's office, the notarial office, and the scrivener's office. Ord. July, 18, 1318. *Isambert*, "Table."

[1] Wrecks and strays were treated as unoccupied property. *Ragueau*, see "Espaves." On maritime wrecks, the seigniorial exaction was called the "droit de bris." The seignior sometimes went to the aid of the ship and the fee for this was doubly onerous. "Tr. Anc. Cout. Norm.," 67, "Gr. C. Norm.," 16 ("de veriscis" varech) 18 (de rebus vaivis, things "guesves," that is to say, abandoned). *Ragueau*, "Gloss.," see "Bris," "Varech," etc. The shipwreck exaction was applied not only to the vessel and its cargo, but to the crew and to the passengers. The popes censured this cruel custom (X, 5, 17, 3). From the time of Henry I it was restricted. *Bracton*, fr. 120, says that if only a dog or a cat survived or even if the merchandise could be recognized by its marks, it had to be returned to its owner on the condition that the latter asserted his claim within a year and a day. 1st Statute of Westminster, c. 24; *Cl. Joly*, "Tr. des restitutions d. grands," p. 69; *Holtzendorff*, "Rechtslexicon," see "Strandrecht"; *Stobbe*, "Handb. d. d. P.," § 149. The "crassus piscis" (certain kinds of fish like the whale and sturgeon) belonged to the king in Denmark, Norway, Normandy, and England. See *Ragueau*, "Esturgeon," "Poisson royal." *Glasson*, "Inst. Anglet.," 3, 70; *Fleury*, "Dr. public," 2, 5, 9; "Olim," I, 848. Above, Maritime laws.

[2] *Loysel*, 279 and following: the king appropriated for himself the fortune and the treasure trove (regalian idea). The gold found belonged to the barons ("Anjou," 61); the other treasures belonged, one third to the justiciary, one third to the owner, and one third to the inventor (Roman idea). In Normandy: 211 and following: the treasure belonged to the seignior of the fief where it was found. "Capit.," 789, 2, I, 69; *Richthofen*, "L. Saxon," p. 181; Edward the Conf., 14; "Schwabensp.," 347; "Sachsensp.," 1, 35, 1. *Stobbe, loc. cit.*

[3] Those who did not leave natural heirs, had for their heir the seignior, but which one? There was a conflict between the feudal seignior over the lands of which the succession was open and the justiciary seignior to which the "de cujus" was amenable. The superior justiciary triumphed ("Paris," 167): this was an incident in the progress toward centralization. "Tr. Anc. Cout. Norm.," 75 ("de bastardia"). "C. Norm.," 146. The communities of inhabitants, the feudal seigniors, and the justiciary seigniors disputed among themselves concerning the possession of vacant lands, of pasturage, woods, etc. *Loysel*, 277, 348.

[4] The constitution "de regalibus" of 1158 ranks among the rights of the king that of exploiting or conceding salt and other mines. *Blondel*, p. 157; "Miroir de Saxe," 1, 35. But the seigniors in fact took possession of them (seigniorial salt, salt tax). *Laurière* on Loysel, no. 240. In France gold and silver mines belonged to the king, upon his paying the owner for the land. The other mines belonged to the owners of the lands, but the king collected the tenth of the revenues. Ord., May 6, 1563; *Isambert*, "Table," see "Mines."

III. From the Church. As protector and advocate of the Church the seignior had certain rights which were confused with those which belonged to him as patron (such were enfeoffed tithes, etc.).[1]

§ 225. **Aids, the "Taille" Lodging and Subsistence ("gîte et procuration").** — 1st, Aids ("auxilia") exacted by the seignior in case of necessity (as in the event of war) were imposed upon vassals; they took the name "taille," "queste," "tolte" ("mala tolta"), "maltâte," and amounted to a forced loan, whenever they were paid by the common people ("roturiers") and the serfs.[2] They may be compared to direct taxes. 2d, By virtue of the rights of lodging and subsistence, the serfs, "roturiers," and even the noble vassals, were required to provide lodging and food for the seignior and his suite whenever they traveled from place to place. These burdensome dues, like various other feudal exactions, were converted into a pecuniary tax.[3]

§ 226. **Taxes on Trade and Industry, Tolls.** — Feudalism did not recognize freedom of trade and industry; trade was carried on and industry was pursued only with the authorization of the seignior. Already during the Frankish period the establishment of fairs and markets was dependent upon the will of the public authorities.[4] The high justiciaries took the place of the State, kept order, collected the dues, and maintained public weights and measures.[5] They sold the right to carry on trades and required of artisans a sort of patent known as the "haufan." They reaped profits especially from tolls, those indirect feudal taxes which were derived from the Roman "portorior"; rivers and highways were dotted with stations where merchandise and travellers were compelled to pay dues which we would call transit fees, octroi, and customs; they were collected under the pretense that they were needed for the maintenance of roads and for policing the same (direction and safe-conduct). But as the seigniors performed both services very badly, it followed that commerce was handicapped in every way and became almost impossible.[6] Here again the

[1] Laical abbés, *cf. Luchaire*, p. 276.

[2] See above, Frankish epoch, p. 557. Cap. "de villis," 3, I, 83. Under certain circumstances, free men made presents to the king, while the inferiors ("colons," etc.) were taxed arbitrarily: from that arose the "aides" and "taille."

[3] *Luchaire*, 207; *Petit-Dutaillis*, "Louis VIII," 377. See also *supra*, 556.

[4] On fairs and markets, *cf. Huvelin*, Thesis, 1897; *D. Vaissete*, 5, 1139, 755, 605; 8, 296; *Blondel*, p. 142; *Ragueau*, see "Foires."

[5] "Gr. C. Norm.," 15; *Beaumanoir*, 2, 26; "Olim," Table, see "Pedagia," "Mercata."

[6] Tolls, market tolls, "leudes" or "leydes" (from "levita" for "levata," thing, sum levied), were derived from the Roman "portorium." The

royal power made gradual progress; the instruction of 1372 proclaimed that to the king alone belonged the right to grant fairs and markets, that those coming and going were under his protection; the police of trades was reserved to him; uniformity of weights and measures was demanded; and tolls themselves were called royal rights by the jurists of the 1500 s, but the seigniors retained them by virtue of royal concessions or by reason of immemorial possession.[1]

§ 227. "**Banalités**" [service monopolies], (mills, bake ovens, wine presses, forges, breweries, bulls, etc.),[2] implied: (*a*) The right of the seignior to require the inhabitants of the seigniory to grind their grain at his mill, to bake their bread in his oven, etc.; and (*b*) the prohibition against any one else having ovens, mills, and the like on his lands.[3] He levied and collected taxes on unfermented wine, flour, etc.; but this monopoly did not imply that his interest alone was involved; it was established also for economic reasons, to prevent competition; it was perhaps a relic of collective ownership,[4] perhaps a creation of the great landowners in the interest of the inhabitants of their domains.[5] Whatever the origin of this monopoly, whether it was an attribute of proprietorship in certain respects, or a right of justice,[6] the

"guidage" was rather a fee paid by travelers to secure protection on the routes. In the 1300 s the king was the sovereign inspector of highways of the kingdom and had the policing of public ways. *Cf. Blondel*, p. 161; *D. Vaissete*, 5, 414, 646, 731, 862, 1261, 1292; 8, 331, 296, 527, 1160, 1292. Exemptions, for example, for the profit of the Church, of the abbeys. *Boutaric*, p. 292; Declar. of January, 1663.

[1] "Et. de Saint Louis," I, 148; *Ferrière*, "Dict. de droit" (and the other authors cited). The toll seigniors were obliged to keep in repair bridges, passages, and public roads (Ord. Orléans, 107; Blois, 282) and to keep them in safe condition. No seignior could impose a new toll without the permission of the king. In Forez, along the Loire and the Rhone, the toll was still a seigniorial and not a royal right. Code Henry III, 10, 38. *Champion*, "La France d'ap. les Cahiers de 1789," p. 152.

[2] "Banalité," from the word "ban," right of the seignior to issue an injunction under a penalty. "Banlieu," territory where this right was exercised. *Cf. Hauban*, Ban of vintage, etc. *Guyot*, "Inst. féod.," p. 256.

[3] There were "banalités" from the 1000 s. Windmills did not become common until the 1300 s. "Paris," 72. "Tr. Anc. Cout. Norm.," 60; "Et. de Saint Louis," I, 111, 114.

[4] *Viollet*, "Et. de Saint Louis," I, 104; "R. hist.," 1886, vol. 32, p. 86, "L. Baiuw.," 1, 9, 2. Industries necessary to life were organized into a system of agrarian communities, under the form of public services. "Cout. de Prayssas," 1266, Art. 7, 35.

[5] *Thévenin*, "R. hist.," vol. 31, p. 241; Cap. "de villis," c. 18. The mill was considered as private property in many Barbarian laws. "Sal.," 22; "Roth.," 149 and following; "Alam.," 2, 86; "Wis.," 7, 2, 12, and 4, 30.

[6] "Et. de Saint Louis," I, 102: fees for justice; it was not only the tenants of the seignior but those amenable to his courts who were subject to this imposition.

"banalités," unpopular as they were from an early date,[1] were suppressed in many places in the 1500 s[2] but abolished only by the law of July 17, 1793.[3]

Resembling "banalités," properly so called, were: 1st, the bans of vintage and harvest, proclaimed by the seignior, which brought it about that agriculture was no more free than was commerce or industry;[4] 2d, the "banvin" or prohibition against the inhabitants selling their wine before the seignior had sold his;[5] and 3d, monopolies, for example, of money.

§ 228. **Waters and Forests.** — In many places the seignior regarded himself as the exclusive owner of the forests and also claimed for himself the ownership of waters.[6] This particular class of domainal possessions, like the land, consisted of two parts: that which he reserved for himself (the warren, the use of which was prohibited to all others) and that which he assigned to the use of his tenants upon the payment of certain dues. The important fisheries were infeudated and sometimes even maritime fisheries were granted. Over the timber the seigniors claimed various rights of "gruerie," "grairie," "triage," etc., which were only forms of their superior ownership.[7] They also had the right

[1] Because of the annoyances to which it gave rise (obligation to accept poor flour, bread burned or not cooked, long distance to the mill, necessity of waiting three days at the door of a mill without water, etc.). *Champion*, p. 142.

[2] Ord. 1629, Art. 207; *Loysel*, 240 and following. Many coutumes supplanted the "banalités" or attached them to the fief. *Boutaric*, p. 351 (fief or justice).

[3] The law of March 15–28, 1790, vol. 2, Art. 23, allowed certain banalities to remain, among others, those which were established by agreement between a community of inhabitants and a private person, not a seignior. The Council of State considered these as abolished and the Court of Cassation as continuing. Advice of the Council of State, July 3, 1808; Dec. of April, 1809. The communes could not establish new banalities.

[4] D. "de feriis," 4. They wished to assure the good quality of the harvests. During the feudal epoch, these bans served to facilitate the collection of the tithe, and the feudal impositions.

[5] "Fors de Béarn," ed. *Mazure*, p. 216; *D. Vaissete*, 8, 980; 5, 831, 1199, 1051.

[6] "Et. de Saint Louis," I, 121; *Michelet*, "Orig. du dr. fr. Bourbonn," 340. *Boutillier*, I, 73; the large rivers belonged to the king and were treated as royal streams (a question of navigable rivers). The others belonged to the seigniors in the territory through which they flowed. "Gr. C. of France," I, 4, p. 110. The non-nobles could hunt anywhere outside of the warrens (Ord. 1402, Charles VI, waters and forests); *Guyot*, "Inst. féod.," p. 269: the unnavigable rivers belonged, according to the localities, to the superior justiciaries or to the feudal seigniors; *cf. Boutaric*, p. 554; the concession of fishing belonged to the superior justiciary. *Stobbe*, Handb. d. d. P., § 150 and following.

[7] That is to say, jurisdiction, profits of justice, pasturage, share in the wood felled, etc. "Third and danger" means a third of the proceeds of each sale plus a tenth, in all, thirteen out of thirty (Normandy). "Olim," Table, see "Dangerii."

of hunting, not only on their own reserves or warrens, but in the forests and on the lands of their tenants.[1] In all these cases the seigniorial rights were gradually abandoned; the seigniors frequently declared the right of fishing to be free to all, exacted nothing for the use of woods and vacant lands, and acknowledged the ownership to belong to the community. On his part the king claimed the right to navigable rivers and streams suitable for rafting, regulated the rights of the seigniors in respect to the woods, regulated the right of hunting and made it a privilege of the nobles; to the seigniors there remained only vestiges of their

[1] *Viollet*, "Et. de Saint Louis," vol. I, p. 102 (and authors cited); *Du Cange*, see "Foresta," "Garenna"; *Championnière*, no. 53; *De Launay*, "Tr. du dr. de chasse," 1684; Hunting code, 1734; *Freminville*, "Pratique des terriers," vol. 4; *Ferrière*, "Dict."; "Gr. Encycl.," see "Chasse," "Garenne"; *Blondel*, p. 60. On forestry legislation in England, *Glasson*, "Inst. Anglet.," 3, 61; Henry III's charter of the forest, 1712; *Bémont*, "Chartes des libertés angl.," p. 64. The right of hunting may be considered: 1st, as an attribute of the ownership of the soil of which the game was only a product (feudal conception); 2d, or, if one regards the game as "res nullius," something to which every one has a natural right, whether he be the owner of the land or not (Roman conception). Kings and seigniors, in falling heir to agrarian communities, did not take away the liberty of hunting which the inhabitants enjoyed. They were content with creating for themselves "forestæ," warrens, or defenses, that is to say, territories where hunting and fishing were forbidden to others ("nemus bannitum"). During the feudal epoch, the seignior had "garennes jurées," that is to say, reserves and "garennes ouvertes," hunting being permitted in all or in a part of his jurisdiction. The royal ordinances of the 1300 s restricted this last right (1316, 1350, 1355, etc.). In the 1500 s, warrens could not be established without the permission of the king, registered after inquiry upon the marble table. Ord. 1669, 30, 19. *Loysel*, 237. Toward the end of the 1300 s, fishing and hunting tended to become a privilege of the nobility. Ord. Jan. 1396, (*Isambert*, 6, 774). *Cf.* "Cout. Bigorre," Art. 26. According to the ordinance of 1669, vol. 30, common people ("roturiers") did not have the right to hunt except in their own fiefs, if they possessed any; the nobles hunted on their lands and if they did not possess any, then on the lands adjoining their house or on the fiefs of others with the authorization of the seignior proprietors. The superior justiciary had equally the right to hunt in his jurisdiction, by reason of the public power with which he was invested. *Loysel*, 278; *Fleury*, "Dr. public," 2, 6, 13. (The ordinance was poorly observed, for the prohibition of hunting made for the common people and for the periods of the year when hunting was forbidden.) Complaints were made against the right of hunting, which formerly had been of the greatest utility to agriculture: 1st, because the misdemeanors of the chase were punished by severe penalties, atrocious, even during the Middle Ages (Normandy, England); 2d, because its exercise was ruinous to agriculture; the game of the seigniorial warrens wrought the greatest damage. *La Fontaine*, "Le Jardinier et son seigneur." Code Henry III, 16; *Cl. Joly*, "Tr. des restit. des Grands," p. 71; *Guyot*, "Inst. féod.," p. 266, 273, sees in the chase a feudal right; *Boutaric*, p. 523, a right of justice. Then came the revolution. Robespierre was a partisan of unlimited freedom of the chase; Mirabeau wished to reserve this right to the owner. Dec. of Aug. 4 and 11, 1789, April 30, 1790 (in this last meaning, every proprietor could hunt on his lands). *Cf. Isambert*, Table; "Olim," Table, see "Chaciæ," "Piscat."

original privileges: the right of hunting and of maintaining warrens, to which may be compared the right of maintaining dovecotes.[1]

§ 229. **Origin, Legitimacy, and Decadence of Feudal Rights.** — This is an obscure subject àpropos of which two maxims have been drawn upon: "fief and justice are entirely one," and "fief and justice have nothing in common." Neither one nor the other explains the legitimacy of feudal rights. Many of them were established in an entirely regular manner by virtue of contracts in the interest of both parties[2] or through charters of immunity; still others had their origin in violence or usurpation, but to these time and circumstances gave a sanction which was equivalent to the legality of the others. Conversely some feudal exactions which had no original taint became unjustifiable through its consequences. In the main, these exactions were the budget of the feudal State and there is no State without a budget. We may regard them as excessive, unjustly established and out of proportion to the services rendered in the general interest by the seigniors; but it is impossible to condemn them entirely. The feudal tax had great faults; it was often arbitrary, it varied according to the social condition of those upon whom it fell and not according to their ability to pay. Certain classes, like the clergy and the nobility, were almost exempt from it; others were overtaxed; never was the proverbial rapacity of the treasury more reproached. The system of feudal taxation appears to have been organized in the interest of the personnel of the seignior and not in that of the seigniory or feudal State for the maintenance of services of general interest; hence they do not deserve the name of taxes in the modern sense of the word, the tax, properly so called, was in them blended with domainal dues. Under the monarchy and after the establishment of the royal tax, most of the feudal impositions lost their "raison d'être." Some of them were restored to the

[1] The seigniors only had dovecotes "à pied," that is to say, round or square in shape, with pigeonholes or pots along its length designed to accommodate the pigeons. The "fines" or "volets," "volières" (pigeon houses) and the dovecotes on posts, did not have pigeonholes to the ground. Sometimes the "fines" were seigniorial. "Paris," 19, 70; "Orléans," 178, "Britanny," 398. *Guyot*, "Inst.," p. 262. Dec. Aug. 4–11, 1789, Art. 2.

[2] Guests were established on the lands of a seignior, for which they engaged to pay him certain fees; this was a free contract. The same when a seignior erected a bastile or a place of rescue; the inhabitants accepted the conditions that the seignior exacted of them. There was sometimes usurpation without violence, as when the seignior substituted himself for the head of the State; but, doubtless, there was not a large number of acts of violence. *Weanspeare*, "St. d. abusi feudali in Ital.," 1885.

category of regalian fees (redemption, freehold, aubaine, bastardy, coinage, regalia).[1] Seigniorial aids and the seigniorial "taille" disappeared in competition with the royal tax;[2] the same was true of most of the other feudal impositions resembling a tax, with the exception of the ancient tolls which the seigniors retained. They lost the right to reëstablish them; there remained for them the administration of justice with its emoluments together with the proceeds from fines, from confiscated property, banalities, escheats, wreckage, and hunting.

§ 230. **The Product of the Feudal Dues**[3] varied too widely to make a general evaluation possible. It is impossible to give even an approximate estimate of the amount of the revenue of the nobility, or of the extent of the burdens which the feudal exactions imposed upon the people, nor do we know the total amount on which these dues were paid. The rate of assessment hardly ever varied, though the purchasing power of money decreased; more than that, the amount of the quit rents and revenues was fixed in sous at a time when sous were gold coins, in the 1400 s they were silver, and in the 1600 s copper; the amount in sous was always the same, the seignior bore the entire loss. We see from these simple observations how difficult the problem of evaluation is. It has been maintained that on the eve of the Revolution, and even for a long time before, the feudal exactions yielded but little. Some have estimated the amount at about 4 per cent of the revenue, others at 14 per cent. It should not be forgotten, moreover, that the former, which gave scarcely any benefit to the seignior, did not cease to be very onerous (for example, "banalités").

§ 231. **Abolition of Feudal Rights.** — As we have seen, a large number of these rights had already been abolished by the monarchy; those which still remained in 1789 were abolished by the Revolution.

[1] *Cf. Bacquet*, "Lefebvre de la Planche," etc.

[2] The ordinance, 1439, Art. 44 (*Isamb.*, 9, 70), allowed only the tax on the serfs to remain, by reason of their condition, and on the common classes very exceptionally by virtue of a title.

[3] *Taine*, "L'Ancien Régime," p. 531 (Act of division of 1783: 810 arpents paid in the neighborhood of 575 francs). About 1720, a seigniory of 800 hectares in Dauphiny contributed 1686 pounds. *D'Avenel*, "Richelieu," I, 400; "La fortune privée à travers sept siècles," p. 207; "Hist. econom. de la propriété," 1894; *Marion*, "Rev. de la Révol.," 1895 (the twentieth in Languedoc); *Champion*, "La France d'ap. les Cahiers de 1789," p. 133; *Remoudière*, "Charges du paysan avant la Révolution," 1894 (Poitou); *D. Zolla*, "Ann. Ecole sc. pol.," July 15, 1894; *Abbé Mathieu*, *op. cit.*, p. 304.

(A.) **The Constituent Assembly.** *The distinction between dominant and contracting feudalism* [*i.e.* feudalism based on agreement]. Feudal rights were abolished in principle on the night of August 4, 1789; but the law of March 15–28, 1790, passed upon the report of Merlin, distinguished between dominant and contracting feudalism, the latter being regarded as legitimate, the former as being founded on usurpation and injustice. The law, (*a*) abolished without indemnity all seigniorial rights implying the superiority of one person over another (mortmain, feudal seizure, etc.), or the exercise by the seigniors of rights belonging to the public powers (tolls, banalities, etc.); (*b*) useful feudal dues (ground rent, dues in kind, enfeoffed tithes, etc.) were declared to be extinguishable by purchase; it was presumed that they were the price for the use of the land, and the obligation rested upon him who refused to pay them to show that he was not liable.[1]

(B.) **The Legislative Assembly** reversed this presumption. By the law of August 25–28, 1790, it abolished without indemnity seigniorial dues unless the seignior himself was able to prove by referring to the original title that they were the price or condition of the original cession of the land. This was to demand the impossible of them, in at least nine cases out of ten.

(C.) **The Convention** abolished outright all seigniorial and feudal dues and ordered the burning of the title deeds of the seigniors. This did not, however, put an end to the matter. It remained to distinguish between feudal dues, strictly speaking, and those in the nature of land rent which did not imply any feudal relation nor the superiority of one person over another. The task was often a very delicate one because the contracts were not explicit; for more than half a century jurisprudence struggled with these difficulties, and feudalism has fallen into its dotage in this question, which even to the present day is sometimes submitted to the courts. The law of December 18–29, 1790, declared purely land rent dues to be extinguishable by purchase and authorized leases for a period not exceeding ninety-nine years (*cf.* Art. 530 of the Civil Code).

TOPIC 3. TOWNS AND COMMUNES[2]

§ 232. **Introductory.** — The towns ("villes") and the open country were at the beginning of the feudal period subject to an

[1] Dec. May 3, 1790, concerning the conditions of redemption. *Salvioli*, p. 231.

[2] BIBLIOGRAPHY: *Giry*, "Doc. s. les rel. de la royauté avec les villes de France," 1885 (contains a reasonable bibliography); *Raynouard*,

identical régime which was only a continuation of that in force under the second dynasty. The seigniors administered them through their agents, *provosts* (" præpositi "), bailiffs or beadles (" bajuli "), and others. As the powers of these agents were very extensive and vaguely defined, and since the seignior exercised over them only an insufficient control, their authority was easily turned into tyranny; it was frequently arbitrary in law, and always in actual fact.[1]

§ 233. **Emancipation of the Towns.** — By the 1100 s this uniform régime had given place to great diversity. The condition of the townspeople was different from that of the inhabitants of the open country. Almost everywhere, not only in France, but in all western Europe, the towns had obtained certain privileges, a special administration, and undoubted autonomy. It is customary to recognize in France four kinds of towns, so far as the extent of their franchises is concerned: 1st, *provost towns*, which were still subject to the primitive régime; 2d, *privileged towns*, which had a provost but also a charter of liberties; 3d, the *communes*, which had acquired an autonomy almost complete; 4th, *consular towns*, which were only a sort of commune.

§ 234. **What were the Causes?** — So general a fact can be explained only by deep-seated causes, which are the same everywhere; but the forces which have produced it have not always had the

"Hist. du dr. municipal en France," 1829; *Guizot*, "Hist. de la civilis. en France," 1829; *Aug. Thierry*, "Lettres s. l'hist. de F.," 1827; "Consid. s. l'hist. de F.," 1840; "Essai s. l'hist. du Tiers-Etat," 1850; "Tableau de l'anc. France municipale," 1853; *Luchaire*, "Hist. des inst. mon. s. les premiers capétiens," 2e éd., 1891; "Les Communes françaises," 1890; "Manuel," p. 353; *Hegel*, "Städte u. Gilden d. german. Völker in M. A.," 1891; *Glasson*, II, 380, etc.; *Esmein*, p. 286; *Flach*, "Orig. de l'anc. France," II; *Pirenne*, "R. hist.," 1893, 67; Some monographs are: *Giry*, "Etabl. de Rouen," 1883–5; "Hist. de Saint-Omer," 1877; *Labande*, "Hist. de Beauvais," 1892; *Flammermont*; "de Senlis," 1881; *Tuetey*, "Et. s. le dr. munic. en Franche-Comté," 1865; *Klippfel*, "Révol. commun. dans les cités épiscop. de l'emp.," 1869; "Les paraiges messins," 1867; *Rivière*, "Hist. d. inst. de l'Auvergne," 1874; *Soger*, "Et. s. la comm. des hab. de Blois," 1894; *De Maulde*, N.R.H., 1883 (Orléans), t. I (Avignon); *Germain*, "Hist. de la comm. de Montpellier," 1851; *Lambert*, "Rég. mun. en Provence," 1882. *A. du Bourg*, "Cout. communales du S.-O.," 1882; *Dognon*, "Inst. pol. du Languedoc," 1895; The Netherlands: *Wauters*, "Libertés communales," 1869–78. *Vanderkindere*, "Le siècle des Artevelde," 1879; *Pirenne*, "Hist. de Dinant," 1889; England: *R. Gneist*, "La Const. communale de l'Angleterre," 1868; *Glasson*, "Hist. du dr. et d. Inst. de l'Anglet.," *passim*. *Pollock and Maitland*, I, 625. *Maitland*, "Township and Borough," 1898; Italy: *Hegel*, "Gesch. d. Städteverf. v. Ital.," 1847; *Salvioli*, "St. d. dir. ital.," no 123; Germany: *Schröder*, § 51 (detailed bibliog.). *R. Sohm*, "Enstehung d. deutsch. Städtewesens," 1890; *Blondel*, "Frédéric II," 280; *Flach*, *op. cit.*, 215; Add. *Giry*, "Orig. de la comm. de Saint-Quentin"; *Lefranc*, "Hist. de Noyon," 1888; *Bardon*, "d'Alais," 1894.

[1] "Olim," I, 848.

same intensity and have not always operated under the same favorable circumstances; consequently in the movement for emancipation there were variations and different degrees of progress. The urban grouping, which was furthered by the Norman and Saracen invasions and the general insecurity, of itself gave rise to a special condition for the bourgeoisie. Strong by reason of numbers and protected by their ramparts, they had little need for the protection of a seignior, and many of the feudal dues arising solely from grants of land did not affect them. If they did not constitute a political body, they sometimes formed a civil personality possessing property, collective rights, common interests, general assemblies, public solicitors ("procureurs") to represent them, and experts to collect the seigniorial poll tax ("taille"). To the older towns the churches and abbeys after the 1000 s added new ones; these were the asylums or places of refuge for fugitive serfs (even criminals); they had their own markets, their special systems of justice, exemptions from seigniorial dues and from military service. The seigniors imitated them with their "bastides" or charters of settlement. Boroughs ("burgus," fortress) or suburbs ("feris burgus," outside the walls, "suburbium") were established near the ancient town.[1] In these industry and commerce (growing out of the crusades) created a wealth independent of feudalism and the mercantile aristocracy which owned them sought to free themselves from the seigniorial authority by every means: struggles by force of arms, negotiations, and good offices, — which called for concessions of liberty as their reward. Wherever the economic evolution was the earliest and the most marked, as in Italy, on the Rhine, and in Flanders, the political evolution was the more accentuated. Once begun it progressed easily; sometimes, in fact, the seigniors believed it to be for their own interest to compel their towns to take on the communal organization, as did the kings of England in the case of their French possessions.[2]

[1] Subdivisions of the town were: the quarter, the parish, without counting the guilds or corporations of artisans, the hanses, or societies of merchants, and the brotherhoods, or religious associations. The effect of the feudal partition in the old towns was, that not only did the château, the city, and the borough not always have the same seignior, but it was not rare for streets, houses, or persons to have different masters. The parish comprised several seigniories. The town, then, was only a unity in fact; in law, unity did not exist. Moreover, it cannot be said that it always constituted a juristic person. The communal revolution put the law in accord with the fact.

[2] **Special Theories:** We cannot be content with these general reasons; but must look more closely into the genesis of communal liberties.

§ 235. **Fairs and Markets.** — The town was a place of commerce; it had its weekly market, sometimes its annual fair. Markets and fairs could not be held without a special peace which the public authority (king, seignior, church, or commune, depending on the place) assured by means of a system of heavy penalties (retaliation, beheading, amputation). The merchants[1] who at-

Numerous theories have made progress, from those which attributed their origin to the municipal Gallic-Roman régime (which had degenerated before the time of the Barbarian invasion into a régime of oppression and had been replaced by the Frankish administration of the 500 s to the 1100 s) or to the old Germanic institutions which were almost abandoned, to the most recent theories, as those which attribute their origin to the public law ("Staatsrecht," *Arnold*), to the Frankish aldermanic institution (*Heusler*), to the domainal régime (*Hofrecht*) with its agents and its privileges, to the guilds and the trades societies (*Wilda, Gierke*), to the markets and rural communities (*Maurer, Below*), or, finally, to the simple fact of the establishment of a permanent market and the rights and immunities which were a consequence of it (*Schröder, Sohm*). There was in each of these theories some truth, but no one contained the whole truth, even for a single country. Let us consider the last mentioned. The German town was essentially a permanent market; the "Weichbild" or cross of the market, an emblem of royal authority, made the king present, after a fashion, and gave to the town the peace of the royal palace, its right of refuge; the place of refuge supposed the existence of a privileged tribunal. The urban law was the privileged law of the market. The town once established, an administrative organ ("Rath") took the place of the royal judge ("écoutête," "amman," a judge who had cognizance of civil cases). The cross erected over the place bore a glove, a sword, or other symbols of the royal power; in the north of Germany, it was replaced by statues of Roland, Roland wearing, according to tradition, the sword and buckler of Charlemagne. This opinion, explained by Schröder, and systematized by Sohm, did not prevail. *Maitland*, "Domesday Book," 193, and *Flach*, II, 365, oppose it; the law of the market did not last longer than the market; it was not the market which made the town a place of refuge and gave it its franchise; on the contrary, it was the refuge and immunity which established the security of the market. Concerning the ideas of *Flach*, *cf. Pfister*, "R. hist.," 1893, 53, 364. *Pirenne*, *ib.*, 53, 77, and 57, 66, shows that the formation of medieval towns is explained by purely geographical causes (*cf.* America to-day); neither monasteries, nor châteaux, nor fairs and markets determined their formation independently of their situation. Some villages, as Thourout and Messine in Flanders, had fairs. *Huvelin*, "Essai hist. sur le droit des foires et marchés," 1897, p. 220, sustains Sohm's thesis, but only partly; the peace of the town and, consequently, the urban law, was in his opinion derived from the peace of the market, but this latter did not have its source in the peace of the prince; it was a forced consequence of the existence of the market. The point of departure of these theories is found in the book of *Arnold*, "Verfassungsgesch. d. deutschen Freistädte," 1854, that Pirenne compared in importance to the "Beneficialwesen" of *Roth*. Concerning the Roman towns in the first centuries of the Middle Ages, *cf. Flach*, II, 243; *Rietschl*, "Die Civitas auf deutschen Boden," 1894. "R. hist.," 67, 59. On the persistency of the curials, N.R.H., 1898, 782.

[1] On the Carolingian laws concerning merchants see *Waitz*, VG., IV, 44. "Form imper.," 30, "Ed. Pist.," etc. Commerce by caravans from the 700 s to the 1100 s. The primitive bourgeoisie was composed only of merchants. The special juridical condition which they enjoyed as a result of their occupation, as that of noble, from the profession of arms; that of serf, from the culture of the soil.

tended obtained a safe-conduct or safeguard while they were going and returning [1] (through a contract with the seignior at first and later in a general way as a police measure). They were drawn to the fairs by exemptions from transit dues (such as tolls, etc.) and from taxes collected on the occasion of sales of merchandise (as, for example, on wine). They were subject neither to escheat dues (" droit d'aubaine ") nor to the right of marque and reprisal, by virtue of which merchants were stopped and their goods seized for the offenses or debts of their fellow citizens or of their seigniors — debts and offenses of whose existence they often had no suspicion; they even enjoyed freedom from arrest,[2] that is, their creditors could neither imprison them nor attach their goods for previous debts or offenses.[3]

In return, the execution of contracts made at the fair was assured by rigorous measures (often before special judges).[4] The procedure was more expeditious and less barbarous; the seal of the fair was evidence of the authenticity and executory force of all agreements to which it was affixed, those who did not perform their obligations were sent to prison, the goods of the debtor who fled were sequestrated and the proceeds proportionately distributed among his creditors as in modern bankruptcy procedure. To this "jus mercatorum," "jus fori," urban law

[1] *Imbart de la Tour*, "La Liberté commerciale en France aux douzième et treizième siècles. Réforme soc.," 1895, 29–49; "Immunités comm. aux Eglises du VIIe to IXe siècle," "Studies dedicated to G. Monod," 1896, p. 71. The "droit d'étape" ("jus stapulæ") obliged the merchants who passed through a town to put their merchandise on sale in that town; sometimes, they were allowed to sell to or buy only from inhabitants of the town; sometimes, on the contrary, it sufficed if their merchandise was discharged, weighed, and marked, for the levying of the market toll was all that was desired. Like the "jus nundinarum" (fairs), this right conceded by the seigniors during the feudal epoch was regalian during the 1500s and 1600s. *Huvelin*, "Marchés et foires," p. 210.

[2] C. J., 4, 60, "De nundinis," 1, N.R.H., 1884, p. 295. Lorris (1155), 6. Soissons, Ord. XI, 219. "Aigues Mortes," IV, 52. Freedom from arrest was limited little by little and became useless following the disappearance of arrest itself.

[3] Towns of Arrest. This name was given, under the old régime, to towns in which the bourgeoisie had the right to seize the goods or even the person of their foreign debtor, if he did not pay his debts when they were due. "Paris," "Priv." of Louis the Fat, 1134 (Ord. I, 6); "Cout.," Art. 173. — "Orléans," 442, "Reims," 407. The conditions and the regulations governing this right varied according to the epochs. *Collinet*, "Et. sur la saisie privée," 1895; *Huvelin*, p. 446; *Ragueau*, see "Arrest"; *Ferrière*, Dict., see "Villes d'arrêt"; *Isambert*, "Table"; *Bourdot de R.*, I, 510, 554, 768, 995, N.R.H., 91, 186.

[4] Merchant Consuls. *Glasson*, N.R.H., 1897, 1. In Italy the heads of corporations ("consules") sat sometimes surrounded by assessors ("consiliarii") in the house of the corporation ("domus," "curia mercatorum"); it was the custom to submit to them the affairs of the corporation. *Morel*, "Jurid. commerc.," thesis 1897.

owed much, and from it some have concluded that it was the market which created the town, but the contrary is perhaps more exact; generally, the market made its appearance only after the town had already come into existence.

§ 236. **Privileged Towns** (especially in the center of France, for example Lorris in Gâtinais, 1155).[1] In the place of arbitrary exploitation by the seigniorial provost a régime of privileges was gradually introduced in many towns. (*a*) When industry and commerce were more prosperous and the inhabitants more numerous and wealthy, it was to the interest of the seignior to treat them with consideration and to defend them against his own provost; exactions injured him, they led to revolts; or the inhabitants purchased their freedom with money; the petty despot, the provost, was henceforth bound by a charter. (*b*) In the depopulated towns and on uncultivated lands the abbeys, from the very first, and later the kings and the seigniors, opened asylums (places of refuge) and attracted inhabitants to them by the bait of privileges and better conditions than those of neighboring seigniories; thus there grew up numerous "bastides," new towns and free towns were established.[2]

In default of political liberties and of communal autonomy the free town enjoyed important civil liberties which the provost swore to respect at the time of entering upon his duties. Personal liberty was guaranteed (*cf.* habeas corpus); the accused who gave a bond to appear in court could not be seized and imprisoned; every accused person had a right to be tried before his natural judges and it was forbidden to try him outside the town; trial by judicial combat and by torture no longer existed; confiscation was limited. There was no more serfdom; the inhabitants had the right to go and come and to leave the town at will; they had the right to marry and to enter religious orders; their domiciles

[1] *Giry*, "Doc.," p. 113, has edited a new chap. 50 of *Beaumanoir* on "good towns" ("Les bonnes villes"). *Soyer*, *op. cit.*; *Stouff*, "Comtes de Bourgogne," 1899.

[2] A "bastide" (or "bastille") was a wooden construction erected against a besieged place (*Froissart*, 3, 4); this term was also employed to designate towns built on a desert spot, according to a preconceived plan, with streets at right angles and endowed with privileges. Besides the general denominations of "Sauvetés," "Salvetat," "Villefranche," "Villeneuve," "Castelnau," other names were given them: "Saint-Louis," "Villeréal," "Montréal," "Beaumarchais" (name of a royal officer), "Fleurance" (for Florence), "Cordes" (for Cordoue), Cologne, Grenade, Beaumont, etc. Toward 1340, bastiles were no longer built, for the population had become dense, and there were no more waste lands. *Giry*, "Gr. Encycl.," see "Bastide" (Plan of the bastile of Montpazier); *Curie-Seimbres*, "Essai s. les bastides," 1880.

were inviolable; military service was limited, ownership of property was free, and consequently the right to alienate it "inter vivos" and to make wills. The amount and the number of seigniorial impositions were reduced and the "taille" and the "corvée" were abolished or converted into fixed dues. This urban law, having an international character, together with the existing commercial usages, were already in many respects entirely modern. As the town had no corporate character, in case of need the provost summoned and consulted all the inhabitants, or the latter chose syndics to represent them in matters of general interest.

§ 237. **Transition to Communes.** — It was these free towns which had municipal authorities, either with or without judicial competence, and which approximated in character the communes (or consular towns) to such an extent that they were almost confused with them; but there always existed one difference between them: the commune, properly speaking, was not subject to the seignior, but was completely independent of him, whereas the free town had not, like it, succeeded in breaking its bonds of subjection (an example was Beaumont, in Argonne, 1082, and the towns which adopted its law; also many consular towns in southwest France[1]).

§ 238. **"Echevinat" and Guilds.** — The towns which gave themselves an administrative and judicial apparel rarely made it out of whole cloth, but ordinarily were limited to the use of already existing elements. It happened sometimes that the community had occasional representatives for certain collective interests (procurators or mandatories "ad litem," and notables chosen to apportion and collect the seigniorial "taille"); they became permanent officials and their functions were extended. Elsewhere the council of the seignior, or even a group of his officers, was transformed into an exclusively urban organ. The Carolingian "échevinate," half popular in origin, was especially designed, in regions like the north, where it had been maintained, as an independent judicial body, but it acquired administrative powers also. The same was true of the Germanic guild and the religious and commercial associations, houses, corporations, or brotherhoods which ante-

[1] *Cf.* Paris with its merchant's provost and its royal provost. The problem of the origin of these jurisdictions or municipal administrations is the same as for the communes. In England, a centralized State from the time of the Norman Conquest, there were no communes, properly speaking, but only privileged towns with partial autonomy. *Mrs. Green*, "Town Life in the XV century," 1894, distinguishes: towns of the king, towns of the lords, and ecclesiastical towns.

dated the communal movement. The guild was an association for mutual defense, the members of which regarded themselves as brothers and participated in periodic banquets at the common expense; membership assessments ("geldonia") and the requirement of an oath ("conjuratio") were two of their characteristic features. In spite of the Carolingian prohibitions the guilds multiplied because association was the only means by which the weak were able to secure protection at a time when the State did not afford it and when the family was disorganized.[1] In England, in North France, and in the Germanic countries they were very numerous.[2] In South France, it is believed that organizations of artisans or of merchants of the Roman period had existed from the 400 s to the 1000 s; but the fact has not been well established; most of them must have been reduced to servitude. In any case, associations of artisans or of merchants were formed anew at an early day and guilds or other associations were among the most active agents for emancipation of the towns; the administrators of one of them sometimes became the administrators of the entire community (for example, Saint-Omer, Paris).[3]

§ 239. **The Commune.** — Although this word[4] was applied in a general sense to every town constituting a political body and having a municipal organization, and although it may be applied hence even to consular towns, in the strict sense it designates especially "communes jurées" of northern France and of Flanders, — those towns which acquired the greatest number of political rights. Their independence rested on an association formed under oath, a "conjuration" among the inhabitants, which implied mutual defense like the guild and an agreement to put an end to disorders and violence ("pax," "amicitia"); [5] it was sanctioned by a charter

[1] The "gilde" was a fictitious or enlarged "sippe."

[2] The municipality of Paris at first belonged exclusively to the corporation of "water merchants," which recalls the "nautæ parisienses" of the Roman epoch, without the connection between them being established; from that, the vessel which still figures on the coat of arms of Paris and the name of the "Prévôt des Marchands" given to the mayor of Paris. It has been maintained (but wrongly) that in England the commune always commenced by being the merchant guild. *Gross*, "Gild merchant," 1890; *Drioux*, "De la gilde germ.," 1883; *Hegel*, *op. cit.*; *Flach*, II, 376; *Pappenheim*, "Die altdaenisch. Schutzgilden," 1885; *Mrs. Green*, *op. cit.*, vol. 2.

[3] Concerning the relations and the differences between the associations of peace, "communia pacis," and the municipal commune, *cf. Luchaire*, "Manuel," p. 374; *Flach*, *op. cit.*

[4] "Communia," "communitas," are terms which designate the association of the inhabitants, then the town, and even communities in general. The members of the commune were called "jurati communie," "vicini," "amice," "burgeuses." *Cf. Flach*, II, 415; *Mrs. Green*, *op. cit.*, c. 9.

[5] Peace of the local and secular town; the peace of God extended over all the country and had a religious character.

to which the seignior had to give his consent, just as a State is compelled to recognize the independence of one of its colonies; often it followed an insurrection, and sometimes the citizens bought it at a dear price.[1] Besides the civil liberties which the free towns enjoyed[2] the communes had a political organization and constituted a feudal personality.[3]

The internal constitution of these petty States was of various types, from the strictest form of oligarchy to the broadest form of democracy, and from direct government to a representative system. In most instances, as in the cities of antiquity, it evolved, willing or unwilling, as a result of opposition to tyranny (or administrative despotism).[4]

[1] Date, Saint Quentin, before 1077; Beauvais, before 1099; Noyon, about 1108; Amiens, 1113; Soissons, 1126. The communal charters spread from one town to the other; the principal commune was called "chef de sens" and had a kind of jurisdiction over its "filiales." In Germany and Italy, they formed powerful leagues. *Beaumanoir*, 30, 63. There were not only urban communes, but also rural communes. Villages syndicated themselves in order to form collective communes (Pyrenees, Alps, Picardy, Artois, Flanders), for example, commune of Laonnois, formed from seventeen villages having for center Anizy-le-Château, 1128.

[2] *Guibert de Nogent*, "De vita sua," 1, 3, in a passage often cited, makes allusion to the civil liberties and not to the political liberties of the communes: "Commune is a new and detestable word and this is what is understood by the word: taxable men no longer pay to their seigniors anything except an annual assessment; if they commit some misdemeanor, they are acquitted of it by a fine legally fixed, and as for the pecuniary impositions that it was the custom to inflict on serfs, they are entirely exempt from it." The same writer explains the communal reaction by showing the lengths to which the abuse of feudalism was carried in a town like Laon: "massacres and pillage filled the republic; there was no security to him who left his house at night; he ran the risk of being stopped, struck, killed; not a peasant penetrated the walls without being seized and held for purpose of ransom; the serfs, although emancipated, were forced back into their previous condition." "Hist. de France," XII, 249 and following.

[3] It was rare that the entire city was subject to the commune; slaves of all kinds were found; seigniories were subject to the king, to the suzerain of the commune, to private seigniors; the bishop often had jurisdiction of the cloister, of a part of the town, even of the entire city, the commune being established only in the borough. Between these rival seigniories, conflicts were incessant. Another source of conflict was: a number of the inhabitants of the town escaped from the communal jurisdiction; justiciable nobles, from that of the feudal courts, clerks, from that of church courts, serfs, from the jurisdiction of their seignior, the bourgeois of the king, from that of the royal tribunals. The "banlieue" was the territory situated outside the walls of the town over which the commune had the right of ban; ordinarily, it was a league in extent, sometimes more, 5 or 7 (whence the name of "septene"). The "dex" in the south was the limit of communal territory. *Loysel*, 261; "Cout. of Toulouse," *passim*.

[4] One would say a vast field of social experience. Universal suffrage, restricted suffrage, election by several degrees, coöptation combined with the election, seigniorial intervention,—all systems were found. *Cf.* Constitution of Italian towns, as Florence or Venice. At Rouen, *Grand Council of a Hundred Peers*, from which emanated a middle council of twenty-four jurors, subdivided into two little councils of twelve aldermen

§ 240. **General Assemblies. The Great Council.** — The commune sometimes included all the inhabitants of the town without distinction, even the nobility and the clergy, who were constrained to take the oath; general assemblies, where they all took part, decided important questions, imposed the taxes, appointed the magistrates, and enacted ordinances. But in most cases direct government was not practiced, the people did not participate in the administration of public affairs, but only an aristocratic assembly, a sort of municipal senate known as the great Council. The substantial bourgeoisie, enriched by commerce, oppressed nearly everywhere the small artisans, the common people. Nearly everywhere, also, the population was divided into two classes: 1st, the *bourgeoisie* or *citizens* who alone possessed political rights; and 2d, the inhabitants ("incolæ"); the first category formed only a minority of the population.

§ 241. **The Municipal Magistracy** (the petty council) consisted of a body of aldermen ("échevins"), of jurors ("jurés" or "jurats"), and of peers, the chief of whom bore the title of mayor or provost (or the "vierg," as he was called at Autun). Many of them were ancient seigniorial officers. Such was the mayor (or the mayors, because there were sometimes two of them), the provost, and the "vierg" or the "viguier" of the duke of Burgundy.[1] Others, perhaps, had been administrators of communal property, as the mayor and provost were stewards. The "échevins" had a judicial origin, the peers a feudal origin. Their term of office and method of selection were affected by this diversity of origin. The tenure was sometimes for life, sometimes for a fixed period (usually a year). They were sometimes chosen by popular election, either directly or according to a procedure child-

and twelve counselors. The Council of the Hundred Peers designated each year three candidates, from among whom the king appointed the mayor. At Peronne (1368) the twelve trade guilds each elected two persons; the twenty-four elected chose two of the most honest men of the town; these latter added to their number ten more and so attained the number twenty; after which, the twenty added ten more, total thirty. These thirty chose the mayor and the aldermen; besides, there was a council of six persons appointed directly by the chiefs of the trade guilds; this council was consulted concerning the establishment of taxes and added to their number six other members designated by the mayor and the aldermen. *Davidsohn*, "Gesch. v. Florenz," 1893.

[1] Auxiliaries of the municipal magistrates. (A) **Municipal functionaries;** (1) the receivor ("argentier," and in the south "clavaire"); (2) secretary and recorder (clerk of the commune); (3) procurer-syndic, the legal representative of the commune; (4) various clerks; (5) sergeants, bailiffs, and officers of police, porters, etc. (B) **Commissions:** "paiseurs" (justices of the peace for reconciling the parties); "gard' orphènes" (guardians of orphans); etc.

ishly complicated[1] whose mechanical effect did not in the least tend to make chance the sole master of the affairs of the commune. Often they were chosen by coöptation by those whose places they took; finally, instances were not rare in which they were appointed and installed by the seignior alone. Sometimes he was content merely to install them and invest them with the insignia of their office.[2] Their powers included the complete management of the affairs of the town, or there was a division of power between them and the great council, or the popular assembly.

§ 242. **Consular Towns.** — Like the communes of northern France the consular towns of the south were independent and possessed political and judicial organs of their own. Most of them obtained their freedom gradually and without violence. The municipal body was composed of magistrates called **consuls**, as in the Italian towns, from which, it is commonly believed, the consular system was borrowed. But the fact is not well established that Italy preceded France in the institution of these municipal consulates; they were formed on the spot simultaneously in the two countries.[3] The **consuls** or councilors, "consiliarii," "probi homines ad consulendum rempublicam" (at Toulouse, "capitouls," "capitularii," "prudhommes" of the chapter or seigniorial council),[4] were from the notables, not very numerous, "by whose advice a community was administered." They began by being councilors of the seignior or of his beadle;[5] sometimes they were rather "syndics" or representatives whom the corpora-

[1] Designed to remove bribery and corruption.

[2] Concerning the character of these magistrates, *cf.* "R. hist.," 1895, vol. 57, p. 316.

[3] The oldest consulary charters were: Moissac, about 1125; Montech and Castelsarrasin, 1134; Ambialet, 1136. "These dates and the position of the places," says *M. Dognon*, p. 58, "suffice to prove that the consulates did not originate in Italy." The Custom of Moissac proves anterior usages from which it follows that the consulate must have been as old in that town as in Italy where it appeared at the end of the 100 s. *Salvioli*, 216, proves, nevertheless, that Naples, Amalfi, etc., had municipal magistrates elected by the people about the year 1000. *Cf. Haulleville*, "Hist. des comm. lomb.," 1857; *Pawinski*, "Ensteh. Gesch. d. Consulats in Ital.," 1867.

[4] In spite of the legend which gives to Toulouse a republican municipality dating back without interruption to the Roman epoch, this town did not escape the common fate. It was governed first by its counts or by their functionaries, then it received from them certain privileges and it did not delay to give itself a deliberating body, the "commune consilium Tolose," which made, in 1152, ordinances with the count. The members of the municipal body, "capitulum," were designated as "domini de capitulo capitularii." Concerning the vicissitudes of the commune of Toulouse, *cf. Roschach; A. Molinier*, in "Hist. d. Languedoc," VII, 212, 559; BCh., 1882.

[5] *Cadier*, "Etats de Béarn," p. 95; *Dognon, op. cit. Cf.* "R. hist.," 65, 300.

tion appointed to determine a particular matter and whose office became permanent. From this double origin it resulted that in the consular towns the petty nobility often figured side by side with the upper bourgeoisie; the members of these two classes naturally took part in the seigniorial council or the communal syndicate. The consuls were sometimes designated by the seignior, sometimes by the members of the corporation, sometimes even by their predecessors, depending on whether the independence of the town was more or less complete. Ordinarily their term of office was of short duration which might come from the fact that they received no compensation, so the wealthy families bore the expense in turn. The consuls were nearly always assisted by a council whose decisions they merely enforced, and occasionally they had recourse to the general assembly of the bourgeoisie (the Parliament or common council).

§ 243. **Seigniorial Rights of the Communes and Consular Towns.** — The commune ("sensu lato") constituted a seigniory,[1] and, consequently, enjoyed more or less complete sovereign rights like ordinary seigniories. These were:

1st, **The right of peace and of war** (consequently, also the right of arson, that is to say, the right to burn or demolish the house of him who had offended); the commune maintained an armed force which was under the orders of the municipal magistrates and, in case of need, served the suzerain or the king.[2] Watch service was one of the heaviest burdens of the townsmen.

2d, **The right to legislate**, to issue bans, ordinances, and statutes (relating to police, markets, fines, sumptuary measures, price of bread, rate of wages, etc.).[3]

3d, **Right of Justice.** — The townsmen were guaranteed the right of trial by their peers. The municipal courts had a double origin: (*a*) the aldermanic tribunals of the Carolingian period administered justice at first in the name of the seignior, later in the name of the commune; in southern France the same change

[1] In consequence, it was at the same time political person and juristic person. *Vauthier*, "Pers. morales," p. 152; *Gierke*, "Genossenschaftrecht," I, 220 and following; *M. Fournier*, "Statuts et Priv. des Univers. fr.," I, no. 71. Nevers had a numerous population; nevertheless this town did not constitute a "universitas," or body; the inhabitants lived "ut singuli"; they had neither commune, nor seal, nor bell, nor common property, nor a commoh treasury. The greater part of the time, the contrary was the case. *Luchaire*, "Manuel," p. 376. *Cf.* "R. hist.," 57, 303. *Beaum.*, vol. I, p. 316; "R. quest. hist.," 34, 523; *Stouff*, *op. cit.*, 53. [2] Not a glorious rôle for the communal militia at Bouvines.

[3] Revision of the "customs," regulation of industry. *Roisin*, p. 52 and following. No right of ban at Amiens (Art. 54). *Pollock*, I, 644.

often occurred in regard to the "prud'hommes" who assisted the seigniorial bailiffs in the administration of justice;[1] often, also, the seignior retained the right to administer justice wholly or in part.[2] (*b*) In the absence of these tribunals others were established, as a necessary result of the police powers of the communal magistrates. In the associations anterior to the commune there already existed a disciplinary jurisdiction as is the case in every society, and this jurisdiction developed with the independence of the communes and came to exclude every other.[3] There were municipal courts just as there were seigniorial courts; they found in the courts of the king dangerous rivals and by the 1500s there remained to them only a police jurisdiction exercised in the interest of the municipal authorities.[4]

4th, **The right to coin Money and levy Taxes.** — The municipal body established and levied arbitrarily "tailles" or collections; it also established tolls,[5] and compelled the new burgesses to pay an entrance fee. To this source of revenue were added the income from communal property and from the administration of justice, to fill up the common treasury. The **seal** and the **belfry**[6] (the tower containing the bell by which the assemblies of the citizens were convened and the militia summoned) were the symbols of communal independence; "when the king abolished a commune he broke its seal and demolished its belfry."[7] Like the seigniors, the commune sometimes had its vassals and, ordinarily, a suzerain to whom it owed feudal duties, homage, military service,[8] and aids; he, on his part, could give it in pledge for his obligations.

[1] The differences between the Carolingian aldermen or "boni homines" and the consuls of the feudal epoch were: 1st, the first were judges of the hundred and not solely of the "urbs"; 2d, they were not necessarily the same for all affairs, while the latter sat permanently.

[2] Seigniorial justice did not always completely disappear; the seignior often retained jurisdiction of important criminal cases, like murder or suits relating to lands granted by him to bourgeois persons. "Et. de Rouen," Art. 24. Sometimes the commune had only an intermediate or inferior court. *Pauffin*, "Org. munic. d. le Nord et l'Est, et en part. des conflits de jurid.," 1886. *Nicolai*, "Hist. de l'org. jurid. à Bordeaux," 1892.

[3] This was the municipal jurisdiction, properly speaking; the commune also had a seigniorial jurisdiction by virtue of its character as a feudal seignior (over its vassals and its copyholder). *Cf.* above "Parloir aux bourgeois" at Paris, p. 306.

[4] Code Henry III, 3, 15.

[5] *Beaumanoir*, 50. Expenses, particularly fortifications of the town.

[6] Tower of peace, "Berg-friede."

[7] The town remained, however, as a juridical unity with its own custom; in the same way, if a corporation was abolished, its business continued with the rules established by public powers.

[8] The charter of the commune ordinarily fixed the conditions of military service (Arras had to furnish 1000 sergeants or 3000 pounds). In the

§ 244. **The Policy of the Throne in Respect to the Communes.** — A historical tradition, of which we find an echo in the preamble to the Charter of 1814, attributed to Louis VI, the Fat, the enfranchisement of the communes. There is nothing in the tradition, though down to the time of St. Louis the throne favored the communal movement, at least outside the royal domain. It created by this means allies against feudalism; by signing the charter of a commune and guaranteeing its observance, the king had a check upon his vassals. The jurists, reasoning from this, maintained that the communal town belonged to the king. At the close of the 1200 s the theory was established that the king alone had the right to create communes or consular towns,[1] as he had the right to abolish them as a form of punishment or as an act of grace, as for example, when they were bankrupt and unable to support municipal expenses.[2]

§ 245. **The Overthrow of Municipal Liberties.**[3] — From this time dates an opposition policy; the royal power became "the greatest enemy of the communes." They usurped a portion of the sovereignty, and could not be tolerated any more than the feudal seigniories; in the reorganization of the State there was no place for the commune. Occasions were not wanting for the king to interfere in the affairs of the towns: 1st, there were struggles between the popular party and the governing oligarchy; 2d, there was deplorable management of the municipal finances; 3d, there were conflicts of jurisdiction.[4] Beaumanoir had already employed

1200 s in France, this obligation was commuted into a tax paid to the king, and the inhabitants of the town were required to do watch duty only. An ordinance of 1317 (Philip the Long) substituted captains appointed by the king in the place of municipal magistrates as commanders of the militia.

[1] The seignior, by accepting the commune, curtailed his fief; *cf.* theories of redeeming the Frankish fief. Ord. III, 305. Louis VII "reputabat civitates omnes suas esse in quibus communiæ essent." *Beaumanoir*, 50, 2.

[2] In 1296, the commune of Laon was suppressed by a decision of the Parliament. *Giry*, "Docum.," p. 148. Fr. *Funck-Brentano*, "Philippe le Bel en Flandre," 1897.

[3] The communal history of other countries is nearly the same as that of France. The communes of Flanders and the Low-Countries, very flourishing in the 1300 s, underwent a democratic revolution (the "Artevelde"); but from the 1400 s reverses and ruin began to set in. In Germany, they were still autonomous and powerful in the 1500 s; in the 1700 s fifty-one were still in existence, but they no longer had influence (except the large towns of Hanse, Hamburg, etc.). The Italian towns had played the most brilliant rôle; but rivalries and internal strife delivered them to tyrants and transformed them into principalities. While, everywhere else, municipal franchises disappeared, leaving no traces behind, the communes of England gave her a second chamber.

[4] *Sée*, "Louis XI et les villes," 1893; *Langlois*, "Philippe le Hardi," p. 249; *Giry*, "Doc.," p. 120 and following (important passages of Beau-

the modern formula of administrative guardianship ("tutelle administrative"): "there is great need that the communal towns should be succored in every case just as the child under age should be."

An ordinance issued between 1256 and 1261 subjected the financial administration of the towns in the royal domains to the control of the chamber of accounts; the budgets which were shown at that time indicated a considerable deficit and enormous debts (which the heavy fines inflicted on the towns by the Parliament increased still more). The king's men were obliged to visit the towns, reëstablish their budgetary equilibrium, reform their finances, and levy the aid or the royal tax.[1] The public order was disturbed by riots and popular uprisings, due frequently to the fact that the bourgeoisie threw back upon the common people the burden of municipal taxes or "tailles." In certain towns, Marseilles, Arles, and Avignon, "podestas" were appointed, following the Italian practice; they were dictators, strangers to the towns in which they discharged their duties, and, consequently, afforded some guarantee of impartiality. But nearly everywhere it was the king who fulfilled the functions of "podesta"; he adopted measures to put an end to the disorders, sometimes abolished the commune, in all cases exercising control over the municipal magistrates, leaving to the electoral body of the citizens (more and more reduced) only a semblance of liberty.[2] In the 1600 s the offices of mayor and alderman became purchasable and hereditary. The jurisdiction of the municipal courts was attacked by the bailiffs with the help of the same procedure as in the case of the seigniorial courts (royal cases, etc.). At Rouen, in 1278, and at Toulouse, in 1283, the king was obliged to delimit the powers of the municipal judges. By the 1500s they retained only some powers of a police character; in 1563 their commercial jurisdiction was withdrawn, and in 1566 their civil jurisdiction. The system of administrative tutelage reached its zenith in the 1600s with the extension of the power of the intendants; a stone could not be removed, or the expense of a sou incurred without the consent of this officer. It was not, however, merely a return to

manoir); *A. de Boislile*, "Bull. Soc. h. France," 1872, 86; *Bémont*, "Rôles gascons," 1896, c. II.

[1] Edict of Crémieu, 1536. Measures taken by Colbert.

[2] Non-prejudicial letters ("lettres de non prejudice") were a means of attacking communal liberties; they were not respected in a given case, but in declaring by non-prejudicial letters that they would be respected in the future; the precedent was not less established by it. They were employed also in other cases.

a primitive uniformity in the administration of the towns. There remained everywhere numerous vestiges of the institutions of the feudal age, forms and solemnities to which the people held fast; the monarchy did not judge it worth while to destroy this vain shadow.[1]

[1] *Babeau*, "La ville sous l'Ancien Régime," 1880; *D'Avenel*, "Richelieu," vol. IV; *Isambert*, "Table," see "Communes." Edicts of Aug., 1692, January, 1714, May, 1765 (Marly). Decree of the Council of 1778 (Toulouse); *D. Vaissete*, 13, 1249, and 14, 2400; *Dupuy*, "Admin. municipale au XVIIIe siècle," 1891; N.R.H., 1894, 128.

CHAPTER VI

THE FEUDAL PERIOD (*Continued*). STATUS OF LANDS

§ 246. **Introduction.** — The organization of landownership was so closely connected with the political constitution of the feudal world that it is necessary to describe it before passing to a consideration of the status of persons. It is the custom to distinguish between four sorts of lands: 1st, the **fief**, or noble land; 2d, the **copyhold**, or land occupied by the villein or peasant; 3d, lands held by **servile tenure**; and 4th, the **alod** ("alleu") or freehold. But it is necessary to treat separately the alod which was outside the feudal system, the entire history of which consisted in attempts of the seigniors or the king to bring such lands under the feudal régime. The ownership which it implied was nothing more than the "dominium" or individual ownership, full and absolute, of the Roman law. The fief, the copyhold, and the servile tenure, consisted, on the contrary, of lands granted by a seignior to a vassal, to a free tenant, or to a serf subject to the payment of certain charges. The proprietorship was divided between the grantor and the grantee, one having the right of **eminent domain**, the other the right of enjoyment or use, "domaine utile" [usufruct]. This is not wholly exact in the case of the serf, because he had no right of ownership at all; but since we cannot separate him from his tenure, his situation was comparable to that of the villein or free peasant (the "roturier"[1]).

TOPIC 1. THE FIEF[2]

§ 247. **General Notions.** — The fief was a portion of land granted by a seignior[3] ("senior," "dominus") to his vassal ("vassus,"

[1] The term "roturier" was sometimes applied to the serf though usually with a qualifying word. The villein proper was a free man in law but not free in occupation.

[2] BIBLIOGRAPHY: *Glasson*, IX, 273; *Luchaire*, "Man.," 155; *Viollet*, "Hist.," 634; *Beaune*, "Cond. des biens," 1886; *Esmein*, 185; *Laboulaye*, "Hist. du dr. de propr. fonc.," 1839; *Roth*, "Feudalität u. Unterthanverband," 1863; *Homeyer*, "Syst. d. Lehnrechts"; "Sachsensp.," II; *Stobbe*, "Handb. d. d. Privatr.," II, § 116 (bibl.); *J. T. Abdy*, "Feudalism," 1890; *Dramard*, "Bibl. de la bibl. gén. du droit," 1893. It would not be practicable to give even a survey of the ancient literature concerning the fief from the glossarists to Cujas, Dumoulin, etc.; it would be well, nevertheless, to recall that these canonists themselves discussed fiefs, for example, *Hostiensis* in his "Summa Decretalium," *G. Durand* in his "Speculum de Feudis." The greater part of the coutumes discuss fiefs. In the citation "A.C." signifies "Ancienne Coutume"; "N.C." "Nouvelle Coutume" or reformed coutume; "T.A.C." "Très Ancienne Coutume" (very old "coutume"); "Paris," 47, means, new "coutume" of Paris, Art. 47. Concerning Paris, *cf. Buche*, N.R.H., 1884. For the ordinances, *Isambert*, "Table," see "Fiefs"; Lombard Law, *Calisse*, "Dig. ital.," see "Feudo," 136; collection of feudal documents, "Historiens de Fr.," vol. 23, p. 605, 705; *Tenlet*, "Layettes de Trésor des Chartes," vols. II and III; *D'Arbois de Jubainville*, "Hist. des comtes de Champagne," vols. II and V; *Lognon*, "Rôles des fiefs des c. de Champ.," 1249–1252; "Arch. d'Anjou," 1843; "Arch. hist. du Poitou," vol. 4, 7, 8; "Mém. Antiq. de. l'Ouest," 1874; "Arch. hist. de la Gironde"; *D. Vaissete*, "Preuves"; *De Wittasse*, "Aveux et dénombr. Picardie," 1884; *Warnkoenig and St.*, "Inst. de Flandre, Preuves," *Du Cange*, "Gloss." (*Luchaire*, p. 184); *Lex*, "Les Fiefs du Mâconnais," 1897; *Riston*, Thesis, p. 23 (*Lorraine*).

[3] "Fief" comes from the German "fehu" (*cf.* "vieh" = "pecus"). Forms: "feus," "fevus," "feudum," "feodum" (the "d" confuses

"homo") subject to the obligation of fealty and homage and the performance of noble services (military service, etc.);[1] it was capable of being transmitted to the heirs of the vassal but the vassal did not hold it in full ownership. He acquired only a beneficial or usufructuary right (the "**domaine utile**"), the seignior reserving the direct ownership ("**domaine éminent**").[2] It was the Carolingian benefice become hereditary and combined with the personal relation of vassalage,[3] the services owed by the vassal being regarded as the price of the concession. The right of the vassal did not cease to grow stronger and that of the seignior to decrease. The fief was at the same time a political institution and a form of ownership. During the monarchical period it cast off its political character and feudal ownership was abolished by the Revolution.

§ 248. **Division of the Seigniorial Domain.** — The seignior who created a fief thereby dismembered his domain; the part which

philologists; influence of "allodium"?). Provençal: "feu"; Anglo-Saxon, "feoh." *Cf. Blackstone*, 2, 4. German law: "Lehn," *cf.* "Leihe," concession: Spain: "honor," "señorio." The "feodatarius," feudatory, was the grantee. "Beneficium" and "feudum" for a long time were synonymous; *Waitz*, VG, VI, 4. "Feudum" is found in the acts of the 900 s; *Gernier Durand*, "Cart. de l'Egl. de Nimes," year 943, p. 78. *D. Vaissete*, V, 225 (year 959); 241 (year 960), etc. *Du Cange*, see "Feodum." It prevailed in the 1100 s. *Flach*, "Orig.," II, 515. In Sweden infeodation was unknown.

[1] Meaning of the word "fief": 1st, cattle, and, by extension, property in general; 2d, any concession whatever upon condition of any service whatever, for example, prestations in silver, or in kind; in this sense, there were noble fiefs and villein fiefs ("C. of Toulouse," "C. of Normandy"). *Ragueau*, see "Fief noble," from "haubert," abridgment, restraint; 3d, in the sense which prevailed (1200 s) the fief was opposed to the "censive" (fief, villein) tenure upon condition of villein services. "L. Feud.," 2, 23. 2. English law: the tenure by knight's service "pro hommagio et servitio militari," disappeared under Charles II (1660); there remained only tenures in "franc-socage," on condition of fidelity and payment of rent. *Glasson*, "Inst. de l'Angl.," V, 278, 482; *Lehr*, "Dr. Angl.," 177; *Pollock and Maitland*, I, 271. The "franc-socage," *cf.* "fiefferme" and "vavassorie" in Normandy, *L. Delisle*, *op. cit.*, 32, 45, holds middle place between the military fief and the villein tenures. Tenure by "bourgage," *ibid.*, p. 39.

[2] *Hostiensis*, "Summa Decret.," vol. "de feudis," p. 270.

[3] Personal recommendation ("advocatio," "commenda," "captennium") outside of all feudal bonds, particularly in the 1200 s. *Brussel*, II, 859; *Molinier, op. cit.; Flach*, "Orig.," vol. 2; *Esmein*, N.R.H., 1894, 537, shows the normal union of the fief and of fidelity: *Fulbert de Chartres*, "Ep.," 6, 10 (about 1007); *Bourel de La Roncière*, "Vie de Bouchard," c. IX, p. 22 (1032); *Yves de Chartres*, "Ep.," 208; *Pfister*, "De Fulberti Carnot. vità," 1885. During the Frankish epoch, one could be a "vassus" of only one "senior"; during the feudal epoch, fiefs could be received from several (*Secùrs*, "Siet Part.," 4, 26, 3. *Cf.* "behetrias," following); the same vassal frequently had several seigniors; proof of the predominance that the real element acquired. In case of war among the various seigniors, the vassal rendered personal service only to the one of whom he was liege man; for the others he was excused from defending them in this case, or he sent some one in his place. *Cf.* below.

was detached (the "**fief servant**") was said to be in the tenure ("**mouvance**") of the part that he retained (the "**fief dominant**"), that is, dependent upon it; it was to the land rather than to the seignior personally, that the feudal obligations were due, because if the seignior changed they were due to the new proprietor. The fief dominant was itself dependent upon a superior fief (the suzerain fief) over against which the fief servant was an "**arriere fief**" or "mesne-fief" [subfief].[1] During the monarchical period it was generally admitted that all fiefs were "sub-fiefs" of the king; no one in France could hold land without being amenable to the king for it (mediately or immediately).[2] The king, therefore, possessed the right of eminent domain over all land in the kingdom,[3] a universal lordship, an idea which did not, it appears, date from the earliest times of feudalism, because at this time the kings asserted only a right of sovereignty over French soil outside their own domains; it was solely by virtue of their right as sovereigns and not as suzerains that they appeared at the summit of the feudal hierarchy.[4] Supreme suzerainty had been a weapon. which they had employed in their struggles against feudalism.[5]

[1] For example, 1st, Fief A was a dominant of fief B, and suzerain of fief C; 2d, Fief B was a "servant" of fief A, and a "dominant" of fief C; 3d, Fief C was a "servant" of fief B, and an "arriere fief" of fief A. The vassal who had fief B had a right of usufruct with reference to the suzerain, and the right of eminent domain with reference to the "arriere" vassal (or to the copyholder, if there had been constituted a copyhold in the place of a subfief). This regeneration of the right of eminent domain was rather illogical and caused criticism of the feudal theory of ownership. Let us recall the rule: "Vasallus vasalli mei non est meus vasallus." Nevertheless, in many circumstances, there was a direct relation between the seignior and the "arriere" vassal. *Guyot*, "Inst.," 65. To hold "nument," was to hold directly, immediately. In England, the direct vassal of the king held "in capite." *Ragueau*, "Fief en chef" or "Chevel," etc. [2] *Guyot*, "Inst. féod.," 1, 7. *Blackstone*, vol. 2, p. 293.

[3] Of same in England, *Blackstone* says, 2, 4: "The king is lord and universal proprietor of all the lands of his kingdom and no man possessed it or could own the least part of it unless he had received it mediately or immediately from the king." The English law does not admit allodial property.

[4] Dissension between Bulgarus and Martinus. Antonin the Pious designated himself as the "mundi dominus."

[5] At Jerusalem, Amaury I, 1162, caused subvassals of the crown to be considered as liege men of the king. *J. d'Ibelin*, c. 140. They thus became his immediate vassals. Immediatization greatly contributed, very justly, says *Luchaire*, "Man.," p. 227, to the formation of provincial souvereignties, dukedoms, or powerfully organized counties. The principles of feudal law did not permit the suzerain to substitute himself directly in the place of the seignior, but the interest of the suzerain in increasing his troops and his revenues and the interest of the vassal in having a powerful protector struck a blow at the rules. Aside from violent means the method of arriving at the immediatization of subfiefs was the prestation of several homages by the same vassal; by giving himself to two masters, he escaped the weaker.

It was recognized as belonging to them, at least from the 1200 s, and gradually from this time the results became apparent.

§ 249. **The Constitution of the Fief (Infeudation)** was not a simple operation. It was a solemn contract (involving the formalities of fealty and homage) [1] to which was added the formality of investiture or transmission of ownership of the land by the seignior to the vassal.[2] The investiture should naturally have preceded the act of rendering homage since the services of the vassal were the price of the concession, but this order of procedure was not admitted; [3] it was regarded rather as a sort of compensation for the engagements already accepted.[4]

§ 250. **Fealty and Homage** ("fidelitas," "hominium") were two distinct solemnities, the first being derived from the oath of fealty taken, under the first two dynasties, first to the king and then to the simple "senior" by the "vassus"; the second, from the "recommendation." The formalities varied according to the time and place.[5] They all amounted to this: 1st, the vassal

[1] *Esmein*, p. 188, considers this contract as unilateral, but if this was its original aspect, we can see in it a reciprocal act at an early date.

[2] Two forms: 1st, Direct concession; the seignior ceded a part of his land to the vassal; 2d, Transformation of an alod into a fief ("feudum oblatium"); the proprietor of an allod acknowledged that he held his land as a fief from the seignior. *Luchaire*, "Man.," p. 156, rightly criticizes the ideas of Boutaric and Seignobos.

[3] According to the "Loi Feud.," 2, 4, investiture preceded fidelity. But, in general, homage took place before the granting of the fief; it could even exist without fief, as was observed above. *Esmein*, N.R.H., 1894, p. 539, rightly remarks that as a formal contract, it would operate without a "causa," but it did not preserve this character and was transformed into real contract; the "causa" was the concession of the fief, and care was taken to recall it in the acts of homage. *Durand*, "Spec. de feudis," no. 11. X, "de fide inst.," 2, 22, 14. *J. d'Ibelin*, 198: "Sire, deviens vostre home lige de tel fié."

[4] Concerning eventual infeudation, see "Loi Feud.," 2, 26, 3; 1, 3 pr. and following; *Horn*, "De investitura eventuali," 1865. Concerning the "coinvestitura," see "Loi Feud.," 2, 8, 2; 2, 12, pr.; 2, 18; 1, 14, 2. Concerning the "investitura simultanea" or "juris germanici," *Stobbe*, II, 443.

[5] *Du Cange*, see "Hominium," "Ligius," "Manscap," in German. Forms: 1200 s, *J. d'Ibelin*, c. 195; "Jostice," 12, 22, 1. "L. Feud.," 2, 5, 6, 7; *G. Durand*, "De feud.," 8; "Gr. C. Norm.," 39, 27; "Miroir de Souabe," 3, 4; *D. Vaissete*, 8, 686; *Teulet*, "Layettes," II, 328; *Waitz*, VG, 6, 46 and following; *Warnkoenig*, II, 357; 1300 s, *Boutillier*, I, 82; "Gr. C. de France," II; 1500 s, *Loysel*, "Inst.," 555. "Paris," 63: the vassal knelt on the ground bareheaded, without sword or spurs, declared that he would render faith and homage for such fief, etc. *Ragueau*, see "Bouche"; *Dumoulin*, s. "Paris," Art. 3, gl. 3, nos. 15 and following: liege homage was rendered to the sovereign alone, by the vassal with head bared and on his knees; all other homage was taken by raising the hand. *Challine*, "Méth. génér. p. l'intellig. des cout. de France," 1665, p. 52. 1600 s, *Pothier ed. Bugnet*, vol. 9, p. 497; *Fréminville*, "Pratiq. des terriers," I, 207; *Fleury*, "Inst. au dr. fr.," I, 262; *Argon*, 2, 2; *Boutaric*, "Dr. seign.," p. 390.

declared himself to be the "man,"[1] that is, the servitor, of the seignior in consideration of the fief which he had received; he knelt down and placed his hands in those of the seignior, who then accepted him and gave him the kiss of peace[2] ("hands and mouth"); 2d, following this formality the vassal swore upon the gospel and upon the altar, to be faithful to his seignior.[3] Since these ceremonies were performed at the same time, they ended by being confused, as is indicated by the expression, to swear "fealty and homage"; by the same process of simplification the oath ceased to be taken,[4] although the fealty was the most essential thing in the creation of a fief; in the 1700 s even homage itself was scarcely made except upon paper in the form of a "procès-verbal" attested by a notary.[5]

[1] According to Bracton and the old authorities, homage preceded faith. *Du Cange*, see "Fidelitas," "Hominium"; *Galbert de Bruges* ed. *Pirenne*, p. 89. *Cf. Esmein*, N.R.H., 1894, p. 541. "Et. s. les contrats," p. 98 and 104.

[2] In practice the custom of kissing was abandoned; Dumoulin criticizes it as scarcely decent. *Loysel*, 561; *Ragueau*, see "Baiser" (ancient custom in contracts).

[3] All vassals were faithfuls ("fidèles") but not all faithfuls were vassals, for example, ecclesiastics and the bourgeois who took the oath of fealty to the king or to the seignior in the quality of subjects. *Schröder*, 398. Bishops took the oath of fealty, but did not render homage (in the forty days "post susceptionem regalium"). N.R.H., 1894, p. 543. The vassal king did not do homage to any one (*Du Cange*, see "Homagium evanescere"); he indemnified the seignior or furnished a vassal who took his place. *Du Cange*, see "Fidelitas." "Gr. C. de France," 2, 28; *Jacq. d'Ibelin*, 1; *D. Vaissete*, 5, 804, 1126; *Loysel*, 644; *Garsonnet*, p. 377; *Glasson*, IV, 292.

[4] "d'Argentré," *Guyot*, "Inst. féod.," p. 2. *Cf. Laurière* concerning Art. 3, "C. de Paris."

[5] Conflicts of "Coutumes," *Loysel*, 594. Right of "chambellage" paid to the chamberlain or officer of the seignior who figured in the ceremony. *Olim*, I, 130; II, 77; Ord. 1272, I, 296; *Loysel*, 560 and following, *Ragueau*. Fealty and homage had to be rendered, in principle, by the vassal in person, unless the seignior consented to receive him by proxy or if the vassal had an excuse. "L. Feud.," II, 3, 1; *Lecoq*, 301, "Paris," 1, 67; *Loysel*, 558. Homages of the husband, of the "*baillistre*," of the man "living and dead." Homage was rendered to the chamber of accounts for the lands taken from the domain of the crown; to the principal manor of the dominant fief in general. *Loysel*, 555; the seignior was absent when the vassal presented himself: (*a*) ancient law: the vassal kissed the bolt of the manor; (*b*) *Dumoulin*: offers were made and a document prepared, *Loysel*, 559. *Ragueau*, see "Baiser le verroul." In case of combat of fief, that is to say, of contest between two seigniors over the tenure of a servant fief, the vassal not being able to bear faith to one without exposing himself to a disavowal of the other, if the latter was the true seignior, was received in faith by "main suzeraine," that is to say, by the superior seignior, and by "main souveraine," that is to say, by the king (or rather by his officers), when the two seigniors held different suzerains. This last proceeding ended by being employed solely. *Desmares*, 145, "Paris," 1, 60; *Loysel*, 645, 648.

§ 251. **Liege Homage,**[1] which was distinguished from ordinary or plain homage, obligated the vassal to defend the seignior to whom it was rendered against all men; this was due to him of whom the vassal held his principal fief; to other seigniors he rendered only homage "salvo jure prioris domini." This was neither the obligation to render military service for an indefinite period nor the maintenance of the old ceremonial which characterized liege homage, but it is correct to say that these two features occurred more often than otherwise. In regarding the king as the universal suzerain the idea (a false one in the early times of feudalism) came to prevail that liege homage was due only to the king.

§ 252. **The Investiture**[2] (or "livery of seissin"), that is to say, the transmission of the ownership of the fief, took place after the taking of the oath of fealty and homage. The seignior delivered to the vassal a banner, a sword, a staff, a clod of earth, and a pair of gloves and declared that he invested him with the fief; the actual taking possession of it by the vassal completed this symbolic act.[3] Very soon the parties were content with a symbolic investiture, then little by little that too fell into desuetude and "letters of fief" took its place. These were official minutes or records of the act of homage which had actually taken place and of the investiture which should have taken place.[4]

§ 253. **Avowal and Enumeration.** — (A) "Monstrée d'héritage" ("visio," "ostensio terræ") in the earliest times when the seignior

[1] Liege (from which allegiance) from the German "ledig," free, simple, without condition, and not from the Latin "ligare."

J. d'Ibelin, c. 198. Reserved from the beginning of the 1000 s. *Fulbert de Chartres*, "Hist. Fr.," X, 447. The "Cout. of Toulouse" calls the serf "homo ligius" ("de homagiis," 7, 8); *Ragueau*, see "Lige"; *Garsonnet*, 353; *Baudouin*, N.R.H., 1883, 667; *Pollock*, I, 279; *Esmein*, p. 193; "L. Henr.," I, 43, 6; *Britton*, 2, 41; "Jostice," p. 238; *J. d'Ibelin*, c. 140, 148; *Ph. de Nav.*, c. 40, 69; "Clef des Ass.," no. 214; "Liv. au Roi," 38; *G. Durand*, no. 3, *cf. Brussel*, I, 94 (three kinds of homage, the plain, the ordinary, and the liege, the first imposing less obligation than the second, and the second less than the third. From this point of view, other categories may be established). *Du Cange*, see "Homagium"; *Luchaire*, "Man.," p. 189, 197; *Boutaric*, "Le rég. féodal," p. 343 and following; *Loysel*, 555.

[2] *Du Cange*, see "Investitura"; "L. Feud.," 7, 1; 8, 8.

[3] By the first act, the vassal only acquired a right to take possession. Of two vassals, the one who had first been put in possession was preferred. If the lord happened to die before the investiture his successors were not bound to deliver the fief to the vassal. *Cf.* "Loi Feud.," 2. As to the right which it implied, the contrary was the case; the symbolic investiture conferred on the vassal a right to enter upon possession. Concerning the prescription, *cf.* "Loi Feud.," 2, 26, 4; 2, 33. "Cap. extrav." of *Jac. de Ardizone*, 2, 87.

[4] The tendency manifests itself from the 1300 s. *Brussél*, I, 116; *Ferrière*, Dict., see "Investiture." For the "censives" the payment of seigniorial dues took the place of investiture.

feared that the vassal would lessen his fief.[1] (B) In the 1300s the vassal was obliged within the forty days following the act of homage to make a written avowal, that is, a "recognition" that he held his fief of the seignior, and a written enumeration of the rights that he had received from the seignior.[2] The avowal and enumeration, veritable seigniorial title deeds, retained all their importance in the monarchical period.[3]

§ 254. **The Capacity to grant a Fief** belonged in principle only to kings, seigniors, and towns, that is, to those who could exact military service or administer justice.[4]

§ 255. **The Capacity to receive a Fief.** — In the beginning infeudation took place only for the benefit of persons capable of rendering feudal military service; minors, women, villeins, and ecclesiastics were excluded by virtue of the purpose for which the fief was designed.[5] But these incapacities were greatly extenuated or even disappeared in proportion as the principle of the inheritance was applied to fiefs.

§ 256. **The Object.** — As a general rule the fief was a piece of land, a heritage ("fief corporel"),[6] but it might also be a real right, such as an office or an administrative or judicial function,[7] and even a yearly income[8] ("fiefs incorporels"); in this way the seigniors obtained public officers and soldiers.[9] Household goods

[1] "Et. de Saint Louis," 1, 50 (*cf.* vol. 4, p. 323, ed. *Viollet*); "Olim," "Table," see "Monstræ," "Visus."

[2] "Gr. Cout.," 2, 25; "Paris," 5. Enumerations from the 1000s. *Luchaire,* "Man.," 191, cites: "Cart. de Grenoble," no. 46, year 1040; "Cart. de Saint-Père de Chartres," p. 315; "Hist. Fr.," 23, 656; "Rh. dr.," vol. 5, p. 397. The seignior had forty days in which to find fault with the enumeration. *Loysel,* 593 (communication of papers, *cf.* "C. of Toulouse," "t. de feudis"), 598; *Guyot,* "Inst.," 45.

[3] Notarial acts. *Fleury,* I, 163; *Fréminville,* "Prat. des terriers." *Supra,* p. 311.

[4] "Loi Feud.," 1, 1 pr. and 6; 2, 10 "pr. Consuet. Medial.," 27. *Fleury,* "Inst. du dr. fr.," I, 260: the king only, or the great seigniors with his permission could make a fief of what was a villeinage. But there was no seignior who could not divide a fief into several subfiefs.

[5] Add infamous and excommunicated persons. — Invalids. "L. Feud.," 2, 36.

[6] Ecclesiastical property? "Loi Feud.," 1, 6 pr.

[7] "Loi Feud.," 2, 1, 1. *Cf.* English sergeanty, fief of the "serviens" (sergeant, marshal, chamberlain, etc.). The manual trades were equally entailed, such as that of cook; the kitchen could be a fief. *L. Lelisle, op. cit.,* p. 44. Infeudation of tithes, of churches, position of "avoué," courts, etc.

[8] With "assignat" on a landed property or on the revenues of the seignior ("feuda de camera et cavena," "L. Feud.," 2, 1, 1). *Ragueau,* see "Fief de revenue"; *Du Cange,* see "Feudum bursæ." In 1248, Joinville refused to swear fidelity to Saint Louis, because he was not his man; in 1253 he became so by the payment of 200 pounds.

[9] *Guyot,* "Inst.," 9, fief corporal and "fief in the air" (without land reserved by the seignior).

alone were incapable of being held in fief because they were perishable.[1]

§ 257. **Effects of Infeudation.** — Infeudation was at once a contract giving rise to personal obligations and a transfer of property to which the establishment of real rights was attached.

§ 258. **Obligations of the Seignior.** — The seignior was particularly concerned about his rights, but less about his obligations, because of the superior position that he occupied. The principle was that he must return like for like to his vassal under all circumstances.[2] He owed him protection, justice, and assistance,[3] in default of which, during the feudal age, he lost his rights and the vassal was no longer bound except to the suzerain; during the period of the monarchy the seignior having been stripped of his political sovereignty, these obligations no longer had any reason for existence.

§ 259. **Obligations of the Vassal.** — These were of two kinds, one being imperfectly defined and for this reason designated as duties, the others fixed by the custom and designated as services.

A. **Duties.** — The duties of the vassal were summed up in the obligation of fealty;[4] under all circumstances he owed the seignior respect and assistance.[5] During the monarchical period this obligation had no longer any meaning. The vassal sustained the relation of subject toward the State which gave him the protection which the seignior had formerly furnished; in case of conflict between his duties as subject and his fealty to the seignior, the latter had to be sacrificed; it finally amounted to not showing himself ungrateful towards the seignior.

[1] *Cf.* "Preuss. Landrecht," I, 18, 26.

[2] *Fulbert de Chartres*, "Hist. Fr.," X, 463; *Beaumanoir*, 58; 45, 4. *Cf.* "Et. de Saint Louis," ed. *Viollet*, I, 161; *Loysel*, 649.

[3] "L. Feud.," 2, 26, 24. "Prussian Landrecht," 1, 18, 164. It must guarantee to him possession of the fief.

[4] In the oldest acts of homage (900 s) the vassal swore the life and members of the seignior and promised not to take away from him his château. "Forma fidelitatis," taken from letter 58 of *Fulbert de Chartres* (1020), "Hist. Fr.," X, 463, or *Migne*, "Patr. l.," 141, 229, inserted in the "L. Feud.," 2, 6, and in *Gratian*, 2d part, c. 18, c. 22, q. 5: "Qui domino suo fidelitatem jurat, ista sex in memoria semper habere debet: incolume, tutum, honestum, utile, facile, possibile. Incolume, ne sit in damno domino suo de corpore suo; tutum, ne sit ei in damno de secreto suo, vel de munitionibus suis per quas esse tutus potest; honestum, ne sit ei in damno de sua justitia vel de aliis causis quæ ad honestatem ejus pertinere videntur; utile, ne sit ei in damno de suis possessionibus; facile vel possibile, ne id bonum quod dominus suus facere leviter poterat, faciet ei difficile, neve id quod possibile ei erat, faciat impossibile." He could not give information concerning the crimes of the seignior or testify against him.

[5] The vassal had to answer for his seignior ("plivium" or "plegium," "manlevatio," "assecuratio") either as surety or hostage.

§ 260. **Services. I. Military Service,**[1] or service in the host.[2] Upon summons or requisition addressed to him by the seignior[3] the vassal was bound to report in person to the seignior, to arm and equip himself at his own expense,[4] and to serve throughout the whole war against all, even against his own relatives, even against the king.[5] Such was the rigor of the early law.[6] Custom and special agreements greatly modified the manner and duration of this obligation. Thus the service of the host (important military expedition) was frequently reduced to forty days; beyond this period or outside certain territorial limits the service of the vassal was only voluntary and at the seignior's expense. He was allowed to furnish a substitute. In rendering homage he reserved the right not to be compelled to go against the superior seignior and especially against the king (**liege hommage**). The service in the host tended to disappear in consequence of the abolition of private war among the seigniors and on account of its insufficiency when it was for the benefit of the king; the feudal army was undisciplined, it was assembled in an irregular manner, and it could not be relied upon for long expeditions, the seigniors always having good reasons for excusing themselves from the performance of their

[1] Villeins or "roturiers," subjects of the seignior, owed military service the same as vassals (ban); subvassals and mediate subjects owed it also in certain cases, for example, in case of invasion ("arrierè"-ban-reserve, "retrobannum"). *Boutaric,* "Inst. milit.," 1863; "Gr. C. Norm.," 22, 3. *Cf. Boutillier,* ed. *Charondas,* p. 488.

[2] We may distinguish (without the meaning of these words being always well defined) the "ost," or grand military expedition, the "estage" or guard of the seigniorial château, and the "chevauchée" ("cavalcata"), short incursion in the neighborhood. *Ragueau,* h. vis; *J. d'Ibelin,* c. 2, 17, 226. "Livre au Roi," c. 29. A year's service and consequently continual: *J. d'Ibelin,* c. 217, 222. "Clef des Ass.," 268. Sixty years passed, service in person was no longer due. *J. d'Ibelin,* c. 226, 228. "Ass. d'Antioche," H.C., I, 10. Service outside of the kingdom: *J. d'Ibelin,* c. 217. "Livre au Roi," 29. "Assises," vol. II, p. 432. Soudée, *J. d'Ibelin,* c. 224, 226, 80. "Livre au Roi," 27; *Ph. de Navarre,* 58. *Cf.* "Fiefs de soudée"; Life annuities attributed by virtue of fiefs to the mercenaries (hirelings?). *J. d'Ibelin,* c. 59, 62, 63, 243. *Ph. de Navarre,* 70, 211; "Jostice," p. 238; *Ragueau,* see "Fief de corps."

[3] By letter for the great feudatories, by proclamation for secondary vassals and towns.

[4] The vassal also had to be responsible for furnishing the seignior a "roncin de service," that is to say, a horse fit for war. *Viollet,* "Et. de Saint Louis," table, h. vo. *Cf.* the "restor" of the "Livre au Roi," c. 10 and following. *Ragueau,* see "Cheval de service, Traversant. Jostice," p. 238.

[5] "L. Feud.," 2, 27. *Renaud de Montauban.*

[6] The château of the vassal was "jurable et rendable" at discretion, that is to say, it had to be delivered to the suzerain whenever the latter exacted it. The vassal could not without the authorization of the seignior build a château anew. *Loysel,* 654; *Du Cange,* "Diss.," 30 and following; *Joinville,* "Des fiefs jurable et rendable"; *Ragueau,* h. "Jostice," p. 240.

duties. A pecuniary payment ("scutage," "hostenditiæ") was substituted in the place of personal service from the 1100s in England.[1] Of that which had been the essential obligation of the vassal and the reason for the existence of the fief there remained only the **ban** and the **arrière ban**, that is, a convocation of the nobles by the king to render feudal service to him, and this was commuted into the payment of a tax in money.[2]

II. **Court Service.**[3] — This was an obligation imposed on the vassal to attend, upon summons, the court of the seignior ("curia") for the purpose of giving him advice (duty of counsel) and to judge (service of court) with his fellow vassals, his peers. The feudal court thus constituted gave rise to the provincial estates and the States-General. Court service, which was connected, like military service, with the Carolingian usages, disappeared, as we have seen was the case with the seigniorial courts, when the barons ceased to figure in them as judges.[4]

III. **Aids for Four Cases** ("auxilium")[5] were sums of money, equivalent ordinarily to the annual income of the fief, which the vassal paid to the seignior, voluntarily in the earliest times, but later as a debt: 1st, for his ransom when he was made a prisoner; 2d, when his eldest son became an armed knight; 3d, when his eldest daughter was married; and 4th, when he armed himself for a crusade to which the vassal did not accompany him.[6] Aids were not required in the 1600s when there were no longer any crusades, no more knighthood, and when the practice of individual ransom had ceased.[7]

[1] Ord. XI, 351. "Hist. Fr.," 23, 759; *Langlois*, "Philippe le Hardi," p. 362; *Beaumanoir*, I, 428; "Gr. C. Norm.," c. 44. No "scutage" was levied, says Coke, after 1315.

[2] *Boutillier*, ed. *Charondas*, 1603, p. 488; *Ragueau*, h. vo.; *Boutaric*, "Dr. seign.," p. 391; *Guyot*, "Rép.," see *Ban*, *D'Avenel*, "Richelieu," I, 297.

[3] The villeins, subjects of the seignior, were, like vassals, subject to service. Sometimes the obligation was limited to three pleas (Christmas, Easter, and Pentecost), as under the Carolingians.

[4] *Casaveteri*, s. the "Cout. of Toulouse," "t. de feudis."

[5] The "aide," called also "taille," "queste," was levied by the seignior not only on his noble vassals, but on ecclesiastical communities, towns, villeins, and serfs. In fact, vassals did not themselves pay the "aide," but made their villeins or their serfs pay it.

[6] *Glanvill*, 9, 8; "T.A.C. Norm.," 470; Gr. Charter, 12; *Stubbs*, 479; "Gr. C. Norm.," 33 ("de capitalibus auxiliis"), 43; "C. de Norm.," 166 ("aides chevels"); *J. d'Ibelin*, 249, 269; *Bracton*, 50, 36; *Desmares*, 419; *Boutillier*, I, 86, no action; *G. Durand*, "Spec. de homag.," no. 67; action in order to reclaim them. *Ragueau*, "hac voce," *Loysel*, 604 ("loyaux aides"), and following. *Blackstone*, vol. 2, p. 315.

[7] *Pocquet de Liv.*, "Fiefs," p. 24; *Guyot*, "Rép.," see "Aide"; *Ferrière*, Dict., see "Aides Chevels."

§ 261. **Rights of the Seignior and of the Vassal over the Fief.** — (A.) The seignior preserved direct ownership (legal title) and in virtue thereof reclaimed it, alienated it, gave his consent to a change of vassals, exacted payments and received back the fief as a result of disinheritance or escheat. (B.) The vassal had a usufructuary right over the domain, that is, the right of possession and a certain right of disposal (which varied during different periods) so long as it did not involve an infringement upon the rights of the seignior. He was entitled to all the fruits and revenues of the fief; he had the right to manage it as he wished; but in the beginning, if it was too badly managed, the seignior had the right to resume possession.[1] He could lease the fief either for a definite period or for an indefinite time.[2] In case of a suit affecting the fief he had the right to maintain the action either as plaintiff or as the defendant; and the judgment was binding upon the seignior except in case of fraudulent collusion.[3] The maxim of Loysel, "all fiefs are patrimonies,"[4] summed up exactly enough the rights of the vassal; it resulted from this principle that fiefs were hereditary and capable of being alienated, but the inheritance and alienation of fiefs were far from being regulated as in the case of ordinary property. Among other results they gave rise to those perquisites or beneficial rights demanded by the seignior and which, in his opinion, constituted the entire fief, at least to the end of the old régime.

§ 262. **Transmission of Fiefs "Mortis Causa."** — Upon the death of the vassal the fief passed to his heirs;[5] but as a reminder of the epoch when it was a personal concession and only for the life of the grantee the inheritance of fiefs was regulated differently from that of other estates (*e.g.* those of the villein class); the will of the seignior prevailed in some measure in order to insure regard for the purpose for which the fief was designed, since its aspect as a military endowment could not be altered without making

[1] Ancient law, "L. Feud.," 2, 8, 3; 2, 27, 16; 2, 28; 8, 14.

[2] "L. Feud.," 1, 5, 2 and 4; 1, 14; 1 and 2; 2, 1; 2, 9, 3; 2, 45, 1. "Contractus libellarius." Prussian Landrecht, 1, 18, 192. *Cf. Loysel*, 641.

[3] "L. Feud.," 2, 8; 26; 43.

[4] *Loysel*, 552.

[5] In Italy, the Constitution of Conrad II ("L. Feud.," 5, 1; *cf.* 6, 1) consecrated (but did not create) the heredity of fiefs. In Germany, the custom was established in the 1000 s, but only in the sense of inheritance in the interest of the descendants; collaterals succeeded only by virtue of provisions in the contract of infeodation or of local laws (1100 s). *Cf.* for France, *supra*, p. 602; in the 1000 s, the custom of inheritance was recognized. *Yves de Chartres*, "Ep.," 71. Exceptions, *Flach*, "Orig.," II, 514; *Luchaire*, "Hist. des inst. mon. sous les premiers Cap.," vol. 2, c. 2; "L. Feud.," 1, 1. 8, 14; 2, 11, 37, 45, 50, 61. Laws of Frederic II, Dauphiné: mortmain on noble vassals.

it impossible for the vassal to perform his obligations.[1] The peculiarities of feudal succession are explained by the idea of a new grant or of a confirmation by the seignior. Thus the vassal could not regulate by testament the succession to his fief;[2] he had only those heirs whom God had given him ("solus Deus heredes facere potest, non homo," Glanvill). In theory the seignior resumed possession of the fief upon the death of the vassal, so that if the vassal left no heir the fief belonged definitively to the seignior.[3] It was the same if the vassal left only illegitimate issue or heirs incapable of performing feudal service, such as females and minors. Ancestors hardly fit for military service by reason of their age were excluded from the succession in all cases by the seignior, who, if he had desired to grant them the fief, would never have granted it in the first instance to their sons or grandsons. Succession to fiefs therefore never ascended.[4] When a fit heir came into possession of a fief by inheritance he was obliged to go through the formalities of a new infeudation. He took the oath of fealty and did homage within a period of time which varied (forty days, or a year and one day).[5] The seignior, who was bound to grant the investiture,[6] did so only in consideration of the payment of a sum of money equivalent ordinarily to a year's income from the fief;[7]

[1] "L. Feud.," 1, 1, 1 ("beneficium confirmare").

[2] "L. Feud.," 1, 8; 2, 9, 26. *Cf.*, however, theories of reserve and of legitimacy (which follow); except these rights, the vassal could dispose of the fief by testament. [3] "L. Feud.," 2, 50; *Beaumanoir*, 14, 23.

[4] *Beaumanoir*, 14, 16; "Gr. C. de France," 2, 27.

[5] *Beaumanoir*, 14, 16; "Gr. C. de France," 2, 27; "L. Feud.," 2, 55; 2, 26, 12. "Feuda franca, feuda honorata": the vassal was excused from fealty and homage, but not from the duty of fidelity. *Loysel*, 574. *Cf. Ragueau*, see "Fiefs francs," "Jostice," p. 254. The new vassal could not take possession of the fief or exercise the right of complaint without having taken the oath of fealty and homage. ("Gr. Cout.," 2, 1921, 25; "St. Parl.," 28, 14; *Desmares*, 62, 177), *cf.* "L. Feud.," or, at least without having obtained "souffrance" (sufferance) from the seignior. In the 1300 s, the silence of the seignior was regarded as tacit sufferance ("Tant que le seigneur dort, le vassal veille"). *Loysel*, 584, 601; *Brodeau* on Art. 82, I, 627; *De Laurière*, "C. de Paris," I, 171; *Ragueau*, see "Fief ouvert," "Souffrance." The time allowed for performing the obligation to do homage was indefeasible. *Beaumanoir*, 24, 9; *Desmares*, 198; "Paris," 1, 12.

[6] "L. Feud.," 1, 14; 4, 9; *J. d'Ibelin*, 151; "Gr. C. de France," 2, 21; *Desmares*, 177, 193, 285; "Cout. not.," 134; "Regiam Maj.," 3, 28, 1; *Durand*, "Spec. de feudis," 3; *Masner*, 27, 17; *Loysel*, 552; *Ferrière*, "Dictionn.," see "Invest."

[7] The amount was at first arbitrary, and depended upon the will of the seignior. England: Glanvill, 9, 4. "Gr. Charter," 2; Bracton, fo. 84; details in *Pollock and Maitland*, I, 289. Amount of first seizin paid by the heir of the fief held from the king "in capite." France: "T.A.C. Norm.," 47; "Gr. C. Norm.," 32, 3; Ord. 1235, *Isamb.*, II, 244. "Jostice," 12, 6, 1; *Beaumanoir*, 27, 2; *Desmares*, 287; "Gr. C. Fr.," 2, 27; N.R.H., 1891, 178; "Cout. not. Chât.," 138; "Paris," 47; *Loysel*, 564,

this charge for transmission "mortis causa" was called the "**relief**," for the reason that the seignior raised up again, for the benefit of the new vassal, the fief which had fallen from the hands of the former holder; it was also known as the "**repurchase**" ("rachat") because the heir purchased anew the feudal concession.[1] These expressions, exact for a time when fiefs were not hereditary, indicated by their very exaggeration, how far, eventually, the transaction was from being an ordinary succession. These rules were opposed to the old maxim: "le mort saisit le vif" (the dead puts the living in possession). Since, by virtue of this fiction, the deceased himself was supposed to have transmitted his rights to his heir, there should have been no question of seigniorial investiture nor of relief. With some difficulty this was conceded for one class of heirs, namely, direct descendants;[2] they were exempted from the payment of relief,[3] but they were not relieved from the obligation of taking the oath of fealty and homage. As to collateral heirs[4] it was necessary for them to be invested, so long as investiture was a custom; in the 1700 s a third or a fourth of the amount of the relief was remitted to them.

§ 263. **Plurality of Heirs. I. Indivisibility of the Fief. Primogeniture.**[5] — Two reasons led to the establishment of the prin-

566 and following; *Pothier*, "Fiefs," 2, 1; *Luchaire*, "Man.," 205. The rights of justice were excepted as not forming part of the fief.

[1] *Beaumanoir*, 27, 2; *Bracton*, 2, 36; "Gr. Charter," 2; "Jostice," 12, 6; "Gr. C. de France," 2, 19 and 30; *Loysel*, 563; *Ragueau*, see "Relief"; *Teulet*, "Layettes," II, 137, 142, 144; *Tonneins*, 171, etc. "Esporle" ("sportula") at Bordeaux. *Ragueau*, see "Plait" in Dauphiny; "Mi-lod"; Lyonaise, Forez; "Marciage," etc. According to *Guyot*, "Inst. f.," 86, the written law did not recognize the relief (1700 s). Concerning the English "heriot," horses, and arms due the seignior at the death of the vassal, *cf. Pollock and Maitland*, I, 293. Following certain customs, "le fief relève des deux mains," that is to say, the relief was paid at the death of the seignior as at the death of the vassal; but it was exceptional. "Gr. C. Norm.," 32, 9; *Tonneins*, 171 and following; *Desmares*, 193; "Jostice," 12, 15, 6; "Cout. not.," 42, 55, 56; *Bracton*, 2, 36, 5; "Paris," 63; *Loysel*, 588 and following; *Fleury*, "Inst. du dr. fr.," I, 265; *Ragueau*, see "Fiefs q. se gouv. selon la C. du Vexin français."

[2] "Jostice," 12, 6, 1; *Beaumanoir*, 14, 8; "Gr. C. de France," 2, 21, 27, 30; "Cout. not.," 134; *Desmares*, 199, 285, 287; "Paris" (1510), 22 and (1580) 278; *Loysel*, 552, states that every heir, as well as every villein, was seized of fiefs.

[3] *Loysel*, 560 and 563. "Gr. C. de Fr.," l.c.

[4] Concerning the succession of collaterals, "L. Feud.," 1, 1, 2 and following, *Esmein*, p. 202.

[5] 1st, Primogeniture could exist according to the constitution of the family. Hebrews, Gen., xxvii, 29, 39; 49, 3; Hindus, *Maine*, "Ancient Law," p. 440; Greece, *Beauchet*, "Hist. du dr. privé athén.," III, 451; Rome, *Cuq*, "Inst. d. Rom," I, 32. It implied then religious and political privileges rather than a right to exclusive ownership. This right of primogeniture did not exist or no longer existed (*cf. Tacitus*, "Germ.," 32) during the Barbarian epoch. 2d, The feudal right of primogeni-

ciple of the indivisibility of the fief and that of primogeniture, which was a natural consequence of the former (but not a necessary

ture was established in the interest of the seignior, to whom feudal services would be more surely rendered, and in the general interest, the fief being a little State, a political center, the division of which would have been prejudicial to all. 3d, During the monarchical epoch, the seignior's interest disappeared, but the interest of the family still existed; an economic and moral center had been with difficulty established by the effort of several generations, and the right of primogeniture was the means of perpetuating it; it was justified for the family as it was justified for the State, by the principle of monarchical succession. Although family property was not easily alienated, it attained its end; since the obstacles to the disposition of this property had disappeared or become inefficacious, it was necessary to strengthen the right of primogeniture by means of trust substitutions, the custom of which extended to the 1500s. The noble appointed his eldest son as heir, and substituted for him the eldest of the latter's sons, and so continuing in such a way that there was transmission from male to male by order of primogeniture. The entailed property became untransferable in the hands of the eldest of the family. By the side of advantages that are too often forgotten in our time, and which are of a moral as well as material character (assistance for aged relatives, for sick or poor members of the family, a fund for relief, insurance, hospital treatment, maintenance of traditions of honor, etc.), this system offers inconveniences which brought unpopularity on it at the end of the Old Régime: property withdrawn from commerce, withdrawn from business; creditors defrauded by a debtor who seemed to possess great fortune, but who was only a trustee, since he had to transmit it intact to his oldest son; every generation marked by shameful insolvency; unworthy eldest sons, dissipating the revenues of family property, etc. The English corrective, the liberty of making a will, permitting the putting aside of unworthy sons, was not accepted by our ancient law. The will of the father of the family was defied, as it was thought that nature would be mistaken less often than he. Under this form, the institution, not giving the results that were expected of it, was condemned. In our time, the absence of the former family head is filled by the State, by religious or other associations, or by an artificial family that is chosen. In English law, the right of primogeniture was not a privilege of the nobility as in France. Under Edward I, the act "de donis conditionalibus" introduced permanent substitutions. The "estate tail" or "feodum talliatum" (mutilated fief) was a fief of substitution. *Boutmy*, "Dévelop. de la Const. angl.," 1887, p. 93: "The actual régime of 'latifundia' and of entailed estates, did not begin to flourish until after the Restoration." In Germany (*Stobbe*, V, 103) the right of primogeniture did not acquire the importance that it had in France. The collective investiture appeared sufficient to safeguard the interests of the seignior; younger brothers and sisters were not sacrificed, in general. "Golden Bull," 25, 1. "Schwabensp.," p. 57. Beginning from the 1300s, family laws ("Hausgesetze") applied to the "Stammgüter" (ancestral estates) of princely dynasties, the absolute principle of indivisibility and of indefeasibility. Since the 1500 s, in the same spirit of conservation of seigniorial fortunes, substitutions were practiced ("Familienfideicommis"), *cf. Stobbe*, V, 368, § 321. The properties entailed passed: 1st, to the oldest ("séniorat") or youngest ("juniorat") of the family; 2d, to the oldest ("majorat") or to the youngest ("minorat") of the nearest relatives of the dead; 3d, to the oldest ("primogéniture") or to the last born ("ultimogéniture") of the descendants of the latter, and so on, in the same order, primogeniture or "majorat" were the preferred régime. For example: I die, leaving an uncle, a brother, and a grandson. In the system of the "seniorat," the uncle succeeds; in the "majorat," the brother; in primogeniture, the grandson.

result).[1] They were: 1st, During the period when benefices were granted for life, the seignior who reëntered into possession of his property at the death of the vassal did not divide it up among the heirs of the deceased vassal; each one of the parcels would have been unable to render the services that he expected from them, and particularly the military service; his interests, therefore, required that he grant it to one of them alone.[2] *A fortiori*, it was the same in regard to public offices. 2d, The seigniories constituted political centers a division of which would have been attended by the same inconveniences as the dismemberment of a State.[3] Feudal primogeniture was regulated by law only from the end of the 1100 s (Anglo-Norman Customs, Assizes of Count Geoffrey, 1185), but it existed before that time by usage and custom (acts and wills);[4] in the 1000 s it came to prevail, following a struggle with the traditional rule of equal division; it did not,

[1] "L. Feud.," 1, 8 (divided equally among sons, in spite of testamentary dispositions to the contrary). Genesis, xxv; Deuteronomy, xxi, 17. Anglo-Norman texts: L. of Henry I, in *Houard*, I, 340; *Glanvill*, 7, 3; "Très Anc. Cout. Norm.," 8, 2; "Gr. C. Norm.," 23, 5; 24, 34. "Assize" of Count Geoffroy, 1185; *Planiol*, N.R.H., 1887, 145; *J. d'Ibelin*, 192; *Loysel*, 638, 611; *Tiraqueau*, "De jure primig.," 3 ed., 1581; *Luchaire*, "Man.," 161 (bibl.); *cf. Ragueau*, Gloss., see "Aisneté" (Charter of 892), *Aînesse; Cauwes*, "Gr. Encycl.," *Vachier*, Thesis, 1889; *G. d'Espinay*, N.R.H., 1896, 365 (Poitou); *Schulze*, "Recht d. Erstgeburt," 1851. Primogeniture, in the Midi, was general for the large fiefs only at the end of the 1100 s. "L. Feud.," 1, 1, 1 (equal division); *D. Vaissete*, V, 316, 323, 1032; VIII, 289, 462. In the Pyrenees region, primogeniture prevailed in respect of all property, whether nobles or villeins, for the benefit of daughters the same as sons, of collaterals as of descendants, with indefeasibility of family property. "Fors de Béarn," passim. *Barèges*, 1 and following; *Cordier*, "Rhdr.," vols. 14 and 15 ("De l'orig. de la famille chez les Basques"), and vol. 5 ("Le dr. de famille aux Pyrénées"); *Guyot*, "Inst. féod.," 224: the countries of written law were not familiar with the right of primogeniture; if the eldest had the fief, it was by accommodation or ordinance of the father. *Dognon*, 17.

[2] The property of nobles (fiefs, noble allodiums) was divided "nobly" (primogeniture), while equal division was the rule for villeins ("censives") or properties not noble, with the exception of certain customs (Normandy, 235). *Beaumanoir*, 14, 5; 47, 6; "Jostice," 12, 6, and 21; *P. de Font.*, 34, 2; "Gr. C. de France," p. 283, 290; *Boutillier*, p. 46; *Loysel*, 613. The right of primogeniture belonged to the grandson or to the granddaughter as representative of the eldest son, predeceased. The eldest son could renounce his birthright or even the entire succession after the death of his father.

[3] Const. of Frederic I, 1158. *Loysel*, 638. By the Salic Law, kingdoms, duchies, counties, marquisates, and baronies were not dismembered, 639. But the king had to provide an appanage for his brothers and younger male children and husbands for his sisters and daughters; and to dukes, counts, and barons, recompense in other lands. Germany: Golden Bull of 1356, indivisibility of the possessions of electors based on the indivisibility of the electoral voice. *Schulte*, trans. *Fournier*, p. 235.

[4] *Orderic Vital*, "Hist. eccles." (ed. *Soc. hist. Fr.*), II, 26, 48, 76, 86, 129.

however, apply to daughters or to collateral heirs.[1] It was the interest of the seignior and the seigniory that caused the principle of primogeniture to prevail; there was no thought of giving an advantage to one of the brothers over the others; indeed whenever a vassal had several fiefs and several children each of them received one of the fiefs. The idea of creating for him a superior position in the interest of the family which he was charged with perpetuating appeared, on the contrary, in the English law which gave to the eldest son the right to all the fiefs whatever their number.[2]

II. **Division of Fiefs.** — The eldest son keeping the fief must provide his brothers with appanages and his sisters with marriage dowries. A simple allowance for maintenance at first, the appanage later consisted of a portion of the fief in which the brothers had a life interest,[3] and finally a hereditary interest; but the eldest son always had a larger share than his brothers. The Customs ordinarily gave him: (*a*) the chief manor house or principal château with an acre and a half of adjoining land; (*b*) two thirds or a half of the remaining land according as there were one or several children; in the former case the division was by thirds; in the latter case, by fourths. The eldest son had a third or a fourth as a preference legacy (besides the principal manor house), then a third or a fourth as his hereditary portion, and his share of the debts was only in proportion to the latter.[4] Besides, he had precedence over the younger sons and took the family name, the family titles, archives, portraits, emblem, and full arms (without rebatement).[5] The Customs did not ordinarily recognize the right of primogeniture among daughters or among collateral heirs.[6]

[1] *Beaumanoir*, 14, 4 (the eldest of the daughters had the principal manor). "Gr. C. Fr.," 2, 27. "Etabl. de Saint Louis," 1, 12, "Touraine," 273. "Jostice," 12, 6, 34 (no birthright among girls). *Cf. Meynial*, N.R.H., 1892, 421; *J. d'Ibelin*, 150, 182; *Navarre*, 72, 81 (subinfeudation): about 1170. *Loysel*, 632; *Lagrèze*, "Hist. du dr. dans les Pyrénées," 182.

[2] In case there were several fiefs to divide, the eldest chose the best fief. "Gr. Cout. Norm.," 26; *Boutillier*, 76; *Navarre*, 68, 71; *J. d'Ibelin*, 148. Old rule: a man could possess only one fief. Contrary Assize about 1180. *Meynial*, N.R.H., 1892, p. 413.

[3] "Assise du comte Geffroi," ed. *Planiol*. "T.A.C. Bretagne," 209; "Maine," 242; "Anjou," 238. "Const. Châtelet," 65; *Boutillier*, I, 79; *Loysel*, 639. *Cf.* below "Apanage"; *Ragueau*, see "Fief boursal."

[4] *P. de Font.*, 34, 2. "Jostice," 12, 6, 10; *Beaumanoir*, 14, 5 and following; "Artois," 26, 1; *Boutillier*, I, 79, 80; "Gr. C. Fr.," 2, 25, p. 283; *Loysel*, 614 and following, 630 and following. "Olim," I, 527. The "lar" or principal house, *Bayonne*, 12, 8.

[5] *Loysel*, 615; *Ragueau*, see "Cri." The right of justice attached to the fief continued to belong to the eldest, but the other children shared the emoluments.

[6] "Jostice," 12, 6, 14, 15; *Beaumanoir*, 14, 8; *Guy Coquille*, "Inst.," pp. 112, 114. *Cf. Loysel*, 626; 632 (Ord. of the comt. of Troyes, 1212), 633.

§ 264. **By what Title did the Eldest Son and the Younger Sons have a Portion of the Fief?** — (A.) **By parage,** that is, without homage or service. As against the seignior there was no partition. The eldest son (the chief "parager") alone rendered homage and performed the feudal duties. Among brothers ("aparageurs") there was a division as in ancient law, and in this sense, equality; they were peers (from which "parage") since each received a portion of the fief, although this portion was less for the younger sons.[1]

(B.) **By Subinfeudation.** — The portion of the younger son was a subfief in relation to the seignior, and he became the immediate vassal of his eldest brother. The unity of the feudal bond was thus safeguarded.[2]

(C.) **By an Ordinance of Philip Augustus (1209 or 1210),** by which the divisibility of the fief was made complete; each brother was considered as holding his part from the seignior himself; the eldest brother was not at all the seignior of his younger brothers, for they all rendered homage to the dominant seignior.[3]

§ 265. **Women,** being incapable of performing military service, were, in accordance with the rigor of the law, excluded from inheriting fiefs.[4] Men were preferred to them. Unlike the rule of primogeniture, the privilege of masculinity dated from the Barbarian period, where the arguments were already demolished. In feudal practice it disappeared gradually, at first through provisions inserted in the contracts of infeudation admitting daughters to the right of succession. It finally came to be governed by the following rules: (*a*) the sons excluded the daughters; (*b*) in their turn the daughters excluded the collateral heirs; (*c*) among collaterals of equal degree males succeeded to the exclusion of females except in the case of fiefs held by women.[5] A female

[1] "Gr. C. Norm.," 28, 30 and following. *Beaumanoir*, 47; *Ph. de Navarre*, 75; *J. d'Ibelin*, 150. "Etabl. Saint Louis," I, 10 and following, 24, 46 and following; 79 and following, 130. "Jostice," 126 "Const. Châtelet," 65; *Bout.*, I, 89; "Gr. C. de Fr.," 2, 27, 29; *Ragueau*, Gloss., see "Parage," "Fief boursal," "Mirouer." *Loysel*, 611 and following, 622, 628. *Laur.* s., "Paris.," 35 and 51, I, 93. *Brussel*, 3, 13.

[2] *Beaum.*, 14, 5; *Ragueau*, see "Farescheux"; *J. d'Ibelin*, 150; *Ph. de Nav.*, 71; Lignages d'Outre-Mer, 16 (middle of the 1100 s). "Gr. C. Norm.," 27, 7; 28, 1 (beginning from the seventh degree "quod per paragium tenebatur per homagium tenebitur").

[3] Ord. I, 29; *Isambert*, I, 203. Made solely for the king's domain, it soon came to be applied outside of it, but did not become general, however, to the point of causing the other systems to disappear. *Loysel*, 622.

[4] "L. Feud.," 1, 1, 3; 1, 8 pr.; *Loysel*, 637, "T.A.C. of Bretagne," 233.

[5] "L. Feud.," 1, 8, 24; 2, 11, 17, 30, 50. "Sent. de success. mulierum in bonis feod." *Alb.*, I, 1299; *Ph. de Nav.*, 69, 175; *J. d'Ibelin*, 187. "Ass. Romanie," c. 44; "Jostice," 12, 6, 7; "T.A.C. Bretagne," 232;

vassal performed her feudal services through a representative, and her natural representative being her husband, she could not, under penalty of losing her fief, marry without the consent of the seignior. The husband took the oath of fealty and homage for her as if he were the vassal and it is obvious that the seignior was not bound to accept an enemy. Sometimes indeed, as in Palestine, the seignior offered his female vassal three barons from among whom she was obliged to choose her husband; the attainment of the sixtieth year of age afforded a legitimate excuse for failure to marry just as it relieved one from the duty of military service.[1]

§ 266. **Minors.** — If the vassal left a minor child [2] the seignior had the guardianship of the fief, that is,[3] he administered it, appropriated the income from it (except what was necessary for the support of the child) and restored only the principal at the majority of the child. This **seigniorial guardianship** had two defects: it was prejudicial to the minor; sometimes, indeed, it was a source of expense to the seignior. It therefore disappeared and in its place was substituted the **lease** ("bail") [4] by which the seignior gave the fief to the heir presumptive of the minor, who was designated as the "baillistre" and who was required to pay the purchase fee as though the succession were already open to him; this was well enough justified since the "baillistre" was a quasi proprietor who received the fruits and paid the debts of the fief. With such a guardian the life of the minor would be in danger; he was protected by giving to the "baillistre" only the property,

Beaumanoir, vol. I, p. 408 and following; II, 160; *Loysel*, 634 and following; *Bordeaux*, 229, 233; *D. Vaissete*, 5, 316, 323, 1032, 1072. "Et. de Saint Louis," 1, 12; *Hotman*, "De feudis," 15; *G. Rolbagii*, "Certamen masculo-fœmineum," 1602.

[1] *Glanvill*, 7, 9. "Reg. maj.," 2, 48, 5; "Gr. Charte," 8; *Bracton*, fo. 37, 89 (the seignior extended to sons what at first was applied only to women). *Blackstone*, vol. 2, p. 324; *Pollock and Maitland*, I, 299. "Const. Sic.," 3, 21; *Ph. de Navarre*, 72, 79, 86; *J. d'Ibelin*, 171, 175, 187, 217, 227. "Et. de Saint Louis," 1, 51, 63, 67. "Gr. C. Norm.," 33; *Beautemps-Beaupré*, "Anc. Cout. d'Anjou," p. 25; *Viollet*, "Et. de Saint Louis," 3, 357; *Ragueau*, see "Mariage." In case of several marriages, the same fees were paid to each one as in case of a new acquisition.

[2] Feudal majority: boys, 21 years; girls, 15. *Desmares*, 249; "Gr. C. de Fr.," 2, 25; "Paris," 32, "L. Feud.," 2, 55, 2.

[3] *Pollock and Maitland*, I, 299; "G. Ch.," 3; "Gr. C. Norm.," 26, 33; "Et. de Saint Louis," I, 73, 137; II, 18; *Beaumanoir*, c. 15, 16, 17; "Gr. C. Fr.," 2, 41; *Du Cange*, see "Custodia."

[4] 1200 s. "Jostice," 12, 6; *Beaumanoir*, c. 15, 21; *J. d'Ibelin*, 171, 227; Ord. 1246, I, 58; *Desmares*, 281; *Boutillier*, 1, 93; *Loysel*, 176 and following, 191, 581 and following. Minors and tutors did not take the oath of fidelity but the "baillistres" did. *Ragueau*, see "Déport." Formerly the lease was terminated for women only with their marriage. "Gr. C. Norm.," 31, 14.

the care of his person being intrusted to another relative; according to the old maxim: "ne doit mie garder l'agnel, qui doit en avoir la pel" (do not trust the lamb to the person who is entitled to the skin).

§ 267. **Alienation "inter vivos."** — According to primitive law[1] the vassal could not alienate his fief either by sale or gift because this would have been to substitute another in the performance of his feudal obligations, for example, in military service. Thus the seignior who had chosen his vassal, his soldier (or at least his family, when the fief was hereditary), would have been deceived in his expectations if he allowed the vassal to substitute some one else in his place.[2] At least, unless he had previously given his consent, which would have been equivalent to a new grant for the benefit of him who had received it. The vassal who alienated his fief without the permission of the seignior thereby forfeited it ("fiefs de danger," in Burgundy). Nevertheless, the patrimonial idea triumphed and the subsequent development of the law allowed the vassal the free disposal of the fief,[3] but at the same time safeguarded the rights of the seignior, 1st, by feudal redemption; 2d, by profits or fees charged for the right of alienation; and 3d, by a prohibition upon the curtailment of the fief.[4] On his part,

[1] However, the "L. Feud." permitted alienation without the consent of the seignior; the purchaser did homage to the seignior and he could not refuse to accept it. *Cf. Tourtoulon*, "J. de Revigny," p. 45.

[2] "L. Feud.," 252 ("Const. of Lothaire," III, 1136) and 53 ("C. of Frederic," I, 1154 at Roncaglia); "Gr. C. Norm.," 27, 9; "A. C. Bourgogne," *Giraud*, II, 275; *Ragueau*, see "Fiefs de danger." *Loysel*, 552, 646. Concerning the subinfeudation authorized in this system as it differed from sale, exchange, donation, long lease, and mortgage, *cf. Gui Pape*, "Cons.," 214.

[3] "Statut of Milan," "L. Feud.," 1, 13; 2, 9, and 49; 2, 26, 25. *J. d'Ibelin*, 182 and following. Common law of France in the 1200s. In England, the statute "Quia emptores," 1290, authorized total or partial alienation of the fief. *Pollock and Maitland*, I, 318, 310 (theories of Coke and Blackstone on primitive law and historic evolution in matters relating to the alienation of fiefs). N.R.H., 1897, 828. The "obligatio" or "impignoratio" was subject to the same rules as alienation. "Lex Feud.," 1, 5, 2; 2, 55 pr. Priv. Nuremberg, 1219, § 4; *Gierke*, "De debitis feudal," 1860. In principle the fief was not responsible for the debts of the vassal, since the fief was the property of the seignior; at most, the creditor had only the right to take the revenues of the fief in payment of his debts. "L. Feud.," 2, 45. But in a measure as the fief became alienable, its seizure was authorized. For the rest, it was necessary also to make the fief pay the debts contracted in its exclusive interest ("ex versione in rem.," etc.). *Loysel*, 650 and following; *J. d'Ibelin*, 186; *Boutillier*, I, 71. The English law on this point shows a remarkable evolution; in principle the fief was not responsible for the debts of its tenants (*Britton*, 64 b; *cf. Glanvill*, 7, 8; *Bracton*, 61 a); *Lehr*, "Dr. Angl.," p. 155.

[4] Edict of Conrad the Salic, 1037; *Molinier*, *op. cit.*, p. 146, and *Luchaire*, "Man.," p. 217; *Froissart*, "Chron.," I, 141. *Gui Pape*, "Dec. Gratian," 560.

however, the seignior in the end might alienate the fief without his vassal's consent.

§ 268. **Feudal Redemption or Retention.** — The vassal who sold his fief was required to remit it into the hands of the seignior, who might retain it for the price which the purchaser paid for it.[1] By the 1500 s the formalities of disseizin by the seller and of seizin by the purchaser had fallen into desuetude; the seignior exercised his right of redemption no longer by means of retention, but through action, and for this purpose he was allowed a year and a day from the time when the alienation was known to him.

§ 269. **The Mutation Fee.** — If the price of sale was low the seignior took the fief himself, if it was high the interest of the seignior required him to accord the investiture to the purchaser;[2] what happened, in fact, was that his consent was acquired by the payment of an alienation fee, or "right of mutation" proportional to the price, ordinarily a fifth (the "**quint**"), and to this was added in the course of time a fifth of this fifth (the "**requint**").[3] In the 1700 s it was the custom, says Pothier, for the seignior to remit all or a part of this payment.

§ 270. **Dismemberment of the Fief Prohibited.** — The division of a fief was forbidden,[4] that is, a vassal could not make several fiefs out of one without the consent of the seignior, because this would have been a violation of the contract which bound the vassal to the seignior and would have also diverted the fief from its original purpose.[5] But subinfeudation, or releasing of a part of the fief, was generally permitted because these acts did not alter the relations between the seignior and his vassal.[6]

[1] Cod. Just., "de j. emph.," 4, 66; "L. Feud.," 2, 26, 14; 9, 3. "Cout. de la Chapelaude," 1073; *Beaumanoir*, 51, 20; "Gr. C. Fr.," 2, 25; *Desmares*, 204; *Bordeaux*, 128; *Coquille*, "Inst.," p. 86; "Paris," 20, and *Dumoulin* on this Art.; *Pothier*, "Fiefs," nos. 691 and following.

[2] C. J., 4, 66, 3; *Beaumanoir*, 27, 7 (a fifth of the price for the fief, a twelfth for the manor). "Toulouse," 135 ("pax," a twelfth). "Montpellier," 11; "Bordeaux," 128; *Desmares*, 199 and following. "Gr. C. de France," 2, 25, 30; "Jostice," 12, 13; *Loysel*, 572; "Paris," 33. Sanction: feudal seizure, "Paris," 24; "Orléans," 44. *Cf. Pothier*, "Fiefs," § 410. Donation: "relief" was paid as if it were a succession. *Loysel*, 571, N.R.H., 1891, 180. The "relief" and the "fifth" were not cumulative.

[3] *Fleury*, "Inst. au dr. fr.," I, 264.

[4] "Const. Pis.," 1161, c. 4.

[5] *Cf.* division of the fief in case of succession. "Gr. Charter," 32; *Beaumanoir*, 14, 25, 47; "Gr. C. of France," 2, 27, 29; "Paris," 13 and following, 35. "Jostice," p. 238; *J. d'Iberlin*, 185; "Gr. C. Norm.," 27, 9 (right to transfer the third). *Pothier*, 780. Feudal seizure of the dismembered part. "Olim," I, 604, year 1265; "Const. Châtelet," 20, 23 (*Mortet*, "Intro.," p. 17). *Cf. Guyot*, "Inst. féod.," 201. "Add." Ord., 1275; *Ragueau*, see "Dépié de fief," "Foy Démission."

[6] *Brunner*, "D. Rechtsg.," II, 251; *Beaumanoir*, 47, 7; 45, 25 and following; 14, 25 (⅓); *Bout.*, 1, 80, 82; *G. Durand*, *op. cit.*, no. 38; *Loysel*,

§ 271. **Alienation of the Fief to a Villein** ("**roturier**") was not permitted, because such a purchaser was not qualified to render noble services.[1] A fief sold to a villein ("roturier") reverted to the suzerain whose rights were decreased by the alienation, and from him to the superior suzerain for the same reason. Instead of dispossessing the villein, the seignior, in most instances, was content with demanding an indemnity from him. The ordinance of 1275, which established the law on this point, and which was renewed at different times, permitted non-nobles to retain their fiefs, even when divided, by a tenure "ad servitium minus competens," upon payment of a certain sum to the king (two years' income); however, if there were three seigniors intermediate between them and the prince, they owed the king nothing because they had already given enough to the other seigniors.[2] From the end of the 1400s the king exacted the payment of the fee known as "francs-fiefs" of all villeins who acquired fiefs; in the end the intermediate seigniors no longer demanded anything.[3] The "franc-fief" thus entered into the class of regalian rights.

641. In England, the statute "Quia emptores," 1290 (*Stubbs*, "Sel. Ch.," p. 478), prohibited subinfeudation and permitted partial alienation by making the purchasers direct vassals of the suzerain. — In France, theory of the "Jeu de fief." — (A), without abandonment of fealty (without profits); the vassal alienated a part of the fief, two thirds at most, but retained the entire "foi," that is to say, held it as if there had been no alienation. "Vassalli invito domino possunt dividere fundum et non feudum." (B), "avec démission de foi." There was only one fief, but there were two vassals associated and held together for all service. The profits belonged to the seignior. These subtleties had the effect of ruining the old principle. *Beau.*, 14, 25; *Loysel*, 641; *Brodeau*, "C. de Paris," concerning the Art. 51, 52; *Fleury*, "Inst. au dr. fr.," I, 265; N.R.H., 1891, 151. Concerning the "dépié" of fief (Anjou, Maine, etc.) *cf. Ragueau*, h. v., *Guyot*, "Inst. f.," 195. Concerning the sale by auction, the division of the fief, *cf. Guyot*, *op. cit.*, and p. 9. In these matters, the customs were very varied and the feudists very obscure; the right of the vassal was disentangled with difficulty, at least in theory.

[1] "L. Feud.," 2, 4 ("etiam servus investiri poterit"); *Beaumanoir*, c. 48; *P. de Font.*, 3, 4; *J. d'Ibelin*, c. 187; *Marnier*, "Assises," p. 110; "Olim," II, 726; "Ass. des Bourgeois," c. 21; "A. C. Bourges," 28; *Boutillier*, 2. 1; *Brussel*, p. 128; *Ragueau*, see "Fief abrégé," "restraint"; "franc"; *cf.* concerning the "beneficium urbanum," which did not obligate one to military service, *Schröder*, p. 405.

[2] *Langlois*, "Philippe le Hardi," p. 260; *D. Vaissete*, "Pr.," 120, 241. The ordinance of 1275, I, 303 (*cf.* "Olim," II, 213), did not oblige villeins to pay the king when fiefs came to them by succession, by marriage, or if they had owned them for twenty years. *Isambert*, "Table," see "Franc fief." Treaties of Bacquet, etc. *Glasson*, IV, 316; *Esmein*, 224; *Viollet*, 255.

[3] The king, says *Ferrière*, "Dict. h. vo.," had published from time to time (*e.g.*, every forty years) an ordinance of the francs-fiefs and new acquisitions, and created commissaries who determined the amount of money that the villeins had to pay for the fiefs which they held. *Cf.* "Decree of C." of Jan. 21, 1738; *Boutaric*, "Dr. seign.," p. 467.

§ 272. **Alienation in Mortmain,**[1] especially to churches and religious orders, was still more prejudicial to the interests of the seigniors, for not only were the church and religious orders incapable of performing military service but they never died, never alienated their possessions, and never committed felonies, hence, there was never escheat nor other profits from the fief. These dangerous acquirers of fiefs were obliged to pay to the king an amortization fee (one third of the value of the fief, one fifth of that paid by villeins) and to the immediate seignior an indemnity fee (same amount).[2]

§ 273. **Rupture of the Bond between the Seignior and the Vassal and the Sanction of Feudal Obligations.** — The feudal bond was in theory very strong, but in practice it was weak. It was broken in a regular manner by mutual agreement or by the abandonment of the fief;[3] but most frequently it was broken by violation of faith either by the seignior or by the vassal, especially by the latter, who aspired to independence, so it was not judicial powers but war which definitely regulated their respective situations.

Whenever the seignior failed to perform his obligations (for example, by a denial of justice or by an act of felony), the vassal had a right to disavow him; henceforth he held his fief no longer of his immediate seignior but from the suzerain.[4] Sometimes the vassal incurred penalties, of which the principal one, the loss of the fief, became more and more rare.

§ 274. **Forfeiture,**[5] that is to say, revocation, or loss of the

[1] These were our artificial juridical persons; *e.g.* churches, religious communities, brotherhoods, hospices, towns, parishes, universities, etc. *Dumoulin*, on Art. 51, "C. de Paris."

[2] Add "L. Feud.," 2, 109. England, "Stat. de viris religiosis," 1279; *Stubbs*, 457; Mortmain Act of 1736; *Lehr*, "Dr. anglais," 150; "Gr. C. Fr.," 2, 21; *Desmares*, 202; N.R.H., 1891, p. 148; "Styl. Parl.," 7, 47; Ord. 1372; *Boutillier*, 1, 84; *Loysel*, 77, 83; *J. d'Ibelin*, 234, 249; *Jarry*, "Amortiss.," 1725; *Ragueau*, *Ferrière*. After the Edict of May, 1708, religious communities no longer paid the tax on new acquisitions, because they had to declare their real estate acquisitions within the year. *Boutaric*, "Dr. seign.," p. 480, shows that often it was not only necessary to pay the "indemnité," but to make prestation of a "living and dying man." *Cf.* Ord. 1372, V, 480; *Glasson*, IV, 343.

[3] *Brussel*, I, 350. "Arch. hist. de la Gironde," 7, 230. Spain: "behetrias," inheritances of which the owner could change the seignior. "Siete Part.," 4, 25, 3; *Cardenas*, "Hist. de la prop. terr.," 1875 (suppression in the 1400 s).

[4] "L. Feud.," 2, 47; *Loysel*, 842; *Desmares*, 299; "Gr. C. de Fr.," 2, 25; *Boutillier*, I, 39.

[5] Dig., 39, 4, 14. Forfeiture of the fief. The seignior reannexed it to his table. *Teulet*, "Layettes," no. 3778; *Ragueau*, see "Commise"; *Glanv.*, 7, 12, 17; 9, 1; "Gr. Ch.," 39; *Pollock and Maitland*, I, 332; "L. Feud.," 2, 23 and following; 31, 52 and following; *J. d'Ibelin*, 190. "Et. Saint Louis," 1, 52 and following, 86; *Beaum.*, c. 45; "Gr. C. Fr.,"

fief,[1] originally for failure to render homage and refusal to perform feudal services,[2] later on account of: (a) **felony** (every atrocious offense or an attack on the life or honor of the seignior, revolt, or failure to execute the sentences of his court[3]); (b) **disavowal** (by which the vassal knowingly and of set purpose repudiated holding his fief of the seignior).[4] Forfeiture, which rarely took place without contests, hence occurred only as a result of a sentence by the feudal court.[5]

§ 275. **Feudal Seizure.** — By virtue of his private authority[6] the seignior took possession of the fief in order to appropriate its revenues,[7] either because of the refusal of the vassal to render feudal services[8] or because of non-payment of feudal dues. The seizure amounted to a temporary confiscation which could be transformed into forfeiture if the vassal persisted in his refusal, for example, for the period of a year and a day.[9] About the 1500s the institution was transformed, a sergeant now seized the fief upon the order of a judge[10] and this took place in two cases: (a) for default of the man,[11] as where homage had not been rendered within the prescribed period (forty days, for example), the seignior deriving the benefit; (b) for default of enumeration, in which case the benefits went to the vassal.[12]

2, 21. The indefeasible right of the seignior, "L. Feud.," 2, 44; prescriptible, according to the German practice. *Cf.* "L. Feud.," 1, 5; 2, 39. N.R.H., 1891, 149; *Desmares*, 198.

[1] The confiscation of the fief took place for public offenses.

[2] Or in case of the contraction of the fief.

[3] "L. Feud.," 2, 1, 22; "Gr. Cout.," 2, 25; *Loysel*, 842; *Ragueau*, Felon = "malus homo." *Brunner*, D.R., II, 508 ("L. Sal.," "feltroctis").

[4] *Desmares*, 134, 302; "Paris," 43; *Loysel*, 648; *Viollet*, "Et. de Saint Louis," IV, 281 and following, 322; *Ragueau*, h. v.; *Guyot*, "Inst.," 187 (judgment).

[5] "Gr. Charter," 39: "disseisiatur nisi per judicium parium." In primitive feudalism, the seignior retook the fief doubtless without judgment. Prescription of 30 years.

[6] Toulouse, "t. de feudis." *Durand*, *op. cit.*, no. 34.

[7] *Loysel*, 653: "un seigneur de paille mange un vassal d'acier" (a straw seignior eats a steel vassal).

[8] *Boutillier*, I, 83; *Loysel*, 575, 595; "L. Feud.," 2, 24.

[9] "Gr. C. d. Norm.," 23, 4. "Et. de Saint Louis," I, 72.

[10] Nevertheless, says *Dumoulin*, "Feud.," 1, 4, 67, "ad manum Patroni feudum, ponitur."

[11] Default of homage entailed forfeiture at first, even for simple negligence; then it was required that there be fraud which was equivalent to disavowal. "L. Feud.," 2, 54, 24, 52; 1, 22. *J. d'Ibelin*, 191; "Jostice," 22, 17, 3. 1st, the seignior might seize the fief as soon as it was vacant but could not claim the produce of it until after forty days. "Styl. Parl.," 28, 14. "Gr. C. Fr.," 2, 25, N.R.H., 1891, 177. *Lecoq*, 162; *Loysel*, 575, 602. 2d, the seizure was possible only after forty days, and the produce did not belong to the seignior until the day of seizure. *Desm.*, 345; *Beaumanoir*, 14, 17; "Paris," 1, 7. The rule: "souffrance vaut foi," set aside the seizure. *Desmares*, 61, 63; "Gr. C. Fr.," 2, 25, 27; "Paris," 41, 42; BCh., 1876, 51.

[12] "Paris," 44.

§ 276. **By a Fine** (60 sous, for example) for less serious faults or in cases where the seignior having the right of seizure or escheat was content with an indemnity. The fine was a means of redeeming the confiscated or distrained fief. In later law forfeiture, which had become rare, was regarded as a form of revocation of a gift for ingratitude (disavowal and grave injury); feudal seizure was hardly anything more than an act of sequestration, and it did not give the seignior a right to the benefits of the fief.

§ 277. **Conclusion. Abolition of Fiefs.** — (A) Feudal services of a political character (such as aids, military and court service) no longer had any reason for existence at the period of the monarchy since the local sovereignties upon which they were dependent had been extinguished by the royal power; and so they fell into desuetude.[1] The duty of fidelity remained but was regarded rather as a simple obligation of recognition due a benefactor. The fief was regarded as hardly anything more than a form of ownership, the seignior concerned himself only with the payments due him for the use of it (relief, fifths, etc.). It was this proprietary and fiscal aspect alone which appeared in the fief now reduced to the state of a private institution. (B) The Revolution expropriated the eminent domain or feudal rights of the seigniors and gave to the vassal the full ownership of the fief now transformed into an alod; but chiefly it was the copyholder, that is, the villein and not the noble vassal, who profited from the change, because the vassal himself did not cultivate his lands, but rented them. In consequence of the laws of the Revolution his rights therefore disappeared.[2]

[1] Aug. 8, 1789, decree of, March 15–28, 1790.

[2] In England, a statute of 1660 (12 Ch. II, c. 24) abolished knight service and the feudal dues which were the consequence of it, scutage, fees of first seizin, marriage, etc. Thus military feudalism disappeared. *Glasson*, "Inst. de l'Angl.," 5, 278. Fiefs did not disappear until 1812 in Sicily, and 1811 in Spain. Napoleon created twelve of them in Venice and six in the kingdom of Naples. In Germany, *cf.* Act of June 12, 1806, mediatizing, that is to say, suppressing a great number of seigniories; simple fiefs, without sovereign rights, have disappeared little by little during this century. *Holtzendorff*, "Rechtslexicon," see "Rittergüter"; *Laveleye*, R.D.M., June 15, 1867; *Garsonnet*, p. 372; *Salvioli*, p. 231.

TOPIC 2. THE COPYHOLD ("CENSIVE")[1]

§ 278. **In General.** — The copyhold ("villenage," "roture," "fief vilain")[2] was a piece of land granted by the seignior to a villein ("roturier") in consideration of the payment by him of rent and the performance of non-noble services, the seignior reserving the right of eminent domain, leaving the tenant only a possessory right—that is, the right of use and enjoyment. It was called a "censive" (copyhold) because of the "cens" or pecuniary charge which the grantee or copyholder ("censitaire") was obliged to pay the grantor or seignior. In principle it was nothing but the Roman "emphytéose," and the Frankish "precarium" or benefice for which rent was paid, mingled, and feudalized. It was dependent upon a seigniorial manor just as the tenures of the Frankish "coloni" were dependent upon the "terra indominicata"; or these were even sometimes tenures of "coloni" which had become copyholds[3] at the same time that the "coloni" were elevated from the servile class to that of free laborers. In many respects the copyhold, villein land, resembled the fief, or noble land, in being only a replica, the difference relating mainly to its economic purpose; it served to improve the land, to "put it out to pasture," whereas the fief had rather a political object. The seignior who infeudated his lands thereby acquired soldiers; he who leased them for rent secured cultivators, and from them he did not demand fealty and homage, but payments in money or in kind.

The copyhold was found in France under different names;[4] it was the normal type of tenure for the villein class. They were

[1] BIBLIOGRAPHY: *Buche*, N.R.H., 1884, 74; *Serrigny*, "R. crit.," III, 417; *Loyseau*, "Garantie des rentes," 1599; "Déguerpissement," 1613; *Pothier*, "Tr. des cens"; *H. de Pansey*, "Diss. féod.," 1789 (cens); *Garsonnet*, "Hist. des locat. perpét.," 1879; *Lefort*, "Hist. des contr. de loc. perp.," 1875; *Chénon*, "Demembr. de la propr. fonc.," 1881; *Viollet*, "Hist. du dr. privé," p. 695, 729 (bibl.); *Riston*, Thesis, p. 200.

[2] *Beaumanoir*, 14, 7; *Teulet*, "Layettes," I, no. 1556; "Et. de Saint Louis," vol. I, pp. 496, 498 (ed. *Viollet*); "Olim," III, 291, no. 7. Concerning the "hostise," *cf.* below.

[3] So, in England, villein tenure was converted into copyhold tenure. *Cf. Garsonnet*, p. 405. *Merville*, 30 (N.R.H., 91, 591): "res feudales seu emphyteoticariæ."

[4] Germany: the peasant's holdings ("Bauernhoefe") grouped around the seigniorial estate ("Frohnhof") upon which they were dependent (*cf.* above manorial system) and to which they owed services and rents ("Zinse," "Frohnden") were granted sometimes by temporary leases or for life, sometimes as copyholds, or by hereditary leases, sometimes as fiefs, improperly called, upon condition of faith and homage, but with exemption from military service (*cf.* the English "socage"). Alsace: 1st, "Erbpacht," "Erbleihe," hereditary lease analogous to the "censive"; 2d,

not all, however, brought under it. Aside from temporary or life leases, three kinds of grants to villeins can be distinguished:[1] 1. Perpetual leases which conferred only the right of enjoyment, the lessor preserving the full ownership;[2] 2. Perpetual leases conferring the right of use, the lessor preserving his lordship;[3] 3. Per-

"Landsiedelei," "colonat," the lessee had only a real right and not a usufructuary right. In certain cases, "jus palæ, Schauffelrecht" (right of the spade), that is to say, right of the lessee to the improvements that he had made. The Alsatian "colonge" ("colonica") was only a form of the "Frohnhof" and "Bauernhof." *Hanauer*, "Constitutions des campagnes de l'Alsace," 1865, *cf. Garsonnet*, p. 440; *Stouff*, "Régime colonger," N.R.H., 1893, 46. In England, the manor was the territorial unit comprising what the German law called the "Frohnhof," and the "Bauernhoefe" (*cf.* 1200 s, *Pollock and Maitland*, I, 337, 582; *Maitland*, "Domesday Book," p. 119). The tenures which were dependent upon it were the free "socage" conferred on the free man on condition of paying rent and of rendering fealty and homage, the "villenage," or servile tenure, a precarious possession with arbitrary charges imposed on the peasants, but which was transformed by the tolerance of the seigniors and the power of custom into a copyhold (tenants by virtue of a copy or extract from the rôles of the manorial court) of which the custom of the manor (*cf.* German "Hofrecht") guaranteed heredity the greater part of the time (end of the 1400 s). Rent, alienation fees, and the hériot were the principal charges of the copyhold. Long-term leases were also made in England; but since the 1500 s it has been the tenure at will which the common law recognizes — liberty for the master and farmer to break their lease at will. "While the tenants on the continent acquired, if not ownership, at least at an assured possession, the farmers acquired in England only the right to freely quit the land." *Cf. L. Delisle*, "Cond. des classes agric. en Norm.," p. 51 (analogous phenomenon). Concerning dispossessions in mass in the 1500 s, the change that the agrarian régime underwent, and the state of Ireland, *cf. Garsonnet*, p. 462. *Boutmy*, "Développ. de la constit. en Angleterre," p. 227, 314; *P. Fournier*, "La crise agraire en Irlande," 1887. The system of the three F's (fair rent, fixity of tenure, free sale) in which the claims of Irish peasants were epitomized, was realized by the hereditary leases of the Old Régime.

[1] The law of July 17, 1793, maintained the first form of grant, suppressed the second, and declared the third redeemable.

[2] "Bail à locataire perpétuelle" of Languedoc (*Fonmaur*, "Dr. de quint," 1778, no. 536); "Bail à métairie perpétuelle" of Marche and of Limousin, "Albergement" of Bugy. "Bail à complant" (Lower Loire), by which the farmer engaged to plant vines generally and to remit to the proprietor a part of the profits. It was often agreed that after a certain time, five to seven years, half of the land so planted should return to the lessor, the other half remaining indefinitely with the lessee. "Bail à domaine congeable" or "bail à convenant" in Lower Brittany (formerly of long duration, but for a short term since the drawing up of the "coutumes") entailing (*a*) ownership of the soil by the lessor or "foncier"; (*b*) ownership of the surface, constructions, and certain trees, by the lessee or "domainer"; (*c*) power of dismissing the lessee by reimbursing him for the value of the surface. *Henry*, "Une vieille cout. bretonne," 1894; *Chénon*, "L'ancien droit dans le Morbihan," 1894; *Glasson*, IV, 430, N.R.H., 95, 270 ("mote," "quevaize").

[3] Seigniorial lease in general: "Albergement" in Savoy and Dauphiny; "Maniferme," north of France and Belgium (*Du Cange*, see "Manufirma"); "Fiefferme," in Normandy in the 1200 s (*L. Delisle*, "Et. s. la cond. de la classe agric.," p. 45). *Bordelage*, Nivernaise, Auvergne (*Guy Coquille*, "Comm. sur Niv.," vol. 6; *Boucomont*, "Th.," 50) (*Du Cange*, see "Borda," "Bordaria"). Concerning "Champart," which is some-

petual leases conferring the full ownership,[1] the lessor retaining a simple real right.[2] The land for the use of the holder,—such was the end towards which the way led (in spite of deviations like that which was implied in the first category of these acts, more recent than the second).[3]

§ 279. **Formation.** — The copyhold was the result of a contract; it was a lease of land for rent, which differed from infeudation especially by the absence of fealty and homage. Simple consent was not sufficient; the land (or the real estate, the only possible object of contract) had to be leased, that is, the property had to be transmitted to the lessee and it was the custom to prepare a record of the transaction. The copyholder's acknowledgments corresponded to the old feudal avowals.[4] The capacity to lease was limited by the rule: No lease of a lease ("cens sur cens"). The lessee could not therefore sublet his land "à cens" (but he could lease it "à rente" without reserving the right of

times seigniorial, sometimes private, *cf.* below. The "emphytéose" (long lease) was almost merged with the lease "à cens" to which were applied the greater part of the rules. The right of lordship which the lessor reserved was not seigniorial in character, but merely a private right; but there was a theoretical difference here. The "emphyteusis" could only emanate from the possessor of an allodium; constituted by the possessor of a fief, it was a copyhold because the lordship was seigniorial; constituted by a copyholder, it could only be a ground rent lease for he did not have the right to reserve either seigniorial lordship or private lordship. *Garsonnet*, p. 414. The Roman "emphyteusis" was maintained in Italy, under the name of "fitto" ("fictus census," *cf. Du Cange*), "livello" ("libellus," written), "censo" (*Garsonnet*, p. 263, 267). In Tuscany, in the 1700 s, "sistema livellare leopoldino"; the leopoldine "emphyteusis" was more a sale on credit than perpetual location. *Garsonnet*, p. 466; *Salvioli*, 422. It is also probable that the "emphyteusis" did not cease to be practiced in Portugal ("aforamento") and in Spain; but servile tenures predominated there for a long time. In the 1300 s, they resembled the copyhold. *De Cardenas*, I, 258, 341 and following.

[1] Ground rent lease; perpetual tenant, who transferred ownership in Provence (but not in Languedoc).

[2] How identify the transferable leases of ownership? This was a question of fact. Ordinarily, the perpetual lease carried the right of use and enjoyment; however, the lease "à complant" (*i.e.* of a vineyard where the produce was shared with the lessor), although perpetual, did not always have this effect. On the other hand, the lease for life carried the right of use. How can we know if in the transferable leases of ownership the lessor reserved the lordship of the domain or a simple real right? This question, like the foregoing one, was settled by local custom.

[3] *Cf.* the law of the market in the Santerre in Picardy, "mauvais gré" in Hainaut. In these regions where the short-term lease prevailed, as in England, the farmers resisted the process of expulsion, put in the index those who came to replace them, and obliged the proprietors by menace, fire, or murder, to leave them indefinitely in possession. *Cf.* Ireland. *Lefort*, "Le droit de marché," 1892; *Glasson*, IV, 436.

[4] "Paris," 73. Exhibition of titles by the copyholder (and not by the seignior).

eminent domain); he alone was qualified to lease "à cens" who possessed a noble allodium or a fief.[1]

§ 280. **Effects.** — The seignior reserved the right of eminent domain, which included such privileges as the right of hunting and certain beneficial rights. The lessee ("censitaire") acquired the right to use the land (the "domaine utile"); by virtue of this right he cultivated it as he pleased,[2] kept the revenues and had a certain right of disposal. He was obliged to make certain annual payments in money ("cens" "oublies")[3] or in kind ("champart,"[4] "agrier," "terrage") and sometimes to perform compulsory labor in the construction of certain works on the portion of the domain retained by the seignior. These payments were invariable.[5] The rent charge ("cens")[6] did not correspond to the income from the land as is the case to-day in the renting of a farm; it was a very

[1] *Loysel*, 532; *La Thaumassière*, "Com. s. Berry," p. 209. "Bull. Soc. arch. Touraine," VI, 315 (Act of 1290). From the moment when the vassal could subinfeudate, it seems that the copyholder should have had the power to sublease his land. It was doubtless for political reasons that it was denied; the villein "censitaire" was not authorized, as were the noble holders of fiefs, to create for himself honorary rights and to establish a seigniory over another villein. He was only allowed to cede the copyhold in consideration of the payment of rent, which was not contrary to the object of the copyhold any more than if he had farmed it out ("Jost.," 12, 15, 11) when he found it impossible to cultivate it himself. The rent was not seigniorial in character and did not imply honorary privileges, nor superiority of one landed property over another. This operation itself was lawful only with the consent of the seignior, according to *Beaumanoir*, 24, 20. *Cf.* transfer of fiefs. *Guérard*, "Cart. de Saint-Père de Chartres," p. 345 (1100 s). *Beaumanoir* reserves the rights of the seignior, and *Laur.* s., "Loysel," 535, observed that, according to the "Gr. C. de Fr.," 4, 5 (?), the seignior's charges were due in case of alienation. "Jostice," 12, 15, 9 and 10, considered the "cens" as imprescriptible. *Cf. Viollet*, p. 684 (divergent views). In England a copyholder would not have been able to constitute a subcopyhold, but nothing prevented his conferring upon a third party in the exercise of his rights. *Lehr.*, p. 231.

[2] He could change the method of cultivation, even impair the inheritance provided the rent could be collected from it. *Loysel*, 534. *Cf. Pothier*, "Rente," 113.

[3] *L. Delisle*, "Cond. des classes agric. en Norm.," p. 60, 57 ("regards," "respectus," additional rents, chickens, eggs, etc.).

[4] The "tenure en champart" [field rent paid in kind to the seignior] differed but little from the copyhold. (*a*) The "champart" was a part of the crop, and so varied, while the "cens" and accessory payments which were often added to it were fixed; (*b*) It did not cumulate arrears any more than the tithe, that is to say, the seignior could demand only a year's rent, for at the end of a short time, it was difficult to make a valuation of the crop (otherwise in countries of written law); (*c*) It was ordinarily demandable, like the tithe, perhaps because the seignior's excise office must oversee the harvest; (*d*) The tenant did not have the right of modifying the cultivation. *Pothier*, "Tr. des Champarts"; *Merlin*, "Quest.," see "Terrage." "Cart. du Saint Sépulcre," p. 239, 242.

[5] Fixed rent in Ireland for the tenant right of Ulster.

[6] "Census" or "redditus" (rent). *Beaumanoir*, 24, 19; *Mortet*, "Const. Châtelet," p. 72, no. 2, "Cout. not.," 171. "Chef cens," "sur-

small sum (sometimes still less, for example, a "good morning") at Michaelmas, given mainly as a recognition of the eminent domain of the seignior, for the essential characteristic of the "cens" was that it should be recognitory.[1] In this capacity it was indivisible (for recognition could not be divided), imprescriptible (a farmer could not acquire by prescription against his master), "portable" (by virtue of the seignior's eminent situation), and non-demandable by the latter.[2] To it was often added a supplement ("surcens," "cens costier") which corresponded more to the income from the land.[3] In default of the payment of the rent the copyholder at first lost the land (by forfeiture),[4] later the lessee contented himself with imposing a fine [5] upon him and with proceeding against him by way of distraint. The copyholder had one resource that the vassal did not have; the latter was personally bound by reason of his promise of fealty; he could not free himself from his feudal obligations by abandoning his fief; the copyholder did not, strictly speaking, own anything; it was his land upon which the obligations lay, and since he was not attached to it like a serf he could relieve himself from the payment of rent by the quitting

cens," "gros cens," "menu cens": concerning this confused terminology, *cf. Guyot*, "Inst. f.," p. 161; *Luchaire*, "Man.," 337; *Prou*, "Lorris," 58.

[1] The small amount of the "cens" at least for later copyholds indicated that the seigniors considered it only as a mark of honor and superiority, but for the greater part of the copyhold, it had an entirely different cause. The "cens" represented originally the fruits of inheritance, which being often uncultivated, yielded but little and the amount of the "cens" was of necessity small; with time, the value of the lands increased and that of money diminished. Those seigniors who had a stipulated rent in sous and deniers found themselves ruined by the working of economic laws. The copyholders whose rents were fixed benefited exclusively by the increase in the value of the lands; on the other hand, when the rent was stipulated in grain, the seignior shared the benefits. *Argou*, 2, 4; *Fleury*, "Inst.," I, 268; *D'Avenel*, "La Fort. privée à tr. sept siècles," p. 184; *Viollet*, p. 674; *Garsonnet*, p. 405; *Cibrario*, *Lamprecht*, etc., on the political economy of the Middle Ages.

[2] If the inheritance was divided among several persons, the heirs of each portion were held collectively for the payment of the entire "cens." *Pothier*, 8; *Loysel*, 530 and following.

[3] *Viollet*, p. 683: Act of 1289 in "R. docum. hist.," 8, 58; Act of 1202, *La Thaumassière* sur *Beaumanoir*, p. 405; *L. Delisle*, *op. cit.*, p. 60; *Guérard*, "Cart. S. Père," 153.

[4] *Beaumanoir*, 30, 39; *Loysel*, 551. Concerning the long lease ("emphytéose") *cf. Loyseau*, "Offices," 1, 13, 4; "Livre des droiz," 853.

[5] Fine of five sous, "Paris," 85 (except for the city and suburbs). On quit rent seizure, *cf. Buche*, N.R.H., 1884, 65. It differed from feudal seizure which made the seignior the proprietor and provisional possessor of the fief; it was an obstacle to the right of use and enjoyment by the copyholder. *Pothier*, no. 52. Originally, it took the place of private authority. "Orléans," A.C., 105 and N.C., 103. 1500 s: mortgage to the seignior. "Paris," 74, 99.

or abandonment of the copyhold to the lessor;[1] this supposed not only actual abandonment[2] but a declaration, which at first in the 1200 s was made to the seignior-lessor, but which, in the 1500 s, took place in court.[3]

§ 281. **Transmission of the Copyhold.** (A) **Mortis Causa.**—The copyhold was hereditary,[4] like the fief, and more so, because the interest of the seignior did not here require a special order of things, like primogeniture for example; it was not therefore divided according to the law of nobility but in equal parts.[5] In the beginning the seignior resumed possession of his land at the death of the copyholder, and was bound to vest it in the heir, the latter being allowed to enter upon it only after this formality and the payment of the transmission fees (called double "cens" by reason of the ordinary tax or relief, "relevoison," purchase).[6] From the 1200 s the act of investiture was dispensed with, at least in the case of descendants; the dead was accounted as having himself seised his heir and the transmission charge was often not collected.[7]

(B) **Inter Vivos.**[8] — Ancient customary law obliged the lessee who alienated his land to deliver it up to the seignior[9] who had the choice between two courses, 1st, to keep it on his own account by exercising his rights of preëmption ("préemption," "prelation," "retrait censuel")[10] or, 2d, to approve the alienation and to invest the purchaser with it upon the payment by him of an amount proportioned to the purchase price known as "lods et

[1] Except where there was a contrary clause, which had to be formal. The Castillian "solariego" who abandoned his land was incapable of acquiring any other, according to the ordinance of Alcala, 1348.

[2] Ord. 1287, XII, 328. *Glasson*, IV, 409, 2; *Viollet*, 678, 685; N.R.H., 1884, 80; "Cout. not.," 169; "Gr. C. de Fr.," p. 317 and 277; *Loysel*, 549.

[3] He freed himself for the future, but not for the past. "Paris," 109, exacted the preliminary payment of the accrued "cens" and the nearest quarter's rent not due.

[4] The hereditary lease of Alsace was ended by the extinction of the descendants of the farmer.

[5] *P. de Font.*, 24, 12; "Jostice," 12, 25, 7; *Beaumanoir*, 14, 6; "Trust" in Italy, *Garsonnet*, p. 470.

[6] "Luctuosa" (Spain, Portugal). "Bondage," "Besthaupt," right of the seignior at the death of the tenant; "vinicopium," at the entering of the heir (Germany) upon possession.

[7] "Jostice," 12, 5, 6, "Gr. C. de France," p. 367; *Boutillier*, I, 84; *Loysel*, 547. "Orléans," 126; *Pothier*, "Cens," no. 65. For the Italian "emphytéose," *cf. Bartole*, 1, 1. Dig., "de aq. cot."; *Garsonnet*, p. 470.

[8] Foreign legislation; frequent restrictions on the right of alienation, for example, authority was only given to sell to persons of the same status.

[9] Within eight days, "Gr. C. de Fr.," p. 264.

[10] The right of preëmption was exercised before the conclusion of the sale; the right of redemption within forty days after notifying the seignior of the sale. It was supposed, then, that the sale had been validly concluded and that the right of alienation by the copyholder was fully recognized.

ventes."[1] Under the law of the second period the tenant had the full right (or nearly so) of alienation.[2] The right of preëmption by the seignior in case of alienation had gone out of use nearly everywhere.[3] The delivery of the land to the seignior by the seller and the investment of the new purchaser by the seignior survived only in the customs of certain places (for example, Reims, Lille, etc.). This formality was known under the name of "**nantissement**" (pledge, lien) because the ownership was transmitted to the new owner by the formalities of "nantissement" or "vest et devest," administered by the seignior or his officers. Moreover, everywhere the purchaser became the owner solely as a result of the contract:[4] "No one is seized who does not wish to be."[5] A standing clause in the deeds of sale or of gift (the clause "disseizin—seizin," "vest et devest") replaced seigniorial livery of seizin. In the place of a solemn and public delivery was substituted a non-apparent delivery on paper. But this did not result in the disappearance of the right to "lods" and "ventes"; the seigniors at the close of the "Ancien Régime" were content to make remissions. The alienation of copyholds to mortmain persons gave rise to the collection of the fifth farthing ("denier"). If the copyhold charges were not paid, the penalty was seizure of the land and the imposition of a fine.

§ 282. **Ground Rents.**[6] — The ground rent lease was a method

[1] *Beaumanoir*, 27, 6, 7; "Jostice," 12, 13, 1; *Loysel*, 535 and following; "Paris," 76; *Argou*, vol. 2, p. 173; the seller owed the "ventes," the purchaser the "lods" according to certain "coutumes." "Melun," 125; "Troyes," 54. Accessory rights: gloves, wine. "Orléans," 106. Seizin: twelve deniers. "Paris," 82, 130. "Gr. C. de Fr.," "l.c." at the end of eight, twenty, or forty days, the purchaser must pay the dues or demand an additional delay. *Ragueau*, h. v°. In default of payment, seizure ("saisie censuelle,") according to "Orléans," 103, but not according to "Paris." Fine for concealed sales. "Paris," 77. Exchange, differing from sale, was not subject to the payment of feudal profits in respect to "censives" and was only subject to it in matters of fiefs after the 600s. N.R.H., 1891, 177; "Paris," 76 and following; *Loysel*, 535 and following (acts for which "lods" and "ventes" were due), 542 (no "lods" and "ventes" in case of division, sale by auction, and adjudication between coheirs). *Argou*, II, 4, Edict Feb., 1764 and Decl. July 20, 1674, May 1, 1696. Exemptions, *Argou*, II, 169.

[2] *Cf.* in Ireland the same right of alienation in Ulster (tenant right); the purchaser reimbursed for improvements made.

[3] *Desmares*, 204; *Loysel*, 424.

[4] But it was not under cover either of "retrait censuel" nor of "retrait lignager" (which could be exercised within a year from the date of the acknowledgement of the purchaser as a tenant), "Paris," 82, 130.

[5] "Gr. C. de Fr.," p. 265, *n.* 5 (text not dated). "Const. du temp de Charles XII," N.R.H., p. 176. The tradition of the letters sufficed — the seizin of the seignior was not necessary.

[6] The ground rent lease was, according to *Maleville*, *Locré*, "Trav. prep. du C. civ.," VIII, 82, the most widely prevailing tenure in France about 1789.

by which the proprietor of land alienated it upon payment of a perpetual rent; [1] it involved no reservation of the right of eminent domain on the part of the alienator and no superiority of the land which he retained over that which he alienated; [2] the lessor retained over it only a real right which insured the regular payment of arrears somewhat like a mortgage, but with this difference that it rested with the debtor to free himself from the mortgage by paying his debt, while it did not rest with the purchaser debtor for the ground rent to extinguish the latter by paying back the principal. This would have been to dispossess the alienator and one had no more right to do this than to free his property of a real servitude to which it was subject. This was expressed by the saying that "ground rent was not redeemable"; [3] the debtor had, it was said, in return for landed property sold the right to exact arrears, and he could not redeem it. He had only the option of moving off (unless he had renounced that right in advance by means of the clause "to furnish and make good") [4] in this way he exempted himself for the future from the payment of arrears.[5] The decree of December 18–29, 1790, declared ground rents to be redeemable, and the lessor could be dispossessed by means of an indemnity. The tenant of a copyhold was only a half owner but a ground rent tenant acquired the ownership except that it was subject to a servitude; the Revolution freed it from this servitude.[6]

§ 283. **The Law of the Revolution.** — Ancient tenures were in process of decay; for centuries tenants had gradually freed their lands from feudal charges; the Revolution freed them in a definite manner by abolishing copyholds and by declaring ground rents redeemable.[7] In this respect it was an agrarian revolution,

[1] *Cf.* sale; the sale was a "consensuel" contract; the rent lease was a real contract. The purchaser could not avoid the payment of the price by removing; the lessee was obliged not to depreciate the property to such an extent that the payment of the rent was not assured.

[2] If the lessor sold the part of the property that he had reserved, the purchaser did not have the right to the rent. Otherwise, in the case of a copyhold.

[3] Except by agreement to the contrary. Redemption was permitted by certain Ordinances in order to avoid the depreciation of the property whose revenue was absorbed by the rent, 1441, 1539, 1553 (twenty deniers), *Isamb.*, IX, 91 (VIII, 692); XII, 645.

[4] This became a mere formal clause. *Locré*, VIII, 83. [5] *Pothier*, 123.

[6] *Cf.* Art. 530, C. civ. The ground rent lessor of the old régime had a real unredeemable right; the proprietor who to-day leases property for an annuity has only a personal credit which is reimbursable, but guaranteed by a privilege and a right of cancellation which are real rights. *Locré*, VIII, 88; *Merlin*, "Rep.," see "Rente."

[7] Precedents, *Gasquet*, II, 331; *R. Beudant*, "La transform. juridique de la propriété f. dans le dr. interm.," 1889; *Viollet*, p. 729; *Doniol*, "La Révol. fr. et la féodalité," 1874 and 1889.

but it only put the last touch to a movement begun long before; upon that depended the stability of its work. We cannot go to the length of saying that it gave the land to the laborer; those who especially gained by this legislation, the copyholder and the ground renter, did not always cultivate their lands. In their hands tenancy was converted into ownership at the same time that a system of temporary leases[1] was developed for the cultivators.

TOPIC 3. SERVILE TENURES

Lands granted by the seignior to his serfs did not belong to them at all, for he reserved both the right of eminent domain and the use of the land ("domaine utile"); the only right which the serfs had was not to be separated from the land which they occupied. By means of the "taille" the seignior could take their crops or the value thereof and by means of confiscation he could retake possession of the land itself if it had been alienated. Upon the death of the serf his tenement reverted to the seignior by virtue of the right of mortmain. We shall see further on that when serfdom had become mitigated the serf had a quasi-ownership: fixed charges, right of inheritance, and in some degree, the right of alienation.

TOPIC 4. THE ALOD[2]

§ 284. **General Notions.** — The alod[3] was land held in free and full ownership;[4] it did not come to its master through a seigniorial grant and consequently the seignior could require neither fealty and homage, nor services of a noble character, nor the payment of the "cens," nor feudal dues, nor the performance of villein services, nor charges for the use of it ("profits"), nor transmission fees. The owner of an alod was not the tenant of the

[1] "Métayage" [leasing of farms on condition of giving the owner half the produce] especially according to *Arthur Young. Gasquet*, II, 301; *D'Avenel, op. cit.*, 252; *Loutchisky*, "La petite propriété en France avant la Révolution," 1897. "R. hist.," 66, 410. Same movement in foreign countries, *Garsonnet*, p. 535 and following.

[2] *Chénon*, "Et. s. l'hist. des alleux en France," 1888 (with detailed bibliography); *Lanery d'Arc*, "Du franc alleu," 1888; *Glasson*, IV, 466; *Luchaire*, "Man.," p. 147; *Schupfer*, "L'Allodio," 1886; *Salvioli*, p. 375; *Viollet*, "Hist.," 708.

[3] "Aleu," "Franc Aleu," "Aloy," "allodium." *Du Cange*, see "Alaudis."

[4] *Desmares*, 17, 371, "Gr. C. de Fr.," 2, 23. Numerous alods in southern France. Enumeration of 1272, by order of the Duke of Aquitaine, king of England. Southern cartularies. Original alods by grant (by the seignior), by prescription (Lorraine and Barrois) where the "cens" was prescriptible and redeemable.

seignior; he was only amenable to his jurisdiction;[1] this is what Loysel said, 227: "to hold a free alod is to hold from God alone except in matters of justice."

§ 285. **Feudalism and the Alod.** — (A) *The noble alod and the villein alod.* The action of feudalism on the alod was sufficiently strong to half assimilate it to the condition of a fief or a copyhold; alods were classified as noble or villein possessions according as they had or had not a court, or a fief, or a copyhold dependent upon them. Noble alods were treated like fiefs as regards the right of primogeniture, like freeholds as regards the capacity to infeudate, to lease, and for the right to hunt.

(B) *Conversion of alods into fiefs or copyholds*[2] took place, for example, in consequence of offenses committed by the seignior against the allodial owners (allodial infractions) or because the holder needed the protection of the seignior.[3]

(C) There was a maxim: "*No land without a seignior.*" The right of the seigniors to administer justice extended over all lands without distinction and they took advantage of the confusion which came to exist between the right to administer justice and the ownership of land to call themselves owners of lands where they were only judges; thus they claimed the right of eminent domain over allodial lands situated within their jurisdiction. The Customs were divided on this point, but most of them maintained the idea of a universal seigniorial lordship. Many alods disappeared through the application of the maxim: "no land without a seignior."[4] It signified that all land was presumed to be a seigniorial concession, that is, a fief or copyhold, sometimes until the

[1] Unless the holder of an alod was himself a justiciary seignior (for example, by virtue of a charter of immunity). But the alod did not of itself imply the right of administering justice. (In the opposite sense: *Flach*, "Orig. de l'anc. France," I, 205.) Certain alods (for example, the kingdom of Yvetot, until 1553) were even entirely sovereign and constituted independent States on French soil (as in our time, the republic of San Marino in Italy). There were therefore: 1st, alods without the right of justice; 2d, alods with the right of justice; 3d, sovereign alods.

[2] BCh., 22, alliance between holders of alods in the 1100 s.

[3] "Feudum oblatum" fief of resumption: alod returned to the seignior by its owner who received it back as a fief. "Feuda honorata," sometimes free fiefs and fiefs half converted into alods, sometimes alods transformed into fiefs. *Guérard*, "Polypt. d'Irm.," I, 477, 532. *Roupnel*, "Le rég. féodal à Châtillon-sur-Seine," 1896.

[4] *Loysel*, 19, 228. The seigniorial lordship was indefeasible. *Cf.* the German proverb: "Kein Erbe ohne Zins," no inheritance without dues, and the designation "fiefs of the sun" given, sometimes applied to the alods. *Chaisemartin*, "Prov. du dr. g.," 139. In the time of the "Mirrors," there were many alods still in existence in Germany.

contrary was proven,[1] sometimes absolutely, the presumption being irrefutable and the Customs wholly prohibiting alods.[2] In the allodial countries, on the contrary (for example, Languedoc, Dauphiny, etc.), the opposite rule was recognized, "no seignior without a title,"[3] all land being presumed to be held by allodial tenure save the right of the seignior within whose jurisdiction it was situated to prove the contrary by showing his titles. In the estates of Blois, in 1577, the nobility vainly demanded a formal law abolishing this rule.

§ 286. **The Royal Power and the Alod.** — Allodial holders had hardly escaped from the bonds of the feudal system when they found themselves in the presence of a new and more dangerous enemy still, namely, the king, whose jurisdiction encroached upon the alods and who claimed universal lordship.[4] Every estate not amenable to some seignior, said the Code Michau (Ord. 1629, Art. 383) should be considered as amenable to the king. It resulted from this principle that in case of sale or alienation in general, alienation fees were due the king. Of all the allodial countries of France, Languedoc alone resisted energetically this royal encroachment. To the memoir of a royal officer named Galland entitled "Against the Freehold without Title," 1629–1637, an advocate of Toulouse, P. Caseneuve, replied, upon the request of the Provincial Estates, in a learned dissertation entitled, "Inquiry into the Freehold of the Province of Languedoc," 1640–1645.[5] The edict of August, 1692, abolished only the noble freehold without title and left the villein alod undisturbed.[6] In 1789 the question was still in doubt.[7]

§ 287. **The Revolution** converted the imperfect right of the vassal and of the copyholder into full and absolute ownership; fiefs and copyholds were made into, one may say, borrowing the language of the feudalists, villein alods; through the play of

[1] "Paris," 68. It was difficult for the holder of an alod to establish the freedom of his land, since this was the primordial fact; only the concession of a fief or copyhold left traces.

[2] *Beaumanoir*, 24, 5; *Guyot*, "Inst. féod.," 309. England: *Blackstone*, 2, 5.

[3] Ord. 1368 (V, 99), 1484. *Laur.* s. "Loysel," 228, Italy.

[4] Decision of the Parl. of Bordeaux, March 21, 1617, May 14, 1624. Decision of the council, May 22, 1667.

[5] Writings of *Dominicy*, (country of Written Law), of *la Thaumassière* (for Berry), of *Furgole* (for Guyenne), of *Gensollen* (for Provence).

[6] Edict of Aug., 1692. Nero II, 239. Edict of 1703 concerning the "centième denier"; Edict 19 of July, 1704, the alods were formally subjected to the payment of this due. *Isambert*, 20, 450.

[7] *H. de Pansey*, "Dissert. féod.," 1789 (written against the Frankish alod).

political and economic causes the Roman "dominium" therefore reappeared after an eclipse of centuries. But if this revolution had great importance in theory, in fact its importance is somewhat less, since the alienation fees which the State demanded under the "Ancien Régime" by reason of the seigniorial lordship are to-day collected without being contested.[1]

§ 288. **The "Frank-Almoign"** was a piece of land given to the Church for the support of religious services (prayers, etc.). It was therefore a sort of religious fief as contradistinguished from a lay or military fief.[2] Our jurists likened it to the freehold. Religious service was not susceptible, indeed, to the precision which characterized military service, and the eminent domain of the grantor disappeared, more especially as the Church tribunals were alone competent in cases involving this sort of property, at least in the beginning, because the "frank-almoign" did not fail to become dependent upon the royal or seigniorial courts;[3] it did better, it ceased to exist; judicial interpretation did not allow the Church to receive property which was not amenable to some person.[4]

[1] Decree of Aug. 4, 1789, and March 15, 1790. *Merlin*, "Rép.," see "Féodalité"; *Viollet*, "Hist.," 607. The State claimed to have a privilege over the property comprised in successions as a means of securing the payment of succession fees upon death of the owner. But the Court of Cassation set aside these claims and recognized the fact that the State did not have a superior right over private property. Cass. 23 June, 1857, D., 57, 1, 253. The actual inheritance fees corresponded, it is said, to the "centième denier," rather than to feudal profits.

[2] *Cf. Pollock*, I, 219. "Maisons Croisées" in Normandy, *L. Delisle*, p. 39. "Gr. C. Norm.," 32. *Ragueau*, Gloss., see "Aumône." *Loysel*, 84. "C. of Norm." (1583), 41, 139 and following.

[3] Above, Redemption, *Viollet*, "Hist.," 702; *Denisart*, IX, 34; *H. de Pansey*, "Diss. féod.," II, 88; *Glasson*, IV, 344, 484. "Gleysage," in the Midi.

[4] Concerning the price of the lands and the variations of revenue in France, *cf. Levasseur*, "Les Prix," 1893; *D. Zolla*, "Ann. de l'Ec. libre des Sc. polit.," 15 July, 1894 (1600 s and 1700 s); *D'Avenel*, "La Fortune privée à travers sept siècles," 1895; *Arthur Young*, "Travels in France, 1787–1788."

CHAPTER VII

THE FEUDAL PERIOD (*continued*). STATUS OF PERSONS

§ 289. Classes of Persons

§ 289. **Classes of Persons.** — The status of persons corresponded to that of lands without there being, however, an absolute correlation. Thus there was not in France corresponding to the holders of alods a class of free landowners who were outside the feudal body. The German axiom, "Frei Mann, frei Gut" (free man, free property) expressed, no doubt, the primitive state of things; [1]

[1] In Germany, men who were dependent directly upon the Empire or upon a territorial sovereign, and who were consequently free (*Garsonnet*, p. 499) in contradistinction to the "eigene Leute" ("ministeriales," who disappeared in the 1500 s, "Hörigen," "Leibeigenen"). In east and middle Friesland there was no nobility before the end of the 1300 s,

but it early ceased to be true in France. Four classes of persons were distinguished:[1] 1st, the **clergy**, who had always been regarded as the first order of the State and who numbered 80,000 persons in 1789, according to the estimate (much disputed) of Sieyès; the Church, as well as the clergy, considered individually, possessed fiefs, copyholds, lands held by servile tenures, and in the South, "alods"; the "frank-almoign" was the only tenure which belonged to it exclusively. 2d, the **nobility**, embracing all the possessors of fiefs, seigniors, and vassals; at first sovereigns, later constituting the Second Estate; there were about 140,000 nobles in 1789. 3d, the "**roturiers**,"[2] the bourgeois in the towns and the villeins in the country, possessors of copyholds, and subject to feudal obligations, though free; these, as a result of their organization into corporations, communes, and societies, ended by having a political standing; they formed the **Third Estate**, — almost the entire population, which was estimated very arbitrarily at 24,000,000 in 1789. 4th, the **serfs**, or mortmain persons, not numerous at the time of the monarchy, the number being about 150,000 in 1789. These figures show, from the numerical point of view at least, how little removed from equality they were at the eve of the Revolution. The old German rule, "Tell me the man and I will tell you the right," gradually became mitigated, the law came to be the same, and the classes were disappearing.

TOPIC 1. THE NOBILITY[3]

§ 290. **Character and Origin of the Feudal Nobility.** — The feudal nobility did not result directly either from the social dis-

but free peasants. *Schröder*, p. 444. In England, the free "socagers," or yeomen, were not proprietors, but had a more complete political liberty than our tenants. *Garsonnet*, p. 492; *Boutmy*, "Dével. de la Const. angl.," p. 201. The free socagers have disappeared as also most of the copyholders. There remain only short-term farmers.

[1] *Beaumanoir*, 45, 30. The principle of "Ebenbürtigkeit," equality of birth, is in Germany the consequence of the distinction of classes: Judgment by equals and not by inferiors, heredity, guardianship of equals or of superiors, marriage between persons of the same class. *Schröder*, p. 457. [2] See p. 305 for further explanation of the term "roturier."

[3] Ancient treatises of *Poggius*, *Tiraqueau*, etc.; Works of *Loyseau; La Roque*, "Tr. de la noblesse," 1678, 1735; *Isambert*, "Table," see "Noblesse"; *Denisart*, see "Noblesse"; *Chassant*, "Les nobles et les vilains"; *Semainville*, "Code de la noblesse," 1860; *Louandre*, "De la noblesse," 1880; *Maury*, "R. des Deux-Mondes," 15 décembre 1882; "R. hist.," 1883, 21, 291; *D'Avenel*, "Richelieu," 1884; "Mém. de Saint-Simon" (end of the reign of Louis XIV); *Taine*, "L'Ancien Régime"; *Viollet*, "Hist. du dr. privé," 265 (bibliog.); "Et. de Saint Louis," I, 169; "R. crit. de litt.," 1879, 326; *Luchaire*, "Man.," p. 178 (bibl.); *Glasson*, IV, 282, 315; *Salvioli*, 269; *Savigny*, "Verm. Schr.," IV, 1; *Maurer*, "Ueber

tinctions of the Roman Empire, nor from inequalities of race between Romans and Barbarians;[1] the nobles were the "milites" (knights),[2] free men who rendered cavalry service during the time of the Carolingians, when such service was the price for the grant of a fief, and when the fief was hereditary; they were the possessors of fiefs, soldiers by heredity; the contract of infeudation bound them one to another; many of them enjoyed the rights of sovereigns on their lands.[3] At the monarchical period the nobility had lost a large part of its military character; its sovereign rights had degenerated into privileges and these latter had been bestowed upon others than the possessors of fiefs. The nobles no longer constituted anything but a privileged hereditary class, an order of the State. They never had constituted an exclusive class; members of the Third Estate ("roturiers") were admitted to its ranks in early times: 1st, by becoming knights (originally every knight had the right of conferring knighthood);[4] and 2d, by acquiring fiefs and following the military calling.[5] When these two modes of ennoblement disappeared about the 1200 s, the king raised a large number of "roturiers" to the dignity of nobles, so that the nobility appeared to be only an emanation of the royal power, a creation of it.

§ 291. **How One became a Noble.** — One became a noble: 1st, by **birth**.[6] "Gentility must come from the father,"[7] said

d. Wesen d. Adels," 1846; *R. von Schreckenstein*, "Ritterwürde," 1886; "Z. f. Gesch. d. Oberheim," 1887, 288; "Staatslexicon v. Goerres Gesellschaft," "Adel"; *Viollet*, "Inst.," II, 417; *De Courcelles*, "Dict. univ. de la noblesse de France," 1820.

[1] From the 1500 s to the 1700 s, the common opinion was that the nobility had its origin in the Frankish conquest. *Pothier*, "Tr. des pers.," 9. Sieyès asks why the Third Estate did not send back into the forests of Franconia the families which were said to issue from the conquering race. Bismarck to Bluntschli: "1789 is the return of the Celts upon the Franks": we do not stop to refute this opinion.

[2] "Miles," "caballarius," "cavalier," gentlemen. *Dognon*, "Inst. du. Langued."

[3] "Gr. C. de Fr.," 2, 7; *Loysel*, 27 and following; *Du Cange*, "Miles," etc.

[4] Otherwise, 1200 s, *Beaumanoir*, 45, 30 (the king only). "Et. de Saint Louis," I, 134; *Loysel*, 46.

[5] *Seignobos*, "Rég. féod. en Bourg.," p. 83.

[6] And by marriage. *Loysel*, 54. A free woman was ennobled by her marriage, but not a serf woman. "Gr. C. de. Fr.," 2, 16. *Cf. Vitry*, 68.

[7] This principle was not admitted without difficulty. *Beaumanoir*, 45, 15. The children of a noble and a serf could not be knights; neither those of a noble woman and of a villein husband, but they were in fact treated as gentlemen though they could not hold a fief. "Etab. de Saint Louis," I, 173. *Loysel*, 40. Concerning the nobility on the mother's side of Champagne and Barrois, see bibl. in *Viollet*, 253. *La Roque*, p. 141; BCh., vol. 50, 509. The Ord. of Nov. 15, 1370, subjected the children of a noble mother and of a villein father to the payment of "franc fief" dues. *Ragueau*, see "Noblesse." "Jostice," p. 56.

Beaumanoir. In reality, it was a rule that legitimate children[1] took the status of their father; if he was a noble, they became noble; if he was a commoner, they were commoners, whatever may have been the status of the mother. Nobility of race could not be directly proven, because it was necessary to establish that the founder of the race was noble, a thing impossible in fact and in law; in fact, because it would have required a genealogy without gaps or uncertainties, at least as far as the 900 s; in law, because, even with the best-established genealogy, the status of persons was too fluctuating at the time of the establishment of feudalism to warrant definite conclusions. The courts avoided embarrassment by insisting upon the possession of the noble status for only three generations (or one hundred years).

2d, **The Possession of a Fief.**[2] — (A) The possession of a fief, coupled with the profession of arms, conferred nobility, at least during the early stages of feudalism when the noble class was in process of formation.[3]

(B) In the 1200s, the acquisition of fiefs was prohibited, or not easily permitted, to members of the Third Estate; if they were allowed to hold fiefs, they could not render personal military service; consequently admission to the ranks of the nobility was, in fact, denied to them (Ord. 1275 concerning "Amortissements").

(C) The Ordinance of Blois, 1579, Article 258, converted the usual fact into rigorous law: "villeins purchasing noble fiefs shall not become ennobled thereby"; they had to have letters from the king,[4] as the interest of the treasury required.[5]

[1] *Loysel*, 62: A bastard avoué (recognized) retained the name and the nobility of his father's house with the right to place his arms on the left. The Edict of March, 1600, obliged them to take letters, that is to say, to cause themselves to be ennobled by the king. *Cf. Fleury*, "Inst. au dr. fr.," II, 217. *Cf. Loysel*, 27; "Olim," I, 154: from 1261, Parliament judged in this sense. Declar. 1664, 1697, 1714, etc., Normandy: four generations, *Loyseau*, "Offices," 1, 9, 32. *Cf. Fleury*, "Inst. au dr. fr.," I, 217. The king sometimes ordered the verification of titles of nobility in a province, BCh., 1894 (*Bourdalière*, "Maintenues de noblesse en 1714").

[2] *Esmein*, 224: by accepting the villein as vassal, the seignior ennobled him. But it was not so much the will of the seignior as the possession of the fief and the military profession which made him a noble.

[3] *Loysel*, 27 and following. *P. de Font.*, 3, 4 and following (as long as he resided on the fief, the villein was free from the obligations for which he was held in this quality). *Beaumanoir*, 48, 1, 7: "li fief doivent estre as gentix homes par ancienne coustume et par novel establissement," an allusion, not as has been maintained, to a lost ordinance, but to the Ord. of 1275. *Langlois*, "Phil. III," 204; "Jostice," p. 66; *Boutillier*, II, 1, p. 656; "Et. de Saint Louis," I, 147 (ed. *Viollet*, IV, 159): nobility acquired "à la tierce foy," that is to say, when fealty and homage had been taken three times. "Olim," I, 154, 740. Ord. I, 227; *Glasson*, IV, 314; *Britz*, "Dr. belg.," 517.

[4] Except in Béarn, a province reunited to the crown after 1576. *De*

3d, **Ennoblement.** — From the 1300 s,[1] at least, the principle was established that the king alone could confer the status of nobility and legitimacy throughout all his kingdom.[2] Royal letters of ennoblement[3] were granted in large numbers, were lavished, according to the need of the treasury, to such an extent that the ennoblement of villeins degenerated into a mere fiscal procedure.

4th, **The Nobility of Functionaries.** — The titularies of the highest offices of State were so often ennobled that in the end nobility came to be regarded as an incident of these offices by a purely personal title at first, later, for certain offices at the very least, with hereditary privileges. As most public offices were venal (that is, purchasable) this bonus to vanity increased their price. Necker estimated that under Louis XVI there were four thousand noble offices. They included: (A) administrative, and, especially, judicial offices (at the end of the 1300 s the nobility of the robe as contradistinguished from the nobility of the sword): secretaries of the king, treasurers, counselors of the Parliament, etc.[4]

Jaurgain, "Nobiliaire de B.," 1, 3, 1879. The villein who acquired a seigniory drew from it the profits of justice, etc., without being ennobled by it; he was a seignior, but not a noble.

[5] Laws against the usurpation of nobility. Grimandet, in the 1500 s: "sont infinis faux nobles, les pères desquels ont manié les armes et fait act de chevalerie dans les boutiques de blasterie, de minoterie, de draperie, au movlin et aux fermes des seigneurs. Ils veulent se décharger des tributs et leur cote est répartie sur le commun." *Molière*, ".Ecole des femmes," 2, 1. Nobility was not acquired by prescription.

[1] "The emperor makes you free, he cannot make you noble," so it was said to Ebbon, bishop of Rheims, in the time of Louis the Debonair.

[2] The ennobled were detested by the villeins and scorned by the old families: "the kings of France," it was said, "cured villeinage as they did scrofula; but there always remained something of it." "Gr. C. de Fr.," I, 8; *Loysel*, 30; *Viollet*, 256. Previously (and sometimes even after) ennoblement emanated also from the large feudatories. *Boutaric*, "Alf. de Poitiers," p. 496. In 1268, Mgr. Sevestre, new cavalier, in order to be excused from proving his nobility paid 200 pounds. "Olim," II, 144, 166, 191 (year 1280). In speaking of the Count of Flanders, "non poterat facere de villaud militem sine authoritate regis." Germany: nobility granted by the princes was recognized only in their States, while nobility accorded by the emperor was recognized in all the empire, and carried more privileges. The emperors created counts and princes of the empire and even wished to create States of the empire without the consent of the Diet.

[3] *A. de Barthélemy*, "Et. s. les lettres d'anobl.," 1869. The first authentic letters were those of Philippe le Bel, 1285–1290. Did Philippe le Hardi grant letters to Raoul l'Orfèvre in 1270–1285? *Langlois*, "Phil. III," p. 205; *La Roque*, p. 75. These letters were verified by the Chamber of Accounts and by the Court of Aids. *Bacquet*, "Du droit d'anoblissement." Colbert, in 1661, revoked the titles of 40,000 persons who had been ennobled.

[4] After 1350 (*P. de la Forest*). *Cf.* ordinance of 1582. The German axiom, "Office does not ennoble any one," expresses the primitive law.

(B) municipal offices (nobility of the parish or shrievalty) in the great cities, for example, the town councilors of Toulouse.[1] (C) Military offices, villein officers at the end of the 1700 s. (D) Ecclesiastics, bishops and archbishops.

§ 292. **How Nobility was Lost.**[2] — The rights of nobility were lost: (A) by forfeiture which resulted from conviction of infamous crime;[3] (B) by degradation, that is, by following a trade (despicable business, handicraft) incompatible with the profession of arms; but in the latter case the noble status was suspended rather than lost, for as soon as the noble began to live like a noble, he recovered his former status.[4]

§ 293. **Titles of the Nobility.**[5] — Most of the titles of nobility (dukes, counts, marquises)[6] dated from the Frankish epoch, when they were applied to public functionaries and described the offices which they held. The title of "baron" was not a title at the very first; it was nearly the equivalent to that of free man.[7] That of "prince," reserved for the members of the royal family,

Academic nobility, "comitive," *La Roque*, 140. The professors of law after twenty years of service had the right to the title of count; but they do not seem to have taken it after the 1500 s.

[1] *La Roque*, p. 125. Mayors and échevins of Poitiers, from 1372 to 1375.

[2] Neither by time nor by poverty. *Loysel*, 34, 35.

[3] *La Roque*, p. 375 (lèse-majesté, etc.).

[4] "Et. de Saint Louis," I, 64. Edict of Aumale, April, 1450. Ord. 1560, 1567, etc. Ord. of the arch. of Austria for Brabant, Dec. 14, 1616. *La Roque*, p. 340. The notariat derogated in certain provinces but not in Provence and Dauphiny. Glass making commerce on a large scale (Decl. 1669, 1727, 1765), maritime commerce (Ord. 1629, Art. 452) did not involve forfeiture. The noble could work his own lands provided he did not have more than four plows (1407–1720). From the sixteenth century the grandson took letters of rehabilitation without this being absolutely necessary if his father and his grandfather had lost their nobility through derogation; at the end of seven generations, new letters of ennoblement. "La Noblesse commerçante," 1756 (*Coyer*).

[5] Some titles resembled coats of arms, at first personal emblems, then fixed and hereditary signs (from the time of Louis VII); they gave way to the creation of marshals of arms, king of arms, etc. (1487); they were registered under Louis XIV (Edict Nov., 1696, a fiscal measure). "Armorial général de France," by *Ch. d'Hozier*, drawn up between 1696 and 1709. "Armorial des Etats de Languedoc," by *Gastelier de la Tour*, 1767 (*cf. ibid.*, by *L. de Laroque*, 1860). "Armorial général de la France," by *P. d'Hozier* and *A. d'Hozier*, 1738–1768. The "Nobiliaires" contained the genealogies of families. "Gr. Encycl." see "Armoiries," "Blason." *La Roque*, "Tr. du Blason." German adage: "Letters of arms do not ennoble."

[6] *Ch. Mortet*, "Gr. Encycl." see "Comte." *Loysel*, 50, "Comites," companion in the Midi. *Du Cange*, see "Comites." There was only a nominal relation between the borders of the Frankish epoch and the "marches separantes" or parishes with joint tenure between several feudal seigniors. *Chénon*, N.R.H., 1892, 18; 1897, 62.

[7] "L. Rib.," 58, 2: "si quis hominem tam baronem quam feminam." During the feudal epoch, the domains of certain seigniors who did not have titles were called "baronnies." *Loysel*, 32, 638, 639 and following.

was extended in the 1500 s to a few nobles.[1] The king conferred titles: (*a*) originally by infeudation, by granting a fief to which the title was attached; (*b*) by raising certain lands to fiefs of dignity, in the 1300 s (for example, the raising of a simple seigniory to a duchy); (*c*) by personal grant (*e.g.* the marquis of Dreux and the count of Chamillart under Louis XIV). At the same time, the nobles who acquired fiefs took the titles that were attached to them. They were transmitted from father to son according to the rule of primogeniture, like patrimonial property, and as a fixed hierarchy became established among them, an irregular practice was introduced by which the younger brothers added to their family name a title inferior to that of their elder brother; during the life of the father the oldest son did likewise. The noble without children designated an heir under condition that he bear his name and arms.[2] The hierarchy of titles, unknown at first, because the rank of a seignior was determined by his power, became fixed in order to regulate questions of precedence when titles no longer corresponded to an effective sovereignty.[3] In the 1500 s the classification was as follows:[4] duke, marquis (?),

[1] Principalities since the 1500 s; thus the seignior of Monaco was styled prince (in the 1600 s). The king profited by this fact in order to erect lands into principalities. Napoleon I made this the highest of all titles; Loyseau placed princes only after counts; at the end of the Old Régime, they came after dukes.

[2] The transmission of the title in the collateral line or by virtue of testamentary disposition had to be approved by letters of the prince.

[3] The classification of the oldest register of Philip Augustus was: 1, dukes and counts; 2, barons; 3, chatelains; 4, cavaliers (without doubt bannerets, "milites bannerii"); 5, vavassors (nobles of inferior condition). *Cf.* sergent "fieffé," "voyes," "bachelier" ("bacalarius"). "Jostice," p. 67: duke, count, viscount, baron, chatelain, "vavassor," citizen, villein. *Glasson*, IV, 735; *Loysel*, 46, 47. "Dominus," seignior or sire (English, sir) ("dominus Johannes," "dominus Belli Joci," messire Jean, seignior of Beaujeu). "Monsieur" is the equivalent of "dominus." (Monsieur, the king's brother.) Provençal: E.N., N', for "dominus"; N.A., N', for "domina." Spanish "don. Domicellus," "domoiseau," "donzel," a young noble before being esquire. "Domina," dame, noble woman. "Domicella," "demoiselle," daughter of a gentleman; from the 1200 s, married women, or widows; later "noblesse" of the robe, bourgeoisie. Concerning the title of noble man, *cf. La Roque*, p. 209; *Giry*, "Diplomat.," p. 318 (titles and qualities).

[4] Dukes, counts, etc., of the monarchical epoch received their titles from the king. Dukes and peers with the right of sitting in Parliament, hereditary dukes, dukes "à brevet." *Loysel*, 50, 16: there were in France twelve peers, six ecclesiastics (Rheims, Langres, Laon, Beauvais, Châlons, Noyon) and six "laics" (Burgundy, Normandy, Guyenne, Champagne, Flanders, Toulouse). As these peerages were reunited to the crown, the king instituted others from them and in a larger number (Nivernais, Eu, Guise, etc.). The peers of France were present at the crowning of the king, received his oath, promised him obedience in the name of the country, assisted him, and gave him counsel when he held his estates general or when he sat in Parliament holding his "bed of justice." *Luchaire*,

count, viscount, baron, knight (chevalier),[1] and squire.[2] From the titled nobility was distinguished the simple nobility,[3] which no longer exists to-day, the Revolution having destroyed its privileges, although the titles are still protected by law (Code pénal, Art. 259).

"Man.," p. 560; "R. hist.," 54, 382; *Flach*, "Orig.," I, 251; *Langlois*, "Les Orig. du Parl. de Paris," p. 12; *F. Lot*, "R. hist.," 1894, vol. 54, p. 34; *Viollet*, "Inst.," II, 428; *G. de Manteyes*, "Etudes déd. à G. Monod.," p. 189; *Labande*, "Hist. de Beauvais," 1892; *Isambert*, "Table," see "Paris." The French peers were not distinguished originally from the fief peers who attended at the court of the king, as at the court of each seignior. From the 1100 s by these were understood twelve great vassals dependent directly upon the king, forming part of his court, but being separated by their power in fact from the other members. It was decided in 1224 that the officers of the king's palace had the right to sit with the French peers to judge a peer. *Du Cange*, see "Paris." "Jostice," p. 126; "Olim," "Tables," see "Pares." The prerogatives of the peers relative to the coronation of kings does not date back of the 1300 s. The conventional figure of twelve peers (*cf.* twelve apostles) was not always attained. The six ecclesiastical peers doubtless subsequent to the "laical" peers (large territorial divisions of the kingdom, Burgundy, Normandy, etc.), existed in 1216. It is no longer admitted that the peerage was constituted by Philip Augustus "à propos" the process of John Lackland. *Bémont*, "La condamn. de Jean S. T.," p. 59; "Acad. sc. morales," 1893, 83. *Cf. Blackstone*, vol. 2, p. 93.

[1] *L. Gautier*, "La Chevalerie," 1884; *Flach*, "Orig. de l'anc. France," II, 561; "Gr. Encycl." (*Giry*). This institution, of little importance in law ("Gr. C. Norm.," 22) but not in relation to the customs (*cf.* chevaliers-brigands, "Raubritter" of Germany), had its origin in the solemnities of the taking of arms and in the custom of horseback fighting. The "chevalier" was at first simply the cavalier, rich enough to equip himself at his own expense, then possessor of a fief or the son of a fief holder. Military ceremonial, then religious from the 1100s. Following the Crusades, chivalry became an affiliation of all gentlemen to defend Christianity. No knight was born so, not even the king (Francis I, at Marignan). Every knight was able at first to create another knight; then in the 1200 s the rule: "of a villein no one but the king can make a knight." Gold spurs were an attribute of the knight, silver of the squire. *Loysel*, 31–96. At the end of the 1200 s, the legists, civilians, chevaliers of the laws. *Chaisemartin*, p. 74; *Loysel*, p. 31. Military religious orders (1100 s) hospitalers, or Knights of Malta, Templars. Teutonic orders and the court orders (the Order of the Garter; the Order of the Golden Fleece, the Star, in 1351; Saint Michel, 1469; Holy Spirit, Henry III; Saint Louis, 1693; "Mérite militaire," for Protestant officers). The nomination to one of these orders was equivalent to ennoblement. *Loysel*, 31. The younger members of titled families took the title of knight, in default of others, at the end of the old régime (the knight of X, patronymic name).

[2] Squire ("écuyer"), *cf.* "Gr. Encycl." (*Ch. Mortet*), at first a noble filling a subordinate office, then nobles too poor to bear the expenses of knight service, inferior nobles. *Loysel*, 31. In England, "esquire" became synonymous with "gentleman." The son of a knight was born a squire and became knight by virtue of letters of the king. Decl. Jan., 1624, and the "réglement" of Aug. 13, 1667.

[3] Germany: the *high nobility:* (*a*) States of the Empire; (*b*) immediate seigniors of the empire who no longer appeared in the diets, "Hoechstfreie," "Dynastengeschlechter"; (*c*) mediatized families who had been compelled to renounce their claims as States of the Empire. The *inferior nobility* was dependent immediately on the Empire or on some sovereign seignior. English "gentry," *Glasson*, 5, 80.

The particle "de" is not a proof of nobility, as is commonly believed.[1]

§ 294. **The Personal Privileges of the Nobles.**[2] — **During the monarchical period,** the survivals of the sovereign rights of feudal seigniors of former times, or compensation for their loss were of different orders: (*a*) *military*, the higher grades of the army being reserved for the nobility;[3] (*b*) *fiscal*, exemptions from the royal "taille,"[4] from personal "corvées," from "banalités," and from dues on freeholds.[5] (*c*) *judicial*,[6] the nobility had their

[1] At present, it is not allowed to take the particle by adding it to one's name, neither is a division of this name allowed if it commences with "de." This would change the name. Concerning the Roman system of onomatology, *Cf. Girard*, "Manuel de dr. rom.," p. 104; *Cognat*, "Epigraphie," 37. From the fall of the Empire to the 1500 s, it was customary to give only one name at the time of birth or rather at the christening; the Church made it a duty to take the name of the godmother or godfather. This name was personal, not hereditary. To this baptismal name was added at a rather early time a surname, in order to prevent the confusion resulting from homonymy ("N. dictus Puer, Niger, G. non bibens aquam," Le Blanc, Le Petit, etc.). Soubriquets were frequent in the acts of the 1000s. Or indeed, the name was doubled by adding to it that of the father or that of the mother ("Berengarius filius Richardis"; the word "filius" drops easily, for example, "Johannes Andreæ." *Cf.* Arabian names, "ben"; Slav names, "Ivan Petrovitch," son of Peter) or the name of a place (place from which one came originally, or land of which he was proprietor). These surnames or additions to names have served as transitions from individual names, which alone were formerly known, to family names or patronymic, invariable or hereditary names, by a general use; at least since the 1500 s, and the regular tenure of the acts of the civil State. Ord. of 1539, Art. 50, 52; March 26, 1555; 1629, Art. 211. The nobles naturally followed the habit of having their names follow that of their fief or of uniting them by the particle "de"; this explains the common error which considers this a sign of nobility. It was not always so, for villeins used it in taking the name of their lands, and its absence does not prove that a person was not noble or of very old family (the Damas, the Chabots; Jacques Tessart, baron of Tournebu was offended because "de" was added to his old and illustrious name). The edicts restraining the usurpation of nobility aimed only at the abusive use of the title of squire. *Giry*, "Diplom.," 531; *La Roque* in his "Traité de la Noblesse"; *Lallier*, "De la propriété des noms," 1890.

[2] Feudal epoch: judgment by peers, exemption from the "taille," and from the tolls. *Beaumanoir*, 1, 15; 2; 25, 15. "Et. de Saint Louis," I, 63; "Olim," "Tables," see "Nobiles." Legisl. of Louis the Quarrelsome on the privileges of nobility, Ord., I, 551 and following. Edict of Charles VI, Aug. 11, 1408, etc. "R. hist.," 54, 241; *Viollet*, "Inst. pol.," II, 237.

[3] *Ferrière*, "Dict.," see "Nobles"; *Pothier*, "Tr. des pers.," 31; *Merlin*, "Rép.," see "Nobles." Edict of May 22, 1781, *Isambert*, 27, 29. Transformation in tax: rolls established according to a declaration of their income by the nobles. Fortresses. Ord. 1626. *La Roque*, "Tr. du ban et arrière ban" (old rolls).

[4] Ord. Blois, Art. 5. But the equality of all before the tax appeared in new taxes, capitation tax.

[5] Certain offices, certain canonships, and monastic places were reserved for them. By virtue of the Concordat of 1516, the number of years of study was reduced from five to three for nobles (baccalaureate in civil and canonical law).

[6] In the 1200 s, villeins were summoned from morning to evening; nobles every fifteen or seventeen days. *Loysel*, 45. But the time of

own special judges, the bailiffs and the seneschals, and in criminal cases, if there was an appeal, the united chambers of the Parliament; if they were convicted of crime the punishment inflicted upon them was less rigorous,[1] they were put to the torture only in exceptional cases; (*d*) *honorary*, they took precedence over members of the Third Estate; were permitted to designate themselves as squires and to have crested coats of arms; they had the right to bear arms, the privilege of wearing a white plume on their hats, of decorating their roofs with a weathercock, and, as patrons of the churches, they had the right of incense and certain funeral privileges.[2]

§ 295. **The Nobility in 1789.**[3] — Aside from the privileges allowed them by law the nobles enjoyed others in fact. Thus the royal courts dealt less rigorously with them than with "roturiers"[4] and the fiscal administration itself became lenient toward them. The high nobility were the recipients of pensions, court commissions, and fat sinecures;[5] this was the price by which they were paid for their sovereign rights. The feudal dues amounted to little, and they gained more through exemption from the "taille"; they paid taxes, so it was said, with their blood, but this was not exact, since they rendered military service only when they pleased and, moreover, they had the advantage of occupying exclusively the higher grades of the service. The seigniors for the most part did not reside on their lands;[6] they were held re-

summons was fixed by royal ordinances without distinction between nobles and villeins. "Committimus," extra-legal terms and privileges in case of seizure, etc. Ord. 1270, 1302, 1318.

[1] They were properly subjects of the king, that is to say, justiciables of the king only. "Gr. C. de Fr.," 2, 7; *Loysel*, 36; *P. de Font.*, 3; Ord. de Crémieu, 1538; Ord. 1670, 1, 20; *Loysel*, 848–852: the noble was beheaded under conditions where a villein was hung, except in a villein case; the noble paid 60 pounds fine where the villein paid only 60 sols.

[2] Special civil law for nobles: preference in the case of legacies of the conjoint nobles; primogeniture in respect to noble properties; majority.

[3] In England, the feudal nobility had almost disappeared in the 1400 s. The country gentry, peers included, then constituted the superior social class. Concerning the oligarchical régime that it founded, *cf. Boutmy, op. cit.*, 3d part.

[4] The "Great Days," "assises" extraordinary held by royal commissioners when the ordinary courts seemed too feeble to maintain order, often revealed abuses and vexations committed by nobles. Great Days of Poitiers, 1634 (250 capital condemnations — no one was executed). Great Days of Clermont, 1663 ("Memoirs of Fléchier"); a single noble was executed. From 1603 to 1679, sixteen capital edicts against duels; 8,000 letters of pardon to noble duelists.

[5] Concerning these pensions and sinecures, *cf. d'Avenel*, "Richelieu," vol. 1; *Boiteau*, "Etat de la France en 1789."

[6] Arthur Young in 1787 described the prosperity of a village where the seignior lived.

sponsible for the extortion of their farmers, but they were not, as they should have been, the benefactors of the tenants, the agents of agricultural progress, and the administrators and honorary judges of their domains. They were no longer the appointed representatives of the nation, for the very simple reason that there was no longer any political representation, no longer any Estates General.[1] Nothing justified the privileges of this class, which constituted only a very feeble minority, for the nobles in 1789 hardly numbered more than 140,000.[2] The decree of June 19, 1790,[3] abolished the nobility, though Napoleon I attempted to reëstablish it in 1808.[4]

TOPIC 2. "ROTURIERS"[5]

§ 296. **The "roturiers"**[6] constituted a class of free men intermediate between the nobility and the serf class. They did not have the privileges of the nobles,[7] and as they were the tenants of

[1] *Taine*, "Ancien Rég.," pp. 16, 35; "R. q. hist.," 61, 364; 46, 205.

[2] In 1580, there were 70,000 fiefs or subfiefs in France, according to the "Secret des finances" of *Froumenteau*. *Champion*, "La France d'ap. les cahiers de 1789," p. 85.

[3] Decree of June 19, 1790: "hereditary nobility is forever abolished in France; in consequence, the titles of marquis, chevalier, squire, count, viscount, prince, baron, vidame, noble, duke, and all other like titles may not be taken by anyone nor given to anyone; no citizen may bear any name except that of his family; no one may compel his domestic servant to wear livery, nor may have arms; incense will not be burned in the temples except to honor the Divinity, nor offered to anyone whatever; the titles of monseigneur and 'my seigneurs' will not be given to anybody nor to any individual, so also the titles of excellence, highness, eminence, and grandeur."

[4] New nobility with entail created by Napoleon I, Decree of March, 1808. The Legion of Honor was the "inferior assize of this system of fiefs" (*Viollet*). Napoleon gave to his nobility only honorary privileges. He did not relieve it from public responsibilities. In order to show that titles of nobility did not rest on the possession of land, but on the will of the sovereign, he forbade newly made nobles to take as a title the name of a landed estate. Charter of 1814, Art. 7: The old nobility retook their titles; the new retained theirs. Ord. 8–14 Oct., 1814, Art. 2. When the grandfather, the son, and the grandson had been successively members of the Legion of Honor, the grandson was entitled to a noble title by right, and could transmit his nobility and his title of chevalier to all his descendants (upon the payment of a certain sum and the possession of letters of chancellery). Decree of Feb. 29, 1848, abolishing Decree of Jan. 24–27, 1852, reëstablishing titles.

[5] *Luchaire*, "Man.," 328, 353; *Glasson*, V, 89; *L. Delisle, op. cit.; Seignobos, op. cit.*

[6] *Loysel*, 25, 26. Not nobles. Men "de poeste" or "pôté" ("potestas") a word which also serves to designate serfs. "Roturiers," from "ruptura," those who break the earth.

[7] *Loysel*, 49: "Save a villein from the gallows and he will cut your throat." Prejudice of the nobility against the villein. Judicial duel. *Loysel*, p. 812; summons, p. 743; majority, p. 718; freehold, p. 721.

the latter, or amenable to their jurisdiction,[1] they were subject to feudal dues and justice fees which weighed upon the serfs. But they were not subject to the burdens of "formariage" [a fee paid the seignior by a serf for marrying a woman subject to another seignior] and "mortmain" [right of the seignior to retake possession of the land of a serf who died without heirs]; often indeed for them the burdens of the "taille" and the "corvée" were mitigated or not exacted at all.[2] The "roturiers" who lived in the country were called "villeins" ("de villa"); those who lived in the towns took the name of "bourgeois" (from "Burg," a stronghold). The legal condition of the two classes was originally the same; but the bourgeoisie, enriched by commerce and industry, emancipated for the most part from feudal dues, organized into corporations, eventually came to have a municipal organization and even representation in the provincial Estates and in the States-General. They formed the Third Estate, the third order of the State.

§ 297. **The Bourgeoisie.** — Among the "roturiers" the bourgeois was therefore a privileged person. The rural class of "roturiers" (villeins) organized itself slowly and with difficulty[3] and acquired the right of political representation only during the monarchical period at a time when it had lost all value. The rural parish, which was almost always confounded with the "vicus" or the Roman "villa," acquired from the 400 s a religious

[1] Domicile made the "roturier" amenable to the jurisdiction of the seignior. *Loysel*, 44: avowal involved the man and he was amenable to the jurisdiction of the seignior in respect to body and chattel where he slept; but by the Ord. of Moulins, Art. 35, misdemeanors were punished where they were committed, and he who committed them could not ask to be sent before the seignior of the place where he resided.

[2] *P. de Font.*, 19, 8: "saches bien que, selon Dieu, tu n'a mie plénière poeste sor ton vilein: dont, si tu prens don suen fors les droites redevenance qu'il te doit, tu les prens contre Deu et sor le péril de t'ame, comme robierres. Et ce qu'en dit que totes les choses que vileins a sont son seignor, c'est voirs à garder: car s'eles estoient son seignor propres, il n'auriot quant à se nuile différence entre serf et vilein; mès par nostre usage n'a-il, entre toi et ton vilein, juge fors Deu, tant com il est tes couchans et tes levans." *Loysel*, 49.

[3] Concerning rural parishes, *cf. Imbart de la Tour*, "R. hist.," 1896 and following. Concerning "communities of inhabitants," *cf. Fréminville*, "Traité du gouvern. des biens et affaires des communautés d'habitants des villes, bourgs, villages et paroisses," 1860; *Babeau*, "Le village sous l'Ancien Rég.," 1882. Rural communities were represented in the Estates at the end of the 1500 s. *Babeau*, "Assemblées generales des communautés d'habitants du XIII s. à la Révolution," 1893. A recent English law gives to villages governed until the present time by the squire and the curate, elected councils if they contain more than 300 inhabitants, otherwise they are governed by an assembly of the inhabitants. *Glasson*, V, 162, and N.R.H., 1891, 446.

character. An administrative district known as a "community of inhabitants" was produced by means of dissociation and was superimposed upon the parish or placed alongside of it; this was often only the parish considered in its material interests, or from a lay point of view; it was sometimes a distinct entity formed by a fraction of the parish, or, conversely, by the union of several parishes. Although authority resided entirely in the person of the seignior and was exercised by his officers, it was an old custom for the inhabitants of the village to deliberate, at the conclusion of the mass, concerning their collective interests: the use of common property, police of the fields, maintenance of the Church, means of communication, and apportionment of taxes. These assemblies chose syndics to represent the community before the courts or before the superior authorities and the collectors of the "taille." Gradually the system of representation became permanent; in the 1600 s, however, not all rural communities had syndics. At this time they were subjected, like the urban municipalities, to the tutelage of intendants (Decl. of June 7, 1769). The Edict of June, 1787, substituted the representative régime of councils of notables in the place of the democratic régime of general assemblies, under the pretext that the latter were characterized by tumults and disorders and that the more peaceable citizens neglected to attend, leaving them open to the more turbulent.

§ 298. **How One became a Bourgeois.**—One became a bourgeois of a city just as one became a subject of a State: 1st, by *birth* [1] and by *marriage*,[2] the son inheriting the title from his father and the woman acquiring it from her husband; 2d, by *residence* for a year and a day;[3] 3d, by grant of the freedom of the city;[4] subject, ordinarily, to three conditions: residence, payment of a certain sum of money, and the taking of an oath of fidelity to the city.[5]

[1] "Olim," I, 239; II, 726. "Fribourg," Art. 103.

[2] "Aire," Art. 2; "Bergues," 5, 12; "Bailleul," 3, 3, etc.

[3] "Lorris," Art. 18. *Loysel*, 39. "Fribourg," 41.

[4] "Olim," III, 431, no. 40. "Et. de Rouen," 30. "Beaumont en Argonne," 11. Salon, year 1293, in *Giraud*, "Essai s. l'hist. du dr. fr.," II, 248; Tonneins, year 1301, Art 8 (purchase of land in the town). "Olim," II, 724.

[5] The condition of residence, which was the only thing exacted when there was a question of peopling a new town or of increasing the population of an old town, became of secondary importance when the acquisition of citizenship was sought as a favor. At Toulouse by the old "Coutume," 1285, Art. 155, 156, a person was treated as "civis" by the simple declaration that he wished to go to Toulouse and become joint citizen to the "acceptio itineris." In the 1500 s, Casevieille, for. 62 (1544) granted citizenship only after an inquiry "de qualitate et conditione personarum,"

§ 299. **How One ceased to be a Bourgeois.** — Conversely the bourgeois status was lost by marriage to a non-resident of the city,[1] by acquisition of citizenship in another city, or even by simple change of residence.[2] One could not be a bourgeois of two cities, any more than one could have two countries.

§ 300. **The Personal Bourgeoisie.**[3] — The bourgeois of a city had there both his domicile and his customary residence. The fact that he resided outside the town did not always deprive him of his rights; he often preserved them by fulfilling certain conditions, for example, by coming to stay at his city domicile during the four principal fêtes of the year. With this as a beginning it came about that inhabitants of seigniorial lands were allowed to acquire citizenship in a town of the royal domain, without changing their residence, except temporarily, and finally, without changing it at all; in that case it was no longer necessary to attach themselves to a particular city, they simply avowed themselves to be the bourgeoisie of the king. By the side of the real or ordinary bourgeoisie there appeared an exceptional personal bourgeoisie. Although inhabiting the lands of the seigniors, the bourgeoisie of the king enjoyed the great advantage of being amenable to the royal judges.

§ 301. **The Trade Guilds or Corporations of Artisans and Merchants**[4] represented a transition form between the servile labor of

and possession of a house at Toulouse. In the 1700s, there were exacted formalities, publications, a residence of five years (Soulatges, "Comm. de la Cout. de T.," Ord. 18 Sept., 1731). *Cf. Albi*, 4 (*Giraud*, I, 86). Ord. 1287, I, 314.

[1] "Olim," II, 725, no. 18.

[2] "Ét. de Rouen," Art. 38 (declaration), "Bayonne," 18 (year 1273).

[3] Ord. of Philip the Fair, 1287, I, 34. Ruling for royal citizenship of Languedoc, 27 Aug., 1376, Ord., VI, 214. "Olim," III, 431. *Loysel*, 39; *Ragueau*, see "Bourgeois du roi."

[4] *Blanc*, "Bibliog. des classes ouvr.," 1885; *Levasseur*, "Hist. des classes ouvr.," 1859; *Pigeonneau*, "Hist. du commerce," 1885; *Heyd*, "Hist. du comm. du Levant," 1885; *Fagniez*, "Et. s. la classe industr. à Paris au XIIIe et au XIVe s.," 1879; *Hubert-Valleroux*, "Corpor. d'arts et métiers," 1885; *Flach*, "Orig.," II; *Martin Saint-Léon*, "Hist. des corp. ouvr.," 1896; *Esmein*, 693; *Glasson*, V, 7 s.; *Luchaire*, "Man.," 356. Among other monographs: *Leroux de Lincy*, "Hist. de l'hôtel de ville de Paris," 1843; *Germain*, "Hist. du comm. de Montpellier," 1860; *A. Du Bourg*, "Anc. organis. du travail dans le Midi de la France," 1885; *De Ribble*, "Corp. ouvr. en Provence," 1865, etc.; *Bouchot*, "Hist. anecdot. des métiers," 1887; *Isambert*, "Table," v° "Arts et métiers"; Germany: v. *Patow*, "Zünftethum," 1887; *Gierke*, "Genossenschaftsrecht," 1868; *Schröder*, 630; *Frommhold*, § 116 et s.; Italy: *Alberti*, "Le corporazione," 1888; *Rodocanachi*, "Les Corp. ouvr. à Rome," 1894; "J. des Sav.," 1894, 308; *Goldschmidt*, "Universalgesch. d. Handelsrechts," t. I, 1891; *Fagniez*, "Docum. rel. à l'hist. de l'industrie" (jusqu'au XIIIe s.), 1899 (see the Introduction); *Brentano*, "The History of Gilds"; *Franklin*, "Les Corp. ouvr. à Paris," 1884; "Encycl. Migne," "Dict. des Confréries," 1855.

the Frankish epoch and the liberty of commerce and industry of modern times.[1] How was this social body constituted? Roman tradition is perhaps not alien to it, although we cannot establish a direct connection between the "collegia" of the Later Empire and the corporations of feudalism.[2] The guilds and brotherhoods were transformed into corporations or favored their development. Doubtless most of them were groupings of slaves and of "coloni" of the Frankish period; at that time the artisans of the great proprietors, bishops, or laymen worked for them; they were divided into small groups, each including those who performed the same kind of labor, and were placed under the surveillance of a servant or chief of service; the group was called a "ministerium" (service), craft; thus there was a craft of tailors, a craft of blacksmiths, etc.; from this was derived the word "métier" (craft) in the modern sense. Gradually the artisans became free, were less dependent upon the seignior and his agent, manufactured on their own account and sold their own products; but they remained grouped and organized into crafts.

In addition to these causes, which would have been sufficient in themselves to bring about the creation of the trade guilds, there were precedents, habits, and practices which led toward the corporative system. This system was the necessary reaction against the abuses of the time.[3] Suffering the same evils the members of each craft[4] associated themselves

[1] "Credenze," Italy; "Brüderschaften," brotherhoods; "Einungen," "Innungen," "consortia," unions; "Gilden," "convivia"; "Aemter" (magisteria): "Zunft," law, association ruled by laws; "Hanses," "Genossenschaften" in Germany, Gilde in England, "Tsecks" and "Artels" in Russia (the first of administrative creation, Catharine II; the second, spontaneously born).

[2] At the entry of the king Goutran into Orléans, the trade guild went before him with their banners (*Gregory of Tours*). From the 800s, grouping of artisans by quarters, streets ("Acta Sanct.," féb., III, 105); many streets still have the name of a trade, "rue des Tourneurs," "des Chapeliers," etc. Mention of the oldest corporations: 1112, freedom ("magisterium") of the criers of wine. *Luchaire*, "Louis VI," no. 136.

[3] Liberty of association did not exist under the Old Régime at various times, and the royal authority took measures against the societies which were formed without authorization. (Ord. 1305, I, 428; 1537, Art. 185, etc.) But the corporations had received a tacit sanction from custom. At the accession of each king, they paid a fee in order to obtain the confirmation of their privileges. Edict of 1673 obliging them to take letters of confirmation.

[4] Each corporation should have been able to include all the laborers in the same trade in France or even in foreign countries. But, in fact, it was restricted to the laborers of the town in which it was established, which led to rivalry between different towns (or even in the fairs with foreign merchants). There were collective hansas, like that of London, to which were attached several French towns. The Teutonic Hansa comprised as many as eighty towns from Riga to Bruges.

together to defend their interests. Isolated, they could do nothing; union made them strong. It was not necessary, therefore, to force them into the corporations; the constraint came from without, at least in the beginning. It was in this customary way that the rule was established according to which no artisan or merchant could open a shop or workshop unless he was a member of a corporation.[1] The corporation once established became a closed body, to which admission was difficult. The members exercised a strict and jealous surveillance over one another to prevent any cause of inequality among them; regulations determined the process of manufacture down to the last minutiæ, as if the corporation had had an industrial chief imposing his law upon his workmen. The monarchy sanctioned this rule and at times even aggravated it. The State always claimed the right, and even took upon itself the duty of watching over commerce and industry and public opinion demanded its guarantee.[2] More than this, the State (and it is necessary to understand that the State meant the seignior during the feudal period) did not recognize freedom of labor; it sold the right of engaging in the crafts, and granted them as fiefs.[3] The corporations came to constitute no longer a protection for the individual (whom the State protected sufficiently), but establishments of public utility, labor organizations by the State, a form of State socialism.

§ 302. **Members of the Corporations.**[4] — 1st, The *apprentice*, bound by his master to "his bread and to his soup," lodged, instructed, and corrected in case of need, entered the house of his patron under a contract signed in the presence of the wardens, a contract which the latter could refuse to authorize and under which the freedom of the parties was very limited, because the statutes fixed the number of apprentices and the duration and price of their apprenticeship.

2d, *Artisans* or *Journeymen* (sergeants). After a prescribed time (and an examination, a trial piece, "chef-d'œuvre," which was not required in the beginning) the apprentice became a journeyman and received a salary. He was obliged to swear to observe

[1] Corporative organization existed only in the towns; artisans of the villages and country were not subjected to it for the simple reason that there were no trades when the corporations were formed, and that, accordingly, the treasury would have gained little by enrolling the rural laborers.

[2] Transformation of the statutes and rules of corporations into administrative regulations by public authority (from the 1200 s). Generalization of the corporative system, Edicts of 1581, 1597 (*Isambert*, 14, 509; 15, 155; 19, 91), 1673, 1679.

[3] *Guérard*, "Cart. de Saint-Père," I, 59.

[4] No one could belong to two corporations.

the rules of the craft and to inform against contraventions of the same. The contract which bound him to his master was no more free than that which regulated the relations of apprenticeship, except as to the salary which the parties discussed. The day's labor, according to custom, was from sunrise to sunset; night work was prohibited. The journeyman, often lodged and fed by his patron, was under the latter's tutelage even as regarded his private life; but life in common prevented class hatred, more especially since, the expense of setting up in business being of little importance, every industrious and economical journeyman was able to establish himself on his own account. In the 1400 s admittance to the freedom of the company was closed; the mass of artisans defended themselves against the patronal aristocracy by means of secret associations,[1] journeymanship ("compagnonnage"), or even by strikes.[2] 3d, *Masters* ("magistri"). In the 1200 s the journeyman and the patron were almost on the same footing. After the period of apprenticeship, whoever had the means could open a shop, engage workmen and apprentices, and work on his

[1] "*Compagnonnage.*" The laborers thus constituting a distinct class organized themselves into secret societies (companions in work or "dévorants," society of Gavot, good fellows, etc.). By this means, they were assured aid, freedom of traveling, the ability to issue an interdict against a town or a patron. Initiation: strange ceremonies, costly welcome. The journeyman who traveled, on arriving at a town, went to the hostelry where he made himself known by mysterious signs; he was lodged and informed as to the shops where he could find work (*cf.* "Bourse du travail"); if he was ill, he was cared for, money was loaned him, and when he went away, the other members escorted him; he went from town to town hunting work ("tour de France"). *Freemasonry. Findel,* "Gesch. d. Freimaurerei," 3d ed., 1883; "Gr. Encycl.," see "Franc-maçonnerie," bibliog. The Freemasons began as stone cutters, grouped in corporations, dating from the construction of gothic cathedrals; foreigners were admitted, and it was by these members that they were preserved in England, where they became hotbeds of humanitarian theism. The vogue for mystical societies animated them at the end of the seventh century. Modern freemasonry dates from the foundation of the Grand Lodge of London, June 24, 1717. The customs of the corporations of the Middle Ages were preserved in it, but they served to put into action modern ideas. Constitution of Jan. 17, 1723. From this time, its history is very complicated. We here restrict ourselves to giving an idea of the constitution of freemasonry. It was not a secret society; everything was public except the signs of recognition. The Freemasons had no central organization; they were grouped into independent lodges and in each country formed a federation directed by a grand lodge ("le Grand-Orient"). Nevertheless, freemasonry was one, cosmopolitan, international. All Freemasons were regarded as belonging to the same family (mutual assistance, reception of foreign brothers). Freemasonry had no dogma, but a vague ideal of progress through labor of moral dignity, and of rationalism. ("Statuts de l'ordre de la franc maçonnerie francaise.")

[2] Under Saint Louis, there was a coalition of laborers and of patrons; *cf. Beaumanoir,* I, 429. Strike of drapers to the number of 40,000, in 1697; silk workers in Lyon, 1744. International associations, the Maillotins.

own account.[1] But it was not long before this unique social situation was changed by the separation of labor and capital, of enterprise and workmanship. Already in the "Book of Crafts" of Stephen Boileau appeared the examination and the "trial piece," "an object involving the principles of the craft but for which the difficulties were increased"; and in the 1400 s this was always the price of admission to the freedom of the company; apprenticeship was no longer sufficient to prove ability; the workman was required to undergo a term of preparation, then a test so difficult and so costly that he refused to subject himself to it in most cases;[2] the sons alone of masters were admitted without difficulty,[3] and, in fact, admission to the company became hereditary[4] and the number of masters limited. Not only was a test required of the new master but a professional oath and an admission fee. This fee, in the interest of the corporation, was doubled by the "purchase of the trade" from the seignior or king; "it was the price which the artisans held in the bonds of servitude formerly paid for freedom of labor."

Sons of masters were exempt wholly or in part from these pecuniary obligations. From the 1400 s the king conceded the freedom of the company ("maîtrises") in all the crafts, upon his own authority and without consulting the corporation. This was a simple financial proceeding, for one of two things happened: either the new masters paid him for the concession, or the old ones bought it up in order that their number might not be too greatly increased.[5]

§ 303. **Internal Organization of the Corporation.** — The corporation, like a State,[6] had its constitution, its statutes, its regulations,[7] its budget,[8] its common treasury, its house, its government, and its magistrates. It held its privileges from the seignior or the king. The statutes were framed by the assembly of masters, or at

[1] "The ruined master fell into the class of valets."

[2] Ord. 1673, vol. I and the commentary of Barnier.

[3] Freedom ("maîtrise") also passed as a dot to the laborer who married the daughter of a master.

[4] Heredity was the rule among the butchers only.

[5] Edict May, 1767. *Isambert*, 22, 468. Code of Henry III, 10, 26.

[6] Concerning the civil personality and the capacity of corporations, *cf.* above, pp. 626, 721.

[7] Customary law at first, afterwards written. The "Etabs." of Boileau proposed especially "to present well-determined cases of contravention and to prescribe fixed penalties." Renewal of the old statutes and the drawing up of new ones. Edicts 1581, 1597. Colbert.

[8] Revenues: entrance fees, fines, occasional assessments, property acquired by economy, gifts, or legacies. Expenses: maintenance of the house, expense of representation, food, religious service, mutual succor.

least, were approved by it and confirmed by the superior authority.[1] The wardenship or body of wardens[2] who administered the affairs of the corporation were elected by the masters or recruited by means of coöptation; the seignior or the king (or rather his delegates, the provost of Paris and the great officers of the crown) confirmed the choice or made the appointment themselves.[3] The wardens whose number varied (two, four, or six), sometimes having at their head a master, mayor, or head master and appointed ordinarily for one year, received the masters, settled differences between members of the craft (judgment by peers), collected the revenues of the corporation, distributed assistance, pronounced sentence for infractions of the regulations, and, finally, represented the company before the public authorities, in whose eyes they were responsible for the taxes ("tailles," "haubans," etc.), for the sentinels or night watch, and for the king's "droit de prise."

§ 304. **Diverse Functions of the Corporations.** — They were at the same time societies of mutual aid,[4] religious brotherhoods (each with its patron and its fête),[5] and political organizations,[6] because they participated in the municipal administration,[7] es-

[1] Relation of the corporations with the superior authority: at Paris, the "prévôt" was charged with the general police over the corporations; the chief storekeeper had control of the bakery, the chamberlain had control of the makers of clothing, etc. Here were traces of the early régime where the officers of the king's house directed the distinct groups of laborers. In independent towns, the municipal authorities seem to have displaced the seignior or the king.

[2] Excise officers, jurors, "prud'hommes," juror-guards, "eswards." Consuls in the Midi. King of the mercers (abolished in 1597).

[3] Louis XIV, with a fiscal design, changed the "jurandes" into offices; corporations repurchased them just as the towns repurchased their mayoralties. They rebought also their offices of masters created by the king.

[4] *Supra*, p. 693.

[5] *Flach*, "Orig.," II, 373; *Luchaire*, "Man.," p. 366 (bibl.). They did not always comprise all the members of the corporation; the oldest known were: the "Charité" of Valenciennes, before 1070; and the rural brotherhood of Saint Martin du Canigou, 1195. The director was called: "prévôt" in the North, "maître," "bâtonnier" at Paris, "recteur," "bayle," or "prieur" in the South. *Cf.* above, "Universities"; below, "Avocats."

[6] Political rôle of corporations: Etienne Marcel, the "ecorcheur caboche." Under the League it was said that they played the same rôle as the sections armed with pikes in 1793. *Luchaire*, 365. The seventy-six guilds of London still elect the Lord Mayor.

[7] Colbert unified the industrial regulations, revised the statutes, multiplied the rules and the inspections (1669, drapery; 1671, dyeing). An army of functionaries watched over the execution of these rules, which went so far as to provide for the length and width of pieces of cloth, the number of threads of the chain, etc.: Visitorial offices and inspectors general. Each piece of cloth had to bear the name of the maker and the seal of the town. Everything that did not conform to the official type was destroyed. From this was derived perhaps "the solidity, the good quality, and the good taste of the French products."

pecially through the aristocracy of merchants which, in Germany, formed a "Patriciat" from which the city council ("Rath") [1] was exclusively recruited for a long time. But above all, the corporation was an economic organization. Each one had acquired the monopoly of the industry which it conducted; the foreign workman in the city or the isolated artisan could not apply himself to the exercise of his craft. The seignior, and after him, the king alone, guaranteed this monopoly, and the king considered himself as having the right of eminent domain over all crafts. By way of compensation for the monopoly, the members of the corporation were subjected to strict regulation, established by custom and sanctioned by the State (fine, and destruction of products in case of fraud or bad workmanship). Purchasers were thus assured of articles of good quality; it was a sort of State socialism which secured them the advantages that result to-day from competition.[2] But there were inconveniences, the spirit of invention was discouraged;[3] there were no cheap goods (the State fixed the price only in exceptional cases),[4] there were wrangling and lawsuits without end among neighboring crafts, because it was impossible to determine their rights exactly (for example, the respective rights of hat makers and hosiery makers, shoemakers and cobblers, etc.),[5] and there was oppression and tyranny of the guild over the members. These evils were tolerated in the midst of the disorders of the feudal period because the corporation afforded the only possible protection to infant industries; at the end of the "ancien régime" the general security was too well assured by

[1] At Paris, the business of the water merchants (Act of 1170, *Luchaire*, "Acts de Louis VII," 590) was administered in the 1200 s, by four "échevins" and a master of "échevins," provost of water merchants or "prévôt des marchands." They added to their number twenty-four counselors and sat in the parlor of the bourgeois. *Luchaire*, p. 358. Under the monarchy there were six bodies which were superior to the others: those of the drapers, grocers, mercers, furriers, and goldsmiths; and in the 1500s, the butchers. In Italy, the major arts were superior to the minor arts.

[2] "Masters could not form associations, still less coalitions. The monopoly of raw materials or of merchandise was considered as a crime — no time contracts, no speculation, was legal. If two merchants concluded a sale, any bourgeois whatever always had the right to take part in it, that is to say, to buy himself at the merchant's price a part of the wares or products. The corporative régime looked with suspicion upon intermediaries, agents, and peddlers. The sale must, in principle, be made in the shop within sight and knowledge of passers or in the halls on market days." *Monin.*

[3] For example: teasels could not be replaced by iron cards, dyer's wood by indigo, or madder by cochineal, etc.

[4] The feudal State as well as the monarchical State claimed the right to levy official taxes on merchandise, bread, meat and wages, but it did not always exercise it.

[5] In Paris, the expense of litigation was one million (francs) per year.

the State for the protective function of the guild to be longer useful. One could no longer regard it as anything but an impediment to industrial progress, a troublesome mechanism which was used by the treasury against industrial workers.[1] There is no doubt that they would have been abolished sooner had it not been for the resources which they furnished to the treasury.[2]

§ 305. **Turgot and the Constituent Assembly.** — Turgot abolished the wardenships ("jurandes") and the freedom of the company ("maîtrises") by the edict of February, 1776. This measure, demanded for a long time by philosophers, ran foul of the opposition of the Parliaments. Turgot was reproached above all for having impaired vested rights by expropriating without indemnity the privileges which the masters had had to buy at a dear price.[3] Upon the downfall of this minister the guilds were temporarily reëstablished (by an edict of August, 1776), but were subjected to State control much more strictly than they had been in the past.[4] The constituent assembly speedily took up the work of Turgot.[5] It proclaimed freedom of labor and, like Turgot, prohibited every association and every coalition between artisans or citizens of the same calling[6] (decree of June 14–17, 1791).[7]

[1] Criticism in the preamble of the Edict of Turgot, 1776. *Cf.* "Test. polit. de Colbert," ch. 15; *Dareste*, "Hist. de l'admin.," vol. II, p. 195.

[2] The experience of the corporative régime, having been based solely on the petty industry formerly known, did not prove anything for modern times. Great industries scarcely appeared under the old régime (Colbert). Royal manufactures of Gobelin Saint Gobain, etc., Sèvres, 1750. Here the State was the chief operator of the industry.

[3] It was said that the indemnity was not due, because the king could create as many new masters as he pleased. The measure was unjust in depriving masters of privileges on which they had counted and by reason of which they had bought admission to the corporation. The reasons that are found in the Edict are still weaker, namely: if the masters lost as sellers, they gained as purchasers by the suppression of monopoly. Other grievances against the edict were: the public would not be protected against fraud; laborers would suffer from the depreciation of wages; the corporations had not prevented French industry from attaining a high degree of prosperity. It was subjected again to the trial that it had endured through the revocation of the Edict of Nantes (Saint Etienne lost then 16,000 workers; at Calais of 3,000, only 300 remained; Tours saved only fifteen trades in cloth in place of 250, etc.).

[4] *Isambert*, 23, 370, 24, 74. Ord. or decrees of 1776 to 1785. The assembly of masters no longer elected the "jurés" or syndics; they were now appointed by delegates of that assembly.

[5] It admitted in principle that the charges of the "maîtrises" should be reimbursed; in reality, it does not appear that the indemnity was paid. Patents of invention were substituted for royal privileges.

[6] Law of May 25, 1864, admitted the right of coalition and liberty to strike (without menace and violence). Law of March 21, 1884, recognized professional syndicates (they existed already by fact of numerous associations between laborers and patrons).

[7] In foreign countries, trade corporations have disappeared little by little since the Revolution: Westphalia, 1807; Prussia, 1810, 1811, 1869;

TOPIC 3. THE SERFS [1]

§ 306. **Origin.** — In the 1000 s most of the French peasants were serfs or bondmen.[2] The former were previously freed slaves;[3] the latter were "coloni" or "lides" of the Frankish period. The lower classes of the preceding times had a common origin although there remained traces of original distinctions. The condition of the serf was not very different from that of the "colonus" of the Later Empire; the economic condition of the country had changed so little that it is not at all surprising that the law remained the same.[4]

Austria, 1860; Hungary, 1872; England, 1835; Rome, 1807; Naples, 1826; Switzerland, 1830. The corporative system which had been abolished everywhere has found again some favor in the present time, where there has been opportunity to forget its vices and its oppressive character (Professional syndicates in France: German laws of June 18, 1881, June 11, 1883, July 6, 1884; Austrian law of March 15, 1883). *Cf.* *Howell*, "Le passé et l'avenir des Trades Unions," 1892; *Meynis*, "Des Corporations," 1886; *Levasseur*, "L'ouvrier américain," 1898. (Knights of Labor, etc.)

[1] BIBLIOGRAPHY: *Dunod*, "Tr. de la mainmorte," 1760; *Rivière*, "L'Eglise et l'esclavage," 1864; *Biot*, "Abol. de l'esclav.," 1844; Bibliog. in *Luchaire*, "Man.," 293, 335; *Viollet*, "Hist. du dr. civ.," 327; *Glasson*, VII, 29; *A. Réville*, "Les paysans au moyen âge," 1896; *Hanauer*, "Les paysans de l'Alsace," 1866; *Beaune*, "Condit. des pers.," 1880; *Lecoy de la Marche*, "Le Correspondant," 1884; *Allard*, "Esclaves, serfs et mainmortables," 1884; *Grandmaison*, "Livre des serfs de Marmoutiers," 1864 (Soc. arch. Touraine); *Guérard*, "Polypt. d'Irminon"; "Cart. de Saint-Père de Chartres," etc.; *L. Delisle*, "Classes agric. en Norm.," p. 18; *De la Borderie*, "Serv. en Bretagne"; *Dupré*, "Serv. dans le Blésois," 1867; *Raymond*, "Soc. Pau," 2, VIII, 171; *Cadier*, "Etats de Béarn," 72; *Brutails*, "Et. sur la cond. des popul. rurales du Roussillon," 1891; *Finot*, N.R.H., XII; *Melleville*, "Soc. Laon," XII; *Autorde*, "Serv. dans la Marche," 1891; *Sée*, "Classes serviles en Champagne" ("R. hist.," 1894); "Et. s. les classes rurales en Bretagne," 1897; *Doniol*, "Hist. des cl. rurales," 1857; *Dareste*, "Hist. des cl. agricoles," 1854; "Rh. dr.," 1858, 351; *Perreciot*, "Etat des personnes et cond. des terres," 1845; "Rq. hist.," 18, 381; *Laurière s. Loysel*, 89; *Boucomont*, "thèse" (Nivernais), 1895; *Pollock and Maitland*, I, 337; *Vinogradoff*, "Villainage in England," 1892; *Schröder*, 430; Add. *Seignobos*, "Le rég. féod. en Bourgogne."

[2] "Homo lignis de corpore," Toulouse, 155. "Questan" (queste, taille) in Béarn. "Homines potestatis," Villeins. *Cf. Seignobos*, p. 32; *Du Cange*, see "Conditionati," "Costumarii," etc. Several "coutumes" of the sixteenth century treat of the state and quality of persons (Meaux, Troyes, etc.).

[3] On the theory of B. Guérard (3 phases: slavery, servitude, bondage), *cf. Luchaire*, "Man.," p. 298.

[4] Concerning "hôtes," *cf. Luchaire*, "Man.," 327 (bibliog.); *Flach*, "Orig. de l'anc. Fr.," I, 160, 307; *Du Cange*, see "Hostisia," "Hospites." The "hostise," frequent in the twelfth and thirteenth centuries, disappeared later. It was a little habitation with court, garden and some arpents of land that the seignior granted to foreigners in order to repopulate his domains and put them again in cultivation. The "hôte" was free, but subject to services and rents which often reduced him almost to bondage. Ord., VII, 455; XII, 298. *Beaumanoir*, II, 226.

§ 307. **How One became a Serf.**[1] — One became a serf: 1st, by *birth* (origin). The children of two serfs were serfs. If the father and the mother were serfs of different seigniors, the children were divided between them except where the contrary was provided by agreement.[2] In case of marriage between a free person and a serf, the status of the children varied according to the customs;[3] sometimes they were always serfs by virtue of the old rule the "worse carries with him the good";[4] sometimes they followed the condition of the mother (slaves, "servi" in Roman law);[5] sometimes that of the father (since they were the issue of a legitimate marriage).[6] 2d, by *marriage:* a free woman who married a serf followed the husband's status.[7] 3d, by *convention*[8] or, indeed, by voluntary *oblation* to a Church, or to a religious establishment.[9] 4th, by *residence for a year and a day* on a seigniorial estate in places where the "air enslaves."[10] 5th, by *way of punishment.*[11]

[1] *Beaumanoir*, 45.

[2] Number of imperfect children, delayed births. Undivided serfs. "R. hist.," 1887, p. 276; *D. Vaissete*, X, 962, xi; *Giraud*, "Essai s. l'hist. du dr. fr.," II, 333; *Roupnel*, "Le rég. féod. à Châtillon-sur-Seine," 1896; *Luchaire*, "Inst. mon.," 2, 125, 1 (act of 1152); "Man.," p. 302; *Viollet*, "Etabl.," 3, 289. The king did not divide with any one (except privileges). *Guérard*, "Cart. de Saint-Père," II, 283.

[3] *Loysel*, 41 and following. *Cf.* "Liv. des serfs de Marmoutiers," *passim.* *Chaisemartin*, "Proverbes du dr. germ.," p. 77.

[4] *Ulp.*, 5, 8–10; *Gratian*, 2 p., C. 32, Q. 4, c. 15; *Ragueau*, see "Le mauvais." "Toulouse," 150, 154; "Bourbonn.," 199; "Nivernais," 8, 22. *Viollet*, "Etabl. Saint Louis," I, 42, 178; *Beaum.*, 45, 16: the bastard, being legally without parents, was not a serf.

[5] Dig., 1, 5, 24. X, 4, 10, 1; 1, 18, 10; *Beauman.*, 45, 15; "Vitry," 144; *Viollet*, "Etabl. de Saint Louis," III, 283. Meaux, 75.

[6] "Burgundy," 9, 3. England.

[7] "Liv. des serfs de Marmoutiers," App. no. 6. *Tardif*, "Mon. hist.," no. 629. "Cart. de Saint-Père," I, 91; II, 296, etc. "Burgundy," 9, 8; Fr.-Comté, 91. *Esmein*, "Le mariage en dr. can.," I, 326 and following.

[8] Made originally with the formality of the four denarii placed on the head. "Livre des serfs de Marmoutiers," no. 124. "Toulouse," 155a (Art. not approved in 1286). *Dunod*, "Mainmorte" (1760), p. 28; "Burgundy," 9, 5. *Guy Pape*, "Dec.," 314 and following. In Germany, disappearance of free peasants following the war of 1524, the Thirty Years' War.

[9] *Beaum.*, 45, 19. The lay monk ("oblat") sacrificed his freedom for the salvation of his soul and in order to enjoy the protection of the Church. Formalities: cord around his neck, denarius on his head. *Raymond*, "Cart. de Saint-Jean de Sordes," 1875. *Grandmaison, op. cit.*; *Pasquier*, "Recherches," 4, 5; *Flach*, I, 458.

[10] The greater part of the time (but not always, for example men of service) it was accompanied by occupation through a servile tenure. How did the land impose its condition on the man? At a period when the greater part of the peasants were serfs and the greater part of the lands they occupied were held by servile tenures it must be presumed that the immigrant was himself a serf. Uniformity of condition was the simplest means of regulating his status, all the more so because he had been tacitly accepted by the sole fact of his establishment in a serf country. *Beaum.*, 45, 19. Châtillon-sur-Seine, 1 and following. Burgundy, 9, 5, and 6.

§ 308. **How One ceased to be a Serf.** — In principle the status of the serfs was perpetual like that of the "coloni," but in the progress of this class of men toward freedom, modes of liberation were developed, correlative with the events which reduced to serfdom: 1st, by birth of a free mother, or by marriage of a serf woman to a free man;[1] 2d, by residence for a year and a day in a free place, where "the air makes free";[2] 3d, by disavowal by the seignior coupled with the abandonment of the land (or even of the household goods and property acquired by the serf);[3] 4th, by emancipation.[4]

§ 309. **The Condition of the Serfs** varied widely.[5] At the end of the 1200 s some had hardly emerged from slavery,[6] while

Charroux, 1247, Art. 3 (*Giraud*, "Essai," II). *Chaisemartin, op. cit.*, 46 and following. *Bracton*, 1, 10, 3; *Littlejohn*, 175: it was not the tenure which made the villein. Concerning the delay of a year and a day, *cf.* "Sal.," 45, "Capit.," 825, c. 11. "Freiburg i/B." (1120), Art. 37 (*Giraud*, "Essai," I, 126). Lorris (18) N.R.H., 1884, 452. "Marche," 127 (occupation of servile lands for thirty years).

[11] *Beaum.*, 45, 19. *Cf. Luchaire*, 296, c and d.

[1] "Burgundy," 9, 7; *Beaum.*, 45, 34. Below "prêtrise."

[2] *Nieuport*, in *Giraud*, "Essai s. l'hist.," I, 10; "Freiburg," 37. Ord. XII, 416, "Toulouse," 156; *Beauman.*, 45, 36. In certain places, residence for a year and a day was not necessary; in others, prescription of long duration (twenty years). "Et. de Saint Louis," 2, 31. Ecclesiastical status for ten years. In 1779, Louis XVI abolished the right of pursuit with regard to all serfs established in a free place. *Isambert*, 26, 139. The fear of seeing the serfs leave his domain often kept the seignior from abusing his rights over them.

[3] *Beaum.*, 45, 5. *Giraud*, "Essai," II, 277 ("Burgundy," 46). The disavowal had to be presented first for the body serf in the form of a suit for recovery of his freedom. In certain "coutumes," the serf was authorized to disavow his seignior purely and simply, and consequently to choose between serfdom and freedom. "A. C. Bourg.," 120. *Seignobos, op. cit.*, p. 48 (Charters of 1232, 1236, etc.). The man without a seignior, "without avowal," was no longer treated rigorously as a foreigner. He even sought to keep the ownership of his tenement. "Cout. of Simon de Montfort," *D. Vaissete*, VIII, 631.

[4] Forms of the Frankish epoch. In the 1200 s, they disappeared, and at most, there was ordinarily, without this being necessary, drawing up of a written document. *Beaum.*, 45, 14, "Ass. Bourgeois," 206 and following. Ord. XI, 214. *Luchaire*, "Actes de Louis le Gros," *passim*, *Esmein*, p. 239.

[5] Lay serfs and even free men subjected themselves to ecclesiastical serfdom, which proves that it had its advantages: better assurance of security, greater comfort, for the Church was richer and more pacific than the seigniors. *Guérard*, "Cart. de Saint-Père," Prol. 56; "N.-D. de Paris," I, 223. They were better treated. *Migne*, "Patr. lat.," 189, 146. But *M. Luchaire*, "Man.," p. 311, clearly shows that these advantages have been exaggerated; the Church rarely emancipated serfs, because it was difficult for it to make over its property and it had not the same need of money as the seigniors. *Flach*, I, 462. Concerning the royal serfs, who were in a still better condition, *cf. Luchaire, loc. cit.*

[6] *Beaum.*, 45, 30. "Anc. Us. d'Artois," 57, "A. C. Burgundy," 114, 119. *Du Cange*, see "Quittius." The English "villeins," according to the "Mirror of Judges," could not pursue anything except at the "opus" of their

others had almost acquired equality with the "roturiers."[1] Generally they were subject to the right of pursuit, to restrictions governing foreign marriage, to the "taille," the "corvée," and mortmain dues. In this way the attachment of the serf to the soil was assured, which was for them just as it had been for the "coloni" both an advantage and a burden.[2] It also assured the exploitation of the serf by the seignior. In public law they were scarcely taken into account and hardly had the right to justice (between the serf and his seignior there was no other judge but God).[3]

seigniors (*cf.* "Anc. Cout. Anjou," vol. II, p. 221); they did not know in the evening whom they would serve in the morning. The seigniors could have them beaten with rods, imprisoned and punished at will, keep their lives and entire body. In Palestine, quasi-slavery of villeins. *J. d'Ibelin*, 251 and following. Germany: the "Leibeigene" ("Sachsensp.," III, 32) were sold, exchanged, and arbitrarily punished by the seignior. "Sachsensp.," III, 32. Castille: in 1348 the Ord. of Alcala forbade the killing of laborers. Aragon: "villanos" under the cover of arbitrary exactions, and "villanos de parada" whom the seignior treated well or badly at will.

[1] *Beaum.*, 45, 30: "li uns des sers sunt si souget a lor segneurs, que lor sires pot peure quanqu'ils ont, à mort et à vie, et lor cors tenir en prison toutes les fois qu'il lor plest' soit a tort, soit à droit, qu'il n'eu est tenue à respondre fors à Dieu. Et li autre sunt demené plus debonerement, car tant comme ils vivent, li segneur ne lor poent riens demander, s'ils ne meffont, fors lor cens et lor rentes et lor redevances qu'ils ont acoustumées à paier por lor servitutes." In Languedoc, at the same period, there were body serfs and serfs of "caselage." These latter were held only by reason of their land (or "caselage") and, like a copyholder, freed themselves of their obligations by abandoning their holdings. *Cf.* the German "Hörigen" were attached to their tenement in such a way that they could not leave it and the seignior could not remove them; they were unable to alienate it or to transmit it by succession to others than the tenants of the domain, but they were qualified for the judicial combat, and had a right to the "wergeld." "Sachsensp.," 2, 3; "Schwabensp.," 104. *Blondel*, "Frédéric II," 353. From the English villein arose the copyholder, of whom *Coke* said in 1628: "he is no longer subject to the good pleasure of the seignior, does not tremble at the least breath of wind, eats and drinks tranquilly, and although he regularly performs the service of his tenure, he can leave the seignior to knit his brows, for he has nothing to fear from him."

[2] *Douais*, "Cart. de Saint-Sernin," p. 93: sale of lands with the men who cultivated them. *Viollet*, "Etabl. de Saint Louis," IV, 297. This principle does not seem to have been respected always. The seignior sometimes withdrew his tenement from the serf. "Cart. de Saint-Père, Livre des serfs de Marmoutiers," *passim*. *Cf. Esmein*, p. 226, who does not admit the attachment of the serf to his tenement, but only to the seigniory, and yet in the sense that the seignior could break this bond. England: protection of the king (*Houard, Littleton*, I, 267). *Bracton*, 1, 10, 3, *Britton*, 2, 13.

[3] "A. C. Burgundy," 13, 6: they could neither assemble nor obtrude. *Seignobos*, p. 57. The seignior administered justice, which gave rise to many abuses. Sometimes, they could not be witnesses in the courts except against other serfs. *Bourbonnais*, 205; *Beaum.*, 39, 32 and 66; 63, 1. They held inferior offices. *D. Vaissete*, VII, 553. *Cf.* German, "Hofrecht," *Colonges, Finot*, N.R.H., 1883, 298.

§ 310. **Pursuit.**[1] — (A) Originally this right differed little from the right to recover a fugitive slave; the seignior could reclaim his serf wherever he found him; the latter therefore did not have the right to go and come as he pleased.[2] (B) By the 1600 s the serf had long been in possession of this latter right; the privilege of pursuit was therefore reduced to the right merely to require the payment of the "taille" of the serf whenever he might be found and to claim his inheritance upon his death.[3] There was still a distinction between serfs bound by their persons and serfs bound by the land;[4] the latter, by abandoning the tenement which they had received from the seignior, escaped from all pursuit.

§ 311. **"Formariage" [Marriage between Serfs belonging to Different Seigniors].**[5] — The Church recognized the validity of the marriage of the serf, even when it took place without the consent of the seignior.[6] According to the secular law, however, such consent was required under penalty of a fine and especially in the case of "foris maritagium," that is, marriage outside of the seigniory or with a free woman,[7] because, in such a case, the status of the wife and children gave rise to difficulties.[8] Most generally the permission of the seigniorial authority was purchased by the payment of a tax called "droit de formariage."[9]

[1] "Secta," "sequela," "parata." Cod. Just. 11, 47, 6. — *Beaum.*, 45, 36. Procedure in the 1100 s. Chronicle of *Hugues de Poitiers*. *Luchaire*, "Man.," 307. Treaty of "parcours et d'entrecours," authorizing the serfs of one seigniory to establish themselves on another, and reciprocally. *Du Cange*, *Ragueau*, *Luchaire*, "Louis VI," no. 497. The Russian serf who owed the "obrok," money rent, and not the "brachtina," or service, could go to a town to practice a trade.

[2] "Toulouse," 155; the seignior took his serf and marked him, as an animal bought in the market. Ord. I, 53 (1230).

[3] *Pothier*, ed. *Bugnet*, IX, 16. Edict Aug. 10, 1779, *Isambert*, 26, 139, abolishing the right of pursuit (according to the decree of June 17, 1790, concerning the "requisitoire" of Séguier). *Guyot*, see "Mainmorte."

[4] Old distinction (1100 s, Burgundy, Franche-Comté). *Seignobos*, "Rég. féod. en Bourg.," 48. *Luchaire*, 303. Body serfs: "taille," "corvée" service, independently of all property (Nivernais, 8, 3). The serf with an estate attempted to leave the seigniory without losing the ownership of his tenement. *Loysel*, 89, "Olim," I, 76. The "personal" serfs could free themselves only by abandoning their inheritance and all their belongings.

[5] *Hanauer*, "Cout. matrimon.," "Mém. Acad. Stanislas," 1893. *Cf.* *Glasson*, VII, 160, BCh., 1873, 323. Const. Châtelet, 72. The seignior went so far as to compel marriage. *Cf. Esmein*, p. 232; "Le mar. en dr. canon.," I, 318. [6] Confiscation of property. "Burgundy," 9, 21.

[7] Marriages by exchange, conventions of "parcours et entrecours," N.R.H., 1895, 654. *J. d'Ibelin*, 278, 253.

[8] "A. C. Burgundy," c. IX.

[9] The serf could no longer enter into the religious orders without the consent of the seignior. *Beaum.*, 45, 17, 28. X, "de serv. non ordin." *Loysel*, 80. (He was bound to provide the seignior with a man to do the personal services of his place.)

§ 312. **Dues.** — (A) *"Chevage,"* or capitation tax, was a personal contribution[1] of fixed amount payable annually, which became rare from the end of the 1100 s. (B) The *"taille"* (seigniorial)[2,3,4] was, at first, an arbitrary tax imposed at the will of the seignior, a fact which enabled him to take possession of all of the personal property of the serf.[5] According to the subsequent law, which was in process of formation from the 1100 s, the seignior could not impose a "taille" upon his serf whenever and in such manner as he wished. As a result of the idea that the "taille" must be reasonable,[6] it was gradually converted into a regular tax. Custom required that it be levied only once a year or at fixed times; in the end it became a fixed quota and was confused with "chevage," or was even abolished in consideration of the payment of a fixed amount once for all.[7]

§ 313. **The Seigniorial "Corvée" [Compulsory Labor]**[8] went through the same stages of transition as did the "taille."[9] It was

[1] "Capitagium, cavagium, census capitis: hommes de capite." *Du Cange*, see "Capitale," "Denarius." Rate of four denarii. "Obrok" due by the Russian serf: twenty-five to fifty francs per year.

[2] "Tallia" (1000 s), a notch cut at the moment of the levying of the "exactio" on a stick broken into two equal parts; this primitive mode of proof was still employed by the tradesmen (bakers); the seller kept the "taille," the consumer the duplicate. Code civ., Art. 1333. These terms were also used: "quête," and "tolte" ("maltôte.")

[3] *Loysel*, 909 and following (bibliog.). Concerning the royal "taille," see below.

[4] "Tallia ad voluntatem, ad misericordiam, alta et bassa; talliabiles." *Seignobos*, "Le rég. féod. en Bourgoge," p. 40. The "taille" was a relic of the rights of a master over a slave, and was doubtless connected with Germanic customs in matters of taxes (gifts of the subject to the king, of the vassal to the seignior). "Personal" in principle, it sometimes became "real," that is to say, levied only on the income of servile tenements. "A. C. Burgundy," 100. *Glasson*, IV, 441.

[5] *Beaum.*, 45, 36 ("Cens" and "Cavages"), *P. de Font.*, 19, 8. "Toulouse," 155. In 1422, a seignior met his serf in the streets of Dijon, stopped him, and called upon him to pay a "taille" of 400 écus of gold. *Loysel*, 49.

[6] Conc. Lateran, 1179. Ord. of Saint Louis, cited by *Joinville*, ed. *Wailly*, p. 252. "Gr. C. de Fr.," p. 212. "St. Parl.," 3, 36. "A. C. Nivernais" (1490), 14, 1; N. C. (1534), 8, 1. "Bourbonnais," 190 and following, 345. *Esmein*, p. 229. The "prud'hommes" in order to ascertain the ability of each one, the "taille" being proportional to his ability. Subscriptions or fixed annual tax. "Siete Part., 7 in f.," *Simon de Montfort*, D. *Vaissete*, 8, 630 (recourse to the count).

[7] The abolition of the "taille" was frequent in the charters of enfranchisement. *D. Vaissete*, 6, 782.

[8] *Luchaire*, "Man.," 346, *Glasson*, IV, 454; *Mortet*, "Gr. Encycl.," see "Corvée." Concerning the royal "corvée," see below. *Guyot*, "Fiefs," vol. I.

[9] Concerning the Roman origin of the "corvée," *cf.* above. It consisted: (*a*) in services which the seignior exacted for the cultivation or improvement of the part of the domain that he reserved for himself: keeping up of the château, transportation of the crops, reaping, mowing, etc.; (*b*) in other services, such as summoning parties in judicial actions, escorting criminals, etc.; (*c*) and finally in the performance of labor that

at first arbitrary and at the expense of the serfs.[1] The seignior demanded from them what work he pleased and whenever he pleased. In the 1500 s [2] Loysel said: "Corvées at will are limited to twelve days per year, from sunrise to sunset; not more than three may be required during one month and in different weeks." According to the decisions the seignior was bound to notify those of whom it was required, two days in advance, to feed them, and to allow them sufficient time at the close of the day to return home. It is true that the "corvée" thus mitigated (as well as the compounded "taille") was required during this period as often of villeins as of serfs.[3] In Provence the "corvée" had been bought off since the 1500 s.[4]

§ 314. **Mortmain.**[5] — (A) *Primitive Law.* The estate which the serf had received from the seignior belonged to the latter; nevertheless it could not be taken away from the serf as the savings ("pécule") of a slave could be.[6] The serf held it until his death, or rather he was attached to it like a "colonus"; however, although in fact his children succeeded him in consideration of a fee analogous to the relief or purchase in the case of fiefs and "censives," in law his tenure was not hereditary like that of the "colonus."[7] The seignior took possession of the servile inheritance upon the death of the serf, by virtue of the right of mort-

was formerly done for the State, such as furnishing wagons and relays of horses for the post, maintenance and repair of roads and bridges, etc. *Du Cange*, see "Angaria," etc. Add. Gard of the château and sentinel duty. The Russian peasant worked three days a week on the seignior's lands.

[1] "Toulouse," 155[a] ("de eis se servire").

[2] Only the ancient "corvées" founded on titles were allowed to stand. "Paris," 71. "Blois," 283.

[3] *D. Vaissete*, 8, 631; *Loysel*, 915; *Auvergne*, 18, 25; *Boutaric*, "Dr. seign." p. 390 (Decs. of Toulouse, 1558, etc.). Like the "taille," the "corvée" was sometimes real, sometimes personal; if real, it was due by every possessor of an estate situated in the seigniory, even by nobles and clerks, but the latter furnished substitutes.

[4] Repurchase, from the 1100 s. The "hauban" in the towns was a commutation tax. This word ("halbannum"), properly speaking, means requisition of those liable to the "corvée." Louis the Great and Philip Augustus authorized the craftsmen of Paris to pay an annual "hauban" in place of the "corvée." *Mortet, op. cit.*

[5] *Halthaus*, "Gloss. germ," see "Tote Hand," "Mainmorte," "Mortaille," "Echute" ("Todfall"), "Cattel" (capital).

[6] The English villein could be sold; the lord could take away his land at pleasure. Let us observe that, even in France, the serfs bound to the service of the seignior did not have tenements. In Brittany, *cf.* domain held under tenancy at will, p. 284, n. 2, concerning the right of "mote" and of "quevaize," N.R.H., 1895, 266 (tenures non-hereditary, unlike those of "roturiers," or copyholds).

[7] *Beaum.*, 45, 31; 12, 3: the serf could make his will for only 5 sous ("pro remedio animæ"). *Loysel*, 90, 92. BCh., 1873, 323. In the South: right to make a will in the seigniory. *Faber*, "Inst.," 1, 3, 2, 2.

main,[1] and this right was so characteristic of serfdom, that at the end of the "ancien régime" serfs were scarcely designated otherwise than as in mortmain ("**mainmortables**").[2] The serf therefore had only the use and enjoyment of the land that he cultivated; all right of testamentary disposition was lacking, and of course also the right of disposing it "inter vivos" [3] (sale, donation, etc.).

(B) *Restrictions on the Right of Mortmain.* (*a*) The principle of heredity was introduced under the cover of **family communities**; the community, being a moral person, never died and the family, so long as it was not extinguished, retained its tenement.[4] This was allowed, in particular, for the descendants of a serf, serfs like himself and living in common with him; separated children were, for the same reason, denied the right of succession, but if some of them, even one, remained at the paternal fireside, all profited by their presence, so it was finally decided. From the moment when the right of mortmain ceased to be exercised, all came to share in the division. Finally, the archaic condition of communal life ceased to be a matter of importance. (*b*) Other relatives succeeded equally, but in consideration of a payment [5] or by surrendering to the seignior one head of cattle ("Besthaupt," "mortuarium," bondage), which was also required sometimes of descendants themselves.[6] (*c*) Serfs who occupied estates ("serfs d'héritage"), by abandoning their servile tenure could acquire property over which there was no right of mortmain; on the contrary, all acquisitions by body serfs ("serfs de corps") reverted at their death to the seignior.[7] And so in these different rela-

[1] "Gr. C. de Fr.," p. 287; *Pasquier*, "Inst. de Justinian," ed. *Gir.*, p. 55.

[2] Aside from his tenement the serf could have other property, personal or real, acquired by economy. The ancient law allowed him to dispose only of his personal property as it was necessary for the needs of the administration. At his death, the seignior took everything, except enough to pay the debts of the serf on the acquisitions. *Cf.* "Et. de Saint Louis," I, 126; II, 4, 32. By the law of the second formation the serf was allowed to alienate "inter vivos" or even to dispose of by will property not comprised in his tenement. "Fors de Béarn," 189. *Beaum.*, 45, 33, 37: "pot li sers perdre et gaaignier par marceandise, et se pot vivre de ce qu'il à se volenté. . . . Et tant poent il bien avoir de segnorie en lor coyes qu'il aquierent à grief paine et à grant traveil." The serf could not acquire fiefs and, in the ancient law, "censives" were restricted to "roturiers." "T. A. C. Bourg.," 40 and following.

[3] "Franche-Comté," 13: the tenement alienated without the consent of the seignior reverted to him. [4] *Esmein*, p. 236.

[5] *Loysel*, 92, 101: "Un seul enfant en celle requeust (écarte) la mainmorte." "Celle," "cella," house. "Jostice," 12, 25, 2. *Desmares*, 236. "Bourg.," 9, 17; Nivern., 8, 7. *Esmein*, 237.

[6] *Loysel*, 95: "Argent rachète mortemaine."

[7] *Pothier*, "Tr. des personnes," 42.

tions the incapacity of serfs to transmit and inherit was mitigated. But the incapacity to alienate "inter vivos," at least outside the seigniory, still remained.[1]

§ 315. **Servile Communities,**[2] the débris of ancient collectivism, preserved in the poor and mountainous regions of central France,[3] as evidence of a social and economic state elsewhere vanished, have left their traces even to the present time. These communities supplied the deficiency due to the absence of commerce and industry by the exercise of all the trades; they bought only salt and iron. Whereas the condition of the isolated serf was wretched, they became well-to-do, paid their dues better, and by that means indemnified the seignior for the loss of the right of mortmain.

These communities, said Coquille in the 1500 s, were administered and governed by one alone, the "master of the community," elected by the members of the community. He commanded them, represented them in court, bound the community by his acts for the common interest as far as movables were concerned, and he alone prepared the "taille" and other tax rolls. The community ceased to exist when each had maintained a separate household for a year and a day. It was even said: "one gone, all gone," a rule which rendered the community so unstable that it served as an indication of the decadence of the institution.[4] Still prosperous in the 1500 s, these peasant societies were ruined in the 1700 s, a consequence of the suppression of mortmain and of economic changes. In 1783, in the provincial assembly of Berry, only their shortcomings were disclosed; they were the occasion of quarrels

[1] *Fleury*, "Inst. au dr. fr.," 219. Besides, it is said that the serfs could negotiate and contract freely like the Franks, and their wives had a dower.

[2] "Polypt. d'Irminon," 9. 215. Hamlets of serfs called "cellæ," near to the seigniorial château ("celleneuve," etc.). Phalanstery seen by *Masselin*, "Journal états gen. de 1484": "ego ipse domune unam ita institutam vidi ut essent illic decem matrimonia et septuaginta animæ." *Dareste*, p. 283. Formerly, says *Valin*, s. "la Rochelle," the "taisible" (tacit) community was universal in the kingdom. *L. Delisle, op. cit.*, 2, 33. *Beaumanoir*, vol. I, p. 305. *Loysel*, 92 and following (bibliog.), *Legrand d'Aussy*, "Voyage en Auvergne" (1787). *Dupin*, "Réquis.," vol. VI, 1840. *Doniol*, II, 2; III, 4; *Garsonnet*, pp. 511, 526 (foreign countries).

[3] Nivernais, Auvergne, Marche, Bourbonnais. *Boucomont*, "Mainmortes en Nivernais," thesis 1895; N.R.H., 1897, 766 ("A. C. de Nivern."). *Maron*, "La communauté des Jaults," 1890; *De Cheverry*, "Fermiers du Niv." in "Les Ouvr. des Deux-Mondes" of Le Play, vol. V; *Chartier*, thesis, 1885.

[4] *Loysel*, 75. Nivernais, 8, 9 and 15 and the community of *Guy Coquille*. It is admitted, in spite of the text of the "Coutume," that the community continued when one of the children left it in order to marry or to establish himself, or when he left it, excluded by his own fault.

and of lawsuits and involved the exploitation of some by the others.[1]

§ 316. **Mitigation of the Condition of the Serfs.** — The serfs who lived in communities enjoyed special advantages. As we have seen, from a very early time, servile incapacities disappearing in fragments, the condition of the serfs approached that of the "roturiers."[2] Mitigated serfdom, the only kind that the absolute monarchy had known, was sometimes designated as "mortmain" for the reason that of all the incapacities to which the serfs had been subject, mortmain was the principal one remaining.

§ 317. **How and when Serfdom Disappeared.**[3] — (A) **Individual emancipation** had taken place especially on the occasion of certain events, such as marriages, births, and the death of the seignior;[4] they were accordingly rare and their effect was offset by causes which reduced free men to serfdom; the serfs customarily gained from it only a limited liberty, because services and payments were still exacted from them.[5] Far from favoring them, the feudal law placed an obstacle in the way by not permitting the seignior to emancipate his serfs without the authorization of the suzerain; by doing it he abridged his own rights, prejudiced the rights of the suzerain, and, as in the case of amortization, there was need to purchase the consent of the superior seignior, with-

[1] These defects did not, in former times, prevent the communities from prospering. The true cause of their ruin was found in the change of social and economic conditions.

[2] *Cf.* the various "reductions" of the "Coutume" of Burgundy. In the 1700 s, Bouhier held that the seignior who abused his rights could be deprived of them by law. In 1556, *Dumoulin*, "Cons.," 17, saw the Picardians and the Normans depressed by exactions, although they were not serfs, emigrate to the Franche-Comté, a country of serfdom. *Championnière*, p. 493. In Russia, the serfs of small proprietors were miserable, the others, better treated; a great seignior, like Cheremetief, had as serfs millionaire merchants and he did not exploit them.

[3] *Du Cange*, "Gloss.," see "Manumissio"; *Luchaire*, "Man.," p. 320; *Darmstaedter*, "Die Befreiung der Leibeigenen in Savoyen, Schweiz und Lothringen," 1897; *Sugenheim*, "Gesch. d. Aufheb. d. Leibeigenschaft in Europa," 1861; *Salvioli*, 291. After the 1000 s, there were no more serfs in Normandy. *L. Delisle*, "Classe agric. en Norm.," p. 38. In England, the villeins or serfs also disappeared very early in the 1300 s. They formed a superior class in rural society; the yeomen (paying the electoral "cens" of four shillings of rent in freehold, 1450, etc.) disappeared in the 1700 s.

[4] Testament: free enfranchisement very rare apart from this case.

[5] The effect of enfranchisement varied with the terms of the act so that the serf sometimes gained very little by it and he therefore accepted it reluctantly. Having become free, even without restrictions, he rarely escaped the "taille" and the seigniorial "corvée." *Cf. Luchaire*, "Man.," 325. "Livre des serfs de Marmoutiers." But save for these exceptions, it may be said that he was subject only to fixed charges, like any free man. *Seignobos*, p. 148.

out which the enfranchised became the serf of the latter. It would have been necessary to proceed from seignior to seignior up to the king and to indemnify successively all the intermediate seigniors; but it was customary to stop at the regional sovereign, the grand local feudatory. In time the king intervened; the right of enfranchisement was, in the 1500 s, a royal or regalian right; it was no longer the rule to pay the price to the intermediate seignior, but to the king alone.[1]

(B) **General emancipation**, that is, enfranchisement "en masse" by the king, the Church, or the seigniors. Philip the Fair in 1298 and 1304 by two letters emancipated the serfs of Languedoc.[2] The most general and the most celebrated act was the ordinance of July, 1315, of Louis the Quarrelsome, emancipating the serfs on the royal domain in consideration of the payment of a sum of money.[3] From the beginning of the 1300 s, most of the serfs had become villeins. This was brought about in these ways: (*a*) Sometimes, especially for financial reasons,[4] the king, being short of money, sold liberty to his serfs and compelled them to buy it, as did Louis the Quarrelsome, who ordered that those who refused to purchase their freedom should be taxed according to their means. The seignior, seeing the serfs desert his lands in order to establish themselves in free places, forestalled their emigration by emancipating them.[5] (*b*) Sometimes they were emancipated for economic reasons, servile labor not being very profitable; two reapers of Middlesex, said John Stuart Mill, performed as much labor as six Russian serfs. (*c*) Sometimes they

[1] "Et. de Saint Louis," II, 32. *Beaumanoir*, 45, 18 and 26. *Loysel*, 91. "Droit et Const. of Champaigne," 17. *Cf.* "Livre des serfs de Marmoutiers," no. 73 (900 s); App. no. 1.

[2] Ord. XII, 335. *D. Vaissete*, X, 348, 403. Alphonse of Poitiers had already freed the serfs of Languedoc by testament in consideration of an annual payment.

[3] Ord. I, 653. The preamble was ambiguous concerning the word "Francs" and reproduced the commonplace subject: "according to the law of nature, everyone is born free" ("Inst. Just.," 1, 2, 2. *Beaum.*, 45, 32). The real thought of the king appeared in the mandate which followed the Ordonance. *Cf.* Ord. 1317, I, 653. Edict of March, 1543. *Vuitry*, "Et. sur le rég. financier," n.s. I, 48. The interest which the serfs had in becoming free sometimes led them to pay considerable sums in order to obtain their liberty. *Luchaire*, "Man.," 323; *Demante*, p. 73.

[4] Ord. 1315, etc.

[5] Charter of enfranchisement of the town of Gy by Hugues of Vienna, archbishop of Besançon, in 1347: when the seigniory is free, foreigners will come to establish themselves in it, it will be peopled, the vacant lands will be cultivated; those subject to mortmain are careless about working, because they work for others; the proceeds of mortmain when they come to the seignior are nearly all of little value. *Perreciot*, vol. 3, Proof, no. 126.

were emancipated for religious reasons.[1] Serfdom, which was half slavery, was regarded with the same feeling of reprobation as slavery properly speaking and public opinion demanded its abolition.[2] The movement, however, did not result in complete abolition of serfdom.[3] In 1789 there were still in France about 150,000 serfs, almost all belonging to the Church.[4] The celebrated suit between the chapter of Saint-Claude and the serfs of Mont-Jura, in 1775, led to the Edict of August 8, 1779, which abolished the right of pursuit everywhere in France but abolished mortmain only on the domains of the king.[5] Serfdom did not completely disappear in France until August 4, 1789.[6]

§ 318. **The Peasants in 1789.** — The legal condition of the serfs was ameliorated as the economic condition of the country improved. This condition itself too often varied with the times and places to justify us in considering it here.[7] We may only state

[1] *Beaumanoir*, 45, 32 (confusion between serfdom and slavery): "grant aumosne fet li sires qui les oste de servitute, et les met en francise, car c'est grans maus quant un crestiens est de serve condition." The Church no longer condemned bondage except slavery; according to the principle: "All power comes from God," it regarded slavery as a divine institution.

[2] N.R.H., 1883, 298.

[3] *G. Demante*, "Et. hist. sur les gens de cond. mainmort, au XVIIIe siècle," 1894; *Champion*, "La France d'ap. les cahiers de 1789," p. 218; *Chérest*, "La Chute de l'Anc. Rég.," 1883; *Finot*, N.R.H., 1881, 244 (Cherlieu); 1880, 217 (Luxeuil); *Chassin*, "L'Eglise et les derniers serfs," 1880; *Voltaire*, "Dict. philos.," see "Mainmortables."

[4] Which is explained by the relative mildness of ecclesiastical serfdom ("Il est bon d'habiter sous la croix") and by the fact that the Church, more wealthy than the seigniors, was not obliged to sell freedom to its serfs. Saint-Claude had 40,000 serfs.

[5] *Isambert*, 26, 139 (*cf.* "Table," see "Mainmortable"). Louis XVI persuaded the seigniors to follow his example by freeing their serfs. He did not believe that he was authorized to free them without allowing the seigniors an indemnity, which the state of his finances did not permit him to do. *Volux de Lamoignon*, p. 397. In Lorraine, Duke Leopold abolished serfdom in 1711 in return for a payment.

[6] Upon the demand of the Duke de Noailles and of the Duke de Larochefoucauld-Liancourt. The seigniors did not receive any indemnity, even for the tenements that the serfs kept. *Chassin*, p. 235: the last of the serfs before the National Assembly. Abolition of serfdom in Russia was enacted by the "ukase" of Feb. 19, 1861. This measure suddenly liberated 45,000,000 men, half of them on the domain of the crown, half on the lands of the seigniors. Alexander I gave to the Russian peasants, in addition to personal liberty, the ownership of lots of land corresponding somewhat to those which they possessed, but subject to the payment of an indemnity to the owner of the land, which they could not have done without the advances which they received from the State and which were to be reimbursable in forty-nine years at 6% interest. *Garsonnet*, p. 596; *A. Leroy-Beaulieu*, "L'Empire des Tsars," I, 380; *Kovalewsky*, "Le servage et son abolition en Russie" (N.R.H., 1889, 407). Germany: abolition of serfdom in Prussia, 1773; in Austria, 1781. *Grünberg*, "Die Bauernbefreiung" (Bohemia, etc.), 1894; *Knapp*, "Die Bauernbefreiung," see "Bauer." Italy: *Salvioli*, p. 292 (Piedmont, 1762).

[7] *Boutmy*, "Constit. Anglet.," p. 215: condition of the English peasant compared with that of the French peasant by Fortescue (1400 s).

that so far as the epoch upon which we are best informed is concerned, the end of the "ancien régime," there is much controversy and the evidence is contradictory. La Bruyère and Vauban have portrayed the situation of the rural inhabitants as the saddest at that time; foreigners who visited France in the 1700 s, basing their judgments upon comparison, were impressed with their prosperity (*e.g.* Lady Montague); Arthur Young (1787–1789) spoke sometimes of their misery and sometimes of their comforts.[1]

[1] *Cf.* *Boislile*, "Mém. des Intendants"; *Boulainvilliers*, "Etat de la France," 1727; *Boisguillebert*, "Détail de la France," 1712; *Vauban*, "Dîme royale"; *A. Babeau*, "Le village sous l'Ancien Régime," 1879; "La vie rurale dans l'ancienne France," 1883; *A. de Calonne*, "La vie agricole sous l'Anc. R. en Picardie et en Artois," 1883; *Abbé Mathieu*, "L'Anc. Rég. dans les prov. de Lorraine et de Barrois," 1879; *Brunetière*, "R. des Deux-Mondes," 1883, t. 56, p. 661; *Gasquet*, "Précis d. inst. pol. de l'Anc. Fr.," II, 302 (Auvergne); *Gautier de Biauzat*, "Doléances sur les surcharges que les gens du peuple supportent," 1788; *D'Avenel*, "La fortune privée à travers sept siècles," 1895; "J. des Sav.," 1880, 422; *Mège*, "Charges et contrib. des habit. de l'Auvergne à la fin de l'Anc. Rég.," 1898; *Cf. Baudrillart*, "Les populations agricoles de la France," 1885 et suiv., "Revue sociolog.," 1894, 129; "Journal de Voyage de Mme Craddock" (1783–1786).

CHAPTER VIII

THE PERIOD OF MONARCHY.[1] THE CONSTITUTIONAL MONARCHY

TOPIC 1. THE ROYAL POWER

TOPIC 2. TRANSMISSION OF THE ROYAL POWER

TOPIC 3. ACQUISITION AND LOSS OF THE CROWN

TOPIC 4. EXERCISE OF THE SOVEREIGNTY

TOPIC 5. THE ROYAL FAMILY

TOPIC 6. THE COURT

[1] BIBLIOGRAPHY: *Monod*, "Bibliog.," and *Lavisse and Rambaud*, "Hist. gén." Here are mentioned the purely historical works and documents.

The Feudal Epoch.—Luchaire, "Manuel des Inst. fr." (Capétiens directs), 1892 (bibliog. detailed); "Institutions monarchiques"; *Jourdain*, "La royauté fr. et le dr. populaire d'ap. les écrivains du M. A.," "Mém. Ac. Ins.," 28, 2, 97; *Viollet*, "Hist. des instit. politiq.," t. II; *Glasson*, t. VI, VII. Recent Monographs on the principal kings: *Pfister*, "Robert le Pieux," 1885; *Richard*, "Louis VII," 1872; *Williston-Walker*, "On the increase of royal power in France under Philip Augustus," 1883; *Petit Dutaillis*, "Louis VIII," 1892; *Beugnot*, "Essai s. les inst. de Saint Louis," 1821; *Langlois*, "Philippe III," 1887; *Boutaric*, "La France sous Philippe

TOPIC 1. THE ROYAL POWER

§ 319. **The Constitution.** — The question has been asked whether in former times France had a constitution.[1] Liberal opinion in the 1700 s answered the question in the negative, and to this absence of a constitution was attributed all the evil which existed.[2] It is certain that France had no written constitution; but the constitutional laws, like ordinary laws, may consist of

le Bel," 1861; "Saint Louis et Alfonse de Poitiers," 1870; *Lehugeur*, "Philippe le Long," 1898; *Benoist*, "Charles V," 1885; *de Beaucourt*, "Charles VII," 1881 *et seq.; Vallet de Viriville*, "Charles VII" (BCh., 1872).

The Monarchical Epoch. — *Cf.* the works of theorists like *Bodin, Gregory of Toulouse*, etc., where much information on ancient public law will be found. Consult also the Memoirs and Correspondence of statesmen like *Richelieu, Louis XIV, Colbert*, and others. *S. Goulart*, "Estat de la France s. Charles IX," 1578; *Besongne*, "L'Etat de la France" (since 1661); "Almanachs royaux" (since 1700); *Piganiol de La Force*, "N. Descript. de la Fr.," 1715; *Expilly*, "Dict. géogr.," 1768; *Waroquier*, "Etat général de la Fr.," 1789; *P. Boiteau*, "La Fr. en 1789," 1866 (2 éd., 1892); "Encyclop. méthodique," 1782–89; *Régnier de La Planche*, "Hist. de l'Estat de la France, 1559–60" (éd. P., Paris, 1836); "Respublica s. status Galliæ," 1626; *Fleury* (*l'abbé*), "Dr. public de la France," 1781, t. IV (*cf.* éd. *Darragon*, 1769); *Boulainvilliers*, "Hist. de l'anc. Gouvern. de la France," 1727; "Etat de la France," 1727; *Le Laboureur*, "Hist. du Gouvern. de la Fr.," 1743; *D'Argenson*, "Consid. s. le Gouvern. de la Fr.," 1764; *Garnier*, "De l'orig. du gouv. fr.," 1765; *Gautier de Sibert*, "Variations de la monarchie fr.," 1765; *De Brancas*, "Essai de Constitution," 1771; "Maximes de dr. public fr.," 1775; *Chabrit*, "De la monarchie br.," 1783; *Buat*, "Orig. de l'ancien Gouvern. de la Fr.," 1789; *Moreau*, "Principes de dr. public 1777–89"; "Expos. et déf. de la Constit. mon.," 1789; *Clos*, "Analyse des lois et usages du gouv. des Francs," 1790; *Sénac de Meilhan*, "Du Gouv. de la France avant 1789," 1814; *Montlosier*, "De la monarchie fr.," 1815; *Mlle de Lézardière*, "Théorie des lois politiques de la monarchie fr.," 1844; *P. Mesnard*, "Projet de gouvern. du duc de Bourgogne," 1860; *Lémontey*, "Essai s. l'établ. monarch. de Louis XIV," 1818; *Dareste* (de la Chavanne), "Hist. de l'administration en France, depuis Philippe-Auguste jusqu'à Louis XIV," 1848; *Chéruel*, "Hist. de l'admin. monarchique," 1855; "Dictionn. des Institutions," 1880, 5e éd.; "Admin. de Louis XIV," 1849; *Caillet*, "L'admin. en Fr. sous Richelieu," 1857; *D'Avenel*, "Richelieu," 1890; *G. Hanotaux*, "Hist. de Richelieu," 1893; "Tableau de la France en 1614," 1899; *P. Clément*, "Le gouvern. s. Louis XIV," 1848; "La Police," *id.*, 1866; *Lacour-Gayet*, "L'éducation politique de Louis XIV," 1898; *De Carné*, "Les fondateurs de l'Unité française," 1855; "La monarchie fr. au XVIIIe s.," 1859; *Capefigue*, "Hist. constit. et admin. de la Fr.," 1831; *Chérest*, "La chute de l'Anc. Régime," 1884–7; *Sépet*, "Prélimin. de la Révolution," 1890; *Rocquain*, "L'esprit révolution. avant la Révol.," 1878; *Raudot*, "La France avant la Révol.," 1841, 2e éd.; *Tocqueville*, "L'Ancien Régime et la Révol.," 1857; "Etat de la France en 1789," 1836; *Taine*, "Origines de la Fr. contemp.," t. I, 1875; *Pizard*, "La France en 1789," 1882; *Gasquet*, "Précis," 1885; *Canet*, "Les éléments de l'anc. Constit. fr.," 1885; *De Broc*, "La France s. l'Anc. Régime," 1886; *Kovalewski*, "Orig. de la démoc. fr.," 1895.

[1] *Esmein*, "Elém. de dr. constitutionnel," p. 391.

[2] For a contrary view, see *Joseph de Maistre*, very hostile to written constitutions.

customs, as is the case in contemporary England.[1] And so it was formerly in France. The French were not at all subject to a despotism like that of Turkey, although the contrary was sometimes affirmed; this would have implied that the caprice of the monarch was the only law.[2] This will be considered later. We may note here merely that all were in agreement in recognizing the existence of certain fundamental laws [3] to which the king himself was subject (for example, the rules of succession to the throne, the inalienability of the royal domain and independence as against the Church and the Empire, expressed in the rules: "the king is emperor in his kingdom" (Baldus) and "he holds only from God and by his sword"),[4] but they ceased to agree when it came to making a list of them; the absolutists reduced the number while the liberals increased them.

The vagueness, concerning which there was complaint, would have disappeared if tradition had given place to a charter, as, in general, written law was substituted for custom. But the drawing up of a constitution could not fail to be, whether this was desired or not, the occasion for profound reforms; yet instead of reforms there came the Revolution. We shall give a sketch of this constitution of monarchical France, confining ourselves to facts rather than to theories. Inconsistencies will not be lacking, because in

[1] Except for certain acts, 1679 ("habeas corpus"), 1689 (bill of rights), 1700 (act of settlement).

[2] *Loysel*, 19 (ed. *Dupin*): "Qui veut le roi, si veut la loi" ("What the king wills is law"). This does not mean that all that the king willed was law, but that there was no law contrary to the will of the king; such is, at least, the liberal interpretation of commentators upon Loysel. *Lacour-Gayet*, p. 401. De Bonald tries to show that the old régime was that of a liberal government.

[3] In considering as such only those which belong logically to the absolute monarchy, or which accommodate themselves to it, the enumeration given in the text is limitative. Concerning these laws, *cf. Le Bret*, "Souver. du roi," I, 4; *Dareste*, "Hotman," p. 75–87; *Savaron*, "De la souv.," 29; (*Lepaige*), "Lettres," 1753.

[4] The universal monarchy renewed by Rome in the Holy Empire went counter to the nationalist tendencies; the king of France did not acknowledge a superior. "E. de Saint Louis," I, 83; II, 14; *Loysel*, 20; *Innocent III*, X, 4, 17, 13: "Rex (Franciæ) superiorem in temporalibus minime recognoscit." Gloss: "de facto, de jure tamen subest Romano imperio." In this sense, the Gloss and Bartolus, concerning the law "Hostes D. de capt.," *Baldus*, 7, C., "de prob.," 4, 18, *Boutillier*, 2, 7 and the greater part of the French jurisconsults rejected the thesis of the dependence upon the empire; but the question was still disputed by *Le Bret*, "De la souv.," I, 3, at the beginning of the 1600 s. Louis XIV preoccupied himself with it in his "Memoires," ed. *Dreyss*, III, 451. *Degrassalius*, "Regal Fr.," I, 6; *P. Fournier*, "Bull. crit.," 1895, 544; *Viollet*, II, 40; *Esmein*, p. 339. So, also, the king of England. *Glasson*, IV, 78. *Cf. J. Bryce*, "The Holy Roman Empire"; *Bodin*, "Républ.," I, 9.

the constitutional practice of the "Ancien Régime" several tendencies made progress, none of which fully triumphed.[1]

Feudal monarchy, absolute monarchy, limited monarchy — such are the three political systems that one meets in France and in Europe.[2] The general tendency was in the direction of concentration and absolutism; the small federal States of the feudal period united to form great unified States, and in all these latter were established strong monarchies of an absolute type and a complicated administration. This evolution was sometimes very slow of realization (for example, in Sweden); sometimes it seemed to have made no progress and the feudal dismemberment lasted almost to our day (as in Germany). The ancient kingdom of Palestine perished from its feudal law, and long afterwards, Poland was disemembered because it had preserved these superannuated political forms. France is the type of a centralized and unified State. But at the very moment, when absolutism there attained its most complete development, England introduced a system of political liberty which was the point of departure for the public law of our day: Parliament always has the last word; the king reigns but does not govern.[3]

§ 320. **The Feudal Monarchy.**[4] — In the system of which the kingdom of Jerusalem offered the most perfect type, the king was rather the keystone of the feudal edifice than the sovereign of the kingdom; he was "primus inter pares," the chief of a federal State. Neither the territory nor the regalian rights were his exclusive property; they belonged equally to the seigniors. What did the king possess which did not belong to the seigniors? A

[1] *Cf.* the theorists cited.

[2] *Lavisse*, "Vue génér. de l'hist. polit. de l'Europe." *Cf.* the democratic or aristocratic régimes of the Italian republics, Switzerland, and Netherlands. Concerning German public law, *cf.* the collections of *Seckendorf*, 1694; *Schmauss*, 1722; *Moser*, 1737; *Mylius*, 1736; and the writings of *Hippol.*, of *Lapide* (Chemnitz), of *Monzambano* (*Pufendorf*), *Lavisse and Rambaud*, VI, 586, and VII, 944; *Camus and Dupin*, II, 623.

[3] *Cf. Pologne:* Const. "nihil novi," 1505: the king could not introduce innovations without the consent of the Senate and of the nuncios or deputies.

[4] *Luchaire*, p. 457; *Dodu*, "Inst. mon. d. le roy. de Jérusalem," 1894, shows the insufficiency and vices of the feudal State of Palestine. In Germany, the centralizing tendency failed; little by little the emperor found himself reduced to impotency; authority passed to the princes and the local sovereign.

[5] Some fiefs were dependent on the Empire (*P. Fournier*, "Le royaume d'Arles"); others were independent (kingdom of Navarre). The junction of the first to a unitarian State like France led to the severing of the feudal bonds that bound them to the Empire. *Esmein*, p. 315. Concerning the vassal king, *cf. Viollet*, II, 183.

title, memories,[1] and the support of the clergy; he drew his real strength from the extent of his domain. Furthermore it was the policy of the Capetian kings to annex to their possessions the domains of the great feudatories, independent fiefs.[2] Where they were not successful in substituting themselves in the place of the seigniors they despoiled them of their rights; in this way were gradually reconstituted the territorial unity and the rights of the State. In the prince, the feudal person, who was in the foreground in the beginning, effaced himself before the royal person. Even then the theories of feudalism were not without influence upon the public law: the king always considered himself as the chief of the nobility, the feudal sovereign, the universal overlord; by virtue of this title he dispossessed the seigniors of various rights (amortization, freehold) and secured for himself important seigniories (through confiscation, escheat, etc.); fiefs being patrimonial he was able to acquire them by purchase, marriage, and succession, as in the case of a private patrimony.[3]

§ 321. **The Absolute Monarchy.**[4] — The Roman idea of the unlimited power of the prince, of the concentration of all public authority in his hands, had not completely disappeared with the feudal system; thus the Church was influenced by it in attributing monarchical omnipotence to the Holy See. This idea came to the surface in French public law with the revival of the Roman law, and with the extension of the territorial domain which gave to the kings of France the material power without which their rights would have been reduced to vain pretensions, as were often those of the German Emperors. It was supported upon grounds of practical necessity and upon religious considerations. 1st, unity of command, indispensable during the long years when the national existence was at stake, made the people lose the habit of political liberty, and determined the destruction or humiliation of the rival powers, the nobility, the Church, and the communes. It was foreign politics which consolidated the monarchical power in

[1] In the legacy of the Carolingians one will understand the "arrière-ban" and the appeal to all the inhabitants when the country was in danger, and the guardianship of all the churches of the kingdom. *Esmein*, p. 343. *Cf.* England, "Prærogativa regis," under Edward III, *Glasson*, III, 65 (Inst. of Eng.).

[2] *Lognon*, "Atlas hist. de la Fr."; *Brunet*, "Abrégé chronol. des grands fiefs," 1769.

[3] *Himly*, "Hist. de la form. territ. des Etats de l'Europe centrale," 1876; *Dufayard*, "R. hist.," vol. 54 and 55; *Viollet*, II, 237.

[4] Theorists of absolute monarchy: *Bodin, Hobbes, Bossuet. Hanotaux*, "Et. hist. sur le 16e et le 17e s.," 1886 (Toulouse school and the diffusion of absolutist ideas). *Cf.* "Mémoires" of *Louis XIV*.

France. 2d, it was a tradition that royal authority came from God: the king was the vicar of God in temporal affairs as the pope was in spiritual matters;[1] but the authority of God being absolute, it appeared natural enough to regard the royal power in the same light. The person of the king was sacred; he was accountable only to God; his subjects had no more rights against him than the creature against its creator; but by an insufficient compensation, religion enjoined the king to devote himself to his subjects and it forbade him to oppress them.[2]

§ 322. **The Limited Monarchy.**[3]—Though the system of absolute monarchy by right divine prevailed until the Revolution, care was taken not to carry it to its extreme lengths. It was never a pure despotism, that is to say, one in which the arbitrary will and caprice of the king were imposed upon all without restrictions of any sort. By the mere fact that the territory of France was very extensive, the royal will encountered material obstacles which often rendered it powerless. The functionaries were not held to passive obedience to the same degree as they are to-day; they did not always execute the orders of the king,—sometimes from a spirit of independence, but more often through negligence. It was the same with subjects;[4] to such a degree was this true that the most absolute kings were less well obeyed than the humblest functionaries of the present day. It was therefore necessary to confirm, to recall to mind, to reiterate their edicts if they did not wish to see them remain dead letters.

A whole network of laws fettered the will of the king. It rested with him to abolish them, but the necessities of good administration and the interest of the king himself were opposed to this; the arbitrary will and caprice of the king therefore moved in a fairly small circle, outside which he was inspired only with the public interest, and conducted himself according to the general desire and not according to individual whims. Finally, the *fundamental*

[1] *Lacour-Gayet*, pp. 289 to 356; *Lavisse and Rambaud*, VI, 152 and following.

[2] *Viollet*, BCh., 1869, V, 129 (Instr. of Saint Louis to his son); *Cros.*, "Vrais enseign. de Saint Louis."

[3] *Loysel*, ed. *Dupin*, 1: hereditary monarchy limited by laws. Did the limited monarchy succeed the feudal monarchy as a transition to absolutism? Did it last from Philip the Fair to Henry IV? *D'Avenel*, "Richelieu," vol. I, and *Esmein*, p. 344. The facts scarcely admit of an affirmative answer, and I limit myself to saying that there were tendencies to establish it almost at all times. *Cf. Viollet*, II, 188, who cites *Fortescue*, "Govern. of England," c. 1 to 4.

[4] Public opinion was not without force: songs, riots, and barricades. *Tixier*, "Théories s. la souver. aux Etats de 1484," 1899.

laws, which may be compared to our constitutional laws, imposed restrictions upon the kings themselves.[1]

Other sources of resistance to the royal will, the clergy, the nobility, the cities, had retained, in the form of important privileges, the remains of their former rights, and new bodies of royal creation, like the Parliaments,[2] had likewise acquired prerogatives. If the king might in theory attack them, he most often in fact respected them. Out of these elements an attempt has been made to construct a true political system; not without difficulty, because on all points there were contradictory precedents. The liberal legists, like Guy Coquille, and the independent parliamentarians have maintained: 1st, that the king did not alone possess the legislative power, only those laws were valid which were made by the king during the sittings of his Estates or published and verified in the Parliaments; 2d, that taxes could be legally imposed only under the same condition.[3] These propositions were sometimes in accordance with the facts; in general, however, the royal authority succeeded in escaping from the control which the great organized Estates attempted to exercise over it.

§ 323. **Extent and Character of the Sovereignty.**[4] — In the absolutist system, the royal power, being an emanation of the divine power, had no other limits than the latter; the king, like God, had unfathomable designs; he allowed himself to be guided by reasons of State (régime of good pleasure).[5] The sovereignty

[1] *Loysel*, "Inst. Cout.," ed. *Dupin*, 1 and 19; *Pithou*, "Libertés de l'Eglise gallic"; *Bracton*, I, 8; "rex sub Deo et sub lege"; *Fortescue*, "De laudibus legum Angliæ," c. 9: the king of England could not change the laws of the kingdom without the consent of his subjects nor levy extraordinary taxes, *Glasson*, IV, 63.

[2] [Once for all, the reader may here be reminded that the French provincial "Parlements" were not legislative bodies, but appellate courts of justice primarily. — TRANSL.]

[3] *Loysel*, ed. *Dupin*, nos. 3, 14, 23; *Seyssel*, "La grande monarchie," 1541. Other more vague limitations upon the royal authority were the divine law and natural law. *Isambert*, XIV, 606.

[4] *Le Bret*, "De la souveraineté du roy," 1632; *F. Pithou*, "Tr. de la grandeur des droits des rois de France," 1587; *Savaron*, "Tr. de la souveraineté du roi," 1615; "Examen," 1615; *Savaron*, "Erreurs de l'examen," 1616; "De la souv. du roi," 1620; *L'Hommeau*, 1, 1; *De Paule la Garde*, "Tr. hist. de la souver. du roi," 1754 (same ed.); "Tr. hist. des droits du souverain en France," 1767, *Viollet*, II, 184.

[5] Personal power: secret diplomacy of the king (*De Broglie*, "Le secret du roi," 1879), "lettres de cachet" (arbitrary warrants), reserved justice, etc., *Loysel*, 19. Concerning the formula "du bon plaisir," *cf.* BCh., 1895, 226 (*V. Mortet*); *Cauvière*, "Le rég. du bon plaisir," 1893. Spain: "Es mi merced.," *Viollet*, II, 187, n. 2; *Lacour-Gayet*, p. 401; *La Bruyère*, "Du souverain." The secrecy of State affairs was explained in England, for a long time, by the fact that the parliamentary debates were not published; until 1771, only stolen reports could be made of them. *Boutmy*, "Dévelop. de la Const.," p. 157.

which he exercised was absolute, inalienable, and indivisible; it was not optional with him to divide it or to surrender it; he could only delegate the exercise of power which formed a part of it and the delegation could neither be perpetual nor complete.[1] This constituted a remarkable reaction against the feudal ideas regarding patrimoniality, and regarding the division and alienation of regalian rights. Of the principal attributes of sovereignty,[2] the right of peace and of war,[3] legislation,[4] military command, and, in general, the executive power, appointment of magistrates, the administration of justice, the pardoning power, the coining of money, the levy of taxes, and police of the Church,[5] not one belonged fully to the feudal king. He made few laws and those which he issued were hardly ever enforced outside the royal domain; he had no national army; outside his own domain he did not administer justice, or levy taxes, or appoint magistrates, or coin money (countries under the dominion of the king, countries not under the dominion of the king).[6] However, his mission, as it was set forth in his oath, solemnly pronounced at his coronation and such as the Carolingians had been able to draw up, required

[1] Fleury maintains that no officer had all the public power over a portion of territory; a separation of powers made headway on this account in the interest of the king, through hate of feudalism, and in the interest of the subjects, through fear of abuse.

[2] Ord. May, 1372 (V, 475): Instrs. concerning the royal rights in the town of Montpellier. *Lavisse*, "R. hist.," 26, 233; *L'Hommeau*, "Maximes," 1, 1; *Loysel*, "Inst. cout.," ed. *Dupin*. (At the head, the editors had enumerated the principal articles of the customary constitution of monarchical France.) *Cf. Le Bret, Degrassalius*, etc.

[3] Diplomatic relations: *De Villiers-Hotman*, "L'Ambassadeur," taken from the treatise of *Ch. Pascal* on this subject (*Colomiès*, "Op.," 1709, p. 472). *Dumont*, "Corps diplom. et du dr. des gens," 1726; *Flassan*, "Hist. de la diplom. fr.," 1808.

[4] *Beaum.*, 35, 29; *Loysel*, 19; *Luchaire*, p. 487; *Esmein*, p. 476; *Petiet*, "Le pouvoir legisl. en Fr. dep. Philippe le Bel jusqu'à 1789," 1892; *Viollet*, II, 189; *A. Babeau*, "Préambules des Ord.," 1896 (Ac. sc. mor.).

[5] Add. *Grotius*, "De imperio summæ potest. circa sacra," 1648. *Luchaire*, p. 565 (bibliog.); *Perrens*, "L'Eglise et l'Etat en France sous Henri IV," 1882; "Recueils des Edits, etc., pour l'extirp. de la R. P. R.," 1885 (ed. div. 1686 to 1752); *Talon*, "Autor. des rois touch. l'Eglise," 1700; *Fra Paolo*, "Les droits des souverains," 1721 (French translation).

[6] "Pays d'obéissance du roy et Pays hors l'obéissance du roy" ("Etabl. de Saint Louis," I, 11). The countries subject to the king were the region over which Hugh Capet was feudal suzerain before being king: the duchy of France, the king being here immediate feudal seignior, according to the feudal law itself. The country not subject to the king comprised chiefly the six large fiefs, Normandy, Burgundy, Aquitaine, Toulouse, Flanders, and Champagne. In these feudal principalities, the king was only mediate seignior in relation to the vassals of the great feudatories; he did not have direct right over them. *Luchaire*, II, 29, criticizes this distinction. It was equivalent, in sum, to the distinction between the domain of the crown and that of the great fiefs which were almost independent, in fact, of the king. *Viollet*, "Et.," IV, 384.

him to protect the Church, to render justice (and by consequence, to maintain order and peace),[1] and, finally, to defend the kingdom.[2] The first Capetians were far from carrying out this program, after all rather vague. We have seen how, gradually, the rights of the kings grew and were bound together into this inseparable pile of which Bodin and the imperialists constructed the "majesté" or sovereignty.[3] From the 1500 s, the king, the incarnation of the State, had, both in theory and in fact, all the attributes of supreme power ("I am the State").

To the two essential functions of the State, defense without and justice within, the monarchy added police power,[4] or surveillance over morals (sumptuary laws,[5] prohibitions on games of chance, etc.) and over the events of economic life (regulation of commerce, industry, etc.).[6] What was the extent of this right? It had no legal limits; the Carolingian legislation touched many matters which appear to us as falling within the domain of individual liberty. The "Ancien Régime" did not forbear to conform to this tradition.

§ 324. **Political Rights.** — Subjects had no share in the exercise of sovereignty; they possessed no political rights;[7] it was to the

[1] Where the royal authority was powerless, there were established institutions like the Spanish "Sainte Hermandad" (brotherhood, confederation of towns) to maintain peace, and to repress brigandage. *Cf.* "Capitul," 2, 46.

[2] *Cf.* German, *Blondel*, "Fréd. II," 35; England, *Bracton*, 3, 9, etc.; *Boutmy*, "Dévelop. de la Const. en Anglet."; *Glasson*, IV, 78, and V, 1° (analysis of the royal prerogative): the king cannot do wrong, he is irresponsible, he cannot be incapable of governing, therefore, he cannot be a minor, he is the sole owner of the English soil, he summons and dissolves Parliament, appoints peers, converts bills into laws by his sanction, appoints public officers, he is the visible head of the Church, he is deemed to be present in all the courts of justice, suits cannot be brought against him by any one, he is head of the army, etc.

[3] Bodin reasons juridically; he does not perceive the genesis of his doctrine, of which he makes a kind of geometric theorem.

[4] *Fleury*, p. 99; *De La Mare*, "Tr. de la Police," 1707–38; *Fréminville*, "Dict. de la Police," 1756, 1775; *Lemoyne*, *id.*, 1786; *Peuchet*, *id.*, 1789.

[5] BCh., 3d cent. V., 176. *Baudrillart*, "Hist. du Luxe," 2d edit., 1880; Theses: *Dubost*, 1888; *Bauthion*, 1891, etc.; *Isamb.*, "Table."

[6] The Old Régime had its state industries like the post office. Edict of Louis XI, June 19, 1464. *Dareste*, II, 187. Post office established by Cromwell, 1657. In Germany the postal service was granted "en fief" to the seignior of Taxis, 1615. *Schulte*, p. 313. Royal manufactures, *Dareste*, II, p. 216. *Cf.* Monopolies of the commercial companies of the colonies. *Pauliat*, "Louis XIV et la Compagnie des Indes or.," 1886; *Fagniez*, "L'industrie en France sous Henri IV"; "R. hist.," 1883; "L'Econ. sociale de la France s. Henri IV," 1887. State monopolies were numerous and were found in most countries: Spain, monopoly of alcohol under the Bourbons, monopoly of tobacco; England, under Elizabeth, monopolies so numerous that complaint was made.

[7] *Cf.* Etats gén. *Challomel*, "Hist. de la liberté en Fr.," 1886; *De Carné*, "Hist. de la liberté politique en France."

king that all these rights belonged. The passive obedience (" nicht raisonniren ") to which they were held was closely enough allied with the divine right.[1] They did not even have the right of individual or collective resistance against the king when he failed in his duties. In England, on the contrary, they had: 1st, political rights, a share in the government, thanks to the representative system;[2] 2d, the right of insurrection or resistance against arbitrary acts of the royal authority.[3]

§ 325. **Individual Rights.**[4] — In France the individual not only did not enjoy political rights, but he lacked those necessary intangible liberties with which the Revolution has since endowed our country and which England took care to preserve and develop. Liberty and property, said Voltaire, were the invention of the English; they are well worth " Montjoye et Saint Denys." In France, security was afforded by a powerful administrative organism; the English relied more upon themselves and less upon the State. Neither the English nor the French possessed civil equality.

1st, **Individual liberty**[5] had no guarantees against arbitrary

[1] Without being a forced consequence of it, for God could divide the power.

[2] *Cf.* (" Les monarchomaques ") French ed. p. 404. *Douarche*, " de Tyrannicidio," 1888. After the revolution of 1688, the king had to convoke Parliament every year in order that it might vote the budget for the maintenance of the army; he alone could neither make the laws nor suspend the execution of the laws voted by Parliament. This organization rendered useless the right of resistance recognized by the Great Charter (Art. 61) (right of the barons and the country to seize the castles, the lands, and the goods of the king) and the right which Blackstone accorded to every English subject whose rights were attacked, to complain to the judges, to petition the king and Parliament, and finally to procure arms for his legitimate defense and to use them in case of need (*cf.* insurrection of the English colonies of America). In Hungary, the oath of the king recognized the right of insurrection by subjects.

[3] Junius Brutus held that subjects did not owe obedience to the orders of the king when they were contrary to the law of God, that insurrection was a right and a duty of the subject, not only in this case, but even against the king who oppressed the state (usurper, tyrant "absque titulo"), and even against the legitimate king who abused his power (tyrant "ab exercitio"). *Touchard*, "De politica Hub. Langueti," 1898. *Treumann*, "Die Monarchomachen," 1895.

[4] *Esmein*, "Dr. constitut.," p. 369; *Hauriou*, "Droit admin.," 3d ed.

[5] *Cf. Lacour-Gayet*, p. 426, concerning the question whether the king had the right of life and death over private individuals. *Lavisse and Rambaud*, V, 659 (Spain).

Article 39 of the Great Charter forbade the seizure or imprisonment of a free man or the taking of his property or exiling him. The king could proceed against him only "per legale judicium parium suorum vel per legem terræ." From that time, there were no arbitrary arrests, no specially created courts. The most simple means for one who was arrested arbitrarily was to apply for or to cause application to be made for a writ of habeas corpus, to the High Court of Justice. The writ was so called warrants of imprisonment ("lettres de cachet"),[1] arbitrary arrests,[2] justice by commissioners,[3] or accusations for "lèse-majesté."[4] There was nothing which resembled the inviolability of domicile of the English law.[5]

2d, **Private property** was no more sheltered than the individual from arbitrary measures: general confiscation,[6] expropriation without indemnity, excessive taxes[7] and dues demanded by the king in pursuance of his right of eminent domain. Nor did anything guarantee to individuals respect for their mutual engagements. In maintaining that the king had no right to take the property of others or to violate private agreements[8] Bodin invoked

because it began with these words: "Habeas corpus ad subjiciendum"; it was necessary, in reality, to produce the detained person before the Court, in order that it might pass upon the validity of the arrest. *Coke*, "Inst.," 4, 182. The Act of Charles II removed the objections of the judges and the jailers which rendered the "habeas corpus" too often illusive (immediate liberty, or, at least, provisional liberty under bond); it allowed opposition to it in case of sequestration by private individuals or public officers, and even on the order of the prince. An Act of George III extended these rules of arrest to cases of misdemeanors or arrests under all other pretexts (abduction, confinement in a lunatic asylum). At times of crises, Parliament has sometimes suspended the application of these laws (*cf.* State of siege). Connected with "habeas corpus" was the prohibition of compelling an Englishman to leave the kingdom (except soldiers and sailors). Parliament alone could banish any one. On the other hand, for a long time, the king could forbid his subjects to leave England without his permission. *Cf.* "R. hist.," 1892, L. 1, "Abjuratio regni."

[1] Issued for political motives or in the interest of families. Under the ministry of La Villière, they were sold for twenty-five louis. *Malesherbes*, "Remontr. de la C. des Aides," 1770: No one was great enough to be shielded from the hatred of a minister, nor small enough not to be worthy of that of a tax farmer's clerk. *Joly*, "L. de cachet de la Génér. de Caen," 1889; *Marion*, "Ac. sc. mor." (there exists in the Nat. Arch. a file of "lettres de cachet" in white), 1898. BCh., 1894, 227, 361 (Bastille). Concerning the Bastille, *cf.* *Ravaisson*, "Archives de la Bastille," 1868–86; *Bournon*, "Notice s. la Bast.," 1885; *Funck-Brentano*, "Légendes et Arch. de la Bastille," 1898; "Bibliog. crit. de la Prise de la Bastille," 1899.

[2] Bassompierre, Lauzun, the Count Mattioli or the Mask of Iron (minister of the Duke of Mantua, accused of having revealed our State secrets to our enemies and arrested in a foreign country). *R. de Maulde*, "Procéd. polit. s. Louis XII," "R. hist.," 31, 111, and 43, 100. Assassinations of Concini, Monaldeschi.

[3] Marshal de Marillac, etc.

[4] *Cf.* Law of suspects, incivism under the Revolution.

[5] The tempest may beat upon it and the rain may penetrate the cabin of the English peasant, but the king cannot enter it. (Lord Chatham): "My house is my castle."

[6] Abolished by the Charter of 1814, Art. 66, this punishment affected innocent people, the family of the culprit, and it was abused, for "after having confiscated one's property because he was condemned, he was condemned in order that his property might be confiscated."

[7] *Cf.* "Finances" *infra* and my study on "Cl. Joly," p. 39.

[8] *Cf.* above "Alod," p. 291. Had the king the ownership of the land of the state as he possessed sovereignty over it? If he did, the consequence would have been that he could have taken possession of it in a general way

natural law; but the positive legislation did not afford in a like case any means of defense to subjects against the king.

3d, **Freedom of labor, of commerce, and of industry** existed only imperfectly; it was shackled by a multitude of regulations.

4th, **Liberty of conscience** unknown, State religion, persecution of non-conformists, tutelage of the Gallican Church in such a manner as to transform the parish priests into administrative agents; — such was the "Ancien Régime."[1]

5th, In place of **liberty of the press** the "Ancien Régime" did not cease to push to excess a system at once preventive and repressive; previous authorization was required for publishing every writing,[2] a censorship was exercised by the Parliaments, the Sorbonne, the clergy, and the council of State, and heavy penalties imposed[3] against libels. The violation

by arbitrarily increasing the taxes, and specially, by appropriating for himself the lands at his convenience. The first question alone concerns us. A passage in the "Mémoires" of Louis XIV has been misconstrued as affirming that the king was the universal owner: "The kings were absolute lords, and naturally had full and free disposition of all property, secular as well as ecclesiastical, and the right to use it according to the needs of the State." (Ed. *Dreyss*, I, 177; II, 288.) Louis XIV wished simply to protest (as appears from the context) against the claims of the clergy to be relieved from contributing to the expenses of the State. He did not speak with the precision of a lawyer. If he had believed that the property of his subjects belonged to him, it would not have been understood that P. Tellier had affirmed his pretensions in order to destroy the scruples that had arisen in his mind against the imposition of the tax of the tithe. The anecdote related by Saint Simon must be true, in the main. As for the words of P. Tellier, it was a current phrase, to which it is necessary to add the following in order to be exact in law: "in case they were indispensable for the needs of the State." The view of the jurists of the Sorbonne is not known. *Saint Simon*, "Mém.," IX, 44 (ed. 1829). Villeroy to the infant Louis XV: "the people are yours," a phrase of a courtier, from which one would be wrong in drawing judicial conclusions. See, concerning the question, *Lacour-Gayet*, p. 426. In England, the king had the eminent domain over all lands without exception.

[1] The English law was no more tolerant: witness the oath of supremacy (of the State over the Church) under Elizabeth, 1562; persecution of Catholics and Puritans; Test Oath Act, 1673 (whoever aspired to a public office was forced to renounce the dogma of transubstantiation), and the Act of 1661 by which no one could be mayor, etc., if he had not taken communion in the year, according to the rites of the Anglican church. For the "draconic" Acts against the papists, *cf. Blackstone*, IV, 55, and the treatment inflicted on the Protestants in France. Catholics were not relieved of the incapacities by which they were excluded from office until 1829.

[2] In 1631, Théophrastus Renaudot founded the "Gazette" (a weekly journal) which Richelieu supported and directed. *Isambert*, "Table," see "Imprimerie," "Librairie," etc.; *D'Avenel*, I, 145; *Peignot*, "Essai hist. s. la lib. d'écrire," 1832; *De Luçay*, "Sécrét. d'Etat," p. 470.

[3] Same rigorous régime in England. Milton wrote against the censorship of the press, but that institution was suppressed only in 1695. Penal laws against libel fell into desuetude, the judges always acquitting, and private persons hesitating to invoke the protection of such laws because of the outrages to which they gave rise. Thus was established liberty of the press. *Boutmy*, 152.

of the secrecy of correspondence had always existed since the establishment of the postal service.[1]

6th, With greater reason the "Ancien Régime" did not recognize the right of association, of assembly, the liberty of instruction, etc.

TOPIC 2. TRANSMISSION OF THE ROYAL POWER[2]

§ 326. **Transmission of the Royal Power.** — The Capetians, who came to the throne by election, abolished this system by associating their eldest sons with themselves on the throne[3] (*cf.* the Roman Empire, Augustus and Cæsar); this association was practiced until the time of Philip Augustus, that is to say, during two centuries. From this custom arose the rule of monarchical heredity. The system of election left traces only in the ceremonies of consecration.[4] The question was no longer disputed, except for a moment in the 1500s by the pen of Hotman and in the doctrines of the Leaguers.[5] However if the exercise of royal power was a public function, a magistracy, the exercise of which implied a certain capacity, election would seem to be more suitable than heredity.[6] The latter principle supposed the patrimoniality of

[1] Louis XV created a special organ to inspect letters, chiefly in order to obtain information concerning scandalous letters ("Black Cabinet"). Decis. of the Cons., Aug. 10, 1775. Suppression July 9 and Aug. 22, 1790. But after 1791, it reappeared for international correspondence. Concerning the present law, *cf.* "Gr. Encycl.," see "Cabinet." In England, a statute of Queen Anne forbade violation of the secrecy of letters.

[2] *Du Tillet*, "Recueil des rois de Fr.," 1618; *Duchesne*, "Les antiquités des rois," 1669; *Le P. Anselme*, "Hist. généalog. de la maison royale," 1726.

[3] *Luchaire*, p. 464; *Viollet*, II, 22 (bibl. p. 262). *M. Sepet*, "R. q. hist.," 1870.

[4] *Esmein*, p. 317, and the other authors whom he cites. *Yves de Chartres*, "Ep.," 189, considered the monarchy as being at the same time hereditary and elective.

[5] *Isamb.*, XI, 25; Jourdain, "La royauté fr.," Mém. Ac. Inscr. 28, 2, 97. *Hotman*, "Franco-Gallia," 1573, held that the crown of France had been elective (Carolingians, Capetians) and showed that in the Middle Ages, election was still the common law of Europe (Germany, Sweden, Denmark, etc,). *Cf.* England, *Glasson*, IV, 67. At Jerusalem, the king was elected by an assemblage of seigniors and prelates. The same was true of the election of the Emperor, but beginning with the 1300s, the electors were reduced to a closed college of seven members. "Saxon Mirror," "Lehnr.," 42; *cf.* "Landr.," 3, 52. The "Golden Bull," c. 2. For the Empire, heredity was combined in a certain measure with election; at Jerusalem, it was in the end done away with. *Dodu*, "Inst. du roy. de J.," p. 106. The elective principle had been a cause of weakness, as in Poland, where the Const. of May 3, 1791, introduced heredity; until then, it is said, this country was "an anarchy tempered by confederations." Concerning the Empire, *cf. Blondel*, "Fréd. II," p. 28; *Schulte*, p. 199; *Schröder*, p. 466 (bibl.).

[6] The elective monarchy was reproached with enfeebling the royal power, because the person elected depended upon the elector (Ex: "Wahl-

the crown; the kingdom, considered as the personal property of the sovereign, was transmitted from father to son like an inheritance (*cf.* patrimoniality of fiefs).[1] Nevertheless, the succession to the crown differed in certain respects from ordinary succession; the idea of office was combined with that of patrimoniality, to establish in the interest of the dynasty certain rules to which the king could not go contrary:[2] the indivisibility of the kingdom, the right of primogeniture and the exclusion of females. It was not permissible to him to disinherit his natural heirs ("non habent ab ipso patre, sed a consuetudine regni"), nor to dispose of it by testament for the benefit of strangers; nor had the heir the right to renounce the crown during his lifetime.[3]

§ 327. **Indivisibility of the Kingdom.** — According to the Salic Law, said Loysel (p. 638), the kingdoms, duchies, counties, marquisates, and baronies could not be dismembered. The Salic Law could have been here only the old French custom, dating from the treaty of Verdun in 843 and allied in different epochs with different ideas, — the unity of the imperial title, the theory of the

capitulationen" in Germany, "Pacta conventa" in Poland, etc.), with weakening the kingdom, because the elections were a pretext for dissensions and quarrels. *Guy Coquille*, in *Loysel*, ed. *Dupin*, no. 1, said: The monarchy was confered by lineage and not by election, which is fortunate, for elections often engender civil wars, and ordinarily are characterized by plots and bribery, where the strongest and shrewdest and richest ordinarily have more power than the best and most generous men. Hugh Capet was king by legitimate vocation. Guy Coquille finds two arguments with which to support the rights of the Capetians: 1st, the consent of the princes and seigniors and of the people of the three orders; 2d, their descent in the direct masculine line from the Merovingians who had established the monarchy by true conquest, while Charles Martel was a usurper. (*Duplessis-Mornay*), "Disc. s. le droit prétendu du duc de Guise sur la couronne de France," 1583; *Bodin*, 6, 5; *Greg. Tolos.*, 73; *Lacour-Gayet*, p. 390.

[1] Heredity created traditions of government which the royal family preserve: it assures a political education and a preparation for public affairs which are lacking in other systems; if the reigning prince governs only in theory, the royal family often directs him in fact; the vexatious effects which the hazard of birth sometimes produce are thus corrected. In France, it facilitated the constant growth of the royal domain and strengthened the royalty against rival powers. *Cf. Germany*: *Blondel*, "Et. comp. s. le dévelop. constitutionnel de la France et de l'Allemagne" ("Rev. int. de l'Enseign.," 1891).

[2] *L'Hommeau*, "Maximes," 6: not held for the debts of their predecessors.

[3] The ancient successoral system of private law also led to these conclusions: the patrimony was the property of the family rather than of the individual; disinheritance, testament, renunciation of future inheritance were not recognized. But when the private law was changed, these rules were maintained for political reasons in public law. On this last point, *cf. Esmein*, p. 323; *Dumoulin*, s. "Paris," 1, 13 and following; *Viollet*, II, 85. On the case of Charles VII, *cf. Isambert*, VIII, 650; *Du Tillet*, "Rec. de Traitez," ed. 1602, p. 197.

fief, the association (of the living heir) with the occupant of the throne (constantly practiced for the profit of one alone), and the modern conception of the State.[1]

§ 328. **Right of Primogeniture** (an ancient rule in England and Spain; more recent in Germany; Prussia, "dispositio achillea," 1473; Austria, 1584). From the time when the kingdom became indivisible it was necessary to restrict the succession to one alone of the relatives of the deceased king.[2] It was conferred upon the eldest of his legitimate sons[3] in preference to any of the younger brothers who had only appanages.[4] The right of primogeniture was established by custom, the first Capetians having always followed the practice of associating their eldest son with themselves on the throne. The right of representation was allowed without limit in the direct as well in the collateral line; thus the most distant relative of the eldest branch was preferred to the nearest member of the younger branch.[5]

§ 329. **Exclusion of Women (Salic Law).**[6]—The kingdom did not descend by the female line,—another rule founded on custom only, but more ancient than primogeniture. Under the first two dynasties no woman ever put forward a claim to the crown; this old custom was strengthened under the third dynasty through the practice of association on the throne of the eldest son. The custom was supported by debatable considerations like the following: in manly hands the royal authority would seem stronger; if women were permitted to succeed to the throne there would be danger of the crown passing to a foreigner through marriage.[7] The question of the right of women to succeed was raised for the first time

[1] *Cf. Bodin*, 6, 5.

[2] Otherwise one would have had to admit the existence of a comonarchy, *cf.* coseigniories.

[3] "Regna non ascendunt": no succession of ascendants. *Cf.* above, Fiefs. *Dumoulin*, s. "Paris," 1, 13, 1; *Bodin*, 6, 5. *Greg. Tolos.*, 7, 5.

[4] *Loysel*, 611. *Cf. Majorat, Séniorat*, above. *Viollet*, II, 53. "Tanistry," p. 433.

[5] *Loysel*, 326. Henry IV was preferred to his uncle, the Cardinal of Bourbon; he was the son of the cardinal's older brother and consequently a distant relative of Henry III. Writings of *François* and of *Antoine Hotman*. *Dareste*, "Hotman," p. 86.

[6] *Laboulaye*, "Condit. des femmes," book 5. "Bibliog." in *Viollet*, I, 247; II, 55; *Servois*, "Bull. Soc. hist. Fr.," 1864. *Esmein*, p. 318. *Cf.* following, from 1311, exclusion of women from succession to appanages.

[7] The history of other countries throws doubt upon the value of these reasons given by our former jurisconsults. *Cf. Viollet*, II, 81: "If the French heir had been a relative through women, and the English pretendant a relative through males, our public law, modeling itself on the interests of the country, would not have failed to proclaim the right of women." Rights of women at Jerusalem, *Dodu*, p. 120; *Rolbag*, "Certamen masculo fœmineum," 1602; *Bodin*, 6, 5; *Greg. Tolos.*, 7, 11.

in 1316 at the death of Louis the Quarrelsome; three times within a few years, 1316, 1322, and 1328, it was decided for the exclusion of women, and in 1328 males were excluded whose right to succeed was derived through the female line[1] (the agnatic system);[2] Philip of Valois, first cousin of Charles IV, the Fair, by his father Charles of Valois, brother of Philip the Fair, was preferred to Edward III, king of England, nephew of Charles the Fair by his mother Isabella, daughter of Philip the Fair, although the latter was the nearest relative. The assemblies of barons and prelates, the University of Paris, and even the papacy itself (1340) pronounced in favor of these principles by adhering to the old usage.[3] Nevertheless, the succession of women was admitted in the case of fiefs,[4] and they enjoyed the right of succession to the crown in various countries (Navarre, Jerusalem, England, Castille, etc.) without its being a source of weakness to the State.[5] But it may be remarked that they have always been excluded from the succession to the Empire.

§ 330. **Extinction of the Dynasty.** — Such a case never having arisen in France, it is difficult to say whether the leaning would have been toward the system of patrimoniality which would have allowed the king to adopt a successor and designate him by testament, or whether a return would have been made to the elective system. In default of selection by adoption or by testamentary designation, the latter method would have been the only one possible.[6]

[1] "Lib. Feud.," 2, 11; *Beaumanoir*, 14, 28; *Loysel*, 325. "Vindiciæ gallicæ," 1639. Where the mother had no rights, the children likewise had none. In order to understand this idea recorded in the chroniclers, it is necessary to remember that, according to the old law, the woman left her natural family by marriage; she thereby lost all right of succession, and her children belonging also to a different family, had no more rights than she.

[2] Feudal law, German princely law: 1st, the agnatic system, excluding women and descendants through the female line, or cognates. However, in default of males, the crown passed to the "Erbtochter" but the succession immediately became again agnatic (Maria-Theresa); 2d, subsidiary succession of women, in default of men of the same degree; 3d, cognatic succession, where women and descendants through the female line succeed the same as males.

[3] "Songe du Verger," I, c. 142 (Fr. text). "Memoirs of the Pope," *cf. Viollet, op. cit.*

[4] *Viollet*, II, 58 (Louis X admitted that the daughters of Philip the Long should succeed to his appanage by virtue of natural law).

[5] England, *Glasson*, "Hist. des Inst. de l'Angl.," IV, 67; V, 67.

[6] *Dumoulin*, s. "Paris," 1, 13, 3, 9; *Bodin*, 6, 5; *Greg. Tolos.*, 7, 12.

TOPIC 3. ACQUISITION AND LOSS OF THE CROWN

§ 331. **The Coronation.**[1] — The crown being hereditary should have passed "ipso facto" without formality from the dead sovereign to his successor. There was, however, a widespread belief that the king became really king only by coronation (Charles VII and Joan of Arc). In the act of coronation usages persisted which gave rise to changes of dynasty and the intervention of the Church and of the people. An accident (for example, the extinction of the reigning family) would have sufficed to give it the significance of an ecclesiastical investiture or of a popular election. But far as it had been from being such, the ceremony of coronation degenerated more and more into a simple formality, a solemn installation of the new king, already invested with his title.[2]

The coronation[3] included three parts: (*a*) the supposed *election* by the clergy, the nobility, and the people assembled together;[4] the archbishop of Rheims proclaimed as king the heir to the throne ("elegit eum in regem") and the spectators acclaimed him: "laudamus, volumus, fiat." The bishops never failed to ask the spectators if they accepted the heir to the throne as their king; but at the coronation of Louis XIV in place of the acclamations there was a respectful silence.[5] Before being thus proclaimed the

[1] *Luchaire*, no. 249 (bibliog.); *Leber*, "Du sacre," 1825; *Clausel de Coussergues*, "Du sacre," 1825; *Dupuy*, "Majorités," p. 11; *Prou*, "Gr. Encycl.," see "Couronnement" (and the bibliography, particularly for foreign countries); "Hist. des sacres," 1721; *Th. and Denys Godefroy*, "Le cérémonial français," 1649; *Du Mont and Rousset*, "Cérémonial des cours de l'Europe," 1739; BCh., 1893, p. 45; *Viollet*, II, 50.

[2] *Loyseau*, "Offic.," 1, 10, 58. "Vind. gall.," 63. *Du Tillet*, "Rec. des rois de Fr.," p. 261: the beginning of the reign was at first reckoned from the day of coronation and not from the death of the predecessor. *Dupuy*, "Majorités," ch. 2. In the 1500s, the deputies of the Estates wished to withdraw under the pretext that the king who had convoked them was dead. Charles VI, Decl., April 1404; Edict of Dec. 26, 1407; Decree of 1498; *Lucius* (*Duluc*), "Placitorum," 3, 3; *Loysel*, 21; *Isambert*, XI, 33. *Cf.* concerning the importance of the coronation in Germany, *Blondel*, "Fréd. II," p. 33.

[3] Minutes of the coronation of Philip I ("Hist. de Fr.," XI, 32). "Mitth. d. Inst. f. oest. Gesch.," vol. 19; *Linder*, "L'electio et la laudatio" (in France and in Germany). *D. Martène*, "De antiq. Ecclesiæ rit.," II, 596; *Langlois*, "Phil. III," 55.

[4] Convocation at the coronation of prelates and barons: what was the procedure? what personages were convoked? During the monarchical epoch, the "baillis" and seneschals proclaimed the solemnities of the coronation, in order that the municipal magistrates of the town might attend. A delegation from the Parliaments was sent to the coronation of Henry IV. There was never present a regular representation of the State, although numbers of the three Estates attended.

[5] The consent of the people was demanded by the bishops. Coronation of Charles the Bald in 869. "Capit.," II, 337. *Cf. Viollet*, II, 51, 1.

king took an oath[1] to preserve the rights of the Church and to render justice to all.[2] (*b*) *Anointment* with oil from the holy phial,[3] consecration of the king, as if the royalty were a sacrament or a priesthood.[4] (*c*) The *coronation* proper, the actual taking

[1] The oath of the king contained two principal clauses: 1st, to preserve the honor of the Church, according to the terms of the Capitularies; 2d, to render justice. Saint Louis, the first, swore to exterminate heretics, which signified expulsion rather than putting to death (however, both were done). *Cf.* "4th council of the Lateran," 1215, c. 3. Louis XIV and Louis XVI swore not to pardon duellists. *Cf. Isamb.*, XV, 3, 22. Charles X, Napoleon I. Oaths of the kings of England: they bound themselves to preserve the rights of the Church and the integrity of the kingdom, to maintain good order and render justice and to preserve the laws and customs. Since the reign of William and Mary, they have sworn to maintain the Protestant religion. The relations between the sovereign and subjects is derived from the oath of allegiance that every Englishman must take after he is twelve years old, but which he scarcely ever takes until he accepts an office. On his side, the king takes an oath at the time of his coronation; if he refuses to take it, the refusal is considered as equivalent to an abdication. The single fact of failure to take the oath does not necessitate the deposition of the king; the jurisconsults demand a combination of circumstances for deposition, such as that which brought about the downfall of James II (it was a precedent): attempt to overthrow the constitution, violation of the fundamental pact, abandonment of the kingdom. The conversion to a religion other than the State religion involved the loss of the throne; also, marriage to a Catholic woman; this was equivalent to an abdication. *Cf. Isamb.*, 44. Arragon: "we make you king on condition that you maintain our liberties; otherwise, not."

[2] "Hæc populo christiano et mihi subdito in Christi promitto nomine: In primis ut Ecclesiæ Dei omnis populus Christianus veram pacem, nostro arbitrio in omni tempore servet. Item, ut omnes rapacitates et omnes iniquitates omnibus gradibus interdicam. Item, ut in omnibus judiciis æquitatem et misericordiam præcipiam; ut mihi et vobis indulgeat suam misericordiam clemens et misericors Deus. Item, de terra mea ac jurisdictione mihi subdita universos hæreticos ab Ecclesia denotatos pro viribus bona fide exterminare studebo. Hæc omnia supradicta firmo juramento: Sic me Deus adjuvet et hæc sancta Dei Evangelia." *Clausel de Coussergues* ("Coronation of Louis XIV"), p. 494 et seq (xxxii). *Cf.* "Hist. de Fr.," XI, 32 (coronation of Phil. I). *Godefroy, I*, 76. *Savaron*, "De la souv.," p. 38. Under Charles V, clause: "et superioritatem, jura et nobilitates coronæ Franciæ inviolabiter custodiam et illa non transportabo nec alienabo." *Bodin*, I, 8 (p. 136, ed. 1580). Balde asks if the king of France may alienate a city of the kingdom "invitis civibus"; "respondeo non," he says, "secundum Hostiensem." *Savaron, ibid.*, p. 168 (texts). *Degrassalius*, p. 37.

[3] The coronation took place ordinarily at Rheims, where Clovis was baptized. The oil (or "balm") of Saint Ampoule was reputed to have been brought from heaven by an angel for the baptism of Clovis. Rhul, a delegate to the National Convention, publicly smashed the holy vessel, in 1793; but it was claimed afterwards that a small part of this holy ointment had been saved, and it was used for the coronation of Charles X. *Clausel de Coussergues*, p. 93. *Cf. Degrassalius*, "Regal.," 10 and following. "Vindiciæ gallicæ," c. 2 and following.

[4] *Cf.* the coronation of the bishops, *Chérnel*, "Dict. des inst.," see "Evêque," "Chrême." The person of the king was sacred and inviolable in France as well as in England (*Glasson*, "Angl.," IV, 78; he could not be sued in the courts. *Cf. Bodin*, p. 158. A consequence of his doubly holy character: cure of the king's evil ("Ecronelles"). "Gr.

possession of the crown: the king clothed himself with the insignia of his dignity which were borne with solemnity by the principal seigniors.[1]

§ 332. **Seizin.** — The maxim of the private law: "the dead puts the living in possession," had its analogy in the axiom of public law: "the king never dies," or, "the king is dead, long live the king."[2] The new king succeeded his predecessor without interruption; he acquired immediately the enjoyment and exercise of his rights. The association on the throne of the eldest son practised by the first Capetians favored the adoption of this rule. The inconvenience resulting from a vacancy on the throne caused it to be accepted even in elective monarchies; the new king was considered to have succeeded his predecessor from the moment of the latter's death.

§ 333. **Effects of the Acquisition.** — 1st, The successor had the same titles[3] and the same rights as his predecessor; as a matter of law his person continued. The acts of the king were considered as those of the State; consequently they bound all those who occupied the throne and there was no need to confirm them at the accession of the new prince. But this did not prevent the successor from modifying the existing laws. In this respect there was no "lex in perpetuum valituva." From the moment that the royal power was regarded as an office these very simple principles were introduced with some difficulty. The successor to the throne did not always respect the engagements of his predecessors, and he was therefore frequently called upon to confirm them.[4]

2d, The union in full right of the lands which belonged to the prince at the time of his accession with the crown domain was a necessity, since this domain was also his patrimony and the same

Encyc." *Guibert de Nogent* speaks of it regarding Louis the Fat. The kings of England, having taken the title of kings of France, touched scrofulous people ("les scrouelles") (from the time of Henry IV to Queen Anne).

[1] Under the 3d dynasty, ecclesiastical peers and laics supported the crown (from what time?) while under the 2d dynasty the bishops alone crowned the king. At the coronation of the king of England, the office of Lord High Steward was revived for one day, also that of High Constable. The king receives the homage of the bishops and peers. *Isamb.*, XI, 273.

[2] *Loysel*, 21. In England, it seems that at first the taking possession of the throne by the heir was required; but as he was, at a given moment, in Palestine, the course of justice was interrupted until his return. Veritable anarchy prevailed. The old rule had to be abandoned. *Cf.* for the papacy, Clement V, 1307; *Dupuy*, "Major." I.

[3] Titles of the king, *Viollet*, II, 96.

[4] *Cf. Esmein*, p. 324, n. 1, and other authors whom he cites; *Bodin*, 1, 8; 4, 4; 5, 6; *Loyseau*, "Offices," 2, 2, 34; *Isamb.*, XII, 1. Privileges conceded on the occasion of a happy event. *Isamb.*, XIV, 3; *Greg. Tolos.*, 9, 1, 34.

person could not possess two.[1] But when the sovereign and the private person were distinguished in the prince, and when the State was no longer regarded as his personal property,[2] the private domain of the prince and the domain of the crown would have to be distinguished, as is done in modern public law (that is to say, the possessions acquired in the manner of an ordinary individual and those acquired as king).[3] Under Louis XII and under Henry IV an attempt was made to introduce this distinction but without success;[4] the tradition swept it aside (Edict of 1607) and the system of annexation of fiefs, which had increased the royal power, operated in this case. It was on the principle that everything the king acquired belonged to the crown.

§ 334. **Loss of the Crown.** — The title of the king was not ineffaceable like that of a consecrated person, although it was sometimes claimed to be. The crown could be lost in certain cases: 1st, by **abdication**; (*a*) through refusal of the dignity of king by him who was called to succeed;[5] (*b*) by abdication, properly speaking, of one who had been king; this might be unconditional (this is the only kind permitted in modern law),[6] or with the reservation of certain rights (which was contrary to the theory of the indivisibility of the sovereignty), or, finally, in favor of some one else (which was equally inadmissible, because the principle of heredity could not be modified even by an absolute king, since this would have been the suicide of the monarchy[7]).

[1] *Chopin*, "De doman.," 1, 2, 13; *Le Bret*, "Souverain.," 3, 1; *De Beloy*, "Dissert. s. l'Edit de 1607"; "Dict. des Domaines," II, 83 and following; *Brillon*, "Dict. des Arrêts," see "Dom.," Mémoires of 1738, 1760 which are here cited. *Cf.* below, "Domaines"; *Esmein*, p. 332 (divergent views); *Bodin*, VI, 2, p. 866, ed. 1588.

[2] The distinction is made, for debts, by *Bodin*, I, 8; *L'Hommeau*, I, 6.

[3] The appanagist becoming chief of the dynasty, there was greater reason for uniting the appanage possessions with the crown; these lands had been detached from it. The Ord. of Dec. 31, 1316, applied this idea. *Isambert*, III, 150; Ord. XI, 444. *Luchaire*, p. 485. It will be observed, moreover, that the greater part of the lands of princes of the royal family were derived from the crown.

[4] Louis XII, 1509; Henry IV, letters of 1590, 1596; Edict of July, 1607 (*cf.* Ord. 1413), Decree July 16, 1567; Jan. 9, 1679. *Cf.* in modern times, property of Orléans given by Louis-Philippe to his children at the time the crown was bestowed on him (Aug. 7, 1830). Will of the duke of Bourbon, the last of the Condés, in favor of the duke of Aumale (1829).

[5] If done when the reigning king was alive, it would be void.

[6] According to which, the royal authority is an office and not a patrimony.

[7] Tacit abdication: renunciation by the prince when the constitution requires that he be the adherent of a particular confession. Charles the Fifth, Marie Stuart, Napoleon, Charles X, Louis-Philippe. *Cf. Isamb.*, XII, 237. (Francis I, prisoner at Madrid, issued an edict that the Dauphin would be anointed and crowned.)

2d, by **deposition.** Deposition was incompatible with hereditary right. There was no superior power, like the Church, which could release subjects from their oaths of allegiance. As for the nation represented by the Estates of the kingdom, it no more had the right to depose the king, under the pretext, for example, that he did not fulfill his duties, than it had the right to elect him.[1]

TOPIC 4. EXERCISE OF THE SOVEREIGNTY

§ 335. **Exercise of the Royal Power.** — The king governed personally and could not delegate the sovereign power.[2] However, if he was incapable, in law or in fact, of exercising his authority[3] a regency was established. The case in which the king was a minor was distinguished from the more abnormal cases in which he was ill, insane, or absent. Even mental incapacity and physical weakness are matters of degree, and a procedure had to be organized for the purpose of deciding upon the necessity of a regency or for its cessation; there existed nothing of the kind during the "ancien régime."[4] If the disability was of short duration (absence or illness) no regent was appointed but the king charged his successor or a minister to replace him temporarily; this representative had only limited powers which were always revocable, and he could act only in accordance with the instructions which he had received.[5] Sometimes the royal power was exercised by a usurper, in which case all his acts were binding upon the legitimate dynasty like those of a regent, unless they were directed specifically against the lawful dynasty and against its rights.[6]

§ 336. **The Majority of the King**[7] had been fixed at the begin-

[1] In 1327, deposition of Edward II by Parliament. In 1830, deposition of the duke of Brunswick for incapacity. *Franqueville*, "Gouv. brit.," I, 199.

[2] At least as a whole; the functionaries had only partial delegations of authority and could do nothing more than execute the will of the king.

[3] Grave infirmities, incurable disease, and madness were at first causes of exclusion from the throne. "Golden Bull," 6 to 25. As to tender age, *cf.* Charles the Simple and "Eudes.," *Greg. Tolos.*, "De Repub.," 7, 6. Vicars of the Empire in case of vacancy on the throne. *Schulte*, p. 211; *P. Fournier*, "Roy. d'Arles," p. 477.

[4] *Cf.* modern constitutions. Madness of Charles VI.

[5] The Dauphin replaced Louis XV, at the time of the "attentat" of Damiens. In times of crises, a lieutenant general of the kingdom was found, *e.g.* Guise, after the battle of Saint Quentin, 1558; Mayenne at the time of the League. Louis Philippe bore this title from July 29 to Aug. 7, 1830. *Isamb.*, XI, 6, 276.

[6] These acts could not be annulled (*e.g.* laws, treaties) without producing the most inadmissible consequences; the life of a nation cannot be interrupted.

[7] *Dupuy*, "Tr. de la majorité de nos rois et des regences du royaume," 1655, 1722; *Guyot*, "Offices," I, 77; *Bréquigny*, "Mém. Ac. Inscr.,"

ning of the fourteenth year, after some hesitation [1] (1271, 1374).[2] If this was a precocious age it was a means of avoiding the inconveniences of long regencies,[3] with the troubles which they involved and the dangers to which the legitimate heir was exposed by the ambition of the regent.[4]

§ 337. **The Appointment of the Regent.**[5]—Following the example of private guardianship, which was legitimate, conferred by law, will, or appointment, the regent was selected: 1st, according to the law of blood relationship, the heir presumptive to the crown (the nearest agnate);[6] 2d, by will,[7] or by letters of the king to the queen mother,[8] to the princes of the blood, or to certain seigniors;[9]

50, 520; *Luchaire*, 468; *Glasson*, V, 293; *Viollet*, II, 86 (bibl., p. 262). *Cf. Hotman*, "Franco-Gallia," c. 19.

[1] Under the first two races it was twelve and fourteen years respectively. There was no fixed rule under the first Capetians. Saint Louis attained his majority at twenty-one years ("regna feudis æquiparantur"), as did the nobles). The "roturier" majority of fourteen years was preferred (*cf. Waitz*, VI, 215). At Jerusalem, it was fifteen years. *Dodu*, p. 123. Ord. dec. 1271 (I, 295). Const. of 1791, 2, 1: eighteen years.

[2] Ord., XI, 349; VI, 26. Same motive for preferring the beginning of the year to the end of the year. (Ord. 1271.) *Dupuy*, II, 64, referred to the "L. ad. rempubl." Dig., "de muner."

[3] Must the coronation take place at the time of the attainment of the prince's majority or at the time of his accession? There was some hesitation. Ord. 1374. But conforming to the principle of seizin, Charles VI, April, 1403, declared that the king would be crowned at the earliest moment. Variations afterwards. *Dupuy*, I, 13.

[4] The declaration of the majority of kings in a "bed of justice" (*e.g.* Charles IX) was not indispensable.

[5] Law of 1842 concerning the regency. *Isamb.*, "Table," see "Régence." *Dupuy*, vol. II, p. 415 (bibliog.). In England, since the (1700s), the office of regent has been filled by Parliament. *Franqueville*, "Gouv. britann.," I, 179.

[6] *Cf.* for Jerusalem, *Dodu*, p. 124 (queen, agnate, election). Duke of Orléans, 1715–22. Uncle of Charles VI, 1380–85. Charles reigned during the captivity of John the Good. Germany, "Golden Bull," 7, 4: the nearest major agnate. Prussian const., Art. 56. Several constitutions exclude women from the regency (*e.g.* Prussia and Saxony). The greater number leave the rights to the mother or to the grandmother, sometimes in default of agnates (*e.g.* Bavaria and Würtemberg), sometimes in preference to agnates, at least if they have not remarried (Gotha). *Isamb.*, XI, 24.

[7] The agnatic system is followed in several German States without regard to the will of the defunct king; in default of agnates, the regency is provided for by law. In England, Parliament does this.

[8] The queen-mother has the care of the person of the king and of his education; it is natural enough that she should exercise the regency, the more so, as there is no fear that she will attempt to take possession of the throne, for women are excluded from it. Was she regent by right to the exclusion of princes of the blood (*cf. Dodu*, p. 124)? Controv. *Le Bret*, I, 6, Grandmothers, aunts, sisters of the king were likewise regents. *Laboulaye*, "Condition des femmes," 1841. Francis I, going to Italy, appointed his mother regent by Letters patents, 1515, *Isamb.*, XII, 38, 210; XIII, 340.

[9] *Beaudouin* V, Count of Flanders, tutor of Philip I ("regni procurator et bajulus").

3d, the same persons following designation or confirmation by great governmental bodies.[1]

§ 338. **Powers of the Regent.** — Private law distinguished the trust organized in the interest of the ward, from the temporary right giving to the holder almost all the rights of a proprietor. A similar distinction is found in public law.[2] (A.) The regent governed in his personal name,[3] made ordinances in his own name, and affixed his seal to warrants and pardons. The guardianship of the king's person did not belong to him (except when the queen was regent).[4] (B.) The declaration of April, 1403, and the Edict of December 26, 1407, established a different system. The minor king exercised the royal powers[5] as far as possible; it was in his name that acts of government were performed. Already before this time, the institution of a council of regency had served as a means by which the kings limited the authority of regents.[6]

[1] Assembly of Etampes: *Suger*, 1147. In 1316 an assembly of barons and prelates gave the title of regent to Philip the Long. Estates of Tours, 1484. In 1610, Parliament gave the regency to Marie de Medici, according to the probable wish of Henry IV; in 1643, it annulled all restrictions upon the power of Anne of Austria; the duke of Orléans was lieutenant-general of the kingdom; in 1715, the duke of Orléans also caused to be annulled, in the same way, the will of Louis XIV; Saint Simon maintains that an assembly of peers ought to have intervened. *Cf. Viollet*, II, 91.

[2] *Loysel*, 21. The title of regent ("regens regnum") seems to have been borne for the first time by Philip the Long. Ord. 1357. *Cf. Loysel*, 176.

[3] "Golden Bull," 7, 4. In 1614, the Elector Palatin being a minor, the guardianship belonged to the duke des Deux-Ponts, his uncle, who acted as though he were himself the Elector. *Dupuy*, c. 5. Pledge, oath, *cf. Dupuy, passim.*

[4] In 1374, Charles V intrusted the guardianship to the queen, and the regency to the duke of Anjou, his brother. According to the will of Louis XIV, the duke of Maine was given the guardianship and the duke of Orléans the regency. *Cf.* Modern constitutions. Ordinarily, the King could by will arrange for the guardianship of his minor heir.

[5] Louis XIV at the age of four years personally supported a rule in regard to the "taille." Louis XV, some days after the death of Louis XIV, held a "bed of justice" in which he confirmed the rights of the regent. In English law, the king is never a minor. *Cf. Bodin*, p. 158.

[6] Testament of Philip Augustus, 1190 (limitations of the regency). *Cf.* Louis VII and *Suger*. 1270: thirteen persons, 1374, 1392. "Procès. verb. du C. de régence de Charles VIII," unedited document, 1836. Testament of Louis XIV, eleven members, but the regent modified the composition of it. *Cf. Dupuy*, "Preuves," II, 263. *Isambert*, XVII, 1°. *Cf.* Modern constitutions. In Bavaria, the council of regency was composed of all the ministers; in Wurtemberg, of all the major princes. The powers of the regent were also formally limited here; they were less than those of the king.

TOPIC 5. THE ROYAL FAMILY

§ 339. **The Royal Family**, a close community, often having a special and archaic law, was composed of the reigning prince, his wife, princes, and princesses who were connected with the royal house by bonds of legitimate relationship, their wives and their widows. The princesses left it on marrying to become members of the families of their husbands.[1] The head of the reigning house exercised over all its members an authority analogous to the domestic power of the head of the family in ancient law. His consent was necessary before they could marry.[2] He instituted and supervised the guardianship of the incapable, and exercised control over the court of the princes and princesses. He had the right to take the necessary measures to maintain the peace and honor of the reigning family. On such an occasion he exercised over the members a disciplinary power the extent of which was fixed by custom.[3]

§ 340. **The Queen.** — (*a*) During the life of the king she was not the equal of her husband; however, to a certain extent she shared the crown;[4] she was consecrated[5] and crowned like him, had a seal, a house, officers, and revenues, but she did not intervene officially in the affairs of the kingdom.[6] (*b*) Upon the death

[1] It is especially in Germany that the internal constitutions of princely families ("Hochadelige Familie") have been studied. *Gierke*, "Die jurist Personlichk. d. hochadl. Hauses," 1862; *Schulze* in the "Rechtslexikon" of Holtzendorff. In that country, family law is better regulated than in France, where it is very vague. In Germany, the head of the family has fewer rights. A family council, composed of all major agnates limits his authority; it intervenes in cases where family discipline is involved, it watches over the conservation of the family patrimony, and authorizes the transfer of it, decides upon the establishment of guardianship over incapables, legislates on family rights, etc. ("Hausgesetze").

[2] *Le Bret*, "Souverain.," I, 8. *Cf. Isambert*, XI, 447.

[3] Prohibition of misalliances ("Ebenbürtigkeit," equality of condition): there was no misalliance in a marriage between members of reigning families (or formerly reigning) in Germany or outside of Germany (the Bonapartes, the Bernadottes, for example). Each house could act contrary to the principle of "Ebenbürtigkeit" and transform a misalliance into a regular marriage. In Russia, Statute of March 20, 1820. In England, *cf.* "Royal Marriage Act" of 1772 (no question of misalliance).

[4] Under the first races, she had the custody of the treasure, and the direction of the palace as mistress of the house. *Cf.* for the Capetians, *Luchaire*, p. 477; *Viollet*, II, 87; *Isamb.*, 12, 18. England, *Glasson*, IV, 71 (the queen was a "feme sole"). *Cf.* the situation of the prince consort in England.

[5] With special cream. "Capit.," II, 426.

[6] However, under the first Capetians, she signed the royal charters, as well as the heir presumptive. Some honorary prerogatives were: precedence, she could plead by attorney like the king; she had days by turn in the Parliaments as did dukes, peers, etc.

of the king the widow was often guardian or regent; she received certain lands as a dowry, but (according to the old law) did not live in community of goods.[1]

§ 341. **The Dauphin.** — The eldest son of the king of France[2] bore the title of Dauphin after 1349,[3] the date of the annexation of Dauphiny to the Crown.

(A) *The system of association with the crown.* The first Capetians regularly associated their eldest sons with themselves on the throne, and had them crowned during the life of the king, in order to avoid any attempt to change the dynasty through election.[4] The powers of the associate king[5] were not well defined, but, officially, he was almost the equal of his father. (B) The dynasty once consolidated, at the end of the 1200s, the policy of association on the throne was abandoned; the prince royal henceforth played no official rôle; he could be regent and could govern when the king was a prisoner; and he attended the council of the king upon the attainment of an age fixed by the king. But he was a subject;[6] "the king had no companion in his royal majesty."[7]

§ 342. **Other Members of the Royal Family (princes of the blood).** —The younger sons received an appanage,[8] the daughters a marriage portion or dowry in money. The only right recognized as be-

[1] *Isambert*, "Table," see "Reines." *Loysel*, 111. Ord. of Blois, Art. 350, 352. *Fleury*, p. 350; *Laboulaye*, "Cond. des femmes," p. 193; *Donet d'Arcq.*, "Comptes de l'argenterie des rois de France," 1874; *Luchaire*, p. 480; *Le Bret*, I, 6.

[2] Concerning the determination of the eldest son, *cf. Dumoulin*, on "Paris," I, 13; *Greg. Tolos.*, 7, 9.

[3] *Prudhomme*, BCh., 1893, p. 429. In Auvergne and in Dauphiny, the word "Delphinus," employed first as the Christian name, became a patronymic name, then a title of dignity (about 1282). The county of Vienna and of Albon became the "Delphinatus Viennensis"; the county of Clermont, the Dauphiny of Auvergne. England: Prince of Wales. *Glasson*, VI, 25; IV, 73.

[4] *Luchaire*, p. 465: sometimes the coronation was preceded by a solemn "designatio," participated in by the bishops and grandees. (Louis the Fat), Rôle of the "designatio" in Germany, *Waitz*, VI, 129.

[5] His name appears on the royal charters; the grandees swore fidelity to him, as also to the queen. *Cartellieri*, "Philipp, August," 1899, vol. I.

[6] The son of Louis XIV was the first to be called "Monseigneur." Saint Simon says also that, in assemblies of the clergy, the bishops "Monseigneuri-saient," contrary to the old custom that required one to say "Monsieur." *Chéruel*, "Dict. des Inst."

[7] *Loysel*, 22, *cf.* 2. "Mém." of Louis XIV, ed. *Dreyss*, II, 10; *Le Bret*, I, 7.

[8] *Cf.* following "Apanages." BCh., 4th s., IV, 473. From the time of Gaston of Orléans, brother of Louis XIII, the first brother of the king was called "Monsieur." His wife was called "Madame." All the daughters of France were called "Madame" (for ex., "Madame Royale," etc.). *Fleury*, p. 152; *Isamb.*, XI, 447. Dotations in England.

longing to them[1] aside from honorary prerogatives and the power which came from their appanages, was to hold the regency.[2]

Topic 6. The Court

§ 343. **Its Composition.** — The court was composed of two elements: 1st, the court nobility and the functionaries of the central administration. Centralization caused the nobility to desert the provinces and flock to the court, the only place where privileges, pensions, and dignities could be obtained.

2d, The household of the king (and of the queen and the princes) was subdivided into a civil and a military household[3] and included the various services attached to the person of the king.[4]

§ 344. **The Ceremonial.**—For this numerous body of courtiers and servants discipline was necessary. The etiquette or ceremonial[5] was nothing more than this discipline, but with a rigidity and minutiæ which would have made it grotesque if the service of the king had not taken on the aspect of a cult. The king himself was the slave of etiquette; it was a means of keeping him away from the crowd of subjects (" major e longinquo ").

[1] *Cf. Isamb.*, XI, 20, 24; XIII, 465; XVII, 11. *Le Bret*, 1, 7; *Degrassalius*, p. 320: the sons of the king did not pay taxes, as the king and queen did not. *Cf.* below, "Capitation."

[2] Illegitimate children were not members of the royal family. Louis XIV declared the Duke of Maine and the Count of Toulouse princes of the blood, Aug. 2, 1714, and the 23d May, 1715, sons of France. *Greg. Tolos.*, 7, 8; *Dumoulin*, s. "Paris," 13, 1, 33.

[3] The civil household, at the end of the 1700 s, did not comprise less than twenty-two departments (with a personnel of 4,000 men). It included the almonry, the grand house, the king's chamber, the king's wardrobe, the king's cooks (pantry, butlery, etc.), large stables, small stables, the kennel, falconry, wolf hunt, etc. The offices of the king's house were very much sought after; in 1789, the Prince of Condé was grand master, the Duke of Bouillon, grand chamberlain, the Duke of Richelieu, first gentleman of the chamber. Concerning the king's household ("hospitium regis") in the 1200 s, see *Luchaire*, p. 531 (bibliog.); *Boiteau*, ch. VI.

[4] Concerning the courtier, *cf. Castiglione*, 1528; *Gracian*, 1687; *Faret*, 1636; *du Refuge*, 1617. *Spanheim*, "Relation de la Cour de France," 1690.

[5] Concerning the juridical side of the ceremonial, see *Ihering*, "Zweck im Recht." Details in *Monin*, "Gr. Encycl.," see "Etiquette." The ceremonial was very ancient (the Egyptian king Pepi I allowed his general Ouna to keep his sandals on in his presence) but it was developed in Europe with the triumph of the absolute monarchy. The Castilians, naturally formal, were the first to abolish familiarity from the life of princes. At Washington, when the President of the United States holds a reception, any one who looks respectable may go and shake hands with him. *Comtesse de Genlis*, "Dict. des etiq. de la Cour," 1818; *Th. Godefroy*, "Le Cérémonial fr.," 1649.

§ 345. **Political Rôle of the Court.** — Without official character and without official rights, the court had none the less an occult power, as also the family of the king; it produced by its intrigues the downfall of ministers, it set itself against reforms (Turgot had no more implacable adversary), and it ruined the budget. In 1789 many persons attributed to it all the evils from which France suffered.[1]

[1] *Cf. Montesquieu*, "Esprit des lois," 3, 3; *D. Argenson*, etc.

CHAPTER IX

THE MONARCHICAL PERIOD (*Continued*). THE STATES-GENERAL AND THE PROVINCIAL ESTATES

TOPIC 1. THE STATES-GENERAL

TOPIC 2. ASSEMBLIES OF NOTABLES

TOPIC 3. THE PROVINCIAL ESTATES

TOPIC 4. PROVINCIAL ASSEMBLIES

§ 346. **The Legislative Power** [1] of the king was greatly limited in the beginning of the feudal epoch: 1st, the law being mainly customary, there was little occasion for legislation (except for the granting of privileges and the making of some police and administrative regulations); [2] 2d, outside the crown domain, the law, which was the exclusive work of the king, was not binding; the great feudal lords, themselves giving laws on their own domains, could receive or reject the king's law; moreover, it was not unusual to secure their consent in advance; [3] 3d, finally, the king took up very few important matters without consulting the officers, barons,

[1] *Viollet*, II, p. 189 (bibliog., p. 264); *Esmein*, p. 476; *Petiet*, "Du pouv. législ. en France dep. Phil. le Bel, jq. 1789;" 1891; *Flammermont*, "De concessu legis . . . XIIIe s.," 1883; *Luchaire*, p. 487; *A. Babeau*, "Préamb. des Ord.," 1896 (Ac. sc. mor).

[2] *Viollet*, II, 199.

[3] *Petiet*, p. 79 and following; *Viollet*, II, 192. Ord., I, 44; XI, 291. Concerning the Ord. of 1223, *cf. Petiet*, p. 48. "Et. de Saint Louis," I, 26. *Beaumanoir*, "Const. du Châtelet."

or prelates who formed his court ("de consilio baronum," "prælatorum").[1] By the 1500 s the principles were quite the opposite.

1st, The king legislated upon all matters, and written law was developing and encroaching more and more upon customary law. From the time of Philip the Fair, legislation in the form of ordinances had become very abundant (relating to questions of public utility and reform of the kingdom).

2d, The royal laws were binding throughout the kingdom and the seigniors lost local legislative authority. (A) There was a tendency toward the first result by the time of the 1200 s when Philip Augustus directed that his orders should be proclaimed in Champagne. His successors undertook to compel the great feudal nobles to execute certain of their ordinances even when the latter had not accepted them. Beaumanoir affirms that in his time the general enactments of the king should "run everywhere throughout the kingdom." This was the formula of the future law and it came to accord more and more with the facts.[2] (B) Statutes ("établissements") or general laws were rare; by making them obligatory upon the lands of the feudal lords the king reduced their legislative power, but they retained the right to make special or local laws analogous to those enacted by the king for his own domain. By the 1500 s even this right had disappeared, and there remained only insignificant vestiges of it.[3]

3d, The laws were regarded as the personal work of the king. This last point, however, calls for some observations.

According to the Roman principle, so often invoked during the Middle Ages, "quidquid principi placuit legis habet vigorem," legislative authority resided entirely in the person of the king.[4]

[1] *Tardif*, "Cout. de Norm.," vol. II, p. 3. N.R.H., XI, 120. "Cout. de Simon de Montfort," 1212. *D. Vaissette*, VIII, no. 165. "De consilio venerab. domina," etc. (archbishops and barons), *cf. Petiet*, p. 51. *Cf. Viollet*, II, 190; *Dodu*, p. 160. At Jerusalem, the court of the lieges, or High Court (composed of the only liege vassals of the kingdom) had, in reality, legislative power (with prelates and the bourgeois); the king's vassals had the right to refuse him military service and even to rise in insurrection against him if he violated his oath. *Flammermont*, p. 5.

[2] 1215, 1223, 1230, 1308. Ord., I, 35, 48, 53, 449. *Beaumanoir*, 34, 41; 35, 29; 48, 4; 49; 61; 25. *Boutillier*, II, 1; *Loysel*, ed. *Dupin*, 1.

[3] "Coutumes" officially compiled by the authority of the Dukes of Burgundy, 1459; of "Bourbonnais," 1493, etc. Barons, according to *Beaumanoir*, 49, could make laws in time of famine, etc. *Loyseau*, "Seign." ch. IX: statutes of police. In the 1700 s, *Dunod*, on "Burgogne," I, 39: the offices of the seigniors had only an inferior police power (*e.g.* over bake ovens and chimneys, etc.). Concerning Germany, *cf. Le Bret*, I, 9.

[4] *P. de Font.*, App. IX; "Jostice," p. 4; *Petiet*, p. 185; *Dumoulin*, "De

But this was a theoretical rule little in accord with the facts, for at no time did the king alone exercise this power. Beaumanoir, in translating the Roman rule, maintained that the general enactments should be made by the "most great council" and for the common good.[1] This vague formula might as well mean the advice of the king's court, or of his council, as that of the States-General, which soon made its appearance, or the assemblies which had preceded it. The royal acts were really prepared for the most part in the council of the king; and from the 1300 s to the 1500 s the States-General was frequently convoked to deliberate upon the laws.[2] Not even the University of Paris was without some political rôle at the time. When the States-General ceased to meet, the *Parlement* [a judicial body], which for a very long time had had some part in the legislative power by means of general orders,[3] multiplied its remonstrances and refusals to register the royal edicts. Although it lacked the power to initiate laws, it acquired a sort of right of veto of which the king at times was compelled to take account.[4] The other sovereign courts intervened in like manner in legislative matters, each in its sphere. There will be elsewhere a discussion of these bodies; we shall consider here only the States-General; and as the Provincial States were formed according to the same type, we shall occupy ourselves equally with them, although they were concerned rather with administration than with legislation.

leg. et priv. regni. fr.," Art. 12; *Guy Coquille*, "Inst.," etc.; *L'Hommeau*, I, 5; *Loyseau*, "Seign.," c. 1 and following. *Le Bret*, I, 9: "if one asks whether the king may make and publish all changes in the laws by his sole authority, without the advice of his council or of his sovereign courts, the answer must be yes, for the king alone is sovereign in his kingdom and the sovereignty is no more divided than is a point in geometry. However, it will always be fitting that a great king cause his laws and his edicts to be approved by his parliaments and the principal officers of the crown." *Cf. Bucherellus*, "Inst.," p. 13 *et seq.*

[1] *Langlois*, "Philippe III," p. 286. *Beaumanoir*, 49, 6, adds that if the new "establishments" were made contrary to God or contrary to good customs, the subjects (of the king) ought not to submit to them. *Cf.* Ord., I, 35 (1215) and 390.

[2] *Cf.* below. *Dareste*, "Hotman," p. 70; *Bodin*, "Rép.," I, 8, p. 142.

[3] *Petiet*, p. 272: table of the decisions of the Parliament of Paris. *Cf.* p. 222.

[4] *De Maulde La Clavière*, "Les orig. de la Révol. fr. au commenc. du XVIe s." (cited by *Viollet*, II, 198).

TOPIC 1. THE STATES-GENERAL[1]

§ 347. **Origin.**[2]—The kings of the third dynasty did not content themselves with consulting their principal officers and their immediate vassals, who frequently gathered about them and formed their habitual suite, their court; they consulted more numerous assemblies ("cours plénières") in which the great feudatories and the most powerful prelates participated with their ordinary "entourage" (*cf.* the Carolingian assemblies). There was no fixed rule either with respect to the organization or the convocation of these assemblies; their power was not defined. The great lords had places of honor at the coronation of the new king, and it was customary for the crown to obtain their assent to important measures which it was obliged to take (such as expeditions, enactment of laws, etc.), and most of the time the feebleness of the monarchy made this custom a necessity. The king was not obliged to summon the feudal body, but if he failed to do so he limited his means of action and ran the risk of raising a dangerous opposition on the part of the barons.[3] In the course of the 1200 s the king addressed himself to a new feudal person, the cities, which sent representatives to him. But he did not assemble at the same place, or on the same day, in solemn sessions the Three Estates of France (clergy, nobility, and bourgeoisie), and the assemblies

[1] BIBLIOGRAPHY: Documents: "Recueil général des estats," 1651; "Forme de la convocation et tenue des Ass. nation.," 1789; *Mayer*, "Des Etats Généraux," 1789; "Rec. de pièces concern. la tenue des Etats Gén.," 1789; *Masselin*, "Journal des états de 1484," ed. *Bernier*, 1835; *Bodin*, "Journal du tiers," 1575; *Bernard*, "Procès-verbaux des Etats de 1593," 1842; BCh., 1849; *Fl. Rapine*, "Etats de 1614," 1651; *Savaron*, "Chronologie des Etats Gén.," 1615; *Hérelle*, "Doc. inéd. s. les Etats Gén.," 1789; *Isambert*, "Table," see "Etats"; *Zampini*, "Degli Stati di Francia," 1578; *Boulainvillers*, "Hist. de l'anc. gouvern. de la France," 1727; *Landine*, "Des Etats Gén.," 1788; *Bergier et D. Verdier*, "Rech. s. les Et. Gén. et s. l'orig. des Etats Prov." *H. de Pansey*, "Des Ass. nation. en Fr.," 1829; *Thibaudeau*, "Hist. des Etats Gén.," 1843; *A. Thierry*, "Hist. du Tiers Etats," 1853; Histories of the Estates General by *Rathery*, 1845; by *Boullée*, 1845; by *Desjardins*, 1871; by *G. Picot*, 1872 (2e éd., 1888); by *Jallifier*, 1885. "Gr. Encycl.," see "Etats," "Assemblées"; *Beugnot*, "Ann. Soc. hist.," 1840; *Barral*, "Etats gén. de 1576," 1874; *Viollet*, "Les Etats de Paris en 1358," 1894. *Cf.* below, "Provincial States." *Glasson*, V, 406.

[2] *Boutaric*, "La France s. Phil. le Bel," 1861; BCh., 1, 1; *Luchaire*, "Inst. mon.," 1883; *Manuel*, p. 502; *Hervieu*, "Rech. s. les 1ers Etats Gén," 1879; *Froidevaux*, thesis (Philip Augustus), 1891; *Bayet*, "R. hist.," vol. XVII; *Callery*, "Hist. de l'orig. des pouvoirs des Etats Gén. et Prov.," 1880; *Luchaire*, "Ann. Bordeaux," 1882; BCh., 5e s. 1, 21. *Cadier*, "Etats de Béarn," p. 3.

[3] *Cf. Luchaire*, p. 492; *Yves de Chartres*, "Ep.," 209: "fœdus illud" (marriage of the king) "consilio episcoporum et optimatum cassabitur." *Abbon*, "Hist. de Fr.," X, 627; *Callery*, "Rev. des quest. hist.," 29, 87: Extra feudal measures.

which he held had no regular organization; there were as yet no States-General.[1]

The assembly summoned by Philip the Fair in 1302, on the occasion of his controversy with Pope Boniface VIII, was the first to which the name "States-General" may properly be applied. To the summons for a council at Rome, Philip the Fair responded by summoning the States of the kingdom in order to ask their aid and counsel. There was not in this act, however, as some have believed, a radical innovation, for these Estates were feudal assemblies modeled on those which had preceded them.[2] The essential difference was, that in 1302 there was a *simultaneous convocation on a large scale* of the clergy, the nobility, and the Third Estate (that is to say, the bourgeoisie of the cities).[3] The creation of this new political organ was not an isolated fact. In most of the countries of Western Europe (England, Germany, Spain, etc.) there appeared about the same time parliaments, diets, cortes — assemblies composed likewise of the three orders of the State[4] and of which the crown asked aid and counsel as in France, and especially the vote of taxes. The same needs and the same precedents gave rise to the same institution; the Estates, evolving out of the Carolingian assemblies and the feudal courts, permitted the crown to exercise over the feudal world a more vigorous control.

[1] *Cadier*, p. 31: the plenary courts (1000 s to the 1300 s) were derived from the feudal courts, the Estates of the Plenary Courts. *Cf. Froidevaux*, p. 89.

[2] We must guard against the belief that the practice was well established from this time: sometimes the king sent commissioners into the provinces to obtain voluntarily or by force the adhesion of the feudal powers (seigniors, towns); sometimes in place of going from town to town, his commissioners summoned the Provincial Estates and, finally, sometimes they went so far as to convoke a solemn meeting of the States-General.

[3] *Cf. Langlois*, "Philippe III," 146, 150. Assembly at Senlis of 1301 ("à propos" of Bernard Saisset). *Dupuy*, "Actes du différend entre Boniface VIII et Phil. le Bel," 1651, p. 629. *Esmein*, p. 485.

[4] In Germany: The individual States had their local diet ("Landtag") where the "Landstaende" met. The Empire had its imperial diet ("Reichstag") resembling a congress of sovereigns, where all the States of the Empire were represented in three colleges: electors ("Kurfürsten"), princes, towns; unanimity was necessary except upon religious questions, where there was a schism between the "Corpus catholicorum" and "Corpus evangelicorum"; upon separating, the Diet published its decisions sanctioned by the emperor or "Recesse" ("Reichsabschiede"). *Frommhold*, p. 187 (bibliog.); *Blondel*, "Frédéric II," p. 43. In Spain: "Cortes" (Courts) of Leon and of Castile, 1188 (?); Catalonia, before 1283; Navarre, 1300 s; in England, the Parliament was definitely organized in 1297. Variable division: two orders in England, Hungary, Poland (magnates and prelates, nobles and towns); in Germany, three orders (of which two were noble, the high and the low nobility); in Sweden, four (clergy, nobility, bourgeoisie peasants). No part of the isolated chambers formed a complete organ; they had to be united, convoked, and dissolved by the same act; they could not make a decision without the assent of each order.

They were, or rather they began by being, auxiliaries of the royal power.

§ 348. **History.** — Concerning the history of the States-General from 1302 to 1789 we will observe only: 1st, that under King John, from 1355 to 1358, the representative régime was on the point of being established; the Ordinance of 1355 and that of 1357 have been compared to the Great English Charter of 1215;[1] 2d, that, except at this moment, the Estates constituted only advisory assemblies; the most important were the Estates of 1413, followed by the "Cabochienne" ordinance (May 26, 1413), the Estates of Tours of 1484, which are known to us by the journal of Masselin, the Estates of Orléans of 1560, of Blois of 1576 and 1588, and, finally, the Estates of 1614. The number of sessions gradually decreased; there were thirteen in the 1300 s, eight in the 1400 s, five in the 1500 s, one in the 1600 s. After 1614 the Estates were almost forgotten, but the political agitation at the end of the reign of Louis XVI made their convocation the first article of the reform program of the bourgeoisie.[2] No more in France than in most of the other States of Europe did they succeed in becoming a normal organ of government; assembled intermittently, without autonomy, they played only a secondary, and in a certain way, an unusual, part in fiscal matters. It was otherwise only in England.[3]

§ 349. **Election.**[4] — (A) *The Old System.* To attend the Estates

[1] Ord., vol. III. *Perrens*, "Etienne Marcel," 1860; *N. Valois*, "Le gouv. représentatif en Fr. au XIXe s." ("Rev. des quest. hist.," 37, 63).

[2] Their convocation was already demanded by Fénelon and Boulainvilliers.

[3] The English Parliament which had, in theory, only the character and functions of the primitive States-General, played a very different rôle. It is an extraordinary assembly summoned and dissolved by the king; but, in fact, its meetings are periodical; it assembles every year to vote taxes. It is divided into two chambers — the one personal, the other representative; but as the House of Commons alone votes the taxes, it is preponderant; equal in theory, the two chambers are unequal in fact. The representatives, although private individuals, are inviolable like public officers; although agents, they are not bound by instructions; although elected by shires and boroughs, and consequently representing a locality, they deliberate and vote as though they represented the entire nation.

[4] *Cf.* the procurations, records of the elections, journals, etc. The electoral law changed from province to province, from session to session. The place of meeting was sometimes Paris, sometimes another town, Tours, Blois, Orléans, etc. The number of deputies varied greatly: in 1308 there were 1200 or perhaps 1500; in 1356, more than 800, more than 400 being deputies of the Third Estate; in 1484, 284; in 1560, 440, of which 107 were representatives of the clergy, as many representatives of the nobility, and 224 representatives of the Third Estate; in 1588, 505, of which 134 represented the clergy, 180 the nobility, 191 the Third Es-

was to render feudal service, court duty,[1] and not at all to exercise a right or a privilege. Penalties were imposed upon those who did not appear. The king summoned individually the most important seigniors and the prelates who possessed temporalties and the right of administering justice (bishops and abbots);[2] they attended in person to perform the duty of giving counsel[3] except when prevented and then they sent a proxy[4] with their excuses. Religious communities (chapters and abbeys), the "good" cities, that is, the most populous and most notable cities and boroughs, sent delegates[5] furnished with credentials of authority and allowed them an indemnity for the performance of their duties (representative element).[6] The open country, which was not distinguished politically from the seigniories, was not represented, or if so, only by seigniors.[7]

Summing up, each seigniory, each feudal group, participated in the Estates. Each having its own independence, the decision of the majority did not necessarily make law; each could stipulate only for itself.

tate; in 1614, 464, 140 for the clergy, 132 for the nobility, 192 for the people. The representatives of the First Estate were always less numerous, 80 in 1596, 50 in 1617, etc.

[1] In 1302, Philip the Fair summoned the Council of the three orders "ut dominus et amicus." The deputies were under the safeguard of the king.

[2] Nobles and prelates were summoned rather arbitrarily by the king (as the towns themselves were formerly). These latter sat more in the quality of seigniors than by their spiritual authority; same observation for chapters and abbeys. *Cf. Boutmy*, p. 111. In Sicily the "feudal arm" of Parliament comprised only nobles, possessors of fiefs "in capite"; the "ecclesiastical arm" appeared only under the kings of Aragon.

[3] Women who possessed a fief could be represented.

[4] English system: each county elected two deputies, each town or borough, the same. The boroughs fell into decay, but preserved the right of representation. Old Sarum, which had only a farm, sent Pitt to the Chamber. In the parliaments of Sicily, the "domainal arm" comprised the deputies of the communes or the lands of the royal domain.

[5] Elected, ordinarily, by the municipal body, where there was one; where there was none, by the entire community, or by certain of its members invested with the electoral function. *Hervieu*, p. 34.

[6] This explains the unpopularity of the Estates. *Cf. Cadier*, p. 247. The indemnity voted at the time of election varied according to the rank of the deputies: deputies who were archbishops received 25 francs per day, and deputies of the open country 6 francs per day. Following the Estates of the League, Bernard claimed an indemnity of his electors: "no one owes you anything for the beautiful work that you have done," they replied. BCh., vol. X, 1849; *Aubertin*, "L'Elog. polit.," p. 123; *Bernard*, p. 772, 804.

[7] Nevertheless, in the Estates of 1308, there were procurations (powers of attorney) emanating from the people of the country. *Cf. Babeau*, "Assembl. générales des com. d'hab.," p. 65 (and the authors that he cites on this point). *Bernier*, "Essai s. le tiers état rural (Basse Norm.) au XVIIIe s.," 1891.

§ 350. **The Definitive System.**[1] —Toward the end of the 1400 s, the Estates, instead of being a meeting of the feudal persons of the kingdom, became the representation of the three orders of the nation. The change was owing to the fact that political feudalism was decayed; seigniories and cities no longer formed petty independent States whose chiefs appeared in person (or by plenipotentiaries) at a sort of Congress. Nobles and ecclesiastics no longer sat individually in virtue of a personal obligation; they were represented collectively and sent deputies in imitation of the Third Estate (1484);[2] if their representation was distinct from that of the Third Estate, it was because they formed distinct classes in the nation. The country districts, emancipated, like the cities, from the seigniorial authority, became independent political bodies and acquired the right of being represented directly.[3] And, in a general way, to attend the Estates became a right, because in each class the majority imposed its will upon the minority[4] and for a stronger reason upon those who were absent. The latter no longer had, as in the past, the expedient of opposing measures to which they had not consented; it was therefore to their interest to be summoned and represented in the Estates. The election unit was the bailiwick, the only important administrative division of the old period (as in England it was the county). Cities and country districts were united in each bailiwick and formed only a single electoral body;[5] the nobility and the clergy acted by themselves. Whatever its population, each bailiwick had the same rights; the number of its deputies was of little importance.

[1] *Taillandier*, BCh., 1845. "Arr. d. Cons.," July 5, and Oct. 5, 1788. "Réglement" of Jan. 24, 1789. *Picot*, "Ac. sc. mov.," 1874 (Elections to the Estates). *Saripolos*, "La démocratie et l'élection proportionelle," 1899, p. 93. *Gregor. Tolos.*, 24, 4, 8.

[2] In all times, prelates and barons were able to have themselves represented by agents, and in order to reduce the expense of traveling and of residence, which was charged to them, it often happened that several were represented by the same person. This custom facilitated the transition to a system of elective representation. *Esmein*, p. 488.

[3] In 1510, at the time of the official compilation of the "Coutume" of Paris, the rural country was not yet represented. *Cf. Esmein*, p. 490; *Viollet*, BCh., 1866 (Estates of 1468, 1484).

[4] *Cf.* the Polish "Liberum veto," Aragon, Netherlands. Concerning the decisions of the majority of the English Parliament, *cf. Fischel*, II, 189.

[5] In England, counties, towns, boroughs, and universities have a distinct representation. This was the old French system. In 1413, the University of Paris had representatives. In 1593, it was affirmed not to be the custom for the *Parlement* [a judicial body] to send deputies to the Estates; *Bernard*, p. 14; *Esmein*, p. 492, n. 4: the royal bailiwicks alone were represented; so Brittany did not participate in the Estates of 1484: a bailiwick erected into an appanage lost its representation. "Mém. sur. les états gén.," p. 73. But *cf. Mayer*, XVI, 86.

Instead of individual summonses where the performance of a duty was demanded, the letters of the king were addressed to the bailiffs and seneschals, issued by these officials with the date of the general assembly of the bailiwick, and transmitted to the inferior judges and to the parish priests, who were charged with making them public in the sermon after the parish mass.

§ 351. **Nobility and Clergy.** — The election of the deputies of these two orders took place on a day fixed by the bailiffs and seneschals at the chief place of the bailiwick and of the seneschals' district.[1] At the same time they proceeded to the preparation of a list of grievances which the deputies should lay before the Estates. The electoral body of the clergy was composed of the bishop, the parish priests (curés) or ecclesiastics having a benefice in the district, and of delegates from the chapters and religious communities. All the nobles having fiefs in the bailiwick were electors.[2] Each order elected its deputies separately[3] and by direct suffrage, but voting by proxy was permitted.

§ 352. **The Third Estate.** — (A) *Important Towns.*[4] The electoral body was almost the same as for municipal elections (notables, and deputies of the trade guilds). (B) The *country and small towns* were grouped together and the purpose of the election was to give them a common representation. It took place in two or three stages: (*a*) in the ordinary parish assemblies in which all those took part who paid the "taille," even the women when they were heads of houses (unmarried or widows); in these assemblies the lists of grievances were prepared and the deputies selected;[5] (*b*) sometimes these deputies proceeded directly to the chief place of the bailiwick, sometimes they assembled in the neighboring city and chose delegates;[6] (*c*) the deputies elected directly

[1] The day of election in the bailiwick was not necessarily the same for the three orders. *Meyer*, XVI, 48. For a stronger reason the day was different among different bailiwicks. *Cf.* the English elections. *Cf. Mavidal and L.*, "Arch. Parl.," vol. I; *Duveyrier*, "Procès-Verbal," 1790; "Gr. Encycl.," see "Ass. des électeurs de Paris en 1789." Concerning the English High Chamber, *cf. Fischel*, II, p. 212.

[2] In memory of the time when each seigniory was represented.

[3] In 1484, a single electoral body embraced the nobility, the clergy, and the Third Estate. BCh., 6e s. 2, 31; *Viollet*, BCh., 1886.

[4] In 1789, Paris alone had special deputies. *Cf.* the "Réglement" of 1789, Jan. 24, details concerning these elections and "état annexe" of the towns, bailiwicks, and seneschals' jurisdictions, with the number of their deputies. *Cf.* English system, *Fischel*, II, 223.

[5] Presided over by the judge of the place, the attorney of the king (procureur), or the notary. "R. hist.," 21, 91. Often several parishes elected the same delegates.

[6] *Esmein*, p. 497: it seems that this was regularly the case when the inhabitants of the parishes were not directly amenable to the jurisdiction

and by almost universal suffrage, or the deputies of the second degree, assembled at the chief place of the bailiwick under the presidency of the royal judge; there took place the fusion of the lists into one and the election of the deputies who were to sit in the States-General.[1]

§ 353. **Sessions of the Estates.** — 1st, *The king convoked and dissolved the Estates.*[2] This is still the rule in respect to the English Parliament. With this principle it was hard to reconcile the periodicity of sessions, — often, but vainly, demanded in France. It would not have failed to be established, nevertheless, had budgetary and legislative rights been conceded to the Estates;[3] it did exist in the case of the Provincial Estates.

2d, *Verification of the credentials of the deputies* was made separately by each order,[4] which certified that the deputies were bearers of official mandates; also a president and speakers were elected (*cf.* the Speaker of the English House of Commons).

3d, *Opening of the session* ("os apertum"). After these preliminaries, the deputies of the three Estates met in a joint session presided over by the king, who said a few words and charged the chancellor with developing his ideas. This was what we call the

of the bailiwick tribunal but of another inferior court. The rural electors were also associated with the electors of the small neighboring towns through considerations of economy, in order to avoid the expense of special delegates. In 1789, reduction to a fourth.

[1] Two from each bailiwick. Secret or public vote, "scrutin de liste" or series of individual votes, absolute or relative majority. Sometimes, as in Provence, the deputies were elected by the Provincial Estates. *Esmein*, p. 500.

[2] The same for the Provincial Estates. *Le Bret*, "Souver.," 4, 12. In the Estates of 1484, the chancellor declared, on the 11th of March, that the deputies could withdraw; they refused; on the 12th, they were informed that beginning on the 14th, the daily indemnity that they received would cease to be paid to them; on the 14th they had all departed. In 1614, the closing session was held without anything having been done; the next day, the deputies found the hall where they sat closed. One of them exclaimed: "Are we those who yesterday entered the hall of Bourbon?" These were the words of Sieyès's in 1789: "We are to-day what we were yesterday: let us deliberate." In 1614, the deputies withdrew almost immediately.

[3] In Sicily, the Estates met every three years, and in the interval of the sessions, a commission elected by the Parliament administered the funds voted to the king, and watched over the rights of the nation. English system, *Fischel*, II, p. 242 and following.

[4] *Esmein*, p. 500: each order verified the regularity of the election and of the mandate of the deputy: the king's council determined questions of law which the election raised. *Cf. Mayer*, XVI, 82: the king's council decided whether a locality had a right to a deputy. *Cf. Astre*, "Admin. publ. en Languedoc avant 1789," 1874. In Languedoc, the Estates disputed the proofs of nobility furnished by the barons, excluded from the assembly every officer of the king, and watched over the liberty of the elections of the Third Estate (to avoid the king's intervention by means of "lettres de cachet," and that of the supreme court by decisions).

speech from the throne, making known the reasons for the summoning of the Estates and explaining the projects that it was proposed to submit to them; the speakers of the clergy, the nobility, and the Third Estate then replied.[1]

4th, *Deliberations and votes.* The three Estates deliberated separately (already in 1302), but it was customary for each to send deputations to the others to make known their views; even joint sessions were sometimes held at which the respective speakers made known the results of their deliberations. The voting took place by Estates.[2] In each Estate the voting was by bailiwick and not by head, each bailiwick had only one vote which was determined by the majority of its deputies, with the result that it mattered little that the number of deputies varied among the bailiwicks. Fairness required that when taxes were to be voted the clergy and the nobility who did not pay taxes should not be reckoned as constituting a majority against the deputies of the Third Estate.[3] It may even be said that in general two Estates acting in accord could not make law for the remaining one, because each was regarded as a distinct nation.[4]

5th, *Mandate of the deputies.* The sessions, very short at first, were never very long. Electors and deputies were consulted only on a small number of matters.[5] If in the course of the session new and unforeseen matters arose, the deputies were sent back to the electors for instructions. If the deputies exceeded their powers, their acts were disavowed by the electors. They rendered to the electors an account of the acts of the Estates and received from them a pecuniary reimbursement.[6] The deputies were

[1] In the Estates of Blois and in those of 1614, the speaker of the Third Estate had to address the king on his knees; in 1560, he began his address on his knees as did the speakers of the clergy and of the nobility, but as for the latter, the king made him rise after he had spoken a few words.

[2] At least, in general (from 1302). In 1308, voting by head, in 1413, by provinces. In 1484, the three orders sat together and were divided into six regional bureaus. *Mayer*, XVI, 63. In 1356 there was a commission composed of delegates of the three orders.

[3] Ord. 1560, Art. 135. *Isambert*, XIV, 95. *Cf. Fischel*, vol. II, p. 183.

[4] In 1789, it was a question of voting by polls or by Estates. *Champion, op. cit.*

[5] In 1302, Philip the Fair commanded the towns to send "procureurs, having power to hear, to do, and to consent, each and all, to the things that the king will order." This formula gives an idea of the rôle of the first Estates-General. *Cf.* oath of the deputies in 1614, *H. de Pansey*, "Ass. nat.," p. 371.

[6] The deputies bore a power of attorney in form; letters were exchanged between the communities and the assembly. Deputies sometimes returned to their constituents for instructions; sometimes they bore a mandate "ad audiendum et referendum," without power to adopt resolutions definitively.

therefore only mouthpieces of the electors; they had no powers of their own and were under a strict obligation to conform their action to the will of their constituents. This idea was a consequence of early law; the prelates and barons finding it impossible to appear in person at the assembly sent proxies to make known their views.[1] With the new system of representation of the estates of the nation, the imperative mandate should have been abandoned. But if in theory the old principle was adhered to, the deputies in fact enjoyed a considerable independence, and it does not appear that they were recalled because of disagreement with the electors.[2] These facts thus prepared the way for the modern theory of political representation.[3]

6th, *Closure of the session.* In a solemn session which was the counterpart of the opening session the lists of grievances were laid before the king by the three Estates.[4] It was in this way that the right of parliamentary initiative was exercised, not a very efficacious initiative, since there was no means of compelling the king to examine the petitions of the Estates, or, "a fortiori," to grant their demands.

§ 354. **Powers of the Estates.**[5] — Although it was a principle

[1] Members of the English Parliament cannot resign. But, when a member wishes to retire, for example, because he is not in sympathy with his electors, the crown confers on him an official sinecure which is incompatible with the mandate of a member.

[2] *Cf. Esmein*, p. 499. "Journal" of *Bodin*, p. 224.

[3] They were not supposed to represent the nation, but only the class and the bailiwick which elected them. *Cf. Fischel*, "Const. d'Anglet.," vol. II, p. 188.

[4] Remonstrances, *cf.* BCh., 1890, p. 432 (Estates of 1413); 1844 (Marion) were registered after 1468 at least, in the "cahiers" of complaints from 1484, each order submitted a "cahier" (and even in 1484, the three "cahiers" were merged into a single one). *Mayer*, XVI, 54. "Rec. des Cahiers gén. des trois ordres, 1560 à 1614," 1789. *Prudhommes*, "Rés. des Cahiers des états gén." *Chevalier*, "Et. s. les Cahiers des états de Blois," 1877. *Mavidal et Laurent*, "Arch. parl.," 1876 ("Cahiers des états gén. de 1789"). *Cf. Monod*, nos. 4385 et suiv. *Abbé Allain*, "Cahiers des états de 1789" (Inst. publ.), 1886. *Gégout*, "Les Cahiers de la Lorraine aux Etats de 1789," 1889. *Chassin*, "Cahiers de Paris en 1789"; "Le génie de la Révolution," "Les Cahiers des curés"; *Champion*, "La Fr. d'ap. les cahiers de 1789," 1897. Concerning English bills, *cf. Fischel*, II, 313.

[5] The political rôle of the Estates was defined in various ways by the writers of the 1500 s. The most extreme absolutists saw in them only an emanation of the royal power, an assembly called by the king and without power of its own. Others, less radical, conceded to the Estates the right to vote taxes and desired to have them consulted on fundamental laws. There were some who went as far as the limited monarchy: the king could not issue laws of general interest without the advice of the representatives of the nation. Finally, it was writers, like Boulainvilliers, who saw in the Estates, the old, sovereign aristocracy which had retained a part of its rights and was found associated with the government of the date. *Cf. Dareste*, "Hotman," p. 69; *Le Bret*, 4, 12.

that the Estates could deliberate only upon matters, (*a*) submitted to their examination by the king, and (*b*) those mentioned in their mandates, they had to occupy themselves with all sorts of political and administrative measures, with the constitution, the budget, and the laws. In 1302 and 1308 Philip the Fair consulted them in regard to questions of foreign policy (the imbroglio with the Holy See and the affair of the Templars);[1] in 1314 he invited them to grant subsidies to the crown in accordance with the principle: "After the service of counsel, the service of aids." The vote of subsidies was henceforth the essential object of the deliberations of the Estates, but they were not long in joining to them, as the price of these subsidies, demands for reforms: the redress of grievances (1351). Under King John the Estates succeeded for a moment in gaining control of the government and administration,[2] but they speedily fell back into the position of a consultative assembly. The *right to vote taxes* belonged to them until the establishment of the permanent "taille" by Charles VII.[3] The king, whose power to levy by his sole authority a contribution upon the whole kingdom was not recognized, demanded aids and subsidies of the Estates. The latter never renounced formally and by express act their right to vote the tax; it disappeared as a result of the growth of the royal authority and from the custom on the part of the taxpayers of regularly paying the tax. In vain and repeatedly, the Estates protested and demanded its restoration (1441, 1484), but contented themselves, when they could not do otherwise, with denying the right of the king to levy new taxes (except in case of urgency)[4] (1560, 1576, 1588).[5] The legislative power of the Estates was con-

[1] In the Estates assembled by Philip the Fair, there was neither deliberation, discussion, nor vote; the king demanded "an imposing manifestation of fidelity" and obtained it by force if necessary; far from thinking of inaugurating a régime of control and public liberty, he planned to strengthen the royal power. "Procès des Templiers," 1841.

[2] Principles admitted by the Ord. of December 28, 1355: equality of all in respect to taxes, right of the Estates to vote subsidies, to designate agents charged with collecting them, and superintendents to direct the financial administration, regular meetings of the Estates (they voted subsidies for only a year and fixed, themselves, the date of their meetings), unanimity of the three orders for the validity of their acts. *Perrens*, "La démocratie au XIVe s.," 1875.

[3] *Infra:* "Finances."

[4] Importance of this reservation in English history (Stuarts).

[5] In 1560 Catherine de' Medici acknowledged the right of the Estates to vote the tax. In 1576 *Bodin* caused a subsidy bill to be rejected under the pretext that the assembly, instructed by experience, should demand that reforms be made first. In 1588, a demand was made to allow the taxpayers to resist by armed force any one who collected taxes without the consent of the Estates. *Duval*, "Un juriste républicain au XVIe s. Joachim du Chalard et les Etats de 1560," 1871.

nected strictly with their budgetary power.[1] It had the same fate; by losing the one they lost the other because they had no other means of securing a redress of grievances than the refusal of subsidies. On different occasions they attempted without success to make laws to remove their grievances (1576), or to compel the king to do so by not granting subsidies (1588); legislative right and budgetary right escaped them equally. Nevertheless, the Estates always deliberated upon the most important questions of public law:[2] the ratification of treaties, the cession of territory, the alienation of the crown domain, the establishment of a regency, and, indeed, even the election of a king in case of vacancy on the throne.

§ 355. **Conclusion.** — The classic comparison between the English Parliament[3] and the States-General of France raises a difficult question: how is it that with the same elements, a political assembly having the same origin, the same constitution, the same principle that the king could not levy taxes without its assent, and the same right to present its grievances to him, France and England should have reached opposite political systems, — here

[1] *Cf. Cadier*, p. 364. In the 1400s the Spanish Parliament (Cortes) did not allow the king to levy taxes until he had redressed their grievances. The Cortes was more like a congress of petty sovereigns than a consulting body. Unanimity was required for the validity of their decisions. Philip II avoided all discussion and tutelage by not calling them together. England, *cf. Fischel*, II, 326.

[2] In 1484 and in 1560, the organization of the regency. The Estates of 1420 ratified the Treaty of Troyes (crown of France bestowed upon Henry V); in the same way, in 1593, they provided for the vacancy on the throne, the heir, Henry IV, being a heretic and therefore unworthy (*cf.* decree of the Parliament of 1593 on the Salic Law). Edict of July, 1717. In 1468, the Estates declared that Normandy could not be separated from the domain of the crown. The Third Estate demanded, in 1614, the vote of a declaration that the king held his sovereignty only from God, that no spiritual or temporal power had any right over the kingdom, that subjects could never be released from their oath of fidelity to the king. In consequence of the opposition of the clergy, this proposition was rejected.

[3] Occasions were not lacking in which the States-General played a preponderant political rôle. The original sin with which they were reproached, that is to say, of having been only an auxiliary organ of royalty, which paralyzed in advance any attempt of resistance on their part, was also met in the English Parliament. It is paradoxical to maintain (as does De Lolme) that the excessive power of the English kings brought about, by reaction, the liberties of England where the upper classes leagued themselves with the commoners, in order to resist the royal power. The three orders in France, regarding the king less redoubtable, wasted their strength in vain quarrels. *Boutmy*, p. 119: From the 1300s, three principles characterize the Parliament of our States-General: 1, The division into two chambers where the orders were mixed; consequently, they could not isolate themselves and act as classes; 2, the union in the lower chamber of the urban element with a rural element very old and very powerful, originally attached to the baronetcy; 3, the predominantly lay character of the high assembly.

absolute monarchy, there a representative system and public freedom?

There were two principal causes of the difference: 1st, The national temperament of tenacity and habit, among the English, maintained the institution of Parliament even when it no longer rendered any services, and thus they were enabled to utilize it later; the French spirit showed itself less conservative; the States-General had flashes of great brilliancy, then complete eclipses. 2d, The disasters of the Hundred Years' War, by keeping France for a long while in a state of war and putting in jeopardy the national existence, imposed upon our country the most striking features of military organization, absolute power and centralization. In England, the Reformation and the struggles which it brought about gave new life to the old instinct for independence and to traditional liberty. In France the only partial success of the Reformation failed to have the same result. Wherever this leaven was lacking, as in Italy and Spain, public liberty perished. In the whole of Europe, save in England and Holland, the evolution was in the direction of absolute monarchy; representative institutions proved abortive.[1] The same general causes, wars, reaction against feudal partitions, contributed to this result.

Although the States-General did not endow France with a representative system, they rendered certain services: 1st, they affirmed important principles of public law (such as the independence of the crown as against the Holy See, the inalienability of the public domain, and the indivisibility of the national territory); 2d, they inspired certain administrative reforms; their lists of grievances were like preparatory studies for the Royal Ordinances (*e.g.* the Ordinance of L'Hopital and of Blois); 3d, they contributed to the maintenance throughout the nation of an attachment to public liberty. If the monarchical government did not degenerate into a kind of Turkish despotism, this was partly due to the States-General. In some degree the honor belongs to the protests of Stephen Marcel, of Robert le Coq, of Philip Pot,[2] of Masselin, of Jean Bodin, of Savaron, and of Miron. In 1789 they could serve as the " vehicle " for the Revolution.

[1] The kings freed themselves from the troublesome control of the States by all sorts of methods: corruption of deputies, menaces, violence, delay in summoning the States, and, finally, by ceasing to summon them at all. Castile revolted in 1523, and Charles the Fifth profited by it to oblige the Spanish Cortes to vote the taxes before they submitted their grievances to him.

[2] Discourse (in the Journal of Masselin, p. 140): "regnum dignitas est, non hereditas . . .; rempublicam rem populi esse." *Aubertin,*

TOPIC 2. ASSEMBLIES OF NOTABLES

§ 356. **The Assemblies of the Notables,**[1] not very numerous, and arbitrarily chosen,[2] were consequently supple enough to allow the crown to dispense with the States-General without the appearance of breaking with liberal tradition;[3] the king seemed to appeal to public opinion. Thus Henry IV was able to say at Rouen in 1596 that he had put himself under guardianship ("en tutelle"), "a desire which rarely came to graybeards or victors."[4] But neither Louis XIV nor Louis XV preserved this shadow of representation. With the approach of the Revolution, the important assemblies of 1786 and 1788 announced and prepared the way for the reassembling of the States-General.[5]

TOPIC 3. THE PROVINCIAL ESTATES[6]

§ 357. **Origin.** — The Provincial Estates[7] or assemblies of the three orders of a province were, like the States-General, an

"L'éloquence politiq. en France," 1882. *Tixier*, "Théories sur la souveraineté des États de 1484," 1899.

[1] *Cf.* above, Bibliog. des états gén. *De Beaurepaire*, "Louis XIII et l'Ass. des notables en 1617," 1883. "Coll. des Mémoires prés à l'Ass. des not.," 1787. "Procès-verbal de l'Ass. des not.," 1788. "Réimpr. du Moniteur, Introd. historique."

[2] Same elements as in the States-General; but the latter were distinguished by their elective character, whereas the notables were chosen by the king.

[3] In 1558, according to Saint-Quentin, they voted a forced loan; in 1526, according to Pavie, they declared Burgundy inalienable; in 1596 they voted subsidies. Out of 151 notables convoked in 1596, 70 attended.

[4] Concerning the counsel of reason, *cf. N. Valois*, "Invent. des arr. du Conseil d'Etat," XCV.

[5] December 29 and 30, 1786: fourteen prelates, forty-four nobles, twelve counselors of State, thirty-eight magistrates, twelve deputies of the "pays d'Etats," twenty-eight premier magistrates of the towns. *Cf.* following.

[6] BIBLIOGRAPHY: *A. Molinier*, "Gr. Encycl." (bibl.). *Cf. supra*, Bibliog. des états gén., p. 359, n. 1. *Bergier*, "Rech. hist. s. les États d'Auvergne," 1788; *Laferrière*, "Ac. sc. mor.," 1860; *A. Thomas*, "Etats prov. de la France centrale," 1879; *De Beaurepaire*, "Etats de Norm. sous la domin. angl.," 1859; "Cahiers des Etats de Norm." ("Soc. hist. Nom.," 1876–87); *Canel*, "Soc. Antiq. Norm.," t. X; *Coville*, "Etats de Norm."; *De Carné*, "Etats de Bretagne," 1868.; *Trouvé, Id.; B. du Kerorguen*, "Rech. s. les Etats de Bretagne" (1736), 1851; *Rossignol*, "Les anc. lib. de la Bourgogne"; *Clerc*, "États gén. en Franche-Comté," 1882; *Baudel*, "Ann. du Lot," 1881; *Cadier*, "Etats de Béarn," 1888; "Livre des syndics des états de Béarn," 1885; *Faye*, "Etats de la vicomté de Turenne," 1894. Concerning the Estates of Languedoc, besides *D. Vaissete*, "Hist. de Languedoc," *passim*, *cf. Monin*, "Essai s. l'hist. admin. du Lang.," 1885; *Gachon*, "Les états de Lang. et l'Edit de Béziers," 1887; *Dognon*, "Institutions de Languedoc," 1895; thèse lat., 1895; *Astre*, "Administr. publiq. en Languedoc avant 1789," 1874; *Rives*, "Attrib. financières," 1884 (thesis); (*Albisson*), "Loix municipales et économiques du Languedoc," 1780–87.

[7] "Landstände" in most of the German countries, Austria, Prussia, etc.

extension of the feudal courts. Some grew directly out of the courts of the great barons (Provence, Brittany, etc.);[1] the others were formed under the direction of the king, who, in case of need, joined into a single body the assizes of several bailiwicks or seneschal districts (Languedoc).[2] The institution existed only during the 1400 s; the crown summoned the Provincial Estates as it did the States-General, by reason of financial need; these curtailed assemblies were more tractable and easier to call together, for example, in case of invasion by an enemy;[3] and it was the war with England that explains the kind of division made by Charles VII into the Estates of the langue d'Oc and of the langue d'Oïl.

§ 358. **The Composition of the Provincial Estates** recalled the early composition of the States-General (prelates and barons sitting individually, the country regions not represented).[4] In Languedoc the clergy participated in them at first through the bishops, the abbots, and the delegates of cathedral chapters and important colleges; later the bishops and archbishops of the twenty-three dioceses of the provinces alone attended. It was the same for the nobility; the principal nobles were at first summoned in varying number; afterwards, the crown was content to summon twenty-three, some always attending (regular baronies), the others by turns (baronies by turn).[5] The Third Estate was represented by delegates from the "good" towns, that is, the most populous towns and boroughs, and noted communities. In the

[1] Whether a single court constituted the Estates, or whether, as frequently happened, the same suzerain, having several seigniories, formed the States-General of his domain by the union of the particular courts of the latter, *cf.* "R. hist.," 1879; *Cadier*, p. 3 (examination of the thesis of M. Callery); p. 14 (criticism of the ideas of M. Thomas).

[2] Ord. July, 1254: the seneschal of Beaucaire could not prohibit the exportation of cereals without the advice of an assembly composed of prelates, barons, and representatives of good towns. These seneschal district assemblies were the point of departure of the Estates of Languedoc; in the 1300 s, the deputies of the three seneschal's districts of Languedoc were reassembled at the same place. *Dognon*, p. 195.

[3] *Cf. Dognon, op. cit.*, p. 205 and following.

[4] Béarn: large bodies (clergy, barons, "gentius") and the Third Estate. In Burgundy the Third Estate had seventy-two deputies against seventy for the clergy and three hundred for the nobility. In Provence, according to Richelieu (1630), there remained only one deputation composed of delegates elected by the towns to which were added two bishops and two noble owners of fiefs; the representatives of the Third Estate found themselves in the preponderance; in 1787, the ancient Estates were reëstablished, which was for the advantage of the nobility and clergy; it is well known what troubles this measure led to.

[5] In Brittany, after 1567, all the nobles sat in the Estates (not merely those who owned a fief, as formerly); there were as many as 1300; such assemblies could not avoid being tumultuous; they obtained the right to vote by head, the measure being carried easily over the other orders.

end the number of regular places and places by turn was determined as equal to the seats of the other two orders. The delegates were elected, sometimes by the people, sometimes by the municipal body, and they ended by being incumbents of municipal offices now become purchasable. They therefore, like the bishops, held by appointment of the king.[1]

§ 359. **Powers of the Estates.** — In the countries of election ("pays d'élection") the administration was entirely in the hands of agents of the central power. In the countries having Estates ("pays d'états"): 1st, the taxes were voted, at least in form, by the Estates; 2d, they were apportioned and collected by their agents, or, at least, under their supervision; 3d, the Estates had the right to levy special contributions for the construction of the necessary public works in the province; 4th, they also had some part in the administration; 5th, and finally, they had the right of remonstrance and exercised it by sending delegations to the king. During the intervals between sessions each assembly was represented by a committee elected from its own members (permanent commission, general representatives, etc.).[2] We must, however, guard against exaggerating their power.[3] In reality, in spite of appearances, the tutelage of the intendants did not leave much freedom of action in the countries having Estates. Every deliberation in relation to finances was subject to the prior authorization of the royal council ("Réglement," 1768).

§ 360. **The Estates of Languedoc.** — They voted[4] the sum of money demanded by the king; the commissioners of the king dwelt upon the forbearance of the government. Though it could have commanded, it consented to treat with the province; they enumerated the charges upon the treasury and pointed out the duty of the country; the archbishop of Narbonne, president by right, replied by picturing the misery of the province and gave assurances that the assembly would do its best. But these rhetorical exercises did not deceive anybody; the assembly had no

[1] In the 1500s, it was the custom to delegate to the Estates the first consul of the place. "Hist. de Languedoc," XIII, 154, 692.

[2] *De Lucay*, "Ass. prov.," p. 109. *Cf.*, concerning Burgundy, *Thomas*, "Une province sous Louis XIV."

[3] In Béarn, for a long time, the Estates and their syndics were the true masters of the country. In the Netherlands the grand pensionary, a simple registrar or secretary of the Estates of Holland, became the head of the United Provinces.

[4] *Cf.*, for Béarn, *Cadier*, pp. 295 to 372: vote, apportionment of the tax, control of the seigniorial administration, nomination of the tutor or viscount, advice concerning the marriage of the sovereign, declaration of war, etc.

notion of opposing the will of the king. The tax that had to be paid to the king (free gift, etc.) was apportioned by a commission of the Estates among the dioceses, and in each of them by an assembly called the "assiette," a reduced form of the Estates,[1] among the communities. The collection was likewise intrusted to agents of the Estates. The amount which was voted for the needs of the province was applied to enterprises of public utility (roads, the port of Cette, the canal of the two seas, etc.). They did not separate without adopting a list of grievances which a deputation was charged with presenting to the king. In the interval between sessions the Estates continued to function, after a fashion, by standing committees and by their syndics, charged with pleading for the province and looking after the preservation of its privileges and of its rights.[2] Furthermore, the Estates might give the illusion of a liberal and even democratic institution; they met regularly every year[3] at a place fixed by the royal summons; the three orders deliberated in common and voted by heads; as the Third Estate had as many representatives as the clergy and nobility together, it had the last word, provided its members were united (this was what it demanded of the States-General in 1789). In spite of all this, they were dependent upon the intendants.[4] Their defective and superannuated mode of

[1] The diocesan "assiette" appeared in the 1400s. Until that time the financial unit was the "viguerie" or "jugerie"; ordinarily, the principal town appointed a receiver and sent "mandes" or tax lists to the communities. In 1360, "aids" for the ransom of John the Good were collected by the diocese. This was the beginning of the transformation. The assemblies of the "assiette" may be compared to our Councils General. The word "assiette" comes from the fact that the assembly had to sit, to assess the tax. Little Estates in the Vivarais, the Velay, the Gévaudan, "Réglement" of 1658, 1724. "Hist. de Lang.," XIV, 997. *Cf.* Special Estates of the Maconnais. *Rossignol*, "Petits états d'albigeots," 1875.

[2] Commissions: 1. for affairs extraordinary (*e.g.* new taxes); 2. for impositions and public works of the diocese; 3. for public works of the province (this commission was permanent); 4. for manufactures; 5. for agriculture; 6. for accounts, etc. (In Béarn, it was an "abrégé" of the Estates, commission of grievances, auditors of accounts.) The officers of the Estates were: 1. syndics, general agents; it was upon their advice that the Estates most often deliberated; 2. recorders (they kept the minutes of the meetings); 3. attorneys at the sovereign courts; 4. receiver (1522) or treasurer of the Bourse. *Cf. Cadier*, p. 277. It was the Estates of Languedoc which undertook to have the general history of this country written out.

[3] The Estates of Brittany met every two years, those of Burgundy, every three years.

[4] Before the session, the intendant had the deputies meet him, whereupon he informed them of the straight way, and warned them that they must not trifle with the king. Through the power of the intendant to determine upon the legality of their election, it was not difficult to eliminate those who opposed or the indifferent ones. However, the deliberations took place in the absence of the commissioners of the king, and they were secret.

selection made it impossible to regard them as a true representation of the province. But at least they had the advantage of being in contact with people, of having the same interests, and of being better situated than the clerks of the ministers to judge intelligently of local affairs; they formed a useful administrative organ at a time when they had lost all political pretensions.

§ 361. **Decadence.** — In the period of the 1400s we find Estates in most of the provinces of the royal domain and in the great fiefs. But in 1789 (France was divided into "pays d'états" and "pays d'élections"). The "pays d'états" were not very numerous and included only outlying provinces or those which had remained independent for a long time: Languedoc, Provence, Navarre, Bigorre, Béarn, Brittany, Artois, and Burgundy.[1] How was it that the right which was common at the beginning of the 1400s had become the exception at the end of the "ancien régime"? There we have an episode in the progress toward centralization. For the levy of the "taille," the king, who knew how to free himself from the control of the States-General, shook off also the restraint of the Provincial Estates, although it was lighter; neither the one nor the other was popular, because they meant expenses to the taxpayers and scarcely offered any guarantee for the safeguard of their interests. They were assembled again in the 1500s for the official compilation ("redaction") of the **Customs**; after that they ceased to be summoned;[2] some were even formally suppressed by a royal act.[3] This was an evolution which the historians have judged differently; it was a misfortune in the eyes of Fénelon, Montesquieu, and their contemporaries, according to whom the "pays d'états" were more prosperous than the "pays d'élections."[4]

When a vote took place by written ballot, the ballots were torn up after the vote. The oath not to reveal anything accorded rather poorly with the custom of rendering an account to the electors. The deputies could not be arrested for debt or any civil suit, either in going to or returning from the Estates, nor during the session. *Cf. Roschach*, "Hist. de Lang.," XIII, 915.

[1] Add Hainault, and Cambresis, Flanders, Metz, Gex, Bresse, Bugey, Valromey, Foix, Marsan, Nébouzan, Labourd, Quatre-Vallées, Soule, Lower Navarre.

[2] From the end of the 1400s, no more Estates met in central France. Suppression in Dauphiny, 1628 to 1637; in Normandy, 1638, 1655; in Auvergne, before 1624, about 1680; in the Franche-Comté, 1679; in Alsace, in spite of treaties.

[3] Thus, the Czar has just suppressed the Estates of Finland, April, 1899. The logic of autocracy required it. *De Ferron*, "Inst. munic. et prov. comp.," 1884.

[4] *De Luçay*, "Ass. prov.," p. 133; *Mis de Mirabeau*, "Mém. s. les Etats prov."; *Tocqueville*, "Ancien Rég. et Révol.," p. 313; *Mémoire de Necker*, 1778; *Roschach*, "Hist. de Languedoc," XIII, 915.

TOPIC 4. PROVINCIAL ASSEMBLIES

§ 362. **Provincial Assemblies under Louis XVI.**[1] — The intendants in whose hands was concentrated the local administration were far from being popular; clergy, nobility, and supreme courts, which had had to bow before them, were jealous of them; and there was a widespread notion that everything good came from the king and everything bad from the intendant.[2] It was proposed to associate with these agents of the central power in the countries of election ("pays d'élection") representatives of the nation, as there had been in the countries having Estates ("pays d'états").[3] Turgot, in his "Mémoire sur les municipalités," presented a general plan for the organization of assemblies in four degrees: municipalities of cities and parishes,[4] of districts,[5] of provinces,[6] and municipalities of the kingdom — all to be elected without distinction of orders by an electoral body based on landed wealth and charged to deliberate upon the apportionment of taxes (but not to vote them), upon the construction of public works, and upon the police of the poor.[7] Necker, shrinking before a general measure, made some attempts in certain provinces: in Berry, 1778,[8] and in Upper Guyenne in the same year.[9] The ex-

[1] Procès-verbal des Ass. prov. (*cf. Stourm*, "Bibliog. des finances"); *Condorcet*, "Essai sur les Ass. prov.," 1788; *Mme de Staël*, "Consid. s. la Révol. fr.," 1818; *Chérest*, "La chute de l'Ancien Régime," 1884–87; *De Neymarck*, "Turgot et ses doctrines," 1875; *De Luçay*, "Les Ass. prov. sous L. XVI," 1857, 1871; *Semichon*, "Les Réformes sous Louis XVI," 1876; *L. de Lavergne*, "Les Ass. prov. sous L. XVI," 1864; *F. Mège*, "L'ass. prov. d'Auvergne," 1889; *Flandin*, Thèse, 1878; *De Girardot*, "Ass. prov. du Berry," 1845; "Gr. Encycl.," see "Ass. prov."

[2] Boulainvilliers and Marquis de Mirabeau attacked them.

[3] Fénelon had already proposed it in his plans for reform. *De Luçay*, p. 139.

[4] Every citizen having an annual income of 600 francs was to have a voice in the parish assembly; above 600 francs, as many votes in proportion to his wealth, below 600 francs, a fraction of a vote. For the town assemblies, the rate was to be higher, 1500 francs.

[5] The district or arrondissement was to be formed by a grouping of the towns and parishes, two deputies being allowed for the capital of the province, and one for the town or parish.

[6] The municipalities of the provinces were to be formed by the deputies of the arrondissement municipalities, the national municipality by those of the provincial municipalities.

[7] *Tocqueville*, "Mél.," p. 161. The "Memoir of Turgot," 1776, was the work of *Dupont de Nemours*. *Cf. Le Trosne*, "De l'adm. prov.," 1779. *Condorcet*, *op. cit.*

[8] "Arr. of the Council," July 12, 1778. Composition: twelve ecclesiastics, twelve nobles, twenty-four members of the Third Estate (one half for the towns, one half for the countries); the king appointed sixteen members, who chose the thirty-two others; but it was proposed to recruit the assembly, in the future, by election. The archbishop of Bourges presided. Voting was by head, and by loud voice, but by rotation (one ecclesiastic, one noble, two members of the Third Estate, and so, one

perience seemed conclusive enough and Calonne and Brienne renewed the attempt after the downfall of Necker. The Edict of June 27, 1787, established provincial assemblies in all the "countries of election" upon the following principles: the doubling of the Third Estate, voting by heads, permanent commissions during the interval between sessions, deliberations in respect to assessment and the reapportionment of personal and real estate taxes, and upon the expenses of the province, syndic proxies acting in the name of these assemblies and inferior assemblies of "elections" and of parishes; here we find the principal characteristics of the assemblies of Estates.[1] The institution endured for too brief a period for one to pronounce judgment upon its merits. It was sharply attacked; some reproached it with transforming the provinces into republics in a monarchical State and for disorganizing the public service by provoking conflicts among the local authorities;[2] others saw in these assemblies lacking initiative, only a vain shadow of liberty.[3] But at least this attempt at administrative decentralization prepared the way for the later Remonstrances (Cahiers) and determined the personnel of the Revolution.

after another). The assembly sat every two years for a month, and in the interval between sessions it was represented by a commission which controlled the acts of the administration. It was occupied with the apportionment and the levying of direct taxes; it replaced the unpopular "corvée" by an increase of the "taille," carried out the project for the construction of the Berry canal, and interested itself in the erection of public works and in public assistance.

[9] The assembly of Upper Guyenne (Montauban) also made useful reforms. Elsewhere, in Dauphiné, Bourbonnais, and the Franche-Comté, these assemblies failed because of the opposition of the Parliaments, divisions, survivals of the old estates, progress of new ideas, and the agitation that followed it.

[1] Edict of June 22, 1787, and "Réglement" of June 23, 1787. *Isambert*, 28, 366. The king appointed half of the members (24) on recommendation of the intendant, and these chose the others. But afterwards, the assemblies had to be renewed by means of new elections (one quarter every three years). *De Lavergne*, p. 100; *De Luçay*, p. 183. By a real revolution Dauphiny established in its assemblies of Vizille and of Romans the type of the future national assembly. *De Lavergne*, p. 372; *F. Faure*, "Les ass. de Vizille et de Romans in 1788," 1887.

[2] Expenses occasioned by these assemblies: transportation, installation, maintenance of deputies. "Encore de nouvelles mangeries," was said at Orléans, and this phrase gives the measure of the popularity of representative assemblies. The deputies of Metz and Caen refused all reimbursement.

[3] According to Necker, these assemblies were not instituted as legal representatives on the part of subjects sent to treat with the sovereign; it was the sovereign who charged them with watching over the interests of the taxpayers. In any case, they improved the collection of the "taille" and of the capitation tax, obtained subscriptions to the twentieths, occupied themselves with means of communication, and in this connection, with the suppression of the corvée, adopted measures in favor of agriculture and commerce, organized bureaus of charity, etc.

CHAPTER X

THE MONARCHICAL PERIOD (*continued*). THE CENTRAL ADMINISTRATION

TOPIC 1. THE DELIBERATIVE ORGAN, THE COUNCIL OF THE KING

TOPIC 2. THE EXECUTIVE ORGAN. THE MINISTRY

IT was physically impossible for the sovereign to exercise alone all his power. He was obliged to associate auxiliaries with himself, some to aid him in arriving at decisions (a central deliberating organ), others to prepare and execute them (agents of execution, a double organ, central and regional).

TOPIC 1. THE DELIBERATIVE ORGAN, THE COUNCIL OF THE KING[1]

§ 363. **The Council of the King. Origin.** — The Council was but a reduced form of the "curia regis" of the first Capetians.

[1] BIBLIOGRAPHY: Detailed bibl. to 1876 in *Aucoc*, "Le Conseil d'Etat avant et depuis 1789," 1876, p. 263 *et seq.; Fasquier*, "Recherches de la France," II, 6, et p. 167; *Guillard*, "Hist. du Conseil," 1718; *L'Escalopier*, "Rech. s. l'orig. du Conseil du roi," 1765; *H. de Pansey*, "Tr. de l'autorité judiciaire," 1810; "Styles du Conseil du roi," *Du Crot*, 1623; *Du Chesne*, 1662; *Gauret*, 1700; "Règl. du Conseil" by *Tolosan*, 1786; *Denisart*, h. v°, 1786; MS. treatises on the council of the king by *Marillac* (?), 1630; by *Lefevre de Lezeau*, 1667; on the order of Colbert, 1670; by *Lisle de Hérissé*, 1703; *cf. infra*, "Ministère," bibliog.; Works of *Pardessus* and others on judicial organization; *Chéruel*, "Mémoires de Lef. d'Ormesson"; *Baudry*, *Id.* of *J. Foucault; P. Clément*, "Lettres de Colbert"; *R. Dareste*, "La justice admin. en Fr.," 2e éd., 1898; *De Vidaillan*, "Hist. des Conseils du roi," 1856; *A. Maury*, "L'Administration fr. avant la Révolution," 1874; *Decrue*, "De consilio regis Fr. I," 1885; *N. Valois*, "Invent. des arrêts du C. d'Etat" (Henry IV): Intro-

This feudal court, with a rather inconsistent composition, in which prelates, barons, and officers of the royal household participated, gave rise to: 1st, a small council composed especially of officers of the king and of councilors or clergy attached to his person, it was an ambulatory council which followed the king from place to place and was consulted especially in regard to current affairs; 2d, a larger assembly for exceptional affairs, — a plenary court, or the States-General.[1] The Carolingians already had councilors; and though the feudal king was content at first to take the advice of his officers,[2] the multiplicity of affairs which were submitted to him, and the impossibility of frequently assembling the full court, led to the formation of a new political organ, a central governmental council, which began as a private gathering of the confidants of the prince and which acquired an official existence only about the 1200 s.[3] This council itself was soon divided by a very simple application of the law of the division of labor into three bodies: the *Council*, strictly speaking, or a political and administrative body, the *Parlement* or Court of Justice, and the *Chamber of*

duction; "Le Conseil du roi aux XIVe, XVe, XVIe s.," 1888; *De Boislisle*, "Les Conseils sous Louis XIV," t. IV, VI, VII, éd. of *Saint-Simon*, 1881–90; *Luchaire*, p. 538; *Esmein*, p. 459; *Ch. Mortet*, "Gr. Encycl."; *Glasson*, V, 377; *H. Da Gama Barros*, "Hist. de l'admin. publique en Portugal du XIIe au XVe siècle" (in Portuguese), 1895; "R. hist.," 1889, t. LXXI, p. 328 (Netherlands).

[1] *Cf.* English law: the sovereign, says *Blackstone*, I, 5, is surrounded by four councils: the House of Lords, Parliament, the judges, and the Privy Council. This statement was hardly exact in Blackstone's time, but it recalls the common origin of these political bodies. The evolution of the English law offers here a strong analogy to that of our own legislation. The common council of the kingdom became the Parliament. The judicial courts such as the court of the King's Bench became detached from the others. There remained only the Privy Council, of which the Cabinet was legally only a part. *Franqueville*, "Le gouv. et le Parl. britan." vol. I, p. 399. *Nicolas*, "Proceedings and Ordinances of the Privy Council," 1834–7 (from Richard II to Henry VIII).

[2] For example, the kingdom of Jerusalem.

[3] Secret councilors of the German Emperor. *Isaacsohn*, "De consilio regio a Frid. II instituto." In the 1300 s, the English Council, *cf. Glasson*, 4, 74: five ministers, two archbishops, and several lords. The system of Councils of government was general in Europe, but it presented varieties according to the country. First, in the constitution of the Council, sometimes independent of the king, sometimes without influence and without authority apart from the royal power. The Polish and Hungarian senates and the Swedish Council were composed of high dignitaries taken from the nobility, and who depended rather upon the Diet than upon the king; formerly, the Council was composed only of creatures of the king. England had only a single council, the king's Privy Council. Almost everywhere, on the contrary, plurality of councils was the rule. In Spain and in Austria, countries formed by the consolidation of several States, the local councils were subordinate to a superior Council (*e.g.* the Councils of Aragon, of Castile, of the Indies, of Netherlands, etc.). Ordinarily, special Councils, war, finance, etc., were coexistent with a superior council; specialization was extended more or less, according to the country.

Accounts or court of finance. From the reign of Saint Louis the change began to operate;[1] Philip the Tall organized the council of the king (1316–1318), but to the very last there remained traces of the primitive unity of these bodies.[2]

§ 364. **From the 1300 s to the 1400 s.** — Two elements may be distinguished in the council of the king, one of feudal origin, the other professional: (A) Members by right: (*a*) princes of the blood and peers of France; (*b*) the great dignitaries upon whom the king had conferred the right to sit in his council but who, no more than the former, attended it regularly;[3] (B) Nominative councilors, bound by oath and by pledge, appointed and removed by the king; these attended constantly and formed the nucleus of the council. From the earliest times certain members were taken from the ranks of the bourgeoisie. The clergy were a part of the council in every period, but in the 1500 s, under Charles IX, complaint was made of their presence. On different occasions the States-General tried to intervene in the choice of councilors.[4]

[1] *Luchaire*, p. 534; *Esmein*, p. 489. The terms "Consilium" and "Magnum Consilium" were applied more specially to the King's Council about the commencement of the 1300 s. On the meaning of the words "Grand Council," "Council étroit," "Privy," "secret," *cf. Valois*, "Intro.," p. 17. Oath of the councilors under Louis IX or Phil. III, *Valois, op. cit.*, p. vii (correcting an error of Boutaric).

[2] Until the 1500 s, the terms used for the latter two bodies were, respectively, "The Council sitting in the Chamber of Parliament" and "The C. sitting in the Ch. of Accounts." The members of these three bodies were called King's Councilors. They met sometimes in full assembly, sometimes in partial assembly. Certain magistrates sat in the Council by virtue of letters from the king. To the members of the King's Council was given the right to sit in the Court of Accounts and in Parliament, (Ord. Feb. 5, 1388, restricted this right, and Henry II, 1157, allowed it by means of letters and an oath; *cf.* "Régl.," 1644); the king sent them to sit in the Parliament in order that its decisions would be such as pleased him; the Parliament resisted, of course. The rivalry between the Parliament and the Council was only one of the aspects of the strife between royalty and the Parliament. In the main, the Council prevailed over the Parliament; it prepared the laws that the Parliament had merely to apply; it was given the power of reversal over the decrees of the Parliament; originally, it even participated in the nomination of councilors. *Cf.* "Etat Register" of July, 1316. *Valois*, p. 9; *Guyot*, "Off.," II, 230.

[3] Ord. May, 1413; av. 1547. *Guillard*, p. 38. *Cf.* concerning the English Privy Council, *Fischel*, "English Constitution," vol. II, p. 245; *Glasson*, 4, 74.

[4] Ord. Jan., 1285; July, 1316. *Cf.* Ord., II, 330. Concerning the choice of councilors, their number, and their quality, *cf. Valois*, p. LXXX. Concerning the clerks, *ibid.*, p. CIX. *Ferrière*, see "Conseiller-Clerc" (he cites: *Petipied*, "Droit des ecclésiastiques dans l'administration de la justice séculière," 1715). On the intervention of the Estates (1357, 1484, 1576, etc.), *cf. Valois*, p. LXXXII; "R. q. hist.," 1885, p. 63. Analogy in *Bémont*, "Simon de Montfort," 1884, p. 111. Appointed by letters patent, then under Charles IX by simple brevet, the councilors in the end, after Marillac, received letters patent. The act was called

They were assisted by the masters of petitions ("maîtrés des requêtes")[1] who were charged with aiding them in their work, and, in particular, with making reports upon affairs submitted to the council. The powers of this body were most vague: government, administration, administrative controversies, and the administration of justice, in fact everything.[2] It did not hesitate to encroach upon the domain of the chamber of accounts or upon that of the Parliament; it pronounced judgment upon financial questions, and rescinded the decisions of the Parliament,[3] or took suits from its cognizance by removal.[4] This practice, if contrary to the division of functions, was justified upon the idea that the plenitude of judicial and financial power resided in the person of the king and consequently in his council which was the immediate organ of his will. Nevertheless, it was not without difficulty that the jurisdiction of the council was recognized; there was resistance, especially in the 1500 s, on the part of the States-General and the Parliament (as in England, where the Parliament obtained in 1640 the abolition of the Star Chamber and the suppression of the judicial powers of the council). The protests of this latter body burst out at the time of the Fronde (Decl., July 7, 1648); but Louis XIV put an end to them and compelled the Parliaments to respect the decisions of this council (Arr., July 8, 1661), which was "established to keep an eye upon all the other jurisdictions and to retain jurisdiction of affairs which, for reasons of State, ought not to be settled otherwise."

"retenue" because of the formula: "retinentes in nostrum consiliarium"; after the time of Henry III, one said: "élire et ordonner" instead of "retenir." *Cf.* formulas in *Valois*, p. cx.

[1] Formerly the clerks were charged with receiving petitions, with transmitting them to the king, and responding to them with him or in his name; they were called judges of "courts at the gates," "followers of the king" (under Louis the Quarrelsome), masters of petitions. When the King's Court was divided, some formed the Court of Petitions of the Parliament (petitions of the Palace), others remained attached to the Council ("requêtes de l'Hôtel). Ord. Nov., 1317; Dec., 1320; 1418, etc. Concerning admission to the Council, *cf. Valois*, "Intr.," cxvi.

[2] *Cf.* Letters of April 21, 1407.

[3] Ord. March 25, 1302, Art. 12: "Si aliquid erroris continere viderentur (arresta curiae seu communis consilii), correctio, revocatio ad nos vel nostrum commune consilium spectare noscantur, vel ad majorem partem consilii nostri, vel providam deliberationem specialis mandati nostri, et de nostra licentia speciali super omnia antea requisita servetur." Ord. 1331 and 1344.

[4] The Letters of July 22, 1370, restricted the practice of evocations [removal of cases to the Council [*cf.* the American writ of certiorari], but they were without effect. From the 1300 s, the Council played the triple rôle of Court of Cassation, of supreme administrative tribunal, and of judicial Court (1318, 1319). *Valois*, p. xxvi. On the conflicts with the Parliament, *cf.* authors who have written the history of the Parliament; *de Bastard*, *Mérilhou*, etc.

In 1497 a new sovereign Court was detached from the council of the king, under the name of the **Grand Council**, for the exercise of the judicial powers which the king had not delegated.[1] For a long time in course of preparation, accomplished before Charles VIII, this separation was completed under this prince (Ord. Aug. 2, 1497) and under Louis XII (Ord. July 13, 1498). It ended by becoming only an extraordinary tribunal, hardly ever occupying itself with anything more than cases concerning ecclesiastical benefices, and was retained only for reasons of policy in order to lessen the power of the Parliament. It could not be otherwise; the Grand Council detached from the crown was no longer a supreme court; appeal could be taken from its decisions to the king, who was the fountain of all justice. The council which remained attached to the person of the king resumed in a little while the right to quash the decisions of the sovereign courts and even to order the removal of certain cases (Chancellor Poyet, 1538).[2] In the 1500 s the number and diversity of affairs submitted to the council increasing, a new division of labor took place; but it did not lead to a dismemberment of this body; three sections were formed within it connected by close bonds, although each had its own name and powers: the Council of Affairs (political), the Council of Litigation (justice), and the Council of Finance.[3]

§ 365. **Definitive Organization** (1600 s). — The two essential reforms due especially to Richelieu and Louis XIV consisted: 1st, In the reduction of the personnel with a view to specializing its work; prelates, nobles, and members of the Parliament, those who sat as of right were eliminated. By excluding all these independent elements the council was made an "assembly of clerks." 2d, In a better apportionment of affairs in such a manner as to separate the political government from the administration of justice.[4] The different sections which were distinguished under

[1] Its jurisdiction embraced: disputes relative to benefices whose holders were appointed by the king, royal offices; evocations; appeal from the sentences of the masters of petitions of the household; conflicting decisions; and conflicts of jurisdiction between the Parliaments and the Presidiaux. *Valois*, "Introd.," p. xxv. Valois held that the Grand Council was not established upon the petition of the Estates of Tours; for a contrary view, see *Fleury*, p. 85.

[2] *Fleury*, p. 86. *Ferrière*, see "Grand Conseil." *Isambert*, "Table," h.vo.

[3] On the obscure history of the Council of State in the 1500 s, *cf. Mortet, op. cit.; N. Valois*, p. xi.

[4] Various decisions (*cf. Aucoc*, p. 50), 1547, 1582, 1585; *Chéruel*, "Hist. de l'admin.," vol. I, app. 2, Decis. of May, 1615, 1627, 1644. Ord. 1629, Art. 38 and 202. "État de la France," 1656, 1658 (five sections). In 1662, four sections. Decis. Jan. 9, 1673.

Louis XIV corresponded to our council of ministers, to our council of State, and to our Court of Cassation.[1]

1st, *The High Council of State*[2] presided over by the king and composed of ministers of State, persons upon whom a patent of the king conferred with this title a pension and a right to sit in the council (there were seven of them in 1789).[3] The constitution of 1791 still designated as the council of State the council of ministers held under the presidency of the king.[4] The council was occupied with affairs of government, with the direction of internal policy, and with foreign affairs. For the most important matters the kings, without doubt, had almost always had a small secret council (Council of Affairs under Francis I) in which there were only a few intimate councilors.[5] This was the origin of the High Council.

2d, *The Council of Dispatches* (so called because its decisions were contained in the dispatches or missives signed by a secretary of State), presided over by the king, was composed of members of the High Council, of secretaries of State not having the patent of ministers, of the chancellor, and of the princes of the blood (twelve members in 1789). It was a council of administration and had jurisdiction over questions of general police (discipline of the clergy, questions of the judicial order, warrants of imprisonment — "lettres de cachet" — etc.), and administrative questions (relations with the provincial estates, instructions to the intendants, etc.). It also gave advice in respect to ennoblements, naturalization, etc. Thus we see that it played the rôle of our

[1] **Special Councils:** In the sense of a more complete division of functions there were only attempts. *Cf.* modern ministries: 1, the Council of war until 1677; 2, the Council of marine; 3, Bureau of prizes, after 1676; 4, Council of conscience (charged with distributing benefices in the time of Mazarin); at the end of the reign of Louis XIV, the king's confessor disposed of all such appointments; the Council of conscience reappeared for a short time under the reign of the Polysynod. The bureau of ecclesiastical affairs was only one of the commissions of the Privy Council. Add. Council of religious affairs, 1684, 1701; 5, Direction of commerce (Council, Bureau), 1601, 1606, 1626, 1664, 1695, 1700, 1715, 1722, 1730, 1787 (C. of commerce and finance). England: technical councils of the same kind: exchequer, chancery, admiralty, board of trade, etc.

[2] *Ferrière* distinguishes the "C. d'Etat" and the "C. d'En Haut." According to *Boislisle*, V, 438, "C. d'Etat" was the official term, "C. d'En Haut," the current expression.

[3] "Hist. des Ministres d'Etat sous la 3e race," 1688. *J. de Silhon*, "Le Ministre d'Etat," 1631–43. *P. Boiteau*, p. 115.

[4] It was not until 1800 that the Council of State was actually designated by this name.

[5] Mentioned under Philip the Tall, *Valois*, "Intr." *Cf.* "Geheimrath" in Austria and Prussia, the Russian senate of Peter the Great, Council of "Despacho" in Spain, under the Bourbons (Foreign and Interior affairs).

Minister of the Interior because all administrative affairs were centered in it.

3d, *The Council of Finance*, presided over by the king or the chancellor (or even by a chief as a substitute for the latter), was composed of the comptroller general of finance and of a number of councilors of state (eleven members in 1789).[1] Its competence extended to all questions of the budget: the management of finances, the creation of offices, the issue of public loans ("rentes"), the control of accounts, controversies concerning the public domain, etc.[2]

4th, *The Privy Council or Council of Litigation.*[3] This section of the king's council, the most numerous of all, the only one in which all its members were assembled, and the one in which their rank was fixed, was, first of all, a court of justice. It included: (*a*) *members of right*, the chancellor president, the ministers and secretaries of State (who rarely attended), and the comptroller general of finances;[4] (*b*) *councilors of state*, thirty in 1673, three from the Church, three from the army, and twenty-four from the judiciary, recalling the primitive composition of the council since the three orders were represented in it (but with a marked superiority over the Third Estate); the king recruited them from among the masters of petitions ("maîtres des requêtes"), presidents of the sovereign courts, the king's gentlemen attached to these courts, the provosts of the merchants of Paris, etc;[5] although they did not buy their commissions like the "maîtres des re-

[1] It existed from 1563. *Cf. Valois*, "Intr.," p. lx. To the royal council of finance was attached the great and petty direction. Austria: in the 1500 s three councils, Domain ("Hofkammer"), War, Chancellery.

[2] The administration of the crown domain, agriculture, and public works was divided between the Council of Finances and the Council of Dispatches.

[3] *Valois*, "Intro.," p. xlvii and lviii. "Conseil privé" in contradistinction to the "Conseil commun" (the Parliament or a commission taken from Parliament and the Council). "Conseil des parties," because private persons could here assert their rights (because the judges were parties here, it was jocularly said). *Cf.* Judicial Committee of the English Privy Council.

[4] After 1657, the intendants of finance, dukes, and peers also had, but only in theory, the right to sit, but they did not avail of it.

[5] The title of "Conseiler du roi," purely honorary after the 1500 s, was borne by the counselors of Châtelet, the "baillis," presidents of sovereign courts, etc. The grand officers of the king's household, governors of provinces, the presidents, and first presidents of the Parliaments, and the king's men near the Parliaments, etc., designated as "Conseillers du roi en ses Conseils"; admitted formerly to the king's Council, they were excluded from it in 1673. The members of the Privy Council, designated as "conseillers au Conseil d'Etat et privé," had certain privileges, namely: their titles of nobility were transmissible to the first degree, they took precedence over their colleagues except over princes, cardinals, dukes, and peers; they accompanied the king when he attended a bed of justice ("lit de justice"), and were allowed to wear a special costume.

quêtes," they were in fact irremovable; (c) *the maîtres des requêtes* (eighty in 1789)[1] were charged with the preparation of business and the making of reports; it was from among them that the intendants of the provinces[2] and the intendants of finances were almost always taken; their posts, although purchasable and hereditary like those of the magistrates, did not procure for them the same independence as for the latter because this service was a sort of term of probation for higher employments; it was a position which one entered only in order to quit it, said Daguesseau; (d) *assistants,* secretary-recorders, who prepared the official records of the proceedings of the sessions and preserved the minutes of the decisions; (e) *advocates* before the council of the king (160, 170). Edict, Sept., 1643.[3]

§ 366. **Powers of the Council in General.** — It had no powers of its own; its acts were considered as the acts of the king and its different sections were only advisory bodies to which the king addressed himself, if it pleased him, but whose advice he was not bound to follow.[4] However, the Privy Council, in its judicial rôle, deliberated and judged in complete independence, although its decisions were rendered in the name of the king. It served as a bond with the other sections, inasmuch as its members formed commissions in which they acquainted themselves with a portion of the business which fell within the competency of the other sections.[5] Certain acts were even elaborated in the plenary assemblies held with the Privy Council. Through its general orders the council or its sections exercised a large share in the legislation of the monarchical period.[6] It was due to this Council that there could be agreement between the government and the administration and a certain regularity in the application of the laws.[7]

[1] Salaries 150 to 200,000 francs. Ord. 1644, 1674, etc. *O'Reilly,* "Clade Pellot," 1881; *Boislisle,* "Corresp. des Contr. g.," I, 542–558; *Loyseau,* "Off.," I, 7, 57. Edict Nov. 1683. *Isambert,* "Table."

[2] *Cf. Aucoc,* p. 71; *Dareste,* p. 90. They also assisted the chancellor in the use of the seal and they had a special jurisdiction called "Requêtes de l'Hôtel" which embraced cases involving officers admitted to the king's household and other persons enjoying the "committimus" (appeal to the Parliament), contests concerning the titles of royal officials, instances in execution of the decisions of the Private Council, etc.

[3] *Bos,* "Les avocats au C. du roi," 1880.

[4] *Bodin,* "Rep.," III, 1, p. 365. Formula: "by the king in his council." *Cf.* attributes of the English Council. *Franqueville,* I, 427.

[5] Sometimes, the king added to his councilors members of the Parliament, barristers, or even other persons.

[6] *Cf. Des Cilleuls,* "Orig. et dévelop du rég. des travaux publics en Fr.," 1895.

[7] Concerning the work of the council, *cf. Aucoc,* p. 80; *Tocqueville,* "Anc. Rég. et Révol.," II, ch. II; *Fleury,* p. 88.

§ 367. **The Powers of the Privy Council.** — (A) *Preparatory examination of administrative affairs.* The members of the Privy Council formed committees, or bureaus, charged with examining a portion of the administrative affairs depending upon the other councils (those which were submitted to it by these councils or by the comptroller general).[1]

(B) *Contentious jurisdiction.*[2] The Privy Council was, first of all, a tribunal; the chancellor submitted first to its commissions or bureaus the litigation within its powers. The bureau thus consulted rendered a decision admitting or rejecting the suit, and, in case it was admitted, it was sent back to the council with a report. The powers of the council, which was derived from the idea of justice reserved by the king,[3] embraced three principal categories of cases: administrative affairs, removals, and appeals and conflicts.

1st, *As a superior administrative court* (*cf.* our Council of State). The Council of Litigation had jurisdiction of appeals from the judgments of the intendants, for redress against the acts of the Council, or acts of grace emanating from the chancellery (ennoblement, legitimation, patents of offices, etc.). But the other sections of the king's council participated in the exercise of these contentious powers; the Council of Finance, to which were submitted contentious questions relating to the royal domain and to the taxes, and appeals against the decisions of the Court of Aids.[4]

2d, *As an extraordinary tribunal.* It gave decisions upon the removal of cases ("évocations") to the council, or at least upon those which entered, as it were, into the circle of ordinary affairs and for which there was a settled judicial law. If the king called the case up personally, the affair was judged by the High Council; removals on their own motion went to the Council of Dispatches (which in that way sheltered the officeholders from the jurisdiction of the ordinary tribunals).[5]

[1] *Cf. Aucoc,* p. 60. "Code voiturin," 1748 (judgments of the commissioners of the bureau of posts and messages).

[2] "Règlement" of June 28, 1738, on the procedure of the King's Council. *Cf.* June, 1597, Feb., 1660, June, 1787. *Valois,* p. lix: "The procedure in the Council of State was more simple than ordinary procedure. The 'règlement' of 1738 was still applied to the Court of Cassation and served as a model for the Decree of July 22, 1806, on the procedure in the Council of State."

[3] Also one could not appeal from a decision of the council, except by petition or writ of error, or by opposition, if the judgment was rendered on simple petition. *Valois,* p. cxxv. *Cf. Dareste,* p. 105.

[4] *Cf. infra,* Finances; also *Dareste,* p. 71.

[5] Evocations of full right for questions of finance interesting the king, for domainal affairs, claims of officeholders against the State, liquidation

3d, *As a supreme court* (*cf.* our Court of Cassation). Falling within its jurisdiction were decisions as to the competency of courts,[1] removals from one court to another on account of relationship, revision of criminal judgments,[2] and quashing of judgments for violation of the law or evident injustice;[3] after annulment, the case was sent back to another court, or the council retained it through the process of removal in order to judge it itself.[4]

§ 368. **Polysynods.** — In 1715 (Decl. of 15 Sept.), the secretaries of State and the comptroller general, — these five kings of France whose bourgeois tyranny exasperated the great seigniors like Saint Simon, — were replaced by seven councils (foreign affairs, war, marine, finance, internal affairs, conscience, and commerce). Of the council of the king there remained only the Privy Council, under the presidency of the chancellor. This system, abolished in 1722, made the mistake of conferring upon the same council the double function of deliberating and executing; on account of the inexperience of the nobles the deliberations led to exciting and useless discussions (one could not hear the thunders of heaven, said d'Argenson); and besides, a collective administration could not act in harmony and with promptness.[5]

§ 369. **The Law of the Revolution.** — In 1791 (27th April, 25th May)[6] the Council of Ministers under the name of the Council

of indemnities due in case of the abolition of an office, provision markets, questions of rights of authors, cases to which the Company of the Indies was a party, etc. *Dareste*, p. 75; *Fleury*, p. 88.

[1] In case of conflict between judges holding their powers from the king he only could terminate it. *Dareste*, p. 68 and following. An exception was made in the case of conflicts between the Parliament and the "Presidiaux" and between criminal lieutenants and provosts of marshals, — cases in which the Great Council was competent.

[2] The right of revision was open to all condemned persons without delay or special conditions; the condemned or his representatives could use all the means calculated to establish his innocence. Concerning the procedure, *cf. Dareste*, p. 70, "Calas affair."

[3] *Le Bret*, p. 157; *Esmein*, p. 433; *Fleury*, p. 88. Concerning the allowance of appeal, *cf. H. de Pansey*, "Tr. de l'autor. judic.," which cites extracts from the two memoirs of *Gilbert de Voisins* and *Joly de Fleury*, 1762. The violation of the law signified alike a breach of the Roman law and of the Coutumes as of the Ordinances. The reasons upon which decisions of the Parliament were based not being given, reversal was rare. The "demandes en contrariété d'arrêts" were taken to the Great Council, if it was a question concerning the decisions of the Parliament or of the sovereign courts; otherwise to the Council of State.

[4] The Council did not keep registers of its decrees (notwithstanding the "règlement" of Jan. 18, 1630, and the formula: "extrait des Registres" . . .). The minutes of its decrees are in the National Archives; following the report of the councilor, a secretary wrote down the decision and the councilors present, or at least the principal ones of them, signed it.

[5] This system was introduced into Russia by Peter the Great (1718).

[6] Reforms on the eve of the Revolution, *Aucoc*, p. 85. *Cf.* "règl." of August 9, 1789.

of State became the sole auxiliary of the Chief of State in the preparation of the laws. The superior jurisdiction in administrative matters belonged to the king in his Council of Ministers, each in his own department.[1] Thus we see that the revolutionary legislation was not progressive; it confused the contentious jurisdiction with administration, and caused the disappearance of useful machinery in the central organism. But it had the merit of establishing a tribunal of reversals as a Supreme Court (Law of 27th Nov.–1st Dec., 1790). The constitution of the 22d Frimaire, year VIII (1800), restored to the government the organ that it had lost (Art. 52).

Topic 2. The Executive Organ. The Ministry[2]

§ 370. **The Public Functions.** — The administrative office-holders had a share in the public power, but for different reasons; the evolution was in the direction of greater and greater dependence upon the king. The public function was at first a fief, then an office, and finally a commission.[3] But fiefs and offices constituted

[1] Art. 15. *Cf.* "Loi.," Sept. 11, 1790, origin of the existing system of administrative jurisdiction.

[2] *Vincent de la Loupe,* "Liv. des dignités, mag. et offices de France," 1551; *Bodin,* "Rép.," 3, 3; *Du Tillet,* "Recueil des rois de Fr., des rangs," 1601; *Cl. Fauchet,* "Orig. des dignités et magistrats," 1600; *Favin,* "Tr. des 1ers officiers de la couronne," 1613; *Girard (et Joly),* "Trois livres des Offices de France," 1638; *Loyseau,* "Du droit des offices," 16, 10; *Guyot,* "Tr. des dignités et offices," 1786–89; *Le P. Anselme,* "Hist. généalog. de la m. royale, des pairs, gr. officiers," etc., 1726; *De Luçay,* "Orig. du pouvoir ministériel en France," 1881. Concerning England, *cf. Glasson, Fischel, Boutmy, Franqueville,* and the authors they cite.

[3] *Loyseau,* IV, 5; *Ferrière,* see "Office." *Cf. Pothier,* "Traité des personnes et des choses," no. 276, and the treatises on the distinction of properties. *Infra:* Judicial organization. We shall speak only of administrative functions or offices of the government, as they were formerly called. Financial and judicial offices tended, by an inverse evolution, toward the principle of irremovability and of independence; they constituted, for the most part, "offices" "stricto sensu." In a general way the law of the monarchical epoch distinguished between not purchasable ("non-vénal") offices and purchasable ("vénal") offices. The latter were divided into "casuels" and domainal offices. I. *Offices not purchasable,* which Pothier called "purely personal," were entirely at the disposal of the king. The principal ones were, according to *Loyseau:* 1. Offices of the crown, that is to say, the principal offices of the State (high constable, châncellor, first president of the Parliament, etc.); 2. Offices of the king's household (councilors, secretaries of State, secretaries to the king, etc.); 3. Military offices (governors, etc.); 4. Commissions in general. These offices remained outside of commerce [*i.e.* they were not for sale] either because of their importance, because they were, as *Loyseau* said, "part and parcel of the State," or because their incumbents were too near the king for him not to reserve complete liberty in choosing them. From this, it results that they could neither be seized, nor mortgaged, nor divided. At the death of the incumbent, the king alone had the right

veritable property rights of which it was difficult to dispossess the incumbents and which procured for them independence of the superior authority; the *commission*, on the other hand, was only a delegation of authority revocable "ad nutum," and conferred only the right to exercise public power; it was granted to persons without prestige who were supple instruments in the hands of the

to name a successor; they were not alienable nor hereditary ("service de prince ne tombe en héritage," *Loysel*, 554). However, we must not believe that this principle was always respected; for many of these offices, the successor was often designated in advance, the king having granted a reversion or a patent of retention, or having allowed the incumbent to sell his office during his lifetime.

II. *The purchasing of public office* was regularly practiced after the time of Francis I, 1522, at first in the case of the financial offices, a fact which was somewhat explainable, then for the judicial offices, which was more open to criticism and which was practiced only for fiscal reasons. We shall show later how the practice of selling offices was introduced and what its advantages and its disadvantages were.

(A) "Casuel." *Venal offices.* These offices were regarded as being in commerce (*i.e.* salable); they were alienable and hereditary, but there was a distinction. The right to exercise a public function, *i.e.* the "office," was not salable; the State was not deprived of it in theory. But the "income," that is to say, the right of presenting to the king a subject capable of filling the office and of making him pay for it in consideration of the presentation, was part of the patrimony of the incumbent. The king was not forced to accept the candidate presented nor to give reasons for rejecting him; but when there were no motives for refusing to accept a particular candidate, the king granted him the provision of the office; without which, the incumbent would have been obliged to present an indefinite number of candidates; the liberty of choice, intact in appearance, was found in fact to be strongly restricted. The appointee was then received in his office (after the king was informed concerning his life, habits, and religion, and assured that he had been examined and judged capable, but the examination was reduced to a mere formality). The "réception" and the "provisions" alone gave him the character of a public officer, and the right to exercise its powers. The incumbent could not be deprived of it except in three cases: death, resignation, or forfeiture. But the king could retake possession of the office by reimbursing him for the price paid. Purchasable offices became hereditary in consequence of the decision of the Privy Council of the 7th and by the Declaration of the 12th of December, 1604, rendered on the opinion of Charles Paulet, secretary of the King's Chamber. On condition of paying the "Paulette," or annual fee, the incumbent acquired for his heir not exactly the right to exercise the function of the office that he occupied, but the income of the office, that is to say, the right of presentation; and there was no opposition to the heir's exercising this right for his benefit if he possessed the qualifications and met the required conditions. If the "Paulette" was not paid, the office fell to the "Parties casuelles": the king disposed of it at his will, without having to pay an indemnity; from that came the name "Offices casuels," given to this category of purchasable offices.

(B) Domainal Offices were more completely venal than ordinary venal offices, which can be understood without difficulty, since they were recorder's and scrivener's offices. They were alienable and hereditary, with no tax to pay to the king and no necessity for taking the "provisions" of the office, consequently without the consent of the king. Loyseau connects them very properly with feudal offices; originally they were regarded as a kind of fief. In the 1500 s, they were regarded as having been relinquished by the king, in consideration of the grant of a portion of his domain to which an office was attached as accessory; the prinking (secretaries of state, intendants). The general administration included two branches: a central organ and local organs, the latter being united into a regular hierarchy, creating secondary centers connected with the principal centers; this was a necessity if the territory were at all spread out. The multiplicity of affairs and the increase of the powers of the State involved a more and more marked specialization of functions; justice, finance, and the army were in turn detached from the administration properly so called. There was a tendency toward the establishing of uniformity in all the branches of the administration, because it facilitated the action of the central power and made control more certain. The energetic mechanism thus established crushed the petty local tyrannies, destroyed the feudal abuses, encroached upon privileges, and prepared the way for the leveling process of the Revolution. It was reproached for not being very well adapted to satisfy local interests — a point which is debatable — or for annihilating individual initiative, and for alienating even the superior classes of the population in the provinces and making them unfit for political life — a criticism which was better founded — but perhaps it was the price necessary to pay for national unity.

§ 371. **The Ministry.** — The "ancien régime" had no ministry in the modern sense of the term, that is to say, no coherent group of high officials jointly liable and directing the administrative machinery. But there were ministers; we use this term, although it was not formerly used in this sense, to designate the high officeholders of the central administration, the chancellor, the comptroller general of finances, and the secretaries of State. These were "chargés d'affaires" of the king — although to-day the cabinet is the "chargé d'affaires" of the Parliament. The ministers, in former times, were responsible to the king, who could remove them as one may revoke an agency; they were also responsible to public opinion. According to the English axiom "the king can do no wrong" the people readily believed, under an absolute government, that every bad thing came from the ministers; there was much truth in this idea, because, although the king was supposed to do everything, in reality he did very little by himself. The theory of

ciple of indefeasibility of the domain was different in that the abandonment was in perpetuity. It was considered as a mortgage of the domain with a perpetual right to repurchase. It was then allowable for the king to repurchase the office, but until that time, he did not possess the right, provided the mortgagor filled the office or had it filled. Add. certain offices hereditary by privilege and resembling feudal offices: forestry offices, chafe-wax, of the grand chancellery, etc.

the responsibility of the king and, consequently, the irresponsibility of his agents, all of whose acts were done by his order, was in complete discord with the facts. The truth was, the ministry reduced the royal power, as, moreover, the bureaus reduced that of the ministry. The king often reigned without governing, but so did the ministry also. The bureaus created a tradition, a sort of judicial practice; they were criticized for their faults, complications, slowness, expense, and red tape, but on the whole they prevented the greatest of all evils, arbitrary action.

§ 372. **Offices of the Court during the Feudal Period.**[1] — (A) At the Court of the Capetians, as at those of the great feudatories, were to be found the same offices as at the Carolingian palace.[2] According to old usage, the administration was confused with the personal service of the king, but gradually the two were separated; certain officers of the palace were elevated to the rank of State dignitaries; the others remained at the head of the royal household (" maison du roi ").[3]

(B) The feudal, or semifeudal, character of the great officers of the crown made them almost independent of the royal authority; they were displaced for the most part to the advantage of a new stratum of inferior servitors, simple agents of execution, whose origin brought them more strictly under the control of the king. As to those who were not suppressed, for example, the chancellor, since the crown could not dismiss them but was obliged to leave them in office during their lives, it took from them their essential powers; they had only a vain title; thus the Chancellor was supplanted by the Keeper of the Seals (minister of justice). We may observe, also, that they were appointed by the king, and were irremovable, but their offices were not hereditary.

[1] *Luchaire,* "Ann. de Bordeaux," 1881; "Manuel," p. 518 *et seq.* *Viollet,* II, 104. BCh., 51, 265; 55, 613. *Le Féron,* "Hist. des connétables, chanceliers," etc., review by *D. Godefroy,* 1658. *Lepage,* "Les offices des duchés de Lorraine," 1869. *Borrelli de Serres,* "Rech. s. div. services publics du XIIIe au XVIIe s.," 1895. *Glasson,* V, 290.

[2] *Luchaire,* I, 160: in the 1000 s there was no order in the enumeration of the officers mentioned in the Charters: in the 1100 s, a hierarchy was established. At Jerusalem, there were four grand life officers but who were revocable: the seneschal, the high constable, the marshal, and the chamberlain. *Dodu,* "Inst. de Jérus.," p. 156, 177. The chancellor, inferior to these, was usually an ecclesiastic. Empire: seneschal, marshal, cupbearer, chamberlain (and pantler, 1200 s), archchaplain, count-palatin, master of the hounds. These "ministeria" were attached to the fief and like it hereditary. *Frommhold,* p. 121, 186. "Subministeria," hereditary also. "Golden Bull," c. 21, 29.

[3] Division necessary by the extension of the king's powers, and the growth of the "Hospitium regis." *Isambert,* "Table"; *Boiteau,* p. 129, 144; *Lemonnier,* "De min. cubic.," 1887.

The office of *Count of the Palace* [1] had become purely honorary by the 1100 s (the counts of Champagne). The important position of *seneschal* [2] ("senescallus," "dapifer"), including the service of the table, the judicial functions of the Count of the Palace, the intendancy or administration of the royal domain, authority over the provosts and the military command, became vacant at the end of 1191. The *Constable*,[3] chief of the royal stables, took over the military powers of the seneschal; by the 1300 s he was at the head of the army (in time of war); [4] the marshals were his subordinates; he left to the grand equerry the care of the royal equipages. The office of constable was abolished only in 1627. The superintendence of the royal palace passed from the seneschal to the *Grand Master of France*. The *Chancellor* in office (as contradistinguished from the archbishop of Rheims, who was honorary chancellor) added the judicial powers of the seneschal to his own powers as keeper of the seals and chief of the notaries. This secretary of the king became secretary of State (although he did not bear the title) and was placed at the head of the administration and of the judicial system, until the personal secretaries of the king or privy clerks came to dispute with him a portion of his powers.

The *Cupbearer*, charged with the administration of the royal treasure, with the police regulations concerning food and the trades at Paris, as an accessory of his original functions somewhat as the grand pantler had supervision over the bakers, abandoned his domestic rôle to the first or grand cupbearer and became, in the 1300 s, president of the chamber of accounts.

The *Grand Chamberlain* [5] charged with the maintenance of the palace had hardly more than an honorary title in the 1200 s and the position was abolished in 1545. From that time the domestic services of the court were confided, under the direction of the grand master of France, to the grand chamberlain, the grand pantler, the head cook, the marshal of the mews, the master of the hounds,

[1] *Luchaire*, 519; *Brussel*, "Us. d. Fiefs," I, 370.

[2] *Luchaire*, "Hugues de Clers" and the "De Senescalcia Franciæ" (Bibl. "Fac. lettres de Paris," 3d fasc.). *Cf. Bémont*, "Mélanges Monod."; *Luchaire*, "Man.," p. 521; "R. hist.," vol. 37, p. 258.

[3] BCh., 5th s. II, 498. *Cf.* I, 352. *Guérin*, "Thèses Ec. Chartes," 1867. Jurisdiction of the high constable over military persons. *Isambert*, "Table," h. v.

[4] Although there was no permanent army; and even when there was one.

[5] *Lemonnier*, "De ministris cubiculi" (Charles V), 1887. *Cf. L. Delisle*, "Catalogue des Actes de Phil. Aug.," Intro. *Isambert*, "Table."

the grand almoner, and the grand provost of the palace.[1] These officers played only a feeble rôle in the administration.[2]

§ 373. **High Functionaries of the Absolute Monarchy.** — The *Chancellor*[3] was irremovable,[4] thus differing from the secretaries of State.[5] 1st, Of his seigniorial functions he had preserved the direction of the chancellery,[6] the custody of the royal seal, and the care of affixing it to the royal acts. This made him, said Loyseau, the controller and the corrector of all the affairs of France, since, the affixing of the seal did not take place without examination and consequently without possible remonstrances and opposition. There were chancellors who made use of this right to the point of embarrassing the royal authority; they could not be dismissed because they were irremovable; they were therefore deprived of their powers, which were intrusted to a *Keeper of the Seals* ("ex officio" after 1551).[7]

2d, By virtue of being the first officer of the crown he presided over the king's council in the absence of the sovereign, even when there were princes of the blood. He expounded the will of the king at the beds of justice ("lits de justice"), and at the opening of the States-General; he received the oath of fidelity from the officers of the crown,[8] and fealty and homage from the direct vassals of the king.

3d, As the head of the judiciary he was honorary president of the Parliament and of the judiciary;[9] he exercised surveillance over

[1] Other great offices subsequently created were: grand admiral, grand master of archers, then grand master of the artillery in the 1400 s, colonel, and general of the infantry, 1500 s (abolished in 1667). *Luchaire*, p. 527.

[2] BCh., 6th s. IV, 21 (right of the grand officers over the trades of Paris).

[3] *Luchaire*, "Manuel," p. 522 (bibliog.); "Gr. Encycl.," h. v. Cf. *supra*, p. 540; *P. de Miraulmont*, "De la Chancellerie," 1610; *Duchesne*, "Hist. des chanceliers," 1680; *Godefroy*, "Hist. des connétables, chanceliers," etc., 1688; *Tessereau*, "Hist. de la chancellerie," 1710; BCh., 1892, 682; *Cougny*, "G. du Vair," 1857; *Kerviler*, "Le chancelier Séguier," 1874. List of Chancellors in *de Luçay*, p. 639; *cf.* p. 467, 474, "lettres de provision de Meaupou," 1768; *Dupré-Lasale*, "L'Hospital," 1875; *S. Luce*, "R. hist.," 16, 95; *Isambert*, "Table," h. v.

[4] He did not wear mourning upon the death of the king.

[5] Salary of 220,000 pounds including the emoluments of the seal (in 1750).

[6] The English Lord Chancellor, sometimes both "justiciarius" or Grand Judge (office abolished in the 1400 s) and keeper of the great seal (always, since the time of Elizabeth), is president of the House of Lords, of the Court of Chancery, appoints (under certain conditions) the judges, and may revoke them all, etc. Under the Chancellor are two law officers of the crown, the attorney-general, and the solicitor-general, and the Lord Privy Seal.

[7] Meaupou, exiled after 1774, held his office until 1790, when it was abolished. *Isambert*, "Table," see "Garde des Sceaux."

[8] He himself took oath between the hands of the king.

[9] Nevertheless, the relations between the head of the State and the judicial bodies fell within the province of the secretaries of State. *De Luçay*, p. 468.

the magistracy and prepared regulations for its police and discipline.[1] Men like L'Hospital and d'Aguesseau, as chancellors, drew up the royal ordinances.

§ 374. **The Superintendent, later the Comptroller General of Finances.**[2]—The higher administration of finances, after having for a long time belonged to the treasurers and to the treasurers general, passed in the 1500 s, when the latter became local functionaries, to intendants of finances (1523). About 1564, the president of the intendants, the superintendent,[3] was a veritable minister of finance. Upon the downfall of Fouquet, in 1661, the office of superintendent was abolished. The powers which had been attached to it passed to the comptroller general, an agent created in 1547 to verify receipts and to exercise a surveillance over payments made into the royal treasury.[4] From the time of Colbert he administered much more than he supervised;[5] he had the exclusive direction of the financial administration, and was occupied with the increase and reduction of taxes and with their direct collection by the administration or by the farmers of taxes. No expenditure was made without an order; no order was paid without the warrant of the comptroller general.[6] As he passed upon the expenditures of the other ministers he interfered in all their affairs.[7]

[1] Office and director of the bookseller proceeding under his authority to the examination of books. *De Luçay*, p. 469 (details on the press).

[2] "Gr. Encycl.," see "Contrôleur"; *De Boislisle*, "Corresp. des contr. gén. avec les Intendants," 1874–83; "Annuaire de la Soc. de l'hist. de Fr.," 1881, 225; *Depping*, "R. hist.," X, 285; XI, 63; *Montyon*, "Particul. s. les min. des fin. 1610 à 1791," 1812; *Esnault*, "Chamillart," 1884; *De Luçay*, p. 541; list, p. 635; *P. Clément*, "Lettres de Colbert," 1861–8; *Isambert*, "Table," see "Contrôl. g., Finances"; *Boiteau*, p. 132.

[3] *Cf. D'Avenel*, I, 70. The word is older than the office; the superintendents of finances were simply the superior agents of the financial administration. *Loyseau*, IV, 249. From 1623 to 1643 almost all the superintendents were dishonest and incapable. Concerning the case of Fouquet, *cf. C. Rousset*, "R. des Deux-Mondes," Dec. 15, 1890. *Chéruel*, "Vie et Procès de Fouquet," 1864.

[4] Necker was the director of finances only because he was an adherent of the reformed religion. The First Lord of the Treasury in England is nearly always the first minister, but as this title does not exist officially, he ranks below the secretaries of State. He formerly held the Court of Exchequer, a kind of court of accounts, and was occupied with questions of public finance, but at present he is obliged to devolve these functions on the second Lord of the Treasury or Chancellor of the Exchequer.

[5] *De Luçay*, p. 542: commission of Terray. Salary about 200,000 pounds (Terray).

[6] Under his orders were six intendants of finance each at the head of one of the following bureaus: 1, farm and "régie" general; 2, domain and "parties casuelles"; 3, bridges, roads, hospitals, and prisons; 4, lotteries, gunpowders, the Company of the Indies, etc.; 5, manufactures, tolls, fishing, pastures, etc.; 6, treasury.

[7] Interior, public works, commerce, posts, relations with supreme courts, and extraordinary affairs of war. *Cf.* rôle of Colbert, Turgot,

He tended to become the prime minister, as in England the First Lord of the Treasury became the chief of the cabinet.[1]

§ 375. **The Secretaries of State.**[2] — From the group of clerks or notaries of the chancellery, there were detached at the beginning of the 1300s, under the name of privy clerks,[3] certain scribes attached to the person of the king (secretaries of the king) one of whom was charged with keeping the records of the sessions of the council (1316–1320). They received, to the exclusion of all others, the power of signing papers in financial matters.[4] This function won for them a preponderant situation, which was accentuated in the 1500s[5] in proportion as the great feudal offices died out. In 1547 they numbered only four and were called the private and financial secretaries of the king, having charge of the dispatches in his affairs of State.[6] This long title was soon changed to that of secretaries of State.[7] With the new title their powers were modified. From simple dispatch clerks they were elevated to the rank of ministers. On the occasion of the drawing up of the

Necker. *A. des Cilleuls*, "Orig. et dévelop. des trav. publics en France," 1898; *De la Mare*, "Tr. de la police," 1713; *Peuchet*, "Coll. des lois de police dep. le XIIIe s.," 1818.

[1] This great king continually paid court to his comptroller general, said *Ponchartrain*, in speaking of Louis XIV. Abolition, April 27, 1791.

[2] *Luchaire*, p. 534; *Campardon*, "Essai sur les clercs, notaries et secrét. du roi"; *Fauvelet du Toc*, "Hist. des secrétaires d'Etat," 1668; *De Luçay*, "Les Secrét. d'Etat," 1881, p. 577; *Viollet*, II, 140; *Esmein*, p. 448; *Boiteau*, p. 125.

[3] Secrecy was the rule under the "Ancien Régime" for all affairs of State. *Viollet*, II, 140, n. 1. (The Ord. of 1309 was in reality of 1316, according to *Langlois*.) *Isamb.*, III, 11. Ord. Nov. 17, 1317.

[4] Ord. 13 Nov., 1373, Art. 9; 1381, Art. 6; 1388; 1413, Art. 219. Edict 1478.

[5] Personal influence of Florimond Robertet, "the father of secretaries of State" (under Charles VIII, Louis XII, Francis I). *Robertet*, "Les Robertet au XVIe s.," 1888. *Esmein*, p. 449, cites *Chassanœus*, "Catalogus gloriæ mundi," 1692. Under Louis XI, they signed the king's letters; under Charles IX, they signed for the king. The "réglements" of 1570, 1588 show them in a high position. *D'Avenel*, I, 59. In memory of their origin, the secretaries of State being a part of the body of royal notaries had to be provided with the title of secretaries of the king; they drew up marriage contracts for princes of the blood. Concerning these secretaries, *cf. Loyseau*, V, 3; *Girard*, II, 5; *Ferrière*, h. v.; *Isambert*, "Table."

[6] "Réglement" of 1547.

[7] In the treaty of Cateau-Cambrésis, 1559, L'Aubespine would have taken this title, following the example of the secretaries of the king of Spain. *Esmein*, p. 450, maintains that the change was earlier (at least, 1557) according to *Du Tillet*, "Rec. des rangs des grands de Fr.," 1601, p. 107. In England an ecclesiastic (clerk) served as secretary to the Norman kings. He became a member of the Privy Council after the time of Henry VI. Henry III had two laymen for secretaries. In 1794, there were three secretaries: foreign affairs, interior, war. Each one could replace the others, and the sovereign had to be accompanied by one of them on his travels. Every act of the crown is countersigned by a secretary. The name of secretary of State dates from 1601.

king's orders they were consulted, their advice was taken, they were charged with overseeing the execution of these orders, and were themselves permitted to dispatch them (at the end of the 1500s).

In appearance the secretaries of State were below the king's council;[1] in reality they had almost superseded it and the initiative came from them. "Nothing could be done without them, nothing except by them."[2] They could do everything and answered for nothing; they closed the mouths of those who complained by pleading the name of the king; yet often their will was only that of their clerks;[3] the bureaucracy was already a power.[4] They were not invested with an official title, but had simple commissions which were always revocable. Taken from the ranks of the "roturier" class, for a long time, it was only under Louis XV that one saw men like Choiseul and d'Aiguillon, belonging to the high nobility, attaining these high stations. The principles of reversion and heredity were introduced in spite of the revocability of their titles; Colbert bought the superintendency of the marine and the secretaryship of the king's household, and transmitted them to his son Seignelay.

In the 1600s there were four secretaries of State and their

[1] *Dareste*, "Just. admin.," p. 66. The same in England: "in theory, the Privy Council is the only legal council of the Crown; all acts of sovereignty must be performed in Council; the king in Council declares war, concludes peace, etc."

[2] Saint Simon called the comptroller and the secretaries of State "the five kings of France who exercised their tyranny at will, under the real king and almost always without his knowledge." Under the Regency, the ministers were for a time suppressed in consequence of the reaction of the privileged classes, against what Saint Simon called "a long reign of vile bourgeoisie."

[3] A "réglement" of 1589 created bureaus (bookkeepers and clerks).

[4] Centralization led as a consequence to bureaucracy; affairs submitted to the ministers multiplied, and the ministers found it necessary to leave their work to the bureaus, that is to say, to clerks who became masters. D'Argenson, the Court of Aids in its remonstrances in 1775, and Necker in 1778, vainly protested against this new power. Complaint was also made of the great number of administrative formalities and the consequent long delays; complaint is also made of them in our time, as we complain of the complications of procedure. *Tocqueville*, "Ancien Régime et Révolution," 1, II, ch. VI: "Toward the end of the 1700s there could not be established a bureau of charity in the most remote part of a distant province without the comptroller general's keeping watch over its expenditure, drawing up regulations for it, and determining its location. If poorhouses be established, he must know the names of the mendicants who present themselves, he must be informed exactly when they came and when they went. In order to be able to manage everything from Paris and to know everything there, it is necessary to invent a thousand methods of control. The mass of papers is already enormous. The slowness of administrative procedure is so great that I have never noticed that less than a year passed before a parish could get its bell restored or its presbytery repaired; oftener two or three years pass before the request is granted."

powers were of two kinds: 1st, they gave instructions and orders in the name of the king to the functionaries of the provinces who were classed rather arbitrarily as in their department;[1] formerly their functions were limited to that and the apportionment of business among them was made on geographical lines (1547); but a specialization of administrative work took place[2] and other powers resulted therefrom. 2d, each of them was exclusively charged with affairs of a certain kind for which he was competent throughout all France; thus the foreign policy and relations with ambassadors belonged to the Secretary of State for Foreign Affairs; religious affairs, pensions, and the issue of "lettres de cachet" fell within the competence of the Secretary of State for the King's Household, who seemed to aspire to become a minister of the Interior, so great was the number of provinces with which he corresponded. The army and military affairs, the constabulary, and the postal service were assigned to the Secretary of State for War.[3] To the Secretary of Marine, aside from naval affairs properly speaking, were assigned affairs relating to the colonies, the consulates, and the fisheries; but he had no correspondence with any province, not even with those of the seacoast, doubtless for the sole reason that he came too late and there remained none with which he could be put in relation when his office was created.[4] The distribution of administrative services was never very regular;[5] some of them were shifted from one ministry to another according to the hazard of circumstances; thus Louvais assumed the direction of fine arts upon the death of Colbert; sometimes a service was detached in order to form a superintendency (*e.g.* fine arts, fortifications).[6] A rational distribution of

[1] Geographical divisions of France ("Règlement" of March 11, 1626): 1, Foreign affairs: Guyenne and Gascony, Normandy, Berry, Champagne and Brie, Dombes; 2, royal household: Paris, Languedoc, Provence, Foix, Béarn, Bigorre, Nébouzan, Burgundy, Brittany, Picardy, Touraine, Marche, Poitou, Auvergne, Limousin, Bourbonnais, Nivernais, Orléanais, Angoumois, Saintonge, Aunis; 3, war: Trois-Evêchés, Lorraine, Artois, Flanders, Hainaut, Cambrésis, Alsace, Franche-Comté, Dauphiny, Roussillon, Corsica. These latter were the frontier provinces and it was logical to connect them with war. But Béarn and Provence were left out. *De Luçay*, p. 551 and following.

[2] From 1570, royal household; 1589, foreign affairs; marine, 1669. *Cf.* "Règlement" of March 11, 1626.

[3] *De Luçay*, p. 477 (details on diplomacy); p. 493 (the clergy); p. 483 (war); p. 533 (marine).

[4] Council of Commerce of Marseilles, a sort of ministry of marine, for the Mediterranean with its own resources (customs), and expenses for salaries of consuls.

[5] Cumulation of ministries: under Louis XV, Choiseul directed at the same time, the ministries of War, Marine, and Foreign Affairs.

[6] Being given this unmethodical distribution, there was no difficulty in

the offices of State was scarcely considered, or at all events was never realized.[1]

§ 376. **Lack of Unity.** — During certain periods there were personages who played the rôle of prime ministers, — Richelieu, Mazarin, Fleury, — having an almost absolute authority over the secretaries of State; but the ministry was not organized in a normal manner so as to be directed by a sort of viceroy or grand vizier. The policy of Louis XIV, who wished to be his own prime minister and "to keep the eyes of the master upon all affairs," served as a model for his successors. But they imitated him badly; the secretaries of State did not act in concert; each was master in his own department.[2]—The English system of cabinet government[3] was decidedly superior in this respect: the members of the cabinet are jointly responsible (Walpole); this comes from the fact that they represent a single party and are taken by the king from the majority in Parliament instead of being chosen in discretion. One of them, the president of the council, is the leader of this majority, and he is the one charged by the king with forming the ministry. As the king is not free to choose the ministers, he is not held responsible to Parliament for their acts; he is inviolable; his ministers, on the other hand, can be charged, and a vote of want of confidence by Parliament puts them under an obligation to resign. This modern form of the ministry, which was brought about by the revolution of 1688, owes a little of its success to accidental circumstances, such as the accession in England of a foreign dynasty rather inclined, in consequence, not to govern directly; but the preponderance of Parliament over the throne was the real cause. Moreover, it required not less than a century for cabinet government to become organized; this essential piece of machinery in the political mechanism of England did not work well until after the Revolution of 1789, and even to-day, legally speaking, the cabinet does not exist.

1763 in creating a new department for Bertin, with very varied powers: manufactures of porcelain, studs, school of veterinary medicine, agriculture, societies of agriculture, apportionment of pasturage, irrigation canals, mines, coaches, barges, public conveyances, dépots of charters, lotteries, certain provinces. *Le Luçay*, p. 525.

[1] England: high dignitaries (treasurer, admiral, chancellor) directed the services of finance, of marine, and of justice; secretaries of State had duties which were specialized later, foreign affairs, interior, war; certain departments, like commerce, and public instruction, were confided to committees of the Privy Council; post and public works were still attached to the treasury.

[2] *Le Luçay*, p. 307. D'Argenson, in 1749. Mme. de Tencin to the Duke of Richelieu in 1741.

[3] So called because the king assembled in his office (cabinet) a little group of intimate councilors.

CHAPTER XI

MONARCHICAL PERIOD (*continued*). LOCAL ADMINISTRATION[1]

[1] BIBLIOGRAPHY: Concerning the different offices, *cf. Girard et Joly*, "Offices," p. 825; "Supplement" to "Tr. des Aydes cont. l'estat des généralités, élections," etc., 1645; "Nouveaux dénombr. du royaume par généralités, élections, paroisses, feux," 1735; *Dumoulin*, "Descr. gén. du royaume div. en généralités," 1762–67. Concerning the admin. divs. of ancient France, *cf. Monod*, n^{os}, 296 *et seq.; Luchaire*, "Et. s. l'admin. de Louis VII," 1885; *A. Molinier* in *D. Vaissete*, t. VII; *Roschach, ibid.*, t. XIII et XIV; *Allard*, "De l'admin. des provinces av. 1789," 1885; *Paquet*, "Inst. provinc., comm. et corp.," 1835; *Monnet*, "Hist. de l'admin. en Fr.," 1885; *Borrelli de Serres*, "Rech. s. div. services publics du XIIIe au XVIIe s.," 1895; *Esmein*, p. 355; *Glasson*, t. V, p. 460; *Ricard*, "Les instit. judic. et admin. de l'anc. France" (Gex), 1885; *Krug-Basse*, "L'Alsace avant 1789," 1877; *Amelot*, "Dénombrement de la province de Bourgogne," 1790; *L. Maître*, "Le Maine s. l'Anc. Rég.," 1869; BCh., 5e s., 4, 183; *Peyre*, "R. hist.," 41, 94; *A. Babeau*, "La Province sous l'anc. régime," 1894; *Gounon-Loubens*, "L'admin. int. de la Castille au XVIe s.," 1860; *Bourinot*, "Local Govern. in Canada," 1867.

§ 377. **In General.** — The political and administrative divisions of France are of different origins and dates: 1st, one kind, somewhat feudal, corresponding to the large and small seigniories, the *bailiwicks* and "*seneschalships*," were divided into *provostships* and magistracies ("*vigueries*"); 2d, others, another kind, arising under the monarchy, *governments* or *provinces* (1500 s), were identical with or analogous to the great fiefs and were in strict relation to the geographical configuration of France; 3d, finally, the more modern and more artificial division was that of *generalities* and *elections*. Within these limits cities and communities of inhabitants formed special units in which was maintained for a more or less long time a régime of self-government recalling to some extent that of England (*cf.* also the "pays d'Etats").

TOPIC 1. THE BAILIWICKS AND SENESCHALSHIPS

§ 378. **Provosts (North) and "Viguiers" (South).**[1] The royal domain was at first administered by provosts ("præpositi"),[2] a sort of intendant having, like Carolingian functionaries, the most varied powers: military commandants, inferior judges, and collectors of fines and revenues of the king. They held their office sometimes as a fief, sometimes by farm,[3] and the independence which this system brought them, added to the extent of their powers, permitted them to make exactions and abuses to which it was necessary to put an end. This was accomplished: 1st, by charters of franchises; 2d, by the substitution of the warden ("regie," administration) in the place of infeudation or farmage (Stephen Boileau under Saint Louis);[4] 3d, by the control of the seneschals and bailiffs. The ordinance of August 26, 1493, definitely made the provost a paid royal officeholder.[5] The bea-

[1] Or viscounts, chatelains, solicitors.

[2] Instituted, perhaps, in imitation of the "præpositi" of the monasteries. The Capetians feared to create rivals for themselves by giving to their subordinates the titles which they had borne. Hugh Capét created, however, a count at Paris ("comes regalis"). "Prévôt" of Orléans, Oct. 2, 1057. *Cf.* Ord. 1115, 1254, 3 and 4. *Brussel*, "Us. des Fiefs," 2, 139; list of royal provosts in 1202. BCh., 1892, 638. *Luchaire*, p. 539.

[3] *Borrelli de Serres*, "Rech. s. div. services publics du XIIe au XVIIe s.," 1895. *Giry*, "Doc. s. les rel. de la royauté," p. 48. Ord. 1303 (I, 358); 1320 (XII, 449). *Isambert*, "Table," see "Prévôtés."

[4] *Joinville*, "Vie de Saint Louis," c. 141, § 715 (*cf. Borrelli de Serres*, p. 531). Provosts who bought their offices allowed to go unpunished the crimes of their relatives and of rich men. Saint Louis desired that the office of provost should no longer be sold; he gave it, with good pay, to a man who did "bonne et roide justice." *Et. Boileau.*

[5] *Is.*, XII, 214 (*cf.*, however, Ord. Blois, 1498, Art. 60). Oath, etc.

dles and "viguiers" of the south were only provosts under another name.[1] In the 1600 s both were reduced to the exercise of judicial functions almost exclusively; they became inferior royal judges.[2]

§ 379. **Bailiffs (in the North), Seneschals (in the South).**[3] **Origins.**—The grand seneschal, an officer of the court who watched over the royal provosts, disappeared, and even had his office been maintained, the extension of the royal domain would have rendered his control ineffective.[4] The king was under the necessity of sending Palatins into the provinces with missions which recalled those with which the "missi dominici" were formerly invested; these delegates were designated by the name of bailiffs ("ballivi," "baillivi," "bajuli").[5] They belonged rather to the central than to the local administration. By a "processus" analogous to that which transformed the masters of petitions ("maîtres des requêtes") into intendants (1500 s and 1600 s), the bailiffs became local agents having a fixed post, a definite district formed of a group of provostships, and served as hierarchical intermediaries between the provosts and the king.[6] In the testament

[1] *Béarn:* seventeen "vics" (1200 s) or bailiwicks (1300 s); inferior officers of the "baile," messengers, "beguers" or "viguiers," a sort of bailiff; "talhers," "arciuters," fiscal solicitors, toll gatherers, collectors. *Cadier*, "Etats de Bearn," p. 119 and following. *Cf.* English coroners, constables.

[2] *Ferrière*, see "Prévôts"; *Fleury*, "Inst. au dr. fr.," I, 114; *Guyot*, "Répert.," h. vo., enumerates various functionaries bearing the name of "prévôt," among others, the provost of the hôtel, or grand provost of France, who exercised a certain jurisdiction over the Louvre and the royal household; the provosts of the marshals (thirty-three in 1789) charged with surveillance over the great roads; the provost of Paris, chief of the Châtelet or provost and viscount of Paris, who had the same jurisdiction as the bailiffs and seneschals, and who was a royal functionary, differing from the provost of merchants, a municipal officer, head of the bureau of the city of Paris (and of Lyon).

[3] Bibliog. in *Luchaire*. "Man. des Inst.," p. 543; *Cf. Tixier*, "Essai sur les baillis et sénéch. royaux," 1898, p. 185; *Du Cange*, see "Baillivi," "Olim," "Table, h. vis"; *Ferrière*, "Dict." (bibl.); *Isambert*, "Table"; *A. Molinier*, "Corresp. admin. d'Alfonse de Poitiers," t. I, 1894; *De Rorière*. "L'Assize du bailliage de Senlis" (N.R.H., 1891); *Cf.* above, "Etats gén.," "Etats prov.," p. 809; "Traités des offices," p. 855; and *infra*, "Judicial Organization," etc.; *Pardessus*, "Organis. judic.," 1851. *Vuitry*, "Et. s. le rég. financ.," 1878–83; *Luchaire*, "Inst. monarch.," t. I, 1883; *Everat*, "Sénéch. d'Auvergne," 1886; *Laborde*, "Thèses Ec. Ch.," 1854; *L. Delisle*, BCh., 1859; "Soc. Antiq. Norm.," t. 19, p. 61; *Quénault*, *ibid.*, t. 25, p. 125; *Lefèvre*, BCh., 1860; *Furgeot*, "Thèses Ec. Ch.," 1878; *Beautemps-Beaupré*, "Acad. sc. mor.," t. 134; "Mém. Arch. Senlis," 7, 119.

[4] *Cf.* Seneschal of Normandy. *Glasson*, "Inst. de l'Anglet.," vol. II, p. 339. Tours through the country; right to dismiss the bailiffs. "Gr. Cout. de Norm.," c. 4. Circuit judges in England.

[5] *Du Cange*, "Bailli" means guardian, protector.

[6] England (like Normandy) was divided into counties; the viscount or sheriff ("shire gereva") corresponded to the French "grand bailli."

of Philip Augustus, or ordinance of 1190, the existence of these permanent functionaries was already stated as a previous fact;[1] the institution was regulated in the 1200 s.[2] The seneschals of the West and the South, feudal officers who were transformed into royal functionaries by the annexation of fiefs, played the same rôle as the bailiffs of the North.[3]

Among other facts which accorded well with the origin which we have attributed to the bailiff we may mention their strict dependence upon the central power: they were appointed and removed by the king; they held their offices in wardenship and not as fiefs or by lease; they were taken from among the members of the court; and they came regularly to render their accounts to the king.[4] The Parliament never ceased to require them to give

The subordinate bailiffs became simple doorkeepers or ushers ("huissiers"). The sheriff was originally elected by the free men of the shire; the elections being disorderly and resulting in the election of poor functionaries, Edward II suppressed them; at the same time, it was decided that sheriffs should own in the shire sufficient landed property to assure their responsibility.

[1] *Brussel*, "Us. des fiefs," I, 505, wrongly attributes the creation of bailiffs to the Ord. of 1190; ch. Art. 2: "In terris nostris baillivos nostros posuimus qui in bailliviis suis singulis mensibus ponent unum diem qui dicitur assisia, in quo omnes illi qui clamorem facient, recipient jus suum per eos et justitiam sine dilatione, et nos nostra jura et nostram justiciam et forefacta, quæ proprie nostra sunt, ibi scribentur." The bailiffs who are here under consideration and whom modern writers designate under the name of "grand baillis," are distinguished from another category of bailiffs, sometimes called "petits baillis," slightly different from provosts. *Cf. Girard* and *Joly*, "Offices," vol. II; *Brussel, loc. cit.* Normandy, *Léchandé d'Anisy*, "Rôles de l'Echiquier," 1846, p. 104 and following. "Baillivia" indicated at first the function rather than the circumscription, which was not fixed. *Luchaire*, "Man.," p. 545. It was not until about 1234 (in the shires) that bailiffs were designated as bailiffs of a certain place. The short term of office of the bailiff (at least in principle, three years, Ord. 1256; *cf.* p. 287, *Beaumanoir*) is in harmony with the theory of origin that we have accepted. *Cf. Petit-Dutaillis*, "Louis VIII," p. 364; *Bor. de Serres*, p. 195. Concerning the ideas of the latter, see *Esmein*, p. 354, n. 3.

[2] Ord. 1254, 1256, 1302, 1320, etc. *Isambert*, "Table," see "Bailliages." Oath of "baillis," 1254, 1363 (*Girard*, II, 903). "*Tixier*," p. 66. *Cf.*, concerning appointment of "baillis," Ord. Feb. 5, 1388; Jan. 7, 1400. *Isamb.*, VI, 644, 859.

[3] *Esmein*, p. 354. (In 1137, maintenance of the seneschal of Poitou, after the marriage of Louis VII to Eleanor of Guyenne.) Did the institution of "baillis" have its origin in this particular fact? M. Esmein thinks so. *Cf. Luchaire*, p. 550 (bibliog.). *Beautemps-Beaupré*, "Cout. de l'Anjou et du Maine," 1890–97; *A. Molinier*, BCh., 1873, 164; *Cadier*, "Etats de Béarn," p. 121.

[4] Bailiffs often sat in the Parliament during the 1200 s; was it as judges or as those amenable to justice ("justiciables")? According to *Beugnot*, "Olim," II, p. XXVII, it was as judges, because they were only members of the Parliament "in mission"; when their decisions were submitted to this body, they were then both judges and parties. The Ord. of 1291 prohibited them from serving as judges, at least from forming part of the council, and after 1302, they no longer sit in the council while perform-

an account of their administration; councilors informed themselves on the spot concerning their acts; and finally, under Saint Louis and under Philip III, "*inquirers*" were sent by the king into the provinces in order to redress wrongs committed by the bailiffs and officers subordinate to them (judges, bayles, notaries, and sergeants).[1]

§ 380. **Powers of the Bailiffs.**[2] — The bailiff represented the king; he was a sort of viceroy; he commanded in a very extended district; his powers were almost those of the king, or at least they were modeled upon those of the king and were limited only by the intervention of the king, always possible, and by the responsibility which he himself incurred. (*a*) As an **administrator** it was his business to execute the orders of the king and to superintend the inferior officeholders, to make police regulations and to maintain peace in the bailiwick, to publish the ordinances of the king and to issue them himself in case of need;[3] (*b*) as **military chief** (and consequently he was a soldier and always a layman) he summoned the king's men for service in the army,[4] put himself at the head of the contingents of the provosts, defended the bailiwick, and exacted the fine or tax due in place of military service; (*c*) as **justiciar** he was charged by the ordinance of 1190 to render justice to all; thenceforth he rendered judgment in cases of denial of justice by the provosts, he had even the power to call up before himself cases which were submitted to them just as the king could do; and as he was charged with the oversight of the domain, domainal cases naturally went to him; in time his jurisdiction increased, as we shall see later; he became a judge in cases of appeal from sentences pronounced by the provosts, and jurisdiction of

ing their duties (*cf.* Ord. 1296). *Cf. Tixier*, p. 122. The Ord. of April, 1453, prescribed that the bailiffs should appear in the Parliament in case of appeals from their bailiwick.

[1] They were far from possessing all the virtues that *Beaumanoir* required of them, Ch. I. In providing for these inquiries, Saint Louis seems to have generalized a former custom. *Langlois*, "Phil. III," p. 329; *Luchaire*, p. 553. Inquiries in the South, 1247, 1255, 1277. "Layettes du Tr. des Ch.," vol. II, 4202 and following; vol. III, 3627. *A. Molinier* in *D. Vaissete*, vol. VII, p. 500; X, pr. c. 141. Inquiry of 1317 concerning a "bailli" of Cotentin, *L. Delisle*, "Antiq. Norm.," 1851. *Cf.* BCh., 28, 609; 34, 166. "Olim," *passim*, instructions or reproaches of the Parliament, I, 437; II, 78, 103, etc. *Glasson*, V, 401. *Cf.* "Réformateurs" of the 1300s. *Isambert*, "Table."

[2] *Beaumanoir*, I, 20. *Cf.* the English sheriff, who like him lost, in time, many of his early powers. *Fischel*, "English Constitution," vol. II, p. 21; *Glasson*, VI, 490. In North Germany, the solicitor ("Vogt," "Gaugraf," "Schulze") was both administrator and judge. In the west, administration and justice were separate. *Schröder*, p. 600 ("Amtmann").

[3] *Beaumanoir*, II, 293; *D. Vaissete*, X, pr. c. 174.

[4] *Cf.* English "posse comitatus." *D. Vaissete*, X, pr. c. 125.

cases involving the nobility [1] was reserved to him in the first instance; (*d*) as **financial agent** he collected the fines and judicial fees ("droits de justice") to which his judicial functions gave rise; he collected extraordinary dues like mortmain and regalian fees, although ordinary and less variable revenues went to the provosts who farmed their offices and paid a lump sum ("forfait"); he farmed them out to the provosts and centralized their receipts; he administered the royal domain; he paid the local expenses, such as the salaries of inferior officers, and, finally, he turned over to the royal treasury the funds that he received.[2] In the accomplishment of these various duties, the royal bailiffs found themselves in connection and in almost continual conflict with the feudal powers, the Church, the nobility and the communes; the royal authority had no auxiliaries more ardent or less scrupulous.[3]

§ 381. **Same: Decadence of the Institution.** — More numerous and more and more varied, the powers of the bailiff could not fail to disintegrate; this began to occur about the beginning of the 1300s. 1st, In the **matter of finances** he was supplanted by **receivers**, his clerks at first, but (1320) eventually independent royal officers.[4] For the collection of taxes levied during this period a special administration was created. 2d, His **judicial powers** passed to **lieutenants** who were more competent than he.[5] 3d, His military powers lost much of their importance in consequence of the creation of a permanent army (1400s), and what was left passed to the governors; in the end, he retained only the power of convoking the vassals for feudal service ("ban" and "arrière-ban"). 4th,

[1] *Fleury*, p. 76; *cf.* below, "Judicial organization."

[2] *Cf. Langlois*, p. 327; *Petit-Dutaillis*, p. 363; *Borrelli de Serres*, p. 299. Concerning the accounts of the provosts and bailiffs, *cf. Brussel*, II, cxxxix; *Petit-Dutaillis*, p. 522.

[3] *Bardoux*, "Les Légistes," 1877.

[4] Ord. Jan., 1319; March, 1319; May 27, 1320. *Cf.* also Ord. Nov., 1323, Art. 27, and June, 1333. *Decretal*, 1335. *Isambert*, "Table," see "Receveurs." The receivers appeared first in the South (1247 at Carcassonne, etc.). *D. Vaissete*, VII, 500; *Glasson*, VI, p. 91; *Cadier*, "Etats de Béarn," p. 124. At Paris, 1285. *Borelli de Serres*, p. 221. The administration of waters and forests was withdrawn from the bailli at the end of the 1200s. Ord. 1292; 1333; 1346. *Cf.* Germany, the "Rentmeister," subordinate to the "Vogt" or "Amtmann." *Schröder*, p. 602.

[5] At the end of the 1200s, the seneschal at Toulouse judged only when assisted by a chief justice who was a graduate in law and appointed by the king, and who had the right to sit in the absence of the seneschal. *Boutaric*, "Phil. le Bel," p. 187. In the North, the Ord. of Feb. 5, 1388 (*Is.*, VI, 645), allowed the "baillis" to have lieutenants to replace them in case of necessity; Ord. 1498, Art. 47, the bailiffs could not dismiss them; and in the 1500s, the bailiffs were not allowed to act as judges. From the end of the 1200s the king's solicitor had replaced the bailiff in the defense of the royal interests. *Cf.* below, and *Guyot*, "Répert.," see "Bailli," etc.

His administrative functions in the end were inherited by the intendant and his subdelegates; these newcomers, more compliant, more dependent on the will of the king, were preferred to the bailiff, a man of arms, invested with a venal office (from the time of Francis I), who was irremovable and whose office was even hereditary after 1693.[1] The bailiffs of the 1600 s and 1700 s were chiefs of the local nobility;[2] personages of pageantry and almost of comedy, without real powers. In 1789 the bailiwicks and seneschalships were no longer anything but judicial and electoral divisions.[3]

TOPIC 2. THE "GOVERNMENTS"[4]

§ 382. **The Governors**[5] began as military commanders with extraordinary powers; they were placed at the head of several bailiwicks or seneschal districts in such a way as to concentrate their forces and to defend them more efficaciously (1300s); they were entitled lieutenant generals of the king, governors and lieutenants for the king, and had only temporary authority. From this beginning there grew up in the 1500s a regular permanent institution (edict of May 6, 1545).[6] Lieutenants of the king, taken from the high nobility, their situation and functions gave them great powers;[7] the civil wars rendered them quasi-inde-

[1] Edict, Oct., 1693 and Jan., 1696. Ord. Blois, 1579, Art. 263. "Arr. Council," Dec. 16, 1759. Heredity was abolished by orders of the Council of Oct. 26, and Dec. 26, 1719 (according to *Boiteau*, p. 334). *Cf. Loyseau*, "Off.," 4, 4, 66.

[2] Decree of the Council of 1761. Judgments were rendered in their name. They determined on the first instance personal differences among nobles or clerks.

[3] It is admitted that there were 829 of them. *Cf.* "Ann. Soc. Hist. de France," 1850, vol. 14 (1768). *Boiteau*, p. 82-334, "Etat des bailliages et sénéschaussées," Jan. 24, 1789.

[4] *Loyseau*, "Offices," IV, 4, 26; *Ferrière* (bibl.); *Guyot*, "Répert."; *Ch. Mortet*, "Gr. Encycl.," see "Gouvernement," "Gouverneur"; *Marion*, "La Brétagne et le duc Aiguillon," 1898; *Babeau*, I, 253; *Hippeau*, "Gouv. de Norm."

[5] The ordinary estimate in 1789 was thirty-two government districts, plus eight petty districts. A distinction was made between governors of the provinces, lieutenant generals, lieutenants of the king, special governors of the towns, captains or governors of the châteaus. List of the provinces with the date of their union to the crown in *De Luçay*, "La décentralisation," 1891, p. 97. *Isamb.*, XXIII, 436.

[6] *Fischel*, II, 29. After the time of the Tudors, the military powers of the sheriff passed to an aristocratic functionary, the Lord Lieutenant, still to-day invested with the most important honorary office of the shire.

[7] *Cf.* Letters patent by which they were appointed (for ex., *D. Vaissete*, XIV, 43; *Babeau*, "Villars," II, 273): "They must repress disorders, cause transgressors of the laws to be punished by the judges, summon the three Estates, direct functionaries, mayors, sheriffs, officers of the army, exercise surveillance over the commissary," etc.

pendent; and there came a time when these viceroys appeared to be the masters of their provinces.[1] We know how Henry IV and Richelieu destroyed their authority.[2] After them the governorships were sinecures liberally paid and given to courtiers.[3] The governors lost all control over the civil administration, which passed to the intendants; their military powers belonged equally to these latter officials and to the **lieutenants general** placed near them by Henry IV and who were rather, as was said, "countertenants"; they were dependent only upon the secretary of State for War and upon the marshals of France. Many of them resided at court; "in the space of twenty years Villars passed only three months in his government of Provence." When they came to their provinces it was to summon and preside over the Estates and to represent the king in the public ceremonies and fêtes; it was to this rôle of pageantry that the monarchy had reduced them. They were not able to exercise their functions without special permission from the king.

TOPIC 3. TAXING DISTRICTS ("GENERALITIES")[4]

§ 383. **The Intendants**,[5] as the term is here used, were the intendants of the provinces, — intendants of justice, of police, and

[1] On several occasions, the royal power was in real danger, during the religious wars, at the beginning of the reign of Louis XIII, in the time of Mazarin (Condé had succeeded his father in the government of Burgundy; from his brother-in-law, the duke of Longueville, he held Normandy; he also asked the queen for Provence for his brother, and Languedoc and Guyenne for himself).

[2] Henry IV reserved for himself the appointment of the governors of towns and of fortified places; until that time, the right of appointment belonged to governors of provinces.

[3] *Languedoc*, 150,000 pounds; Guyenne, 100,000, etc. Besides this fixed stipend, there were gratuities, a part of the octroi tax, etc., which amounted to as much or more. The governors had only a commission (for three years under Louis XIV), but for some great families, at least, it was renewed indefinitely, except in case of disfavor, so that the incumbents could sell their offices. "Mém. de Louis XIV," II, 570 (ed. *Dreyss*). *Cf. Loyseau*, no. 44 (in his time, there were no real salaries; if they were paid, it was as military officers, or because they received a pension).

[4] *Guyot*, "Offices," 1786, t. III, p. 115–449; *Gauret*, "Stile des Conseils du roi," 1700, p. 359 to 462; *Depping*, "Corresp. admin. de Louis XIV," 1850–1855; *P. Clément*, "Lettres de Colbert," 1861–8; *De Boislisle*, "Corresp. des contrôleurs gén. des fin.," 1874; "Mém. des intend. s. l'état des généralités," 1881; "Chevauchées d'un maître des requêtes en Provence" ("R. d. Soc. sav.," 1881, 159); *R. Dareste*, "Justice admin.," 2e éd., 1898; *G. Hanotaux*, "Orig. de l'inst. des intend. de province," 1884; *Ch. Mortet*, "Gr. Encycl.," see "Int.," "Généralités" (bibl.); *Astre* (Languedoc), "Ac. Sc. Toulouse," 1859; *Monin*, "Basville," 1885; *Boyer de Sainte-Suzanne*, "Amiens," 1865; *Thomas*,

[5] Other functionaries bore this title, for example, the Intendants of finances. *Guyot*, "Répert.," *Ferrière*, *ibid*.

of finance. These functionaries, who were the most active agents of administrative centralization, were habitually taken from the council of the king (maîtres des requêtes). They were put in charge of divisions of financial origin and known as **generalities** (there were seventeen under Louis XIII and thirty-three in 1789),[1] and these were in turn subdivided into "**elections**" at the head of each of which was a **subdelegate** (from 1637) appointed and removed by the intendant.[2]

§ 384. **Origin.** — If Richelieu did not create the intendants,[3] as is customarily said, it was from him that the institution received its definitive character. He made of them resident functionaries and through them caused the action of the State to be felt everywhere with a force and regularity unknown up to that time. The institution had two sources: 1st, the *circuits* (or tours of inspection) of the masters of requests (1551, 1553, etc.), who were commissioned to receive complaints addressed to the council of the king, whether in regard to the rendering of justice or in regard to the levy of taxes, to give information about crimes, abuses, or violation of the ordinances; to make a report on these things to the chancellor, and to repress summarily violations of the laws by means of executory sentences in spite of opposition or appeal, etc.;[4]

"Bourgogne," 1844; *Marchand*, "Lebret" (Provence), 1889; *Baudry*, "Mém. de Foucault," 1868; *Duval*, "Alençon," 1890; *Dumas*, "Tours," 1894; *D'Hugues*, "Turgot," 1859; *Foncin*, "Essai s. Turgot," 1877; N.R.H., 1889; *D'Arbois de Jubainville*, "Champagne," 1880; *Legrand*, "Sénac de Meilhan," 1869; *Raymond*, "Invent. des Basses-Pyr." (Béarn), 1869; *Galard de Magnas*, "Adm. de la prov. d'Auch, en 1787," 1890; *Henry*, "Bosquet, intend. de Guyenne et de Languedoc," 1888; *Roschach* in *D. Vaissete*, v. XIII and XIV; *Cohendy*, "Admin. dans la prov. d'Auvergne," 1856; *Babeau*, II.

[1] Paris, Amiens, Soissons, Orléans, Bourges, Moulins, Lyon, Riom, Poitiers, La Rochelle, Limoges, Bordeaux, Tours, Auch, Montauban, Languedoc, Dauphin, Provence, Roussillon, Franche-Comté, Burgundy, Champagne, Rouen, Caen, Alençon, Brittany, Metz, Alsace, Flanders and Artois, Hainaut and Cambrésis, Dombes, Lorraine, Corsica. Alphabetical list of generalities and the departments of which they were formed, in *De Luçay*, "Les Assembl. prov.," 1871, 2e éd., p. 443; "La décentralisation," 1895, p. 155, *cf*. p. 101.

[2] The subdelegate had variable powers; he gave advice, caused the orders of the intendant to be executed, and judged cases which were sent to him. The intendant had under his orders secretaries, clerks, commissioners of the "taille," excise officers, and mounted police. In Paris, the administration comprised various bureaus with a numerous personnel (secretariat, record office, police, architecture). *Babeau*, II, 25.

[3] The Edict of 1635 (revoked in 1637) did not create intendants, as has been believed, but presidents of the bureau of finance. "The intendants originated not by a general measure, but by individual commissions of different dates." *Dareste*, p. 97; *Isamb.*, XVI, 442.

[4] *Cf*. the "Enquêteurs" of Saint Louis, Reformers of the 1300 s and 1400 s. The circuits ("chevauchées") had originally the same boundaries with the Parliaments, Edict, Aug. 1553; from 1555, with the administra-

2d, the missions of the **intendants of justice**, extraordinary commissioners, who were sent wherever troubles or disorders arose to assist the military authorities in the capacity of civil functionaries (1555, 1565, etc.).[1] These two commissions merged into a single one, whose incumbent was called the **intendant** or commissioner intrusted with the execution of the orders of the king. Instead of a temporary mission the intendants had a permanent charge.[2] But for a long time they were "militant officials" who have been compared to the legates of the Holy See during the Middle Ages[3] and before whom every one bowed down: municipalities, nobility, governors, and Parliaments.[4] The saying of Law gives an apt idea of their rôle: "Know that the kingdom of France is governed by thirty intendants; you have neither Parliaments, nor Estates, nor governors; there are thirty masters of petitions upon whom depend the happiness and unhappiness of the provinces." [5]

§ 385. **Powers.**[6] — The intendant, a delegate of the king, united, like him, widely different powers, the principal ones being specified in the commission which he received at the time of his appointment,[7] the wording of which had become purely formal.[8] They may be grouped under three principal heads: justice, police, and finance.

tive divisions (généralities) "in order that they could more easily serve and assist justice and finances." Ord. Orléans, Jan., 1560, Art. 33; Moulins, Feb., 1566, Art. 7; Blois, May, 1579, Art. 209; 1629, Art. 58 (powers). *Fleury*, p. 88. Concerning the tours of the intendants, see *Babeau*, II, 62.

[1] *Cf.* representatives of the people sent to the armies during the Revolution.

[2] This change passed unperceived, because it was made little by little, the masters of requests prolonging more and more their sojourn in the provinces and because new intendants were frequently displaced, as in the time when their functions were temporary. *Dareste*, p. 97; *Chéruel*, "Hist. de l'admin.," II, 145; *Ferrière:* the intendancies were given ordinarily for only three years; and the intendants retained the domicile they had acquired in Paris, even in case of prolonged absence.

[3] *Cf. D'Avenel*, IV, p. 206.

[4] Remonstrances of the Parliament from 1626, *Chéruel*, "Hist. de l'admin.," I, 292. Suppressed by the declaration of July 18, 1648, on demand of the sovereign courts, June 30, 1648, the intendants were almost immediately reëstablished.

[5] *Tocqueville*, p. 54 (according to the "Mémoires of d'Argenson").

[6] *Dareste*, p. 100, cites a long memoir Ms. written in 1738 by a former intendant, M. d'Aube ("Bibl. Nat.," no. 422). *Tocqueville*, 1, II, c. 2 and 6; *Babeau*, II, 79.

[7] *Caillet*, p. 487; *Guyot*, vol. III, p. 132, gives forms of commissions. That of Turgot, 1761, is in the "R. hist. de dr.," 1889, p. 775. For the colonies, *cf. Moreau de Saint Méry*, "Rec. des lois des colonies fr. de l'Amérique Sous-le-Vent," I, 318. "Edits et ord. du Canada," 1856, vol. III.

[8] The king could modify them and issue him extraordinary commissions. "Ex.," *Guyot*, III, 132.

1st, **Justice.** — The intendant had a share in the administration of ordinary justice;[1] he was authorized to preside over all the courts of justice except the Parliaments; he watched over the magistrates and in case of need suspended them from the exercise of their functions and inquired into abuses committed in the administration of justice (such as useless actions, false expenses, etc.) and especially into cases of unpunished crime; judicial police was largely in his hands.[2] But the justice of the intendant was especially **administrative**; it was a sort of accessory of his powers of finance and of police ("contentieux administratif").

§ 386. 2d, **Police**, that is to say, administration understood in a very large sense.[3] Under this head, the intendant occupied himself: (*a*) with the levy of the militia, the lodging and maintenance of the soldiers, and with the service of military storehouses and convoys;[4] (*b*) with public works,[5] the service of highway administration, "corvées," police of wagon transportation, and navigation, and with the post and packet services; (*c*) with administrative guardianship of cities, communities, and mortmain, establishments (revenues, liquidation of debts, authorizations to plead);[6]

[1] Origin: the king reserved to himself and to his Council jurisdiction of all matters for which judges had not been provided; from that time, in each generality, they were confided to an intendant, a member of the king's Council, with right of appeal to this body. *Dareste*, p. 106; *Fleury*, "Inst. au dr. fr.," 1665, I, 85, 94; *Guyot*, "Répert.," see "Roi."

[2] Arrests, investigations of office, surveillance of prisons and poorhouses, execution of "lettres de cachet," police of towns, and of public roads.

[3] *Paul Lagarde*, I, 273.

[4] *Infra:* Military organization. The intendant apportioned among the parishes the quota of the generality (previously fixed by the Council), decided questions concerning exemptions, and granted leaves ("Regl.," 1722; Ord. Nov. 27, 1765, Art. 20; Ord. Dec. 1, 1774, IV, 10); he had jurisdiction of disputes relative to the levy of sailors (Ord. Dec 13., 1778, Jan. 3, 1779). Concerning the storage houses and convoys, *cf.* Edict, July, 1716, "Arr. Cons.," Oct. 3, and Dec. 31, 1778. He regulated the price of provisions required to be furnished by the inhabitants to the troops on the march, decided the disputes that arose in connection therewith, watched over the service of military hospitals (Ord. Feb. 26, 1777). He conducted suits against soldiers when they caused disorders (those affecting civil society, while the councils of war repressed infractions of discipline). Ord. 1651, 1718 (Art. 42), 1750 (III, 4), 1768 (IV, 4).

[5] Concerning public works, *cf.* below, "Finances." He instigated edicts of concession for roads, public edifices, drainage of marshes, etc. He issued decrees on the execution of public works, the regulation of indemnities, etc.

[6] As will be seen below, § 4, towns and communities required the authorization of the intendant in order to impose an extraordinary tax upon themselves, to alienate, to borrow, to plead, to choose a schoolmaster, etc. The intendant watched over the liquidation of debts of the communities, and had also the establishment of their receipts. Hospitals and establishments of public instruction could not acquire real estate without the authority of the king given on the advice of the intendant, nor construct buildings without the authority of the intendant. Had

(*d*) with agriculture,[1] with industry,[2] and with commerce;[3] (*e*) with religious worship;[4] and (*f*) with poor-law relief.

§ 387. 3d, **Finances.**[5] — (A) In the countries of election ("pays d'election") the apportionment of the "taille" among the "elections" and among the "communities" passed from the elected representatives and from the treasurers to the intendants; they supervised, through their commissioners, the apportionment of the "taille" among the taxpayers, at times even imposed taxes "ex officio"; there remained to the elected representatives only the contentious administration and that not wholly. In the countries having estates ("pays d'etats"), where the assessment of the "taille" was within the province of the Estates, contentious questions arising thereunder were a part of ordinary justice, they never ceased to complain of the usurpations of the intendants. In the countries of imposts ("pays d'impositions," newly conquered provinces),[6] there were neither elected representatives nor

church "fabriques" the right to plead without authority? Controv. Decl. Oct. 2, 1703. *Cf. Guyot, op. cit.* Concerning public instruction, *cf.* below, "Finances."

[1] Encouragement of agriculture, premiums, breeding studs, nurseries, authorization or interdiction of certain crops, circulars concerning agricultural methods, quarantine, etc. They were judges of violations of agricultural regulations (prohibition of vine planting without authorization, "Arr. Cons.," June 5, 1731; hunting of wolves, "Arr. Cons.," Feb. 28, 1773, etc.), of crimes committed by the farmers in order to preserve their farms (Cambrésis, Picardie, etc.). *Dareste*, p. 138. Agricultural societies after 1757, Agricultural committees, etc.

[2] Execution of regulations concerning industry, of penalties against the judges of negligent manufacturers, the litigation concerning these regulations; authorization to plead to the syndics of precentorships and wardenships, suits relating to their accounts and to the right to exercise the freedom of a company; prohibition of workers from emigrating without permission, from appropriating waste materials, from exporting certain crafts, contests over the hiring of workers of the ironworks, creation of workshops, etc.

[3] Regulations concerning the grain trade ("Arr. Cons.," Dec. 23, 1770, Oct. 12, 1775) and the entry and exportation of merchandise. *Dareste*, p. 139.

[4] Quarrels between parishioners and their curés, surveillance over dissenting cults (Edict Aug., 1553, Art. 6) and the enforcement against Protestants of the rigorous measures following the revocation of the Edict of Nantes (galleys for those relapsed into heresy, Decl. May 14, 1724; sequestration of the property of fugitive Protestants, "Arr. Cons." Jan., March, 1688, Edict, Dec., 1689, "Arr. Cons.," July 20, 1700, Oct. 23 and Dec. 8, 1703, Sept. 14, 1745, Jan. 1, 1779; *cf.* legislation, 1792, on emigrants; authority to sell the property of Protestants remaining in France, "Arr. Cons.," Feb. 28, 1714). *Cf.* "Memoires of Basville" (Languedoc). Prohibitions on Alsatian Jews from acquiring houses, from assembling, from electing syndics, from levying taxes upon themselves without his authority ("L. Pat.," July 10, 1784).

[5] *Cf. Dareste*, p. 107 ("textes"). Below, "Finances."

[6] Alsace, Flanders and Artois, Franche-Comté, Hainaut and Cambrésis, Lorraine and Barrois, Metz and Trois-Evêchés, Roussillon, Corsica.

Estates; the administration and the contentious jurisdiction in regard to "tailles" belonged to the intendants.

(B) The capitation tax, the "twentieths," and new taxes were alike within their power, as to assessment, collection, and appeals.

(C) In respect to aids and domainal dues, they had jurisdiction of controversies as to dues which had been farmed out since the 1600 s (gauger-agents for the trade in beverages, fees on cards, paper, etc., lists, registration, amortizations, lotteries, 1776).

We see from this long enumeration that if the intendants were a sort of prefect [1] with very extensive districts, they also filled the place of our judges, of our financial officers, of our recruiting commanders, and of our local assemblies.[2] Like the high office-holders of our day, they were in constant correspondence with the ministers and kept them informed of everything.[3] They legislated by means of special ordinances and sometimes by general regulations. Against their decisions in contentious cases appeal was possible to the Privy Council; against their administrative acts there was no recourse before the ordinary judges, but the case could be removed to the council, so that the royal council could always override their acts (*cf.* administrative guarantee).

§ 388. **Estimate of the Rôle of the Intendants.**[4] — The intendants, taken from the ranks of the bourgeoisie, without personal influence, having everything to fear and everything to hope from the royal authority, were docile and devoted agents in its service. They introduced and caused to prevail in all the provinces the spirit and the views of the central authority. It was they who gave security to all and subjected the privileged classes to the common law, a task before which the ordinary judges and the

[1] The subdelegates of the subprefects, the first secretaries of the secretaries-general.

[2] Salaries: approximately 12,000 francs under Louis XIV: in 1789, 15,000 with a supplement of 8,000. Pensions and retirement allowances. Lodging at the expense of the towns, provinces, and the State. *De Luçay*, "Ass. prov.," p. 46.

[3] Statistics, memoirs, public documents concerning lands and crops. *Cf. Pigeonneau and de Foville*, "L'admin. de l'agriculture, 1785–7," 1882. Inquiry of 1697 instituted by the Duke of Burgundy; analysis of the memoirs of intendants in *Boulainvilliers*, "Etat de la France," 1727; *cf. de Boislisle*, "Mém. des Int.," 1881.

[4] *Tocqueville*, "Anc. Rég. et Révol.," 1, II, c. 2 and 6; *Babeau*, II, 320 (*cf. passim* analogies with our administration in numerous details): p. 1, he shows how the creation of intendants was imposed upon the country: the governors were too powerful, the magistrates too independent, the treasurers (finances and public works) seemed to wish to oppose all orders that they received; the provincial estates were little disposed to uphold the central power. *Cf. ibid.*, p. 82.

local authorities had too often shown themselves powerless. We owe to them the erection of great public works and useful encouragement to agriculture and industry (Turgot in Limousin, etc.). In many respects their action was enlightening and beneficent.

It has been contended, however, since the Revolution, that the system of administrative despotism which they established did more evil than good through the abasement or systematic destruction of liberty and of local autonomy; their guardianship "atrophied public spirit and killed individual initiative"; they made "men both revolutionary and servile" instead of accustoming them to proceed by prudent reforms. Their unpopularity in the 1700 s was testified to by Voltaire, d'Argenson, and Mirabeau. The remonstrances of the Court of Aids in April, 1771, included a sharp criticism of their absolute authority. Under the pressure of public opinion, which demanded administrative reforms before political reforms, Louis XVI conferred upon the provincial assemblies a share in the local administration and gave them a certain power of control over the intendant. The Constituent Assembly abolished the office of intendant, divided France into departments, and placed at the head of each elective bodies or directories. But the prefects of the year VIII (1800) continued the administrative traditions of the intendants; with them were associated the Council-general in matters of deliberation and a council of prefecture for the decisions of administrative controversies.

§ 389. **Police.**[1] — Police "sensu stricto" (that is to say, the maintenance of the public peace, sanitary measures, etc.), which formerly belonged to the ordinary judges and to the municipal officers,[2] was made at the end of the 1600 s a distinct branch of the administration. From the office of civil lieutenant of the provost of Paris there was detached in March, 1667, for the benefit of La Reynie, the office of lieutenant of the provost for police, or simply the **lieutenant of police.** In 1699 the institution was generalized and lieutenants-general of police were created in the

[1] *Isambert,* "Table," see "Police"; *Guyot,* "Rép."; *Ferrière,* see "Juges de Police"; *Boiteau,* p. 475.

[2] England: the functions of police belonged to the sheriff; to the coroner, originally a delegate of the sovereign, to-day elected by the assembly of the shire, and charged with inquiring into all cases of sudden death, (with the aid of a jury, ordinarily from fifteen to eighteen members); to constables, formerly officers of the military administration, inspecting the arms of the inhabitants and having supervision over petty constables, their subalterns, the former heads of boroughs and hundreds. Each parish had a constable and each parishioner had to fill the office of constable for a year (except the nobility and the gentry). *Fischel,* "English Constitution," II, 52.

principal cities of the kingdom with commissioners and recorders for the divisions under their orders. "The intendant of the province had the right of control over them which he exercised over all officeholders."

§ 390. **The Provosts of the Marshals,**[1] so called because they were originally only military judges under the orders of the marshals of France, became under Louis XI officers of permanent police established in all the provinces and having under their orders troop of constabulary. Their jurisdiction was extended naturally from the soldiery and vagabonds who followed the army to all men without occupation; they had to scour the country to prevent disorders and to seize vagabonds, brigands, and highwaymen. They were restricted to imprisoning ordinary criminals caught while committing flagrant offenses or taken in consequence of a public outcry; their right to judge was recognized only in what were called *provost cases,* that is: crimes committed by persons without occupation, vagabonds, habitual criminals; excesses committed by soldiers; illegal assemblies; thefts committed on the great highways; burglary and counterfeiting. As they were soldiers, they were obliged to take counsel with the judges of the inferior courts or advocates. There was no appeal from their judgment. This expeditious justice, which too well explained the violent customs of former times, gave rise to many abuses.

TOPIC 4. CITIES AND VILLAGES

§ 391. **The Cities.**[2] — Contrary to modern law, which has attempted to reconcile two apparently incompatible things, central-

[1] Edict, 1564; Ord. 1670; Decl. Feb. 5, 1731. *Fleury,* p. 83; *Ferrière; Guyot; Isambert,* "Table"; *Esmein,* "Hist. de la procéd. crim. en France," p. 41.

[2] *Supra,* p. 243, 256 and 307 (bibliog.). Add. *Ferrière,* "Dict.," see "Corps" and "Communautés"; *Brillon,* "Dict.," see "Communautés"; *Guyot,* "Répert.," h. vis.; *Boileau,* "Régl. et Rech. concern. les municipalités," 1785; *Leber,* "Hist. du dr. municipal," 1828; *De Calonne,* "La vie municipale au XVe s. dans le Nord de la France," 1880; "R. hist.," II, 222; XI, 419; *A. Baveau,* "La Ville sous l'anc. Régime," 1880.

Documents: Bonnardot, "Rég. des délib. du bureau de la ville de Paris," from 1409, 1885 *et seq.;* "Archiv. municip. de Bordeaux, Jurades de Bergerac, d'Agen," etc.; "Registres consulaires de Limoges," 1504–1788, 1869–84; *Roserot,* "Rég. d. délib. du C. de ville de Troyes," 1885.

Monographs: Grün, "La Vie publique de Montaigne," 1855; BCh., 4, 147 (*Delpit*): 1, 522 (*Dareste*); *Cardevaque,* "L'adm. munic. d'Arras," 1880; *Debidour,* "La Fronde Angevine," 1880; *Miron de l'Espinoy,* "Miron et l'admin. munic. de Paris sous Henri IV," 1885; *Carré,* "Admin. de Redon s. Henri IV," 1888; *Laronze,* "Rég. munic. en Bretagne," 1890; *Stouff,* "Le pouv. temporel et le rég. munic. de l'Ev. de Bâle," 1891; *Charléty,* "De B. Villario," 1896; *Tholin,* "Ville libre et barons," 1886.

ization and municipal liberty, the old monarchy, by reaction against the excessive independence of feudal times,[1] sought to destroy all local autonomy and to introduce some uniformity into the administration of the cities. In addition to the systematic abolition of their privileges, the régime of administrative tutelage to which they were subjected showed itself everywhere by the intervention of the State in municipal elections, in the management of finances, in the administration of public affairs, and, finally, by the almost complete abolition of municipal justice.[2] The city of the Middle Ages was extraordinarily heterogeneous, with its citizens or inhabitants of the city, its burgesses or inhabitants of the borough, simple inhabitants, aliens or foreigners, and in each of these classes instead of individuals with equal rights, there were professional groups; the clergy, the nobility, officers of justice, craft guilds, all having special privileges. They fell short in 1789 from attaining modern unity, but nevertheless they were on the way toward it; in many places the burgess, the citizen, and the inhabitant mingled with one another;[3] but that

[1] *Cf.* English "self-government." Besides the authors already cited, and particularly *Gneist*, *cf. Vauthier*, "Admin. locale de l'Anglet.," 1888. English self-government rests on the former division of territory into counties, hundreds, and tithings. The local officers, of which the principal one was the justice of the peace (appointed by the king from 1327) belonged to the gentry, that is to say, to the landed proprietors and received no stipend; they administered according to the customs and statutes and not according to the instructions received from superior officials. The English law does not distinguish between town and country. "City" was formerly a town, the seat of a bishopric; "town" ("ville"); "borough" ("bourg"); "village" ("ville"); "hamlet" — all agglomerations submitted, in principle, to the authorities of the county, but certain ones constituted bodies corporate, were subject to a privileged régime, and had a municipal organization. The borough sent deputies to Parliament. *Cf. Jannet*, "Etats-Unis contemp.," 1879.

Germany: Bibliog. in *Schröder*, p. 608; *Gierke*, "Genossenschaftsrecht," I, 249, etc.

[2] Loss of commercial jurisdiction in many towns in consequence of the establishment of consular judges (at Paris, Edict 1563). *Isamb.*, "Table," see "Juges de commerce"; *Glasson*, N.R.H., 1897, 5; *Valsen*, "Jurid. comm. à Lyon s. l'Anc. Rég.," 1881. The Ord. of Moulins, Feb., 1566, Art. 71, took away from them their civil jurisdiction; there remained to the municipal magistrates only an inferior criminal jurisdiction or simple police. *Isamb.*, XIV, 208; *Babeau*, p. 329. They also retained a very limited ordinance power and the right to issue police regulations, *cf.* the by-laws, laws, or local statutes of the guilds, parishes, and towns in England.

[3] *Babeau*, pp. 1 to 20. Authorization to reside in the towns was still necessary in some places in the 1700s and it was paid for; the price of citizenship was higher than that of residence, when they differed from each other. *Loyseau*, "Ordres," 8, 8; *Loysel*, "Inst. cout.," 21. Germany: *Schröder*, p. 622. The bourgeoisie sometimes had privileges: exemption from the "taille" (at Lyons), from "aides" (Havre), freeholds (Paris, Toulouse, etc.; Decl. June 1, 1771, abolished); right to bear arms, to fish, to hunt. "Towns of Arrest": the inhabitants had the privilege of arrest-

which most distinguished the urban community of those times from that of our day was that the former was an "aggregation of associations." The crafts guilds [1] were always petty rival States, constantly at war (the lawsuit between the shoemakers and the cobblers at Lyons lasted for two hundred years); the monarchy, substituting itself in the place of the municipalities, imposed regulations upon them, increased or reduced the number of guild masterships (a good pretext for levying taxes), and adopted measures to prevent merchants and artisans from escaping from the obligation to be members of a corporation. Under Louis XIV the positions of syndics and of wardens were even made into venal offices; but most of the corporations bought them back and always elected their chiefs; [2] the assembly of masters was reduced, instead of all members participating in it they had to send deputies (24 for 300 masters, 36 for a greater number).[3]

§ 392. **Municipal Elections.** — As late as the 1600s and even in the 1700s the most varied electoral systems were in operation: universal or restricted suffrage; direct suffrage or indirect to two or three degrees; elections of delegates by parishes, by quarters, or by corporations; the use of lots or nomination by arbitrators charged with the selection; voting *viva voce* and by secret ballot.[4] The principle of election had, to be sure, survived, but almost everywhere the municipal authorities were chosen by a bourgeois oligarchy, the general assemblies [5] having been reduced to simple meetings of notables in order to avoid tumults and disorders. Formerly, the seignior, later the king, frequently confirmed the elections; from confirmation and indirect nomination they came, by pressure of financial necessity,[6] to direct appointment.[7] The

ing their foreign debtors ("arrêt personnel") or of seizing their personal effects ("arrêt réel") on condition that they or their effects were found in the town; this survival of old institutions (see my, "Private Law") disappeared in part by the Edict of Aug., 1786. *Isamb.*, XXVIII, 230; personal arrest was abolished because it was no longer in harmony with the customs (*cf.* the disputable historical considerations of the preamble of the Edict), *Ferrière; Ragueau*, see "Arrest." *Guyot, ibid.*, N.R.H., 1884, 348.

[1] *R. Eberstadt*, "Magisterium et Fraternitas," 1897; "Das franz. Gewerberecht," 1899; *A. Babeau*, p. 22. *Cf.* England, *Fischel*, II, 61; Germany, *Schröder*, p. 630.

[2] *Guyot*, "Rép.," see "Maîtrises"; *Brillon*, IV, 185. Edicts of 1581, 1587, 1673. *Isamb.*, XXIII, 374.

[3] Edict of Aug., 1776; *Isambert*, XXIV, 74, Jan., 1777, etc.

[4] Details in *Babeau*, p. 40 and following. *D'Avenel*, IV, 221, 235.

[5] Presided over by the local judge, in memory of the former authority of the seignior of whom the judge was the representative.

[6] *Desjardins*, "Corresp.," LXXXII, p. 587; *Babeau*, p. 70. Recommendation and official candidacy, nomination sometimes by "lettre de cachet."

[7] The decision of municipal election controversies belonged to the royal judges and to the Parliaments. Edict, May, 1765, Art. 41. Complaint was

Edict of August, 1692, made the mayoralties of the cities purchasable offices; this was, so it was said, a means of preventing cabals and disorders and of giving to the cities administrators having more impartiality, more experience, and more competence.[1] In 1706 alternate mayors were provided for and, a little later, the principle of purchase was extended to "échevins," "jurats," and "capitouls." The cities bought back these offices repeatedly because they clung to their electoral rights and to their customs; the State showed no more scruples in accepting these redemptions than in reëstablishing the principle of purchase, so that in the 1700 s election and purchase followed one another almost regularly. The Edict of Marly, in May, 1765, decreed that the mayor should be appointed by the king from a list of three candidates;[2] four "échevins" and six councilors (not counting a syndic-receiver and a secretary recorder) constituted the municipal authorities and were elected by the assembly of notables from among the notables themselves.[3] The cities whose population was below 4,500 had a similar organization though less complete; for example, those below 2,000 had no mayor and but two "échevins" and three councilors. In November, 1771, there was a return to the system of venality after the same reproaches had been made against the system of election as in the past.[4]

§ 393. **The Town Corporation.** — The municipal administration, everywhere collective,[5] was vested in a body composed of a mayor,

made of the encroachments of the intendants. *Thomas*, "Une province sous Louis XIV," p. 416. Decl. April 6, 1717 (Languedoc): authorization of intendants was required for appeals against consular elections.

[1] Concerning the effects of this Edict, *cf. Babeau*, p. 76: it established mayors in many places where they did not exist, and increased the prerogatives and rights of municipal magistrates, stating them precisely.

[2] A very old custom, *Isamb.*, II, 278, *cf.* "Etabliss. de Rouen," and widely prevalent in the 1500 s. *Babeau*, p. 71.

[3] The assembly of notables embraced at first the members of the corporation, then fourteen notables taken one from the general chapter (clergy), one from the nobility, one from the bureau of finance, one from among the officers of other jurisdictions, two from the officers or the royal household, advocats, physicians, and bourgeois living "nobly," one from the community of notaries and royal solicitors, three from the wholesale merchants, two from the artisans (representation by classes). The electors chose the deputies eight days before the election; these were the deputies who elected the notables for four years from among persons at least thirty years old and residents for ten years. The mayor was elected for three years, the "échevins" for two years and the councilors for six; each year, two "échevins" and one councilor were replaced. The syndic and the recorder did not have a deliberative voice; the recorder could not even be present at the deliberations except when he was sent for.

[4] Edict of Compiègne, Aug., 1764, and of Marly, 1765. Edict of Fontainebleau, 1771. *Isamb.*, XXII, 434, 539.

[5] In the 1600 s, *Babeau*, p. 107, distinguished three types: 1. The "syndicate" (small towns and villages); one or more royal solicitors

"échevins" (in the North), or consuls (in the South), and of other officers such as the recorder, the syndic-attorney, and the collector.[1] The municipal tenure was ordinarily one year, a system not without its inconveniences, because these annually elected magistrates had little experience in public affairs; under Louis XIV the tenure of the mayors became perpetual (1692), but in 1706 alternates were created to share the authority with the actual incumbents; in 1765 the mayors were appointed for three years. The shortness of the municipal tenure accommodated itself well with the obligatory and gratuitous character of the service; on this latter point, however, we may observe that the rule was not rigorously followed; the custom was introduced of giving presents to municipal magistrates and of indemnifying them for their expenses; they were presented with tokens for payment or were given wine and liquors to insure their attendance at the sessions, to such an extent that there were no "deliberations without collation and without refreshment." In addition to these advantages they enjoyed certain prerogatives which were not uniform, such as a particular costume, noble rank, the right to have guards. The edicts of 1692 and of 1706 exempted the mayors from the dues of the "taille," watch, guard duty, and the payment of the octroi. At the same time the edicts defined their powers; these were: the summoning of the urban assemblies, receiving the oaths of municipal officers, custody of the keys to the city gates, jurisdiction over the police and over the bourgeois militia, the presiding over adjudications and over the rendering of accounts, independence of the local judge and of the officers of finance. The monetary value of the new

or syndics executed the decisions of the general assembly which appointed them; 2. The consular or "échinival" régime; the administration with police powers, which did not belong to the syndics, was exercised by the consuls or "échevins"; 3. The mayoralty; a chief, the mayor, was added to the "échevinate." Variable qualifications for voting (wealth, rank, ability). *Dareste*, p. 142. Special administration for Paris. The jurisdiction of the intendant was devolved in part upon the bureau of finance, in part, upon the lieutenant of police (who judged, with the right of appeal to the Council). Jurisdiction of the "hôtel de ville," town hall (Edict, Dec., 1672), embraced: controversies concerning the subject of municipal stocks, police of ports, wharves, and markets, disputes relative to the provisioning of Paris by the Seine, poll tax, appeals to the Parliament in general, to the council in the matter of taxes, and to the court in matters relating to octrois. *Cf. Mercier*, "Tableau de Paris," 1782. Concerning Lyon, *cf. Isamb.*, XXII, 417.

[1] Until near the middle of the 1400 s, the kings confided the administration of the English towns to the guilds, which represented, in their eyes, the entire urban commune. *Fischel*, II, 61. Aristocratic régime since the Stuarts: mayor or bailiff, aldermen, and common council. In 1725, London received the aristocratic constitution by which it is still governed.

offices created by the king and thrown on the market was thus doubly augmented. In the exercise of their functions the mayor and "échevins" had as auxiliaries: the **syndic-attorney**, later the king's attorney, a sort of public prosecutor close to the "échevin" judges, and who was charged with proposing and demanding everything which concerned the public utility, and having a salary and deputies; the **recorder** (in the 1700s the secretary, who was keeper of the archives) who was the recorder of the proceedings of the municipal assembly, and a hereditary office-holder (Edict of 1690); the **receiver**, whose position was also raised into an office in 1690; and also the highway inspectors charged with the construction of public works, local police officers, and tithing men, chiefs of the militia, sergeants, and marshals, etc.

The **City Council**[1] assisted the mayor and the "échevins" (magistrates) in their deliberations. It was composed of members, elected according to the procedure described above, and of members by right, such as ex-mayors and "échevins." In the 1700s the position of city councilor was erected into an office. The Edict of 1765 fixed at six years the term of this office, and provided that the incumbents should be taken from different classes of the population.

§ 394. **Municipal Revenues and Expenses.** — The finances of the cities were at first subject to the control of the bailiffs and of the court of accounts, later chiefly to that of the intendants and the King's Council.[2] Measures were taken for the conservation of their domains, and their alienated properties were restored to them.[3] Colbert had found the cities burdened with debts and he endeavored to discharge these and to prevent them from contracting debts in the future.[4] The municipal budget had to be approved (and consequently regulated) by the superior authority.[5] The

[1] The "Stadtrat," "consilium," "consules," in the 1200 s in Germany; *Schröder*, p. 625. Contentions between the patrician and inferior classes, and afterwards, about the 1400 s, various types of municipal organization.

[2] Edicts of Crémieu, 1536, etc. Municipal regulations, BCh., V, 139.

[3] Decl. of June 22, 1659.

[4] The correspondence of the intendants shows the waste of which the municipal magistrates were guilty. *Dareste*, p. 133; *Guyot*, "Offices," vol. III, p. 299; *La Fontaine*, "Fables," 13, 7. Negligence in presenting accounts.

[5] The intendants, says M. d'Aube, passed upon the question of the utility of enterprises undertaken by the communities; their deliberations had to be approved by the intendant. *Dareste*, p. 133. Commission of Turgot, Art. 4: to verify the debts of the communities, judge of their validity, of the suits relating to them, to grant extensions of time and suspensions, to compel the presentation of accounts and documentary evidence, etc. They likewise controlled the sources of income of the communities; adjudication of leased lands, choice of receivers, etc.

cities could not incur any expense [1] nor maintain suits in the courts, nor impose taxes upon themselves, nor alienate nor acquire property, without the authorization of the intendant (or that of the King's Council). The town corporation, although it had its hands tied, retained a wide field of activity in the erection of public works,[2] the organization of fêtes, the bourgeois militia, the accommodation of troops, poor-relief,[3] instruction,[4] regulation of commerce and of industry, and relations with the clergy.[5]

[1] Expenses: indemnities to municipal officers and salaries of their agents (200,000 livres at Paris in 1779), presents to the governor and to the intendant, maintenance of the ramparts, expenses of the bourgeois militia, constructions and other public works, assistance, instruction, worship, and interest on the debt. The increase of expenses, very noticeable at the end of the 1700 s was explained by the increase of the population, new needs, and the diminution of the purchasing power of money. "The same causes have for a hundred years increased tenfold the municipal expenses, and consequently the taxes, which it is necessary to levy in order to provide for them." *Babeau*, p. 225; Edict, 1683; *Isamb.*, XIX, 421. Municipal budget: 1. Common funds or revenues from common property; 2. Octroi, duty on wines, ciders, brandy, meat, cheese, vegetables, eggs, etc. *Isambert*, "Table." In 1647, Mazarin gave the proceeds of it to the State; Colbert restored half of it to the towns in 1663. Their imposition had to be agreed to by the inhabitants and authorized ("octroyée") by the king (from which their name).

[2] "The transformation which took place from the 1500s to the 1700s in institutions, likewise took place in the construction and maintenance of cities. The central power executed what the municipal spirit had not been able to do. It was the state chiefly which had the streets enlarged, constructed wharves, opened vast squares, laid out promenades and which contributed most toward making the towns more regular and healthy." *A. Babeau*, p. 360. Régime of alignment; competence of the intendant. Concerning fire engines, *Babeau*, p. 386; playhouses, *ibid.*, p. 391.

[3] As regards public assistance, the State was at first subordinate to the ecclesiastical authority, and later to the municipal authority; general hospitals under Louis XIV; he did not go so far, however, as to exclude either from the administration of almshouses; the mayor, like the curé, was a member of the administration by right (Decl. 1698).

[4] Primary instruction given in the parochial schools by laical masters under the direction of religious authority was undertaken, in certain directions, by the municipalities; they paid the salaries, and furnished supplies and a lodging for the schoolmaster. The corporations of schoolmasters struggled for their privileges, notably against the brotherhood schools founded by J. B. de la Salle (lay brothers), schools entirely free, while in parochial schools, gratuity existed only for the indigent. The edicts of 1698 and 1724 (imperfectly applied) made primary instruction obligatory, with a view of converting young Protestants. Concerning the colleges, *cf.* the "règlement" of 1763. The municipalities assisted them and had a share in their direction. Nearly everywhere, secondary instruction was free. The royal administration did not intervene in the establishment of schools before the end of the 1600 s; and, again, it was the desire to give Catholic instruction to Protestants that led to it. The intendant did not appoint the schoolmasters, but confirmed the agreements entered into between them and the communities and, in last resort, pronounced on their removal.

[5] Municipalities, like the civil authorities in general, were auxiliaries of the clergy; they looked after the observance of Sunday and of fast days; prohibited the eating of meat during lent (prohibition upon butchers

§ 395. **Communities of Inhabitants,**[1] parishes, villages, and hamlets,[2] had at first only an existence in fact[3] and, forming an integral part of the seigniory, were subject in every respect to the authority of the seignior and to that of his officers.[4] From an early time, however, in many places, their independence and their personality emerged.[5] Three principal causes contributed to this change: the defense of their common interests, the support of the church, and later the levy of royal taxes.[6] The general assembly of the inhabitants had to meet under certain circumstances with the assent of the seignior to adopt necessary measures and to appoint a syndic,[7] a mere agent charged with the execution of its decisions; unlike the officers of the cities, his office was revocable.

and hotel keepers). The municipal magistrates took part in processions and had a seat in church. Vows, fasting, public prayers in times of epidemics. The towns furnished the parish priests with a parsonage and contributed to the construction of churches. Religious communities could not be established in towns without the consent of the inhabitants; but the latter often yielded before the letters patent of the sovereign. No religious order encountered more resistance than the Jesuits; Rennes litigated thirty years in order to compel their superior to receive each year a kiss from all the newly-married women; he had commuted this feudal right into an impost of a weight of wax worth five sous. *Babeau*, p. 469.

[1] *Isambert*, "Table," see "Communautés," "Communes," "Paroisses"; *Ferrière, Guyot*, h. vis.; *De Fréminville*, "Traité du gouvernement des biens et affaires des communautés d'habitants," 1760; *Denisart*, "Coll. de décis.," IV, 737, éd. 1786; *Jousse*, "Gouv. spirit. et temporel des paroisses," 1769; *A. Babeau*, "Le village," 2e éd., 1879 (bibl., *passim*); *Beugnot*, "Municip. rurales, Rev. fr.," 1838; *Serrigny*, "Dr. public et admin. rom.," Appendix, 1862; *Tailliar*, "Villages dans le Nord de la France," 1860; *Normand*, "Rel. de l'Etat et des comm.," 17e, 18e s. (Saint-Quentin, 1882); "R. de Gascogne," XVII, 436; *Robiou*, "Popul. rurales en France," "R. hist.," 1875; *L. Delisle*, "Cond. de la classe agric. en Normandie," p. 137 *et seq.; Hidé*, "L'admin. et la jurid. munic. de Bruyères," 1861; *Fauché-Prunelle*, "Anc. instit. des Alpes briançonn."; *Guyot*, "Dict. des postes," 1754.

[2] At the time of the Revolution there were estimated to be 43,915 municipalities. *Babeau*, p. 43, n. 5. Languedoc had 2,800 "communities."

[3] To what extent, in France and elsewhere, were the "communities" and parishes the successors of the village communities? As for the English system of the frank pledge, which united the inhabitants of the same place by rendering the tithing to which they belonged responsible for their offenses (at least if they were not more closely attached to the neighboring seignior), it does not seem to have worked in France.

[4] *Luchaire*, p. 552, mayor, sub-provost in the villages.

[5] From the 1100s, *Beaumanoir*, I, 317 (*cf.* I, 80): (where there was no commune). *Du Cange*, see "Baticium." "Ville" in the 1200s was rather a village, ordinarily as contradistinguished from cities, châteaux, and boroughs.

[6] *Babeau*, p. 16. "Tailles" for the repair of the church, *ibid.*, p. 361. Ord. 1358 (*Isambert*, V, 32): "liceat . . . communitatibus se congregare . . . pro taillando et congregando dictas summas." Ord. Nov., 1379 (*ibid.*, V, 516). By apportioning the "tailles" by parishes and by making the inhabitants conjointly responsible for their payment, the "communities" were officially recognized.

[7] Dig., 50, 4, 18, 13; *Du Cange*, see "Syndicus."

Little by little autonomy was assured and these rudiments of organization were developed. The seignior, who was nothing more than a subject of the king, the chief inhabitant, ceased to be an administrative officer.[1] The assemblies met without his leave, upon the summons of the syndics, chosen by them and now permanent; these latter officials were not judges, but subaltern administrators responsible to their electors and to the superior administrative authorities.

§ 396. **The Assemblies**[2] met at the conclusion of mass under the church porch or in the open air near by. The peasants and inhabitants of the place had the right to take part, and especially the heads of families, sometimes widows and perhaps even married women; sometimes there did not seem to be any condition as to age, rating, or even as to domicile. It was, with numerous variations, the democratic practice of universal suffrage. The intendants consented to admit only those who were inscribed on the list of the "taille" payers, thus excluding domestics and beggars. For the validity of their deliberations the presence of at least ten inhabitants was ordinarily required ("ten make a people"). The absent were fined (five livres in the 1700 s). The powers of these assemblies included all matters which concerned the community. The inhabitants assembled in a body, voted the expenditures, and made appointments (subject to the approval of the intendant). They passed upon sales, purchases, exchanges, location of communal lands, the repair of churches, parsonages, public edifices, roads, and bridges; besides their syndics they appointed their schoolmaster, their herdsman, their keeper of vineyards, their sergeant, and the collectors of tithes and of "tailles." All these acts had to be clothed in authentic form and written out by the recorder of the judge who presided over the assembly, or in case of his absence, by a notary. From 1722 on they were subject to an audit. On the eve of the Revolution these acts could be written out by a special secretary who was often the schoolmaster.

In the 1500 s the rural communities acquired a political status; they were represented in the Provincial Estates at the writing out of the Customs and participated, through their delegates, in the elections to the States-General.

[1] It was of little consequence to the seignior that the inhabitants appointed the collectors, for he did not pay the "taille," or that they deliberated concerning the maintenance of the church and the parsonage, for he did not contribute to the expense of either.

[2] *Babeau,* "Ass. gén. des comm. d'hab.," 1893.

§ 397. **The Syndic,**[1] (*a*) as an agent of the inhabitants caused the assemblies to be called, or summoned them himself, presided over them in the absence of the local judge, and later, even when he was present, received and expended the funds of the community, rendered an account to the inhabitants and to the subdelegate, maintained actions on behalf of the community, and had the custody of its papers and archives; (*b*) as the agent of the administration (1700 s) he played a rôle in the levying of taxes, the recruiting of the militia, and the royal "corvée"; he supervised the repair of roads, looked after the lodging of troops in transit, the destruction of caterpillars, the quarantine of epizoötics, and informed the intendant of all happenings which could affect the service of the king or the public tranquillity (epidemics, etc.).[2] The duties of the syndic, although lasting only a year, were onerous and little sought after. No one was permitted to decline them. The expenses which followed were poorly compensated by some pecuniary indemnities and advantages, such as a relief from part of the "taille" and exemption from the watch. In case of neglect of their duties they were frequently subjected to heavy fines. The Revolution gave to the mayor, who took the place of the old syndics, or syndic-attorneys, their municipal functions, some of the police powers of the local judge, and the keeping of registers of the civil status formerly intrusted to the parish priest.

§ 398. **Revenues and Expenses.** — (A) The revenues of the communities were derived principally: (*a*) from the produce of communal property, the lopping of forests, dues paid by each inhabitant for the right of cutting wood, and the renting of pastures; (*b*) from communal impositions; in order to prevent the levying of these contributions from prejudicing the royal tax, expensive letters of assessment (ratified by the treasurers of France and by the elected representatives) were required; for a levy of 300 livres, this expense amounted to 100 livres. The intendants delivered gratuitous authorizations and compelled the privileged classes, nobles and priests, and the aliens or foreigners in the com-

[1] *Babeau*, p. 66. *Cf. Fréminville*, p. 60.

[2] 1200 s: attorneys ("procureurs") of the "bateices" cities were appointed by the seignior and the community. In general, it was the régime of election which prevailed for municipal offices, *cf. Domat*, "Loix civiles," XVI, 4, 4. Attempt, under Louis XIV, Edict March, 1702, to create perpetual syndics; but if in the towns the municipal offices were found attractive, they were not so in the country; an edict of 1717 returned to the elective system (very diverse electoral customs). But the liberty of elections was abolished by the intendants; they gradually assumed the right to confirm the election of syndics, that of recalling them, and even that of appointing them to office in certain cases.

mune, to pay their share of the contribution; (*c*) from the proceeds from loans, which had to be voted by the inhabitants and approved by the intendant.[1]

(B) Local expenses formerly voted entirely by the assembly of inhabitants ended by becoming, some obligatory and others optional; the intendant *ex officio* inserted in the budget the obligatory expenses: the salary of the schoolmaster, the fees of the subdelegate, indemnities for the syndic and collector, the expense of mustering the militia, the maintenance of the nave of the church, construction of the parsonage, and the inclosure of the cemetery. Among other expenses we may mention lawsuits for which, from the time of Louis XIV, administrative authorizations were necessary.[2] The accounts of the communities were submitted to the subdelegates and to the intendants.

§ 399. **Councils of Notables.** — Although the villages, after the cities, had fallen under the guardianship of the intendants,[3] they had retained the right of assembling and of electing their agents. But in the 1700 s the general assemblies disappeared in many places to make way for bodies of notables; in the place of direct government was substituted the representative régime, that is to say, the modern municipal system.[4] There was complaint (by Turgot and others) that the popular assemblies were tumultous, that they accomplished nothing, and that the wealthiest and most intelligent men had no influence and remained away.[5] In 1776 the Intendant of Champagne took the initiative by creating councils of notables in many localities. Regulations ("règlements")

[1] Concerning these properties, *cf.* preamble of the Ord. of 1667; Decl. 1659; Edicts 1677, 1702; "Arr. Coun.," 1689; *Fréminville*, "Pratique des Terriers," III, 282. Louis XIV had the property of the communities restored to them, forbade their alienation in the future, and prohibited the Third Estate from disturbing them. *Cf. Jousse*, p. 129. Division from the 1500 s. *Clément*, "Les comm. d'hab. en Berry," 1890; in the 1700 s they were multiplied. "Le produit et le droit des communes," 1782. *A. Babeau*, p. 82. Question of the uses of marshes in Picardy and Artois, competency of the intendants until 1764, of the States since 1769; in Walloon, Flanders, where they were divided in 1777, controversies on this subject were submitted to the intendant; in Artois, to the Estates; in Burgundy, to ordinary tribunals. *Legentil*, "Legisl. des portions ménagère," 1854; *Guyot*, "Offices," III, 307.

[2] *Denisart*, see "Comm. d'hab.," IV, p. 742. Edicts April, 1683, Aug. 2, 1687, Oct. 2, 1703; Ord. Aug., 1764 (*Isambert*, 22, 415). Decl. April 13, 1761.

[3] Of the judicial power and elected representatives formerly, Decl. June 7, 1659 (minor communities), Edict April, 1683, and Decl. Aug. 2, 1687.

[4] In the South, political councils were found a long time before this date. *Trouvé*, "Etats gén. de Languedoc," I, 305.

[5] *Cf. Babeau*, p. 51 (facts in this sense).

issued in pursuance of the Edict of June, 1787, providing for the creation of provincial assemblies, established municipalities in the countries of election (*e.g.* the Regulation of June 23, 1787, for Champagne). The seignior and the parish priest were members of right; the seignior presided and in his absence the elected syndic; three, six, or nine members (according to the number of households) were elected by ballot by the parish assembly, which was attended neither by the seignior nor the parish priest, but in which all the inhabitants paying 10 livres of land or personal tax participated.[1]

§ 400. **The Parish** and the community were very often confused with each other, although it might happen that several communities formed a single parish, or that one community formed several parishes (as in cities).[2] In the 1700 s the two organizations, religious and secular, became dissociated. The parish priest, the chief of the parish, was, like the seignior, without great influence upon the assembly of inhabitants.[3] He belonged, however, to the administration, as an officer of the civil state because he made public the acts of legal authority.[4] The church wardens, the agents of the parish as the syndics were of the community, at times even exercising the same functions, elected by the general assembly of inhabitants (in the cities by an assembly of notables), and required to render their accounts to it, collected the receipts of the vestry boards (endowments, cutting of trees in the cemeteries, revenues from seats, the receipts from collections, concessions of burial places, etc.),[5] and applied them to the expenses of worship and the upkeep of the church.[6] Important questions were submitted to the assembly of inhabitants (in the towns to the municipal bodies), such as those relating to burials, the price of pews, acceptance of legacies, etc. Control by the administration was

[1] *Isamb.*, XXVIII, 365. *De Lavergne*, "Ass. prov.," p. 108.

[2] The English parish had always constituted a secular district. Fixed residence made the parishioner, and every parishioner had the right to take part in the communal assembly, also, he had to pay his part of the local taxes. This assembly received the name of "vestry," because it met in the vestry; from the time of the Stuarts, distinction was made between the general assembly of the parish, which appointed the church wardens and levied the church tax, and the "select vestry," a restricted committee which became more and more important.

[3] *Jousse, op. cit.* Ord. 1695, Art 22; *Isamb.*, XX, 249. The inhabitants lodged him and furnished his house. *Babeau*, p. 138.

[4] At the time of the sermon, reading of the ordinances, acts of adjudication, excommunications, monitories.

[5] *Boutillier*, I, 17.

[6] Ord. 1695. *Isamb.*, XX, 249: the nave of the churches was in the care of the inhabitants, also the inclosure of the cemetery, and the lodging of the curé; the choir, in that of the tithe owners. *Fréminville*, p. 444.

extended to the parishes and to the vestry boards as well as to the communities; nevertheless, it may be said that the parish administered itself by means of its elected representatives, although to-day "the parishioners are no longer occupied with the temporal affairs of the local body; these matters are intrusted to church wardens chosen without the participation of the parishioners and whose accounts are rendered and verified behind closed doors."

CHAPTER XII

THE MONARCHICAL PERIOD (*continued*). JUDICIAL ORGANIZATION [1]

[1] BIBLIOGRAPHY: *Fleury*, p. 71; *Jousse*, "Tr. de l'admin. de la justice," 1771; *Pardessus*, "Essai hist. sur l'org. de la justice," t. XXI, Ord; *Brewer*, "Gesch. d. franz. Gerichtsverf.," 1837; *Ricard*, "Inst. judic. de l'anc. Fr." (Gex), 1885; *Sadoul*, "Inst. judic. de Lorraine," 1898; *Baudouin*, "Org. jud. du Limousin," 1890; *Meyer*, "Esprit des inst. judic. des principaux pays de l'Europe," 1818–23; *Esmein*, p. 349.

TOPIC 7. AUXILIARIES OF JUSTICE

TOPIC 1. IN GENERAL

§ 401. **All Justice Emanated from the King**[1] was an undisputed axiom in the 1500 s. But it had been the reverse of the reality in feudal times; as a matter of fact, there had been not less than four jurisdictions administering justice in the name of different authorities: the Church, the Seigniors, the Communes, and the King. The legists, proceeding upon the idea that the right of administering justice was held as a fief of the king,[2] secured recognition for his benefit of "a right of eminent justice" over the whole kingdom. Bailiffs and seneschals struggled to strengthen the royal jurisdiction and by slow progress it prevailed in the end; the theory of the "royal cases," the system of appeal by writ of error, and the right of recourse which permitted appeal from all tribunals to the Court of the King, all led to this result. In 1789 the church courts still existed, but they had almost no cases; one could hardly speak of municipal courts; the seigniorial tribunals had disappeared from the cities, and those which had not been bought up and which remained in the villages were subject to the régime of the royal jurisdiction.[3]

Everywhere, except in the courts of the Church, justice was rendered in the name of the king, by virtue of an express or tacit delegation of authority, — a fact which permitted the king to suppress them in case of abuse.

The ordinary royal courts were: 1st, the Parliaments; 2d, the inferior courts and those of the bailiwicks and the seneschalships; 3d, those of the provostships and local justices.[4]

[1] *L'Hommeau*, "Maximes," 1610; *Ferrière*, see "Juges royaux."

[2] *Beaumanoir*, XI, 13: "All lay jurisdiction is held of the king in fief or in subfief." In a sense, this was a dangerous formula for the royalty, for if a recognition of the superior right of the king resulted from it, it also implied that the administration of justice had become a right of the seigniors of which they could not be deprived.

[3] According to the Ord. 1693, every officer of seigniorial or ecclesiastical justice must receive the investiture from the king.

[4] **List of royal courts:** I. **Ordinary courts:** the *Parliaments*, the *presidials*, and those of the *bailli*, the *seneschal*, the *provost*, and the *justice*. II. **Extraordinary courts:** (A) those for privileged persons: consul-judges, the conservator of the privileges of the University of Paris (the *provost* of Paris), grand provost of the Hôtel, "requêtes" (claims) of the Palace and of the Hôtel for those who enjoyed the right of "com-

There were in addition, extraordinary, administrative, and military courts.[1] But aside from these two categories of tribunals there was still an exceptional court, which had no regular organization and which was justified on the theory that the king was the sole holder of the judicial power;[2] all the courts received jurisdiction by delegation (**delegated justice**); but he had the right to deprive them of it, he had not prohibited himself from judging cases himself nor from conferring upon whomsoever he pleased the right to judge such cases as he wished (**reserved justice**). He could not have avoided it if he had desired to do so, because to render justice was an essential attribute of the royal power; it was a duty as well as a right.

§ 402. **Reserved Justice.** — In the 1200 s the king intervened in the deliberations of his court, amended its judgments, or obliged it to revise them.[3] Not content with thus controlling his judges, he even administered justice in person (Saint Louis at Vincennes) with the assistance of his council; "courts at the gate" were held by some of his councilors, the future masters of petitions ("maîtres des requêtes") of the palace.[4] It gradually came to

mittimus"; (B) those for certain causes: 1. **Supreme**: the *Court of Accounts*, the *Court of the Treasury*, the *Court of Aids*, the *Court of the Mint*, the *Grand Council*, the *Privy Council;* 2. **Superiors**: the "*marble table*," which included three courts: the *Court of the High Constable*, that of the *Admiralty*, and that of *Waters and Forests* (the name came, says *Fleury*, p. 82, from the large marble table at the end of the hall of the palace at Paris, burned in 1618, and which was used for solemn feasts). 3. **Inferiors**: elections, "greniers" of salt, admiralties, special masters of waters and forests, mints, provost of the marshals. III. **Exceptional Courts**: (by commission), *commissioners*, *chambers of justice*, and *intendants*. Supreme courts, like the Parliaments, ordinarily judged cases on appeal, and their decisions, from which no appeal was allowed, could, at most, only be annulled by the king's council, for extraordinary reasons; but this body did not constitute a distinct degree of jurisdiction. *Cf. Fleury*, "Inst. au dr. fr.," I, p. 95.

[1] The *grand provost of the Hôtel* exercised a disciplinary power over the king's retinue which made him the judge of civil cases among the inferior officers of the court, including the police and criminal jurisdiction of acts committed at the court (assault of Damiens upon Louis XV); in his judicial functions, he assisted the judges taken from the king's council. *Clos*, "Hist. de la prévôté de l'Hôtel," 1790.

[2] Concerning the Carolingian conception of the king justiciar, *cf. Langlois*, "Philippe III," p. 266: "rex a recte judicando." This conception, which was in accord with the judicial system of the Roman Empire, was violated, or else eliminated, by feudalism. On this point, as on all the others, it was necessary to reconstruct the State. At Jerusalem, the king had only an arbitral jurisdiction, or perhaps gave a decision in urgent cases, without the intervention of the High Court. *Cf. infra*, "Origins of the Parliament," *Blondel*, "Fréd. II," p. 53.

[3] *Beugnot*, "Olim," III, 132, 261, 283, 1435, 1543.

[4] *Joinville*, 57 *et seq.*: "mes sires de Neelle et li bons cuens de Soissons, et nous autres qui estiens entour li, aliens oïr les plaiz de la porte, que on appelle maintenant les requestes. . . . En estei il se aloit seoir ou bois de Vin-

pass that the king devolved upon a section of his council the task of judging cases that were submitted to him for his personal attention; this section became a new judicial court.[1]

(A) This personal and quasi-patriarchal justice gradually disappeared and, during the monarchical period, instead of administering justice himself, the king ordinarily appointed **commissioners** who were charged with judging particular cases, — a tribunal regarded with suspicion, because those who composed it were less judges than executors of the will of the king or of his ministers, and since then an odious tribunal suited for the trial of political cases. The **chambers of justice**, composed of members of the supreme courts,[2] were almost always formed to examine the acts of financial agents (peculation, embezzlement, and extortion), and criminal courts (**chambers "ardentes"**) to try State criminals.[3] This was a convenient means of getting rid of political persons, either suspected or troublesome, and at the same time of saving appearances.[4] But the king had a more effective instrument still: the personal order, or arbitrary warrant, the "**lettre de cachet.**"[5]

(B) Most of the other forms of reserved justice were rather modifications of normal procedure; they tended to become regularized and to lose in a large measure their arbitrary character:

ciennes apres sa messe, et se acostoioit à un chesne, et nous fesoit seoir entour li. Et tout cil qui avoient afaire venoient parler à li, sanz destourbier de huissier ne d'autre. . . . Et lors il appeloit mon signour Perron de Fonteinnes et mon signour Geffroy de Villete, et disoit à l'un d'aus: 'Delivrez-moi ceste partie.' Et quant il veoit aucune chose à amender en la parole de ceux qui parloient pour li, ou en la parole de ceux qui parloient pour autrui, il meismes l'amendoit de sa bouche." *Cf. Guill. de Saint-Pathus*, "Vie de Saint Louis," ed. *Delaborde*, 1899, p. 135.

[1] *Langlois*, "Orig.," p. 113: In England, the "rex in concilio" relieved himself little by little of his extraordinary equity jurisdiction for the benefit of one of the members of the Privy Council, the chancellor; from that originated the chancellor's court, a rival of the courts of common law. Like them, it was the result of a delegation of the powers of the king, but a more recent delegation. The chancellorship and the great council were institutions of the 1300s and 1400s. *Cf. Dicey*, "The Privy Council," 1887; *Franqueville*, "Syst. judic. de la Gr. Bretagne," 1893.

[2] Ord. Blois, 1579, Art. 98. *Le Bret*, "Souveraineté," 2, 1; *Isambert*, "Table," see "Commiss."

[3] "Gr. Encycl." (bibliog.); *Weiss*, "La Ch. Ardente," 1889.

[4] The English Parliament could render a decision, by special law, on the life and property of the citizen; it could pass a bill of attainder or of proscription, punishing acts to which the law did not attach a penalty (Catherine Howard, Strafford). The House of Lords acts as political high court to judge criminals of State impeached by the House of Commons (impeachment, trial of accused ministers, and high State functionaries).

[5] Abolished March 16, 1790. *Cf. Esmein*, p. 439. It is certain that blank letters of cachet were issued; in what way were they employed? *Marion, F. Funck-Brentano*, "Légendes de la Bastille," 1898.

1st, **Letters of Grace and of Justice** by which the king, following the example of the Roman Emperor, granted ("octroyer") privileges and dispensed with the execution of the laws in particular cases.[1] The "letters of grace" corresponded to both the pardon and the amnesty of modern criminal law.[2] The "letters of justice" were a means of attacking a judgment (bill of review), a contract (fraud, unfairness), or of obtaining a privilege, such as the privilege of inventory. It was under the form of a particular act of grace that these methods of procedure, borrowed mostly from the Roman law, were introduced into our old legal system as a means of softening its rigor;[3] practice applied for them and welcomed them; on account of their own worth, the king granted them for the pecuniary advantages which he derived from issuing them (they were no more, says Loyseau,[4] than a tax on procedure); thus justice and the fiscal interests were in accord.[5]

2d, The **Evocations**[6] and letters of "**Committimus**" altered the jurisdiction of tribunals by depriving the ordinary judges of their jurisdiction for the benefit of the King's Council or the Court of Requests. The privilege of "**Committimus**"[7] consisted in the

[1] *Esmein*, p. 434, and the authors he cites: *Beaumanoir*, 48, 8; 45, 30. *Loyseau*, "Seigneuries," 3, 16; 5, 42; 14, 51; *Le Bret*, "Souver.," c. 3. *Cf.* dispensations in canonical law. *Giry*, "Gr. Encycl.," see "Lettres." *Isambert*, "Table."

[2] *Esmein*, "Hist. de la procéd. crim.," p. 254. Various sorts of letters of grace: *abolition* and *pardon*, depending upon whether or not the crime was punished by death; *commutation* of the penalty; *rehabilitation*, restoration of civil capacity: *remission* in cases of involuntary homicide or in case of legitimate defense, that the ancient law punished. *Boutillier*, 1, 2, vol. 40. Formulas in the "Nouveau style de chancellerie." *Ferrière*, "Dict. de droit." The Penal Code of 1791, I, 7, 13, abolished the grace.

[3] *Beaumanoir*, 35, 29. "Anc. Cout. of Artois," 2, 8.

[4] The judges had to make an examination to ascertain whether the conditions requisite for their granting existed. *Fagniez*, "Fragm. d'un Répert. de jurispr. paris.," no. 133 (year 1396). *Cf. Ferrière*, "Dict.," see "Entériner," that is to say, to verify and approve. Ord. 1579, 190, and 1670, XVI. 14.

[5] "Seigniories," 14, 53.

[6] "Textes": *Isamb.*, "Table"; *Aubert*, "Hist. du Parl.," I, 130; *Fleury*, p. 88, distinguishes between the evocations of justice (relationship or alliance, *cf. Ferrière*) and the evocations of grace (*cf. Guyot*). The council of the parties examined the cases on which evocations could be founded, and ordinarily sent the affair to another tribunal, for example, to the Great Council (competent before the Ord. 1669, for all evocations), but most ordinarily to another parliament. In case of reference to another tribunal on account of relationship, the "presidials" sent it to the nearest tribunal of the same order. Before inferior tribunals, procedure was by recusation. Reference to another court on account of relationship was often used as a pretext for avoiding trial by a particular court, the parties claiming relationship to one of the judges. Removal of the cases from the courts of the justices of the peace by the English high courts (by means of the writ of certiorari).

[7] During the Frankish epoch, the king's tribunal judged the cases of counts, of bishops, of officers of the king. "Olim," I, 904, LVII; *Imbert*,

right to bring suit in the first instance before the Claims Court of the Palace and of the Hôtel[1] in personal, possessory, or mixed matters, and to cause to be transferred thereto cases begun before the other tribunals, provided that the issue had not yet been joined. The privilege belonged to a large number of persons (officers of the king or persons placed under the royal protection) including: (*a*) princes of the blood, dukes and peers, officers of the crown, king's councilors, officers of the regiment of the guard, officers admitted to the royal table, etc.; (*b*) members of the Parliament, of the Chambers of Accounts, of the Courts of Aids, of the Courts of the Mint, the Provost of Paris, the provost of the merchants, etc. Although the laws and the jurisprudence of the courts constantly limited the application of the "committimus," it constituted none the less an important derogation from the common law and a source of abuse. It was justified on the ground that it was necessary to permit officeholders to prosecute their claims without leaving the place at which they were obliged to reside for the performance of the public service or that of the king.

3d, **Reversal ("Cassation").**[2] — Reversing or breaking the decisions of the supreme courts by the King's Council for violation

"Pratique," I, 28; *Loyseau*, "Offices," I, 9; *Guyot*, "Formula." Enumeration of persons who enjoyed this privilege in *Ferrière*, *Guyot*. Communities, churches, and abbeys obtained it as did individuals. *Vintry*, "Et. s. le rég. finance de la France," n. s. I, 396. Philip the Fair gave the bishops the right to carry their suits directly to the parliament. *Langlois*, "Textes," no. CVII. Distinction (at what date?) between the "committimus" of the Great Seal, and the "committimus" of the Little Seal; in the first case, the privileged person lured his adversaries to Paris before the Masters of Petitions; in the second case, he drew them before the "Requêtes" of the provincial parliaments without bringing them before the inferior judges. Among other restrictions to which the privilege was subjected we may note the following: the "Caboçhienne" Ord., Art. 218, refused it to all except officers serving the king at Paris. *Aubert*, "Le Parl.," II, 19. There were no real actions nor criminal trials. The privileged person who summoned his debtor before ordinary judges, renounced his privilege by this act. The "committimus" applied only to tribunals of exception, like the Great Council, the Chambers of Accounts, etc. The letters of "committimus" ceased to be valid after the year of their issue. *Fleury*, "Inst.," I, 125. This privilege did not exist in certain provinces, Artois, Flanders, Dauphiny, Brittany, Alsace, etc.

[1] [See *ante*, § 401, Note on Lists of Courts. — TRANSL.]

[2] Before Cassation, properly speaking, there was another procedure, the *writ of error* (see *supra*, § 219). The Privy Council, after having decided that an error had been committed by the Parliament, ordered this body to revise its sentence. Details on this complicated procedure in *Fleury*, "Inst. au dr. fr.," II, p. 269, where it is said that this procedure was not resorted to for forty years. *Cf.* "Textes" cited by *Isamb.*, "Table"; add. Ord. March, 1498, Art. 88, and Ord. 1667, vol. 35, Art. 42. *Ferri`re*, "Dict." Error of fact in the judges' findings could only be availed of on appeal if it was based on fraud. Error of law could not be invoked except under form of an appeal for reversal to the King's Council. A decree of the council determined in advance the question

of the ordinances or customs, at first a simple favor granted at the will of the king, later became a regular and normal procedure.

TOPIC 2. THE PARLIAMENTS [1]

§ 403. **The Parliament of Paris.**[2] **Rise** (until the time of Philip the Fair).[3] The Court of the King (" curia," " consilium," " colloquium," etc., in the 1200 s " parlamentum ") [4] from which emerged the Parliament of Paris, included two elements: the vassals of the king who were bound to him by homage, and the liege men who were bound to him by an oath of fealty; it was at the same time a feudal court and a royal court.[5] It had no

of the admissibility of the appeal. *Ferrière*, see "Cassation"; *Fleury*, *ibid.*; *Isambert*, "Table"; *Guyot*, "Regulation of 1738," IV, 21; *Chénon*, "Orig. de la cass.," 1882, *Esmein*, p. 432; *Girard*, "Offices," p. 357; *Isambert*, "Table"; *Glasson*, "Gr. Encycl."

[1] BIBLIOGRAPHY: *Isambert*, "Table," h. v.; *Marillac*, "Tr. des Parl. de France," 1628; *Laroche-Flavin*, "Parl. de France," 1617; *Girard et Joly*, "Offices," 1645; "Encycl. méthod.," see "Parlement" (*Boucher, d'Argis*); *Dufey*, "Hist. et remontr. des Parl., Ch. des comptes et Cour. des aides," 1826; *De Bastard*, "Parl. de France," 1858; *Desmaze*, "Curiosités des Parl. de France," 1863; *Mérilhou*, "Parl. de France," 1863; *Lespinasse*, "Les Parl. de Fr.," 1878; *Simonnet*, "R. hist.," IV, 159; *Bataillard*, "Mœurs judic. de la Fr. XVIe au XIXe s.," 1878; *Glasson*, "Gr. Encycl.," see "Parlement."

[2] Bibliography in *Langlois*, "Textes," p. xxvi. *Taillandier*, "Mém. s. les registres du Parl. " (Henry II), 1842; *Pasquier*, "Rech. s. l'hist. de Fr.," II, 3; *Dupuy*, "Des prééminences du Parl. de Paris," 1655; *Miraulmont*, "Orig. du Parl. et autres jurid. royales estans dans l'enclos du Palais royal," 1593, 1612; *Gibert*, "Mém. Ac. Inscr.," XXX, 587; *Gautier de Sibert*, *ibid.*, XLI, 583; *Clos*, "Hist. de l'anc. Cour de justice de la maison de nos rois," 1790; *Gérard*, "Hist. du Châtelet et du Parl. de Paris," 1847; *Aubenas*, "Hist. du Parl. de Paris," 1847; *Desmaze*, *ibid.*, 1860 (2e éd.); *Rittiez*, "Hist. du Palais de justice de Paris et du Parl.," 1860; *Fayard*, "Ap. hist. s. le Parl. de Paris," 1877–8; *Cougny*, "Et. s. le Parl. de P.," 1879; *Lot*, see "Parl.," in "Dict. hist.," of *L. Lalanne; Aubert*, "Le Parl. de Paris de Philippe le Bel à Charles VII," 1887–90; "Hist. du Parl. de Paris," 1894; N.R.H., 1888, 432; *Isambert*, "Table," see "Parlement," "Pouvoir judiciare," "Organisation judiciare," "Justice," "Actes du Parl."

[3] *Langlois*, "R. hist.," 1890, t. 42, p. 74; "Philippe III," p. 305; *Luchaire*, "Instit. monarch.," 1883, l. III, c. 2, 3; "La cour du roi sous Louis VI"; "Manuel," p. 556. *Wallon*, "Saint Louis," II, 18. *Boutaric*, "La Fr. s. Phil. le Bel," VIII, 3.

[4] "Parliament" means assembly; in the 1200 s, the word was understood to mean a judicial body in France and a political assembly in England. In 1239, Saint Louis held a Parliament in Paris. One spoke of the Parliament of the "Chandeleur," or the Parliament of Christmas of such a year.

[5] *Dodu*, "Inst. de Jérus.," p. 261 and 160. In Palestine the High Court, a strictly feudal assembly, was both a council of the government and a court of justice; the king was only executor of its sentences. Germany: the emperor held, until the 1200 s, "Reichstage" or general diets which were only a continuation of the Carolingian assemblies, and "Hoftage," or special diets which the grandees of the country attended; it judged cases of the grandees, and pronounced the "sententia imperii" with the consent of the assembly.

fixed place of meeting, no regular sessions; it met wherever the king happened to be and traveled about the country with him. On the occasion of great fêtes, such as Christmas, All Saints' Day, and Pentecost, the attendance was large; in ordinary times, there was hardly any one except the officers of the palace. Those palatines, who sat regularly and who, as a result of their experience, played a considerable rôle from the first, were distinguished from the end of the reign of Philip I from the rest of the liege men. Gradually, they formed a body from which was detached, by a division of labor, a group of judges, magistrate councilors, like those who surrounded Saint Louis.[1] If the king pronounced the judgment, it was only after discussion and by the advice of the court.[2] In order to determine its competence it is necessary to distinguish between the fact and the law. In law, from the 1000 s, no one in the kingdom could deny its authority, neither vassals, nor simple liege men, for we find there, at least in the grand assizes, the principal vassals of the crown and the principal liege men where "each was faced by his peers." But until the time of Louis the Fat many seigniors refused to attend; it had only theoretical rights over the great feudatories. Under Louis VII it judged the most powerful of these, the duke of Burgundy, for example. From the 1200 s, in addition to suits between the king and his vassals and those involving denial of justice of the vassals of the

[1] The personnel of this body varied from one meeting to another, according to the importance of the cases; if a suit involved great personages, the chancellor, the peers, and prelates attended the Parliament. But twenty or thirty of the king's clerks sat in it regularly from the 1200 s and received pay. "Arr. Parl.," 1224 (*Boutaric*, "Actes du P.," I, 303, 13): peers contended that in cases in which they were parties, the great officers of the court ("ministeriales hospitii regis") could not sit. Regulation, Jan., 1278. *Langlois*, "Textes," no. 72.

[2] *Langlois*, "Textes," p. 15 (year 1136): "Curiæ nostræ judicio decretum est"; p. 21 (year 1153): "judicio Curie judicavimus," etc.; p. 32 (year 1216): "judicatum est a paribus regni," etc., "nobis approbantibus judicium." The court already had its practice, its "usus." The exclusive authority of the king in judicial matters was evolved only under the influence of Roman ideas and with the increase of royal power (*cf.*, however, *Langlois*, p. 91). In this way is explained the fact that the decisions of the Parliament had for the king only the value of simple advice. This was no more true in the beginning for the King of France than for the Emperor of Germany or for the King of Jerusalem. The king could no more judge without the court than the court could judge without the king. The king was, without doubt, a justiciar, "but he rendered justice according to the law, and the law obliged him to render it only by the intermediary" of his court. The king alone was authorized to convoke his court, and to fix the place and date of its meeting. But what clearly shows the independence of the court is the fact that it pronounced an opinion in cases in which it was interested. *Dodu*, p. 264. Likewise, the Emperor of Germany refrained from presiding over the "Reichshofgericht."

king, which were within its cognizance as a feudal court, and in addition, also, to appeals from the decisions of inferior judges, which belonged naturally to it, the Parliament had jurisdiction of cases affecting the Churches and the abbeys,[1] of differences between communes and seigniors, of cases between great feudatories, of cases involving a denial of justice by a great feudatory to his vassals, and of violations by the former of their obligations toward the king.

The extension of the authority of the king's court brought about a distinction among its members during the reign of Philip Augustus; "all were not equal in rank or power." It happened naturally when the lesser gentry entirely predominated, that the principal members of the king's court (all peers among them as co-vassals or co-liege men) reserved for themselves alone the title of peer.[2] This group of great feudatories acquired the privilege[3] of sitting in the court of the king whenever one of them was involved by reason of his peerage; at any rate, they had to be summoned in order that the judgment might be regular.[4] The **Court of Peers** was only the king's court "decorated" with the peers of France. The number of these was fixed at twelve only at the beginning of the 1200 s;[5] in 1789 there were thirty-eight lay peers, the peerage being nothing more than a distinction conferred upon the high nobility[6] and which was fated to disappear with the Revolution.

[1] Ord. of 1205 and 1215 (*L. Lelisle*, "Catal. des Actes de Philippe-Auguste," nos. 927, 928, 1530): *P. Fournier*, "R. qu. hist.," 27, 1437 (conflicts from 1180 to 1328); *Langlois*, p. 86.

[2] Concerning the peers, *cf. Langlois*, "R. hist.," vol. 42, p. 85; *Glasson*, "Acad. sc. mor.," 1893, p. 83; *Isambert*, "Table"; *Kervyn de Lettenhore*, "Le procès de Robert d'Artois" ("Ac. roy. Belg.," 2ᵉ s. 10 and 11); *Luchaire*, p. 560 (bibl.). *Cf.* Germany: the college of electors which was detached from the imperial pleas. The princes of the empire from the 1100 s claimed the right to be judged by princes.

[3] In 1153, the Duke of Burgundy was judged by an assembly that cannot be regarded as a court of peers. *Langlois*, "Textes," p. 20. In 1216, the peerage certainly existed. *Teulet*, "Layettes," I, no. 1182. Concerning the false act of 1171, *cf. Luchaire*, "R. hist.," 541, 382. Concerning the case of John Lackland, *cf. Beugnot*, BCh., 2ᵉ s. V, 1; *Bémont*, "R. hist.," vol. XXXII (1886), and BCh., 1899, p. 363. *Guilhiermoz*, *ibid.*, p. 45.

[4] "The Parliament under Saint Louis and Philip the Fair got the principle to be accepted that the presence of a single peer sufficed to render valid a decision of the court, that the presence of peers was not even necessary when a question involving the rights of the peerage was not raised, and that the court alone had the power to decide whether peers should be consulted or not." *Langlois*, "Textes," p. 49.

[5] *Cf. Langlois*, *op cit.*, p. 86, n. 2; *Isambert*, 3, 143; 150, 165; 4, 395; 5, 150. Conjectures in *Guilhiermoz*, *op. cit.*

[6] "The English peerage was the body of 'barones majores' which received the hereditary right of being summoned to the political parlia-

The Court of the King,[1] both a council of the government and a judicial tribunal, began to disintegrate, about the time of Saint Louis, into three parts: the King's Council, the Chamber of Accounts, and the Parliament. The formation of a judicial section[2] was gradually accomplished and was a result of the fact that the cases submitted to the King's Court, particularly appeals from the bailiff,[3] became each day more numerous.[4] The date at which the Parliament became an independent body cannot be fixed, but it seems to be proved that, if Philip the Fair did not create it, as was long believed, it was during the reign of this prince that it

ments." The High Chamber was both a privileged tribunal for the trial of peers, and the supreme court of appeal.

[1] England: The courts of William Rufus, whether they were derived from the Anglo-Saxon "witenagemot" or from the feudal courts of the dukes of Normandy, were held three times a year: at Christmas, at Easter, and at Pentecost; "their vague composition and their indefinite competence recall those of the Capetian courts of the same epoch." Under Henry I, the court of justice, with its regular judges, "justiciarii" "was a tribunal of the first instance for privileged persons, a court of appeal for all subjects, and an administrative tribunal for financial disputes"; the sheriffs appeared before it to render account; from it set out the itinerant judges who went to preside over the local tribunals and to compel them to accept the decisions of the court. In 1178, Henry II separated the fiscal tribunal or Exchequer ("Scaccarium") of the judicial body, from the King's Bench; but the latter court judged only with the king until the time of Henry VI, and was, consequently, an ambulatory court; the Great Charter of 1215, Art. 17, instituted the Court of Common Pleas, for the trial of civil suits between private persons, in order to relieve them from the obligation of following the King's Bench on its circuits. From the commencement of the 1200 s, England had its three courts of common law. The Chancery Court, with its equity jurisdiction, was of the 1300 s. "If the English kings organized their royal tribunal with so much regularity, at such an early time, it was because they were all powerful from the time of William the Conqueror; to plead before the 'Curia regis' was, from the beginning, a favor that was dearly bought, instead of being, as in France, a duty often eluded. From an early time, a 'writ de præcipe' emanating from the royal chancery sufficed to carry any case whatever to the county courts and to the seigniorial courts. With these vast powers the English court had to be divided into special sections." *Langlois*, p. 83; *Maitland*, "Select Pleas of the Crown," 1888.

[2] In the same way, the Parliament of Navarre resulted from the dismemberment of the old plenary court of the viscounts of Béarn (1080). The "Cour majour," created in 1220, was composed of twelve hereditary "jurats" or barons charged with rendering justice. In the 1500 s, it disappeared and was replaced by a sovereign council transformed into a Parliament (1620). *Cadier*, "Etats de Béarn," p. 51; *Frederichs*, "Le Grand Conseil ambulant des ducs de Bourgogne," 1890 ("Bull. comm. hist. Belg."); *Brabant*, "Conseils des ducs de Bourg." (*Ibid.*)

[3] Concerning appeals, *cf. Luchaire*, p. 570 ("bibliog."); *Aubert, op. cit. Cf. Dupond*, "Appels de Guyenne" ("Pos. Ec. Chartes," 1887). Ord. 1344, Art. 12: presence of "baillis" in the Parliament when appeals from their bailiwicks were before it.

[4] It was even necessary to restrict its jurisdiction by excluding cases of little importance, by the "Règlement" of 1278; like the Statute of Gloucester, 1278, in England depriving the court of common pleas of cases in which the amount involved was less than forty shillings, and leaving them to the county court. *Langlois*, "Orig.," p. 101.

received its definitive constitution.[1] It became stationary, with its seat fixed at Paris instead of being ambulatory and following the king in his movements. The sessions were no longer short, but continued throughout the year, except during the Easter vacation and from September 8 to November 15. As the procedure became more technical, the feudal element, barons, prelates, and officers of the crown, were gradually eliminated (without wholly disappearing, however);[2] professional jurisconsults, "magistri curiæ," "consiliarii regis," almost entirely made up the court (which, in the 1300 s, was half lay and half ecclesiastic.)[3] The "esprit du corps" changed; the legists, imbued with the principles of imperial law, transformed the Parliament into an instrument of domination at the service of the absolute power, or, to speak more accurately, into one of those forces which worked for the reconstitution of the State.

In the history of the formation of her great judicial bodies France was behind England; in the former country the evolution was made rapidly and through legislation; in England it was slow and imperceptible.[4] The organization of the Parlia-

[1] The Ord. of March, 1302, Art. 62, which enacted that there should be held each year two parliaments in Paris (*cf.* Ord. 1190), two exchequers at Rouen, two "Great Days" at Troyes, and one parliament at Toulouse, did not regularize the institution of parliaments and did not fix the king's court at Paris; after 1282, there were two sessions a year; from 1291 to 1296, one; in 1296 Philip the Fair prescribed the holding of two sessions, an order which was no more observed after 1302 than after 1296. Finally, the Parliament of Toulouse was not summoned to meet. *Langlois*, "Textes," p. 161, 174. Ord. of Philip the Fair concerning the Parliament: 1291, 1296, 1303; 1310 (the last mentioned was reproduced in 1318 by Philip the Long). *Langlois, ibid.*, p. 183.; *Isamb.*, III, 190, 254.

[2] *Beugnot*, "Olim," Préf. Klimroth, "Trav.," II, 87. Philip the Fair ordered that there should be regularly at the head of his Parliament some great barons and some bishops (1296, 1303). These presidents or chiefs did not direct the debates or render the decisions; there were senior councilors who exercised that function; but they had a preponderant voice in case of division; the police of the hall belonged to them. At the beginning of each session, they organized the divisions of the parliament; the notaries of the court were under their orders. *Langlois*, p. 108. At Jerusalem the High Court was never composed of any members except the liege vassals of the king.

[3] In 1258, Gui Fouquois, in 1298, Guil. de Nogaret, P. de Belleperche are mentioned in the "Olim" as clerks of the king. Ord. 1278. *Langlois*, "Textes," see "Conseilers." *Aubert, op. cit.* "Baillis" and seneschals were removed from the Parliament in 1303; after 1291 they could sit only if they were chief councilors, and yet, in this case, they could retire if the affair concerned them. *Langlois*, "Textes," p. 158; 164; 173. "In 1319, Philip V forbade admission to the Parliament to every prelate who did not form part of the Great Council."

[4] *Cf.* Germany where the jurisdiction of the emperor was exercised chiefly through the tribunal of the palace ("Reichshofgericht") presided over by the prince, or after 1235, by a "justitiarius curiæ regiæ." The jurisdiction of this functionary, which extended to all affairs submitted

ment was chiefly a matter of custom and until the last days it preserved some characteristics of its primitive condition: seigniors sitting by the side of councilors in commemoration of the courts of vassals and liegemen; the intervention of the Parliament in political matters, as formerly when the judicial court and the political court were not distinguished one from the other; special summons, at the beginning of the 1300 s, for the assembling of each session of the Parliament;[1] and for a long time confirmation of the Parliament at the beginning of each new reign.[2]

§ 404. **Internal Organization.**[3] — The Parliament, that is, the judicial section which had become detached from the "curia regis," was itself subdivided into several sections for the more rapid dispatch of the increasing business which was submitted to it. At first provisional committees were formed, and these, becoming permanent in time, were constituted into courts (1278),[4]

to the emperor, except the "causæ majores" which were taken before a "Reichstag" or a "Hoftag," lost its importance in consequence of special grants to the privileged classes ("de non evocando, de non appellando") and of the quashing of its decrees. In 1450, the "Reichshofgericht" ceased to sit. It had already been supplanted by the emperor himself, who exercised personal justice with his councilors. From this originated, in 1495, the Imperial Chamber of Justice, the "Reichskammergericht," with a fixed seat (Frankfort, 1495; Wetzlar, 1693–1806) composed of judges appointed in part by the emperor, in part, by electors and the estates. It had jurisdiction of violations of the public peace, of suits in fiscal matters, of suits of those seigniors who held immediately of the Empire, and, finally, appeals and cases involving denials of justice. The "Reichstag" had the right to revise the decisions of this chamber (only a suspensive effect after 1555). The institution of the Imperial Chamber did not take away from the emperor his personal right of administering justice; he exercised it with his council, which ended by being divided into a political body, the privy council ("Geh. Rath"), and a judicial body, the aulic council ("Reichshofrath"); after having commenced by preparing the cases which had to be submitted to the decision of the emperor, it became a tribunal independent of him, at least in a certain measure, for it was always possible to defer the judgment to the emperor ("votum ad imperatorem"). The members of the privy council were excluded from it. The emperor could be asked to revise his decisions. The competence of this tribunal was twofold; it had jurisdiction of the same cases as the Imperial Chamber; and it determined exclusively feudal questions, criminal actions against the seigniors who held immediately of the empire and cases involving imperial privileges. — Concerning the putting under the ban of the empire, *cf. Schröder*, p. 816. Bibliog. *ibid.*, p. 539, 811; *Blondel*, "Fréd. II.," p. 33; *Franklin*, "Reichshofgericht," 1867; "De justitiariis Cur. imp.," 1860.

[1] Because, at each session, it was necessary to establish a list of service; it was only when this list did not vary, so to speak, that the Parliament adopted the practice of meeting at the expiration of its vacations. During these periods the Parliament believed itself under the necessity of having royal authority in order to judge.

[2] At each new reign, it was deemed to be dissolved.

[3] *Klimrath*, "Trav.," II, 104; *Aubert.*, *op. cit.; Ferrière*, "Dict.," see "Chambre"; *Boiteau*, "Etat de la France en 1789," p. 323.

[4] "Règlement" of 1308; Ord. Dec., 1320.

namely, the Court of Inquests ("chambre des enquêtes") and the Court of Requests of the palace ("chambre des requêtes")—alongside the Great Chamber in which everything was originally concentrated.[1] Under Charles XII it became necessary to create a second Court of Inquests, in 1789 there were three; at the beginning of the 1500 s the "Tournelle" (Criminal Chamber) ceased to be a delegation from the Great Chamber.[2] The number of members which composed the Parliament and each of its chambers varied greatly.

§ 405. **The Great Chamber** or Chamber of Pleas, "camera placitorum,"[3] always retained an unquestioned preëminence over the other chambers. It was there that the king came to sit; there sat the peers; it alone had jurisdiction of cases concerning the crown or the royal domain, the appanages, the peers, the University of Paris, and the communities under the protection of the king; for a long time it delivered the judgments of the Court of Inquests, revised them or reversed them, and likewise revised or reversed those of the Court of Requests. About 1308 it was composed of eleven masters or clerical councilors, and eleven lay councilors in addition to the presidents; in 1789 there were ten presidents, twenty-five lay councilors, and twelve clerical councilors.[4]

[1] "Auditoire du droit écrit": a commission instituted after the annexation of Languedoc to judge suits arising in the countries of written law. Ord. 1278, Art. 17. After some vicissitudes, it disappeared about 1318. *Aubert*, "Parl.," I, 7, 35.

[2] Delegations of the Vacations (after 1276) and of the "Marée." The Chamber of Vacations composed of a president and a certain number of councilors, designated in turn by the first president, judged the cases which required celerity. A commission of the king had always been necessary in order that it might be constituted and that it might hold its sessions. *Ferrière*, "Dict." In the 1300 s, the "Requêtes" and the "Inquêtes" frequently served the Chamber of Vacations. *Girard*, p. 203.

[3] The case was introduced by a counsel's speech to the Great Chamber, which not ordinarily, being able to pronounce judgment itself, sent it to the Chamber of Inquests; the parties furnished the "articles," or indications of the points on which it was necessary to be informed; the chamber, after the examination, designated the commissioners, to proceed with the inquiry; these betook themselves to the locality and, the inquiry being closed, returned to Paris; the Chamber of Inquests had to see if the results of the inquiry permitted a judgment, or if a supplementary inquiry was necessary; in the case where the inquiry was received, the documents were given again to a reporter, who read them and proposed a decision, the text of which adopted by the Chamber of Inquests was pronounced by the Great Chamber.

[4] Further, according to Ferriere, the councilors of honor, four masters of the requests of the Hôtel; princes, dukes, peers, the chancellor, councilors of State; the archbishop of Paris and the abbé of Cluny took part in the sitting. *Cf. Boiteau*, p. 382.

§ 406. **The Court of Inquests**[1] ("chambre des enquêtes") owed its origin to the practice of conducting inquiries at the place where the affair originated — a necessity in most of the matters submitted to the Parliament. Certain masters were charged with making these investigations,[2] or instead, they were intrusted to the bailiffs and seneschals. Of the examining masters, certain ones, the **auditors**, proceeded to the locality to investigate the case and to take the testimony of witnesses; the others, the **observers** ("regardeurs"), and **hearers** ("entendeurs") tried the case after the inquiry by the auditors.[3] From this arose the distinction between reporters and judges which lasted for a long time. Constituted as a special chamber, the Inquests took cognizance of all cases decided by inquiry, or more generally by documents.[4] The masters designated by the presidents to conduct the inquiries were called Commissioners ("Commissaires"); the clerk of the court delivered the papers relating to the examination to the designated reporters.

§ 407. **The Court of Requests** ("chambre des requêtes") originated in the jurisdiction known as the "courts at the gate." Masters detached from the king's court received the petitions addressed to him, delivered them to him in case they were applications for pardon; if not, the parties were sent before the bailiff.[5] When the court became broken up into several bodies, some of them, the **Masters of Requests of the Mansion**, attached themselves to the king's council;[6] the others, **Masters of Requests of the Palace**, to the Parliament, where they formed a special chamber

[1] Nine masters in 1308; sixteen "judgers" and twenty-four reporters in 1319; three presidents and thirty-two councillors in the 1700 s. *Isambert*, "Table," see "Enquêtes."

[2] "The inquiry decreed by mandate of the king and executed in the locality by commissioners appointed by him, began to be generalized under Philip Augustus." It made the king's court present in the provinces and facilitated appeal. *Luchaire*, p. 559. The inquiry or "information" did not consist simply in the hearing of witnesses, but in the search for information of all kinds and in the examination of written documents and papers. *H. Sée*, "De judiciariis inquestis," 1892; *Guilhiermoz*, "Enquêtes," 1892.

[3] "Règlement," Jan. 7, 1278; Ord. 1291, 1303, 1316, etc. Under Charles VI, the judgments rendered by the Chamber of Inquests were still pronounced by the Great Chamber, which had the right to correct them and to annul them.

[4] *Aubert*, "Hist du Parl.," II, 30, *i.e.*, suits decided by inquiry ordered by the Parliament or arising on a report from a magistrate requiring confirmation; furthermore, incidental motions, petty criminal cases, and cases referred by the Great Chamber.

[5] This distinction between voluntary jurisdiction ("gracieuse") and contentious jurisdiction was made by the Ord. of Jan., 1278, Art. 16. *Cf.* Ord. 1291, 1306, 1318, etc.

[6] *Aubert*, "Hist. du Parl.," I, 29; *Girard*, p. 56, 263, 658.

(1291–1296).[1] Its competence extended to two principal categories of cases: (*a*) the examination of petitions and the delivery of **letters of justice** (authorizing, for example, the bringing of a case before the Parliament, or pleading by means of an attorney);[2] (*b*) the rendering of judgment in the first instance in the case of persons enjoying the right of **committimus** (under Charles V at least).[3] We may add that in early times it played often enough the rôle of a Chamber of Vacations.

§ 408. **The "Tournelle,"** or criminal chamber, for a long time a mere temporary assignment of councilors of the Great Chamber charged with the investigation of criminal affairs,[4] had become in 1446 a permanent assignment; in 1515 it was styled a "chamber"; the councilors who composed it, all laymen, were taken in turn[5] from among the members of the Great Chamber and from those of the Chamber of Inquests.

§ 409. **The Chamber of the Edict** (of Nantes, Art. 34) of the Parliament of Paris upon which there was a councilor of the reformed religion, and the mixed Chambers, composed, half of Protestants and half of Catholics, established in connection with certain provincial Parliaments (Castres, Nérac, Grenoble), judged actions involving members of the Reformed Church, upon their demand; an edict of 1669 abolished them and left to the latter persons only the right to challenge two or three judges.[6]

§ 410. **Judicial Powers of the Parliament.** — The judgments of the king's court were the work of both the judges who composed it

[1] *Cf. Glasson*, "Gr. Encycl.," see "Parl."; *Fleury*, "Inst. au dr. fr.," I, 125, ranks among the extraordinary tribunals: 1. the "Requêtes" of the Hôtel; 2. the "Requêtes" of the Palace. *Isambert*, III, 259 and following; V, 224.

[2] Ord. Nov. 17, 1318. *Cf.* royal "Indiculus" of the Frankish epoch.

[3] In competition with the masters of requests of the Hôtel, for privileged persons ordinarily had a choice between these two courts. *Cf. Ferrière*, see "Requêtes."

[4] Priests, gentlemen, and officers of justice accused of crime could demand to be judged by the Great Chamber, and the "Tournelle" together (Ord. 1566, Art. 38); the councilors of the Parliament and the king's men, by all the chambers assembled. *Ferrière*, see "Chambres assemblées."

[5] From that, according to some authorities, originated the name of this chamber. It was desirable, says Bodin, that its composition should change in order to prevent habitual sentencing from making the judges inhuman. In reality, its name was derived from the fact that it held its sessions in the "Tournelle" or little tower of Saint Louis. *Aubert*, "Parl.," I, 19, no. 3. There was, for some time, a civil "Tournelle" (1667–1690, 1735) established in order to relieve the Great Chamber. *Girard*, p. 34.

[6] *Isamb.*, XIV, 285, "Table," see "Parlement" ("Cours de"). *Ferrière*, h. v. *infra*, p. 643. *Cambon de Lavalette*, "La Ch. de l'Edit de Languedoc," 1862; *Sacase*, *id.* ("Acad. lég.," II, 282). *Brun-Durand*, "La Ch. de l'Edit de Grenoble," 1873. *Girard*, p. 39.

and of the king who presided over it.[1] Once the Parliament became detached from the king's court, it acquired by that very fact a power of its own and an independent jurisdiction. Its judgments were its exclusive work.[2] Nevertheless, the king was always in theory the chief of the Parliament, and it rested with him to come to sit in it[3] as well as to revise its judgments.[4]

§ 411. **What Cases did it Judge?**[5] — We have seen above what had been the original jurisdiction of the Parliament;[6] this grew along with the royal authority (privileged or crown cases, prosecution, appeal), and, under the absolute monarchy, this court brought about (in a measure too limited, but in a certain measure, nevertheless), uniformity of decisions in the countries of the customary law ("pays coutumier") just as the council of the king brought about administrative unity in the whole of France.

It was especially a tribunal of **Appeal.** It heard appeals from the judgment of the bailiffs and the seneschals, from those of the seigniorial courts of the royal domain, and those from the courts of the great feudatories, although these latter had high independent courts,[7] and from the ecclesiastical courts (appeals for excess of powers). Even the decisions of many special jurisdictions were submitted to it, such as the judgments of the court of the high constable, the judges of the universities, etc.[8] As a court of first

[1] *Cf.* concerning the judges of the feudal courts, *supra*, p. 223, and *Dodu*, "Inst. de Jérusalem," p. 261; *Degrassalius*, p. 168: in the Parliament it was said: "curia ordinat"; in the Council of the king: "le roy ordonne." The Ord. of 1302 declared the decisions of the court to be sovereign. Philip III rarely sat in the Parliament.

[2] Concerning the procedure of the Parliament *cf. supra*, p. 189 *et seq.; Beaudouin*, "R. qu. hist.," 1893; *Bordier*, BCh, 2e s., I, 396; *Tardif*, "La procéd. aux XIIIe et XIVe s.," 1885. *Tanon*, "L'ordre du procès civil au XIVe s.," 1885; N.R.H; *Aubert*, "Hist. du Parl.," t. II.; *Glasson*, IV, 172; *Esmein*, p. 507; *Guilhiermoz*, N.R.H., 1889, p. 21; *Langlois*, "Textes," *passim*. The Chambers of Inquests and of Requests had their particular procedure. *Du Crot*, "Le vrai style du Conseil privé, de la Cour de Parlement, de la Cour des Aides," 1633. *Girard*, "Offices," 288 to 323. Ord. 1344, 1446, 1453, 1535 (Provence), 1536 (Bretagne), etc.

[3] *Aubert*, "Parl.," I, 186. The chancellor was the head of it, after the king; he presided over the annual opening. In England, the king lost the personal presidency of the King's Bench and the Common Pleas.

[4] *Langlois*, p. 113, no. 3. Philip the Fair annulled wholesale, in 1309, all the decisions of his court which were contrary to certain favors accorded by him. "Arch. hist. Poitou," X, 144.

[5] BCh., 5e s. III, 171; *Aubert*, "Hist. du. Parl.," I, 263; and especially, "Le Parl. de Paris de Ph. le Bel à Ch. VII, sa compétence, ses attrib.," 1890.

[6] Ord. of Blois, 1499, Art. 81.

[7] *Dupond*, "Appels de Guyenne" (1200s and 1300s), 1888; *Aubert*, "Hist. du Parl.," I, 270.

[8] The "prévôts" of the marshals and the intendants judged without appeal; likewise the consular judges to the amount of 500 livres. Against these arbitrary sentences, recourse could be had to the ordinary judges.

instance[1] it had jurisdiction of actions relative to the domain[2] or to the rights of the king (" regalia "), cases of peers, princes, the grand feudatories, seigniors holding immediately of the king, those of dignitaries enjoying the right of committimus,[3] and cases brought before it by removal from another court (" évocation "). It judged likewise appeals from its own decisions, at least on writ of error, and on bill of review (" requête civile ").[4]

§ 412. **Conflicts with the Other Supreme Courts.**[5] — The competence of the Parliament, derived from that of the ancient court of the king, was so extensive and so vague that it did not fail to come into collision with other supreme courts in the exercise of its jurisdiction, and even with royalty itself in the exercise of its other powers. An edict of 1559, and an ordinance of February, 1569, attempted to provide against conflicts between the Court of Aids, the Chamber of Accounts, and the Parliament. In January, 1495, it was enacted that appeal in criminal cases should be permitted from the Court of the Mint to the Parliament. As regards the King's Council, the royal authority sustained it and upheld his rights as over the assented sovereignty of the Parliament. The conflicts between the Parliaments were settled by the king in council.

§ 413. **Administrative Powers of the Parliament.** — Although the Parliament was above all a judicial body, its powers were far from being confined to the administration of justice.[6] We see it, without there being any precise text to determine its functions, behaving like a high administrative authority, watching over the administration and the victualing of Paris, controlling the administration of the communes, reforming the universities, and occupying itself with highway administration, with public monuments, with

[1] The appeals "omisso medio" from an inferior judge to the Parliament without passing through the degrees of intermediary jurisdiction, and "a priori" the transfer direct to the Parliament, without previous instance, were forbidden by royal ordinances, after having been practiced too often.

[2] Ord. XIV, 202, 284.

[3] The registers of the Parliament gave the list of them.

[4] We may add, actions concerning the salaries of advocates, attorneys, etc., practicing with them, and offenses committed in the Palace inclosure.

[5] *Aubert*, "Hist. du Parl.," I, 280. Ord. Jan. 3, 1320; Feb. 26, 1465 (*cf.* Feb. 5, 1462). *Ibid.*, I, p. 320. Struggle of the Parliament against ecclesiastical jurisdiction.

[6] The Parliament had a disciplinary power over its own members and over those of the inferior courts in its district; it intervened in the choice of many functionaries, for the letters of provision of their offices had to be registered by its recorder; it received their oath, and required them to undergo an examination. "It could determine the boundaries of the bailiwicks in its province."

hospitals, and with the police;[1] it sent its members to visit prisons; it assured the execution of the regulations of the craft guilds; it prohibited fairs and markets in times of epidemics; it forbade certain plays at the theater, suppressed books, and, in 1606, established a tax for the benefit of the poor. Whether we see here a survival of the primitive functions of the Council of the King or an extension of its judicial authority, the Parliament of Paris had, in the 1400s and 1500s, a large share in the administration of public affairs. Specialization of services caused it to return little by little (but never completely) to its true sphere.

TOPIC 3. PARLIAMENTS OF THE PROVINCES[2]

§ 414. **Causes which led to the Creation of Provincial Parliaments.** — Originally the jurisdiction of the Parliament of Paris extended over the entire royal domain, but when the domain had grown much larger through the annexation of great fiefs after the Hundred Years' War, provincial parliaments had to be created. A single sovereign parliament would not have succeeded in dispatching rapidly all matters coming before it and, besides, it would have been too far removed from the suitors. The practice of holding **Great Days** or assizes in which justice was dispensed by a commission taken from the Parliament, a system which was applied particularly in the district of the Parliament of Paris, could only alleviate these inconveniences.[3] To these necessities was added the

[1] *Luchaire*, p. 572; *Aubert*, "Parl.," II, 52, and "Hist. du Parl.," I, 290; *Langlois*, "Orig.," p. 37; *Callery*, "Attrib. fin. du Parl. et de la Ch. des comptes" ("Fr. jud.," IV, 287); *Babeau*, "Province," I, 218.

[2] Hist. of the Parliaments: of Bordeaux, by *Brives-Cazes*, 1875; by *Boscheron des Portes*, 1877 (same, "Registres secrets," 1867; "Chronique" by *Métivier*, 1886–7); of Navarre, by *B. de Lagrèze*, 1873; by *Delmas*, 1899; of Toulouse, by *Lapierre*, 1875; by *Dubédat*, 1886 (*cf. Amilhau*, "Nos premiers présidents," 1882, and *Fons*, "Acad. Législ.," VII, 17; XXV, 75. See also *De Bastard*, *op. cit.*); of Bourgogne, by *Palliot et Petitot*, 1649; by *de La Cuisine*, 1864; by *Des Marches*, 1733–90, 1851; of Metz, by *Michel*, 1845; of Normandy, by *Floquet*, 1840–9; by *Lair*, 1589–94, 1861; of Lorraine, by *Krug-Basse*, "Ann. de l'Est," 1898; "Conseil souverain d'Alsace," by *Neyremand et Pillot*, 1860; of Flanders, by *Pillot*, 1851; of Franche-Comté, by *Estignard*, 1892; of Britanny, by *Bossard*, 1860; by *Carré*, 1888 (*cf. De la Borderie*, "La revolte du papier timbré en Bretagne," 1884); of Provence, by *Cabasse*, 1826; by *Giraud*, 1842; N.R.H., III, 471. *Desmaze*, "Curiosités des Parlements de France," 1863. *Cf. Glasson*, "Gr. Encycl.," see "Parlement." *Girard*, "Offices," p. 325 to 620. *Gaillard*, "Le conseil de Brabant," 1898. "R. de législ.," IV, 489.

[3] The assizes of the "Great Days," held by virtue of the king's letters patent which determined their competence, had for their purpose the bringing of judges and suitors closer together, and especially to reëstablish order in regions where the ordinary courts had proven powerless. "Great Days" of Poitiers, 1454, of Bordeaux, 1456, etc. They became

political interest involving in continuing the high feudal courts already in existence in the great seigniories; many of these new parliaments were new in nothing but name. The first one to be created was that of Toulouse,[1] in 1443 (after sundry attempts in 1303(?)–1420); then came that of Grenoble, 1453; Bordeaux, 1462; Burgundy, 1476 (former "Great Days"); Brittany, 1495, 1553; Normandy, 1499, 1515; Aix (Prôvence) 1501; Trevaux, 1538; Béarn, 1620; Metz, 1633; Besançon, 1676; Douai, 1709 (Tournay, 1686); Nancy, 1775.

To these we must add the **Supreme Councils** of Alsace, 1657, of Roussillon, 1660, of Artois, 1677, and of Corsica, all of which had the same powers as the parliaments. Even after the creation of the provincial parliaments, the Parliament of Paris embraced within its jurisdiction a third of the kingdom, or about ten million persons subject to its authority; Toulouse, Bordeaux, Rouen, and Rennes had from two to three million each; the others many less; thus there was flagrant inequality.

§ 415. **Equality and Indivisibility of the Parliaments.** — The parliaments maintained, nevertheless, that they were equal in law, and even that they formed only a single body of which the Parliament of Paris constituted the first division. This asserted unity, conceived during periods of struggle against the royal power for the purpose of strengthening the opposition of the judicial bodies, had scarcely any support in the history of the creation

rare after the 1600 s, because suitors did not willingly accept the decisions rendered by them, and because the parliaments saw in them a step toward the creation of new sovereign courts. At the end of the 1200 s, delegations of the Parliament of Paris held the exchequer in Normandy and the "Great Days" in Champagne, 1454, 1455. Ord. March, 1499, Art. 72. Ord. Blois, 1579; Ord. 1661; "Memoirs of Fléchier" on the "Great Days" of Clermont, 1665–6; "R. hist.," VI, 1, 272; *Boutiot*, "Rech. s. les Grands-Jours de Troyes," 1852; *Pasquier*, "Les Gr. Jours de Poitiers," 1875; *Baudouin*, "Journ. s. les Gr. Jours de Languedoc, 1666," 1871; *Brives-Cazes*, "Les Gr. Jours du d. duc de Guyenne, 1469–72," 1867; *Chevreux*, Thesis, 1880; "R. hist.," VI, 1, and 272; *Aubert*, "Hist. du Parl.," I, 271; *Isambert*, "Table," see "Gr. Jours"; *Babeau*, "Province," I, 216; *Girad*, p. 204.

[1] Alfonse of Poitiers governed, like Saint Louis, with the aid of a council of clerks and chevaliers, which was at the same time a court of justice (ambulatory, sessions at certain times of the year, variable composition). In 1270, a delegated section of this court sat at Toulouse (there is an unpublished collection of its decisions, *Boutaric*, p. 416). Under Philip III, temporary assizes were held by commissioners of the king, delegates of the Parliament. *Cf.* Ord. 1303, Art. 62, which was not executed. Finally, a parliament was established at Toulouse by letters of March 20, 1420, transferred to Béziers in 1425, and reunited to the parliament of Poitiérs in 1438. On the "volu" of the Estates of Languedoc, the Ord. of 1437 prescribed its reëstablishment; in 1443, it was definitely organized. *D. Vaissete*, X, 2207.

of the Parliament of Toulouse or in the royal declarations authorizing the members of this parliament to sit at Paris when they happened to be there (and reciprocally).[1] In regard to the equality among the parliaments, a logical result of their unity, it could have been conceded independently of the question of their solidarity. The truth is, the provincial parliaments were equal among themselves and independent of that of Paris, but that the latter had certain special privileges. Each parliament was supreme within its own district; the décisions of one could be enforced within the district of another only by writs of subpœna ("lettres de pareatis").[2] It frequently happened that an ordinance registered by one parliament was not registered by another; a number of laws thus enforced in one part of the kingdom were unknown in the rest of it. The principal privileges of the Parliament of Paris (apart from its location) were: supreme jurisdiction over the courts of the great feudatories, jurisdiction of suits involving peers, those of princes of the blood, and of great officers of the crown, and of actions relative to the royal domain, to the regalia, and to the organization of the regency.[3]

TOPIC 4. THE POLITICAL RÔLE OF THE PARLIAMENTS[4]

§ 416. **Registration and Remonstrances.** — The participation in the legislative power by our old parliaments was exercised at first by means of general orders ("arrêts de règlement") which we have already considered;[5] later by refusing to register the royal

[1] The members of the Parliament of Paris in the 1500s claimed the right of "entrée" to the other parliaments, without the latter having reciprocal rights. *Isambert*, "Table," see "Parlement de Toulouse."

[2] Dispatched from the royal chancellery in order to render the decisions executory throughout the entire kingdom, from the local chancelleries, in order to render them executory within the limits of their districts, and by the judges, in order to render them executory in their jurisdictions. *Ferrière* and *Guyot* say nothing of a privilege that the Parliament of Paris would have had by virtue of an ordinance of 1474. *Glasson*, "Gr. Encycl.," see "Parlement." There is also cited an edict of 1560, to which they make no allusion. Needless to say, one parliament could not encroach on the jurisdiction of another.

[3] *Cf. Dupuy*, "Majorité des rois," in-fo.; *Joly*, "Offices," I, 1. *Ferrière*, see "Parl. de P." (bibl.).

[4] *P. Picault*, "Tr. des Parl. ou Etats gén.," 1679; "De la nature et qualité du Parl. de Paris," 1652; *Boulainvilliers*, "Lettres s. les anc. Parl.," 1753; *Lepaige*, "Lettres hist. s. les fonctions du Parl., le dr. des Pairs, les lois fondamentales du royaume," 1753; *Voltaire*, "Dict. philos.," see "Parlement"; "Hist. du Parl. de Paris," 1769; *Aubenas*, "Acad. des Sc. mor.," XI, 147; *Desjardins*, *ibid.*, CXII, 478; "Henri IV et les Parl.," 1879; *Flammermont*, "Remontrances du Parl. de Paris au XVIIIe s.," Doc. inéd., 1892; *Aubert*, "Hist.," I, 347; "Parl.," II, 187.

[5] *Petiet*, "Pouv. legisl. en France," p. 272; *Aubert*, "Le Parl.," II, 215 (*cf.* "Hist. du Parl.," I, 357) cites the oldest which are found in the "Olim"

ordinances and by remonstrances. Since the Parliament kept registers, it was the custom to inscribe upon them the royal acts and especially the ordinances. The other supreme courts adopted the same practice in respect to acts falling within their spheres and so did the bailiffs and the seneschals. This was only a formality intended to complete the reading of the royal acts and the publicity which had been given them;[1] their execution was better assured by the Parliament (or the tribunal) preserving them in this way and having always at its disposition a correct copy.

But before inscribing the royal act the Parliament had need to assure itself of the authenticity of the act; it verified it and ordered it to be registered only after deliberation as in the case of ordinary decisions. If necessary, it addressed to the king petitions or remonstrances in regard to the inconveniences which could result from the measures he had taken. The ordinance of March, 1303, Article 21, recommended to the bailiffs and the provosts not to execute the orders of the king which were contrary to the law or too difficult of enforcement; they should refer such orders to the prince, who, it was supposed, had been badly informed.[2] Much more plausibly might the Parliament, as a detached section of the King's Court, proceed in like manner. It did so, either upon the formal invitation of the king, or to comply with their own private desires, whether it was a question of ordinances properly so called, or of special orders of the king.[3] From this practice arose its occasional refusal to register even in spite of the will of the king, and the theory according to which the ordinances were obligatory only after they had been registered.[4]

In the 1300 s the king "recommends" the Parliament to register his acts (without believing himself obliged to do so, and without

(I, 748, 23; II, 74, 9; 613, 11; 38 and following; 269; 303, etc.); the greater number relate to questions of procedure (1268, attorneys and advocates; inquiry by "turbe"); other matters: amortization, 1291; abolition of the right of procuration, 1412.

[1] *Langlois*, "Orig.," p. 112: publicity of the proceedings of the royal court was esteemed for a multitude of extra-judicial acts, for example, for the taking of the oath of homage. The Valois sent to the Parliament acts of all kinds, treaties of peace, testaments, etc., because of the authority of the court, said the registrar Nicholas de Baye in his journal.

[2] *Cf.* Ord. 1319, 25, *Isamb.*, III, 238 ("Ch. des Comptes").

[3] "Monuments précieux de la sagesse de nos rois," 1753 (textes). Ord. 1318, Art. 25; 1344, Art. 10. Same right of remonstrance for the chancellor and the high functionaries, *Bodin*, III, 4. The university also addressed remonstrances, notably in 1413.

[4] The refusal of the parliaments to register certain acts is evidence of the late date of this theory. The "règlement" relating to the examiners of the Châtelet, issued in Sept., 1483, was not registered until Aug., 1609.

a thought that their validity depended upon their being registered).[1] In 1390 the Parliament refused to register an act of Charles VI granting a privilege to Notre Dame, under the pretext that it was prejudicial to the king and contrary to the ordinances. In 1392, Charles VI ordered it to be registered. Were these, as has been said, the first remonstrances and the first letters of royal command? Next we see it refusing to register, under the pretext that the act was not done in the presence of the regular councilors of the king or that it was contrary to the honor of the king. When registration by the Parliament was done under compulsion, the formula "de expresso mandato regis, pluries facto" was added; but this was rare; registration nearly always took place as a matter of course (Ord. 1493, Art. 70). Many things were needed, historically, for building up eventually this doctrine of the right of resistance, — the connivance of the king, the long custom of registration, the very extensive authority which the Parliament derived from its origin, the habit of consulting the Parliament[2] whether the king called it as a council or whether it came to deliberate in his presence with the princes of the blood and the councilors of the crown, the encroachments which were favored by periods of trouble, such as the reign of Charles VI, and especially the religious wars. Purchasability and heredity of judicial offices gave new force to this bundle of precedents.[3] Thus there appeared in an absolute monarchy, by the simple fact of the separation of powers, an organ of resistance and of control.[4] The Parliament, recruited from the higher middle class, claimed to be the guardian of the fundamental laws of the kingdom and considered itself as a moderating power designed to curb the excesses of royal absolutism.

[1] According to Voltaire, "bed of justice" ("lit de justice") in 1374.

[2] Concerning the relations between the Parliament and the council of the king, see above, § 364, note 1 and § 412.

[3] The judicial bodies, strongly organized, like corporations, could own property and have a common treasury; in 1689, the Parliament of Burgundy offered the king a sum of 200,000 francs that it had borrowed by guaranteeing repayment from salaries of the councilors.

[4] The "justicia" of Aragon pronounced the judgment delivered by the king and his court; the king appointed him, and it was the rule that he should be taken from among the simple nobility; he did not have to be a great feudatory. This mouthpiece of the king became a mediator between him and the nation; he was transformed into a defender of the laws who guaranteed the rights of every one. *Cf.* "Privilegio general," 1283, kind of great charter for Aragon. Catalonia did not have a "justicia," but a "Tribunal suprême des proviseurs des griefs," which repressed all abuses of power by the royal officers. This tribunal seems to have been a sort of annex of the Cortes. These institutions disappeared with the progress of absolute power.

§ 417. **Theories concerning the Rights of the Parliament.** — If we take a sweeping glance at the claims put forth at different times by the Parliament, we shall see that few political and administrative matters would have escaped from its control if the royal power had consented to it: examination and interpretation of treaties (*e.g.* treaty of Madrid), application of the fundamental principles of public law (*e.g.* the Salic Law, inalienability of the royal domain, etc.),[1] annulment of the testaments of kings (*e.g.* Louis XIV) and the organization of the regency, verification of fiscal edicts,[2] and, in general, legislative acts, here remonstrances, and there meddling in the affairs of the government, actions against officeholders (*e.g.* the duke of Aiguillon) or against corporations and communities (*e.g.* the Jesuits) and interference in the administration; it touched everything. But it had only a sort of veto; it possessed no initiative nor does it appear to have demanded any.

According to the monarchist theory the remonstrances had only the import of simple observations addressed to the king at his request; the Parliament had no rights as against the king. From this principle arose the rule imposed by Louis XIV compelling the Parliament to register his edicts as a preliminary to addressing remonstrances to him (1673). The theories of the parliamentarians were varied and even contradictory.

(A) Some maintained that the Parliament was an epitome of the Estates of the kingdom (Du Vair) — they saw in it an image of the nation with the three orders which composed it and were represented by it, — an altogether fictitious representation, since the Parliament had never received a delegation of authority and had never been anything but a body of officials appointed by the king, or who had bought their commissions. The Parliament itself did not always accept this thesis; at times it regarded itself as superior to the Estates, under the pretext that it was the judge of that which they had enacted by grace of its right of verification. The parliaments, it was said, were mediators between the people and the kings.

[1] The Parliament increased the number of these laws and notably the right of registry and of remonstrance. At the end of the 1700 s, it affirmed that the nation was above the king, as the Church universal was above the pope, and that no new tax could be established without the consent of the States-General.

[2] However, the right of remonstrance was never exercised on one principal point, namely, the fixing of the amount of the "taille." The Parliament protested against the creation of new taxes, but did not concern itself with old ones.

(B) According to others, the Parliament was only a section of the King's Court; but the latter was as old as the king; it had always shared with him the exercise of the legislative power (in such a way that it had gained a prescriptive right thereto).[1] Or again, according to other theories, bordering on these and less justifiable, the Parliament was only the ancient Court of Peers whose consent had always been regarded as necessary for all important measures; it was a continuation of the national assemblies of the first two dynasties.

§ 418. **Measures of Constraint against the Parliaments.** — The attempts to establish in France a liberal political régime did not succeed; at the point where the States-General had been stranded, the Parliament also, and for greater reason, was fated to run aground, since the inevitable progress of the specialization of functions was bound to have the effect of confining it within its judicial rôle and of depriving it of its political rights.[2] The royal authority resisted its claims and used every means to overcome its opposition; letters of command ("**lettres de jussion**") containing an express order of the king to register his edicts;[3] and the "bed of justice" ("**lit de justice**")[4] when letters of command were ineffective. The latter institution was a solemn session of the Parliament at which the king, surrounded by the princes of the blood and the chief members of his council, sat upon a seat in the form of a divan, and himself gave the order to register his acts; finally, he resorted to arbitrary arrest ("**lettres de cachet**") of the leaders, and if necessary, to banishment of the entire body.[5]

§ 419. **Historical Survey.** — It was especially after the last years of the 1400 s that we see the Parliament assuming to play the rôle of

[1] *Cf. Hotman* and others, who translated the formula: "quia tale est nostrum placitum" as: "so has our Parliament willed," and not "such is our good pleasure." *Dareste*, "Hotman," p. 59.

[2] J. de la Vacquerie under Louis XI and L'Hospital under Charles IX state that the Parliament was only a judicial body. Ord. of Moulins, 1566, Art. 1. Edict Feb., 1641: prohibition of knowing in advance the affairs of State. *Isamb.*, XVI, 529. *Hotman* ("Franco-Gallia") was hostile to the parliaments.

[3] "Lettres de cachet," as elsewhere, previous orders to register.

[4] Name from the second half of the 1300 s. *Aubert*, "Parl.," I, 196; *Langlois*, "Orig.," p. 114: "Several ordinances of the Valois kings regulated the ceremonies of royal audiences. When the king held a session a canopy was taken to the Great Chamber in the open air with covers and pillows of velvet sown with golden lilies, bearing the arms of France, to decorate the bed or divan of the king. The bed was installed on a platform in a corner of the inclosure or hall, and isolated in such a way that the king could enter secretly with his attendants." *Isambert*, "Table."

[5] *Babeau*, "Le Parl. de Paris à Troyes en 1787," 1871.

guardian to royalty. In the following century it struggled against the States of the League by decreeing the Salic Law to prevail (1593) and by annulling all their acts (1594). It settled the regency at the death of Henry IV, Louis XIII, and of Louis XIV. In 1615 it addressed remonstrances to the king in regard to the bad condition of the administration of the kingdom. In 1648, taking a bold initiative,[1] it allied itself with the other supreme courts (the Chamber of Accounts, the Court of Aids, and the Great Council) and attempted to reëstablish the unity of the deliberating bodies which were the outgrowth of the King's Court (Decree of union, of March 13, 1648).[2] It revolted against the royal authority at the very time when the latter experienced a serious check in England. For this attempted rebellion, Louis XIV, on coming of age, punished the Parliament by a fifty year sentence of silence.[3] Upon his death the Parliament had its revenge: it annulled the last will and testament of the great king; and then, when the Regent, in whose favor it had dared do this, had restored to the Parliament the right to make remonstrances before registering the royal edicts (Decl. of Sept. 15, 1715), this body employed the right by making an almost systematic opposition to the government of Louis XV (à propos of the Bull Unigenitus, letters of Confession, and the case of the Chalotais).[4] The Parliament of Paris, uniting with the other parliaments of the kingdom, claimed to form with them only a single body, in which it occupied the first place. In a "bed of justice" held in 1770, the king forbade it to make use of expressions of unity or of classes, to send memorials to other parliaments, to discontinue its duties;

[1] The meeting of the supreme courts was regulated by tradition (*cf. Savaron*, "Souv. du roy," p. 82), but it took place only upon the king's order.

[2] A delegation of the four supreme courts drew up a political program containing articles like the abolition of "lettres de cachet" and the suppression of intendants. *Isambert*, 17, 72 and following.

[3] An edict of 1665 took away from the Parliament the title of "sovereign court" and substituted that of "superior court," Parliament having no part of the sovereignty. The Edict of Feb., 1673 (*cf.* Ord. 1667, tit. I), ordered immediate registration pure and simple and did not allow remonstrances except during the week of registration. *Isambert*, XIX, 70. The anecdote which represents Louis XIV entering the Great Chamber in 1655 wearing boots and with a whip in his hand is false.

[4] The Duke of Aiguillon, governor of Brittany in fact, although he did not have the title (*Marion*, "La Bretagne et le duc d'Aiguillon," 1898), having caused La Chalotais, attorney general of the Parliament of Rennes, to be judged by a commission, the Parliament of Paris treated it as an attack upon the rights of the members of the judiciary, and instituted a suit against the Duke of Aiguillon for arbitrary and tyrannical acts; the king annulled the proceedings; the parliaments resisted. The result was the Edict of Dec. 7, 1770.

to resign in a body, or to delay registering his edicts, under penalty of dissolution. The Parliament resisted and was banished (1771). Justice was then provisionally dispensed by the Councilors of State and the Masters of Petitions ("maîtres des requêtes"); later, superior councils were established, which administered justice gratuitously, without receiving fees, and without the right to sell their office.[1] Suitors and advocates, sympathizing little with these reforms, which were, however, entirely to their advantage, formed a coalition against what was called the **Parlement Maupeou**, from the name of the chancellor who had established it, and went on a strike; the administration of justice was thus interrupted. Since the king, nevertheless, was unwilling to yield, the public, grown weary of the struggle, began to address itself to new tribunals, but the accession of Louis XVI to the throne saved the Parliaments from certain ruin by restoring them all their rights (Nov. 12, 1774). "He had no reason to be proud of this; they opposed all the useful reforms attempted by Turgot, Malesherbes, and Necker; through their opposition to the establishment of new taxes and their desire for popularity, they urged on the summoning of the States-General (demanded it even in 1787) and thus contributed to their own downfall by precipitating that of the monarchy."[2] The Constitutional Assembly gave them an indefinite vacation November 3, 1789, and abolished them October 4, 1790.

TOPIC 5. SECONDARY JURISDICTIONS[3]

§ 420. **The Provosts and "Viguiers."**[4] — The provosts were the ordinary judges for the "roturiers" and the serfs; cases in

[1] The reforms of Maupeou were good in principle (thus, the too extensive district of the Parliament of Paris was divided among the superior councils, the effect of which was to bring litigants into closer relationship with their judges), but only one thing was seen in them, namely, the abolition of the last check upon the arbitrariness of the king and ministers. *Flammermont*, "Le chancelier Maupeou et les Parlements," 1884. *Cf.* Edict, May 8, 1788. *Cf. Monod*, nos. 4395 and following; *Dareste*, "Ac. sc. mor.," 89, 323; *Bloch*, "Meaupou," 1887. Suit Beaumarchais. *Everat*, "Sénéch. d'Auvergne," 1885.

[2] "Lit de justice," of May 8, 1788 (*Isambert*, 28, 562): the registration of the laws taken away from the Parliament was confided to a plenary court (a supposed resurrection of the old "Curia regis"), composed of the princes of the blood, peers of France, prelates, and delegates of the sovereign courts. The Parliament protested: a decree of the Council of Aug. 8 suspended the execution of these measures.

[3] *Isambert*, "Table," see "Organisation judiciare," "Justice," "Pouvoir judiciare," etc.; *Fleury*, p. 75; *Trevedy*, N.R.H., 1893, 192 (Brittany); *Beautemps-Beaupré*, "Inst. judic. de l'Anjou," 1897.

[4] *Joubert*, "Une famille de prévôts d'Auvergne," 1889; *La Garde*, "Souv. duoi," ch. II; *Isambert*, "Table," see "Prévôté"; *Guyot*, *Ferrière*, etc.; "Jostice," p. 68, 345; *Girard*, p. 825; "R. qu. hist.," 1900, p. 235.

which the king's vassals were parties, were, on the other hand, submitted to his court (and eventually every noble was amenable to the bailiffs). Appeals from their judgments were in the 1200 s brought before the bailiffs. They sat, assisted by peers of the parties, elders and jurors; but as the duty of sitting in the assizes was onerous and involved a loss of time and fines when the judgment was amended upon appeal, the peers of the parties fell into the habit of not attending upon the summons of the provost, so that he alone acted as judge.[1] At times, however, the assize was converted into a permanent court, the notables furnishing proxies and always choosing the same persons as their substitutes. The Edict of April, 1578, authorized assessors to sit with the provosts. The "viguiers" and judges of the South corresponded to the provosts of the North.[2]

§ 421. **The Bailiffs and Seneschals**[3] of the king held assizes in the most important places of their districts,[4] at which the pro-

[1] Ord. 1302, Art 9: prohibition on the "prévôts" to fix the amount of the fine; only the seneschals and "baillis" were authorized to do that. *Isambert*, V, 265.

[2] In the South, there were three kinds of inferior tribunals (not counting the consular judges): 1. "Vigueries"; 2. "Bailies"; 3. "Jugeries." The "viguier" and "baile" were assisted in the exercise of their judicial functions by jurisconsults (1203 at Toulouse); these assessors became officers of justice and ended by taking the place of the "viguier" and "bailli." The judge or the court of the "viguier" judged even instead of and at the place of the "bailli," for example at Béziers. In the "sénéchausées" of Toulouse and Albigeois, Alfonse of Portiers appointed judges with judicial power in several "bailies"; from this originated the "judicatures" or "jugeries." The number of "bailies" did not permit a judge to each one. The "bailes" even retained in certain places, a part of the civil jurisdiction. *D. Vaissete*, VII, 195, 519; VIII, 1389; XIII, 151. Frequent conflicts at Toulouse between the consular court and the court of the "viguier." Philip III, in 1283, established a common court, or at least required the "viguier" or his lieutenant to preside over criminal trials, for it does not appear that the "viguier" had lost all his competence (thus, he alone had jurisdiction of offenses committed by the king's representatives). In 1335, this was still the case; eventually, the consular judges were separated from the "viguier." Limits or "Dex" of Toulouse fixed in 1226. *Bordot de Richebourg*, IV, 1065; *Du Cange*. The "agrimensores" called "decus," "decussis," a cross of Saint Andrew, carved on the trees or stones to mark the limits. "Dex" is a Roman form of this word. "Cart. du Saint-Sépulcre," nos. 71, 155.

[3] *Isambert*, "Table," see "Bailliages," and the authors cited, p. 401; *Beaumanoir*, c. 1. "Gr. Cout.," p. 599; "Jostice," pp. 69 and 336. Ord. 1319, 1388, etc. Letters of 1419. Edict, 1543 (*Is.*, VIII, 616 and 671); *Girard*, p. 825; *Gavet*, "Gr. Encycl.," see "Bailli"; *Bémont*, "Rôles gascons," "Doc. inédits, etc.," 1896 (list of the seneschals of Aquit., 1242–1272).

[4] "Gr. Cout. Norm.," ch. X. *Beaumanoir*, I, 29, 23 (ed. *Beugnot*). Were the "assises" of the "bailli" held only once a year, as *Rozière* thinks, N.R.H., 1891, p. 737? If so the "bailli" would have held audiences without ceremony, for ordinary affairs, throughout the whole year. The ordinances (after 1190) prescribed twelve, six, four "assises" per year. *Cf. Beaumanoir*, I, 29; *Boutillier*, I, 3, tells us that they were poorly ob-

vosts, and, in general, the judicial officers of the place participated.[1] As their court was a feudal court it was composed also of the vassals of the king having fiefs in the district. They judged principally complaints against the provosts either on account of denial of justice or other causes, matters affecting the rights of the king and his domain, and feudal cases. Their jurisdiction, like that of the King's Court, which they represented, had no exact limitations and apparently they were authorized to take jurisdiction of cases submitted to the provost. In the 1200 s the theory of crown cases and that of appeal were important feeders of their jurisdiction; aside from matters which were reserved to them, such as the suits of the nobility, they ceased to dispossess the provosts of their jurisdiction. At this time there were places where they never held court alone (*e.g.* the county of Clermont in Beauvaisis) but with the men of the fief;[2] there were others where the judgment

served. *Cf. Tixier, op. cit.*, p. 74. *Ferrière* declares that up to the 1700 s, the assizes were rarely held, and he describes them thus: "The 'baillis' had all the judges assigned to their districts, royal as well as 'seigniorial,' to hear the reading of the ordinances, to listen to the complaints of subjects against judges and officers of justice, to correct abuses, to impose fines upon those who were in fault, to judge and dispatch during their sessions civil as well as criminal cases which were pending and to be judged in these subordinate courts." *Cf.* sessions of the English justices of the peace: the sheriff of the county summoned a grand jury, sheriffs, justices of the peace, personnel of the grand and petit juries, keeper of rolls, high constables, bailiffs, coroners, jailers. The secretary of the county, clerk of the peace, presents the act of accusation to the grand jury which acts as a court of indictment. The session is opened by the cry: Oyez! oyez! oyez! The inhabitants of the county are taxed, obligatory regulations are made, and various other administrative measures are here taken.

[1] In Germany, justice was rendered by attorneys of the Empire ("Reichsvogt," "Landvogt") assisted by officers ("Schultheissen") and by "ministeriales"; these judges were appointed by the emperor who often sent to them appeals addressed to him. Their competence was limited in the 1400 s and little by little they lost all importance. For a long time Westphalia had "Freigerichte," tribunals for free men ("Vehmgerichte") the judges of which were appointed by the archbishop of Cologne; in the 1200 s and 1300 s, they assured public security; in decadence after the 1400 s, they were transformed into seigniorial courts. *Schulte*, § 115 and following; *Schröder*, p. 568. Germany: "Notgerichte," convoked by public cry in case of flagrant offenses and held by the count or by inferior judges. *Schröder*, p. 553. Germany: the "echte Ding" was held three times a year, and, in case of need, there were extraordinary pleas.

[2] In Germany every free man could take part in the determination of the judgment; this principle was followed for a long time in certain regions; in others, the judgment was rendered by elective or hereditary "schoeffen" (lay-judges; seven or twelve). In the "Vehmgerichte," "schoeffen" chosen from among free men, from the simple peasant to the emperor. Concerning these "Schoeffenbaren," *cf. Schulte*, § 85. *Schröder*, p. 554: in general, ownership of land was a condition required for holding the office of "schoeffen." *Hermann*, "Altdeutsch. Schoeffeng.," 1881. In Jersey, in the 1200 s, twelve jurors appointed for life were given to the governor of the island as assessors; with them, sat the free tenants or direct feud-

was given by the bailiff alone; but even in this case it was the custom to take counsel of "good and wise men" and to conform the judgment to their advice.

In time these ambulatory judges became stationary, the composition of their tribunal was modified, and its jurisdiction precisely delimited. These changes, some of which date back to an earlier time, were not completely realized until the 1500 s. There were, as a rule, no more assizes; the bailiff sat at the chief place of the district.[1] According to the general rule the lawyers superseded the military men on this court. The practitioners, the advocates or prosecutors of the place where the bailiffs were accustomed to consult,[2] were elevated to the rank of permanent assessors,[3] true judges (Francis I).[4] Furthermore, the bailiff himself, in his

atories of the crown. Pleas of judgment: seven jurors and the "bailli" reformed the sentences rendered by a less number. *J. Havet*, "Les Cours royales des îles norm.," 1878 (BCh., vol. 38, 39).

[1] "Assise" of the provost of Paris at Corbeil in 1496. *Fagniez*, "Extr. des Registres du Châtelet de Paris" ("Mem. Soc. Hist. Paris," vol. 17, no. 83); *Freminville*, "Prat. des terriers," vol. II. Languedoc: great "assises" were held five times a year at the chief place of the "sénéchausée" and ambulatory assizes in each judge's district.

[2] *Chassanæus*, "Catalogus gloriæ mundi," part VII, cons. 27 (cited by *Esmein*, p. 361); *Fleury*, p. 75. Esmein rightly considers as a survival of the old practice, the rule according to which: "advocates were called in the order of seniority to complete the tribunal."

[3] In the South, the seneschal, like the "viguier," was replaced by a judge ("judex major," so called to distinguish him from the inferior judges of the "viguier") or even by several judges, a judge of the first instance, and a judge of appeal ("judex appellationum," 1260, at Toulouse).

[4] The English jury, whose rise has been explained by *Brunner*, "Entstehung d. Schwurgerichtes," 1871 (*cf.* "Rev. gén. de droit," 1881, résumé by *Samuely*), was originally only a jury of proof, an assembly of witnesses; no one could be punished by reason of a criminal accusation unless twelve jurors declared him guilty. This jury of proof was transformed into a jury of judgment, and was divided into a grand jury composed of freeholders domiciled in the county, to the number of twenty-three in general, which acted as a court of accusation (indictment), following the preliminary inquiry by the justices of peace, and a petit jury, or jury of judgment composed of twelve members taken also from among the freeholders, but having a certain rating. Every year, the county clerk called upon the high constables to have the jury lists prepared and these intrusted the preparation to the church wardens and overseers of the poor. The justices of peace verified these lists, after which all the names were inscribed on a register. The sheriff appointed from forty-eight to seventy-two jurors for each circuit and assigned twenty-four of them to the sessions of the justices of peace. Half of the jury had to be composed of foreigners when a foreigner was to be judged. The jury of twelve honest men, trying in public and free to take testimony, with judges limited by a very strict theory of evidence (no one could be condemned for false oath or for high treason on the evidence of a single witness, unanimity of verdict), presented great guaranties against arbitrariness. England had not only the criminal jury; it had also the civil jury. *Cf. Pollock and Maitland*, II, 595; Acad. sc. mor., "Le jury anglais," by *Franqueville*, 1890.

capacity as a military man, was eliminated from his own tribunal.[1] From an early time he found it impossible, in consequence of the multiplicity of his duties, to exercise his judicial powers in person, and he was therefore represented by substitutes, vicars, or lieutenants, mere delegates appointed and removed by him at will.[2] Gradually it came to be the lieutenants who acted most frequently as judges; the king, and he alone, appointed and removed them; from being lieutenants of the bailiff they became lieutenants of the king, that is, royal officers (Ord. 1498, 47 s.).[3] The bailiff no longer had the right to take part in the determination of the decisions, although his name always appeared in them; he sat in the court, but without a deliberative voice.[4] The lieutenants of the

[1] *Fleury*, p. 89. In England, the sheriff (chosen by the crown from a list of candidates made out by the Chancellor of the Exchequer, the chancellor, the judges of the high courts and some members of the Privy Council), since the Great Charter no longer exercised criminal justice (except in matters of police). The establishing of the county courts (1846) has taken civil cases from him; he can take jurisdiction of them only exceptionally, by the aid of a jury, and by virtue of a writ from the chancery called "venire facias" (to constitute a jury), "nisi justitiarii prius venerint." In England, the justices of the peace (elected formerly by the assembly of the county, since 1327 appointed by the king) are taken from the gentry having a landed income which has varied according to the time; the aristocracy of landowners perform this service gratuitously. The sovereign can appoint as many justices of the peace as he pleases; their duties cease at his death and they can be recalled. They see to the keeping of the peace (that is to say, they suppress disorders, etc.); a special commission called a quorum authorizes certain of them with the aid of a jury to try felonies. Appeal from their decisions may be taken to the quarter sessions, then to the High Courts, and finally by a writ of "certiorari" the case may be carried to the King's Bench. The magistrates of correctional police everywhere have summary jurisdiction. The members of the High Courts of justice (King's Bench, Exchequer, Common Pleas) were detached from it from the time of the Platagenets, in order to hold courts twice a year in the circuits or judicial districts of the kingdom. There are ordinarily two for each circuit. They are charged, by the terms of a commission which dates from the time of Edward III, to make inquiry into all wrongs committed by the king's agents; they receive the complaints of the inhabitants through the organ of the grand jury; while they are traveling on circuit ("justices in eyre"), local jurisdiction is suspended. Among other commissions they receive that of "oyer" (to hear) and "terminer" (to terminate), that is to say, to try crimes, to empty prisons, either by releasing the prisoners, or by having them indicted (which puts an end to preventive detention twice a year), that of holding assizes, and that of "nisi prius" for cases of lesser importance ordinarily confided to the sheriff.

[2] Ord. 1254, Art. 10. *Beaumanoir*, I, 26, and "Jostice," I, 19, 8, find in the Roman law the justification of this practice, according to which the ordinary judge was authorized to delegate his jurisdiction. Dig. I, 21. *Cf.* concerning the composition of the Châtelet of Paris, "R. hist.," 63, p. 232; *Girard*, 1104, 1120.

[3] After having received a salary from the king (Ord. 1453. Art. 89 and following). *Cf.* citations in *Esmein*, p. 359.

[4] With exception Ord. 1453, 1498, 1579 (Art. 262). *Guy Coquille*, "Œuvres," 1666, I, 396, cites a decree of 1550 in this sense.

bailiff were required to be doctors or licentiates in law from some famous university. Each bailiwick in the end became the seat of a sort of court (parliament) on a small scale;[1] it had a lieutenant (general) in criminal matters (1522), a lieutenant (general) for civil affairs, several special lieutenants supplementing these,[2] councilors, royal prosecutors, substitutes, and the ordinary auxiliaries of justice.[3]

The court of the bailiff decided: (*a*) in the **first instance** cases concerning the royal domain (assigned ordinarily to the Chamber of the Treasury in the 1700s), crown cases ("lèse-majesté," etc.), cases involving benefices, and suits in which the nobility were parties; (*b*) **upon appeal**, from the judgments of inferior judges (royal, seigniorial, or municipal).[4] Charged with supervision over these inferior judges, they were themselves under the supervision of the Parliament (in that which concerned justice) from the administrative point of view under that of the council and the intendants extraordinary, and from the financial point of view under that of the Chamber of Accounts. For a long time they attended the Parliament when appeals from their judgments were before it and we have seen that in the 1200s they sat in it by virtue of their character as judges.[5]

[1] Personnel of the bailiwick court at the end of the old régime: 1st, the "bailli"; 2d, the lieutenant general of the sword, if there was one (Edict Oct., 1703, 1753); 3d, the lieutenants of the long robe, general, special, and criminal; this last office was created in 1522 (Decl. Jan. 15), and then the lieutenant general took the name of civil lieutenant; the criminal lieutenant, that of the short robe, 1554; 4th, inquirers ("enquêteurs") (Ord. Feb., 1514; March, 1583; 1693); 5th, councilors (twenty in the large bailiwicks of the 1700s); 6th, two advocates of the king and one procurator of the king; two recorders; 7th, advocates; 8th, bailiffs, sergeants, etc. [2] *Aubert*, N.R.H., 1894, p. 520, n. 3; *Girard*, 1104, 1120, 1226.

[3] Other auxiliaries of justice: "commissaires enquêteurs" or examiners, advocates and practitioners upon whom the royal judges devolved the duty of making inquiries; the position was erected into an office in 1514, 1588; after the Ordinance of Moulins, the inquiries became rarer, and the commissioners gave instructions in criminal matters, received complaints, prepared the preliminary acts of procedure, etc. No more commissioners in the sovereign courts or in the seigniorial courts. *Fleury*, p. 95; *Ferrière, Guyot; Isambert*, "Table," see "Enquêteurs"; *Girard*, 1467, 1328, 1319. "R. hist.," 63, 241 to 251.

[4] The Châtelet of Paris, a tribunal of the "prévôt" of Paris, first "bailli" of France, was a court of first instance at Paris and in the suburbs and heard appeals from the castellany of the viscount of Paris and from the seigniorial courts of the town and its environs. Ord. 1320, 1327, "R. hist.," 62, 227. *Girard*, p. 954, 1413; *Isambert*, "Table"; *Ferrière, Guyot, ibid.; Pardessus*, p. 292; *Beugnot*, "Olim," III, 1514; BCh., 5th s. III, 173. *Gérard*, "Hist. du Châtelet," 1844; *Desmaze*, "Le Châtelet de Paris," 1867; *Aubert*, "Hist. du Parl.," "Table." In the 1700s the châtelet was composed of a "presidial," a provostship, with a civil chamber, a police chamber, and a criminal chamber. At the audience of the provostship were published the ordinances and edicts. Concerning the "prévôt" of merchants, *cf.* "Ac. Inscr.," 1890; *Isambert*, "Table."

§ 422. **The Inferior Courts ("Présidiaux")** [1] created by Henry II, January, 1551, in the principal cities of the kingdom judged: 1st, in the last resort cases in which the maximum amount involved was 250 livres principal or 10 livres in interest or rent; [2] 2d, provisionally, upon security, where the amount involved was as much as 500 livres principal or 20 livres in interest (so that in this case the appeal, when permitted, did not suspend the execution of the judgment).[3] Seven judges were necessary for the validity of their judgments. The judges of the inferior court formed, moreover, only one and the same company as that of the bailiwick and of the seneschals' district; new magistrates had simply been created by the side of these latter officials.[4] The reason for the creation of these tribunals intermediate between the bailiwick courts and the parliaments was the desire to bring judges and litigants nearer together and to render more expeditious the dispatch of judicial business; [5] the treasury gained thereby new offices to sell.

TOPIC 6. THE JUDICIAL PERSONNEL

§ 423. **The Recruitment of the Parliament** [6] belonged originally to the king alone (save the right of the peers). Before each session

[5] Concerning the period when they ceased to sit here, *cf. Tixier*, "Essai s. les baillis," 1898, p. 122; *Borrelli de Serres*, "Rech. s. div. services publics," 1895.

[1] *Isambert*, "Table"; *Ferrière, Guyot; Jousse*, "Jurid. des presidiaux," 1757; *Laurain*, "Essai s. les presid.," 1896 (N.R.H., 1895); *Girard*, 1428, 952.

[2] Before 1551, the bailiwick courts were designated as "presidiaux." *Fleury*, "Inst. du dr. fr.," I, 112.

[3] Cases which they could never determine in last resort were: those involving the royal domain, waters and forests, seizin and fines, ecclesiastical cases and cases of minors, questions of feudal tenure, capacity of heirs, and interpretation of the "coutumes." *Ferrière, op. cit.*, and the authors whom he cites.

[4] The same officers determined: 1, ordinarily, cases that were beyond the power of the "presidiaux"; 2, those "presidially" in the two chiefs of the Edict of 1551.

[5] *Fleury*, "Dr. public," p. 76, estimated that there were in the entire kingdom, sixty-three "presidiaux," fifteen bailiwicks, ten seneschals' districts, 633 inferior seats, not counting the village courts. In 1789 there were 102 "presidiaux," according to *De Luçay*, "La Décentralisation," 1895, p. 139.

[6] *Borjon*, "Des offices de judicature," 1683; *Jousse*, "Tr. de l'admin. de la justice," 1771; *Glasson*, "Origines du costume de la magistrature" (N.R.H., 1884, p. 109); "Ac. Sc. mor.," 1897, "Journée d'un conseiller au Parlement de Paris, XVIe s." *Foisset*, "Le président de Brosses," 1842; *Blanchard*, "Les présidents à mortier du Parl. de Paris," 1647; *Aubert*, "Le Parl.," I, 48, 107; "Hist. du Parl.," I, 44; *Babeau*, "R. hist.," 1887, t. 37, p. 31; N.R.H., VIII, 109; *De Bastard*, I, 105. Textes: *Isambert*, "Table," see "Magistrats"; *Girard*, p. 19.

he prepared the list of councilors of the next Parliament.[1] When the composition of the Parliament no longer varied, the custom was introduced of allowing the members of the Parliament to prepare a list of candidates from which the king had to make his choice. This right of presentation, formally recognized in 1343, was not slow in becoming a right of election, the king contenting himself with merely ratifying the choice of the Parliament (Ord. of Feb. 5, 1389, Art. 5).[2] The election took place by secret ballot; but the bribery and intrigues to which it gave rise were such that it was abandoned for the system of public voting. The results of the system of election were not such as might have been expected; the king too often violated it by imposing upon the Parliament candidates of his own choice, or even the Parliament itself failed to reject the unworthy or to prevent a secret traffic in the offices (with frequent resignations in the 1400 s). At the end of the reign of Charles VII the usage was established by which the Parliament designated three candidates for each vacant seat and the king chose one of the three.[3]

§ 424. **Purchasability and Heredity of Judicial Offices.**[4] — After the 1300 s and 1400 s it was not rare to see the incumbent of a public office (following the example of the holders of ecclesiastical benefices) disposing of it for the benefit of a third party by the indirect method of a resignation in his favor. This practice suited well enough the morals of the time; it was in harmony with feudal ideas, with the practice of farming out various offices, and with the custom of making presents to the king on the occasion of an investiture of an office. Public office was already in many respects purchasable; there was a regular trade

[1] In England, the fifteen (formerly twelve) judges of the High Courts of Westminster are not taken from among the inferior judges of the towns and counties, but from the order of barristers, or jurists of great reputation. They receive a very high salary, their tenures are permanent "quamdiu bene se gesserint" (in case of misconduct they may be removed by the crown upon an address of the two chambers). They receive neither titles nor decorations, and can aspire only to become chief justice or chancellor. The chief justice swears that if illegal writs come before him, he will advise the king of them and continue to do right, notwithstanding these writs. The independence of the upper magistracy is thus fully assured.

[2] Same vicissitudes for the nomination of presidents. *Cf.* "R. hist.," 16, 91.

[3] Ord., XVI, 441; *cf. Picot,* "Le Parl. de Paris s. Charles VIII" ("Ac. Sc. mor."); Ord. Blois, 1499, Art. 30 *et seq.*

[4] *Savaron,* "Tr. de l'annuel et vénalité des charges," 1617; Treatises on offices by *Loyseau,* etc.; *Fleury,* p. 63; *Aubert, op. cit.; Guyot,* "Offices," t. III (art. of Merlin); *Louis-Lucas,* "De la vén. des off.," 1882; *Theureau,* "Abol. de la vén. des offices," 1868; *Isambert,* "Table," see "Offices"; *Durand,* "Offices," 1863.

in offices. The needs of the treasury led to the regularization and the legalization of the practice.[1] Francis I ran an open shop, first for the sale of financial offices, then for the judicial offices themselves;[2] after him and until the end of the "ancien régime" there was no budgetary expedient to which the ministers recurred more frequently than the creation of new offices. Obviously, they had to recognize the right of the purchaser to resell the office he had bought, in order to obtain a higher price from him; and as the treasury did not wish to lose any opportunity for gain, the right was granted only upon the payment of a fee into the exchequer; on this condition Charles IX admitted the legality of resignations (Ord. of Nov. 12, 1567). Nevertheless, up until 1597, an oath continued to be demanded from the incumbents of judicial offices that they had not bought their offices directly or indirectly; it was also required that they should possess certain conditions of capacity (age, titles, and the passing of an examination, which was reduced to a mere formality). Contemporary jurists taught: 1st, that the office itself was not a salable commodity; the king was not deprived in theory of the right of appointing to office those who were fitted; 2d, that the right of presenting a successor and of compelling him to pay for this presentation was a consideration which constituted a part of the patrimony of the incumbent. The salability of public offices had serious consequences, such as the irremovability of the judges, heredity of judicial offices, and regulation of their fees.

§ 425. **Irremovability of the Judges.**[3] — He who bought his office could not be deprived of it without serious cause established by a judicial process. If it rested with the authority which had appointed him to remove him arbitrarily from his office, it would have been only a fool's bargain. From the 1300 s it was the custom to leave the magistrates in office for life, in the interest of the service. Different royal acts (1344–1467) seem to have established in law the principle of irremovability;[4] but in reality it existed

[1] *Loyseau*, "Offices," III, 1. Louis XII, in 1498, made the offices of finance venal in imitation of the Venetians.

[2] Called the "Office of Escheats," from 1522. The price of the offices was deemed to be loaned to the king; loaned never to be returned, says Loyseau! Concerning this price, *cf. Babeau*, "Province," I, 207.

[3] *M. Sarzeaud*, "Ac. lég. de Toulouse." XXX, 325; *Aubert*, "Hist. du Parl.," I, 84.

[4] The Ordinance of 1344 was only an emergency measure. Louis XI by letters of Oct. 21, 1467, sought simply to attach himself to his officers: "Henceforth," he said, "we shall not give any office if it has not become vacant by death, resignation or forfeiture." It was merely a moral engagement which Louis XI himself did not respect. On their accession,

and was fully recognized only as a consequence of the practice of salability.[1] The independence of the magistracy, therefore, was born of an abuse.

§ 426. **Heredity of Offices.** — If the incumbent died suddenly without having disposed of his office [2] (or, what amounted to the same thing, if he died within forty days after resignation),[3] the king took possession of the office and sold it for his own benefit; the treasury found in this procedure a somewhat immoral opportunity for gain, — an opportunity often relinquished, however, by the granting of reversions,[4] which were revoked without scruple.[5] A decree of the council in 1604, made upon the proposal of Charles Paulet, secretary of the king, inspired by this practice and regulating it, assured to the magistrates the heredity of their offices subject to the payment of an annual fee which amounted to one sixtieth of the price of their office and which was commonly called the "Paulette" from the name of the author. In suspending this measure the king reserved the right to put an end to the practice of heredity of offices, but he did not use this means except to reimburse the purchase price in order to abolish the system of venality; the treasury was always opposed to abolition.

Finally, the system of salability had the result of favoring the old practice of judicial fees ("épices").[6] About the end of the 1300 s gold and silver were substituted in the place of presents in kind, and, from being optional, judicial fees became obligatory

the successors of this prince confirmed in their offices the councilors who occupied them, which would have been useless if they had been irremovable.

[1] Maupeou did not reimburse the councilors of the Parliament for the price which they paid for their offices.

[2] Rule of the pontifical chancellery for ecclesiastical benefices. *Dubois*, "Hérédité des offices," 1893 (Thesis).

[3] Because death so soon after resignation created the suspicion that the resignation had taken place following a serious illness with a view to defrauding the king of an almost certain gain.

[4] Revocations in 1521, 1541, etc. Ord. Blois, 1579, Art. 111.

[5] Heredity. Edict 1568, 1574, 1576, 1586. Edict of December, 1604, concerning the forty-day dispensation. The payment of the annual tax reduced by half the tax levied in case of resignation during the life of the incumbent.

[6] After the middle of the 1300 s, justice ceased to be free; "fees" were paid to the bailiffs and to the clerks; *Girard*, "Textes," p. 149 (Edict of the governor of Numidia of 361–3). Nov. *Just.*, XV, 6 and LXXXII, 9. During the feudal epoch, game, small presents, fruit preserves, etc. Philip the Fair took care that the councilors of Parliament did not receive either gifts or pensions. *Langlois*, "Textes," no. CXIX. Ord. Feb. 22, 1234 (Ord. II, 97). The misfortunes of the Hundred Years' War compelled Charles V to cease paying salaries to the masters of Parliament, the judges' fees therefore reappeared. Concerning the expenses of justice in the 1300 s, *cf. Lot*, BCh., 1872, p. 592; see "Epices," Dict. of Lalanne; *Aubert*, "Hist. du P.," I, 112; *Van Schoor*, "Les épices," 1891; *Girard*, p. cxxvii; *Isambert*, "Table."

(1395–1402). The judges had no legal claim to enforce the payment of fees; the suitor handed them to the recorder after the decision, and the total amount was divided among the judges after each session according to the number and importance of the cases which they had decided.[1] The exorbitant price of the judicial offices and the extreme smallness of the salaries the judges received did not at all justify the collection of these fees, but they explained the practice and constituted extenuating circumstances in favor of the old magistracy.[2]

There was hardly any abuse with which the "Ancien Régime" was more strongly reproached than the purchasability of public offices. Our early jurisconsults, Loyseau and Bodin, were agreed in condemning it. It gave the preference to wealth instead of merit, and the one who bought an office was too often a speculator to whom every means for reimbursing himself for his outlay seemed legitimate.[3] The evil, however, was less than one might suppose; the magistracy, although the method of selection was open to sharp criticism, was distinguished for its integrity, its industry, its learning. In any case the system of purchasability was preferable to favoritism and bribery which would not have failed to take its place had the system of venality been abolished.[4]

TOPIC 7. AUXILIARIES OF JUSTICE[5]

§ 427. **Advocates ("Avocats").**[6] — The corporations of ad-

[1] Edict of August, 1669. *Jousse*, "Comm. s. l'Ord. août 1679" (1775). The peasant code of the revolutionists of Brittany, 1675, demanded the suppression of these fees; this was accomplished for a brief period by Maupeou. The product of fees was valued at twenty-nine millions per year toward the middle of the 1700s. — Solicitations addressed to the judges, question of self-respect of the judges. *D'Avenel*, IV, 37.

[2] The office of president of the Parliament cost from 500,000 to 1,000,000 livres; the office of councilor, 300,000. In the 1600s, a president received only 6,000 livres salary, a councilor, 2000; the penury of the treasury led it to oppose the payment of higher salaries. — Privileges of the members of the Parliament, *cf. Aubert*, "Parl.," I, p. 141; "Hist. du Parl.," I, 121.

[3] This was observed especially in the inferior tribunals. *Dareste*, "Hotman," p. 62: "A butcher buys a beef on foot, cuts it up and sells the pieces in the market; in the same way, the judge buys his office in lump, and sells justice by retail."

[4] *Richelieu*, "Test.," 1, 3. Jan. 15, 1618, the annual tax was abolished; the first offices which became vacant were given to valets and to light cavalry; it was necessary to reëstablish the rule of heredity two years later. We may recall, in the same sense, the words of Beaumarchais à propos of an office: "If an accountant was necessary, a dancer obtained it."

[5] *Cf.* works cited in the preceding sections. *Fleury*, p. 92.

[6] *Loysel*, "Dialogue des avocats," 1602. Sur. J. des Mares, *cf. Bourquelot*, "Rdr. fr.," 1858, 244 ("Lettre sur l'estat d'avocation d'Eust. Deschamps"). *Cf.* works on procedure by *Tancrède*, I, 5, etc.; *Isam-*

vocates of the Later Empire,[1] which had disappeared after the invasions [2] and which the "fore-speakers" or "prolocutores" [3] replaced after the 800 s arise again about the end of the 1100 s in connection with the Church Courts and later in connection with the Parliament [4] before which they had the monopoly of pleading; [5] about the middle of the 1300 s they formed with the public prosecutors the brotherhood of Saint Nicholas whose chief bore the bâton or banner (whence the chief's name "bâtonnier"). The advocates separated themselves from the prosecutors at the end of the 1400 s and in the 1500 s they were designated (following

bert, "Table," see "Avocat"; *Ferrière, Guyot,* h. vo. (bibl.). *Bouchel,* "Biblioth. du dr. fr.," h. vo. *Boucher d'Argis,* "Hist. abrég. de l'Ordre des avocats," 1753, 1778; *Fournel,* "Hist. des avocats," 1813; *Dupin,* "Prof. d'avocat," 1832; *Fournier,* "Officialités," 32, 204; *Delachenal,* "Hist. des avocats au Parl. de Paris, 1300 à 1600," 1885; *Dareste,* "J. des Sav.," 1888; *Langlois,* "Textes," *passim.* "Gr. Encycl.," h. vo.; *Lefort,* "R. gén. de dr.," 1887, p. 308; *Aubert,* "Hist. du Parl.," I, 205; "Le Parl.," I, 232; *Nicolaï,* "Hist. de l'org. judic. en Guyenne et du barreau à Bordeaux du XIIIe au XIXe s.," 1892; *Saulnier de la Pinelais,* "Barreau du Parl. de Bretagne," 1897; *Giraud,* "Parl. et Barreau de Provence," 1842; *Ribbe,* "L'ancien barreau du Parl. de Provence," 1889; "R. hist.," 63, 251. N.R.H., 1886, 97; 1887, 524; *Rendu,* "Avocats d'autref.," 1874; *Froment,* "Eloq. judic.," 1874, 1875; *Garsonnet,* I, 398; *Gaudry,* "Hist. du barreau de Paris," 1866; *De Bastard,* I, 72.

[1] The "advocatus," "avoué" represented parties who, by exception, were not compelled to appear in person (bishops, priests, etc). The "defensor," "causidicus," was a councilor.

[2] In England there are three classes of advocates: 1st, barristers at law, admitted to the Inns of Court, four corporations which have existed in London since the Middle Ages, and which are administered by the oldest members; these latter decide upon the admission of candidates (with right of appeal to the judges of the superior courts) after a probation period of from three to five years, a purely formal examination, the payment of an admission fee and attendance at certain dinners given by members of one of the Inns; 2d, sergeants at law, barristers raised to this dignity by their colleagues after a long practice; the crown lawyers are recruited from among them; 3d, doctors of law who have the privilege of pleading before the Church courts; they are admitted by a college presided over by the Dean of Arches. The "Grand Cout." of Normandy, c. 63, knew only "prolocutores," commonly called "narratores"; below them, were the apprentices who in time became barristers. *Glasson,* "Inst. Angl.," III, 276.

[3] "Règlements" borrowed from the Roman law of the Later Empire; they passed from the ecclesiastical courts to the secular courts. Ord. 1274, 1291. Règl. of 1360. Ord. 1345. *Langlois,* "Orig. du. Parl.," p. 98: the "amparlier" described in sermons and in fables, greedy of gain, brutal and cunning. Philip III required that they be laymen like the procurators in order that the King's court might exercise a disciplinary supervision over them which the clerks would have been able to decline by invoking the immunities ("Textes," LXIX); Ord. 1274 obliged the advocates to bind themselves by an annual oath to defend only just cases and to charge as their honorarium only thirty livres (currency of Tours, worth about ten pence) at most. Oath and assessment for procurators.

[4] Of the Châtelet and other courts. Advocates before the King's Council, 1643.

[5] Ord., II, 10, Feb., 1327. Concerning the cumulation of the conduct of the suit and the pleading, *cf. Isambert,* XIV, 112.

Roman example) as an order. Certain ordinances and decisions of the Parliament regulated their organization, the conditions of inscription on the rolls [1] (*i.e.* capacity,[2] the taking of an oath [3]); their classification into consulting barristers, pleaders, novices or licentiates; their internal discipline and rights (exercised under the control of the Parliament).[4] The advocates [5] were not limited to pleading [6] but gave advice and prepared legal papers.[7] The decree of September 2–11, 1790, abolished the order of advocates and left each litigant to plead his own case or to select some one to represent him. However, litigants were permitted to have recourse to "official defenders" (January 29, 1791); a simple certificate of citizenship took the place of titles, but their employment was not obligatory upon suitors. The roll reappeared

[1] The ordinance of 1345 mentions for the first time the roll or list upon which they were inscribed in the order of their admission. "Bancs" or "barreaux": after the benches upon which were seated the members of the Parliament, representatives of the king, the "baillis," and the seneschals, the bench of the advocates was placed.

[2] A license was required by the civil and canonical law. Ineligible were: those afflicted with physical infirmities, women, judges, notaries, sergeants, and members of religious orders; secular clerks could plead.

[3] Ord. 1274. Costume: a long black robe, furred mantle and hood.

[4] The disciplinary power which at first belonged exclusively to the Parliament as well as the usual ordinance power, was finally assigned in part to the Council of the Order of Advocates which replaced the General Assembly, which had become too large (1662).

[5] In civil matters private individuals could not plead without advocates. A decree ordinance of 1693 divided the duty of preparing written papers between them and the procurators. The Parliament sometimes delegated its powers to advocates to make inquiries, to make sales by auction, and to judge certain cases. The dean of advocates took the place, in case of absence or of legitimate challenge, of the judges of inferior courts in the district of the Parliament. Judicial assistance already existed in early times. Advocate of the poor. *Lot*, BCh., 1872, 592. The "assignment of counsel," or the designation by the court of advocates (or procurators) frequently took place, either because the suitor did not know an advocate, or because he could not agree with an advocate, or because the advocate was afraid of incurring the enmity of some great personage. On the Roman and feudal origin of this custom, *cf. Delachenal*, p. 66. The custom ceased completely in the 1500 s because of the great number of advocates. Interdiction of contingent fees "de quota litis parte," as well as of purchase of rights of action and acceptance of donations; but advocates were authorized to receive legacies. They could exercise judicial functions, administer the estates of an abbey, etc. Privileges of advocates: "committimus," safeguard of the king, exemption from the "taille," etc. The profession of advocate did not confer nobility.

[6] We have no barrister's speech prior to the 1500 s; until that time, there were only analyses inserted in the pleadings (after 1364).

[7] The honoraria of advocates could be recovered by judicial process. Maximum of thirty livres, according to the Ordinance of 1274 (not enforced). For a long time, the advocates gave receipts; the custom having ceased, the Ordinance of Blois, 1579, Art. 161, and a decree of 1602 reëstablished it; thereupon the advocates went on a strike and the court had to yield. The "Dialogue des avocats" of Loisel was composed on this occasion.

in the year XII (22 Vent.) and the order of advocates was reëstablished December 14, 1810, with a monopoly of pleading.[1]

§ 428. **Attorneys**[2] ("procureurs") like the modern ("avoués") represented the parties before the courts, whereas the advocates both then and now merely assisted them. The right of being represented in court proceedings had not always existed for private individuals, and there had not always been officers professing this duty and invested with a monopoly by the State. The rule of the feudal law, which was the same as that of the Frankish law,[3] was: "No one in France may appear by attorney save the king."[4] But the prohibition upon appearing by representatives, which did not exist in the procedure of the Church Courts,[5] ceased in fact long before it was formally abolished by the Ordinance of January 15, 1528. Legal procedure had become a difficult art;[6] from the

[1] *Delon de Mézerac*, "R. des Deux-Mondes," 1893, p. 573. "Avoués," 27 Vent., year VIII, then advocates, 1806, for the court of cassation; advocates for the court of cassation, 1806; Ord. 1817 made them advocates at the court of cassation and at the Council of State (to the number of sixty).

[2] *Bataillard*, "Origines de l'hist. des proc.," 1868; "Mœurs judiciaires," 1878; and *Nusse*, "Hist. des procureurs," 1483–1816, 1883; *Tardif*, "La procédure aux XIIIe et XIVe s.," 1889; *Aubert*, "Hist. du Parl.," I, 205; "Le Parl.," I, 249; *Langlois*, "Textes," table, h. vo.; *Darras*, Thesis, 1884; *Lot*, see "Procureurs"; "Dict. hist." *de L. Lalanne*, "R. hist.," 63, 251; *Fournier*, "Offic.," p. 36; *Theureau*, "Off. minist.," 1893; *Beaumanoir*, c. 4; "Gr. Cout.," p. 393, 432; *Isambert*, IV, 470.

[3] During the Frankish epoch, representation was permitted only with the king's authority (*Marculfe*, I, 27) or exceptionally. Consequently, the profession of "avoué" did not exist. During the feudal epoch, "lettres de grace" were necessary in order that the parties might be represented by counsel. It seems that at a rather early time counsel was allowed the defense and public persons, churches, towns and seigniories. The old oral and formal procedure scarcely lent itself to representation by attorney; on the other hand, with the introduction of written and learned procedure at the close of the 1200 s, no private person could afford to incur the risk of conducting his own case; thus he obtained a procurator, who had to be a layman.

[See the article by *Heinrich Brunner*, "The Early History of the Attorney in England," translated in "Illinois Law Review," III, 257. — ED.]

[4] *Fleury*, p. 93. The king appeared by attorney; private individuals in their own name.

[5] In the Church Courts, the attorney gave security "de rato" if he was the attorney for the plaintiff, unless his mandate was incontestable; the attorney for the defense furnished security "judicatum soli." *Fournier*, "Officialités," p. 40.

[6] Exceptions in the 1200 s: gentlemen, clerks, members of religious orders, and women, if they were defendants; for plaintiffs, letters of grace were necessary to enable them to plead by attorneys; juristic persons (churches, communes, etc.) were exempt, from the necessity of having attorneys, also officers of the king, tutors, curators, executors, and testamentaries. *Beaumanoir*, IV, 2. "Gr. Coutumier," p. 433. The letter of grace was valid for a year. *Aubert*, "Parl.," I, 250. It was necessary to show it at the same time with the letter of procuration containing the mandate. Suppression at the accession of Charles VIII. Representation by counsel ceased to be a privilege and became a right.

middle of the 1200 s the employment of attorneys became frequent. There were organized at each court corporations of men who made a business of receiving mandates "ad litem." [1] The profession of attorney was regulated,[2] then it became an office (originally purchasable). The assistance of attorneys ("procureurs") was rendered compulsory; [3] there was no need of an express authorization to empower them to enter a suit.[4] Attorneys did not attain the consideration which advocates enjoyed.[5] The law of March 20, 1791, punished them for their disrepute by depriving them of the proprietorship of their offices and substituting for the title of attorney ("procureur") that of solicitor ("avoué"), a title borne until that time mainly by those whom the Church had charged with administering its temporal properties. The Convention (3 Brum., year II), more radical, decreed that the parties should be allowed to appear in court themselves or be represented by some one else; agents furnished with a certificate of citizenship took the place of solicitors ("avoués") and managed to make even the latter regretted; but solicitors were reëstablished by the law of 27 Ventôse, year VIII (1800). The system of purchasability in respect to their offices reappeared in 1816 (Law of 28 April, Art. 91).[6]

§ 429. **The Public Attorney.**[7] **[Public Prosecutor, "Ministère**

[1] In the Parliament, brotherhood approved in 1342. Ord., II, 176. Inscription on the roll, oath, no incapacities. *Cf.* Advocates. Letters of Nov. 19, 1393. Office, 22 July, 1572. *Isambert*, XIV, 255; *cf.* Ord. 1620. [2] Ord. 1344: oath, limited number. Tariff for salaries.

[3] Except in the inferior courts (Ord. 1620), where the agents who replaced them ruined the suitors.

[4] The "procureurs" were also advocates, at least in the courts of lower instances (*cf.* Ord. 1560 and to-day's procedure) and even judges in the subordinate courts. Concerning the "Clercs de la Basoche," or community of the clerks of the Parliament of Paris, see "Royaume de la Basoche." *Cf. Ferrière*, "Dict.," "Gr. Encycl.," and bibliography; *A. Fabre*, "Les clercs du Palais," 1875. The clerks of the Chamber of Accounts formed an association of the same kind, "l'Empire de Galilée." *Aubert*, "Hist. du Parl.," I, 214; *Van Schoor*, "La Basoche," 1892.

[5] The "Gr. Cout. de Normandy," c. 64, speaks of the "attourné." *Du Cange*, see "Atturnatus" (same sense as procurator); *Cf.* "Sollicitator curiæ"; *Ragueau*, see "Attournez," "Proctors," of the ecclesiastical tribunals. *Aubert*, "Hist du Parl.," I, 228: in the middle of the 1400 s, "solliciteurs," business agents, directed the suits, paying the advocates and "procureurs."

[6] Practice had reëstablished it in fact and legislation partly (D. of Oct. 6, 1791; L. 25 Vent., year XI), by assignment of the minutes of the notaries, the briefs of the avoués, the "repertoires" of the bailiffs; only the assignee could profitably solicit the office since he alone possessed the papers which permitted him to exercise its functions. *Garsonnet*, I, 377.

[7] *Aubert*, "Hist. du Parl.," I, 141; "Le Parl.," I, 201, n. 1 (bibliog.): N.R.H., 1894, 487; *Delachenal*, "Avocats au Parl.," p. 166; *Coumoul*, N.R.H., 1881, 300; *Ferrière*, *Guyot*, see "Gens du roi," "Procureurs généraux," etc. *Esmein*, "Hist. de la procéd. criminelle," and "Manuel,"

public"]. — The communities (cities, etc.) [1] and the seigniors had attorneys ("procureurs") to represent them and advocates to maintain their rights before the royal courts; as did the king of England, duke of Guyenne, who could not appear in person before the Parliament of Paris. The king had no need of being represented before higher tribunals, since there were none, while in his own courts his bailiffs and provosts guarded his interests. It seems singular that these latter should be at the same time judges and parties in the cases in which the interests of the king were involved. The division of labor had an effect also at this point, so that about the end of the 1200 s the king had his attorneys and advocates appearing and pleading for him before his own tribunals.[2] The attorneys of the king were sometimes special, sometimes general, that is to say, they were intrusted with one particular case or with all cases which came before the court at which they exercised their functions. About the beginning of the 1300 s [3] they became public officials, and in the end they were prohibited from undertaking the cases of private individuals.[4] All the attorneys of the king were attorneys-general in their districts. There were some in all the bailiwick courts and finally in all the extraordinary tribunals.[5] At the same time, with the extension of the royal authority and the substitution of the inquisitorial system of procedure for the accusatory system, the attorney no longer occupied himself solely with the fiscal interests of the king, with his rights, and with the integrity of the royal domain,[6] but

p. 397; *Guyot*, thèse, 1894; *cf. Serrigny*, "Dr. public rom.," II, 29; *Daremberg*, "Dict. des Antiq.," see "Advocatus fisci" (agent who was concerned particularly with the administration of property). "Mém. Acad. Bel.," XLV; *Tierenteyn*, "Officiers fiscaux près des Conseils de justice"; LII, *Alexandre, id.; Garsonnet*, "Tr. de procéd.," I, 273; Add. *Girard*, p. 63, 1240; *De Bastard*, I, 295; *Isambert*, "Table," see "Ministère public."

[1] "Gentes domini regis," 1277. BCh., 1885, 445.

[2] *Aubert*, "Parl.," I, 201; "Olim," II, 112, n° 8 (1278); *Tanon*, "Just. des anc. Eglises de Paris," p. 360. "Procureurs," "Avocats," pensioners of the towns. Chuches and seigniories. Ord. 18 July, 1318, Art. 29. *Beaumanoir*, 30, 90, supposes always private accusation.

[3] *Esmein*, p. 398; "Hist. de la proc. crim.," p. 101; *Aubert*, "Parl.," I, 202. The Ordinance of March 23, 1302, required them to take an oath like the "baillis" and seneschals. When they prosecuted offenses they took the oath of calumny, like private individuals, which corresponded well with their origin.

[4] Ord. 1498. Ord. 1579, Art. 115.

[5] But not before seigniorial courts where the seigniors had fiscal attorneys.

[6] Advice concerning the alienation of the royal domain, the registration of privileges, the collation of benefices, the exercise of regalian powers; control of titles taken by the seigniors; the creation of high seigniorial courts; those of the universities; discussion of treaties of peace, inquests ("enquêtes"), letters of grace; control of appointments to high offices;

with the general interests of the State, and the maintenance of public order; he handled officially the repression of crime ("délits");[1] he defended the interests of the absent, the rights of wards, of the poor and of the weak;[2] he gave information concerning the probity and the fitness of new officials and watched over the conduct of all; he compelled the observance of the laws and ordinances, the canons of the Church, the police regulations, and the special discipline of the judicial bodies. Once the office was established it was organized as follows: the attorneys of the king for the courts of the bailiwicks and the sénéschausées, formerly independent, became deputies, that is to say, subordinates of the attorneys-general; under this latter title were designated the attorneys before the Parliaments(or other supreme courts).[3] The attorneys of the Parliaments and the inferior courts being unable to do everything themselves had deputies to make up the deficiency, — mere delegates at first,[4] but later public officers taken from among the advocates and practitioners of the place (1586–1616). They were assisted by advocates whose history is almost the same as that of the attorneys; originally ordinary advocates, having among their clients the king, they became officials who pleaded only for him. The advocates-general were distinguished from the simple advocates of the king as the attorneys-general were distinguished from the attorneys of the king. At the bar the advocate ranked above the attorney. In criminal courts ("parquet")[5] the contrary was the case; there the advocate was

the choice of "baillis" and seneschals; supervision of the Church courts, and of the acts of the bishops, etc. *Aubert*, "Hist. du Parl.," I, 147.

[1] "Olim," II, 616 (1314); the case of Robert of Artois, 1329. Letters of Feb., 1335 (Ord., II, 106). Ord. of May, 1579, Art. 184; *Aubert*, "Hist. du Parl.," I, 147; *Delpon*, "Essai sur l'Hist. de l'Action publ. et du min pub.," 1830. *Fleury*, p. 93.

[2] Concerning his rôle in civil matters, see *Aubert*, *op. cit.*, p. 165. Police of Paris.

[3] "Stylus Parlamenti," 4, 14 (decree of 1325). *Esmein*, p. 398; *Fleury*, p. 94; *Aubert*, "Hist. du Parl.," I, 143: the texts always say "procureur-général du roi"; the "procureur"-general of the parliament would mean the "procureur" of the pleaders. According to *Garsonnet*, I, 277, the "procureurs"-general appointed the king's "procureurs" until the ordinance of 1522, which instituted the offices of the latter and made them independent. The Ord. 1522 (*Girard*, "Offices," p. 1241) said simply that henceforth there should be royal "procureurs" for the inferior courts, as there were already for the principal bailiwick tribunals.

[4] Ord. March 23, 1302, Art. 20. *Faguiez*, "Fragm. d'un Répert. de jurispr." ("Mem. Soc. Hist. Paris," 18, nos. 15, 131, year 1425, 1396.) The expression "avocat-général" is frequent in the 15th century. Appointment by the king, then, in the 15th century, election by the Parliament; at the end of the reign of Charles VII, appointment by the king; sixteenth century, it became an office.

[5] A part of the court room reserved for the king's representatives.

the subordinate of the attorney because the latter was the representative of the king.[1] The "men of the king,"[2] the term by which all these functionaries were designated, were subject to the orders of the chancellor; nevertheless they shared, by virtue of their irremovability (purchase and heredity of office), the independence of the Parliament.

"We have to-day," said Montesquieu,[3] "an admirable law, by which the prince has an officer at each tribunal charged with prosecuting in his name all crimes; the public prosecutor watches in place of the citizens; he acts and they do nothing." This admirable law, however, does not exist in England. The rule in that country is even yet that each individual, and for a stronger reason the crown through its law officers,[4] may prosecute offenses. Scotland has a mixed system in which public accusation and popular action coexist; this is the wisest method, because we cannot see why individuals should not be allowed to act at their own risk and peril in case of negligence or partiality of the public prosecutor.

Save for the monopoly of the prosecution of crimes, which is a debatable question, the institution was justified in all respects; it was only a happy application of the division of social labor; moreover, it arose spontaneously and not of set purpose. It has had, however, some opponents; it has been said that it was not without dangers for the public liberties, because it might be a powerful weapon in the hands of the executive power; and it has been added that it destroyed the equality between the prosecution and the defense. But granting that there were such risks

[1] The seigniors had fiscal "procureurs" at their tribunals, and there were "promoteurs" at the ecclesiastical tribunals.

[2] The denomination "gens du roi," given at first to all the royal officers, "baillis," etc., was restricted to those who constituted the staff of the public prosecutor. The "procureur" general was appointed by the king in the 1300s, and elected by the Parliament in the 1400s; afterwards, the office became salable. The same for advocates-general. On the appointment of the "procureurs" of the king, *cf. Aubert*, "Parl.," I, 204. After the time of Charles VIII, 1493, the "procureurs" general and the advocates-general held Wednesday conferences, "mercuriales," to recall the members of the Parliament to their duties. The "gens du roi" had the same privileges as the members of the Parliament. They were independent of the judges. Did they form a single and undivided body? Yes, if one may infer from the primitive organization of the institution. *Cf. Garsonnet*, I, 278.

[3] *Montesquieu*, "Esprit des Lois," 6, 8.

[4] The attorney-general, who is the general and fiscal "attorney" of the crown; the solicitor-general, his substitute; the King's Counsel, who gives his advice on questions of Roman and canonical law. *Fischel*, "Const. d' Angl.," I, 395. *Garsonnet*, I, 273.

[For a comparison of the French and the English system, see Esmein's "History of Continental Criminal Procedure," Vol. V in this Series, pp. 338, 596. — ED.]

the good exceeded the evil, because private prosecution assures impunity to a great number of crimes. Although England was able to dispense with the public prosecutor, only her rugged spirit of individualism rendered this defect tolerable.

§ 430. **Notaries**,[1] mere scribes without official character at the close of the Frankish epoch and at the commencement of the feudal period,[2] often attached themselves to the tribunals and were charged with keeping a record of the proceedings; they were then recorders, but recorders who at the same time prepared documents for private individuals. This function became divided into two parts, giving rise to the clerk's office and the notary's business. From the 1100s **notaries public** were found in the south of France, that is to say, officers who gave authenticity to the papers which they drew up by attaching their signature; they acted in their personal name and not in the name of the tribunal of the district in which they drew up deeds; they acquired, however, a part of its powers; sometimes, in fact, they performed acts of non-contentious jurisdiction, the appointment of guardians and curators, emancipation, and authorization of the sale of property belonging to minors.[3] Whoever had power to hold court had also the right to institute notaries to act in his district: kings, seigniors, justiciaries,[4] communes, and bishops;[5] much more the pope and the emperor,

[1] BIBLIOGRAPHY: *Rivier*, Z.S.S., G.A., 1892, 356. Z.R.G., IV, 190; *Stephanus Marcilletus*, "Doctrinale florum artis notariatus," 1492; *J. Fichard*, "Ars notariatus," 1539; *Isamberi*, "Table," h. vo.; *Ferrière*, *Guyot*, h. vis.; *Loyseau*, "Offices," II, 5; *Langloix*, "Droits des notaires," 1738; *Ferrière*, "La science des not.," 1753 (éd. *De Visme*, 1761–71); (*Blondelot*), "Connaiss. nécess. à un not.," 1772–90; *Berge*, "Hist. du notariat," 1815; *Coppin*, "thèse," 1884; *Fournier*, "Officialités," 1880; *Durando*, "Il tabellionato," 1897; *Aubert*, "Hist. du Parl.," I, 229; "Le Parl.," I, 267; *La Garde*, "Souv. du roi," ch. XXII; *Girard*, p. 123, 1647; *Fréminville*, "Dict. de police," see "Notaires"; "Ar. giur.," 64, 141.

[2] The prohibition upon clerics from being notaries was explained on the part of the Church by the desire not to distract them from their religious ministrations, on the part of the State, by the privilege of the clergy which made them almost irresponsible. The prohibition, however, was poorly respected. *Migne*, vol. 216, p. 486. "Capitulaires," I, 79, 115, 121.

[3] From this was derived the name "Judices chartularii" sometimes given them.

[4] In the end, the right to institute notaries was accorded only to seigniors, high justiciars, who were chatelaines (except by right or immemorial possession). Decl. Feb. 24, 1537. "Cout. of Blois," 17; of Tours, 75. It was admitted, however, that this was only by royal tolerance.

[5] The Edict of November, 1691, provided for royal and apostolic notaries in all the dioceses; from that time, it was no longer the bishop, but the king who appointed them. *Cf.* Edict, Feb., 1693. "Science des notaires," 1, 16, c. 21. They ceased to be able to prepare legal instruments in temporal matters. *Fleury*, p. 98.

who, having universal jurisdiction, conferred upon them the power of drawing up legal instruments in all places, "ubique terrarum."[1]

Philip the Fair regulated the profession of notary in the South by an ordinance of July, 1304.[2] During the monarchical period the right to appoint notaries belonged to the king alone or to those to whom he had granted it.[3] In the north of France[4] the notaries remained longer as mere auxiliaries of the court; their acts were authenticated by affixing the royal, seigniorial, episcopal, or communal seal, according to the authority which had established them.[5] The separation between the functions of recorder and notary was not well completed before the Edict of March, 1542.[6] The organization of the notarial profession was complicated (mainly for fiscal reasons after Philip the Fair)[7] by distinguishing between the following: 1st, the notaries, who were merely sworn scribes charged with drawing up documents; 2d, the scriveners ("tabellions") who engrossed these protocols in a large hand and gave them authenticity; 3d, the keepers of the seals, who affixed the seal of jurisdiction on the engrossed copy (and even, 4th, the "garde-notes" in 1575). In the course of time and after many vicissitudes, these offices became hereditary and were united with the profession of notary ("garde-notes," 1579; "tabellions," 1597; "garde-scels," 1708); the notaries themselves sealed their documents and gave them authenticity personally (Edict of July, 1706–1708).[8]

[1] The number of imperial and apostolic notaries was multiplied; ignorant and scarcely honorable, they were unpopular, and, in the end, were suppressed.

[2] Ord., I, 416. *Isambert*, II, 818; *Giry*, p. 827 (details concerning it at the end of the 1200s and beginning of the 1300s). *Cf.* Ord. 1291, XI, 371. Secret notaries of the king, *Girard*, pp. 819 and 680.

[3] *La Garde*, "Souv. du roi," ch. II, LXI.

[4] The notariat, properly speaking, did not exist in England; but the attorneys drew up the acts of the parties; special notaries drew deeds and legal documents (especially in commercial matters) and gave notice of protests. Proctors at the Church Courts were also designated as notaries.

[5] A deed accepted without proof was a deed sealed with an authentic seal, that is to say, with a seal widely enough known to be easily recognized; gentlemen, seigniorial and royal officers, and ecclesiastical judges ordinarily had authentic seals. *Cf. Beaumanoir*, 35, 18; "Olim," II, 251. Ord. 1299, 1300 (I, 344). The oldest royal seals of jurisdiction date from the time of Louis VIII.

[6] The Edict of Nov., 1542, created scriveners officially in all the kingdom. At the same time it forbade judges and recorders from drawing up private deeds; the monopoly of notaries was thus established. *Cf.* Ord. July, 1493. Until 1789, notaries exercised the functions of recorders for the seigniorial courts.

[7] Seigniorial scriveners' offices were anterior to the royal scriveners.

[8] On the notariat during the Revolution, *cf. Duvergier*, "Coll. des lois," vol. III, p. 463 (textes cited); Dec. 29 Sept.–6 Oct., 1791 (abolition

§ 431. **Recorders ("Greffiers").**[1] (A) **Notarius Causæ.** — The fourth Lateran Council (1215 c. 38) having required the presence in every trial of a "publica persona" with a view to drawing up an authentic report of the proceedings and of the decisions of the judges, it became the custom to charge in turn one of the notaries attached to the court with the keeping of the record of each case (rough draft, "schedula"; register, "memoriale," "manuale"). This notary even received sometimes the duty to proceed wholly or in part with the inquiry; he also verified obligations under the form of acknowledgment or "recognitiones" (*cf.* notaries); finally, he caused the decisions of the court to be executed.

(B) **Recorders.** — At the beginning of the 1300s the notary "deputatus ad acta scribenda" had become a functionary keeping the register of the court, a true recorder[2] for the ecclesiastical courts and for the secular tribunals.[3] The recorders received in court the ordinances and decisions of the judges and delivered copies to the parties.[4] From an early time (1302) the recorder's position was farmed out; Francis I made it formally an office in 1521.[5] The Decree of March 20, 1791, abolished the ministerial offices which again became salable in 1816.[6]

§ 432. **Other Officers.** — The **Sergeants,**[7] in court of bailiffs, seneschals, and provosts, and the **marshals**[8] ("huissiers") in the supreme and the presidial courts, maintained order during the session of the court, carried summonses, made levies, and performed other acts of execution. In the exercise of their functions they bore the wand ("verge"), the symbol of power. For a long

of the principle of salability; system of public competition for the recruitment of the notariat). L. 25 Ventôse, year XI. L. 2 Nivôse, year XII (chamber of notaries).

[1] *Luchaire*, p. 568 (bibl.); *Glasson*, N.R.H., t. V (Sources of civil procedure). *Loyseau*, II, 5 and following; *Fleury*, p. 97; *Ferrière, Guyot*, h. vis.; *Isambert*, "Table," see "Greffier," "Greffe." *Lot*, "Org. du greffe au Parl. de Paris" ("Pos. Ec. Chartes," 185–78); *Fournier*, "Officialités," 41; *Aubert*, "Hist. du Parl.," I, 229; "Le Parl.," I, 267; *La Garde*, ch. VII; *Girard*, p. 73, 1359.

[2] "Greffier" means scribe: "graphium," "graphiarius."

[3] *Domat*, "Loix civiles," 2, 2, 5, 1.

[4] On the recorders of presentations, *cf. Aubert*, "Hist. du Parl.," II, 43.

[5] Except the recorders of the supreme courts, *Ferrière, loc. cit.*

[6] On the revolutionary period, *cf. Garsonnet*, I, 353.

[7] "Servientes," "ledelli," "apparitores," "nuncii," "valeti curiæ," "ostiarii"; *Luchaire*, p. 553 (bibl.); *Loyseau*, "Offices," II, 3; *Fleury* p. 96; *Ferrière, Guyot*, h. vis.; *Isambert*, "Table," h., see "Stile des huissiers," 2e éd., regular sergeants, with hereditary office; *cf. Loysel*, 50: Sergeant of the king is peer of the county. "R. hist.," 63, 258; *Trevedy*, "Sergents féodés," 1898, *cf. Beaumanoir*, c. 29.

[8] *Aubert*, "Les huissiers au Parl. de Paris" (BCh., XLVII, 370; "Hist. du Parl.," I, 249; "Le Parl.," I, 300; *Girard*, p. 234, 1539.

time they made only a verbal report of what they had done ("procès-verbal"). In the end, the sergeants were subordinated entirely to the marshals; they announced and caused to be executed judicial and extra-judicial acts; the marshals were charged with the service of the court rooms.[1]

[1] *Jousse*, II, 558. Dec. March 20, 1791. *Cf.* Dec. June 14, 1813. See *Duvergier*, for numerous laws on their subject.

CHAPTER XIII

THE MONARCHICAL PERIOD (*continued*). FINANCIAL ORGANIZATION[1]

TOPIC 1. RECEIPTS AND EXPENSES

TOPIC 2. THE ROYAL DOMAIN

TOPIC 3. ESTABLISHMENT OF TAXES

[1] BIBLIOGRAPHY: Feudal Epoch. — *Luchaire*, "Manuel," p. 578 (bibl.); *Vuitry*, "Et. s. le régime financier de la France," 1878–83; monarchical epoch; *Monod*, "Bibliog. de l'hist. de Fr.," p. 97; *Stourm*, "Bibliog. des finances au XVIIIe s." ("Ann. Ecole sc. polit.," 1886–7); *N. Froumenteau*, "Le secret des finances de France," 1581 (Pseudonym Barnaud?); *Hennequin*, "Le guidon général des finances," 1585, 1644, etc.; *Sully*, "Œconomies royales," 1658; *Boisguillebert*, "Détail de la France," 1696; *Vauban*, "Projet d'une dîme royale" (1696), 1707; "Les oisivetés," 1842; *Desmarets*, "Mém. s. l'admin. des finances," 1708 to 1715; *Du Hautchamp*, "Hist. du syst. des finances," 1719–39; *Dutot*, "Réfl. s. les fin.," 1738; *Forbonnais*, "Rech. s. les fin. de la Fr.," 1595 to 1721, 1758; (*Coquereau*), "Admin. des fin. sous Terrai," 1776; *Le Trosne*, "L'admin. provinc.," 1779; *Moreau de Beaumont*, "Mém. s. les impôts," 1785; *Necker*, "Compte rendu au roi," 1781; "De l'admin. des finances," 1784; *Bourboulon*, "Observ. s. les opér. de Necker," 1781; "Encyclopédie méthod.," see "Finances"; (*Mathon de la Cour*), "Collection de piéces concern. les finances de la Fr., 1708 to 1757," 1788; *Waroquier*, "Etat de la Fr. en 1789," 1789; *Boiteau*, *ibid.*, p. 410; *Jacqueton*, "Doc. rel. à l'admin. fin., 1443–1523," 1891; *Isambert*, "Table," see "Finances," "Impôts," etc.; *cf. Ferrière*, *Guyot*, h. vis.; *Pastoret*, "Ord. des rois de Fr.," t. XV to XIX; *Bresson*, "Hist. fin. de la France," 1829 (2e éd. 1847); *Bailly*, *ibid.*, 1839; *De Nervo*, "Les fin. franç.," 1863; *De Parieu*, "Tr. des impôts," 2e éd., 1866; *Clamageran*, "Hist. de l'impôt," 1867; *Noël*, "Et. hist. s. l'org. fin. de la Fr.," 1882; *Oberleiterer*, "Frank. Finanzgesch. u. L. XVI," 1866; *Clergier*, "Impôts et revenus de l'Anc. Rég.," 1882; *Stourm*, "Les finances de l'Anc. Rég.," 1885; *Fournier de Flaix*, "La réforme de l'impôt," 1885; *Ducrocq*, "Et. d'hist. financ. et monét.," 1888; *Bouchard*, "Syst. fin. de l'anc. monarchie," 1891; *Gomel*, "Causes fin de la Révol.," 1892–3; *L. Say*, "Dict. des Finances," 1894.

TOPIC 4. DIRECT TAXES

TOPIC 5. INDIRECT TAXES

TOPIC 6. THE PUBLIC DEBT

TOPIC 7. FINANCIAL ADMINISTRATION AND JURISDICTION

TOPIC 8. CONCLUSION

TOPIC 1. RECEIPTS AND EXPENSES

§ 433. **Receipts.** — The feudal monarchs had hardly any different resources than those which the seigniors enjoyed, namely, the revenues from their domain.[1] Taxes, which were considered for a long time as extraordinary resources, did not come to be added to the domainal revenues until the end of the 1300 s, and in the 1500 s loans formed a third chapter in what we would call the

[1] Fleury still called them "finances ordinaires" in opposition to "finances extraordinaires," or those derived from aids and "tailles" (1600 s). *Cf. Esmein*, p. 545. The concern of the Estates of the 1500 s was to avoid the alienation of the domain, in order that it would not be necessary to levy taxes. In England, extraordinary revenues depend on a vote of Parliament.

budget of receipts.[1] Corresponding to the two principal classes of resources were for a long time two distinct administrative organizations: the treasurers of France and the generals of finance.

§ 434. **Expenses.** — The feudal monarchs did not have, so to speak, any public expenses,[2] because the public services were cared for in large part by the seigniors, the Church, and the communes.[3] But in the 1600 s this was no longer the case and the expenses of the State were grouped into two classes: 1st, **ordinary** expenses, which included the maintenance of the royal household, salaries of royal officers, the navy, local offices, pensions[4] (which were

[1] Receipts according to *Necker*, "Admin. des finances," I, 35: "twentieths," 76 millions; "taille," 91; capitation, 41½; local impositions, 2; farmers-general, 166; general administration ("aides"), 51; domains, 41; seals, 1; posts and messenger service, 10½; moneys, 500,000; powders, 800,000; royal lottery, 11½ millions; casual revenues, 5,700,000; "marc d'or" (duty paid the king by the titularies of certain offices), 1,700,000; free gifts from the "pays d'Etats," 10½; clergy, 11; octroi, 27; "aides" of Versailles, 900,000; taxes of Corsica, 600,000; taxes of the French guard, etc., 300,000; various objects, 2; "corvée," 20; "contraintes," 7,500,000; sums recovered by the princes, 2,500,000. Total, 585 millions.

[2] Expenses under Saint Louis: A. Ordinary: 1. In the provinces, "liberationes," or pay of the king's agents; "feoda," or rents for the benefit of certain laicals; "eleemosinæ," or gifts to the Church; "opera," or expense of construction, etc.; "minuta expensa," or various expenses. 2. At Paris: Expenses of the king's house. B. Extraordinary: coronation of the king, knighthood for his sons, marriage of his daughters, dowries, "solde" (military pay), crusades, ambassadors and pensions for sovereigns. These expenses increased with the inevitable development of the administrative and diplomatic services: "If the amount of the royal revenues in 1314 was almost double what it was in 1270, the expenses necessitated by the local and central administration increased in triple measure; the deficit was permanent." Under Saint Louis, on the contrary, there was an excess of receipts. *Luchaire*, 584, 601; "Hist. Fr.," 21, 22; *De Wailly*, "Hist. Fr." XXXI; *Langlois*, "Philippe III," 30; BCh., XIV, 27; *Douet d'Areq*, "Comptes de l'hôtêl des rois de Fr., XIVe, XV s." ("Soc. Hist. Fr."); *Brussel*, "Usage des Fiefs," I, 464.

[3] On the subject of public assistance, *cf. Prudhomme*, "L'Assist. pub. à Grenoble," 1898.

[4] The abuse of pensions never ceased to increase, throughout the period of the "ancien régime," the budgetary deficit. They were reduced from time to time, but in vain. Necker, in 1776 and in 1780, suppressed for the future, the "croupes," and parts of interest in the farms and in the "regie." Edicts of Dec. 22, 1776, Nov. 8, 1778, Jan. 7, 1779, and Aug. 8, 1779. *Cf.* the Law of 22, Aug., 1790, which introduced the principles of Necker's legislation in respect to pensions. The 5th of May, 1789, Necker estimated the cost of pensions to be twenty-nine millions; Calonne at thirty-two, of which seven million were not justified. The Constituent Assembly, after having tried to make public abusive favors by the publication of the "Red book" and the "Etat nominatif de toutes les pensions," found itself under the necessity of suppressing or revising all the concessions of the old régime; neither it nor the assemblies which followed, succeeded; in short, the greater part of the pensions, even the most justifiable ones, ceased to be paid in whole or in part. *Stourm*, II, 125 and following.

variable),[1] and loans for the city of Paris; 2d, **extraordinary** expenses: those on account of war, gifts, public works,[2] buildings.[3] Agriculture,[4] industry,[5] commerce,[6] and the colonies them-

[1] Under the "ancien régime," pensions and gratuities were only State favors; in modern law they are, or tend to become, real rights of functionaries. The Constitutional Assembly made itself the judge of whether they should be granted (Law 1790). Not being able to count on the State, the employees of the various administrations organized themselves into syndicates for the creation of retiring pensions by means of deductions from their salaries the amount of which was put into a common treasury apart from that of the State. The law of June 13, 1853, united all these funds in the hands of the State. The precedents for the existing legislation are found in this practice and in the regulations of the old form. (Delib. of Feb. 21, 1768, "Encyclop. méthod.")

[2] For a long time, public works were regarded as a purely local affair; they were executed by the seigniors, towns, corporations, and communities (the towns and corporations receiving by way of compensation the right to levy tolls and local taxes). The king undertook the construction of these public works only as an ordinary seignior on his own domain; the domainal administrators, "baillis," etc., at first, later the treasurers had at the same time the care of public works. Under Charles VII and Louis XI great public works were undertaken by companies of merchants under the supervision of the State (*e.g.* the Seine was rendered navigable). In the 1500s, the rôle of the State was increased (in 1553 there was an order to plant elms along the chief roads; later an order prescribing their width); under Henry VI, there was a centralization of the service of bridges and causeways, which was placed under the direction of Sully, who was called the "grand voyer de France," 1599. There were important companies, for example, for the draining of marshes. Conflicts between local powers and the "grand voyer" brought about the suppression of the office of the latter in 1626. Colbert organized the administration of public works in the "countries of elections": director general, inspectors, and engineers. The expenses of public works were still borne by the provinces, towns, and contracting companies. The administration itself determined the indemnity due the owners on account of expropriation, subject to the right of appeal to the council of the parties.

A. des Cilleuls, "Origine et dévelop. du régime des travaux publics en France," 1895; *Saint-Marc*, "Etude sur l'entreprise du canal du Midi," 1888 ("Ann. univ. Bordeaux"); *Babeau*, *op. cit. infra*, p. 847, 856; *Ravinet*, "Code des ponts et ch., 1729"; *Davenne*, "Rec. des lois s. la voirie," 1824; *Vignon*, "Et. hist. s. l'adm. des voies publiq. av. 1790."

[3] *Fleury*, p. 184; *Dareste*, II, 185; *De Laborde*, "Comptes des bâtiments du roi," 1878; *Guiffrey*, "Comptes des bâtiments du roi," doc. inéd., 1881.

[4] The State adopted general measures in the interest of agriculture only under Sully and Colbert. The Physiocrats (economists who believed that wealth is founded on agriculture) in the 1700s. *Dareste*, II, 191. Premiums were given for early marriages, and to fathers of families containing ten children (1666).

[5] Industry on a large scale scarcely appeared in France until the 1500s; the kings encouraged it by privileges (exemptions from taxation, freedom from tolls and local taxes, temporary monopolies), advances of funds, etc. Colbert established a great number of royal manufactures (tapestries at Beauvais, etc.); he gave to the great industries regulations for manufacturing as minute as those that were imposed on corporations, and, in 1665, he created a comptroller of manufactures; the rigor of the legislation on this point is explained by the fact that it was a question of

[6] During the feudal epoch, the State occupied itself with commerce only in so far as it concerned privileges which the merchant corporations

selves [1] remained for a long time outside the sphere of action of the State and only exceptionally encumbered its budget.

establishing new industries; but it was not without influence on the quality and good taste of the products of our factories. However, it fell into disuse when the industry was established. *Dareste*, II, 214. *Des Cilleuls*, "Hist. et régime de la grande industrie en France au XVIIe et XVIIIe s.," 1898 (Board of Commerce).

---

enjoyed (*e.g.* the water merchants of Paris). It organized fairs and markets, protected foreign merchants attending, and instituted special judges for them (guards of the fairs in Champagne). The absolute monarchy multiplied these privileges, created consular courts, converted professions formerly free into royal offices (courtiers, bankers), created chambers of commerce (central chamber at Paris in 1601, provincial boards), issued the Ordinance of 1673, granted to gentlemen the right to engage in marine commerce without its involving their degradation, created intendants of commerce (1700). Commerce now formed the object of a new branch of the administration. — External commerce, exportation, was at first forbidden, because it was feared that the country would become impoverished by the enrichment of its neighbors; in the 1400s, treaties of commerce (1415, 1498, etc.) encroached upon this principle without destroying it; it reappeared soon to be enforced against the powerful rivals of France, Spain, Holland, and England (Edict of 1659 which recalls the Navigation Act in England, establishing a tax of fifty sous a ton on foreign ships, tariffs of 1664, 1667, etc.); the prohibitive system was applied so rigorously by Colbert and was generalized to such a point under his ministry in consequence of reprisals exercised against France, that it has frequently been designated by the name of "Colbertism." Colbert also organized in a uniform manner consulates designed to protect our subjects in foreign countries. Before this time the consuls were appointed by the merchants themselves or by the towns from which they came. The State appropriated this institution; but there were no consuls appointed by the king before the treaty between Suleiman and Francis I. Colbert "conferred on them in a definite manner the character of agents of the State, and prohibited them from engaging in trade on their own account." At the same time, he exacted of them information concerning the commerce of the country where they resided. *Pigeonneau*, "Hist. du commerce," 1890; *Masson*, "Le commerce français en Orient," 1894.

[1] The colonies (State domain, monopoly of commerce) were not at first exploited by the State, but by great companies (1604, Canada; in the time of Colbert, Company of West and East Indies; Louisiana, 1714, etc.), to which the State accorded privileges, among others, the monopoly of commerce. It would take too long to describe the colonial régime in the time of these great companies, and the transformation they underwent afterwards. We shall limit ourselves to saying that the companies were quasi-sovereign, with the power of raising and maintaining troops, treating with States friendly to France, appointing the greater part of the functionaries, etc.; but their statutes had to be approved by the State and the mother country intervened in the administrative organism with which it endowed the colonies. They succumbed one after another (for ex. 1674, the Company of the West Indies in consequence of the withdrawal of its monopoly), and the State took their place; the administration of the colonies was confided to three authorities often hostile, the governor, the intendant, and the supreme council, and was modeled more and more on that of the mother country. The colonies were forced, in the 1700s, to throw off a little of the too heavy guardianship of the State and the constraint of the prohibitive system. *Isambert*, "Table," see "Colonies"; *Dareste*, II, 225; *Paulliat*, "L. XIV et la Cie des Indes," 1885.

TOPIC 2. THE ROYAL DOMAIN

§ 435. **What it Embraced.** — The domain of the crown[1] included two parts:[2] 1st, the **corporeal domain**, that is to say, the lands which the king held in full ownership just as a private individual, a seignior, or other person might hold them, and, furthermore, those which are to-day classified under the head of the public domain of the state[3] such as the highways, rivers, and navigable streams, shores of the sea, and the walls and moats of fortified towns;[4] waters and forests were at an early time detached from

[1] BIBLIOGRAPHY: *Cf.* the treatises on public law. Bibliog. in the "Gr. Encycl.," see "Domaine" (*Ch. Mortet*); *Camus et Dupin*, nos 1599 *et seq.* *Jacqueton*, "Doc., Table," h. vo., and especially p. 205; *Ferrière*, "Dict.," see "Dom.," citing a comment of Charondas on the Ord. 1566. See especially the treatises of *Chopin* (1572, 1605, 1612), *Lebret* ("Souver. du roi," 1632); *Bacquet* ("Œuvres," éd. 1744); *Loisel* ("Opusc.," 1652); *La Garde* ("Tr. histor.," 1753); *Lefèvre de La Planche* (1764); *Henrys*, 1, 2, 4. "Dict. de Brillon," h. vo.; (*Bosquet*), "Dict. des domaines," 1762; *Isambert*, "Table," see "Domaine," "Bâtiment," "Rivages," "Voirie," etc.; *Pollock and Maitland*, I, 366; *Blackstone*, I, 8; *Cf.* "Seigniorial finances," *supra*, § 222. Add. *Luchaire*, "Manuel," p. 267 (bibl.); *L. Delisle*, "Revenus publics en Normandie au XIIe s."; *Lefèvre*, BCh., XVIII (Champagne). Inventories des Arch. Pas-de-Calais, Bouches-du-Rhône, Côte-d'Or, etc. *Richeré*, "Thèses Ecole des Chartes," 1890 (Flanders); *D'Arbois de Jubainville*, BCh., XXVI (Champagne). *Stouff*, "Le régime communal, forme de l'exploitation seigneuriale," 1899; *Coville*, "Les finances des ducs de Bourgogne," 1897; *H. Sée*, "Ac. Sc. mor.," 1899, t. 51, p. 508 ("Orig. des dr. dom."); *Sagnac*, "Thèse," 1899.

[2] The divisions of the domain were: I. The **Fixed** as contradistinguished from the "**Casuel**," that is to say, uncertain, like the products of the "droit d'aubaine," escheat, etc. II. **Mutable**, the product of which varied (the amount of the "farmage" changed, *e.g.* recorders' fees and tolls), and **Immutable** ("cens," rents, etc. always the same in principle). A subdivision of the fixed domain. III. **The Grand** (seigniories having the right of justice) and **Petit** (detached parcels). The property comprised in the "casuel" domain passed of full right into the fixed domain at the end of ten years of administration by royal officers or was so classified by edicts or declarations. By this means it became inalienable. The petty domain, the exploitation of which would have been too expensive, was alienable. The private or individual domain of the king comprised the property possessed by him before his accession to the throne; it became incorporated in the royal domain as a result of his accession, but remained alienable for ten years; this was a period of proof, a kind of stage before being classified in the great or petty domain. *Bapst*, "Hist. des joyaux de la couronne," 1889. *Supra*, p. 347.

[3] In Roman law, was the State the owner of property which could not belong to private individuals because it was designed for the use of all, or did it have over such land only a right of sovereignty? The point is debatable. *Girard*, "Manuel de dr. rom.," p. 233 (2d ed.); *Saleilles*, N.R.H., 1889. In classical law, a tendency is observed to separate the public domain of the State from its private domain (that is to say, ordinary property, susceptible of private ownership, lands, etc.). On the contrary, feudalism, making little distinction between ownership and sovereignty, united under the same title all the rights of the State in its domain. The distinction outlined at Rome reappeared under the monarchy to be sanctioned finally by modern law.

[4] Among the dependencies of the domain were also ranked territorial seas, the islands and accretions formed in these seas as well as the streams

the ordinary domain; 2d, the **incorporeal domain**,[1] that is to say, the dues ("droits") collected by the king: (*a*) in the capacity of seignior (feudal dues); (*b*) in the capacity of suzerain or sovereign (domainal dues); (*c*) by reason of his right of general police.

The corporeal domain ordinarily included: (*a*) lands ("in allodio," "in fisco") cultivated by copyholders ("censitaires") or serfs; (*b*) fiefs granted to vassals, — this was the ordinary division of every seigniorial domain.[2] The management was intrusted to the provosts and royal bailiffs who were under the control of the superior courts of finance. The domain was increased gradually at the expense of feudalism in the most diverse ways: purchase, marriage dowry, inheritance, confiscation, and conquest. Having acquired his kingdom in this fashion the king was sufficiently justified in regarding it as his patrimony. Incorporation of lands in the domain took place expressly, in consequence of a declaration (*e.g.* return of an appanage, confiscation, feudal withdrawal) or tacitly, as in the case of land held and administered by the royal officers for a period of ten years; it took place also by means of merger of rights when the proprietor became king.

Waters and forests[3] received, at the end of the 1200 s, a special administration: 1st, special directors; 2d, verderers or "gruyers";

and navigable rivers (whose beds consequently belonged to the king), barren and waste lands, buildings on public places (*cf. Loysel*, 277). *Loysel*, no. 232 and following: the small rivers and ways belonged to the seigniors of the lands through which they flowed, the brooks to the individual tenants. The right of fishing in navigable rivers belonged to the king, but navigation of them was free. The public roads, the width of which was determined by regulations (seventy-two feet), could not be changed except by order of the king. *Cf. Ferrière, Guyot*, and *Isambert; La Garde*, ch. IX.

[1] The incorporeal domain should have comprised all the rights of the public power; but in it were included scarcely any except the old seigniorial rights; the greater part of the taxing power remained outside of the domainal authority, for which no explanation could be made except their origin. *Cf.* German theory of the "regalia": public ways, navigable streams, forests, hunting, mines, monies. On the formation of this theory and the character of the king's rights, *cf. Heusler*, "Inst. d. d. Privatr.," II, 368 (§ 74); *Schröder*, §§ 48, 50; *Stobbe*, "Deut. Privat.," I, 529. For England, see *Blackstone*, I, 8.

[2] The domainal administration never got so far as making an exact and complete register of the rights of the king. England: "Liber Rubeus" (about 1230), (Aquitaine, 1137, Champagne, 1285, etc.); succession (Burgundy, 1002, county of Toulouse, Quercy, Rouergue, 1271, etc.); feudal seizure, confiscation (Normandy, 1203, etc.); conquest (Lower Languedoc, 1226, etc.). The "pariages" between the king and the churches or secular seigniors prepared the way for complete union with the crown. *Isambert*, "Table," see "Territoire"; *Lachapelle*, "Code des terriers," 1761. "Titres de la maison de Bourbon," 1864–74.

[3] *Fleury*, p. 144; *Isambert*, "Table," see "Eaux et Forets," "Garennes," etc.; *Sainctyon*, "Eaux et forêts" (lois), 1610; *La Garde*, ch. VIII; *Chauffourt*, "Instruction," 1609, 1642; *De Froidour*, "Instr. pour les

3d, keepers or sergeants (1291), with a superior court, the "Marble-Table" (1346) and a sovereign master and reformer (1302–1318) who presided over the latter body and had the general direction of the administration (1384). The unity of direction, abandoned in the 1500 s, was reëstablished by Sully, who created a superintendent of waters and forests. Colbert reorganized the masterships and to him belongs the credit for the **ordinance of 1669**, the basis of our existing forestry law.[1] From his forestry domain the king derived numerous revenues: proceeds from the sale of cuttings, from the adjudication of acorn pasture rights ("pannages"), from the sale of acorns and from pasturage in forests, from fees on the sale of cuttings by private individuals ("gruerie," "grairie," "tiers et danger"), and from license fees for the privilege of hunting.

§ 436. **Indivisibility and Inalienability of the Crown Domain.**[2] —What the kings acquired on the one hand through the property nature of fiefs, they often lost on the other, because this same system authorized them to dispose of their lands and to dismember the domain, and this was done by the kings of the first two dynasties. It was as much to the interest of the kings, however, to preserve the lands which they had already acquired as to acquire new lands; prudent statesmen were conscious of this and could not fail to be impressed by the example of the Church, which forbade the alienation of its property and whose patrimony never ceased to increase. At the same time, the Roman theory of sovereignty put an obstacle in the way of the abandonment of the rights of the State.

(A) The royal authority proceeded at first according to circumstance; when they found themselves at the end of their resources the kings of the 1300s revoked the alienations already made, only to make them again a little later. These alternations of revocations and sales hardly tended to reassure purchasers and to strengthen the credit of the State.[3] (B.) The 1500s proclaimed as a principle of public law that which had seemed to be only a financial expedient (Ord. Moulins, 1566).[4] We see in it an en-

ventes,"—with notes by *Berrier*, 1759; *Paquet*, "Lois forestières de la France," 1753; *Baudrillart*, "Tr. des Eaux et F.," 1821; *Maury*, "Les forêts de la Gaule," 1865; *De Dionne*, "Hist. du dessèch. des bois et marais avant 1789," 1891; "Recueil des eaux et f.," 1753.

[1] The forests of the State were valued at 1,350,000 livres in 1792, the salt marshes and mines at fifty millions. *Stourm*, II, 453.

[2] *Desjardins*, "De l'alién. et prescr. des biens de l'Etat," 1862.

[3] 1318, 1322, 1357, etc. *Isambert*, "Table," see "Domaine."

[4] Ord. Feb., 1402. Ord. Cabochienne, 1413, Art. 89. Charles VII, 1425. Roll. of the Parliaments and of the Chamber of Accounts. *Viollet*, II, 167; *Aubert*, "Le Parl. de Paris," 1890, p. 203. Ord. June 30, 1539.

dowment of the kind indispensable for the fulfillment of his functions ("dos ipsius regni"), the patrimony of the crown, of which the king was not the owner, but only the administrator. Impoverishment was almost a forfeiture of the crown, while the greatness of the royal power coincided with the increase of the royal domain. The more extensive the domain, the greater were the king's revenues and the fewer were the contributions necessary from his subjects. Besides, the principle of the indivisibility of the kingdom, which was not clearly distinguished from the royal domain, contributed toward the acceptance of the new principle. Inprescriptibility followed as a necessary consequence.[1]

The principle of inalienability was applied to the incorporeal domain as well as to the corporeal domain, but the text of the Ordinance of 1566 did not appear to apply to the rights of the public power; they were none the less regarded as inalienable and frequent applications of this idea had to be made in the course of the long struggle against feudalism; so when the provinces were annexed successively to the crown domain, and so when the seigniorial rights were taken over by the royal sovereignty.

§ 437. **Exceptions to the Rule.** (A.) **Appanages.**[2] — By an appanage we understand a portion of the royal domain set aside for the children of the king in order to provide them with the means of subsistence and the means of maintaining their dignity.[3]

On the acts previous to 1566, *cf. Isambert*, "Table," see "Domaine." Oath of the king on his accession. Legend in "Fleta," 3, 6, 3 (*Houard*, "Traites s. les cout. anglo-norm.," vol. 3, p. 397): a solemn assembly of all the sovereigns of Europe held at Montpellier in 1275 proclaimed the inalienability of the domain of the crown. If the fact is not so, it is at least about that date that the principle began to appear (James, king of Sicily in 1325). *Isambert*, I, 660; *Viollet*, II, 162 (same regulation for the other States). England: acts of resumption and a statute of Anne, I, 1, 4, annulled the grants made for more than thirty-one years or for more than three generations.

[1] Nevertheless, property which had not passed the stage of ten years was prescriptible. The Dec. of Dec. 1, 1790, permitted the prescription of domainal property after forty years. Civil Code, Art. 2227.

[2] *Du Tillet*, "Recueil des rois," p. 286, 1618; *Dupuy*, "Rec. des droits du roi," 1655 (ch. IV); *Bouchel*, "Bibl.," p. 198, 1667; (*Du Vaucel*), "Essai s. les apanages," s. d. "Gr. Encycl.," h. vo.; "Recueil d'Edits," 1714; *Isambert*, "Table," see "Apanages"; *Camus et Dupin*, nos 1607 *et seq.* *Infra*, p. 792; "Comptes du roi de Nav.," 1884.

[3] Dowry or marriage portion ordinarily in money for girls: dower for the widow. *Isambert*, "Table," see "Donaire." The system of appanages reëstablished feudalism, but prepared the way for the union of the provinces to the crown and their assimilation. *Cf. A. Molinier*, "Corresp. admin. d'Alf. de Poitiers," 1896. *P. Guerin*, "Arch. hist. du Poitou," 1881, p. 17. Quota of appanages variable: under the first Capetians, extended domains (for ex. the duchy of Burgundy); then, as a result of reaction, small fiefs; from the time of Louis VIII (*Luchaire*, p. 482) there was a return to considerable dotations, but measures were taken to insure their return to the domain of the crown. *Du Tillet*, p. 290.

Originally, the younger sons had the same rights as the eldest; but once the system of primogeniture was established [1] it became the custom to provide a dowry for the younger children.[2] The régime of appanages which was established for their benefit passed through two phases:

I. The appanagist had full ownership of the appanage, sovereign rights, and the power of disposing of it "inter vivos" and even of bequeathing it to his collateral relatives. The appanage was reannexed to the crown domain only in exceptional cases, such as disinheritance, or succession of the reigning prince to the appanagist or inversely.

II. With the principle of the indivisibility and inalienability of the domain there appeared a tendency to give the holder of the appanage only temporary rights,[3] a sort of usufruct transmissible only in the direct line.[4] (*a*) The appanage could no more be alienated than could the royal domain; the king received it back free from debts after the fashion of a substitution.[5] (*b*) In the successions to the appanage male collaterals were excluded (from Louis VIII) as well as daughters (Philip the Fair) so that it reverted to the crown upon the extinction of the direct male line.[6] During

[1] *Loysel*, 639; *Du Cange*, see "Apanamentum." German law: "ubi primogenitura, ibi apanagium." The right to an appanage existed only for those who were excluded from the succession by virtue of birthright. There was no appanage in the lifetime of the father (however, the oldest son sometimes received it at his majority), but a simple right to maintenance. The appanage was sometimes assigned to the dynasty, sometimes to the individual and for life. It was due from the state, if the king had a civil list, or from the reigning prince when he had a patrimony. (Prussia): *Holtzendorff*, "Encycl. d. Rechtsw.," p. 1277 and the bibliography. "Apanagium," hereditary rent, was opposed to "Paragium," endowment in landed property with ordinary sovereign rights (which amazes recent laws).

[2] *Loysel*, 639: "doit le roi apanage, mariage." But this was doubtless only a moral obligation; there was no means of compulsion to insure its execution. In German law, there could be recourse to the family council. "Decisions" of the "Parlement," 1284. (*Boutaric*, "Actes du Parl.," I, 388): "non possunt petere, sed primogenitus quantum vult et quando vult eis confert." *Viollet*, II, 157; *Luchaire*, p. 485.

[3] Was it for this reason that appanages were larger in extent from the time of Louis VIII? Was it not rather because they were in harmony with the extension which the domain underwent?

[4] Ord. Oct., 1374 (VI, 54. *Isambert*, V, 459). It did not fall by disposition nor to the female line. [5] *Guyot*, "Répert.," vol. II, p. 330.

[6] The appanage returned to the crown if the appanagist died "sine herede proprii corporis," without direct heirs. Louis VIII so stipulated in the case of the appanage of the Count of Artois. *Teulet*, "Layettes du Tr. des Ch.," no. 1710. Application in 1268, 1284. *Cf.* appanage of Philip the Tall (*Viollet*, II, 57): Act of 1314 excluding daughters and the posterior act of Louis the Quarrelsome recalling them to the succession, because the natural right required that they should inherit in default of males. "Invent. Arch. Pas-de-Calais," I, 91.

their lives the appanagists lost, following the example of the seigniors, a part of their sovereign rights.[1] Each appanage had its particular law,[2] and its code in the edict by which it was created.[3]

(B) **Pledge, or Charge.**[4] — The domain might still be alienated for ready money to meet the expenses of war, by letters patent enacted and published by the Parliaments, in which case there was perpetual power of repurchase. In spite of the formal terms of the Ordinance of February, 1566, Art. 1, alienation, in such a case, took the form of a simple pledge to guarantee the reimbursement of a loan; the purchaser was designated as a mortgagee ("engagiste") and the king preserved the ownership of the part of the domain of which he was disseized.[5] The exchange did not offer the dangers of alienation, since the domain was not diminished. It was authorized without constituting an exception to the rule of inalienability, upon the condition of certain formalities (Edict of Oct., 1711).

The monarchical law began by regarding the royal domain as the property of the king; later it made the domain the in-

[1] The king reserved for himself the rights of sovereignty and of jurisdiction, of faith and liege homage, the guardianship of churches and cathedrals, jurisdiction of "royal cases" and of cases which the king knew by prosecution ("prévention"), nomination to many offices, etc. *Du Cange*, see "Regalia." From 1246, Saint Louis reserved for himself the regalia of the churches ("regalia civitatum"), and even royal regalia. The holder of the appanage was bound to care for the forest, as a good father would care for his family, cutting the high trees only to repair edifices. Code Henry III, p. 957. *Augeard*, vol. II, ch. XC; *Despeisses*, I, 7, and II, 313; *Ferrière*, Dict.

[2] Creation of the council of the appanage of the Duke of Orléans, July, 1786 (*Isambert*, 28, 218); comptrollers general (*ibid.*, 27, 265).

[3] The Constitutional Assembly declared (22 November, 1790) that real appanages should no longer be granted. Idea of the reduction of the appanage to an annuity, Ord. Oct., 1374, 1 and 4 (VI, 35), 1486. *Viollet*, II, 161; *Vuitry*, I, 474; *Desjardins*, *op. cit.*

[4] *Isambert*, "Table," see "Dom. engagés."

[5] *Fleury*, p. 153. 1st, The prince upon whom the appanage was settled was called, for example, Duke of Orléans, etc.; the "engagiste" (tenant of crown lands) seignior by pledge of such duchy, etc. 2d, The first received in his name faith and homage and exercised all the feudal rights as proprietor of the dominant fief; he was charged only with transmitting to the Chamber of Accounts in duplicate the acts of faith and homage, etc., in order to preserve the rights of the king. The "engagist" exercised these rights in the name of the king as a simple usufructuary, held only the right of usufruct; the king's officers received from him faith and vows. 3d, Justice was rendered in the name of the holder of the appanage; after 1668, in his name and in the king's name. In domain of the "engagist" justice was rendered in the name of the king only; the renter did not even have the honorary rights of high justiciar. 4th, The officers of the appanage were appointed by the prince with the approval of the king. On "engagist" lands, the king had the full right of provision, if the power of disposing of the offices was not especially included in the terms of the "engagement"; but on all others the officers were always royal. *Cf. Ferrière*, Dict., see "Engagistes."

alienable patrimony of the State. The Constitutional Assembly distinguished in the national domain: 1st, the **public domain** of the State, including: (*a*) property which was used by all (rivers, ports, and roads); (*b*) the rights of the public power.[1] 2d, the **private domain**, composed of all property or rights belonging to the State such as would belong to a private individual. The first alone were made inalienable, by reason of their nature or purpose. As to the others, the so-called **national property** (property of the State and of the Church), the Constituent Assembly ordered their sale: 1st, in order to cover the deficit; 2d, because it was not believed to be wise for the State to be a proprietor and to exploit land. By alienating the lands which it possessed it parceled out and commercialized the soil — an advantage both economic and political, since the lands would be better cultivated and the mass of purchasers would be attached thereby to the new régime. In a general way the property constituting the private domain was declared to be alienable by act of legislature.[2]

§ 438. **The Incorporeal Domain. — (A) Seigniorial Dues,**[3] such as the "cens" and rent,[4] "banalities," profits of justice, fines,

[1] Among the national possessions, the alienation of which the Revolution prohibited, this valuation was made: 1st, three billions, the property of the clergy and crown; 2d, 2½ billions, the property of "emigrés" and refugees (Dec. of Feb. 12, 1792; March 12, 1793). Total: 5½ billions, small pay for the forty-five billions of assignats that were issued. *Cf.* on this estimate and on the exaggerations of the Revolutionary period, *Stourm*, II, 445. Inquiry of 1825 à propos of the billion belonging to the emigrés, *ibid. Bourgain*, "Et. s. les biens ecclés. avant la Revolution," 1891. In its valuation of the property of the clergy and that of the crown, the Constituent Assembly took as a basis the prices of leases and sales in 1790. *Stourm*, II, 450. *Cf.* Report of Cambon of Oct. 17, 1792. *Lavoisier*, "Richesse territ. du roy. de France," 1791.

[2] Law of Nov. 22–Dec. 1, 1790; the alienations previous to 1566 were definitive unless they contained an express requiring return; those made after that date were revoked. The dispossessed holders of appanages received an annuity from the State; the "engagiste" could be deprived of the land, but only in consideration of reimbursement for the amounts he had actually paid to the State; buyers saw their titles annulled in case of irregularity in form, for fraud, or for wrong. In default of power to reimburse their creditors, they were allowed to remain in possession. The Decree of 10 Frim., year II, dispossessed purely and simply all holders of the domain, but it was suspended (22 Frim., year III). The law of 14 Vent., year VII, definitely regulated the situation of all possessors whatever ("engagistes," "échangistes," and even donees); they became incommutable owners upon condition that they paid a fourth of the value of the property received by them. *Cf.* Law, March 12, 1820.

[3] *Isambert*, "Table"; *Ragueau*, "Indice des dr. royaux et seign.," 1620; *La Garde*, ch. XI. In the 1200s: "domaina," "cens," "taille," etc.; "expleta," judicial revenues; "vendæ boscorum," wood cutting; "sigilla," chancellery fees; "racheta," reliefs (Ord. 1235, 36), etc.; "forefacturæ" and "escheeta," confiscated property or successions collected by the king. *Luchaire*, 578; *Coville*, "Finances des ducs de Bourgogne," 1897. *Dodu*, 245. [4] *La Garde*, ch. XI: dues on fiefs, censives, and allodes.

confiscations,[1] disinheritances, wrecks, vacant lands,[2] tolls,[3] etc.

(B) **Regalian or Domainal Dues** (that is to say, seigniorial dues, which had become the exclusive property of the king and formed a part of his domain):[4] amortization, new acquisitions, "francs-fiefs," allodial fees, right of escheat, bastardy, ennoblement, naturalization, legitimation, regalia, etc.[5] The sale of offices, the right to the golden mark ("marc d'or") paid by every one who obtained from the king a public office or a favor, the gift "for a happy result," paid for the confirmation of offices and privileges, the sale of letters of freedom of a company, — all belonged to the same order of ideas.[6] Likewise monopolies, coining of money, salt springs, the business of operating stagecoaches,[7] gunpowder and saltpeter,[8] and tobacco [9] (numerous monopolies in Palestine and in England, 1580, of iron, gunpowder, vinegar, paper, etc.).

[1] Seigniorial courts continued, the profits of justice remained for the seigniors. On confiscation, *cf. Loysel*, 839 and following ("Lèse majesté," then the king took everything). *La Garde*, ch. II and VIII. Rights and emoluments of recorders, *ibid.*, ch. VII.

[2] The king and the seigniors disputed over these fees; some held that domainal or regalian dues should be put in this class. *Loysel*, 277 and following. *Cf. Esmein*, p. 584. On the exploitation of the Jews, *infra*, p. 678; *Luchaire*, "Man.," 582, 599; *Lazard*, "Cond. des Juifs de le dom. royal." In England, débris of shipwrecks if the owner did not present his claim, "bona naviata," or wrecks, estrays, or lost animals, vacant and confiscated lands or escheat ("deodand," the forfeiture of all animals or instruments that had caused the death of a man). *Glasson*, IV, 125.

[3] Tolls, as well as judicial fees, were considered as a concession of the king to the seigniors; the latter could not establish them anew, and the king had the right to suppress the old ones. *La Garde*, ch. XX.

[4] Instr. of May 8, 1372 (*Isambert*, V, 371): definition of regalian rights (*cf. ibid.*, VI, 545). *Blondel*, "Fréd. II," p. 141.

[5] On these various rights, *cf. infra*, 679, *Bacquet, La Garde*, ch. IV, *Ferrière, Guyot, Isambert*, "Table," "Bastardy," *id.* "Francs-fiefs," etc., *La Garde*, ch. XII and following. In England the temporal of vacant bishoprics; in our time these revenues are restored to the new bishop.

[6] *Isambert*, "Table"; *La Garde*, ch. XV; *Vuitry*, "R. Deux-Mondes," 1883.

[7] *Isambert*, "Table." *Rothschild*, "Hist. de la poste aux lettres," 1879. Louis XI organized the postal service in the exclusive interest of the king (1464). The comptroller general of posts was a veritable contractor ("entrepreneur") who bought his office with a view to deriving profit from it; he conceived the idea, under the minority of Louis XIII, of putting "courriers" at the service of private individuals, who, until that time, were compelled to have their letters taken by messengers of the towns or universities. Later the administration of the posts passed completely to the State. A superintendent in the place of a comptroller, 1630; privileges of the masters of post; monopoly, 1672, tariff, 1673; Edict, Jan., 1692 put the post "en régie" (appointment of all the agents by the king). Jurisdiction of intendants. *Lequien*, "Us. des postes," 1720; *Belloc*, "Les Postes fr.," 1886.

[8] *Isambert*, "Table," see "Poudres" and "Salpêtres." Edict Nov., 1340, 1601. "Régie" in 1775.

[9] Tobacco was taxed in 1629; the monopoly established in 1674 passed to the farmers-general in 1730. It brought in about thirty mil-

§ 439. **Money.**[1] — (A) From the 1300 s royal money prevailed and in the end completely excluded seigniorial money.[2] Monetary unity preceded the unity of weights and measures by a long time, for a political reason, since the right to coin money was regarded as a visible sign of the independence of the seigniors, and for an economic reason, since the régime of a plurality of coins excluded any guarantee of good coinage and constituted a constant impediment to trade.[3]

(B) The organization of the monetary monopoly evolved merely applications of the law of the division of labor: (*a*) mints in the principal towns with mint masters and subordinate officers; (*b*) general officers of the mints attached formerly to the Chamber of Accounts, constituting later the Court of the Mint at Paris, erected into a supreme court in 1551.

§ 440. **Mines.**[4] — The mineral industry was subject to the system of previous license. No one could open mines upon the

lions. Regulations analogous to those of to-day. The culture of native tobacco was prohibited except in certain provinces recently annexed, Franche-Comté, Flanders, Hainaut, Artois, Alsace, Cambrésis (line of customs, tobacco zones at a reduced price). The Constituent Assembly suppressed the monopoly, and allowed free cultivation, manufacture, and sale of tobacco (20–27 March, 1791). Tax on manufacture of tobacco under the Directorate and Consulate. Reëstablishment of the monopoly in 1810 (Dec. 29 December) and authorization of native cultivation under the supervision of employees of the administration. *Stourm*, I, 361; *Isambert*, "Table," see "Tobacs," *Larchevêque, thesis*, 1887.

[1] *N. Oresme*, "Tr. des monnaies," éd. 1854; *Leblanc*, "Tr. hist. des monnaies," 1690; *Fleury*, p. 115; "Confér. des Ord.," 11, 6, 1; *La Garde*, ch. XVII; *De Bezingheu*, "Tr. des monnaies," 1764; *Monod*, "Bibliog.," nº 158 *et seq.; Isambert*, "Table," see "Matières d'or et d'argent," "Marqué," "Monnaies," etc.; *Luchaire*, p. 270 (bibliog.) et p. 591; BCh, 1876, 145; *Engel et Serrure*, "Numismatique," t. III, 1899; *De Saulcy*, "Doc. rel. à l'hist. des monnaies," 1879; *Necker*, "Adm. de f.," III. For Germany, *cf. Schröder*, p. 519; *Blondel*, "Fr. II," p. 153; *Dudu*, "Inst. de Jérus.," 243.

[2] Reform of Saint Louis. Ord. May, 1263: the king's money had exclusive right of circulation in his domain and outside of it in competition with seigniorial money. The king alone had jurisdiction over infractions of the ordinance committed in the seigniories. Philip the Fair controlled seigniorial money so rigorously that the seigniors sold him their right of coinage. Progress toward monetary unity was so rapidly accomplished that it brought about the annexation of the fiefs to the crown. *Fleury*, p. 119; *Loysel*, no. 9 (ed. *Dupin*); *L'Hommeau*, I, 12. *Cf. Esmein*, p. 584.

[3] Right of seigniorage for the king. Alteration of moneys: profit: 1. by mixing copper with gold and silver (counterfeit money); 2. by recoining money in circulation; 3. by raising or lowering the nominal value of money in circulation. (Philip the Fair proceeded in this manner, BCh. 1876, 145.)

[4] Cod. Théod., 10, 19; Cod. Just., 11, 6. L. Pat. Charles VI, 30 May, 1413 (pretended Ord. 1321); *Isambert*, "Table," h. vo.; *Fleury*, p. 117, 122; *La Garde*, ch. X; *Dareste*, II, 183; *Lamé-Fleury*, "Législ. min. sous l'anc. mon.," 1863; *Aguillon*, "Législ. des mines," 1886; *Krug-Basse*, thesis, 1888; Add. *Blavier*, "Jurisp. des mines," 1825; *S. Luce*, "R. qu. hist.," 21, 189; L. 21, July, 1791.

lands of private individuals without the permission of the king;[1] the grantee ("entrepreneur," company) indemnified the proprietor and paid a tax of a tenth to the king.[2]

§ 441. **Various Dues** were collected by virtue of the police power of the king: inspection, registration, and the hundredth farthing ("centième denier"), fees relating to mortgages, prescription and stamp taxes, and various other dues (marks on metals, gaming houses, blacksmith shops, etc.).[3]

TOPIC 3. ESTABLISHMENT OF TAXES

§ 442. **Subsidies and Impositions.**[4] — The domainal revenues of the feudal monarchy were not taxes, that is to say, contributions exacted of each individual as his share in the expenses of the general interest (defense of the country, internal order, etc.). It was not as king, but as proprietor, seignior, or suzerain that the king collected most of them. It resulted from this: 1st, that the amount fixed by usage could not vary, as it should have done, with the needs of the State; 2d, that outside his own domains the king could not deprive the seigniors of rights of the same kind; this would have been to expropriate them. However, expenses increasing more rapidly than revenues in consequence of long wars and the augmentation of the public services, the king was forced to find extraordinary resources,[5] temporary expedients designed

[1] In England only gold and silver mines were royal. Germany, *Schröder*, p. 533: regalia of mines and of salt (Act of 940); all metals were subject to the Bergregal. *Cf.* constitution, "de regalibus," 1158. "Golden Bull," 1536, Art. 9. *Blondel*, 157.

[2] The system of domainality of mines prevailed during the feudal epoch (except in certain countries, for example, England, where the ownership of mines belonged to the owner of the surface); one can scarcely see in this a "res nullius" susceptible of being acquired by occupation; but the State did not exercise its right to exploit mines; it authorized private persons to do so. *Cf.* on the Law of 1810, *Aguillon*, "Législ. des mines," 1886.

[3] *La Garde*, ch. X, XVIII, Add. ch. XVI; the "marc d'or," or tax paid by royal officers when they were appointed to their office.

[4] *Potherat de Thou.*, "Rech. s. l'orig. de l'impôt," 1838; *Boutari*, "La France sous Phil. le Bel," 1863; *Callery*, "Du pouvoir royal d'imposer," 1882; "R. qu. hist.," 26, 419; *Flammermont*, "De concessu legis et auxilii," 1883; *Luchaire*, "Inst. mon.," I, 126. *Isambert*, "Table," see "Aides," "Subsides."

[5] Domainal revenues under Saint Louis amounted to about 200,000 livres; local expenses aggregated about 70,000 livres; expenses of the king, about 70,000. Under Philip the Fair, extraordinary resources produced about 500,000 livres, and the royal domain, 400,000. After the death of Charles V, the receipts increased to 1,800,000 livres, of which 300,000 were for ordinary revenues. In 1514, 4,500,000 livres of extraordinary resources, against 300,000 livres for the domain. *Cf. Viollet*, II, 163.

to provide for exceptional expenses, contributions levied with a view to meeting the expense of a fixed enterprise (for example, a war), and which ceased to be exacted when this enterprise was completed.

(A) **In the 1300 s.** — The king, as the universal suzerain, demanded of his vassals, seigniors, or communes the feudal aid,[1] at first, to enable him to engage in a Holy War (the Saladin tithe under Philip Augustus, 1188),[2] later, to carry on wars in general[3] and for other purposes.[4] The aid in the latter case was no longer obligatory for vassals; it was voluntary and constituted a free gift.[5] The king had to ask for it and the vassals could refuse it;[6] sometimes he negotiated individually with each of them; sometimes he consulted the provincial Estates or the States-General (first time in 1314).[7] The view is erroneous, however, that " ac-

[1] Ord. I, 534. *Isambert*, III, 15 (marriage).

[2] In 1146, crusade of Louis VII. Ordinance of Philip Augustus, 1185 (the King of France and the King of England, acting in common, decreed the establishment of a "dîme" in order to supply the needs of the crusade to the Holy Land). Ord. 1188, "dîme saladine": whoever refused to engage in the crusade paid a tenth of his income for a year. This last ordinance could not be enforced, and the same was doubtless the case with the first. *Luchaire*, "R. hist.," 72, 334.

[3] Ord. June, 1319 (I, 692): the nobles of Auvergne, on the demand of the king, granted "benevolently and graciously" an "aide" for the war with Flanders; this gift was made of their free will and special grace; it was not expected of them except by "pure grace"; the granting of it did not influence their successors. Each noble having 2,000 livres of rent paid the wages of a man under arms for a year; the others in proportion to their income. Their word or their oath was taken as to the value of their rents. The amount of the gift was fixed and levied by the deputies of the commune and of the nobles of the bailiwick of Auvergne. The nobles were not held for any "ban" or "arrière ban" during that year, and if they wished to follow the king, they received wages. Ord. Dec., 1355 (*Isambert*, IV, 758), Art. 20: if the three Estates did not agree to furnish him a suitable "aide" the king returned to his domain the moneys and to others rights that he had abandoned (forfeited). *Isambert*, II, 781. *Cf. Luchaire*, p. 271.

[4] Saint Louis and Philip III levied "aides" and received free gifts. Ord. 1295 (XII, 333): levy of a fiftieth of the value of the property for the defense of the kingdom, on clerks and laymen, with the exception of nobles who had to serve in person and at their own expense. We thus reach the subsidies of the 1300 s, "local, unequal, sometimes refused, sometimes accorded by grace." *Luchaire*, I, 120; *Vuitry*, I, 169.

[5] In Germany the first taxes were called "Beden" or "Beten" ("petitiones," "precariæ") because they were exacted, not by virtue of a right, but asked as a favor in certain circumstances. *Cf.* "Benevolences" in England. Other taxes "pro conservatione imperii," 1274, 1290. *Schröder*, p. 536.

[6] Ord. June, 1456 (XIV, 387; *Isambert*, IX, 278): Languedoc granted a subsidy of 116,000 livres instead of 130,000 asked by the king.

[7] By reason even of the right of "arrière ban" or of the levy "en masse" (*Du Cange*, see "Retrobannum"), Philip the Fair asked for "aides" on account of wars. BCh., 5e s. 1, 24. Philip the Fair and the Estates of 1314. His successors addressed themselves rather individually to the seigniors and to the towns (1319, 1350, etc.).

cording to the feudal law no tax was legitimate unless those who had to pay it gave their consent." The aid, voluntarily granted, had no feature of a tax which the taxpayer was under an obligation to vote if it was necessary: and it was not the payer who granted it, but the seignior or the commune, who levied it upon those subject to them and who transmitted the amount to the king. The king attempted, it is true, to undertake the collection of the sum, which was onerous and without profit to the seigniors; half through negligence and half through feebleness the seigniors often allowed the agents of the king to collect the taxes on their domains, expecting that they would be able to do it more effectively.[1] Nevertheless, neither Philip the Fair nor his immediate successors succeeded in depriving the aid of its character as an extraordinary local and temporary resource; it required the calamities of the Hundred Years' War to transform it into a general and permanent contribution upon all men of France.

Subsidies were always free gifts and often the granting of them was an occasion for the redress of grievances; there would be a treaty between the Estates and the king, the Estates agreed to furnish the aid, the king in return promised to take into consideration the demands made of him by the Estates.[2] Grievances and subsidies —

[1] Secret instructions given to the royal commissioners for the levy of a subsidy at the time of the war with Flanders (Ord. I, 350, 370). *Isambert*, II, 781: "And against the will of the barons taxes cannot be levied on their lands and this ordinance shall be kept secret . . . because it would work too great an injury if they were aware of it." *Cf.* p. 928, n. 3.

[2] *Gasquet*, "Précis," I, 325: under Philip the Fair, the "aide" became almost an annual tax, in reality; it assumed all forms, was imposed on all classes, and all precautions were taken to cause it to pass into custom. The war against Aragon was considered as a crusade; the "décimes" were levied at this time on ecclesiastical benefices; nobles and the "good towns" had to respond to the royal summons or pay the ban. Carcassonne gave the king 1,000 livres (Tours currency) in order to be exempted from military service. In 1292, a tax of one "denarius" was levied on the sale of all merchandise; this tax was called the "maltôte" because of the vexations without number to which it gave rise. The population of Paris and of Rouen took up arms; and fearing that the tax would become perpetual, the two cities purchased an exemption, one for the sum of 100,000 livres, the other, for 10,000. In 1293, a forced loan from the rich bourgeois of the "good towns" produced 680,000 livres. In 1295, the king levied an extraordinary tax of one per cent on land revenues; in 1296, a tax of two per cent which was renewed the following year. The terrible war with Flanders made new supplies necessary (1302–1303). The king had to ask the seigniors for their part of the contributions levied on their tenants. In 1304, the feudal "aide" was levied on the occasion of the marriage of his daughter Isabella to the king of England; in 1313 for the accoutrements of his three sons as knights. We note only by way of memorandum, the alterations of money, extortions inflicted on Jews, and Lombards; the purchase for 20,000 livres, of all the Jews of Valois; the confiscation of all debts due Jews under pretext of usury, and the appropriation of the proceeds by the royal treasury. The clergy was not

the English needed no other weapons than these to win their political liberties.[1]

In short, the public tax evolved from the feudal aid; it became, also, to a certain extent, the price of exemption from military service; from the time of Philip Augustus the obligation of military service was transformed more and more into a pecuniary payment: one either paid it in advance, or paid off the fine incurred after the event.[2]

(B) **From the Year 1355.** — The principal taxes, the "taille," the aid, and the salt duty were known, but there was neither order nor regularity in their assessment, nor uniformity in their collection. They were established definitively only at the meeting of the States-General of 1355 and 1356.[3] The latter "proclaimed at the same time the liability of all persons to the payment of taxes,[4] the periodicity of the vote of these taxes, and the necessity

spared any more than the rest of the nation. It paid taxes upon the lands occupied by its "roturier" tenants and paid the "décimes" for its benefices. The purpose of this contribution was to defray the expenses of the crusades. Everything became a matter of the crusades. The complaints of the clergy were carried to the pope, who claimed that his consent was necessary for the taxation of the clergy. Boniface VIII issued his Bull "Clericis laicos," then authorized the perception of a double "décime" for the king, who granted him, in return, the right to collect a "décime" on the clergy of France.

[1] *Isambert*, IV, 633 (year 1350), etc. Especially, the Ord. of Dec., 1355, IV, 734.

[2] *Vuitry*, "Etudes," II, 1; I, 119; *Callery*, "R. qu. hist.," 26, 419. *Cf.* *Langlois*, "Philippe III," 349; *Borelli de Serres*, "Recherches." The estimates of "roturier" service. *Isambert*, II, 782: nobles who wished to be exempted from performing military service had to pay the half, the fifth of the annual revenue of their lands; the non-nobles, the tenth or the fiftieth. *Cf.* IV, 633 (1350), etc. While admitting that the tax was in commutation of military service in certain cases, it was not always so; it was also an "aide." But the bond between the tax and the military service serves to explain the exemption from the "taille," of nobles bearing arms or who had ceased to be able to bear them.

[3] Ord. Dec. 28, 1355 (*Isambert*, IV, 734): the Estates of "Langue d'oïl" allowed a tax to be levied on salt and an imposition of eight "denarius" per livre on everything sold (except inheritances). The administration of this "aide" was confided to elected persons and to general superintendents. The proceeds from it had to be used exclusively for the purposes of war. The accounts were rendered to the Estates. The "aides" lasted only a year and were levied without prejudice to the rights and franchises of the Estates. Nobles and clerks, the king himself, paid these "aides." In return for the "aides," the king renounced the practice of altering monies and abolished various abuses. The "aides" and the salt tax not having appeared sufficient and not being agreeable to everybody, the Ord. of March 12, 1355, created the "taille." *Isambert*, IV, 764. *Cf.* V, 8 (1358); *Lavisse*, "R. hist.," Nov., 1884.

[4] According to the Ordinance of Dec., 1355, Art. 20, the clergy and nobility could not bind the Third Estate in the matter of "aides." The privileged orders did not succeed in obtaining a general exemption from "aides" or indirect taxes. But it was not the same in the case of the "taille": in the 1400 s the nobles were exempt from it for the simple

of a responsible administration placed under the permanent control of the nation." Of these rules not one remained in force; the financial organization established by the Estates alone endured, but by passing into the hands of the king. In the 1400s without there having been a single royal act which established the principle, and without the Estates having accepted it, the permanence of the subsidies was established for all time. The Ordinance of 1435 regulated aids and the Ordinance of 1439 (from which is dated, without good reason, the permanent "taille")[1] prohibited the seigniors from levying "tailles" on their subjects without the authorization of the king;[2] the king then established free companies, the "first permanent army."[3] The permanence of the army could not fail to lead to the permanence of the subsidies. Under these conditions, the voting of subsidies by the Estates degenerated into a simple formality. The king levied them of right throughout the whole kingdom; he imposed them on his subjects; henceforth they are no longer called subsidies but taxes ("impôts") or impositions.

The royal right of levying taxes was thus established: 1st, as a result of custom; 2d, in consequence of the extension of the king's authority and of the influence of the Roman doctrines.[4] One was hardly aware in France of the revolution which had thus taken place.[5] The States-General afterwards attempted, without

reason that they alone were subject to bear arms (while formerly it was necessary that they should be actually in the king's army). Nothing justified this exemption, unless it was the fear of encountering resistance; the nobility, says de Toqueville, had the baseness to allow the Third Estate to be taxed, provided that they themselves were exempted. The clergy obtained the same favor, to a lesser degree.

[1] *Cf. Thomas*, "Etats prov. de la Fr. centr.," 1879.

[2] For example, Flanders, 1296. Ord. XI, 382; *cf.* 1302, *ibid.*, I, 350. The non-nobles paying the "aide" to the king were not liable for the tax to their seignior.

[3] In Germany, after the beginning of the 1500 s, regular contributions were paid for the maintenance of the imperial army, but the princes were too little taxed, the towns and counties too much. Reform in 1541–1545, Diet of Ratisbonne.

[4] From the 1300 s, certain Roman doctrines appeared in Pierre Jacobi (cited by *De Grassalius*, "Regalium Franciæ," p. 106). *Cf.* the comments on Law 1, c. "Nova Vectig. imponi non posse." *Esmein*, p. 549. *J. Lecoq*, q. 60 (it was "lèse-majesté" if one pretended that the king needed the consent of his subjects to levy taxes). The "Songe du Verger," 1, 135. *Cf. Viollet*, II, 163. *De l'Hommeau*, I, 11.

[5] *Cf. Limnæus*, "Notitia regni Franciæ," about 1640: "regnum Galliæ est pratum florentissimum, in quo pascuntur infiniti ovium greges, aureis velleribus, quæ tonderi possunt quoties pastori libuerit" (cited by *Dareste*, II, 121). The Venetian ambassador in 1561 said: "In France, the subjects of the king not only profess great obedience and affection for their prince, but they venerate him, they adore him; their property, the products of their labor, their life, all that they have, can be laid under contribution

success, to recover the budgetary right which they had lost;[1] the provincial Estates alone preserved it in the parts of France where they survived, and even there it was reduced to a mere shadow. Some theorists, like Bodin, protested on the ground that since taxation involved the taking of private property it presupposed the consent of the owners; to this it was replied that the king was the owner of the property of his subjects.[2] England became the founder of modern budgetary control, and the philosophers of the 1700s ranged themselves as its advocates.[3]

§ 443. **English Budgetary Law.** — When Charles I, at the end of his resources, in spite of the Petition of Right which he had signed, June 7, 1628, and without consulting Parliament, undertook to levy again a tax on ships (ship money), formerly levied in time of war in certain counties, he encountered the liveliest resistance. Hampden refused to pay it and maintained in court that the tax was illegal. The judges condemned him, but the Revolution of 1648 marked the triumph of the cause which he had defended, and, in 1688, the Bill of Rights recognized anew, and, this time in a more definite manner, the old rule: " to the representatives of the coun-

by him without fear that they will revolt; it is as if they were slaves. This devotion was worth being remarked as a unique thing in the Christian world." Hist. Doc. of France Reports of the Venetian ambassador in the 16th century (*ibid.*).

[1] *Isambert*, IX, 108 (1441): the Estate of Nevers asked the king not to impose the "taille" without the consent of the Estates; Charles VII replied that by his royal authority, for urgent reasons, he could levy the "taille," as no one else could without his permission; there was no need to assemble the three estates, for it would be only a burden for the poor people who paid the expenses of those who attended; several notable seigniors had asked that the Estates be no more summoned. Charles VII, says Commines, who gained his point of imposing the "taille" at his pleasure without the consent of the Estates, greatly burdened his mind and that of his successors and inflicted upon his kingdom a wound which bled for a long time. — Disregarded in fact, the right of the Estates persisted in the public opinion; it was asserted constantly (Estates of 1483, 1576, 1579, etc.). *Fénelon*, "Examen de conscience sur les devoirs de la royauté": formerly, the king did not take anything from the people on his authority alone; the assembly of the nation accorded him the funds for the extraordinary needs of the State.

[2] *Dupont de Nemours*, Corresp. with J. B. Say: It is a narrow and peevish idea, like that of the English, that it is necessary to determine every year the amount to be granted the government and to reserve the right to refuse the tax. *Stourm*, "Le Budget," p. 33.

[3] Delib. of the sovereign courts, June, 1648 and Decl. July 13, 1648, declaring that in future there should be no new impositions except by virtue of edicts duly verified. *Isambert*, XVII, 74, 84. But this had no reference to what we call indirect taxes; it had reference only to direct taxes like the "taille." In 1787, the "parliamentarians" recognized the fact that to the States-General alone belonged the right of granting the tax: "the constitutional principle of the French monarchy was that impositions must be consented to by those who had to support them." *Stourm*, "Le Budget," p. 38.

try belong exclusively the right to permit the levying of taxes." From this moment the funds intended for the use of the crown and left to the free disposal of the king were distinguished from those which were to be devoted to the public service and which had to be expended under the direction and control of Parliament.[1] The budget is never voted beyond a year, and in the House of Commons must originate the imposition of all taxes.

§ 444. **Forms of Taxes.** — "The problem [of taxation] consists in making each individual contribute in proportion to his resources, but the great difficulty is to reach these resources, which are very diverse; they are a sort of Proteus which takes innumerable forms and disappears." In the 1300 s people were not concerned with the question whether it would be better to establish a single tax or multifarious taxes, a tax on capital or a tax on income;[2] nobody cared, provided the necessary funds were obtained. There were created, therefore, in order to be more sure of success, two sorts of taxes: the one, including the "taille" and the "fouage,"[3] corresponding to our direct taxes; the other corresponding to our indirect taxes and consisting of taxes on the sale and circulation of merchandise: the aids and the customs duties ("traite foraine").[4]

[1] The first constituted the **civil list**, so called because they had to be used for the expenses of the royal household and for the reward of certain civil employees; to-day, the civil list serves only for the expenses of the royal household. The civil list came to us from England; so also came the **budget** or act of prior approval of the public receipts and expenses. This word, in spite of its exotic aspect and its only recent use in France, formerly belonged to the French language: "bougette" = "pochette."

[2] The imposition of eight farthings per livre and the tax on salt were granted to King John; but the question was asked, would these "aides" be agreeable to the people and would they suffice for the expenses of war? The Estates of 1355 replied by levying the "taille." Estates of Tours, 1484 (*Isambert*, XI, 47): if it happened that the domain could not contribute or that there was no need to levy a subsidy, it seemed to the Estates, that without their "taille," the impositions, salt taxes and equivalents, would amount to more than was necessary. The Estates demanded the abolition of the "taille"; they recalled that Saint Louis, in his instructions to his son, recommended him not to levy "tailles" on his people except upon great necessity. They desired, at least, that, if it was indispensable to levy "tailles" it should not be done without the consent of the Estates. The Estates of the Center granted the "taille" to Charles VII, but not the "aides." *Thomas*, "Etats prov.," I, 229.

[3] In the North, "feu" signified household, habitation; in the South, a certain number of households whose revenues could support the imposition levied per household. *Spont*, "Ann. du Midi," 1890, p. 375. Repairing of habitations. Rating of hearth tax, *ibid.*

[4] Here is the full list of the principal taxes of the old régime. Taxes: I. Direct: A. Ancient: (*a*) "taille"; (*b*) "décime," free gifts of the clergy; (*c*) free gifts of the Countries of the Estates. B. Modern: (*a*) corvée; (*b*) poll; (*c*) tenth, twentieth. II. Indirect: A. Ancient: (*a*) "aides" and taxes connected with them; (*b*) salt tax; (*c*) "traites."

TOPIC 4. DIRECT TAXES

§ 445. **The "Taille,"** [1] for a long time a provisional tax levied on account of war and ceasing with the end of the war, became permanent at the same time as did the army under Charles VII (free companies, created in 1439).[2] The twenty per cent increase ("la grand crue") which was added under Francis I and the "taillon" under Henry II were likewise designed for the pay of the army. Afterwards various accessories were added to this and even the "corvée." The proceeds ceased to be applied exclusively to the needs of the army, the king using them for such purposes as he pleased. From 1,800,000 livres under Charles VII the proceeds of the "taille" increased to 52,000,000 under Mazarin and to 90,000,000 on the eve of the Revolution. "In proportion as the burden of the 'taille' increased, the number of those who bore its weight decreased." It was the tax of the "roturier"; the clergy, the nobility, the magistracy, and many functionaries were exempted from it.[3] The nobles were deemed to have paid with

B. Recent: (*a*) stamp; (*b*) "contrôle"; (*c*) "insinuation" and "centième denier." There were also the fees from sales of public office, as a non-regular item.

[1] Concerning the word "taille," *cf. infra*, p. 761, and on the earlier modes of computation, *cf. L. Say*, meeting of the Academy, Jan. 6, 1885; *Charondas*, "Œuvres," II (on the Edict of "tailles"); *Despeisses*, "Tr. des tailles, Œuvres," vol. III, p. 229; *Auger*, "Traité s. les tailles," 1788; BCh. 6th s. II, 189; *Ferrière, Guyot*, see "Code des tailles," 1737. "R. qu. hist.," 32, 41.

[2] Reference here is to the royal "taille," levied by the king in contradistinction to the seigniorial "taille," levied by the seignior: 1, on serfs; 2, and sometimes even on the "roturiers" of his domains, many of whom were only former serfs. In principle, the suzerain could not exact it directly of the serfs or "roturiers" of his vassals, but if he demanded an "aide" of the latter, the vassals themselves, in order to be discharged, collected it of their taxpayers. Having the diversity of feudal relations, it is not surprising that the suzerain himself sometimes proceeded to levy this "taille," whether after an agreement with his vassals, or by virtue of a custom. *Esmein*, p. 553 (and other authors cited). Kings had this way of doing. When the royal "taille" became permanent, the arbitrary seigniorial "taille" was suppressed, or at least restrained. *Boutaric*, "Dr. seign.," holds that it was not due except by virtue of a title (1700s).

[3] *L'Escuyer*, "Instruction général des finances," following the new style of the chancellerie, 1622 (list of exempts). Richelieu estimates at four millions the number of those exempted. According to Avenel, the share of each one would have been forty-five francs under Louis XIII; "to-day, it is eleven francs, and as there are some large quotas (some paying as high as 150,000 fr. land tax), the average figure for the mass is still less." But his estimate of the number of privileged persons is open to question. *Cf. Fleury*, "Dr. publ.," p. 171; *Du Crot*, "Tr. des Aydes, Tailles et Gabelles," 1629 (1636); the "tailles" had to be paid by all indiscriminately, according to the word of God, natural reason, and the ordinances of our kings.

their blood,[1] the functionaries with their services,[2] and the clergy to have paid an equivalent with their tenths and free gifts.[3] But the actual burdens borne by these privileged persons were far from counterbalancing the exemptions which they enjoyed. The free towns or compounded towns [cities which had charters of privileges] like Paris and Rouen, were also excused from paying the "taille," but ordinarily upon condition of paying an equivalent.

The "taille" was real or personal in character. (A) **The real "taille,"** [4] analogous to our real estate tax, was collected on immovables according to their value and this was stated by means of "compoix" or registers of surveys of the lands ("cadastres") [5] prepared at the request of the inhabitants, following an authorization by the Court of Aids by upright men and trusted experts under the direction of local judicial officers. The lands were surveyed, classified, and valued on the basis of their revenue. After that the rôle of assessments or quotas to be paid by each tract of land (so much per acre) was prepared. Only the lands of the nobility and certain landed property of the Church were exempted, so that the nobles and ecclesiastics had to pay for their "roturier" lands. This system, followed in Languedoc and in Guienne,[6] more equi-

[1] Or rather they escaped the tax, because at the beginning it was they who levied it. Let us not forget "that being rich sufficed to make one a noble and one became a noble in order to escape paying taxes." The farmers of the nobles were taxed, a fact which reduced farm rents; in this sense, the "taille" affected the nobles; but the "roturiers" who had farms submitted to the "taille d'exploitation" on the farmers, and paid besides, a tax as owners. *Esmein*, 555, 1; *Fleury*, p. 172; *Condorcet*, "Œuv.," 8, 351.

[2] Principal officers of justice, police, finances, army, professors, etc.

[3] The ecclesiastical "décimes" (a tenth of the revenues of ecclesiastical benefices, verified by the declaration of the taxpayers) were often granted by the popes to the kings after 1188: *Luchaire*, p. 580 (bibliog.), 598; *Vuitry*, I, 404; *Gerbaux*, "Position des élèves de l'Ecole des Chartes," 1881. From the time of Philip the Fair, Rigord, ad. 1188; "décimes" were levied in spite of the pope, and he went so far as to recognize the right of the king to exact them in case of necessity without his consent. On the contrary, the pope needed the authority of the government to levy them on the French clergy. *Necker*, "Adm. d. fin.," IX.

[4] It was the old hearth tax, but it was not apportioned among households, "sénéchausées" and "vigueries"; the "taille" was apportioned by dioceses according to a tariff. *Spont*, "Ann. du Midi," 1890, 377.

[5] "Compoids" (1464) (or estimates), because the weights or valuation of property was made conjointly for all the inhabitants of the same place. "Compoix terrien" or land and "compoix caballiste," containing the valuation of the "cabaux" ("caput," land of trade or traffic) and movables of value, industry, money at interest, pension, rent, cattle. The merchants and inhabitants of the towns were taxed according to the "compoix caballiste" and besides, if they had lands, according to the "compoix terrien." *Cf. Despeisses*, vol. III, s. 1; *Necker*, "Admin. des fin.," chap. IX.

[6] *Despeisses*, vol. II, Art. 14; *Fleury*, p. 170; *Monin*, 89; *Isambert*, "Table," see "Tailles"; II, 654 (1254, Languedoc); V, 374 (1372); XII, 407 (1535); *Spont*, "La taille en Languedoc de 1450 à 1515" ("Ann. du

table than the personal "taille" and less arbitrary, should have been made general and Colbert so proposed.

(B) **The Personal "Taille"** was not, as its name would lead one to believe, a capitation tax or a contribution per head;[1] it was levied on "roturiers" alone, according to the totality of their income (products of landed property, commercial or industrial profits, and wages) as it was known from their declarations. It was in this form that the "taille" was levied in all the "countries of elections" ("pays d'élections").[2]

§ 446. **The Levy and Apportionment of the "Taille."**[3] — Every year, six months in advance, the total amount of the "taille" for all the "countries of elections" was determined by the king in council by means of a general warrant.[4] The apportionment was made according to four degrees: 1st, a **special warrant**, likewise issued by the king in council, fixed the amount of each "généralité."[5] 2d, In each "généralité" this warrant was spread by the bureau of finance to which was added the intendant;

Midi," 1890, 365; 1891, 482); *Dognon, ibid.*, 1891, 340. On the reality of the "taille," *cf.* Ord. XIII, 693. On the apportionment of the "taille," in Languedoc, *cf. Spont*, 1890, p. 484.

[1] *Fleury*, p. 168. *Géraud*, "Paris s. Phil. le Bel," 1837 (list of the "taille"), unedited document.

[2] Ord. March 12, 1355 (*Is.*, IV, 763): Whoever had one hundred livres of revenue, paid four livres; forty livres of revenue, forty sols; ten livres, twenty sols; below ten livres, ten sols (agriculturist laborers); widows, and married children. Domestics who did not earn one hundred sols, and beggars, had nothing to pay. The property of married women was counted with that of their husbands. Concerning personal property, *cf.* Art. 4: it may be observed that the tax of non-nobles was less than that of nobles. The clergy contributed according to its revenues (but with privileged valuation for the property of the Church, and household furnishings were not counted). — Concerning the procedure to be followed for declarations in case of the necessity of an oath by those making declarations, or if they did not wish to swear, the proof by well known commune, *cf.* Art. 10. *Cf. Isambert*, V, 8 [1358].

[3] *Fleury*, 169; *Pizard*, 258. *Cf. Spont*, "Ann. du Midi," 1890, p. 371; *Isambert*, "Table," see "Tailles"; April, 1460; Circul. of General *P. Briçonnet*, Jacqueton, "Doc. s. l'admin. fin.," p. 102; June, 1517; March, 1583, 1663; 1673; July, 1766; Aug., 1776; July 13, 1780 and June, 1788. *Cf. Vauban, Boisguillebert* ("Détail de la F.," 1696; "Factum de la Fr.," 1707).

[4] One of the most serious defects of the old financial system was the indefinite extension of warrants of the "taille"; and the excess of "tailles" in the course of the year. The Parliaments which protested with so much energy as soon as there was a question of the stamp tax or of the "centième denier," did not have any sense of their rights as to the "taille." The declaration of February 7, 1768, fixed definitely and forever the principal of the "taille"; but it did not apply to the second warrant composed of accessories of the "taille." *Necker* (declaration of Feb. 13, 1780) desired that the "taille" be invariable in principal and accessory; changes to be made only by legislative acts submitted to the Parliaments and sovereign courts.

[5] Inequalities among generalities: Riom, nine livres per inhabitant; Rouen, eight; Caen, seven; Bourges, three.

from it were drawn commissions for each "election." 3d, The persons elected, and afterwards the subdelegate, determined the quota of each parish ("mandements"). 4th, Finally, in the parishes, the individual rolls were prepared by assessors and collectors, elected by the inhabitants,[1] a liberal procedure, perhaps, but one which led to the most crying injustices,[2] so much so that finally the apportionments had to be made under the direction of "taille" commissioners appointed by the intendants. These commissioners visited each parish;[3] and there in the presence of the collectors and of the inhabitants drew up an official report of the population and of the state of the parish, adding to it the general declaration of the inhabitants concerning privileged persons and their possessions, and the individual declaration of each person in regard to the landed property which he possessed or cultivated, the income which he received in farm rents, house rent, and income of every kind.[4] Measures (of minimum efficacy) were adopted to assure the truth of the declarations; they provided for the doubling of the tax in case of inaccuracy in the declaration, for the taking of declarations from other persons in case any one refused to give information concerning his fortune, for reading the declarations before the assembly of the people, and, if they were not supported by documentary evidence, for relying instead upon the opinion of the parish, and finally, for a general survey at the expense of those concerned if the intendant suspected fraud.[5]

§ 447. **The Collectors,**[6] or taxpayers charged with collecting

[1] The powers granted in 1355 to the elected officials permitted them to proceed with the apportionment in the parishes; but the abuses of which they were guilty, especially when they were no longer appointed by the Estates, led, by reaction, to the election of "asséeurs" by assemblies of the inhabitants (Ord. Nov. 29, 1379, *Isambert*, V, 515) which was perhaps only the maintenance of a tradition as old as the taxes in the common interest established by the parishes. *Esmein*, p. 560, cites Ord. I, 291 (towns). BCh. I, 455.

[2] *Fleury*, 169: envy of the rich, favors for them, violence of the seigniors to discharge their tenants and domestics, extortion by the officers of finance; the burden fell on the poor. Remedies: the best was a good intendant. Instr. to the commissioners, 1598.

[3] *Pizard*, p. 260. The taxpayers sought to appear poorer than they were, for their declarations were judged by appearances. *Taine*, "Origines de la Fr. cont.," I, 5. *Cf.* the humoristic list of *Marquis de Mirabeau*, "Tr. de la population," II, 50.

[4] Concerning the division of income of the taxpayers into several categories at the end of the old régime, *cf. Esmein*, p. 561 and the authors that he cites: *Auger*, I, 268; III, 1773 (Declaration of Aug. 11, 1776); *D'Arbois de Jubainville*, "L'admin. des intendants," p. 30.

[5] Decl., April 23, 1778 (concerning claims).

[6] *Fleury*, p. 170. At first "asséeurs" charged with preparing the assessment rolls and "collecteurs" who collected the sum total. Later the two offices were united into one. The system of collection practiced

the "taille," showed extreme harshness in performing their duties[1] because they paid the taxes of the insolvent and were jointly and severally responsible for the quota of the whole parish[2] and by reason of this heavy responsibility they were obliged to neglect their own affairs; ruin and imprisonment awaited them as formerly the members of the curia of the Later Empire.

§ 448. **Criticism.** — The "taille" was neither unjust in principle nor always excessive in rate. But it was criticized for being too variable and consequently as discouraging production; for being unequal, since the wealthiest did not pay it and consequently the share of the poorest was increased; and for being disproportionate, thus Riom paid nine livres per capita, Bourges only three. Colbert, who desired to correct the most serious evils by regulating and generalizing the real "taille," succeeded in carrying out only a small part of his program (*cf.* Necker, "Compte rendu," p. 64).

The Constitutional Assembly, by the law of December 1, 1790, established a land tax based on the net income from the land[3] and

by the taxpayers was condemned in the 1700s by Boisguillebert, the abbé of Saint-Pierre, Turgot (*cf. Stourm,* I, 92 and the authors cited). In Limousin, he substituted for collectors, "préposés" (overseers) under bond; a happy innovation that the Assembly of Berry and others were eager to follow, but which the Constituent Assembly was wrong in repudiating. *Stourm,* I, 147. It intrusted the preparation of the register to municipal officers and to the inhabitants of the commune; the collection was awarded by contract. Ten years passed before the rolls were finished; the municipalities paid no attention to the repeated orders which they received; the result was that the taxes remained unpaid. The Consulate found itself under the necessity of creating a special administration by grace of which the law of 1790 was at last, and at the end of a short time, applied (L. Oct. 24, 1799).

[1] Extremely rigorous prosecution of delinquent taxpayers: bailiffs' men or fusileers installed in the homes of the taxpayers, seizure of their furniture, doors and windows, etc. The code of the "tailles" left the agents almost free to act as they pleased. *Stourm,* I, 101. *Boisguillebert,* "Détail de la France," 1696, ch. VI. Capture of villages by assault, deserted parishes. "Croquants" (name given to French peasants who rebelled under Henry IV and Louis XIII) in Guyenne. "Jean-Va-Nu-Pieds" in Normandy, 1639. The Provincial Assemblies proposed several remedies for these evils: substitution of porters of constraint for bailiffs, diminution of expenses, etc. It was proposed to abolish the bailiff's men. (*Cf.* L. Feb. 10, 1877).

[2] An edict of Turgot, Jan. 3, 1775 (*Isambert,* XXIII, 127) abolished constraint solidly, but it reappeared in 1790. *Stourm,* I, 151.

[3] According to the physiocrats (economists who believe that wealth is founded on agriculture), the taxes should be levied only upon landed property and the net produce therefrom. But as it was impossible to determine exactly this product, the Constitutional Assembly adopted only the formula of the physiocrats, and substituted for the net value, the tenantable value of the land. *Stourm,* I, 140. Concerning the subject of the determination of the amount of the land tax (240 millions in 1790; result of the researches of *Lavoisier,* "De la richesse du royaume de France," 1791), concerning the very arbitrary apportionment among the departments, and concerning the determination of a minimum tax (6 one

proclaimed the abolition of privileges and the equality of all in respect to taxation.[1] It contented itself with noting the necessity of a register of land surveys ("cadastre"); the Convention decreed that it should be made, but nothing was done before the time of the Consulate; and the creation of a detailed register was not definitely prescribed until 1807, and was not accomplished until 1845.[2] The law of the 3d Frimaire, year VII (March 23, 1798), formed the point of departure for modern legislation on the subject.

§ 449. **The Royal "Corvée"** (of the great roads)[3] was added in the 1600 s and especially in the 1700 s to the seigniorial "corvée"[4] for the purpose of providing for the construction and repair of the public roads which were badly kept up by the seigniors. It was introduced in imitation of what the seigniors did on their lands and by an extension of the requisitions of men and of horses made in the name of the king in time of war. Sully first had recourse to it and Colbert on a larger scale, but it was still only an excep-

hundredths of the land revenue, above which, the reduction was a matter of right) of which the application led, in time, to an equal assessment; *cf. Stourm*, I, 201; *Condorcet*, "Œuvres," ed. *Arago*, vol. VIII, p. 355.

[1] The "projét" for a territorial tax adopted in 1787 by the assembly of notables, abolished all privileges (Edict Aug., 1787), but the opposition of the Parliaments succeeded in preventing that important reform. Edict of Sept. 19, 1787. *Cf.* result of the Assembly of Peers of Dec. 20, 1788. *Stourm*, I, 114, 133 (extracts from the "cahiers" of the States-General of 1789). Vauban would have had, like the "dîme" levied by the clergy, the tax collected in kind; in 1787, this idea still had its supporters; it was rejected partly because of the greatness of the expense of assessment and the difficulties of execution, and more because it was in opposition to a doctrine of the physiocrats, that taxes should be levied exclusively on the net produce of land; the contribution in kind affected the grass product. The same question was raised in the Constitutional Assembly, which exacted the tax in money, and in the Convention, which introduced the experiment of the tax in kind (1795 to 1797) and demonstrated that it was impracticable.

[2] The so-called "Cadastre," prepared according to the law of 1790, consisted in a simple statement without a survey and map, giving the situation and the approximate size of individual properties with an evaluation of their incomes. It was somewhat like the procedure conceived by the provincial assemblies. It was very inferior to the "cadastre" of the countries having Estates ("pays d'Etats"). *Stourm*, I, 148, "Instr. de l'ass. nation. sur la contrib. foncière," 1790. *Cf. Condorcet*, V, 236.

[3] *Stourm*, I, 221; *L. Say*, "Dict. des Finances," h. vo.; "Dict. d'Econ. Polit.," h. vo.; "Gr. Encycl.," h. vo.; (*Ch. Mortet*) and bibliog.; *Vignon*, "Et. hist. sur l'adm. des voies publ.," 1862; *Hyenne*, "De la corvée," 1863; *Isambert*, h. vo. "Ponts et chaussées" ("Table"); *Ducrocq*, "La corvée et sa suppression," "Rev. gén. du dr.," 1882.

[4] "Corvée" from "corrogatæ" ("corvadæ," "corveiæ"), exceptional labors as contradistinguished from the fixed or "rigæ araturæ." From the Roman epoch where they were chiefly public charges, sometimes, however, private services, they passed with this latter character to the Frankish epoch (*Guérard*, "Polypt. d'Irminon," p. 644) and to the feudal epoch, when the greater part of public works and even the construction of cathedrals were carried out by the "corvée."

tional local measure when the comptroller general, Orry, made it general in 1738 (Instruction concerning the repair of roads, June 13, 1738).[1] He was struck by the fact that good results had been obtained by this method for the maintenance of strategic routes in the frontier provinces; furthermore the treasury had no other resources. The "taille" payers,[2] between sixteen and sixty years of age, living in parishes within three leagues at most from the road to be repaired, were summoned fifteen days in advance and were obliged to betake themselves to the spot with draft animals or beasts of burden, without the right to commute the service into a money payment. There were two summonses a year, one in the spring, the other in the autumn. Moreover, such latitude was left to the intendants[3] that the "corvée" became in their hands the most vexatious of burdens; here the number of days of labor was six, there it was fifty; here the "corvée" service was performed two leagues from home, there, seven; fraudulent exemptions, the exactions of overseers, excesses of subordinate agents and of the constabulary, all contributed to make the institution unpopular. Still, if the beautiful roads which were constructed by it had only been profitable to those who performed the labor! But they connected the great cities with one another, and the local or country roads were almost impassable during the bad season. De Fontette at Caen (1758) and Turgot

[1] A remarkable example of a new tax established by a simple ministerial order.

[2] The syndics prepared every year the list of men and animals subject to the corvée.

[3] The service of roads and bridges which belonged originally to the treasurers of France (Edict 1627) passed little by little for the most part to the intendants (Arr. Con. 1705, 1720, 1721) like the police of wagoning, and that of navigation. *Dareste*, "Justice admin.," p. 122; *cf.* p. 129, no. 2 (in Languedoc: the administration of the public highways belonged to the Estates, the decision of contentious matters to the intendant). *Guyot*, "Offices," III, 333. For the establishment of means of communication, as for that of great public works (canals, draining of marshes), the intendants had to inquire into the usefulness of the enterprise, and the practicability of its execution, give their advice, prepare a plan and an estimate and have it approved by the king (concerning the estimates and plans, *cf.* archives of the ancient seats of the intendants). They had to see that the contractors furnished sufficient guarantees to the king (solvency, domicile, etc.). The Edict of concession or awards of contracts made in regard to each undertaking contained formal clauses, from which have come our laws on expropriation and our rules relative to indemnities for damages. In case of expropriation or damages, the amount of the indemnity was determined by experts and had to be paid previously to taking possession. All rights over real estate were transferred on payment of the recorded price. The controversies which arose in connection with works and indemnities were submitted to the intendants, with the right of appeal to the Council of State. *Cf.* Edict of 1607, 1638, *Delamare*, "Police," IV, 361; *Dareste*, 123, n. 2.

at Limoges (1761) made the "corvée" redeemable[1] under the pretext that they were authorized to complete the delayed public works at the expense of those liable to the "corvée." Having become comptroller general, Turgot abolished the "corvée" (Edict of February, 1776) and substituted in its place an additional tax of a twentieth which was badly received by the privileged classes whom it affected. In August, 1776, the downfall of Turgot put an end to the reform. Calonne, in 1787, took it up again, but the money tax which he substituted for the "corvée" was added to the "taille," that is to say, it fell upon the "roturier" class in such a manner as to spare the privileged classes. From the "countries of elections" the system passed to the "countries of Estates." In 1789 the "corvée" no longer existed except in Brittany.[2] The Constitutional Assembly abolished all personal "corvées" (seigniorial and royal).[3]

§ 450. **Direct Taxes of the 1600 s and 1700 s.** — These were, like the "taille," taxes levied for war purposes[4] under critical circumstances, in the same way as was the income tax in England (1798).[5] The capitation tax appeared in 1695 after the war with the League of Augsburg; was abolished in 1697 and reëstablished in 1704, this time to endure permanently. In 1710, during the war of the Spanish Succession, an income tax of a tenth was added; the amount varied, it was in the end a twentieth, later two (1756) and even three twentieths (1760–1763, 1783–1786).

§ 451. **The Capitation Tax,**[6] included during the feudal epoch with seigniorial dues,[7] took its place among public taxes under

[1] The real "corvées," due by reason of the ownership of land, were purchasable [commutable into pecuniary payments]. They represented, like dues, the price of the land grant. "Trudaine, the director general of the service of roads and bridges, also encouraged, with all his power, the system of redemption."

[2] Bourgeois "corvée" at Metz, Châlons, and Troyes, for streets and rural roads.

[3] Quesnay, Dupont de Nemours, and the Marquis of Mirabeau protested against the "corvée." *Condorcet*, 8, 407. Fault was found with it because it was not an economical tax, for those subject to it worked but little. *Cf.* prestation, Arr. consul., 4 Therm., year X.

[4] The "corvée" was connected, in a certain sense, with war, because it was only a continuation of the construction of strategic routes.

[5] Concerning the English income tax, *cf. Fischel*, I, 339.

[6] *Isambert*, "Table," see "Capitation." "Réglement" of March 12, 1701 (*ibid.*, XX, 381); *Boislisle*, "Corresp. des contrôleurs gén.," I, 565. Edict Jan. 18, 1695; suppression in 1698; reëstablishment in 1704. Product in 1789: 42,192,000 livres. "Gr. Encycl.," see "Capitation"; comparative legislation. "Klassensteuer" in Prussia in 1820 (about 44 millions, more than a million prosecutions). *Necker*, "Admin. des fin.," ch. VII; *Moreau de Beaumont*, II, 421.

[7] *Esmein*, 562, sees in the capitation tax a tax on the income, for the tax imposed on all persons in the same class was fixed according to their presumed income.

Louis XIV (1695, 1704). The taxpayers were divided into twenty-two classes according to their wealth and their profession. The dauphin, by himself, formed the first class and was taxed 2000 livres; simple workmen, day laborers, and servants, who formed the last, paid one livre each. But the tax lost its original form. Among the peasant class ("roturiers") it was fixed in proportion to their share of the "taille" ("capitation taillable") and became an accessory of the "taille." The nobility, the clergy, and the cities acquired privileges of such a sort that in the end the capitation tax fell for the most part upon the "taille" payers.

§ 452. **"Tenths" and "Twentieths."** [1] — Appropriating the ideas of Vauban in his "Dîme Royale," the comptroller general, Desmarets, by the Declaration of October 14, 1710, levied a tax of a tenth on the declared income of the taxpayers; [2] but while Vauban took care to substitute this tax in the place of all others, Desmarets abolished no other. The "twentieth" was superimposed upon the already existing taxes. The amount varied widely: a "fiftieth" over and above was added in 1725; after 1749 (Edict of May) it was styled the "twentieth," then a second (1756), and a third twentieth, then four sous per livre in addition (in all sixteen per cent of the income).

Theoretically, the "twentieth" was imposed upon all incomes, in fact, it was levied almost entirely upon incomes from landed property (among which were included interest and in particular debentures). Necker (November 2, 1777) abolished in the boroughs ("bourgs") and in the country districts the "twentieths of industry" (income from manufactures, commerce, and offices), leaving them in existence only in the cities. At the same time he made the quota unalterable for twenty years in order to avoid the troubles resulting from incessant revisions, a consideration, which, during our century, has always given way before the equal distribution of the land tax.

This tax was criticized for its vexatious and odiously inquisitorial character. There were no frauds which the taxpayers did not

[1] *Isambert*, "Table," see "Impôt"; *Houques-Fourcade*, "Hist. du Dixième et du Cinquantième," 1889; *Marion*, "Les rôles du Vingtième dans el Toulousain," "Rév. fr.," 1894; *Machault*, 1892. *Cf.*, on *Vauban*, *Michel*, 1878; *Mellion*, 1886; *Lohmann*, 1895; *A. de Boislisle*, "La proscr. du Projet de Dîme royale," 1875.

[2] Saint Simon relates that at the time of establishing the tenth, Louis XIV had some scruples about his right to impose new taxes on his subjects; but his conscience was put at ease by P. le Tellier and by consultation with the Sorbonne which declared that all the property of his subjects was his, and that it was a favor for him to leave them what he did not take. *Supra*, p. 340.

commit in order to escape the tax. The more the rate of the tax varied the more they concealed their wealth; they were afraid of being fleeced without mercy if their wealth was known. Bodin in 1577 maintained that the tax should be real and not personal, and this was the dominant opinion in 1789.

§ 453. **Privileges.** — Based on equality in principle, capitation taxes and the "twentieth" left room for privileges. The clergy in 1710 bought them up at a small cost by paying once for all the sum of twenty-four millions. The nobility subject "ex officio" to the capitation tax [1] and paying only one eighth of their share, obtained also a favorable arrangement in respect to the "twentieths." [2] The "Countries of Estates" ("pays d'Etats") and many cities compounded for theirs. Had it not been for the frauds and exemptions, the income from these taxes would have been double what it was.

TOPIC 5. INDIRECT TAXES

§ 454. **The Aids** [3] ("**auxilia**") [4] were a tax collected on the sale and transportation of merchandise or objects of consumption and especially on drinks.[5] Hardly more than two fifths of the kingdom were subjected to this tax (district of the Court of Aids of Paris and that of Rouen) [6] and there was no uniformity in the method

[1] By the intendant, under the pretext that subordinates would not have dared to tax the nobles rigorously; in reality, the intendant fixed as he pleased the amount of the tax that they had to pay.

[2] Letter from a gentleman to the intendant of his generality: "Your tender heart would never consent to a father of my station being subjected to the rigid tax of the twentieths as it would in the case of a common father."

[3] BIBLIOGRAPHY: *Fleury*, p. 160; *Jacquin*, "Comment. s. l'Ord. juin 1680," 1703; *Lefebvre de la Ballande*, "Traité des droits d'aides," 1770; *Rousset*, "Hist. des imp. indir. en Fr.," 1883; *Jacqueton*, "Admin. fin.," p. 122 (Ord. 1508); p. 170 (Ord. 1517); p. 275 ("Vestige des finances").

[4] By the word "aides" was meant at first feudal aids, or subsidies (supplies) granted the king, then all levies of taxes for the necessities of the State, the "taille," salt taxes, etc. "Sensu stricto," the meaning was limited to that which was paid on provisions and merchandise. *Isambert*, III, 46 (1314); IV, 633 (1350), etc.; V, 405 (1374) · VI, 589 (1383); VIII, 834 (1435). Especially Ord. 1680.

[5] Originally, the "aide" was paid by men of all conditions. *Isambert*, VI, 582; VII, 79; VI, 823. Privileged from the "aide" were: members of the Parliament, of the Chamber of Accounts, clergy (exempt from the "aide" on the produce of Church lands), and the nobles (in case of the sale of wine from their inherited lands).

[6] Outside of these limits there were analogous taxes: the "équivalent" in Languedoc, the "ferme des devoirs" in Brittany, the "masphening" in Alsace, etc. The "équivalent" was the commutation price of "aides" in certain provinces. *Spont*, "L'équivalent aux aides en Languedoc, 1450–1515" ("Ann. du Midi," 1891, 232). "Encycl. méth.," see "Devoir."

of collection;[1] they included the duties on wine sold at wholesale, increases of eighths, fourths, subventions, import duties, "octrois," — in all twenty-five general taxes and as many local dues.[2] In each "généralité," in each "élection" the taxes varied.[3] If we add the customs ("traites") and the tolls ("péages") which were often superimposed upon those mentioned above, we can understand how the price of a hogshead of Bordeaux wine was increased in the north of France to ten times its value.[4]

Sharing the prejudices of the physiocrats against indirect taxes[5] the Constitutional Assembly abolished aids (March 2–17, 1791), but they reappeared in 1804 under the form of taxes on beverages.[6]

§ 455. **The "Gabelle"**[7] or salt tax,[8] levied at first like the aids for extraordinary purposes, became, like them, a permanent tax. Most of the seigniors sold salt to their subjects at a price fixed by

[1] The regulation instituted by the Farmers-General (for which Necker substituted the "Régie") formed the basis of the existing legislation on drinks. *Stourm*, I, 831. Product: in the neighborhood of fifty millions in 1789.

[2] Ordinary "aides": 1st, Tax on sales in gross, 5 per cent on sales certified to by the taxpayer (annual inventory of the crop, preëmption for the farm, etc.). Augmentation, 0 fr. 31 cent. per hectare. 2d, An eighth on retail sales, 2 fr. 01 or 2 fr. 51 per hect., plus a fourth proportional to the price of sale. 3d, Entries for the benefit of the treasury in the principal towns. *Stourm*, I, 326. "Octroi" taxes were also levied by towns on wine or provisions which were brought in or taken out, by virtue of permission given by the king (Letters of "octroi"); the product was divided between the king and the town (Ord. 1647, 1667, 1681, 1758). *Ferrière*, Dict., see "Octroi." Extraordinary "aides," for example in 1639; revolts in Normandy and Languedoc. Taxes annexed to the farm of "aides" ("droits réunis"); gauge and brokerage, 1527; annual, 1577; mark of gold, of silver, of iron, 1626; tax on cards, 1577, etc. *Stourm*, II, 91. "Table," see "Encycl. méth."

[3] These differences which shock our sense of equality had their origin, and to a certain extent their reason for existence, in economic conditions and in the system of decentralization of ancient France. Necker still saw here taxes whose assessment and collection were left to the local authorities.

[4] According to *M. d'Avenel*, II, 160, the increase of the tax on the transportation of drinks interfered more with commerce than did the levying of "aides."

[5] *Dupont de Nemours*, "Projets de droits sur les boissons," 1790; *Condorcet*, *op. cit.*, vol. VIII, 339, 361.

[6] Product in 1789, in the neighborhood of fifty millions. "Régie."

[7] BIBLIOGRAPHY: *Isambert*, "Table," h. vo.; *Brillon*, see "Gabelles"; *Fleury*, p. 164; *Ducrocq*, "Le mém. de Boulainvilliers sur l'amortiss. des gabelles," 1884; *Ramel*, "Finances de la Républ. fr.," "Gr. Encycl.," h. vo. (bibl.); *Jacqueton*, *op. cit.*, p. 226 ("Vestige des finances"); *Spont*, "Ann. du Midi," 1891, 427 (Languedoc); *Tomassetti*, "Le sel et le fouage de Rome au moyen âge" ("Arch. Soc. Rom. d. storia," 1897, t. 20); Germany: *Schröder*, p. 532 (bibl.); "Encycl. méth.," see "Gabelle."

[8] *Du Cange*, see "Gablum" having the signification of "cens," tribute, and "Gaule," "Gablagium," "Gabella vini," "salis," etc. Broadly, the "gabelle" was used to include all kinds of taxes; in the end the word came to mean only the tax on salt. *Cf.*, however, *Hatzfeld and Thomas*, "Dict. de la langue fr.," "Encycl. mét."; "gabel," tribute in Germany?

themselves; the seigniorial monopoly was in time superseded by the royal monopoly.[1] In 1345 the sale of salt was organized throughout the kingdom and the Estates of 1355 adopted the "gabelle" which continued in force until the Revolution. All salt produced had to be carried to the king's salt store houses; there the comptrollers of the salt storehouses bought it from the owners of salt marshes, at first at a price agreed upon by mutual consent, later at a price fixed by a tariff; they sold in bulk (wholesale), and the retailers or hucksters commissioned by them resold it in small quantities at a price fixed by a tariff. The tax was collected at the time of the sale, the king's price being higher than that of the merchant. Finally, in order to be certain that the tax would be paid, the obligation was imposed upon families of buying "duty salt" — that is an amount supposed to be necessary for their needs (at least in the countries of the "grande gabelle.")[2] This tax, questionable in principle, since it was levied upon an article of prime necessity and prevented freedom of sale, was one of the most badly organized of the "Ancien Régime": onerous, unequal, and vexatious for all.[3] The price of salt varied in unbelievable proportions, here selling for 2 livres per quintal, there as high as 60 livres. France was divided in this respect into six principal regions: the provinces of the "grande gabelle," the "petite gabelle," the "quart-bouillon," the "salines," the "redeemed" and the "franches"; the price was not even uniform in each of these parts.[4] Such a system conduced to fraud (dealers in contraband

[1] Ord. 1318. *Cf. Lehugeur*, "Phil. le Long," vol. II. Collection by the method of farming 1500s (1547, general lease for each storekeeper in particular; 1605, general lease for the "gabelles" of France, that is, where the "gabelle" was established in ancient times).

[2] A "minot" (3 bushels) or 39.36 litres for 14 persons. In the "redeemed" countries, the least possible quantity was delivered in order to compel the purchase of an additional quantity at a very high price.

[3] "The fiscal agent examined the cellar, tested the brine, tasted the salt, declared, if the salt was too good, that it was smuggled, because that of the farm, which alone was legitimate, was ordinarily damaged, and mixed with coarse plaster." The salt for industrial uses was tainted. The transportation of salt from abroad was prohibited, without which, the inequalities and privileges could not have been maintained; the production of salt was also limited; agents threw back into the sea that which was formed naturally. *Condorcet, op. cit.*, p. 377; *Champion*, "France en 1789," 110.

[4] In the region of the great "gabelle," the center of France, comprising about two thirds of the territory of France, the price of salt was 1 fr. 25 per kil.; but there were privileged places where the price was 10 centimes per kil. Burgundy was in the region of the great "gabelle" (58 livres per quintal); Dijon was privileged (7 l.); Franche-Comté was in the region of the salines "gabelle" (25 l.); Mâconnais, little gabelle (28 l.); Gex, free province (2 to 7 l.); country "redeemed," 9 l.; in the region of the "quart-bouillon" 16 l. Privileged persons had the right of free sale (royal

salt); an army of agents and the infliction of atrocious punishments did not succeed in preventing it. A third of the galley slaves, said Necker, were smugglers, and there were arrested in an ordinary year for fraudulent smuggling of salt 2300 men, 1800 women, and 6600 children.[1]

Necker desired to remedy the evils of the "gabelle" by transforming it into a uniform tax collected on salt at the time of its extraction. The Constitutional Assembly, animated by the proposals of the assembly of notables and the doctrines of the physiocrats and driven on by the popular tumult, preferred to abolish it and to substitute for it additional direct taxes (Decrees of March 30 and October 26, 1790) which remained unpaid and had to be abolished (June 13, 1794). The tax on salt reappeared in 1806 (Decree of March 16) in the form which Necker had desired to give it.[2]

§ 456. **The "Traites"**[3] (*cf.* customs duties) were derived 1st, from seigniorial tolls which the annexation of fiefs to the royal domain did not destroy; 2d, from old prohibitions on the exportation of articles of prime necessity, such as grain, wine, etc., — a measure of prudence at first justified by the difficulty of exchange; there was the danger of lacking the necessaries of life and it was necessary to make provision for the home supply before allowing exportations; or, again, it was a question of gold, or of silver, or of the munitions of war and there was fear of impoverishing or enfeebling the kingdom.[4] These genuine reasons of former times became by the end of the 1300 s a mere pretext. It was well seen when Philip the Fair in 1305 in the midst of his financial embarrassment forbade the exportation of most merchandise;

officers, and magistrates) that is, the right of purchasing salt at cost price. Nobles and ecclesiastical owners of salt marshes. *Boiteau*, p. 367. *Cf. Taine*, "L'Ancien Régime," p. 469.

[1] Penalties: fines, six to nine years at the galleys, death. Originally, punishments were still more severe; thus, horses and other animals were torn to pieces. Informing was obligatory under penalty of heavy fines. Ord. 1680, vol. 17.

[2] Actual product: about thirty millions; in 1789, about sixty millions plus the benefice from the contract of farmage — eighteen to twenty millions.

[3] *Fleury*, p. 156; *Du Fresne de Francheville*, "Hist. des finances," 1738 (tariff of 1664); *Callery*, "Les douanes avant Colbert," "R. hist.," 1882, 49; *Saulnier*, "Rech. hist. s. le dr. de douane," 1839; *Stourm*, I, 470; II, 1; *Isambert*, "Table," see "Douanes," etc.; *Comte de Butenval*, "Etabl. en France du 1er tarif général des douanes," 1787–91, 1880; Germany: "customs duties," *cf. Schröder*, p. 522; *Dowell*, "Hist. of taxation in England," 1888; *Hall*, "Hist. of custom," 1885.

[4] *Isambert*, "Table," see "Espèces d'or et d'argent," "Exportation," "Grains," "Ports francs"; *Luchaire*, 597; *Vuitry*, II, 143.

five days after having issued this impracticable decree, he created a master of ports and passages in order to sell permits to export. The taxes on "haut passage," the "rêve,"[1] and the "imposition foraine" (levied to pay for the ransom of King John), all of which in the end became confused with one another, were taxes on exportation. From this was derived the name "traite" and "traite foraine" (a tax on merchandise carried out of the kingdom).[2] Taxes on imports, which are so considerable to-day, were slow in being established; while conversely, taxes on exports, formerly very heavy, have been reduced to a mere trifle.[3] Before the 1500 s there was nothing to fear from foreign competition; systematic protection of home industries hardly existed before the time of Colbert (1664).[4] Introduced by the accident of the feudal partitions, multiplied by the rapacity of the seigniors, tolls and "traites" covered the entire country with innumerable barriers, veritable internal customs which hindered all commerce.[5] Colbert was of the opinion, and rightly, that by reducing the general wealth they were prejudicial to the interests of the State; regarding them as in contradiction with the logic of the monarchical system he desired to abolish them; but he only partially succeeded. In consequence of the measures that he adopted France was divided into three regions: 1st, the provinces of the "five great farms" (so called from the five principal taxes leased out at first to five farmers, later "en bloc" to the farmers-general: the foreign "traite," the domainal "traite," the entry tax on spices and drugs,

[1] For "rueve," verbal substantif for "rover" ("rogare"). This word is still used in the southwest of France to designate the rent in silver paid by the small farmer to the proprietor. [2] England: customs duties.

[3] The Estates of 1614 demanded the absolute prohibition of the importation of all manufactured products similar to ours, the suppression of the entry tax on raw materials used in our industries, and finally a prohibition of the exportation of French products suitable for use as raw materials in foreign countries. *Dareste*, II, 218. These grievances were the expression of general opinion under the old régime. "Rec. de régles s. les manufactures," 1730.

[4] *Lavisse et Rambaud*, "Hist. gén.," VII, 680; *Monod*, Bibl., n°s 1345 *et seq.*; *cf.* *Cauwès*, "Econ. polit.," bibliog.; *P. Clément*, "Hist. du syst. protecteur," 1854; *Afanassiev*, "Le commerce des céréales," 1894; *Biollay*, "Et. écon. sur le XVIIIe s.," 1885; *cf.* *Bonassieux*, "Cahiers de 1789 au p. de v. industriel et commercial"; *Le Trosne*, "La liberté du commerce des grains," 1765; "Rec. des lois sur le com. des grains," 1769.

[5] Innumerable local taxes: *cf.* enumeration in Law of Nov. 5, 1790, relating to the suppression of "traites." Let us add about 1,600 tolls belonging to the king or to the seigniors. "Ephémérides du citoyen," vol. V, 1775 (mission of M. Blanchet to buy wine in the South to bring it himself to Paris in order to render an account "de visu" of fiscal collections: from Roanne to Melun, 24 "tolls" or octrois). *Stourm*, I, 473; *Guilmoto*, "Les dr. de navig. de la Seine du onzième au dix-huitième s.," 1889.

on cloth of gold or silk, and on commodities in bulk); [1] this region embraced the twelve provinces of central France and they formed a sort of customs union within which goods circulated freely (tariff of 1664); 2d, the provinces reputed as foreign (notably the South, Brittany, etc.); they formed a second union with a higher tariff (tariff of 1667); 3d, the provinces in imitation of the real foreign countries (Alsace, Labourd, Gex, etc.) which traded freely with foreign countries, but not with France.[2] At the end of the 1700 s the abolition of these taxes became easier with the progress of centralization; their inconveniences impressed all the sensible minds (Trudaine, Turgot's Decree of the Council September 13, 1774, on the liberty of commerce in grains throughout the kingdom,[3] and Necker); [4] an edict of abolition was prepared following the deliberation of the Notables; the Constitutional Assembly had only to adopt it (Decrees of Oct. 30–31 and Nov. 5, 1790). The economists Quesnay and Turgot were not only partisans of the abolition of internal customs duties; contrary to all the accepted ideas, they maintained the principle of freedom of trade. Their liberal theories of trade came to be incorporated in the treaty of commerce of 1786 between France and England and especially in the tariff presented to the Notables in 1787, a tariff which the Constitutional Assembly reproduced in 1791 (with some restrictions).[5]

§ 457. **The Stamp Tax** (Edict of March, 1673, and August, 1674).[6] The document duty (to-day the stamp tax) was imposed upon judicial and notarial instruments, for the preparation of which it was necessary to use paper or parchment stamped with

[1] *Fleury*, p. 156. *Cf.* concerning this enumeration and the number of provinces, "Encycl. mét.," see "Cinq. gr. f."

[2] Contentious jurisdiction: First instance, masters of ports and bureaus of "traites"; appeal, Chamber of Accounts, at first, later the Court of "Aides."

[3] Measures taken by Machault, 1749; Decl. May 25, 1763; Dec. 23, 1770.

[4] Order in Council of Aug. 15, 1779, declaring in favor of the principle of the repurchase of seigniorial tolls, but putting off the execution of this measure until the conclusion of peace. Some seigniors surrendered voluntarily their rights to charge tolls. *Stourm*, I, 477.

[5] But October 10, 1795, the importation of English merchandise was prohibited.

[6] *Bosquet*, "Dict. des domaines," h. vis.; "Rec. d'Edits et règl. concern. les domaines," 1719; *id.*, "le contrôle des actes"; *id.*, "le contrôle des exploits," 1689; *Berthelot*, "Traité des domaines," 1719; "Comment. s. le tarif du contrôle" by *Contramont; id.*, by *Basin; Dupin*, "Instr. s. div. quest. rel. au dr. de contrôle," 1787; *Poisson*, "Confér. sur l'éd. du contr." ("Tr. Régale"); *La Garde*, "Souv. du roi," ch. XXI *et seq.; Salefranque*, "Le timbre à travers l'histoire," 1882; *Stourm*, I, 394; England: *Fischel*, II, 338.

the arms of the king and having models of legal forms ("formules") with only the blanks to fill in. After 1674 the "formules" were changed into a mark or stamp on the sheets used for public instruments. The stamp varied with each "généralité."[1] This tax yielded little, was not imposed upon documents under private seal, and was applied in only a part of France.[2] The Assembly of Notables in 1787 elaborated a plan which developed the tax and which was transformed into an edict (August 4, 1787), but which was revoked by the king in consequence of the opposition of the Parliament (September, 1787). The law of the 17th of February, 1791, was suggested by it but was passed in such ineffective form that the proceeds from the tax were not sufficient to meet the expense. After some reforms the definitive law of the 13th Brumaire, year VII (1799), was enacted.

§ 458. **The "Contrôle," the "Insinuation," and the "Centième Denier"** corresponded to our registration fees. The "**contrôle**" (1693) consisted in the registration of legal instruments by abstract[3] upon a public register and in the certificate of registration which was attached to the instrument;[4] the purpose of it was to give the instrument a definite date as against third persons. The "**insinuation**" (1703) was the copy in full or the mention by abstract of a document (donation, sale, etc.) in a register kept by a sworn officer, who was obliged to give information to all who requested it. Thus "insinuated" documents were brought to the knowledge of the public.[5]

[1] *Guyot*, "Rép.," see "Formule"; *Esmein*, p. 578; Revolt in Brittany in 1675 ("Ann. de Bret.," 1898). Ord. 1680, Declar. June 16, 1691, etc. *Cf.* Nov. 44 of Justinian.

[2] Exemption for Artois, Flanders, Alsace, Franche-Comté, etc. *Isambert*, "Table," see "Timbre."

[3] Containing the names of the parties, character of the act, the date, name of the notary, and the number of sheets. *Cf. Ferrière*, "Science des notaires."

[4] Edict June, 1581, June, 1627, Dec., 1635; but the institution was well organized and generalized only by the Edict of March 1693 (Tariff of 1708), at least for acts of notaries. The purpose was to avoid forgery, antedating, suspicions, contests. Edict August 1669, providing for the registration of the writs of bailiffs (to prevent antedating and falsifying). For acts under private seal, Decl. July 14, 1699, Edict October 1705 (they had to be registered before they could be produced in court).

[5] *Cf.* concerning the "insinuation" tax at Rome, *Girard*, "Précis de dr. r.," 2d ed., p. 918; *Isambert*, "Table," see "Insinuation." Ord. Aug., 1539, Art. 132 (donation: registry under penalty of nullity). *Isambert*, XII, 627. Edict, May, 1553: "insinuation" of acts of sale, donation, and of obligation exceeding 50 livres. Ord. Moulins, 1566, Art. 57. Decl. May, 1645. Ecclesiastical "insinuations" (that is to say the registration of acts concerning the State and possessions of ecclesiastics), June, 1595; Dec., 1691. Laical "insinuations," Edict., Dec., 1703 (that is to say, "insinuation" of acts of donations, legacies, sales, etc). *La Garde*, ch. XXV.

The hundredth farthing ("**centième denier**") was a tax on transfers, collected for the benefit of the king over and above the feudal dues or quitrents paid to the seignior.[1] On the occasion of the "insinuation" of acts transferring the ownership or use of immovables, fiefs, copyholds, or even free alods, the recorder collected one per cent of the price or the estimated value of these properties. It mattered little whether the transfer took place by succession by intestacy, by testament, by donation "inter vivos," or by sale; the tax was due even when there was no written transaction.[2] The high rate of these taxes enlightens us concerning their true character; they were fiscal expedients, and not a means by which the State obtained a just compensation for the expense which it incurred in service of the public, through assuring the preservation of legal documents, their authenticity, and their publicity, and so preventing litigation. There was complaint during the 1700 s, with some exaggeration it appears, of the arbitrariness and the harshness with which the tax was collected.[3]

The law of December 19, 1790, relative to registration fees unified the rules in regard to the subject matter, which was well, but it confused the administration, and this required the substitution of a better law, that of the 22d Frimaire, year VII (1799). This law was merely a revision of the old ordinances of the monarchy bringing them into harmony with modern ideas.

§ 459. **Collection of Indirect Taxes.** — At the end of the 1600 s all the revenues of the king were collected by the process of farming out, except the "taille" and the "bois." This extension of the very old system of tax farming and the preference which

Complete copy of donations, registry by extracts of legacies, etc. *Renaud*, "R. de lég.," 1872; "L'enreg. en Fr. au Moyen âge."

[1] Edict Aug., 1706 (*Isambert*, XX, 488). *Isambert*, "Table," see "Droits de mutation," "Contrôle"; *La Garde*, ch. XXV. Tariff of 1722.

[2] "Insinuation" of the act or declaration of succession in six months. Exception for the transfer in direct line by succession and by marriage contract. "Subscription" provinces, like Flanders.

[3] According to a Memoir submitted to the national Assembly by the Royal Society of Agriculture for the acquisition of immovable property worth 26,000 livres, one paid: 6240 livres for the seignior's fifth; 850 livres for the 100th "denier"; 260 livres for the expenses of the transaction, in all, 7091 livres, that is to say 27 per cent of the price. Remonstrance of Malesherbes in the name of the Court of "Aides," in 1775: "Your Majesty should know that all the taxes of 'contrôle,' of 'insinuation' and of the 'centième denier' which are imposed in legal instruments are regulated according to the whims of the tax farmers or of their agents; that the pretended laws on the subject are so obscure and so incomplete that those who have to pay them never know how much they owe; that often, the excise officer does not know any better, and that they permit interpretations more or less rigorous according as the officer is more or less greedy" (cited by *Stourm*, I, 398).

the "Ancien Régime" showed for it in comparison with excise officers ("régie"), are not inexplicable. 1st, Originally there was little difference between the system of farming and that of excise officers. These officers reimbursed themselves by retaining a portion of the receipts; only what was left reached the king. The tax farmer negotiated for it as a speculation, remitted in advance his share to the king, and kept the remainder for himself. 2d, The treasury suffered from fraud, excessive expenses, delays in the payments, and the insolvency of financial officers; on the other hand, "the amount paid by the tax farmer for his contract went with certainty to the king." A decisive reason, this; but the tax farmer, profiting from the embarrassment of the treasury, fleeced the State as he did the taxpayers.[1] "No pity," said Adam Smith, "ever touched a man whose fortune was derived from the collection of taxes." However, the "Ancien Régime" sought to correct the evils of the system by substituting general leases in the place of special leases which alone were practiced at first. The farmers-general disciplined their agents, made good functionaries of them, imposed minute regulations upon them, and thus prepared the way for the modern system of administration.

§ 460. **The Farmers-General.**[2] — For a long time the collection of each tax was the object of a special lease in each bailiwick (or even in each provostship). The inequalities resulting from this defective procedure, the arbitrary prices of the leases, the few guarantees which the farmers offered, and the practice of subleasing to subfarmers who made bad use of them, led Sully to group together similar taxes in such a way as to make four farms-general which the Council of Finances sold at auction to tax farmers ("traitants") or contractors ("partisans"), so called because they were bound to the king by a treaty ("traité") or by conditions ("parti"). Colbert went a little farther and gave a company of forty financiers, the "farmers-general," the right of collecting throughout all France the entire amount of what we should call indirect contributions (1680).[3]

[1] *Montesquieu*, "Esprit des lois," 13, 20; *cf.* "Encycl. méth.," see "Ferme."

[2] *P. Clément and Lemoine*, "M. de Silhouette et les Anciens f. g.," 1865; *Lemoine*, "Les derniers fermiers généraux," 1873; *Delahante*, "Une famille de finance au XVIIIe s.," 1881; *De Janzé*, "Les financiers d'autrefois," 1881; *Chardon*, "Une direction de l'enregistrement," 1887; *Grimaux*, "Lavoisier," 1888; *Besson*, "Gr. Encycl.," h. vo. "Mémoire justificatif" presented to the Convention by *Lavoisier*. "Mémoire" of *Abbé Terray; Isambert*, "Table," see "Ferme," etc.; *Guyot*, "Répert.," see "Ferme générale"; "Rec. des Ord. des fermes," 1750.

[3] The State gained by this system; besides there was a great simplifica-

The lease for tax farming was made for six years in the name of a straw man, who may be compared with the "manceps" of the societies of publicans at Rome.[1] After having signed the contract with the king this dummy (*e.g.* Jean Fauconnet, 1681, and Laurent David, 1774), often a valet, contented himself with receiving an annual salary of 4000 livres; he had neither part nor responsibility in the management of the company; but the award of the contract, as well as legal actions, took place in his name. The company was, in appearance, only his surety; it gave a bond to the amount of ninety millions furnished in equal parts by its members, each of whom was obliged to obtain from the king a warrant as a farmer-general.[2] At Paris the company had a central administration and it conducted inspections in the provinces; in each "généralité" were found inspectors, directors, controllers, verifiers, and clerks:[3] the actual administration.

The unpopularity of those taxes whose collection was confided to them (the "gabelle" and the "traites") was reflected upon the farmers-general. Voltaire summarized in a satiric sentence the opinion of his contemporaries when he said: "There are in Persepolis forty plebeian kings who hold by lease the Empire of Persia and who pay for it something to the king." The monarch and the courtiers were at least associated in what may be regarded as a system of legal plunder. The indiscretion of a

tion in the method of rendering accounts, and the State received a higher price for the farming of the taxes as a result of the reduction of the general expenses.

[1] *Ferrière,* see "Fermes du roi." Ord. July 22, 1681 concerning the forms of contract. In the 1700 s, the auctioning of the contract no longer took place in public; the controller general of finances discussed the price with the farmers, after which, a decree of the council, called the "résultat," assured them the enjoyment of the contract. *Cf.* "Réglement" of March 27, 1780. "Encycl. Méth," see "Bail." Price of 56,670,000 livres, raised to 162 millions in 1774 ("Gabelles," 35,196,000; "traites" and five large farms, 14,031,300; "Aides," 33,983,200; Tobacco, 22,208,700, etc.).

[2] Appointments depended, then, in a certain measure, on the public authorities.

[3] *Central service:* 1. The section of committees (treasuries, personnel, contentious questions, pensions, "gabelle," tobacco, "traites"). Each department was subdivided into bureaus with chiefs, subchiefs, clerks, a director, and a committee of tax farmers. 2. The section of correspondence; 3. The section of inspection.

Regional Service: 1. A director in each generality; 2. Inspectors; 3. Traveling controllers and verifiers; 4. Clerks (exempt from the "taille," the salt tax, and the duty of lodging soldiers, etc.). Ord. July, 1681, Art. 11. Edict March, 1696. Notaries, "procureurs," and recorders, charged with the collection of the taxes of "contrôle," etc., showed but little zeal: from this, came the institution of supernumeraries, July 28, 1774.

clerk under the ministry of Terray disclosed the perquisites ("pots-de-vin"), the New Year's gifts to the ministers, and the pensions and rake-offs given to courtiers,[1] all of which contributed no little to increase the discredit of the system of revenue farming.[2] Under Louis XVI public sentiment made itself felt by securing the abolition of a bonus of 100,000 gold crowns ("écus") given to the comptroller general upon the occasion of each new lease (Turgot), and by a reform more far-reaching, due to Necker, who allowed only "traites," "entrées" at Paris, "gabelles" and the tax on tobacco to be farmed; aids and domainal dues were confided to general excise commissioners and to the administration of the domains; collected by the State, the proceeds of these taxes doubled (order of January 9, 1780). At the same time the number of farmers-general, which in 1755 had risen to sixty, was reduced to forty, a fact which permitted the purging of the company. But these measures did not save the system of tax farming at the time of the Revolution, nor prevent the tax farmers from being condemned to death by the Revolutionary tribunal, May 8, 1794, under the pleas of conspiracy against the State, exactions, and of poisoning (mixing with tobacco ingredients injurious to health); they were even accused of having retained money which they owed the State, in order to supply it to foreign governments.[3] It was proven ultimately that far from owing the treasury anything, they had in fact made advances to it to the amount of eight millions ("arrêt" of May 1, 1806).[4]

[1] Perquisite ("pot-de-vin") of 100,000 gold crowns ("écus") to the comptroller general at each renewal of the lease, a New Year's gift of 200,000 livres per year to ministers, pensions to courtiers, 400,000 livres in 1776. Mme. du Barry had stipulated with her protégé, Bouret d'Erigny, for a "croupe" of 200,000 livres. The king appropriated for his own use, by means of three "croupes" the proceeds of an entire farmer-general (about 300,000 livres per year).

[2] Ostentatious life of certain farmers, Grimod de la Reymère, Bouret, etc. Popelinière patronized authors without fortune, provided dowries for six poor girls. Rousseau "became as fat as a priest" at the home of a tax farmer named Dupin.

[3] The Constitutional Assembly suppressed "aides," "gabelles," etc., and abolished the "farmers-general" (March 26, 1790, Feb. 19–25, 1791, March 2–17, 1791). The Convention of Sept. 27, 1793, instructed a committee to revise the accounts; on the 4th Frim., year II, it ordered the arrest of the farmers of the last three leases (among others Lavoisier). *Cf.* "Moniteur" of 20 Flor., year III.

[4] Instead of paying the price of the lease to the treasury, the farmer had a current account with it and honored the State's drafts. At the end of the lease, if there was a receipt above six annuities of the farm, the surplus was divided between the farmer and the State. In 1780, there was thus a surplus of thirty millions to divide.

Topic 6. The Public Debt

§ 461. **The Public Debt.**[1] — It was under Francis I (1535) that the first bonds were issued, called the bonds of the City Hall ("Hôtel-de-Ville").[2] The treasury being exhausted on account of the war with Milan, this prince, at the end of his resources, borrowed 200,000 livres (Tours currency) from the city of Paris. His commissioners negotiated with the provost and "échevins" and promised to pay in return for the principal 25,000 livres interest with an assignment for their payment of the proceeds from the aids and other taxes collected at Paris. On their part, the provost and the "échevins" were obliged to ask of the wealthiest citizens[3] the necessary amount to complete the sum of 200,000 livres promised the king. The king did not, therefore, make an individual and direct appeal to the capitalists; he had recourse to the city of Paris, whose credit, better established, served to guarantee his own, and the loan was half forced, because in case of refusal by the citizens there is no doubt that pressure would have been brought to bear to obtain the sum promised by the municipal authorities.[4] From the moment when the city served as an intermediary between the State and the capitalists, the administration of the debt, the payment of the interest, and, in case of need, of the reimbursement, and the decision of controversies which arose, concerned only the municipal authorities;[5] it was at the city hall that the income was paid, hence the name of the bonds.

The prohibition on lending money for interest caused the proceeding to take the form of a settlement of perpetual annuities; this was the customary procedure for avoiding this superannuated rule. The State profited by it, moreover, since it could never be forced to pay back the capital it had received; but it always reserved the right of redemption, that is, the right to extinguish its obligations by reimbursing the lender for the principal received

[1] *L. Delisle*, "Mém. s. les opérations financières des Templiers," 1887 ("Ac. Inscr.," t. 33); *Vührer*, "Hist. de la dette publique en France," 1886; *Le Roi*, "Le contrôle des rentes," "Jurisprud. des rentes," 1762; *Loyseau*, "Tr. de la garantie des rentes" (Works, ed. 1666); *Isambert*, "Table," see "Dettes du roi," "Emprunts," "Caisses," etc.

[2] There was an anterior loan to the Temple from Italian bankers, especially to the towns (loan often forced). *Luchaire*, 582; *Servois*, BCh. XIX; *Delisle*, "Opér. fin des Templiers," 1887.

[3] *Cf.* Tax of the "Aysés," 1553, 1570. *Vührer*, I, 24, 30 and following.

[4] And doubtless a beginning would have been made in that way, had there not been fear that resort to force would have caused capital to flee.

[5] Except the loans of the State to other towns, to the clergy, and to the provincial Estates.

and by fixing the hour and the day which were most convenient for it.[1] From the time of Francis I it was under the form of perpetual annuities that the loans of the State were contracted.[2] However, Pontchartrain procured funds by means of a royal tontine (1689),[3] and by issuing life annuities (1693).[4] In the 1700s recourse was frequently had to the (morally doubtful) expedient of a lottery (1700, 1717, etc.); an order in Council of June 30, 1776, gave it a definitive organization and a special administration.[5]

The history of the public debt reflects little honor upon the old monarchy; it was not dishonesty of which it was guilty [6] but delays in the payment of arrears, deduction of one or more quarters from the unfortunate bondholders, revision and reduction of interest dues,[7] and bankruptcy. The only thing that may be said in exoneration is that the creditors of the State were often little deserving of regard; they were treated as usurers and were compelled to disgorge without scruple because the State had received from them only a small part of the amount for which it acknowledged indebtedness.[8]

[1] Thanks to the subvention granted by the clergy, the public debt would have had to be paid; that was its object, but securities were issued on the expectation of this subvention as they had been on other anticipated taxes, and it served, on the contrary, to increase the public debt. *Vührer*, I, 27, 35, 58.

[2] Concerning the constitutional tax or "denier," *cf.* "Jurisprud. des rentes." The "denier 20" is our 5 per cent, or one livre of interest for twenty of capital.

[3] Conceived by the Italian, Laurent Tonti, who gave it his name, and tried at his suggestion, but without success, by Fouquet, 1653, the tontine consisted in the establishment of life annuities for the benefit of a certain number of subscribers; the survivors had the use of the share of those who died first; at the death of the last one, the capital was returned to the State.

[4] The first public loan in England was in 1693.

[5] The Edict of May, 1539, authorized the establishment of lotteries under the name of "Blanque" in the towns of the kingdom, in imitation of the practice of Italian towns,—on the moral grounds of averting licentious games. The king granted the privilege to every town in consideration of an annual sum. A royal lottery was established by the Decree of the Council of May 11, 1700. *Bouchard*, p. 150. Gambling houses were authorized. Insurances against fire, 1754; life insurance in 1787. Order in Council, July 27, 1788. See "Gr. Encycl."; *Isambert*, "Table."

[6] Reduction by Sully, 1604. Bankruptcy in 1660. Order in Council of 1664. Bankruptcy in 1713. John Law's system, *cf. Monod*, 4432 and following. Bankruptcy under Louis XV, with the Abbé Terray. Program of Turgot: neither loans nor new taxes could be applied. Sinking fund office established by Calonne, Edict Aug., 1784. *Vuitry*, "Le désordre des finances" (Louis XIV and Louis XV), 1885.

[7] In our time, conversions (refunding) are explained by a general lowering of the rate of interest; the State has the right to profit by it, like all debtors whose credit is well established, since it is easy for it to borrow at a low rate and to pay what it owes. Formerly, these operations took place under quite different conditions, although bonds were depreciated by the bad faith of the State and its lack of credit; it was a partial failure.

[8] Perpetual debentures were seizable. "Jurispr. des r.," see "Saisies."

TOPIC 7. FINANCIAL ADMINISTRATION[1] AND JURISDICTION[2]

§ 462. **Personnel of the Administration of Finances.** — Fleury (at the end of the 1600 s) pointed out a distinction in the personnel of the financial administration which made very slow progress and which, as late as 1789, was still very imperfect.[3] He distinguished: 1st, the **drawers of warrants** ("ordonnateurs") who were charged with prescribing the expenses; 2d, the **accountants** ("comptables"), charged with the management of the funds; and 3d, the **judges** to whom was confided the decision in disputed claims.[4] With Fleury we may also divide the history of the administration of the finances under the third dynasty into four periods: 1st, when the king had only the domain; 2d, after the imposition of extraordinary taxes; 3d, after the merging of ordinary with extraordinary impositions; and 4th, after the institution of farmers-general (already discussed above); at this time the official organization was duplicated by an independent organization more and more perfected, almost identical at the end of the "ancien régime" with the mechanism of a State, and entirely ready to become a part of the official organization.

§ 463. (A) **Ordinary Finances. The Domain.** — The administration of the domain was distinguished from the general administration only during the 1300 s. The provosts and the bailiffs, who were at the same time "ordonnateurs," paymasters,

Cf. Vührer, I, 33 (Edict, Oct. 18, 1566). They were exempted from the payment of the tenth and the twentieth. *Cf. Pech de Laclause*, Thesis, 1899. Sinking fund office (Machault, 1749). Bureau of accounts, 1776. Bourse; sixty stockbrokers; the newspapers published the quotations of the Bourse since 1789.

[1] *Isambert*, "Table," see "Aides," "Finances," "Trésor," "Comptables," etc.; *Jacqueton*, "Doc. relatifs à l'admin. fin. en France depuis Charles VII à François Ier," 1891; BCh., 1892, 164, 323, 676-680.

[2] *Pardessus*, "Organis. judic.," p. 210, and *Kovalewsky*, "Essai s. l'hist. de la jurid. fiscale en France depuis le XIVe s. jusqu'à la mort de Louis XIV," 1876 (in Russian); *Isambert*, "Table"; also see *R. Dareste*, "Justice administrative en France," 2e éd.

[3] "If the 'ordonnateurs' had had the handling of the funds, they would have disposed of them in their interest and to the detriment of the treasury; the judges could not be charged with the administration without being at the same time both judges and parties. As simple as these ideas were, it took centuries to put them into practice."

[4] List of financial courts. I. **Supreme Courts**: chambers of accounts, courts of "aides," and the chamber of the treasury; II. **Superior Courts** (of appeal): the court of the mint and the "Table of Marble" (for waters and forests); III. **Ordinary Courts**: courts of "elections," of salt storehouses, bureaus of finances, intendants, masters of ports, and judges of "traites," special masters of waters and forests and courts of mints; IV. **Inferior Courts**: "gruyers" and "verdiers."

and accountants,[1] began by paying the local expenses (salaries of the royal officers, expenses of managing the king's estate, etc.), turning over to the treasury only the net product of the receipts. The masters of waters and forests,[2] officers of the foreign impositions, and the mint masters were regarded as attached to the domain.

§ 464. **The Receivers.** — About 1320, the financial powers of the bailiffs and seneschals passed to **receivers**,[3] clerks or secretaries whom they had removed at will and of whom the State made royal agents with the power of handling the funds. The effect was to establish, at least in the provinces, a separation between the functions of the administrator and those of the accountant. But although the innovation was excellent, an exact reckoning of its import was not taken; it was regarded chiefly as a means of relieving the bailiffs. Instead of confining the receivers to the duty of accounting as should have been done for the good order of the finances, the mistake was made of giving them administrative powers.

§ 465. **The Treasurers of France**,[4] mere custodians or cashiers at first, centralized, under Philip the Fair, the administration of the finances, with the concurrence and under the surveillance of the Chamber of Accounts where they sat. The Ordinance of 1318 already mentioned a **chief** of treasurers, who was a sort of minister of finances, the predecessor of the superintendent. The treasury had no power to make a payment without the order of the king and the ratification of the treasurers.[5] Although the bailiffs retained

[1] Accounts of 1203, *Brussel*, "Us. des fiefs," t. II, CXXXIX; of 1226, *Petit Dutaillis*, "Louis VIII," p. 526, and *Borrelli de Serres*, "Rech. s. div. services publics," p. 299; of 1234, "Hist. Fr.," XXII, 566; of 1238, *ibid.*, XXI, 252; of 1248, *ibid.*, XXI, 260; of 1285, *ibid.*, XXII, 623 (Receipts: "racheta," "domania," "expleta"; Expenses: "feoda," "eleemosynæ," "liberationes," "opera," "minuta expensa"); *cf. Layettes*, III, 4380 (a. 1257); *Léchaude*, "Grands Rôles" ("Mém. Antiq. Norm.") 1846 (a. 1230).

[2] Inferior jurisdiction of "gruyers" and "verdiers"; the "ordinary" of special masters (Ord. 1283, 1291; Feb., 1318; July, 1367, Sept., 1402, etc.); court of appeal of the grand master ("Table de Marbre" in the "Palais de Justice" at Paris). Appeal to the Parliament of Paris (*cf.* L. 22 June, 1394; Ord. Nov., 1508). Afterwards, each Parliament had its "Table de Marbre" (1554). *Cf.* Edict 1704 (executed only at Douai and at Besançon). Its jurisdiction embraced: litigations and violations of law relating to waters and woods of the domain and not to those of private persons or communities. Ord. 1518, 1543, 1669.

[3] Ord. July, 1318; Jan., 1320; May 27, 1320; 1444. *Cf. Isambert*, "Table," see "Receveurs." Ord. Nov., 1323 (not executed). *Luchaire*, p. 602; *Couderc*, "Charles le Bel" (Thesis, "Ec. Chartes," 1886).

[4] *Luchaire*, p. 603 (bibl.); *Raguenet*, "Thèses Ec. Chartes," 1878; *P. Clément*, "Enguerrand de Marigny," 1857; *Fournival*, "Rec. des titres concernant les trésoriers de France," 1655.

[5] "Enteriner," that is to say, to initiate an act: to approve it, to confirm it, to order the execution of it.

the jurisdiction of disputed claims, a distinction was made (Ord. 1389) between : (*a*) the "treasurers in matter of finances," supreme administrators of the domainal property,[1] four in number and with four distinct districts (Normandy, Langue d'oïl, Languedoc, and the country beyond the Seine); and (*b*) the "treasurers in matter of justice," who were judges of domainal controversies;[2] here was the origin of the **Chamber of the Treasury** (end of the 1400 s),[3] the jurisdiction of which was extended over the entire kingdom; appeal from its decisions lay to the Parliament.[4]

§ 466. (B) **Extraordinary Finances. Division of the Kingdom into "Elections" and "Généralités."** — The Estates of 1355 reserved for themselves the collection, the administration, and the litigation of the taxes which they voted.[5] They appointed certain tax officials, taking them from the three Estates and conferring upon them both the power of administration and of jurisdiction.

[1] Under their surveillance an accountant, the "changeur du Trésor," received the domainal revenues, but deduction was made of the sums that the receivers paid, that is to say, "deniers revenants bons," and even deduction was made of the sums paid to liquidate the debts of the treasury against receipts or discharges delivered to its creditors. Closely associated with the accountant, were clerks or controllers of the treasury, who kept a record of receipts and expenses. *Cf.* **Treasury of Savings**, reserve funds for unexpected expenses, in which were deposited the proceeds from casual projects (Francis I, 1522). *Fleury*, p. 190. In case of ordinary or extraordinary financial confusion, all the net revenue of the king was deposited in the Savings Treasury, which was no longer distinguished from the royal treasury.

[2] *Baquet*, "Edits concern. la Ch. du Trésor," 1640; *Dareste*, I, 350; *Ferrière*, h. vo., "Gr. Encycl.," h. vo.; *Fleury*, p. 193; *Pardessus*, "Organ. jud."; *Bourneuf*, "Mém. sur les priv. et les fonct. des Trésoriers," 1745; *Miraulmont*, "Orig. des Cours souv.," 1584; *Jousse*, "Traité de la jurid. des trésoriers de France," 1777.

[3] The insufficiency of this court led Francis I to give the bailiffs and seneschals jurisdiction in domainal matters. Edict Crémieu, 1536; Feb., 1543. The Chamber of the Treasury exercised a rival jurisdiction with them, except in some bailiwicks in the neighborhood of Paris, where it had an exclusive jurisdiction until 1693, when it was suppressed.

[4] *Isambert*, "Table," see "Elections"; *Vieule*, "Traité des Elections," 1739; *Vuitry*, III, 140.

[5] "The generals of finance had, with regard to extraordinary revenues, powers analogous to those of the treasurers with regard to ordinary revenues. They were administrators and ordonnateurs of them and fulfilled, at the same time, the functions of inspectors general of the officers charged with collecting and distributing them. As the treasurers ratified acts relating to ordinary revenues, so the generals joined their seal of judicial ratification to mandates relating to extraordinary revenues, which were all addressed to them. There were four of them, and each had a generality under his direction; the generalities bore the same names and had the same boundaries as the circumscriptions of the treasurers of France." *Jacqueton*, p. xi. The receivers general of finance corresponded to the "changeur du Trésor," there being one for each generality; they paid the assignments addressed by the king to the generals not in specie, but in discharges, on the receivers of the "taille" or of "aides" and on the keepers of storehouses.

These officials were: 1st, nine **general superintendents** ("ordonnateurs") and inspectors charged with assuring the employment of the taxes for war purposes only; 2d, under them were the **elected superintendents**, charged with the apportionment and levy of the tax in each province. Both general and elected superintendents had near them receivers, some general, others special.[1] The subsidies being permanent and the Estates rarely assembling, the appointment of these officers of finance soon passed to the king (Charles V, 1360) and in time the offices became purchasable. By the side of the elective officials for "tailles" and aids [2] there were comptrollers of the salt stores for the salt tax (the "gabelle") [3] and masters of the ports for the tax on foreign goods,[4] all being at the same time administrators and judges (in the first instance).

Over them were placed always the **generals of finance**, divided, after 1388, into two groups, one for the business of finance, that is, they were mere administrators, the other for the administration of justice in financial matters and constituting the **Court of Aids**, 1411.[5] This sovereign tribunal [6] had appellate jurisdiction [7]

[1] *Isambert*, "Table."

[2] "Elections," Ordinance 1452, special "elections" suppressed Aug., 1681 and Jan., 1685. In the 1700s, there were 180 "elections" divided into 20 "generalities." Each one comprised presidents, counselors, procureurs, and recorders. They had administrative jurisdiction in matters of taxes, direct or indirect (except the salt tax and customs). Ord. June 19, 1445. *Cf.*, especially, Ordinance July, 1681. Their jurisdiction was even criminal (rebellion against fiscal agents). Ord. Aug. 26, 1452; summary procedure. Decl. Feb. 17, 1688; April 23, 1778. Jurisdiction of last resort up to an amount which varied: 1552, 10 sols; 1685, 50 livres. *Cf.* Edict 1552, 1578 concerning the administrative powers of those elected. Above, p. 410; *Fleury*, p. 187. In the Countries of Estates, administrative jurisdiction concerning taxes belonged to the ordinary judges, with the right of appeal to the Court of Aids. Concerning Languedoc, *cf.* "Mémoire de Basville sur le Languedoc," p. 148.

[3] Salt storehouses: storekeepers, controllers, "procureurs" of the king, recorder (countries of the "gabelle"): they had administrative jurisdiction of questions relating to the salt tax and the repression of contraventions. Edicts 1553, 1639, May, 1680. Their jurisdiction was maintained in places which were not seats of "elections." Ed. 1685. Concerning Languedoc, *cf. Basville*, "Mémoire," p. 144.

[4] Masters of ports and judges of "traites": disputes and contraventions in customs matters. Jurisdiction of first instance; appeal to the Court of Aides. Edict, 1551; Ord. July, 1681; Feb., 1687; Edict May, 1691.

[5] *Isambert*, "Table," see "Aides," "Cour des aides," "Généraux"; *A. Callery*, "Hist. des attrib. du Parlement de la Cour des aides et de la Chambre des comptes," 1880; *Du Crot*, "Le vrai style du Conseil privé, de la Cour de Parlement, de la Cour des aides," 1633; (*Dionis*), "Mém. p. servir à l'hist. de la C. des aides," 1355; "Mém. p. la C. des aides sur les conflits entre elle et la Ch. des comptes," 1782; (*Auger*), "Mémoire, etc. C. des aides dep. 1756 à 1775," 1779; *R. Dareste*, p. 30.

[6] Conflicts between the parliaments and the Court of "Aides," Edict

[7] Concerning its jurisdiction in the first instance and last resort, *cf. R. Dareste*, p. 35; in criminal matters, p. 36.

in litigation relating to aids, the salt tax, and customs duties, or involving the comptrollers of the salt stores, and also appellate jurisdiction of cases relating to customs and "traites." Like the Parliament this court had the right of addressing remonstrances to the king against edicts concerning taxes. Corresponding to the provincial parliaments there were provincial courts of aids, created directly by the king, or which were outgrowths of the Chambers of Accounts or of the seigniorial courts of aids.[1] After 1390 Languedoc had its generals of finances; after 1437 its court of aids (made stationary at Montpelier in 1467 and united to the Chamber of Accounts in 1629); in 1789 there were only three of them left: Clermont-Ferrand, 1557; Bordeaux, 1637; and Montauban, 1642–1650.[2]

§ 467. **Merger of Ordinary and Extraordinary Finances.**[3] —In the 1500 s the administration of the domain and that of the taxes formed only a single service. Francis I, in 1542, created six receiver-generalships to receive indiscriminately the proceeds of the domains, the aids, "tailles," and the salt taxes; in each of them he placed a receiver-general and a clerk from the treasurers of France and generals of finance. Henry II, in 1551, transformed these positions from commissions into offices; there were seventeen offices of **treasurers of France** who were at the same time **generals of finances**, but in order to have more offices to sell, the treasurers were separated from the generals (1557). Henry III reunited the offices, but multiplied the number for the same financial object and his successors imitated his example. In July,

Dec. 20, 1559, settled by the Great Chamber of Parliament united with the Commissioners of the Court of "Aides"; Ord. Aug., 1669, 11, 12, by the king's council. Above, p. 442.

[1] Paris, the oldest; Montpellier, 1437, 1467 (*Phillipi*, "Recueil sur la Cour des aides de Montp.," 1560), same district as the Parliament of Toulouse, Rouen, 1483.

[2] The greater part had been united to the Parliaments or to the Chamber of Accounts. Rouen, 1450–1705. Pau, 1632. Grenoble, 1638–1658. Dijon, united in 1630; Dôle in 1771.

[3] In the provinces united to the kingdom after the time of Charles VII, Burgundy, Dauphiny, Brittany, etc., there was already a single administration for ordinary and extraordinary taxes: a general and a treasurer or receiver general, *Loyseau*, "Offices," 3, 4; *Fleury*, p. 187. The general inventory or register of finances or "Etat du roi," a kind of budget, was elaborated by the king, the treasurers, and the generals, who, residing at the court while they were not making tours or inspection trips in their circumscriptions, united to form a kind of council of finance; the last word belonged to the Council of the King, but very often, treasurers and generals acted without him. They divided among their districts the resources and the charges established in the general inventory, and so special inventories came to be made. Expenses which were not anticipated in it could be paid only by special order of the king, countersigned by one of his secretaries. *Jacqueton*, p. 243.

1577, he placed in each "généralité" a **bureau of finances** composed at first of five treasurers-general, but who numbered more than thirty in 1775, including presidents, prosecuting attorneys, advocates of the king, and a recorder. The intendants took away from them a portion of their powers; these latter were both administrative and judicial (domainal affairs and highways; *cf.* our councils of prefecture). In the countries with Estates, the authority of the intendants was restrained by that of the Estates; there were no bureaus of finances. The "countries of impositions," recently annexed, had neither bureaus of finances nor Estates; there the duty of apportioning the "taille" and other direct taxes devolved upon the intendants.

The four treasurers of France and the four generals of finance established at Paris [1] disappeared in order to make way for the central bureau of the **intendants of finances** with a chief,[2] the **superintendent**, corresponding to the former grand treasurer of France,[3] and a **comptroller general** "as long as the finances were ticklish" ("chatouilleuses").[4] The downfall of the superintendent, Fouquet, and his replacement by the comptroller general, Colbert, was a case in point. Below them was a **guardian of the royal treasury** who received: (*a*) "the sum remaining to the good of all finances after the charges were deducted"; and (*b*) paid out in ready money upon ordinances signed by the king which were for regular expenses; for the extraordinary expenses the king gave patents or current quittances. The patents in discharge ("acquits patents") were for presents which he was willing should be known to the Chamber of Accounts; they had to be registered if the gift exceeded 3,000 livres. The "receipts on account" or certificates for cash were also letters addressed to the Chamber

[1] Charged, before there were intendants, with the direction of the public services, they retained the registration of acts relating to the domain, the reception of faith from direct vassals of the king for lands the titles to which they did not hold, the ordering of payments, and the supervision of accountants.

[2] Edict 1626. The Chamber of the Treasury was abolished in 1693 in the "generality" of Paris, and the bureau of finance inherited its local powers.

[3] *Jacqueton*, p. XIX: Semblançay was not superintendent of finance in the sense that was given to this word in the 1600s. *De Boislisle*, "Hist. de la surint. de Semblançay" ("Bibl. Soc. Hist. Fr.," vol XVIII); *Spont*, "Semblançay," 1895. On Colbert, *cf. supra*, p. 394, no. 4. *Mollieu*, "Mém. d'un ministre du Trésor," 1780–1815," 1846.

[4] On the origin of comptroller's office, *supra*, *cf.* p. 518, n. 2. General control of finances established in 1554. *Fleury*, p. 190; *Isambert*, "Table," see "Contrôleurs des finances," "Trésor," "Trésoriers." England has had a comptroller general only since the time of William IV; *cf.*, concerning his functions, *Fischel*, I, 268.

of Accounts, but without mention of the name of the parties receiving them, nor of the cause; only the king stated that the guardian of the treasury had placed ready money in his hands for secret purposes, such a sum as he wished to be allowed in his account, without there being a need for further accounting. These secret expenses were the privy purse for the minor expenses of the king (formerly 10,000 gold crowns per month, said Fleury), for the money used for secret negotiations of State concern, gratuities which the king wished kept secret, — material in plenty for fraud. Receipts of this kind were introduced by the favorites of Henry III.[1] Without examining how far this assertion of Fleury is well founded we may say that the practice of receipts on account was in accord with the logic of the absolute monarchy; it was by this means that the personal power of the king expressed itself in the matter of finances.

§ 468. **The Chamber of Accounts.**[2] **Origin.**[3] — Accountants, masters of accounts,[4] appeared in the second half of the 1200 s; they were members of the king's court, charged with auditing and verifying the accounts of the domainal agents (for example, those of the bailiffs), and with judging disputed claims relating to finances.[5] This commission acquired a certain permanence at the end of the 1200 s and constituted, incontestably, a distinct chamber, independent of the Parliament at the beginning of the 1300 s. An ordinance of 1309 was the first act which spoke of the "camera compotorum." The ordinances of July 18, 1318, and of January 3, 1320, organized it definitively. Its composition was analogous

[1] *Fleury*, p. 191. *Infra*, p. 523.

[2] *Cl. de Beaune*, "Tr. de la Ch. des comptes," 1647; *Leufroy, Id.*, 1702; *Le Chanteur*, "La Ch. des comptes," 1765; *Boislisle*, "Premiers présid. de la Ch. des comptes," 1873; *Vuitry*, I, 503; II, 278; *Prou*, "Gr. Encycl."; BCh., 1894, 115; "Hist. de Fr.," t. XXII; *J. Le Grand*, "Instr. s. le fait des finances," 1582; *Miraulmont*, "Mém. s. l'orig. et inst. des Cours souver.," 1584; *Pasquier*, "Rech. de la France," II, 5; *Cl. Gosset*, "Recueil d'Edits et lettres concern. les officiers de la Ch. des comptes de Paris," 1728; "R. de lég.," 3, 71; 4, 105; *Dareste*, "Justice admin.," p. 7 *et seq.*; *Petit*, "Mémoriaux de la Ch. des comptes," 1899.

[3] *Luchaire*, 590, 604; *Beugnot*, "Olim," III, 1508; *Langlois*, "Textes," p. 180; "Phil. III," 303. *Cf.* the Exchequer of Normandy (from the end of the 1100 s), "Hauts renneurs" of Flanders, "maîtres rationnaires" in Provence, etc., *Luchaire*, 269. Exchequer in England, court of fiscal justice, to which the sheriffs rendered their accounts, where their offices were farmed out and where they were revoked; the sheriffs being at the head of the militia, the exchequer gave them orders to assemble it.

[4] Ord. 1256; *Giry*, "Docum.," p. 85, 87. Ord. 1278; *De Boislisle*, "Ann. Soc. Hist. France," 1872.

[5] Ord. 1256, I, 83: "gentes quæ ad nostros compotos deputantur." "Olim," III, 13. Close relations for a long time between the Parliament and the king's council. *Supra*, p. 380, 442.

to that of the Parliament: it had its presidents, its masters, its correctors, its auditors, a king's prosecuting attorney and a king's advocate, its recorders, its prosecuting attorneys, in all two hundred and fifty-seven officers at the close of the 1600 s.

Its **powers** varied widely: I. In the 1300 s the Chamber of Accounts was a council of government and of finances which the king frequently consulted and with which he still deliberated as late as 1498. From this practice the following rights resulted: 1st, the right of registration (legislative acts relative to finances, letters patent for legitimation, ennoblement, amortization, etc.); 2d, the right of remonstrance. It ought to have retained likewise the right of examination and preparation of measures of a financial character; but the monarchical epoch reserved this function to the **Council of Finances.** The Chamber of Accounts was not only a council; it was especially a tribunal, a great administrative court; it was the sole judge of all financial cases.[1] It soon lost many of its powers; the Court of the Mint and the Chamber of the Treasury took over a part of them when they became detached from it. It had a rival in the Court of Aids, and there came a time when the King's Council could reverse its decisions. Although the Exchequer of England, without losing any of its fiscal jurisdiction, became, through a fiction of procedure, one of the three great Courts of Justice of the kingdom, judging civil cases by the same right as the court of the King's Bench or that of the Common Pleas, the Chamber of Accounts of Paris found itself gradually restricted to the field of accounts.

II. There remained to the Chamber of Accounts three sorts of powers:

1st, that of **accounts.** It judged, settled, and audited the annual accounts of all those who had the handling of public moneys;[2] it made sure of their regularity and gave discharges to those whose accounts were found exact. The control which it exercised thereby over the whole financial administration was of

[1] Examples in the "Olim," I, 347; III, 119, 1184, etc. "Ordonnances," II, 144, 321, etc. Ord. 1346, 1383, 1388 (IV, 716; VII, 48, 167). Declaration of March 13, 1390: all things and needs whatever concerning the inheritance of the king will be dealt with in the Chamber of Accounts.

[2] Even the accounts of the "aides," made at first to the States-General, was deferred to it, also the accounts of the subsidies of the clergy. "Regl." March 1, 1388, December 4, 1400, Dec. 23, 1454, March, 1500, Dec., 1511. It also examined the accounts of the communal funds and the funds from the octroi authorized by the king; and if the civil judges controlled the use of patrimonial funds, departures were often made from this rule. The declaration of July 27, 1766, abrogated it. *Fleury*, "Instit. au dr. fr.," I, 214; *R. Dareste*, p. 13.

prime importance.[1] In the Council of the King there was prepared the "state of the king," a sort of budget (very imperfect) of receipts and expenditures; the accountant had to conform his accounts therewith; thus every expenditure not provided for in the "state of the king" (or not ordered by the king himself) had to be stricken out. "At the expiration of each inspection, the accountant presented to the Council 'the true state' ('etat au vrai'), that is to say, a summarized account containing a statement of the real receipts and expenditures." (The epitome of accounts thus rendered was given over to the Council and was also called the "true state.")[2] "It was only after having rendered the account by 'the true state' to the Council that the accountant submitted his accounts, together with vouchers, to the Chamber of Accounts." If an expenditure had been made without an order of payment or if it had been made in pursuance of an irregular order, the Chamber verified it; if a receipted item had not been collected, the Chamber made sure of it; finally, it permitted the state of the treasury to be settled at a given moment, and it furnished thereby points of departure for later accounts. But this was rather what should have been done than what was done in reality;[3] sometimes the Chamber verified accounts fifty years afterwards; the establishment of provincial Chambers prevented it from centralizing all financial operations.[4] Moreover, if it discovered

[1] The Edict of Aug., 1598, and especially the Edict of Aug., 1669, are found almost in their totality in our laws.

[2] *Fleury* calls the "état au vrai" an effective account while the "état du roi" was not so in all respects; there were treasurers who had to make payments outside of the king's "état." *Cf. Chéruel*, "Dict. des inst.," see "Budget" (Colbert's budgets according to the memorandum books of Louis XIV). The custom of "états au vrai" seems to have been very old. Edict, Sept. 25, 1443 (general rule). They had to be presented every year; on the contrary, accountants were allowed delays for presenting their accounts formally (Feb., 1771, etc.).

[3] The Chamber of Accounts did not have jurisdiction: 1st, of expenses ordered directly by the king under the form of receipts for cash; 2d, of accounts called up arbitrarily by the king or the intendants of the council of State or the bureau of finances. Concerning accounting, *cf.* "Inst. s. le fait des finances," 1582. "Rec. de régl. s. le fait des fin.," 1599.

[4] Chamber of Provincial Accounts in 1789 (ancient seigniorial chambers: Aix, Bar, Blois, Dijon, Dôle, Grenoble, Montpellier, Nancy, Nantes, Pau, and Rouen). Add. Lille, abolished in 1691, and the Chamber of Accounts of the appanagist princes and dowager queen (Louise of Savoy, Catharine de' Médicis, etc.). *Cf. Prou*, "Gr. Encycl.," h. vo. (bibliogr.); *H. de Fourmont*, "Hist. de la Ch. des comptes de Bretagne," 1854; *L. Delisle*, BCh., 2e s., V, 268; *Joly*, "Tr. de la Ch. des comptes de Dijon," 1640; *Valbonnais*, "Hist. du Dauphiné," II, 286; *R. Bartholomæus*, "Statuta curie camere regie rationum civ. Aquensis," 1508; *F. de Claperiis*, "Centuria caus. in summa rationum Prov. curia decis.," 1587; *Kowalevsky, op. cit.* (Languedoc), 1876. Add. Bibl. in *Dareste*, p. 17; *Finot*, "Ch. des comptes de Lille," 1887. Certain Chambers had retained a more extended jurisdiction than that of Paris.

the existence of abuses, it was powerless to prevent them;[1] "it could declare an accountant in debt or give him a discharge, but it was beyond its power to enlighten, still less to criticize, the acts of the government."

2d, **Judicial Functions.** — Its jurisdiction, difficult to distinguish from that of the Parliament[2] and the other courts of finances, covered litigation incidental to accounts (controversies among accountants, and litigation between accountants and individuals who must receive from them).[3]

3d, **Domainal Powers.** — The Chamber of Accounts had originally the financial administration (" régie ") and the care of the royal domain. Of these powers it retained the registration of acts relative to the domain (letters constituting appanages and letters of engagement), the revocation of domainal alienations,[4] the reception of oaths of fealty and homage taken by direct vassals of the king, and by the clergy in virtue of their temporal possessions, and a certain power over the officers of the domain and of the treasury (oaths, bonds, etc.).[5]

TOPIC 8. CONCLUSION

§ 469. **Defects.** — The defects of the financial system of the "Ancien Régime" have been pointed out in the course of the account in preceding pages. We may recall here the most striking: 1st, the arbitrary fixing by the king of the total amount of the tax and of the sum total of the public expenditures;[6] inequalities among the provinces; special privileges which placed the burden of taxation

[1] According to *Fleury*, p. 196, it had lost public confidence and the secret management of affairs; the principal acts were done in the King's Council; only the forms were left to the Chamber; it did not concern itself with particular acts of administration and the reasons for the expenses justified by the receipts that were submitted to it were unknown to it.

[2] Conflicts of sovereignty between the Chamber of Accounts and the Parliament, the latter claiming the right to judge upon appeal the decisions of the Chamber of Accounts. Ord. Jan., 1319, Art. 23. Ord. Cabochienne, May 27, 1413, Art. 150. Letters, 1459, 1460, etc. *Cf.* especially *Dareste*, p. 8. The ordinances authorized only recourse in revision to the Chamber of Accounts to which was added several councilors of the Parliament. In the 1600 s, the power of revision was replaced by power of annulment by the Council of the King.

[3] Criminal jurisdiction over accountants, Sept. 13, 1374; Edict, Feb., 1566. Jurisdiction in domainal matters, Edict, Dec., 1460; Ord. Jan., 1319, Dec. 23, 1454. *Denisart*, see "Aven."

[4] *Ferrière, Guyot, Denisart*, see "Chambre des comptes." *Supra*, p. 478.

[5] Suppression, Sept. 2, 1790, Dec. 17, 1791. A bureau of accounts replaced it. In 1807, Court of Accounts.

[6] Sinecures for the clergy and the nobility, pensions, gifts, excessive expenses of the Court. "Code des commensaux," 1720.

upon the poor;[1] harsh, vexatious, and costly methods of collection.[2] 2d, an insufficient budget (that is to say, the "statement of the king"), lack of publicity, lack of control over expenditures,[3] tremendous disorder in the accounts,[4] the system of special charges and consequently of incessant payments by transfers of accounts.[5] 3d, Lack of a special financial administration in the beginning, and, when it was established, the same functionaries were at once directors, accountants, and administrative judges; the division of labor operated only incompletely. In short — bad assessment, bad collection, and bad expenditure.

[1] The general view in 1789 was in favor of the tax on real property, proportional, uniform basis, the same for all; in effect, as Adam Smith thought, the greatest merit of a tax is that it should be certain, and have some fixity, so that taxpayers may know for a rather long period, the amount of charges to which they will be subject. What did the taxpayer pay in 1789? *Taine*, "L'Anc. Régime," p. 543, calculates that on 100 fr. of net income, the State, the nobility, the Church took from him 81 fr. 71, leaving him only 18 fr. 29. "Taille," 18 fr. 10; accessories of the "taille," capitation, twentieth, 35 fr. 05. "Dîme" (seventh of the net revenue), 14 fr. 28; Feudal taxes, *idem.* Indirect taxes are not included in this estimate. But the figures given by Taine are questioned and the result is still more. *D. Arbois de Jubainville*, "Intend. de Champagne," 1880; *supra*, p. 232 *et seq.; F. Mège*, "Charges et Contr. des hab. de l'Auvergne," 1898; *Gautier de Biauzat.* "Doléances sur les surcharges que les gens du peuple supportent," 1788.

[2] The expense of collecting the tax was very great; it is estimated that the expense of collecting the "taille" increased to 25 per cent; to 40 per cent when the tax was farmed; to-day, it is only 5 per cent.

[3] "Acquits au Comptant" (73 to 145 millions per year from 1780 to 1787). By the side of the justified ordinances submitted to the Chamber of Accounts there were ordinances of account which permitted all control and all publicity to be dispensed with; the details were entered by the comptrollers-general with the sign-manual of the king on the "Red Book" (register bound in red Morocco), which the Constituent Assembly ordered to be printed. It is easy to see what abuses were possible in such a system; Turgot, Necker, and the Notables criticized it and attempted to suppress or restrict it. Necker states, however, that the greater part of the expenses which were recorded in the "Red Book" were justified and that there was nothing to fear from its publication. *Stourm*, II, 153.

[4] The "Etat au vrai," a recapitulation of partial abstracts furnished by each accountant, gave a table of the total receipts and expenses for the completed budgetary period; prepared by the comptroller-general and approved by the Council, one would be tempted to regard it as a source of exact information on all points; but this official "état" was incomplete and insufficient because of the faults of bookkeeping. *Stourm*, II, 182: Analysis of the discussion between Calonne and Necker in 1787. *Necker*, "Mémoir en réponse au discours prononcé par M. de Calonne devant l'Assemblée des notables," 1787; "Sur le Compte rendu au Roi en 1781. Nouveaux éclaircissements," 1788. *Calonne*, "Rép. à l'écrit de M. Necker," 1788. *Cf.* for the 1500s the curious table prepared by *Froumenteau*.

[5] For example, the revenues of the domain were used to pay the expenses of the royal household, the "aides," those of war, etc. As there was never an exact balance between each kind of receipts and the corresponding expenses, this system necessitated incessant transfers, which caused very complicated accounting. It had, at least, the advantage of limiting royal arbitrariness; it was difficult for the king to divert an appropriation from the object for which it was specified.

The financial system of the "Ancien Régime" was somewhat like that of its system of legislation; it was an inextricable jumble of measures adopted at different times under the pressure of circumstances; absolute royal power could not succeed in putting it in order; the deficit (nearly sixty millions in 1789) and the bankruptcy, toward which it never ceased to tend (which were owing to its faults no doubt, but also to obstacles of all sorts which it encountered), were the immediate cause of its ruin, and thus "the germ of our liberties."[1]

[1] We may apply to all the institutions of the old régime the saying of *Voltaire,* "Dict. philos.," see "Lois": "The laws are made piece by piece, by chance and irregularly, as towns are built. You see in Paris the quarter of Les Halles, of Saint-Pierre-aux-Bœufs, the rue Brise Miche, that of Pet au Diable, in contrast with the Louvre and the Tuileries; there is the image of our laws. London became worthy of being inhabited only after it was reduced to ashes. The streets after that epoch were enlarged and made over. London became a city by being burned. Would you have good laws? If so, burn yours and make new ones."

Chapter XIV

THE MONARCHICAL PERIOD (*continued*)
MILITARY ORGANIZATION[1]

§ 470. **Feudal Troops, Mercenaries, and the Royal Army.**—The insufficiency of feudal military service[2] and the custom of commutation by pecuniary payments[3] led the kings to make use chiefly of paid troops (as early as Philip Augustus[4] we find mention of veterans, soldiers, guides, men in armor), among whom

[1] Bibliography: *Luchaire*, "Manuel," p. 606 (bibl.); *Daniel*, "Hist. de la milice," 1721; *Fleury*, "Dr. public," pp. 199 to 264: *cf.* p. 123 (marine; exposition of the law of nations, according to *Grotius*); "Règ. et Ord. p. la guerre," 1691; *Briquet*, "Code militaire," 1761; *Boutaric*, "Instit. milit. de la France," 1863; *Rousset*, "Hist. de Louvois," 1861; *Dareste*, "Hist. de l'admin.," II, 219; *Gébelin*, "Les milices nation. av. 1789," 1883; *Duruy*, "L'armée royale en 1789," 1888; *Babeau*, "La vie milit. s. l'Anc. Rég.," 1890; "Le recrut. territ. s. l'Anc. Rég.," 1877; compare by the same author "La Ville"; "Le Village"; *Caron*, "Le Tellier, intendant d'armée," 1881; *Duc d'Aumale*, "Revue des Deux Mondes," 1867. Upon the law of nations compare bibliography in *Bonfils*, "Manuel de droit internat.," 2d ed. by *Fauchille*, p. 519; *Camus*, "Table," see "Dr. des gens," "Diplomatie," "Traités"; *Baltzar*, "Deutsch. Kriegswesen," 1877.

[2] Upon the abolition of feudal and communal troops, compare *supra*, pp. 215, 253; *Luchaire*, 607; Ord. 1274: tariff of fines for those who did not render military service; Ord. 1279: "de jumentis tenendis." Royal garrisons in seigniorial châteaux, 1367. Abolition or commutation of watch-service. Ord. 1451, 1479; Philip the Fair, 1303 (service for four months). Ord. of June 12, 1302, May 29, 1303. Concerning military service by "roturiers," compare *Prou*, "R. hist.," Nov., 1890; *Borrelli de Serres*, "Rech. sur div. services publics," 1895; Ord. 1317, Rolls of the year 1214 (Bouvines) containing the list of those who were compelled to perform military service for the king. *La Roque*, "Tr. du ban et de l'arrière-ban" (continuation of the "Traité de la Noblesse"), 1676. Compare *supra*, p. 268, Ord. of 1355: only the king could create the "arrière-ban"; compare *Dareste*, II, 314 (the insubordination of certain volunteers obtained by this means); Ord. 1484; 1489 (exemptions), 1534, 1548, 1579, Art. 317. BCh., 5th s., 2, 25; 3, 267.

[3] *Supra*, p. 268.

[4] The "ban" and the "arrière-ban" doubtless were already under pay. Ord. 1318; 1338; 1367; 1408. *Supra*, p. 255, n. 3. The choice between military service and a money tax belonged in principle to the king. *Boutaric*, p. 130. In the 1200s, if the "ban" was proclaimed, the seigniors levied troops which they furnished to the king; if the "arrière-ban" was proclaimed, the king himself had the right to levy troops on the lands of the seigniors. The "ban," ordinary summons, and the "arrière-ban," extraordinary summons, were no longer separated in the monarchical epoch, *Fleury*, p. 217.

were to be found the nobility in great numbers. The method of recruiting was that of voluntary enlistment; the captains went with the companies themselves and retained over them rights analogous to those which the seigniors had over their vassals and the militia which they led.[1] The soldiers, obliged to support themselves at their own expense, treated the provinces as conquered countries (in spite of ordinances to the contrary).[2] The superior officers alone were royal functionaries. They were: the constable,[3] the marshals of France,[4] the grand master of archers[5] (later, of artillery, 1500 s), and their provosts or lieutenants. They had both military and judicial power, through the court of the high constable (military offenses, acts committed by private individuals against soldiers, payment of the troops, etc.).[6]

Modern military organization, the creation of a permanent national army entirely under the control of the king and therefore better disciplined, began with Charles VII. This prince organized in 1439 companies of men at arms or companies of heavy cavalry ("compagnies d'ordonnance"), composed entirely of nobles, and in 1448 regular infantry ("francs-archers"). The latter forces were levied like the "taille" through the agency of elective officials; the contingent was apportioned among the parishes; the best-fitted men for military service were selected in each by the elected officials, and were equipped at the expense of the parishes so that there was a strict correlation between taxation and military service. The free-archers disappeared in 1480, but the system of a permanent army of paid soldiers was not abandoned. Although the number of the foreign corps was consider-

[1] Ord. of Jan., 1374. Compare Ord. 1318, 1351 (war treasurers). Ord. 1351 prescribed that the companies should be full (abuse of the fagots, — "passe-volants," — supernumeraries who replaced the soldiers at the time of parades or reviews); the fewer soldiers he had, the greater profits the captain realized, since he was paid as though his company was complete.

[2] Ord. of Dec. 28, 1355; April, 1363; 1374. [3] Ord. of Feb., 1341.

[4] Subordinate to them, camp marshals. Office revocable. Oath of J. Clément in 1223 (*Isambert*).

[5] Commander of special troops (archers, etc., masters of artillery, 1291). Existed under Saint Louis.

[6] This tribunal, composed of the constable, and of the marshals or their lieutenants, sat at the "Table de Marbre" as early as 1356. *Beaufort*, "Recueil conc. les maréch.," 1784. Its powers were very restricted. Military jurisdiction passed almost completely to the Councils of War (Ord. July, 1665) and to the intendants; the Court of "aides" and the king's council had jurisdiction concerning equipment and the service of war, in general. *Pinson*, "Maréchaussée de France," 1679. *Fleury*, p. 230. Compare *supra*, p. 413 ("Prevôts des maréchaux").

able in the 1500 s,[1] Francis I organized in imitation of the free-archers provincial legions (1534) to which the name of **regiments** was given at the end of the 1500 s, and which made up the regular army.[2] In 1688 it was duplicated by a sort of "landwehr" the **militia**,[3] at first temporary but afterwards permanent, which made it similar to regular troops. At the same time, the division of France into **governments** in the 1500 s had the effect of specializing the organization of the army by depriving the bailiffs and seneschals of what remained of their military powers as chiefs of the feudal forces.

§ 471. **Method of Recruiting.** — (A) **The Regular Troops,**[4] who composed the greater part of the army. The levies and recruits (who filled the vacancies) were obtained by voluntary agreements made in pursuance of a royal commission issued to the captains; the soldiers received a very small bounty (*e.g.* 50 livres) [5] and were obliged to serve six or eight years. Violence and fraud too often tainted the enrollment [6] and we may wonder whether the morality of the army was not affected by it.[7]

[1] Privileges, exemption from the "droit d'aubaine" (the right of the State to property of deceased aliens), 1481, etc.

[2] The primitive system of recruiting by the local authorities gave such poor results that it became necessary to substitute for it more and more the action of the State. There remained of the old practice the custom of giving to regiments the name of a province (Picardy, Auvergne), although the men were recruited to some extent from other places.

[3] Compare concerning the "*bourgeoise militia,*" *Fleury*, p. 217; *Babeau*, "La Ville," p. 254. Care should be taken not to confuse this with the national militia organized in 1688. It was the old militia of the communes charged with watch and guard service, reorganized and modeled after the army divisions. The "quartiers" to which the bourgeois belonged became companies; the "quarteniers" became captains, and the "dizainiers" lieutenants. All inhabitants were compelled to perform service in the militia; but the poor were excluded and in the 1600 s the nobility secured exemptions. Compare *supra*, p. 416. In addition to the militia there were formed companies of volunteers ("arquebusiers," etc.).

[4] Ord. 1680, 1686, 1692. The extraordinary troops were under the jurisdiction of the comptroller of finances, and by them was understood troops other than those of the royal household and the "gendarmerie." They were disbanded in times of peace.

[5] Wages were paid from month to month at the time of reviews and were called "monstre"; they were eventually advanced every ten days as advance pay.

[6] "Racoleurs" (recruiting sergeants) and "feurs" (crimping houses), places where young men were slugged and kidnapped, cabarets where they were made drunk. Nicknames used to disguise suspected recruits: "Sans-Raison," "Bel Amour," etc. Barbarous discipline from that time. Cosmopolitan recruiting (notably Swiss) raids among foreigners and vagabonds in France. Deserters in great numbers. The army was only half French, drawing from the nation practically only the criminal and immoral elements.

[7] To form an idea of the old army one has only to remember that before the time of Richelieu and Louvois there were no uniforms, and no commissariat, the soldiers foraged for their living, there was no hospital

(B) **The Militia** after 1688 (infantry reserves, not very numerous) consisted of thirty regiments, which served only under serious circumstances. They constituted, or could have constituted, a national army recruited on the basis of obligatory military service for all; the contingent required of the provinces and of the "généralités" was apportioned among the parishes under the care of the intendant, and in each parish there took place a **conscription** and annual drawing by lot. But the excessive number of exemptions caused the burden of the service to fall upon the poor. Great difficulty was experienced in overcoming the aversion of the conscripts for service in the army. The drawing by lot was the signal for violent outbreaks; the refractory took to the woods and the others pursued them. The militiamen once selected and drilled, it was not unusual for the syndics of the parishes to be obliged to take them by force under the constabulary to the places designated for the muster. Under these conditions it is not surprising that the militia was several times abolished.[1] In 1789 this military service, although so restricted in comparison with that of our day, was denounced unanimously.

§ 472. **Conclusion.** — The monarchy had abolished the former feudal commands and had subordinated the army to a single management, that of the secretary of state for war.[2] In addition to voluntary enlistments it had instituted a system of recruiting militiamen and had established schools for the training of officers.[3] It had devolved upon the State the expense of equipment, of remounting, the maintenance of stores, and the organization of the commissariat.[4] But it made the mistake of not strengthening this organization and of not effacing certain traces of the feudal régime,

service, no pensions, etc. Concerning veterans and invalids, see *Dareste*, II, 310, 324, "Hôtel des Invalides," 1670. When peace was once concluded, the regular troops were often disbanded, with the exception of a few regiments and those of the royal household.

[1] Ord. Jan. 17, 1689, 1701.

[2] The office of constable was purchased at Lesdiguières in 1627, and the purchaser of subordinate offices was reimbursed for the price paid. The authority of the king was exercised with more complete freedom from that time on. The office of colonel general of infantry was abolished in 1661.

[3] Companies of gentlemen or cadets, 1682–1692. Military schools under Louis XV.

[4] The commissary service was established and specialized under Richelieu. Code Marillac. Ord. 1637. Storehouses, markets open to the public, supplies which the inhabitants were compelled to furnish the troops on march. Soldiers lodged by the inhabitants had the right to demand only "trade-implements": a bed with sheets, a pot, a bowl, a glass, fire, and light; in consideration of the payment of a sum of money they were excused, in 1674, from supplying the pot and the bowl, but were still compelled to furnish cover and beds.

for example, the custom of selling regiments and companies (so that the choice of inferior officers belonged exclusively to the colonels and the captains)[1] and the privileges of the nobility for admission and promotion in the corps of officers.[2]

§ 473. **The Marine.**[3] — (A) **The Admiralty.** The admiral of France, one of the great officers of the crown since the 1200 s,[4] had the direction of the marine (commissions to privateers, prize jurisdiction,[5] and various expenditures); he received a share of the prizes and the proceeds of fines which he imposed; it has been said with some justice that he was less a functionary than a contractor ("entrepreneur") of the administration of the marine.[6] It was he who appointed all the subordinate officers. There were, moreover, in the maritime provinces, like Provence, special admiralties prior to the annexation of these provinces to the crown.[7] Appeal from their judgments lay to the "Marble Table" of the neighboring parliament.

(B) **Reforms of Richelieu and Colbert.** The office of admiral of France was bought back in 1626, like that of constable, and the commissions of naval officers came from the king. Though the admiralties continued to exist, with judicial and administrative

[1] In 1787 there were still twenty-seven regiments which were the property of their colonels and for which the colonels appointed the subordinate officers. Rates of prices for regiments and companies were fixed by Louvois.

[2] The officers, whether pupils of the military schools (Brienne, Auxerre, etc.) or soldiers who had risen from the ranks, had to be noble. The "roturiers" rarely attained to the rank of lieutenant (exceptions: Fabert, Catinat, marshals of France). The edicts of the end of the 1700 s further emphasized the preference for the nobility ("Règl.," 1781: four "quartiers" of the nobility). Tendency to equality: the Order of Saint Louis provided for appointments without distinction of class or rank.

[3] *Luchaire*, "Manuel," p. 612 (bibl.); *Fleury*, "Dr. public," p. 231; *Dareste*, II, 327; *Blanchard*, "Compil. des Ord.," 1715; *Bajot*, "Rép. de l'Admin. de la Marine," 1814; *Isambert*, "Table," see "Amirautés," etc. Compare the bibliography in *Monod*, no. 3871; *Camus*, "Table," see "Marine." Concerning international maritime law, compare *Bonfils*, "Man. de dr. internat.," 2d ed., p. 298; *Grotius*, "Mare liberum," 1609; *Selden*, "Mare clausum," 1635. Claims of the English and French to the sovereignty of the seas (since the 1200 s). "Fasciculus superioritatis maris," 1339, which was adopted by English authors of the 1600 s, Coke, Selden, and Prynne. The Admiralty Court in England, about 1340, reorganized in 1525. "Code naval," 1754 (in "l'Histoire de la marine," by *Boismêle*). Concerning the colonies, compare *Camus and Dupin*, p. 370.

[4] *Isambert*, "Provisions of 1322." *Fleury*, p. 232.

[5] *Lebeau*, "Code des prises," year VII.

[6] Compare the Director General of Posts.

[7] Various ordinances, notably those of 1480, 1584. The states of Languedoc complained that the naval service was not centralized, and demanded, in 1456, that the king alone should have authority to issue letters of marque; commerce suffered from reprisals which drew upon it a great number of French corsairs. BCh., 1862, 264 (Office "de piraterie" at Genoa).

powers, they were subordinated to the central authority in the person of the superintendent of navigation and commerce. The navy thus became a national navy. The personnel was recruited at first by voluntary enlistment, and in case of need, by impressment as in England,[1] but the point was never reached when the navy had a sufficient number of sailors. Colbert remedied the evil by **registration** and the **system of classes** (1668–1673), by which all marines were registered and divided into three or four classes, each of which served by turn for the period of a year.[2] In 1673, the navy had, like the army, its councils of war (tribunals in each port); the admiralties, reduced to the position of simple administrative tribunals, judged controversies relative to commerce on the seas and to the police of the merchant marine, as well as the police of the seashores; the decision of maritime prize cases was confided to a council of marine.[3]

[1] Concerning the consuls, who "with respect to foreigners were like residents, and with respect to Frenchmen were like magistrates and entitled to administer justice to them," compare *Fleury*, p. 133. They received their authority from the king. In important cases they were obliged to call into council a number of merchants and were not authorized to render judgment except upon a plurality of votes. Public acts, contracts, and wills were executed before them. Their chancellor served as a notary. *Bonfils*, "Manuel de droit internat.," 2d ed., p. 376.

[2] Ord. Dec., 1670, 1681, 1683, 1689. The inhabitants of the coasts were compelled, as in times past, to perform watch service of the sea, when an invasion was feared. Convicts and prisoners of war performed galley service (service of the convict gang). [3] *Fleury*, p. 260 (naval war).

CHAPTER XV

REVOLUTIONARY PERIOD (MAY 5, 1789 TO MARCH 21, 1804)[1]

TOPIC 1. PRECEDENTS OF THE REVOLUTION

TOPIC 2. PRINCIPLES OF 1789

TOPIC 3. THE EXECUTIVE POWER

TOPIC 4. THE LEGISLATIVE POWER

TOPIC 5. LOCAL ADMINISTRATION

[1] BIBLIOGRAPHY: *Lavisse et Rambaud*, "Hist. générale," t. VIII, p. 115 (bibl. detailed); "Revue de la Révol. fr.," 1880 *et seq.; Buchez et Roux*, "Hist. parlem. de la Révol. fr.," 1833–8; *Chérest*, "Chute de l'Ancien Rég.," 1884–6; *Tocqueville*, "L'Ancien Régime et la Révolution," 1857; *Taine*, "Origines de la France contemporaine," 1878 *et seq.; P. Janet*, "Philos. de la Révol.," 1875; *M. Sepet*, "Préliminaires de la Révol.," 1890; *Des Cilleuls*, "De l'esprit du droit public sous le Consulat et l'Empire" ("Acad. sc. mor." 145, 377). *Cf.* "Rev. de dr. public" edited by *M. Larnaude*.

TOPIC 6. JUSTICE

TOPIC 7. FINANCES

TOPIC 8. THE ARMY

TOPIC 1. PRECEDENTS OF THE REVOLUTION[1]

§ 474. **Political Theories in the Middle Ages,** very daring at times, remained shut up within the schools; the religious revolution of the 1500 s was necessary to give them expression in the world of facts; these abstract theories, animated with life, became forces with which the Church and the monarchy had to reckon. Instead of submitting to the State which persecuted them, following in that respect the example of the early Christians, the reformers claimed the right to oppose the political sovereign in questions relating to faith. Had not the Church throughout all the Middle Ages proclaimed its independence in spiritual matters? Had it not even imposed its doctrines upon kings? Had it not even gone so far as to excommunicate and depose them, under the pretext that they were violating the law of God? The reformers only took up again on their own behalf the theocratic theses of the Holy See. But between the spiritual and the temporal the boundary had always been very wavering and very faint; the Middle Ages exhausted themselves in vain efforts to trace it, neither in books nor in facts did they succeed.

The partisans of the Reformation did not hesitate to pass from the religious field to the political.[2] Arguments justifying the

[1] *Kovalewsky,* "Les origines de la démocratie contemp.," 1898; *Esmein,* "Elém. de droit constitutionnel," 1896; *Sée,* "Idées polit. de Diderot" ("R. hist.," 65, 46); *Decrue,* "Idées polit. de Mirabeau" (*ibid.,* 21, 257); *Rocquain,* "L'esprit révolution. avant la Révolution," 1878.

[2] In the ecclesiastical organization democratic tendencies made progress among the "irregulars" of the Reformation, the peasants of Westphalia, the communist groups of Friesland, the Baptists, millenariums, and the Quakers. The religious character, in the beginning of the movement, appeared clearly in the action of the Independents, and the Levellers in England, and in the Covenant among the Scotch Presbyterians (1643; *cf.* 1581). *Borgeaud,* "Ann. Ec. sc. pol.," 1890, 1891; *Gooch,* "Hist. of

right of resistance to princes were not lacking; scholasticism had forged them. In France, in the Netherlands, in England, and in Scotland in the struggles against kings[1] they seized the familiar ideas of the theologians: the sovereignty of the people and the theory of the social contract, ideas which regarded the prince as an official bound to obey the laws under penalty of forfeiting his crown. Hotman invoked again the old liberties in the name of history; Junius Brutus, in the "Vindiciæ Contra Tyrannos," analyzed the contract which united the monarch with his subjects; the Jesuit, Mariana, systematized the democratic doctrines of the League; before them, in 1548, Knox had affirmed, in Scotland, the right of the people to depose their kings; and at the end of the century Buchanan was prompted by the same thought.

To the religious revolution the Renaissance contributed secular elements, such as the ancient conception of tyranny and the theories of natural law. Yet these were also the theses of the theologians; but, in putting them forth in this sense, political science secularized the movement. From the end of the 1500 s independent thought moved in the double circle of ideas of the Reformation and the Renaissance. If we except the ideas of the absolutists, few in number after Bodin, Hobbes, and Bossuet, most of the political writers elaborated liberal theories starting from natural law; they attempted to construct a secular State upon the idea of justice ("Rechtsstaat"). It will suffice to mention the most illustrious: Grotius, Spinoza, Locke, Pufendorf, and Rousseau. Their absolute doctrine, which is a perpetual defiance of experience and history, had, at least, laid the bases of the citizenship of the future.

At the same time, the English Revolution realized a form of government which was apparently inspired, more or less by these theories: it was an original piece of work by which, from old materials gathered together, an entirely new whole was formed, and which it required not less than a hundred

English Democracy in the XVII Cent.," 1898; the radical writings of *J. Hare*, 1647; *Hartlieb* ("Utopie"); *Winstanbey*, ("Lawfreedom," 1652), *John Rogers* ("Domesday"), *Godwin*, *Payner*, *Goodmann*, *Browne*, etc. Toland has published the most important.

[1] *Cf. Treumann*, "Die Monarchomachen," 1895; "De jure magistratuum in subditos," 1574; *Naudé*, "Bibliogr. politica," 1633; *Danot*, "Politices christiane," 1596; "Index univ. Fabiani Justiniani Genuensis," 1612; *Hub. Langueti*, "Epist. politicæ," 1646; on *H. Languet*, *Scholz*, 1875; *Waddington*, 1888; *Touchard*, 1898; *Vauthier*, "De Buchanani Vita," 1887; *Douarche*, "De tyrannicidio," 1888.

years to achieve. Animated by a spirit of opposition to absolute monarchy, as much perhaps as by a clear notion of its merits, Montesquieu and his school became enamored of the English constitution and made it the fashion. People saw in it, without always clearly understanding it, the ideal of free peoples.

It was from the school of natural rights and from that of Montesquieu that the principles of the French Revolution came,[1] — so far as they were not the logical development of the public law of the old monarchy (for example, the abolition of privileges). In the work of the Revolution there were, in fact, two parts: one, very stable, in which often, without knowing it, the Revolution was the continuer and inheritor of the defunct monarchy; the other, in which it proceeded by trials and gropings, — in which it experimented with foreign institutions and organized abstract ideas accepted as dogmas by the classical spirit.

§ 475. **The National Sovereignty.** — The idea that sovereignty resides in the multitude had been since the time of Saint Thomas Aquinas a commonplace of scholasticism. It rests, above all, on an observation of fact, namely, that in a society, it is the multitude which will have the last word; if it is necessary to resort to force, as in a battle, it is ordinarily with the greatest battalions that the victory rests: an observation which was especially applicable to the small cities of antiquity, all of whose citizens assembled in a public place, and in which, moreover, there were primitive means for getting rid of opponents, ostracism for example, or, as at Novgorod, drowning in the Volga. But there was nothing in the history of a great State like old France to warrant such a view; the Protestant minority in the 1500 s struggled victoriously against the Catholic majority. In default of a positive basis this principle was ascribed: 1st, to **historical traditions**: the Roman people abandoned all their powers to the emperor by the "lex regia," the election of chiefs of dynasty like Hugh Capet; 2d, to **practical necessities**; in case of the extinction of the reigning dynasty, the nation alone appeared entitled to confide the sovereignty to another family; 3d, to **contemporary facts**; popular assemblies in the Italian republics[2] and in the French communes, the participation of the States-General or of the Parliaments in public affairs, of councils in the settlement of religious questions; 4th, to considerations drawn from **natural law**; the public power

[1] Principles which have, besides, only a historical "processus."

[2] *Cf.* constitutions of the Italian republics, especially those of Venice and Florence. *Fazy*, "Les Constit. de la Républ. de Génève," 1892.

being regarded as legitimate only when it rested upon the express or tacit consent of the people.[1]

§ 476. **The Social Contract.** — It was by the social contract that this consent was given. By that two different acts were understood: 1st, the contract by which men agreed to live in society; 2d, the contract by which the political body thus formed gave itself a sovereign. The first of these acts was the social contract properly so called; the second, the "pactum subjectionis." The social contract[2] properly so called assumed that men lived at first in a state of nature or of anarchy, as was sometimes fancied according to the traditions of classical antiquity (golden age, etc.);[3] they escaped from it through the social contract, that is to say, by an agreement in virtue of which they bound themselves to live in society, each man surrendering his rights to the community and promising to obey the sovereign whom it should give.[4] The state of nature and the social contract, — it is upon these chimeras that our modern liberties rest. We may note, moreover, that the theory represents less a real fact than a logical necessity; the social contract was tacit, or if one prefers, it was a quasi-contract imposed upon men by their weakness.

§ 477. **The "Pactum Subjectionis,"**[5] which especially preoccupied the mind of the Middle Ages, has been interpreted in two ways. According to some, like Accursius, Hostiensis, and others, this contract involved an irrevocable alienation of power

[1] *Bossuet* vigorously criticized the idea of popular sovereignty and the theory of social facts that was associated with it. According to him, political dependence arises from the natural relation of things and not from a convention among men. By that, he approached the modern organic theory. The idea of divine right also appeared in his politics like the sovereignty of law which is superior to the all-powerful populace. "The people is that power which alone has no need to be right in order that its acts may be valid. Who, then, will say to the people that they are not right? No one has anything to say to them, or rather, it is necessary for the good of the people, to establish authorities against which the people themselves can do nothing, and there, in a moment, the sovereignty of the people is overthrown."

[2] Bibliog. in *Gierke*, "Althusius," p. 76. *Cf.* in particular, besides *Rousseau*, *Grotius*, "de jure belli," Prol. 15; 1. I, 1, 14, etc. *Wolff*, "Jus naturæ," vol. VIII, § 28, ed. 1766. *Althusius*, *Pufendorf*, *Locke*, etc.

[3] For Hobbes, the state of nature supposed a war of all against all; before the establishment of civil order, there was neither justice nor private property. Locke, on the contrary, considers men as already subject to the natural law.

[4] *Cf. Hobbes*, *Spinoza*, *Bodin*, and his ideas on the family, which was, rather than the individual, the primordal element of society.

[5] Manegold de Lauterbach in the 1000 s. The greater number of subsequent writers analyze the "pactum." Hobbes denies its existence and after him, Rousseau.

to the benefit of the prince (emperor or pope) who acquired thereby absolute and unlimited authority. The people retained no political right and could neither control the exercise of the public power, nor, *a fortiori*, dissolve the contract, by which they had shorn themselves, in favor of the prince. It was only upon the extinction of the dynasty (or upon the death of the king, if the throne was elective) that the popular right reappeared ("princeps major populo"). According to another view (Cinus, P. de Castro, Occam, and others) the "pactum subjectionis" did not imply a transfer of power but a simple delegation; the people abdicated nothing, they retained the pleasure of power and delegated only the exercise of it ("populus major principe").[1] From this it followed, contrary to the ideas of the absolutists:

1st, that the royal power could be limited by laws and by individual liberties. In sacrificing his independence in order to live in society, the individual retained a portion of it, he gave to the State what was strictly necessary, but kept the rest; these rights were anterior and superior to those of the State.

2d, that the king might be under the necessity of obtaining the consent of the people to certain important acts, and that political authority might be divided between him and a parliament, a body of represenatives of the aristocracy or of the people.

3d, that subjects have, as against the king, a right of resistance (individual or collective) in case he should fail in the obligations which he had contracted; insurrection became a right, even a duty; the king might be tried, suspended, deposed.

§ 478. **The Representative System and Parliamentary Government**[2] were of English origin. The starting point was in the practice of not levying taxes without the consent of Parliament; even absolute kings like Henry VIII did not succeed in avoiding it. From the end of the 1200 s (the Model Parliament of 1295) this assembly was divided into a House of Lords or Upper Chamber and a House of Commons or Lower Chamber. An attempt has been made in our day to justify this division upon rational grounds; but when it was established it was only the expression of social differences which separated the Lords from the commons. The

[1] *Rousseau:* "Sovereignty being only the exercise of the national will, can never be alienated; *power* may be transmitted, but *will* cannot."

[2] TEXTS in *Stubbs*, "Select Charters," 1881; *Gardiner*, "The Constit. Docum. of the Puritan Revolution," 1888. — In addition, the well-known works of *Hallam*, *Gneist*, *Bagehot*, *Stubbs*, etc., *cf*. *Anson*, "Law and Custom," 1892; *Todd*, "Gouvern. parlem.," tr. fr., 1900; *Dicey*, "Law of the Constitution"; *Boutmy*, "Dévelop. de la Const. en Anglet.," new éd. 1898; "Etudes de droit constit., 1890."

thought did not occur to any one that two chambers were better than a single chamber. Besides, nothing resembled less a representation of the nation than the group of spiritual and temporal lords summoned personally by the king, and consequently originally chosen by him, later invested with a hereditary right. The deputies elected by the cities, by the boroughs and landed gentry of the counties, were only plenipotentiaries of feudal persons, or of a narrowly restricted constituency. The Parliament began by being only a simple advisory assembly; from the 1300s, in exchange for the grant of supplies which were asked of it, it demanded the redress of the grievances of which it complained. The perseverance and the tenacity with which it followed this policy gave it, in the 1400s, under Henry VI, an active part in the making of the laws; its drafts or bills were transformed into statutes upon receiving the royal sanction. It is true that the king had the right to refuse his sanction. He might even dispense with the application of the laws in a given case; he alone retained the right of issuing ordinances which hardly differed from statutes properly so called. He might even avoid to a certain extent the vote of subsidies by the Parliament; the revenues from the crown lands, the indirect taxes voted at the beginning of his reign for the whole of his life, commercial regulations and the fines which followed their violation, furnished him with resources sufficient for ordinary times. It was allowable for him not to assemble the Parliament, as Charles I did for some time, or to dissolve it when it was assembled; the royal prerogative was still very extensive.

The religious quarrels of the 1600s and the revolutions to which they gave rise in 1648 and in 1688 reversed these rôles: the king passed to the second place, the Parliament, that is to say, the aristocracy, had the last word in political matters; but an entire century was necessary to elaborate and perfect the work of these two revolutions. It was only towards 1789 that the English government had finally acquired the typical form under which it is customarily considered.

The Petition of Rights of 1629 and the Bill of Rights of 1688 laid the foundations of the new political régime by taking care to present them as traditional principles and time-honored liberties: the king could neither suspend the laws nor dispense with their application; he could levy no taxes without a vote of the Parliament; he could neither raise nor maintain a standing army; for the redress of grievances, for the amendment and strengthening of the laws, the Parliament must be frequently assembled. Here were the principal provisions of the **contract** which united the monarch and his subjects. No guarantee was stipulated for the latter; but was it not sufficient that the Parliament had been seen of all men to try the king, to depose him and to dispose of the crown, in order to inspire the new dynasty with respect for its engagements? Far from violating them, the crown resigned itself to the loss of rights which had not been formally taken away from it, such as the veto on legislation, which fell into desuetude after 1707, the power of the king to form the council of ministers, according to his own inclination, to attend its meetings and to impose his will upon Parliament (as was still done by Queen Anne), and the right to govern personally (*e.g.* William III was a true minister of foreign affairs).

The Parliament, having become omnipotent, was supposed to **represent** the English people: a pure fiction, which, even in our own times, has hardly yet become a reality. In fact it represented only an oligarchy, the great landowners, the gentry. There was no relation between the number of deputies and the population; the rotten boroughs retained their electoral rights and were like the private property of a family. Elections were expensive, the electors frequently selling their votes and the members receiving no salary; consequently, the rich alone found their way into Parliament. In the members thus elected one could not fail to recognize a full independence as over aganst the electors, who could neither limit their powers nor recall them. How were they held to account? The debates of Parliament were not public; until 1771 the Houses deliberated in secret.

The **responsibility of the Ministers**, and, in general, of public officials, afforded evidence of the seizure by Parliament of the public powers. The king, considered as irresponsible, was accounted as able to do no wrong; but the ministers whom he chose could be arraigned before the Parliament by the process of criminal accusation (attainder, impeachment); they were made the responsible publishers of the acts of the king; they were such, in fact, most of the time, and became such always in law; every royal act, pardon, diplomatic communication, etc., had to be countersigned by a minister. This first step taken, the solidarity of the ministry followed, and the formation of a homogeneous cabinet, the members being taken from the chambers, whose vote could compel their resignation. The ministers, at the mercy of the Parliament, in fact, were inevitably the chiefs of the majority and no longer the favorites of the king, his intimates. Two parties, the Whigs and the Tories, represented in Parliament, contested with each other for power; their staff officers constituted the ministry.

Representative government and parliamentarism were in no sense one of those *a priori* creations such as the school of natural law writers imagined them to be; they were the work of the English landed aristocracy, of a "syndicate of great landowners" who had known how to profit by the hazards of history and who were far from intending to establish a model political régime for the rest of Europe. These institutions were complemented by certain rights: 1st, those rather political and for the most part of recent acquisition, — the right of petition, of assembly (the first "meeting" was in 1769), of association (there were still rigorous measures against Catholics in the 1700 s), and liberty of the press (the censorship did not disappear until 1695); 2d, others, quasi-personal rights — trial by jury, freedom from administrative jurisdiction placing private individuals at the mercy of officials, "habeas corpus," inviolability of domicile, and the necessity of a special law (mutiny act) to deprive deserters of the right of trial by jury and to arraign them before a council of war (since 1688).

TOPIC 2. PRINCIPLES OF 1789

§ 479. **The Principles of 1789**[1] were based on the idea that the nation is sovereign and that all its members are free and of equal rights. From this starting point there was drawn up a political constitution dominated by the rule of the separation of powers, executive, legislative, and judicial, and by the recognition in the individual of political rights, that is to say, participation in public affairs, and of civil rights, that is to say, liberties as opposed to the State itself, and accorded, unlike the preceding, not only to citizens, but to women and children.[2] A Constitution, written like that of the United States of America (1787), organized these new principles, giving to public law a precision and a fixity unknown

[1] *Laferrière*, "Hist. des principes de la Révolution," 1850 (reëdited in 1852 under the title of "Essai sur l' hist. du dr. fr."); *Th. Ferneuil*, "Les principes de 1789 et la science sociale," 1889; *Joyaux*, "La philosophie pend. la Révolution," 1893.

[2] The views contained in the "Cahiers" of the States General of 1789 were like advance résumés in the "Resultat" of the King's Council, Dec. 27, 1788. "It was on this program that France voted." *Cf.* Royal session of June 23, 1789. *Champion*, "La France, d'ap. les Cahiers de 1789," 1897.

to the "Ancien Régime."[1] It was preceded, like the American Constitution, by a **Declaration of the rights of man and of the citizen** (August 26, 1789),[2] as follows:

"The representatives of the French People, constituted in National Assembly, considering that ignorance, forgetfulness or contempt of the rights of man are the sole causes of the public miseries and of the corruption of governments, have resolved to set forth in a solemn declaration the natural, inalienable, and sacred rights of man, in order that this declaration, being ever present to all the members of the social body, may unceasingly remind them of their rights and duties; in order that the acts of the legislative power and those of the executive power may be each moment compared with the aim of every political institution and thereby may be more respected; and in order that the demands of the citizens, grounded henceforth upon simple and incontestable principles, may always take the direction of maintaining the constitution and the welfare of all.

"In consequence, the National Assembly recognizes and declares, in the presence and under the auspices of the Supreme Being, the following rights of man and citizen:

"1. Men are born and remain free and equal in rights. Social distinctions can be based only upon public utility.

"2. The aim of every political association is the preservation of the natural and imprescriptible rights of man. These rights are liberty, property, security and resistance to oppression.

"3. The source of all sovereignty is essentially in the nation; no body, no individual can exercise authority that does not proceed from it in plain terms.

"4. Liberty consists in the power to do anything that does not injure others; accordingly, the exercise of the natural rights of each man has for its only limits those that secure to the other members of society the enjoyment of these same rights. These limits can be determined only by law.

"5. The law has the right to forbid only such actions as are in-

[1] On June 17, 1789, the deputies of the Third Estate, with some members of the clergy, declared themselves to be the National Assembly; afterwards, "Constituent" was added.

[2] Adopted between the 20th of August and the 1st of October, 1789, with the essential Articles of the Constitution, which was revised in 1791, and which was consequently called the Constitution of 1791 (3–14 September). The subsequent Constitutions, except that of the year VIII, were preceded by a Declaration of Rights; that of the year III added a Declaration of Duties. *Cf.* the English Acts of the same kind, but not of the same character: Petition of Rights, Bill of Rights, Act of Settlement, 1700. *Paul Janet*, "Hist. de la sc. polit.," 3d ed. (Introduc.).

jurious to society. Nothing can be forbidden that is not interdicted by the law and no one can be constrained to do that which it does not order.

"6. Law is the expression of the general will. All citizens have the right to take part personally or by their representatives in its formation. It must be the same for all whether it protects or punishes. All citizens, being equal in its eyes, are equally eligible to all public dignities, places and employments, according to their capacities, and without other distinctions than those of their virtues and talents.

"7. No man can be accused, arrested, or detained except in the cases determined by law and according to the forms that it has prescribed. Those who procure, expedite, execute, or cause to be executed arbitrary orders ought to be punished: but every citizen summoned or seized in virtue of the law ought to render instant obedience; he makes himself guilty by resistance.

"8. The law ought to establish only penal ties that are strictly and obviously necessary, and no one can be punished except in virtue of a law established and promulgated prior to the offense and legally applied.

"9. Every man being presumed innocent until he has been pronounced guilty, if it is thought indispensable to arrest him, all severity that may not be necessary to secure his person ought to be strictly suppressed by law.

"10. No one ought to be disturbed on account of his opinions, even religious, provided their manifestation does not derange the public order established by law.

"11. The free communication of ideas and opinions is one of the most precious of the rights of man; every citizen then can freely speak, write and print, subject to responsibility for the abuse of this freedom in the cases determined by law.

"12. The guarantee of the rights of man and citizen requires a public force; this force then is instituted for the advantage of all and not for the personal benefit of those to whom it is intrusted.

"13. For the maintenance of the public force and for the expenses of administration a general tax is indispensable; it ought to be equally apportioned among all the citizens according to their means.

"14. All the citizens have the right to determine by themselves or by their representatives, the necessity of the public tax, to consent to it freely, to watch the employment of it, and to determine the quota, the assessment, the collection and the duration of it.

"15. Society has the right to require an account from every public agent of his administration.

"16. Any society in which the guarantee of rights is not secure or the separation of powers not determined has no constitution at all.

"17. Property being a sacred and inviolable right, no one can be deprived of it unless a legally established public necessity evidently demands it, and on the condition of a just and prior indemnity."

§ 480. **The Constitution and Declaration** appeared as a new **social contract**; they contained both a statement of the "rights of human kind" and those of the French nation, and corresponded to what was called under the "Ancien Régime" the fundamental laws of the State. From the first day, there was fear that these essential rules would be too easily modified; experience proved that these fears were well founded, since between 1789 and 1804 not less than four Constitutions were adopted: that of September 3–14, 1791; June 24, 1793; 5 Fructidor, year III (1795); and that of the 22d Frimaire, year VIII (1800). In order to forestall the evil (contrary to the English practice), a distinction was made between the constituent power and the legislative power, between the constitutional laws ("lois constitutionnelles") and the ordinary laws; though the nation always retained the right to change its Constitution, it could do so only by following the forms which it had prescribed in the Constitution itself.[1] It is true that these forms were not always respected, and that the Constitution was usually revised by an uprising or a "coup d'Etat" under the pretext that no form could limit the will of the nation. The Constitution of the year VIII (1800) established a body called the "Sénat Conservateur" to guard the Constitution by sustaining or annulling the acts which were submitted to it as unconstitutional (by the tribunate or the government). It is well known how it discharged this duty.[2]

[1] Const. 1791. Following a vote ("voeu") of three legislatures, an Assembly composed of the members of the "fourth" and of 249 supplementary members appointed by the departments proceeded to the revision, but its jurisdiction was limited to the points mentioned in the vote.

[2] Revolutionary laws. As long as the monarchy existed, the law was completed only by the sanction of the king joined to the decree of the Assembly (Constituent or Legislative); so the laws had two dates, that of the decree and that of the royal sanction; we often content ourselves with giving only the first, for lack of space. The texts of the revolutionary laws, besides the convenient collections of *Duvergier*, *de Galisset*, will be found chiefly in the "Collection Baudouin," May 4, 1789, Dec. 27, 1799 (5 Niv., year VIII), in the Collection of the Louvre, July 7, 1788–June 20, 1794 (22 Pr., year II), in the "Bulletin des Lois," created by the law of Dec. 4, 1793 (14 Frimaire, year II), in the "Moniteur universel" (Nov. 24, 1789), which became an official organ only under the Consulate,

§ 481. **The Principle of National Sovereignty** is simple only in appearance; very different political systems were engrafted on this stock:[1] the constitutional monarchy, the rule of the convention with an omnipotent representative assembly and executive committees, Cæsarism or popular monarchy. From 1789 to 1804 France was delivered over to experiments which hardly ceased during the whole of the 1800 s and which bore witness to the difficulty of the problem. Throughout all the Revolution the **representative régime**[2] was almost exclusively in force with a prohibition of peremptory mandate ("mandat imperatif"). Rousseau considered it incompatible with the principle of national sovereignty ("Contrat Social," 3, 15): "Sovereignty consists in the general will and the general will cannot be represented; deputies of the people are only commissioners; they can decide nothing definitely. Every law which the people have not personally ratified is null; it is no law; the English people think they are free, but they are so only during an election of members of Parliament; as soon as their representatives are chosen they are slaves, they are nothing. In the brief moments of their liberty they make such use of it that they deserve to lose it." **Direct government** by the people, which Rousseau advocated in theory, was on the point of being realized in 1793, as we shall see later; the Constitutions of 1793 and of the year III (1795)[3] were submitted to popular ratification as well as that of the year VIII (1800). The Consulate and the Empire drew from this practice the custom of the "plébiscite" or consultation of the people upon a single question (for example whether Napoleon should be consul for life). In this respect, however, the Revolution was influenced less by Rousseau than by Montesquieu, according to whom the people were incapable of managing an affair, incapable of discussing it, but admirably qualified to choose those to whom they should intrust a part of their authority.

7 Nivôse, year VIII. Concerning the differences in the texts of these laws and the gaps which these publications contain, *cf. Duvergier*, Intro. to his "Collection des lois." The general table of this collection forms a convenient "repertoire," to which we may refer once for all.

[1] *Duguit and Monnier*, "Les Constitutions de la France," 1898; *Moreau*, "Précis de dr. constitut.," 1894; *L. Rossi*, "Krit. Vierteljahrschrift," 1898 (bibliography and criticism of recent works on constitutional law). "Rev. de dr. public," eds. *Larnaude and Jèze*.

[2] Concerning the notion of political representation, various views, *cf.* in *Gierke*, "Althusius," p. 213, who analyzes the opinions of Marsiglio of Padua, Occam, Nicholas of Cusa and later in England, the ideas of Locke and Sidney. *De Greef*, "La constituante et le régime représ.," 1891.

[3] Decree of Sept. 21, 1792: there could be no Constitution except that which was accepted by the people.

§ 482. **The Separation of Powers**, legislative, executive, and judicial, had been considered by Montesquieu as the first condition of political liberty: "In order that there may not be abuse of power in the disposition of affairs, power must check power. All will be lost if the same man or the same body of nobles or of the people exercise all three powers. The fear is that he would make tyrannical laws in order to execute them tyrannically; where the judge is at the same time the legislator, the power over the life and liberty of the citizens is arbitrary." (*Cf.* "Esprit des Lois," 11, 4 and 6.) The spirit of independence of our old Parliaments, their opposition to the crown, and the example (which is questionable) of England, counted for much in the formation of this theory.[1] It had been adopted by the Revolution, but not without hesitation and not without restrictions.[2]

There was hesitation in recognizing the judicial power as distinct from the executive power. Although the Constitution of 1791 and that of the year III followed the doctrine of Montesquieu and adopted the system of election of judges, that of the year VIII made the judiciary a dependency of the executive power. Restrictions were found in the relations between the executive power and the legislative power. The initiation of laws and of voting taxes was denied to the king by the Constitution of 1791, and to the Directory by that of the year III; but the king was granted a right of suspensive veto, *i.e.* setting aside a law enacted by the national representatives during two successive legislatures and only yielding upon its adoption by the third legislature. The responsibility of the ministers to the legislative body was organized, after a vague fashion it is true, but nevertheless recognized by the law of April 27, 1791; this struck a serious blow at the principle of the separation of powers. In the year III (1795) a return to this rule was made by deciding that the members of the Directory could not be removed by the legislative body.[3]

§ 483. **Individual Liberties.** — Under this head we understand not only the liberty of person (no more discretion in arrests, no more

[1] Concerning the ideas of Rousseau and Condorcet, *cf. Esmein*, p. 287, 290.

[2] By defiance against "coups de force" it was decided that no body of troops could approach within 30,000 "toises" ("toise" = 3 feet plus) of the legislative assembly without its authority. Const. 1791 and of the year III.

[3] Concerning the incompatibility between the quality of deputy and that of minister, *cf.* Const. 1791, 3, 2, 4, 2; Const. year III, Art. 136. *J. Schwarcz*, "Montesquieu u. die Verantworth, d. Räthe d. Monarchen i. England," 1892. For Sweden, *Esmein*, p. 83, cites *Mably*, "De la législ.," I, 262; *Simonnet*, "Le gouv. parl. et la Constituante," 1899.

"lettres de cachet," and no more discretion in penalties) [1] and that which then appeared as a necessary consequence of this liberty: inviolability of domicile, free ownership of property, and liberty of labor; but also certain semi-political rights: the liberty of conscience and freedom of worship, the freedom of the press, the right of assembly,[2] and of association, the right of petition, and the freedom of instruction (Const. of the year III, 300).[3]

§ 484. **Political and Civil Equality.** — The division of the nation into classes or orders: clergy, nobility, Third Estate or bourgeoisie, and serfs, had long since lost its reason for existence. Privileges and inequalities were accordingly abolished. All became equal before the law, before the courts, and in respect to taxation. There were no more distinctions drawn from birth or affiliation with the clergy; no more privileges arising from the exercise of public functions; no more incapacities resulting from differences of religious faith; [4] the public offices were open to all, political rights belonged to all. The only inequalities which remained among individuals were natural inequalities, strength and intelligence, and their fated consequences, riches or poverty.[5] To each according to his ability and not according to his birth, — such was the rule of justice which was established. If its consequences were beneficent in general, there was one, however, the merits of which were disputed: the obstacles which the privileged bodies, nobility, clergy, and higher magistracy, had put in the way of the action of the State were abolished.[6] Opposed to a very powerful

[1] *Cf. supra,* p. 565, n. 6, law of suspects. Const. year III, Art. 145; year VIII, Art. 46: the executive power can cause to be arrested those who are suspected of conspiracy against the safety of the State; Const. year VIII, Art. 55: the Senate can authorize their indefinite detention.

[2] Liberty of the press sanctioned, but not organized, by the Declaration of Rights, lasted until the 10th of August, 1792. After the "coup d'Etat" of the eighteenth Fructidor, year V, newspapers were placed under the supervision of the police. Clubs or political societies (Jacobins, etc.) were broken up, sixth Fructidor, year III. The Constitution of the year III did not authorize political societies to affiliate among themselves, to designate themselves as "popular," to hold public meetings, or to prepare collective petitions (Arts. 361, 362, 364).

[3] The celebrated device: "Liberté, Egalité, Fraternité," implied still more positive duties at the expense of the State, aid for the infirm, work for healthy persons without resources, free elementary instruction, etc. Const. 1791, Tit. I.

[4] Concerning Jews, *cf.* Law of January 28, 1790; Law of September 28, 1791. Const. 1791, vol. I, *Liard,* "L'enseign. sup.," 1894.

[5] Concerning the negroes and colonists, Laws of March 8, 1790, September 28, 1791, etc. *Deschamps,* "La Constituante et l'organisation coloniale," 1899. Table of *Duvergier.*

[6] *Cf.* system of checks and balances of Montesquieu. Abolition of privileges of the nobility, August 4, 1789, and Decree of August 13, 1789. March 15–28. Order of October 15, 1789, and Decree of June 19–23,

State there was no longer anything but isolated individuals without strength; the groups which they might form were subjected in their creation and in their action to a strict surveillance by the State.

§ 485. **Economic Changes. (A) Freedom of Land Ownership.** — The constitution of land ownership was closely bound up with the ancient social organization; the privileges of the nobility rested on the feudal theory of ownership; the power of the clergy had as its foundation its vast possessions in real estate. The eminent domain of the nobles was abolished without indemnity and with it all the rights which were directly or remotely connected with public office. Simple tenants were raised to the rank of full owners; they acquired the right to dispose of their lands at will without seigniorial intervention. The royal authority had ruined political feudalism; the Revolution completed the task by ruining civil feudalism (Decree of Aug. 4–11, and Nov. 3, 1789).[1] The domains of the crown, of the clergy, and those of the "émigrés"[2] passed, under the name of national property, into the hands of small proprietors. In this respect the Revolution had a very marked agrarian character; it reëstablished Roman ownership; it despoiled the seigniors without indemnity; it put into the channels of trade the mortmain property of the clergy and of the crown and thereby increased the value of a large part of the soil of France.

§ 486. **The Same. (B) Freedom of Trade and of Industry.** — Aside from the harm they did to individual liberty, the trading companies[3] and corporations constituted an extreme embarrass-

1790: abolition of hereditary nobility; titles of nobility could no longer be borne nor conferred; only the family name could be used. Orders of chivalry were also abolished. Privileges like hunting, the keeping of warrens, were abolished August 4–September 21, 1789. At the same time, the rights of primogeniture and of male succession were abolished; entails went, August 25, 1792. The clergy was dissolved as a body, August 4–11, 1789. The State no longer recognized monastic vows. Decree of October 28–November 1, 1789, February 13–19, 1790. Suppression of religious congregations, Decree of August 17, 1792.

[1] *Infra*, p. 554. Feudal dues were suppressed without indemnity. *Ginoulhiac*, p. 807; *Sagnac*, "Dr. civ. de la Rév.," 1899. Decree of March 18, 1793: penalty of death for any one who proposed the agrarian law. Conspiracy of Babeuf (8 Prairial, year V, May 25, 1797) which had as its aim the suppression of private property and the common welfare. *Espinas*, "La philos. du XVIIIe s. et la Révol.," 1898.

[2] Table of *Duvergier* for the laws concerning "émigrés." *Dalloz*, "Répert." Mirabeau held out with great vigor against the laws against "émigrés." After the flight of the king, the free departure of the royal family ceased to be possible; passports were required. Decrees of June 28 and July 4 and 6, 1791. After the 14th of September, the freedom of emigration was for a time reëstablished.

[3] August 14–October 13, 1790, abolition of the Company of the Indies.

ment to trade and industry; taking up the work of Turgot, the Revolution abolished them, prohibited their reëstablishment, and substituted for monopoly the régime of free competition (March 2–17 to June 14–17, 1791). Industrial property, which the "ancien régime" had known only under the form of royal privileges, became a right and was sanctioned by law by means of patents for inventions (December 31, 1790). Free circulation of grain (April 29, 1790), unity of weights and measures (March 26, 1791), and the freedom of loans at interest (October 3, 1789) [1] completed these measures.[2]

§ 487. **The Same.** (C) **Literary Property,** dependent formerly upon obtaining a royal privilege, was now regarded as a natural and civil right inherent in the right of labor; "it is," said Chapelier, "the most sacred and, if one may so speak, the most personal of all kinds of ownership; nevertheless, it is a form of property entirely different from every other kind." (Decree of July 19, 1793, 25 Prair., year III.[3])

[1] This law did not authorize the taking of usurious rates of interest, that is to say, more than that of the Bourse.

[2] Political troubles, the absence of specie, depreciation of paper money having produced a great increase in the price of provisions, the Convention sought to remedy the evil: 1. by the law against forestalling or cornering (July 26, 1793) which affected not only speculators, but merchants who laid in supplies, subjected their houses to domiciliary searches, and permitted communes to fix prices; 2. by the laws on the "maximum" (September 29, 1793, Feb. 24, 1794), "which stopped production and commerce," because it prescribed the alternative of selling at a loss or subjected the owner to penalties of the law; by requiring sales at a low price it happened that the high prices, already excessive, were still further increased. Nothing was gained by fixing the price of merchandise instead of leaving it to be fixed by the law of supply and demand, or the price of transportation, the profits of the producer, of the wholesale merchant (5%), of the retailer (10 %), and of trying to fix legally such variable elements as the prices of things. The requisitions by which the communes or the State took possession of what was necessary for them, before the merchant could sell his merchandise, increased the evil still more. Finally, to cap the climax, the importation of English merchandise was prohibited (October 10, 1795), and the property of foreign countries with which France was at war was sequestered. This led to reprisals and put a stop to the circulation of bills of exchange. After the 9th Thermidor, the law on the "maximum" was abolished.

[3] The decrees of the Council of 1777 and 1778 "had given guaranties to authors, but without detracting from the fundamental principle, according to which the right to print a book was a royal concession, a mere favor. If the privilege was granted to the author, it was hereditary; if it was granted to a publisher, it ended with the life of the author." These decrees did not apply to dramatic works. The Constituent Assembly recognized for these works, as for other writings, the legality of the rights of the author. Decree of January 19, 1791. At the same time, it proclaimed the freedom of theatrical performances.

TOPIC 3. THE EXECUTIVE POWER

§ 488. **The Monarchy** was retained by the Constitution of 1791; upon the king was conferred the exercise of the executive power and a share (very limited) of the legislative power. But he was nothing more than the chief public functionary; if the nation did not have the right to remove him, there were cases in which he was considered as having abdicated and the monarchical form might be abolished through a revision of the Constitution. The royal power was delegated hereditarily to the reigning house; the king was styled king of *the French people* by the grace of God and the constitutional law of the State. His person was sacred and inviolable; the crown was indivisible and was transmitted through the male line according to the rule of primogeniture, females being excluded. During the minority of the king, which ended with the attainment of his eighteenth year, the regency belonged to his nearest male relative twenty-five years of age, and in default of such, to a regent elected by the nation (by indirect suffrage). The king had a civil list of twenty-five millions. Among other prerogatives the king had was that of watching over the external safety of the State; he appointed ambassadors, and negotiated and treated with foreign nations (subject to the ratification of the legislative body); he was the supreme head of the army, but he could appoint only the superior military commanders; he was likewise the supreme chief of the administration, but the appointment of administrative officers did not belong to him any more than did the appointment of judicial officers. We have already pointed out that he had a suspensive veto upon the acts of the legislature.

The king exercised his powers through the agency of a council of ministers appointed and removed by him, taken from outside the legislative assembly; every order of the king had to be countersigned by a minister and the ministers alone were responsible, while the king was irresponsible.

§ 489. **The Republic. The Convention.** — The king having been suspended on the 10th of August, 1792, and the monarchy abolished September 20, 1792, the executive power passed to delegations of the legislative assembly (an Executive Council of six ministers), or of the Convention: the **Committee of Public Safety,**[1]

[1] *Aulard*, "Rec. des actes du Comité du Salut public," 1889. Abolition of the Gregorian Calendar, October 5–November 24, 1793; the Republican Era was dated from the 22d of September, 1792, date of the foundation of the Republic. Abolition of the Republican calendar, January 1, 1806.

composed of nine of its members (later, a larger number, April 6 and July 10, 1793), and the **Committee of General Security**, charged with internal police and subordinated to the first-mentioned committee. In consequence of a reaction against internal dissensions in the presence of the enemy, the revolutionary government organized itself into (Dec. 4, 1793, 14th Frimaire, Year II) a true dictatorship of the Committee of Public Safety, an unstable dictatorship, but one which restored temporarily the authority of the most absolute kings and caused its power to be felt everywhere, by the aid of delegates at large, national agents, revolutionary committees, and Jacobin societies. With the downfall of Robespierre this omnipotence was broken, several branches of the administration being confided to other committees.

§ 490. **The Directory and the Consulate.** — Through reaction against the régime of the Convention the Constitution of the year III (1795) and especially that of the 22d Frimaire, year VIII (1800) separated and strengthened the executive power. The first provided for a **Directory** of five members appointed by the Council of Elders from a list chosen by secret ballot by the Council of Five Hundred and annually renewed by one fifth. Each member of the Directory presided in turn for a period of three months. The Directory had charge of the internal administration, of police, of foreign affairs, the initiative in matters of war and diplomacy, and the conduct of military operations. It appointed and dismissed the ministers and the commanders in chief. The Directors were irremovable. The Constitution of the year VIII (1800) substituted in their place three **Consuls**, of whom two had only an advisory voice, and with whom were associated two deliberative bodies, the **Council of State**, an administrative body, and the **Privy Council**, rather political (*e.g.* ratification of treaties).

Topic 4. The Legislative Power

§ 491. **The Constitution of 1791.** — The legislative power was confided to a single chamber. This system was preferred to the bicameral system of England for two reasons: 1st, the desire to fuse the deputies of the three Estates into a single national assembly; 2d, the difficulty of finding in a nation in which privileged classes no longer existed the elements with which to form an upper and a lower chamber. The legislative assembly should logically have been elected by universal suffrage, since the principle of the political equality of all citizens had just been proclaimed.

The Constituent Assembly believed it a duty, however, to require certain conditions easily met for the exercise of political rights; it therefore distinguished between **active citizens**, who alone had the right to vote, and **passive citizens** (a system based on property with a very low property qualification, so that the number of electors, 4,298,360, was very large in proportion to the population). Voting was in two stages (indirect suffrage); the active citizens assembled by cantons to choose the electors (one for one hundred and fifty), the electors assembled by departments to choose the 745 members of the Legislative Assembly. The deputies were inviolable; they were considered as representatives of the entire nation and consequently were not bound by instructions from their constituents. The Legislative Assembly voted the laws and the budget, decided upon war, ratified treaties, and had the right to arraign before a High Court the Ministers, public officials, and all those accused of attempts and conspiracies against the safety of the State or against the Constitution.[1]

§ 492. **Universal Suffrage. The Mountain Constitution ("Montagnard") of 1793.** — On the 10th of August, 1792, the king was suspended from his functions and the distinction between active and passive citizens abolished; universal suffrage, or quasi-universal suffrage,[2] was introduced but with two degrees. At the same time the people were invited to choose a national **Convention**; by this was meant, in the current language of the time, an assembly of

[1] In order to be an elector of the 1st degree, with the right to vote in the primary Assemblies, it was necessary to be twenty-five years of age, a resident for one year, not to be a hired servant, and to have paid a direct tax equal to the value of three days' labor; to be eligible to the Electoral Assembly of the department, it was necessary to have paid a tax equal to the value of ten days' labor; to be eligible to the National Assembly, it was necessary to have paid a tax equal to the value of a silver mark (about fifty francs), and besides, to be a property owner. The Constitution of 1791 abolished this requirement; it was henceforth only necessary to be an active citizen; but to be able to take part in the Electoral Assemblies, it was necessary to be an owner, usufructuary, or renter of property yielding an income equal to the value of from 100 to 400 days' labor, according to the population of the towns (or analogous conditions). *Esmein*, p. 203, rightly observes that there was a strong analogy between the electoral system of the Constitution of 1791 and that which was in force before the Revolution for the States-General, namely: vote by two degrees, payment of a tax (that is to say, inscription of the electors on the roll of "taille" payers), exclusion of domestics and residence; the calculation of the amount of the tax required in order to be an elector was made like that formerly of the "taille" on industry and the poll tax on artisans and laborers. *Cf.* the Decree of December 22, 1789, which was modified by the Constitution of 1791. Let us add that the taking of the civic oath was also required for the exercise of political rights. The Revolution used and abused the oath.

[2] Decree of August 11, 1792. Exclusion of domestics, and of indigents; age requirement twenty-one years and a domicile of six months.

revision provided by the Constitution of 1791 (VII, 1). The Convention, having assembled, abolished the monarchy (September 21, 1792), and the Republic was thus proclaimed, almost by surprise (September 22, 1792, the vote of the beginning of the Republican Era). It was necessary to put the constitutional laws into harmony with the new situation. The committee of the Convention on the Constitution brought forward, February 15, 1793, through its reporter, Condorcet, a rough draft, which the downfall of the Girondins caused to be abandoned. The one which replaced it became the Constitution of 1793. Universal suffrage, ultimately and completely sanctioned, became direct; voting by two degrees was retained only for the election of members of departmental or district administrations and of the courts. Not content with establishing universal suffrage the Convention introduced a system of referendum or popular veto in respect to the laws. Passed by a single assembly elected for a year, laws had to be submitted to the electorate if, within forty days after the sending of the text to the communes, 200,000 electors so demanded (a tenth of the primary assemblies in half the departments plus one, which represented about 200,000 electors). But the legislative body had the right to issue decrees, a kind of subsidiary laws, without being subjected to the control of the electors.[1] The executive power was assigned to a council of twenty-four members elected by the legislative body from a list of persons drawn up by the electors of the second degree, one for each department. The Constitution was submitted to the nation and ratified by the primary assemblies, July 14 and 21, but in a very irregular manner (oral vote, etc.). October 10, 1793, its application was postponed until the conclusion of peace. The circumstances of war called forth a political régime which was almost the reverse: the **revolutionary government.**

§ 493. **The Constitution of the 5th Fructidor, year III (1795)** took the place of the Constitution of 1793, which remained a dead letter. It marked a reaction both against the democratic tendencies of the latter and against the omnipotence of a unicameral assembly like the Convention, but it retained the system of centralization which, however, was reformed. A restricted suffrage and voting according to two degrees were reëstablished. In order to take part in the cantonal primary assemblies it was necessary to pay a direct tax on real or personal property equal to the value of three days of farm labor (Art. 304); from 1795 inscription on

[1] The Convention also took care to organize the responsibility of the deputies. *Esmein,* p. 272.

the civil register was to be refused to any one who could not prove that he was able to read and write and to carry on a mechanical trade (or farming); hired servants were still deprived of electoral rights. In the electoral assemblies of the departments (2d degree), which elected the members of the legislative body upon a general ticket, no one could participate who had not attained the age of twenty-five years and who was not a property owner, usufructuary, or lessee of property the income of which varied according to the population (the value of 100, 150, or 200 days' labor).[1] The legislative body was divided into a chamber charged with proposing laws, the **Council of Five Hundred**, and a chamber called the **Council of Elders** (250 in number), charged with approving them. No one could be a member of the first chamber who had not attained the age of thirty years, or of the second, who was not forty years of age.[2] Privileges having disappeared, the natural inequality of age seemed to be the only plausible base for a system of two chambers, but whatever may have been its value, it permitted an escape from the despotism of a Convention.[3] The executive power was intrusted to a Directory of five members elected by the Council of Elders from a list proposed by the Council of Five Hundred. There was repugnance to the idea of the direct election of the head of the State by the mass of electors. The directors could be impeached by the legislative power.

§ 494. **The Constitution of the year VIII (22d Frimaire)** gave to the executive power a marked preponderance by making the legislative power excessively complicated and especially by withdrawing too far from the nation the political assemblies which represented it; those who composed it were the elect of the government rather than of the country.

1st, The **Senate** watched over the preservation of the Constitution; it annulled unconstitutional acts; it revised the Constitution by means of organic "Senatus Consulta" (thus it established the Consulate for life, in 1802; the Empire in 1804; and abolished the Tribunate in 1807); and it elected from departmental lists the 300 members of the legislative body, the 100 tribunes, the

[1] The Constituent Assembly decided that its members could not be members of the Legislative Assembly. The Convention desired, on the contrary, that two thirds of the Legislative Assembly should be taken from its members.

[2] Let us add that in order to be eligible to membership in the Council of Elders it was necessary to have resided in France fifteen years and to be married or to be a widower; celibates were excluded from membership.

[3] The Council of Elders had the right to change the meeting place of the legislative body.

Consuls, the judges of the Court of Cassation, and the Commissioners of Accounts.

2d, The **Legislative Body** enacted without discussion (hence, "the dumb body") bills presented by the orators of the government and discussed by the orators of the **Tribunate**. The elections were held according to a very complicated system at the base of which, however, was universal, or quasi-universal, suffrage (twenty-one years of age, residence in France for a year, and not being a hired servant). There were: 1st, communal lists (containing 600,000 names) made out by the primary electors (five or six million in number), from which the executive authority chose the inferior officeholders and judges; 2d, departmental lists (containing 50,000 to 60,000 names) from which the superior officeholders and judges were chosen; and 3d, a national list (6,000 names) from which the Senate [1] chose the members of the legislative body, the tribunals, the Councilors of State, the Ministers, the judges of the Court of Cassation, and the Commissioners of Accounts.[2]

Topic 5. Local Administration

§ 495. **Administrative Divisions.** — In the place of the old administrative divisions, which were irregular, unequal, full of "enclaves," varying according to administrative services, often having no other basis than historical tradition, the Constitutional Assembly substituted a simple division, uniform areas for all services, so as to render the action of the central power both easier and more certain. These divisions were: **departments** (83), **districts** [3] (arrondissements under Napoleon), and **cantons**, embracing a certain number of towns, parishes, or communities to which the Convention gave the general name of **communes** (Decree of the 10th Brumaire, year II). Everywhere a system of self-government with collective administrative bodies chosen by election took the place of the extreme centralization of the "ancien régime."

§ 496. **Collective Administrations. Anarchy.** — Each department and each district had an administrative Commission divided into a Directory or executive section, and a Council or deliberative

[1] The Senate itself, chosen by the Constitution, was recruited by co-optation from lists prepared by the legislative body, the Tribunate, and the First Consul.

[2] *Cf.* "Senatus consulta" of the 16th Thermidor, year X; and of the 28th Floréal, year XII.

[3] December 22, 1789; January 15, and February 26, 1790.

section, elected like the members of the legislative body and renewable, one half every two years. The administration of the department was composed of thirty-six members with a procureur-general syndic; that of the district of twelve members with a procureur syndic. There could be no deliberation until the procureur syndics had been heard. The district assemblies were subordinate to the departmental assemblies; but between these and the government there was no intermediary; if the king could suspend the members in serious cases, or even procure the dissolution of the legislative body, this was an extreme measure to which recourse was seldom had and which did not prevent administrative anarchy.

§ 497. **Centralization.** — The Convention undertook to remedy the evil by sending "delegates at large" (January 26 and March 9, 1793), who were "veritable intendants" with the right to have suspects arrested, to remove officials, and to take urgent measures. The Decree of December 4, 1793 (14th Frimaire, year II), even abolished the hierarchy between departments and districts, at least for the execution of the revolutionary laws and for measures of public safety and general security; the districts, in which the convention placed national agents, were charged with duties of supervision and were obliged to render an account every ten days to the committees of government; they found devoted auxiliaries in the revolutionary committees and the Jacobin societies. The departmental administrations, reduced to their Directories, lost almost all importance. In this way all the local authorities found themselves strictly subordinated to the Committee of Public Safety. After the downfall of Robespierre, on the 28th Germinal, year III, the departmental and district organizations were reëstablished as they had been before the federalist movement whose progress they had seemed to assist.

The Constitution of the year III reduced the departmental administrations to five members (in imitation of the Directory); in each of them, and in each municipality, the Directory appointed a removable commissioner charged with supervising the execution of the laws. The districts disappeared. The small municipalities were merged into municipalities of cantons formed by the municipal agents elected in each commune. The municipal administration was subordinated to the administration of departments and these latter to the ministers. The Directory had the right to remove them all. With the Constitution of the year VIII there was a definite abandonment of the system of collective administration upon which so many correctives had already been brought to bear and which was so discredited. The **executive** function was confided to a single official, a prefect, subprefect, or mayor; that of **deliberation** to an assembly, the council of the department, the arrondissement, or the municipality. The **contentious** jurisdiction, separated from administration, passed to a council of the prefecture. Then only there began again, in a France leveled and equalized, the centralization of the "ancien régime," more absolute than it had ever been before: the same officials everywhere, with the same powers, the same hierarchy, the same instructions drawn up at Paris even in the minutest detail.

§ 498. **The Communes.** — The system of municipal organization, already in force during the "ancien régime," was made general by the Constituent Assembly.[1] The municipal administration, elected for two years, one half renewable every year, of a number proportional to the population, included: 1st, the **municipal body** ("corps municipal") divided into: (*a*) a bureau, one third, and (*b*) a council, two thirds; 2d, the notables, double the number; and 3d, the mayor, the attorney of the commune, and, in important places, a substitute for this attorney (elected for two years, the mayor not being immediately reëligible).

The notables and the municipal body united to form the Council General of the Commune on exceptional occasions when important matters were involved, such as suits, loans, extraordinary taxes, and the transfer of property.[2] The municipal body was subjected in local affairs (administration of communal property, public works, police, etc.) to the surveillance of the district and departmental authorities, but was in complete dependence upon them in matters of general interest, such as the apportionment and collection of taxes. During the Terror, revolutionary committees were established in each commune to execute the laws against suspects. They gradually disappeared after the Thermidorean reaction, without having been formally abolished (*cf.* Decree of the 7th Fructidor, year II).

[1] Decree of December 14, 1789. The Decree of February, 1790, made the communes responsible for damages caused on account of riots; *cf.* Law of the 10th Vendém., year IV. In case of sedition, the municipal authorities made requisitions upon armed forces, hoisted the red flag, and read the Riot Act (martial law, October 21, 1789).

[2] *Cf.* Decree of May 21, 1790, definitively regulating the municipal organization of Paris and dividing that city into forty-eight sections. The rôle which the commune of Paris played during the Revolution is well known.

TOPIC 6. JUSTICE

§ 499. **Defects of Justice During the "Ancien Régime."**[1] — There was complaint of the excessive number of courts (ecclesiastical, seigniorial, administrative, and exceptional); between them the demurring suitor sometimes remained suspended for long years (jurisdictional uncertainties), appeals and petitions leading him from one to another made lawsuits interminable.[2] Frequently those amenable to one court found themselves deprived of their natural judges; frequently, also, the tribunals were not conveniently accessible, so irregular and extended were the judicial divisions of the Parliaments, or so encumbered still was the public law with the débris of feudalism.[3] While the old magistracy as a whole was distinguished for its integrity, the sale of judgeships and exorbitant judicial fees could not fail to throw a shadow over its good name. Justice was sometimes arbitrary (commissioners and "lettres de cachet"), often unequal (removals of cases to other courts,[4] "committimus," decrees of suspension relieving great personages from paying their debts), and always very slow and very costly in consequence of the complications of the procedure. From the time of Beccaria and the appearance of the man of feeling ("l'homme sensible") in the literature of the 1700 s, public opinion was aroused against the rigor of the criminal law (torture, atrocious punishments, branding, the wheel, quartering, etc.),[5] and against a mode of criminal trial which seems to have been directed toward the doom of the accused. In this respect the Revolution had much to reform.

§ 500. **Under the Revolution** the monarchical maxim: "All justice emanates from the king" became "All justice emanates

[1] The Decree of November 3, 1789, suspended the parliaments indefinitely. The seigniorial courts were abolished August 4, 1789. *Cf.* Dec. October 6, 1790.

[2] Sometimes there were six successive appeals. *Fleury*, p. 74: Rameau, Prépalteau, Montigny, Châteaudun, Blois, Parliament.

[3] Near Châlons-sur-Marne was the village of Saint-Memmée, some of whose inhabitants were judged at Vitry, others at Epernay (none at Châlons).

[4] The Marquis of Beuvron, wishing to have the marriage of his daughter annulled, went before the Parliament of Paris, then had the case transferred to Dijon, and to Aix in Provence; seeing that he was going to lose his suit, he obtained a judgment from the Council. *D'Avenel*, "Richelieu," IV, 30.

[5] It is too often forgotten that the savage manners of older days necessitated pitiless repressions; let it be said, although it costs our vanity something to admit it, the security which we enjoy is derived as much from the inhumanity of the old laws as from our own elevation of the moral level.

from the nation." Justice having a single source, a single class of tribunals was organized in which justice was rendered in the name of the State. The English **Jury** presented itself almost as a necessity: was it not, indeed, a form of popular justice? The Constituent Assembly introduced it for the trial of criminal cases (Law of April 30, 1790);[1] if it rejected the jury in civil cases, it was only after a lively discussion, and it came as near as it could by substituting, in the place of irremovable judges, judges appointed for a fixed term (six years) and holding office by election. It created three kinds of tribunals: ordinary or district courts (courts of the departments under the constitution of 1795), justices of the peace, and a Court of Review. Among the **district courts,** there was no hierarchy, the judiciary being an emanation from the people and no district court being regarded as superior to another (Law of Aug. 16, 1790, Vol. V); appeal lay from one district court to another only by an accident (circular appeals).[2] However, below these ordinary seats of justice were the **justices of the peace,** inexpensive tribunals intended to sit in judgment upon the cases of the poor and to try to prevent lawsuits through measures of reconciliation.[3] A supreme court, the **Court of Review,**[4] was charged with insuring the uniform interpretation of the

[1] Selection of the jury; Law of September 16, 1791.

[2] The tribunals of appeal were established by the Constitution of the year VIII, Art. 61.

[3] Besides, the Revolutionists endeavored to accustom suitors to avoid resort to the judges and courts, by encouraging arbitration. The right of arbitration was one of those rights which the legislature was not authorized to restrict. The Law of August 16–24, 1790, concerning the organization of the judiciary, provided for the creation of "family tribunals" to decide disputes between members of the family and near relatives. Likewise, the Law of September 20, 1792, gave an assembly of relatives and friends of the parties jurisdiction of divorce cases. In the place of the judges, properly speaking, the Convention substituted public arbiters, who were elected every year by the electoral assemblies; they had jurisdiction of disputes not settled by private arbiters or justices of the peace; they deliberated in public, delivered their opinions orally; rendered judgment in last resort, without formalities and without expense, and gave the reasons for their decisions (Const. 1793, Arts. 91 to 95). The organization of this patriarchal justice seems to have been prompted by the illusions which Rousseau nourished ("Gouv. de la Pologne," ch. X).

[4] The members, forty-one or forty-two in number, were chosen by the secondary electors for four years, one judge and one supplementary judge for each department; half of the eighty-three departments, forty-one or forty-two alternately, electing one half of them every four years. The king added to them one commissioner and two substitutes. The draft of the Condorcet Constitution, 1793, substituted for them great judges of assizes, called "judicial censors," who made tours of inspection in the departments. The principle of election was retained until the Empire when the judges of the Court of Review were appointed by Napoleon; the tribunal took the name of Court.

law throughout all the State.[1] Thus was realized the uniformity of decisions, a necessary complement of legislative unity — an achievement which the "ancien régime" had not been able to accomplish.[2] A new principle, the obligation of all the courts to give the reasons for their decisions, contributed to facilitate this result. From the simplified judicial organization with which the Constitutional Assembly endowed the country, certain consequences followed, namely: the abolition of exceptional or extraordinary courts (with the exception of the tribunals of commerce), and of jurisdiction privileges; no one could be deprived of his natural judges, and all citizens without distinction were obliged to sue before the same judges and according to the same forms.

§ 501. **The Election of the Judges** was one of the most radical innovations of the Constituent Assembly. This had no precedents in France except in the organization of the tribunals of commerce and the councils of "prude hommes." The Constitutional Assembly, considering the judicial power as one of the manifestations of the national sovereignty, believed that those who exercised it should hold it through election, by the same title as those who exercised the legislative power, or who exercised administrative functions. But since no one could administer justice without having special attainments and without having had a certain experience, the Constitutional Assembly provided that no one could be selected as a judge unless he had attained the twenty-fifth year of age and had practiced for five years the profession of lawyer.[3] The Convention (Decree of October 14, 1792) made all citizens who were twenty-five years of age eligible to judgeships without other qualifications, and thus opened the magistracy to the politicians. The Constitution of the year III fixed the age qualification at thirty years. But already the elective system, though maintained in theory, had been badly battered down in practice. The Con-

[1] Its jurisdiction embraced abuses of the law, the removal of cases from one tribunal to another when challenged for partiality, prize money, jurisdictional conflicts or doubts, and conflicts of ruling in criminal matters. Concerning conflicts of powers, *cf.* the Decree of October 7, 1790, and the Law of 21st Fructidor, year III.

[2] The tribunal of Review could not pass upon the merits of the cases brought before it, but had to remand them for examination to another tribunal than that of which it had reversed the judgment. Thus was avoided the abuse formerly committed by the old factional Council. The interpretation of laws by means of orders taking jurisdiction did not belong to it; the legislative body, in case of necessity, rendered interpretative decrees. Const. 1791, 5, 21.

[3] The district judges were chosen by the secondary electors, the justices of the peace by the primary electors.

vention annulled the judgments of the elected magistrates, tried cases itself, dismissed the judges, and elected new ones. By virtue of a decree of the 14th Ventôse, year III (1795), the committee of legislation was authorized to appoint thenceforth administrative officers, municipal officers, and judges. Various laws permitted the Directory to proceed in the same way by direct appointment in numerous cases, for example, in case of the annulment of elections, when they had not been held within the prescribed period, etc. Thus progress was made toward the abandonment of the elective system. The Constitution of the year VIII, Art. 45, abolished it finally by providing that the first Consul should appoint the judges.[1] However, until the establishment of the consulate for life, the justices of the peace were elected by the cantonal assemblies for three years, and the judges of the Court of Cassation by the Senate for life.

If the elective system for choosing judges is viewed in the light of experience during the Revolution, there is little to recommend it;[2] the results which it gave during this period were hardly satisfactory. By making the judges elective, the Revolution abolished the principle of **irremovability** for the magistracy,[3] that is to say, the independence of the judges. Those who were first elected were wisely enough chosen, but when they tried to apply the laws impartially, they were attacked with the greatest violence by the electors. The Convention purged the magistracy and the new elections were exclusively political. The Constitution of the year VIII reëstablished the rule of irremovability.[4]

[1] No qualifications were required until the Law of the 22d Ventôse, year XII, requiring the grade of licentiate in law (from the 1st Vend., year XVII); the Law of the 20th April, 1810, prescribed two years' practice at the bar.

[2] *Cf.*, however, *Jeanvrot*, "L'inamovabilité de la magistrature," 1882; "Revol. Fr.," Vol. V; and *Martin-Sarzeaud*, "Et. hist. sur l'inamov.," 1881.

[3] It has been said that the principle of irremovability remained, but the terms of the judges were restricted to short periods; neither the electors nor the executive power could remove them. This is true; but thus understood, the rule of irremovability lost all importance. Moreover, no one was deceived. The principle of irremovability was regarded as incompatible with revolutionary ideas. "The judges were not the proprietors of justice," said Dupard in the Constituent Assembly; "what is a life employment, if it is not private property? Life tenure for the judges was a useful institution under another order of things; it was in force during the old régime; analogous to the privileges of bodies and individuals, it served as a barrier for despotism, but like them it was injurious to liberty." "To declare for the principle of irremovability is to work in the interest of bad judges," said Roederer, on his side.

[4] Article 68 retained the possibility of derogating from it by excluding from the magistrature judges *not maintained on the list of eligibles* (which was revised every three years); this power, which was not made use of,

§ 502. **The Principle of the Separation of Powers** produced three important results: (A) Justice could not be administered by the king, nor, in general, by the holders of executive power, nor by the legislative body.[1] (B) Conversely, the tribunals could not encroach upon the administration; while in England public officials may be arraigned before the courts of justice by private individuals on account of their acts and are civilly and criminally responsible, in France the judges were forbidden to cite the members of the administration before them for acts done in their offices (Law of August 16, 1790, II, 13; Decree of the 16th Fructidor, year III); by this means encroachments upon the administration, similar to those of which the old parliaments were guilty, were aimed against. The decision of administrative controversies was intrusted to the administrative bodies themselves (Decree of September 6–11, 1790) until the Constitution of the year VIII, Art. 52, established a superior administrative tribunal, the Council of State, and the Law of the 28th Pluviôse, year VIII, created a Council of the Prefecture in each department.[2] (C) The judges could not meddle in the exercise of legislative power, either by means of orders taking jurisdiction,[3] or by preventing or suspending the execution of the laws;[4] nor could they pass upon the constitutionality of the laws.

§ 503. **Procedure.** — The Decree of August 16–24, 1790, II, 20, prescribed that judicial procedure should be made more simple, more expeditious, and less expensive; but this order was executed only by the Decree of the 3d Brumaire, year II, which reduced to a strict minimum the pleadings of procedure, required that they should be drawn up in a terse style, that magistrates' reports be simplified,[5] that the judges should deliberate in public, and that the

disappeared with the list of eligibles at the time of the consulate for life. Concerning the Empire *cf.* "Senatus Consult" of October 12, 1807, and *Esmein*, p. 343.

[1] The Constitutions of 1791 and 1795 devoted a special chapter to the judicial power. *Cf.* the Constitution of the year VIII, Tit. V, relating to the tribunals. *Cf. Duguit*, "La Séparation des pouvoirs," 1893.

[2] Add: the Law of September 16, 1807, reëstablishing the Court of Accounts.

[3] Decree of August 16, 1790, II, 12. The tribunals requested, in case of need, the legislative body to interpret the law or to make a new one. "Code Civ.," Art. 5. *Cf.* the orders taking jurisdiction by the parliaments.

[4] *Cf.* remonstrances and refusals (of the Parliament) to register the laws. The Decree of August 16, 1790, II, 11, prescribed that the tribunals were bound forthwith and without alteration to enter in a special register the laws which should be sent to them and to publish the same during the week following.

[5] With a prohibition against taking depositions or discovery before suit begun.

profession of solicitors should be abolished. But this decree was repealed on the 18th Fructidor, year VIII (1800). Until the adoption of the Code of 1807 procedure was governed by the Ordinance of 1667,[1] by certain subsequent ordinances, and by some special laws of the revolutionary period,[2] making altogether a very confused collection, the application of which was often impossible.

We have already seen how the advocates were displaced by **official defenders.** By a strange inconsistency, the public prosecutor (commissioners of the king), although appointed by the king and although a mere agent of the executive power, kept the irremovability acquired under the "Ancien Régime." He lost several of his prerogatives; the initiation of criminal prosecutions was reserved to the justices of the peace, the accusation had to be made by a **public accuser** elected by the people. The Constitution of June 24, 1793, abolished the office, but that of 1795 reëstablished it and made the incumbent removable.[3] The public accuser disappeared by virtue of Article 63 of the Constitution of 1800. The Law of September 16, 1791, organized the criminal procedure by distinguishing two phases: 1st, the preparatory examination, made by the justice of the peace [4] under the control of the public accuser, submitted to a civil tribunal, and then to a jury of accusation; 2d, the final examination in the presence of the trial jury; the pleadings were oral and public; the jury voted according to their inmost convictions, and were not fettered, like the magistrates of former times, by a system of technical proofs. Upon the counts framed by the commissioner of

[1] Decrees of October 19, 1790; of April 28, 1791; and of March 6, 1791.

[2] Decree of January 29, 1791, inventories; of the 4th Germinal, year II, nullities; of the 19th Vend., year IV, appeal; of the 9th Mess., year IV, contumacy; of the 11th Brum., year VII, distress on real property. *Cf.* the Decree of the 7th Niv., year IV, of the 14th Prair., year VI, and of the 21st Vent., year VII.

[3] Decrees of August 16–24, 1790; of September 16–29, 1791; of October 20–22, 1792; Const. of 1795, Arts. 216, 261.

[4] The justices of the peace were therefore charged with the maintenance of the public safety. "Elected by the people to exercise the most gentle and consoling of political prosecutions, did they not appear designed to accumulate in their persons everything which could make police tranquilizing for those whom they protected, respectable for those over whom they exercised surveillance, and reassuring for those who were subject to their authority?" "Instruction concerning criminal procedure," September 22, 1791. With two of his colleagues or assessors, the justice of the peace constituted the correctional tribunal, "which, in repressing offenses, must act especially by moral influence." He became a police judge only by authority of the Decree of the 3d Brumaire, year IV. Until then the municipal authority constituted the tribunal of police. Decree of August 24, 1790, 3, 10.

the king, the tribunal, composed of professional judges, pronounced the punishment which resulted from the verdict of the jury. This system gave the defense important guarantees.[1] Arbitrary imprisonment and the unlimited detentions of the "Ancien Régime" were prohibited by virtue of measures such as that which required an examination within twenty-four hours of every man who was arrested.

§ 504. **Criminal Legislation.**[2] — The Declaration of the Rights of Man and the Decree of January 21, 1790, established new principles in criminal matters; only acts injurious to society were declared punishable and not wrongs consisting only in intent;[3] the law could establish only penalties which were strictly necessary, which involved the abolition of the atrocious punishments of the "Ancien Régime." The same penalty was prescribed for all who committed the same offense, whatever their rank or condition; offenses being personal, the family could not be attainted by a punishment inflicted upon one of its members. Penalties were proportioned to the offense[4] and were divided into three classes: corporal and infamous, correctional, and municipal, corresponding to the grades of offense, crimes, correctional, and municipal offenses, and corresponding also to the courts, the criminal court (judges and juries), the correctional police (justice of the peace and two

[1] Decrees of October 8, 1789; of April 22, 1790; and of September 29, 1791. Modifications were made in the subsequent constitutions, in the Code of the 3d Brumaire, year IV, in the Law of the 19th Fructidor, year V, and in the Code of Criminal Instruction of 1809.

[2] *A. Desjardins*, "Les Cahiers des Etats Généraux en 1789 et la Législation Criminelle," 1883; *Esmein*, "Hist. de la procéd, Crim.," 1882; *Schaeffner*, IV, 322; and *Detourbet*, "La procéd. crim. au XVIIe Siècle," 1881.

[3] The law of suspects of September 17, 1793, ordered the arrest of all who, by their conduct, by their relations, by their speech, or writings showed themselves to be partisans of tyranny or of federalism and therefore enemies of liberty. Committees were charged with making the arrests of such persons. That of the 27th Germinal ordered all former nobles to leave Paris, all fortified places, and all maritime parts, under penalty of being outlawed. Popular commissions tried all persons who, having no obvious livelihood, were accused of being opposed to the Revolution. The Law of the 22d Prairial, year II (June 10, 1794), deprived the accused of advocates, abolished the testimony of witnesses, and prescribed the death penalty for all who opposed the government. This law was repealed after the downfall of Robespierre. The law of hostages, 24th Messidor, year III, provided that the legislative body should decide whether, in the departments or communes which were in a state of unrest, the relatives of "émigrés," the above-mentioned nobles, and the relatives of brigands should be held responsible for assassinations and pillages and arrested and held as hostages. Its execution was only begun when the law was abolished during the Consulate.

[4] Decrees of August 16, 1790; of September 29, 1791; of October 6, 1791; and of July 19, 1791.

assessors), and the municipal police (three judges chosen by the municipal officers and from among them). The penalties prescribed by the Code of September 25, 1791, unlike those of the "Ancien Régime," were neither perpetual, nor atrocious, nor arbitrary. The infliction of the death penalty[1] was limited to decapitation (by the guillotine, March 20, 1792); there were to be no more mutilations, nor branding with red-hot irons, nor whipping; honor penance ("amende honorable"), civil death, and general confiscation disappeared. Through hatred of arbitrary punishments, fixed penalties were prescribed which did not permit the judge to take account either of aggravating circumstances or of extenuating circumstances. The right of pardon, regarded formerly as an application of justice reserved by the king and consequently exercised by him, was abolished, but the heaviest penalties, like putting in irons and imprisonment, were no longer perpetual. Conversely, rehabilitation, which was only a favor during the "Ancien Régime," became a right.

The code of offenses and penalties of the 3d Brumaire, year IV (1796), the personal work of Merlin, had especially as its object the regulation of criminal procedure. It was inspired with the same principles as the preceding laws; on some points, however, we may observe "a tendency to return to the old traditions."[2]

TOPIC 7. FINANCES

§ 505. **Equality in Respect to Taxation,**[3] a consequence of equality before the law, was established in principle by the Constituent

[1] The Convention decreed that the death penalty should be abolished at the conclusion of a general peace. Decree of October 6, 1793.

[2] The Decrees of November 29, 1791, against refractory priests, etc., against "émigrés" (November 9, 1791, perpetual banishment; death in case of breaking of a ban; 28th March, 1793. Civil death against all from May 9, 1792). The law of suspects of September 17, 1793, can be viewed only as an emergency measure in contradiction with the principles of the Revolution.

The Revolutionary Tribunal, August 17, 1792, March 10, 1793, Decrees of October 20, 1793, and 22d Prairial, year III, must be regarded in the same way (summary procedure and a single punishment, death, no right of appeal, no right of defense; "to patriots falsely charged the law gives a jury of patriots to protect them; but conspirators shall have no such protection"). The Decree of 12 Prairial, year III, May 31, 1795, abolished this tribunal. *Campardon*, "Hist. du trib. révol.," 1862; *Berriat St. Prix*, "La justice révol."

[3] The principle of proportionality: the Declaration of the Rights of Man, Art. 13; Const. of 1795, Art. 306; Const. of 1793, Art. 101: "No citizen is exempted from the honorable obligation of contributing to the public expenses." Concerning the progressive tax, *cf. infra*, p. 569, n. 3. The Law of March 18, 1793: the National Convention decreed as a principle that in order to attain an exact proportion in the apportionment of

Assembly. Even the term "tax" ("impôt") disappeared, to give place to that of "rate" ("contribution"), a fact which implies the idea of an equal apportionment among all of the public burdens, and the consent of the ratepayer to pay his share. This consent had to be given through the agency of his representative; the legislature had the right to vote the tax; the budgetary decrees were even freed from the necessity of the royal sanction. Instead of the secret finances of the monarchy, under which all sorts of misdoings were possible, there were publicity and discussion of the budget.[1]

The financial system of the old monarchy had all the faults of traditional systems, composed of elements of different dates: want of logic, the existence of privileges, and a complicated system of administration. The Constitutional Assembly simplified it to excess, by taking too much account both of popular prejudice and of the theories of the physiocrats, according to whom land was the sole source of wealth and therefore the only proper subject of taxation. It began by abolishing a large number of unpopular taxes, — aides, salt taxes, tolls, internal customs duties, and monopolies;[2] of indirect taxes only external customs duties on imported articles, stamp taxes, and registration taxes were retained.[3]

The land tax became the principal source of the revenues of the State.[4] Nevertheless, movable property was burdened, as well as real estate, by a proportional tax.[5] By means of patents, which took the place of the old grants of freedom to trading companies, industrial and commercial property was reached.[6] The

expenditures that each citizen must support by reason of his abilities, there should be established a graduated progressive tax on luxury and wealth, land as well as personalty. Sumptuary laws, *e.g.* that of the 7th Thermidor, year III, abrogated by the Law of April 24, 1806.

[1] *Gomel*, "Hist. fin. de l'ass. constit.," 1897; *Marce*, "La Comptabilité publique pendant la Révolution," 1893. The Court of Accounts was abolished because there was a desire to reserve to the legislature the surveillance over the expenditure of the taxes.

[2] Abolition of lotteries, tax on the credulity of the poor.

[3] *Supra*, p. 510. Concerning alienation or transfer fees, and particularly succession fees, which might easily degenerate into spoliation of the individual by the State, *cf.* Decrees of December 5, 1790; of May 27, 1791, and the Law of 22d Frimaire, year VII. *Laferrière*, p. 403.

[4] Maximum: 6 per cent of the net revenue.

[5] The tax was a sou per livre (5 per cent) or a twentieth of the income calculated on the basis of the rental value of houses, this being taken as a sign of real estate wealth. Decree of January 1, 1791. A special effort was made in framing this tax to avoid the arbitrariness against which there was complaint under the old régime. It was for this reason that an external sign was taken as the basis, *i.e.* the size of the habitation.

[6] The patent created by the Decree of March 2, 1791, for commercial and industrial professions was extended by the Law of the 1st Brumaire, year VII, to the liberal professions.

collection of the tax and the administrative controversies arising out of it were put in relation with the new political divisions.[1] A minister of public contributions replaced the comptroller general, and a bureau of general accounts the Chamber of Accounts and of the Court of Aids.

§ 506. **National Property.** — The conservation of the crown domain was one of the fundamental laws of the old monarchy. Following an opposite policy, the Revolution liquidated the enormous patrimony formed by the union of the crown domain, the lands of the clergy, and those of the "émigrés" (confiscation as a penalty; *cf.* the Protestants under Louis XIV).[2] The immediate purpose was the payment of the public debts, but the Revolutionists were equally moved by hatred of mortmain lands; they desired to parcel out and commercialize these lands [3] and to attach to the new régime the great number of purchasers among whom the national possessions would be divided.[4] The Decree of the 14th of May, 1790, ordered their sale for four hundred millions. But as this measure could not be realized immediately, at least not without a great depreciation of the national domain, the State adopted the expedient of acting as if it had received the price set upon them; it issued paper money, known as **assignats**, to the extent of four hundred millions and used it to pay off its creditors.[5] It was thought that these State notes would be used to acquire the national property, and it was proposed that they should be retired from circulation in a short time, when all these lands should be sold; but they were everywhere used as a new kind of national money. This change of object, which was made all the more easily as metallic money had become rare in consequence of political troubles, gave rise to grave dangers; of these the leaders were conscious and attempted to forestall them by decreeing that the issue of "assignats" should never

[1] Concerning the "cadastre," *cf. supra*, p. 499, n. 3, and Decrees of August 4 and 21, and September 16, 1791.

[2] *Supra*, p. 478 and following; a billion belonging to "émigrés" under the Restoration (1825).

[3] *Borie Minzes*, "Die Nationalgüterveräusserung währ. d. franz. Revol.," 1892. *Cf.* "R. d'écon. polit.," III, 208. "R. hist.," 1894, p. 165: *Maisonabe*, "Thèses Chartes," 1895 (Haute-Garonne); *Louchitzky*, "La petite propriété et la Révol.," 1897. In certain departments, at least, the national property seems to have been bought by speculators, and the peasants therefore experienced only a change of proprietors. *Cf.* concerning the numerous laws relating to national property, the "Table" of *Duvergier*.

[4] *Cf.* concerning the division of communal property, *supra*, p. 461, French ed.

[5] "Assignats" on the extraordinary treasury, from which had to be paid the price for national property sold.

exceed the value of the national property and that there should never be more than 1,200,000 livres of them in circulation. But the emergencies and the distress of the treasury were stronger than the laws; from 400 millions the number rose in 1790 to the maximum of 1,200,000, to 2,000,200,000 in 1792; by the end of 1795 there had been issued more than 40,000,000,000. The entire public wealth would not have been sufficient to guarantee their payment; moreover, they had depreciated to such an extent that under the Directory 100 livres in "assignats" were worth less than 4 sous. **Territorial warrants** ("mandats"), with forced circulation and privileged mortgages on the national possessions (28th Vent., year IV), displaced them for a moment and had some success because they represented a real value; but having in their turn fallen below their nominal value, they were retired from circulation in 1797.

§ 507. **The Public Debt.** — The deficit which existed at the time of the Revolution continued to increase even to the period of the Directory. By abolishing indirect taxes, the Constituent Assembly had deprived the treasury of about a third of its revenues; by charging the municipal authorities with the preparation of the rolls of direct taxes, it brought about the ruin of the State, because, the municipalities not performing their duties, the taxes almost ceased to be collected.[1] Like the "Ancien Régime" it made bad use of the forced loan and rendered it progressive. The forced loan and the progressive tax on wealth,[2] established by the Convention (Law of May 20, 1793),[3] were aimed at the luxury and selfishness which were found especially among the enemies of the Republic, the true "sans culottes" (violent Republicans) deeming that it was civic duty to offer their superfluous wealth to the State in its pecuniary distress, through subscriptions or patriotic contributions. But these two expedients were of equal worth, one had no more success than the other; the State, which asked for a billion, obtained almost nothing. The Directory went so far as to organize the poor into juries of equity and to pay them to tax the rich. Metallic money disappeared; worth-

[1] *Stourm*, II, 338 and following.

[2] Without interest. *Cf. Stourm*, 377. May, 1793; 19th Frimaire, year IV; 10th Messidor and 19th Thermidor, year VII. Decree of September 23, 1793 (depôts).

[3] Progression from 10 to 50 per cent up to 9000 francs of income; above that, the State took the totality. The necessary income which escaped the loan was 1000 livres for the unmarried man, 1500 for the married man, plus 1000 for his wife, each of his children, and each of his ascendants. *Stourm*, II, 373.

less paper, "assignats" and other kinds, flowed into the public treasury. Commerce and industry were deeply injured by measures as futile for the State as they were ruinous, arbitrary, and unjust for individuals. In order to avoid the depreciation of the "assignats" and to prevent jobbing, the Convention abolished loan societies and closed the exchange (February 1, 1793).

In spite of these strenuous expedients the State could not escape bankruptcy. But at least this deplorable solution, to which the "Ancien Régime" had too often resigned itself, was preceded by one useful measure. Cambon conceived the happy idea of unifying the public debt;[1] in place of the old securities, difficult to verify, bearing interest at different rates, the principal sometimes demandable and sometimes not, the creditors of the State were now to have only perpetual and irredeemable government stock, maturing at the same time and bearing the same rate of interest; all their securities were converted into inscriptions on a register called the **Great Book of the Public Debt.**[2] Unfortunately the amount of arrearages was very large, 200 millions, but it was reduced to 160 millions by subjecting the interest to a tax of a fifth. In spite of this measure the government, at the end of its resources, was unable to pay interest on the debt; it therefore declared that it was necessary to sell its property like an unfortunate debtor and as an act of good faith. A third of the debt (the **consolidated third**) was inscribed upon a new Great Book and remained charged to the State, the other two thirds (about two thousand millions)[3] were repaid by treasury vouchers which were receivable for the acquisition of national property, but which circulated at only one per cent of their nominal value. The State therefore suffered partial bankruptcy; as every class of citizens had had to suffer from the troubles of the Revolution, the security holders resigned themselves to this loss (September 30, 1797).

[1] *Stourm*, II, 330 and following; II, 202: Necker and Calonne were not able to agree as to the amount of the public debt — "There did not exist a single official recapitulation of the loans; the State borrowed without knowing what it owed."

[2] Sinking fund office, Nov., 1799. Bank of France, January 23, 1800, united with the Current Accounts, founded in 1786.

[3] What were these two billions in comparison with the forty-eight billions of assignats, the two and one half billions of territorial warrants, the three billions of arrear expenses, liquidated like the debt, and bonds without number? *Stourm*, II, 343.

TOPIC 8. THE ARMY

§ 508. **The Army.** — The recruitment of the army took place, as in the past, by means of voluntary enlistment (December 16, 1789, and March 9, 1791). But the appointment of the chief commanders was reserved only in part to the king; a civil oath was required of all, officers and soldiers alike, all armed bodies were forbidden to deliberate, and a code of offenses and military penalties was adopted by the Constituent Assembly. The tricolor was adopted as the national flag. The royal household gave place to a "constitutional guard" and the constabulary took the name of the national police ("gendarmerie nationale"). The militia and the provincial troops were abolished (June 12, 1790, and March 4, 1791) only to reappear on the 29th of September, 1791, in the National Guard (organized by districts and by cantons and not by communes, except in the important cities); to belong to it classed one as an active citizen (Decree of September 28, 1789, 11, 4). From this came the battalions of volunteers of 1792. On the 11th of July, 1792, the country was proclaimed to be in danger and a "levée en masse" was decreed on August 23, 1793. It was by this means that the system of obligatory service for all Frenchmen was introduced. The exclusion of foreigners from the French army gave it a character entirely national.

INDEX

www.ingramcontent.com/pod-product-compliance
Lightning Source LLC
La Vergne TN
LVHW090254210926
848480LV00001B/15
* 9 7 8 1 5 8 7 9 8 1 0 1 2 *